The Puppeteer's Library Guide:
The Bibliographic Index to the Literature of the World Puppet Theatre

Volume I : The historical background of puppetry and its related fields

by

J. Frances Crothers

The Scarecrow Press, Inc.
Metuchen, N.J.   1971

THE PUPPETEER'S LIBRARY GUIDE

A Bibliographic Index to the Literature of the
World Puppet Theatre

By J. Frances Crothers

A Set in Six Volumes, of published and unpublished material
regarding all types of puppets.

Vol. I   The Historical Background of Puppetry and Its
Related Fields.

Vol. II   The Puppet as an Educator.

Vol. III   The Puppet as an Entertainer.

Vol. IV   The Puppet Show in Production.

Vol. V   Published Material about Puppeteers, their
Companies and their Theatres around the World.

Vol. VI   Generalizations on the Material Listed, and Keys,
Abbreviations Used, Sources, Author Index, etc.

Dedicated to
The Puppeteers of the World
and
To My Husband

Table of Contents

Introduction

This bibliography is primarily for the use of librarians, teachers and puppeteers. Emphasis has been placed upon materials useful in "Education" and in "Therapeutics," other divisions do not pretend to be exhaustive in their treatment. This was necessary because of the vast amount of literature on puppetry. It is suggested that each of the sections, with its divisions, be regarded as a strong spring board into further study or bibliographic exploration.

This index is intended to display the types of material which have been written on the subject of puppetry; the amount of serious interest in this type of drama in the United States and throughout the world. It is also intended to show that puppetry is not just for children but is often of use in serious adult drama for satire, dance, music, propaganda, and creative expression; that puppetry in the United States merits national support, much as it is supported in Europe and Asia; and that there are many fields for research in puppetry which would be of great value in the study of art, drama, education, religion and medicine.

Although Dr. Paul McPharlan indicates by the title of his great puppet history, The Puppet Theatre in America 1524-1948 (N.Y. Harper, 1949) that there is material from 1524 on, I was able to find very little, aside from advertisements published in America up to 1785.

I found more items on puppetry in print by 1790, and by 1800 to 1810 frequent American items began to appear. The

9

basic coverage includes American items from 1639 to 1970, and earlier foreign material. The first items dealing with the use of puppets in "Education" started about 1908 and the first items of "Therapeutic" interest appeared around 1923-1925.

This bibliography has been compiled from source material in the following libraries; and with the very kind assistance of the research librarians of those institutions. The libraries are listed in the order in which they were investigated:

The Deering Library, Northwestern University, Evanston, Ill.
The Newberry Library, Newberry Square, Chicago, Illinois.
The Church Medical Library, Chicago Campus of Northwestern University
The John Crerar Medical Library, Chicago, Illinois.
The Chicago Public Library, Main Building, Chicago, Illinois.
Harper Library, University of Chicago Campus, Chicago, Illinois.
Kent State University Library, Kent State University, Kent, Ohio.
The Paul McPharlan Puppet Library, His Home in Ohio, now at Detroit Art Museum, Detroit, Michigan.
Oberlin University Library, Oberlin, Ohio.
Cleveland Public Library, Main Building, Cleveland, Ohio.
Dartmouth University Library, Hanover, New Hampshire.
Hanover Public Library, Hanover, New Hampshire.
Medical Library of Dartmouth, Dartmouth University Campus, Hanover, New Hampshire.
Quebec Public Library, Quebec, Canada.
Ottawa Public Library, Ottawa, Canada.
Canadian State Library, Ottawa, Canada.
Toronto Public Library, Toronto, Canada.
McGill University Library, Montreal, Canada.
Evanston Public Library, Evanston, Illinois.
Austin Fox-Riggs Mental Medical Clinic Library, Stockbridge, Massachusetts.
Chapin Library and Williams College Library, Williamstown, Massachusetts.
Pittsfield City Library, Pittsfield, Massachusetts.
St. Joseph's College Library, West Hartford, Connecticut.
West Hartford Public Library, West Hartford, Connecticut.
Hartford Public Library, Hartford, Connecticut.
Institute of Living, Medical Library, Hartford, Connecticut (For Mental Disorders).

New York City Public Library, Main Building, New York,
  New York.
Library of Congress, Washington, D. C.
Hartford Seminary Library, Hartford, Connecticut.
Trinity College Library & Watkinson Private Library,
  Hartford, Connecticut
Waterloo University Library, Kitchener, Waterloo, Canada.
Jacob Edwards Library, Southbridge, Massachusetts.
Lincoln Center Museum Theater Library, New York, New York.
Harvard University Libraries, Cambridge, Massachusetts.
Yale University Libraries, New Haven, Connecticut.
Yale University Beinecke Rare Book Library, New Haven,
  Connecticut.
British Puppet & Model Theatre Guild Library, London,
  England.

This Index should contain sufficient material to be
used as a working bibliography for any of the sections just
as it stands. To definitively cover and critically analyze
all the divisions was impossible, but suggestions have been
made as to where more material is available, and the student will find it a tantalizing trail to follow when he jumps
off from these lists into his own field of interest. Again, I
do not claim that coverage of any of the sections is complete. Some of it is quite fragmentary. I know there are
still mountains of written material awaiting my search and
it is difficult to cry halt to such adventure.

I have occasionally made a note as to the location of
an item which might be hard to find and, more rarely a
remark as to whether it was significant material. The
generalizations will be found at the end of the volumes, in
Section Fifteen, rather than with each section. This is done
to avoid confusion that might result from their insertion
throughout the books.

Many existing bibliographies and collections cover
short periods of time, usually from five to ten years. Many
are limited to a specific field of work. The two main com-
pilations most often referred to by collectors, were done

11

before 1932. They are, like mine, admitted by their very excellent authors to be, "of current material"[1] and "selective and limited"[2] in nature. Mr. T. E. Stephens' master's thesis, at Washington State University, A Bibliography of Puppetry, closed as of 1940.

In compiling this Index no distinction was made among the terms Puppets, Marionettes, Shadows, Rods, etc. , unless the term was used in the title of the work. If a term was within the title the item was classified under that field and cross-indexed to other sections where it might be sought for other value.

Brander Matthews and a few others would limit the meaning of the word "puppets" to those figures that are animated by the hand of the operator (such as with rods, or on the hand). The word "Puppet" comes from the Latin word "Pupa," meaning doll. The definition of the word "puppet" in Webster's Dictionary is,

> a toy, or one who is under the influence and control of another, a small image in human form often with jointed limbs moved by hand, or by string or wire; ..acting as another wills; a tool.

Both modern and ancient puppeteers generally operate, or did operate both hand and string figures, and they distinguished between them only on a very wide scale. They call all animated figures puppets when speaking of them generally, differentiating only when necessary to make the meaning very clear. As Mr. H. E. Coleman says in his puppetry index,

> It is interesting to know that such a distinction exists but since so few of the authors throughout this bibliography seem to be aware of this differentiation, and puppeteers themselves do not differentiate very often, it would be confusing to the user of the bibliography if any attempt were made to rectify those errors of centuries in the common terminology."[3]

Deep appreciation is expressed for all the time and assistance so many people have given me. Without their help

it would have been impossible to complete this book. This
bibliography really belongs to all puppeteers of the world because it is their work which has made it a reality and which
gives proof of the importance of this great and ancient form of
creative expression.

Notes

1. Grace G. Ransome, Puppets and Shadows. F. W.
    Faxon, Boston 1931.

2. Library of Congress, A Selective List of References
    on Marionette and Puppet Shows, Punch and Judy,
    etc. Div. of Bibliog. No. 940, Washington, D. C.
    Gov. Printing Office, 1925

3. H. E. Coleman, Bibliography of Marionettes and
    Puppets to 1932 (mim). Puppet File, Ref. Room
    Deering Library, Northwestern Univ. Campus,
    Evanston, Illinois.

Key to General Abbreviations
(Key No. 1)

Acad	Academy
Admin	Administration
Ala	Alabama
Am	America, American
Am. Ind	American Indian
Anon	anonymous
Ariz	Arizona
Ark	Arkansas
arr	arranged by
Assn, assn	Association
Bibliog, bibliog	Bibliography
bibliog-end	bibliography at end of book or article
bi-m	bimonthly
bi-w	biweekly
bk	book
Brit	Britain, British
Brit. C	British Columbia
Brit Pupp and M Thea G Newsl	British Puppet and Model Theatre Guild Newsletter
Bros	Brothers
Bur	Bureau
c	close to this date, circa
Calif	California
Cap, cap	Capital, capitalized
Chap	Chapter
Co	Company
coed	coeducational
Col	College
col	column, as in a newspaper
coll	collection, as a collection of plays
Colo	Colorado
comments	interesting comments by author are given for this item
comp	compiler or compiled by
Cond	condensed

Conn	Connecticut
cont	continued
Corp	Corporation
Czech	Czechoslovakia, Czechoslovakian, Czechoslovak
D'De, Du, etc.	for many names beginning with these, see the family name. (De Lamar, see Lamar, De)
D. C.	District of Columbia
Del	Delaware
Dept	Department
Detro. Inst. of Art. Ref. Lib.	Detroit, Michigan, Institute of Art Research Library, the Puppet Collection
diag	diagram(s)
diff	different
div, Div	Division
E	East
Ed	Education, educational
ed	edited by, editor, or edition
Elem	Elementary
Eng	England, English
Exhib	exhibit, Exhibition
Fed	Federal
Fest	Festival
Fla	Florida
Fr	French, France
freq	frequently, frequent
Ga	Georgia
gen	general
Ger	German, Germany
Govt	Government, Governmental
Gr. Brit.	Great Britain
Grades	Grade School or Elementary School
Guide	Meaning this book
Hi	High School
Hon	Honorable
Ill	Illinois
illus	illustrative material, illustrated by, illustrator
Imp	Impression

15

Inc	incorporated
Ind	Indiana
Inst	Institution, Institute
Intern	International, internationally
introd	introductory, introduction
Irr. Public	Irregular publication
It.	Italian, Italy
item	the page number does not refer to article but to an important item on that page
Jap	Japanese, Japan
Jav	Javanese, Java
Jr	Junior
Jr. Hi	Junior High School
Jr. Leag of Am	Junior Leagues of America Organization
jt auth	joint author
Kans	Kansas
Ky	Kentucky
L.C.	Library of Congress
La	Louisiana
Lib	Library
Lieut	Lieutenant
Lit	literature, literary
m	monthly
McPharlin coll	The Paul McPharlin Memorial Library Puppet Collection at the Detroit Museum of Art, Detroit, Michigan
mag	magazine
Mass	Massachusetts
Master's	Master of Science or Arts degree
Math	mathematics
Md	Maryland
Me	Maine
Med	medical
Mex	Mexican, Mexico
Mich	Michigan
Micro	microfilm
Mimeo	mimeographed
Minn	Minnesota
Miss	Mississippi
Mme S. Z.	Madam S. Zlatin's Rare Theatre Book Store, 46 Rue Madame, Paris, 6°, France
Mo	Missouri
Mont	Montana

MS	manuscript form
Mt	Mount
N	North, November
Nat	National
N. C.	North Carolina
N. D.	North Dakota
n. d.	no date
NE	Northeast, Northeastern
Nebr	Nebraska
n. l.	not located
n. p.	no pagination
Nev	Nevada
New Eng	New England
N. H.	New Hampshire
N. J.	New Jersey
N. Mex	New Mexico
N. N. or	New York Public Library, including its
N. Y. Pub. Lib.	Lincoln Center Branch, Theatre Collection
N. Y.	New York State
NYC	New York City
NW	Northwest, Northwestern
No publ	publisher not given
Off	Office
Okla	Oklahoma
Ont	Ontario
Oreg	Oregon
orig	original, originally
Org	Organization
organ	organized
Pa	Pennsylvania
passim	scattered through the work
pl	unusual plate or illus.
prelim p	preliminary paging
Pres	president
print	printing
Prof	academic award
"Prof"	"Professor" an English title given to the Punch and Judy operator
pseud	pseudonym
pt	part of
psychol	psychology
publ	publisher, publishing
Public	publication
Pupp J Public	Puppetry Journal Publication, to be purchased from that office c/o Mrs. Vivien Michael, Ashville, Ohio

"Pupp of Am"	The Puppeteers of America
q	quarterly
Rec	recreation, recreational
Ref	Reference, references
rev	revised, revised edition
revu	reviewed by, review of
R. I.	Rhode Island
Sat	Saturday
S	South, September
S. C.	South Carolina
Sch	school
S. Dak.	South Dakota
SE	Southeast, southeastern
Sect	Secretary
Sem	Seminary
Serv	service
Shak	Shakespeare, Shakespearian
sig m	very significant material
Soc	society
Sq	Square
Sr. Hi	Senior High School
St	Saint, street
Sun	Sunday
Sup	supplement
Supt	Superintendent
SW	Southwest, southwestern
Tenn	Tennessee
Tex	Texas
Thea	Theatre
trans	translated, translation, translator
U. N.	United Nations Organization
UNESCO	United Nations Educational, Scientific and Cultural Organization
UNIMA	Union of International Marionettes Association Headquarters in Prague, Czech.
Univ	University
U. S. Fed	United States Federal etc.
U. S. Fed Thea	United States Federal Theatre Project (1936-1940)
U. S. Lib Cong.	United States Library of Congress

Va	Virginia
Vol	Volume, volumes
Vt	Vermont
W	West
w	weekly publication
Wash	Washington
Wis	Wisconsin
W. Va.	West Virginia
W. P. A.	Works Progress Administration (1936-1940)
Wyo	Wyoming
yr	yearly
Z. C.	Zip Code

Key to Abbreviations of Periodicals Titles
(Key No. 2)

Some books used a great deal are included.

Booklets or periodicals which do not appear very often, or are international items, not easily understood or found, are given in full form in the text and not usually abbreviated.

Action	Action (N. Y.)
Actor	Screen Actors Guild (Hollywood) became Actor c 1940
All Yr R	All The Year Round became All The Year in 1859
American	The American Monthly, 1834 (was The American Mag, in 1829) then returned to American Magazine, later
Am Artist	American Artist
Am City	American City Magazine
Am Childh	American Childhood
Am Collect	American Collectors Magazine
Am Fam	American Family Magazine
Am Girl	The American Girl
Am Home	The American Home
Am J of Dis Ch	American Journal of Disturbed Child
Am J Nur	American Journal of Nursing
Am J of Occup Therp	American Journal of Occupational Therapy 1936-1961 see also: Occup Therap
Am J Orthopsy	American Journal of Orthopsychiatry
Am J of Psychi	American Journal of Psychiatry
Am J of Pschotherp	American Journal of Psychotherapy
Am Psych	American Psychologist
Am Rev of Rev	American Review of Reviews
Am Weekly	American Weekly Magazine
Art Digest	Art Digest 1929-1931, see The Arts 1931
Art N	Art News
Art Notes	Art Notes (London, 1937, also in NYC)
Art World	see Arts and D

L'Artiste	The Artist, French--L'Artiste
Arts	The Arts (formerly The Art Digest)
Arts & Act	Arts and Activities
Arts & C	Arts and Crafts
Art & C Ed	Art and Craft Education
Arts & D	Arts and Decoration, formerly Art World, 1916-1918 combines with Spur and called Art World & Decoration, 1918
Asia	Asia (1858)
Atlantic	Atlantic (1824, followed by Atlantic Monthly)
Atlantic M	Atlantic Monthly, 1858
B & G World	Boys and Girls World (Los Angeles, 1938)
Balt Bull Ed	Baltimore Bulletin of Education
Balt Mus N	Baltimore Museum of Arts News
Beaux A Inst Des Bull	Beaux-Arts Institute of Design Bulletin (N. Y.)
Bellman	Bellman (Minneapolis)
Bet Hom & Gard	Better Homes and Gardens Magazine
Better Farm	Better Farming, see Country Gent
Bibli Lib J	The Bibliographic Library Journal, formerly Dramatic Index
Bk Coll Q	Book Collector's Quarterly
Blackwoods	Blackwood's Edinburgh Magazine (Europe)
Bookman	Bookman (London 1891)
Bost D G	Boston Daily Globe Newspaper
Bost Eve Trans	Boston Evening Transcript Newspaper
Boys W	Boy's World (Eng, 1879-1882; then Chicago, 1902-1935)
Brit J Med Psych	British Journal of Medical Psychology
Brit Pupp & M Thea G Newsl	British Puppet and Model Theatre Guild Newsletter. Later the organization shortened this to B. P. M. T. G. Newsletter
Bull A Therp	Bulletin of Art Therapy (634 A St. S. E. Washington 3, D. C.)
Bull Hi Points	Bulletin of High Points (1931, see High Points)
Bull Menn Clin	Bulletin of The Menninger Clinic
Bull N Y Publ Lib	Bulletin of the New York City Public Libraries, ed by E. Ulman
Bureau Am Ethn	Bureau of American Ethnology Bulletin

Calif Teach Assn J	California Teachers Association Journal
Camp Thea	Camp Theatricals
Can Geog J	Canadian Geographical Journal
Can H J	Canadian Home Journal
Carnegie Mag	Carnegie Institute Magazine (Pittsburgh, Pennsylvania)
Catalogue	Catalogue Magazine
Cath D	Catholic Digest
Cath Ed R	Catholic Educational Review
Cath H J	Catholic Home Journal
Cath Sch D	Catholic School Digest
Cath Sch J	Catholic School Journal (may be same as above, earlier or later)
Cath W	Catholic World
Cavalcade	The Cavalcade Magazine
Cent	Century Magazine (Century Illustrate Monthly)
Ch Sci H Ed	Christian Science Human Educator
Ch Sci Mon	Christian Science Monitor Newspaper, followed by section of country
Ch Sci Mon M	Christian Science Monitor Magazine, followed by section of country
Ch Sci Mon W	Christian Science Monitor Weekly (comes for East, West, etc. parts of the United States of America)
Chambers J	Chambers Edinburgh Journal
Chicago Sch J	Chicago Schools Journal
Child Develop	Child Development
Childh Ed	Childhood Education
Childh Educr	Childhood Educator (change in name for Childh Ed probably)
Child L	Child Life
Child Psy Techn	Child Psychiatric Techniques (Blackwell Scientific Publications, Dr. L. Benter, Toronto) book Abrev.
Child St	Child Study
Childr Act	Children's Activities (now Highlights for Children)
Childrens R	Children's Royal Magazine (became Vogue Fashion, Vogue Pattern Bk)
Christian Cent	Christian Century
Class J	Classical Journal
Close Up	Close Up Magazine (Switzerland 1927-)
Colliers	Collier's Weekly (National Weekly is another name)
Con Stick	Control Stick (The New England Guild of Puppetry Newsletter)

Conn Schools	The Connecticut Schools
Conno	Connoiseur (Absorbed International Studio in 1931)
Consumer Rep	Consumer Reports
Contemp R	Contemporary Review
Cosmop	Cosmopolitan Magazine
Country Gent	Country Gentleman (now Better Farming, 1953)
Craft Horiz	Craft Horizons
Cranbrook Bull	Cranbrook Bulletin; Cranbrook Inst. of Science Newsletter
Creat A	Creative Art
Creat H	Creative Home
CTA J	(See California Teachers Association Journal)
Cue	The Cue
Curr D of Sov P	Current Digest of The Soviet Press (Russia)
Curr Lit	Current Literature (early N. Y. previous to 1913, became Current Opinion) Vol 60-61, 1915
Curr Op	Current Opinion, see Cur Lit
Dalhousie R	Dalhousie Review or Quarterly (Halifax: Dalhouse Univ. Review Publ Co)
Dance	Dance Magazine
Delin	The Delineator
Design	Design Magazine
Detroit Inst Bull	Detroit Institute of Art Bulletin; U.S.A.
Directory	See Pupp of Am Direct
Drama	Drama Magazine (Drama League of America, 1911-1931)
Drama In	Dramatic Index, see Bibli Lib J
Drama L Mo	Drama League Monthly (Drama League of N. Y. 1913 with a subtitle of Little Theatre Monthly & Little Theatre News which some articles may be listed under
Echo	The Echo Magazine, The Echo, Das Echo, Literarishes Echo (French). There may be other versions in other countries. The Echo Magazine is not the same as The Echo.
E. P. A. (Brit)	This is the chosen shortened name for the British group, "Educational Puppetry Association" who publishes many pamphlets and articles. This began to appear c 1960.

Ed Digest	Educational Digest
Ed Meth	Educational Method (1921-)
Ed Outl	Educational Outlook (Philadelphia 1926-)
Ed Pupp Assn Yrb	British Educational Puppetry Association Yearbook which was published in 1950's previous to the "E.P.A."
Ed Screen	Educational Screen and Audovisual Guide
Ed Times	Educational Times (London 1947-1923 then changed to Journal of Education)
Educa	Education Magazine
El Ed Sch	Elementary Education of Schools, became Elementary School Journal
El Eng	Elementary English
El Eng Rev	Elementary English Review, became Elementary English
El Rev	Elementary Review
El School J	Elementary School Journal, see El Ed Sch
Engl Illus M	English Illustrated Magazine (London, 1883)
Eng J	English Journal
Eng J HI Ed	English Journal High School Education (Branch of Eng J)
English Review	English Review (London)
Emer Q	Emerson Quarterly (Boston, 1920)
Era	Era Magazine (England) See New Era Magazine. "Era" absorbed Cinematography and then absorbed Screen and Stage.
Etude	Etudé (France, America, England)
Farm J	Farm Journal
Film A	Film Art (London, 1937)
Film S Gu	Film Strip Guide
Film News	Film News Quarterly (1939, became Films in Review)
Films R	Films in Review, see Film News
Film S Prog	Film Society Programme (1925, 1934, 1930 a quarterly)
Fortnightly Rev	Fortnightly Review (London)
Four Arts	Four Arts (Virginia Art Alliance, Richmond: 1934 and from London, much earlier, 1863-1867)
France Illus	France Illustrée (Paris, A Literary, Scientific and Religious Journal, do not confuse with L'Illus or Illus.
Fraser's	Fraser's Magazine (London, 1882)
Gebrauchs	Gebrauchsgraphik (German)
Gen Psy Monog	Genetic Psychology Monographs (Provincetown)

G N Y Pupp	
G Newsl	Greater New York Puppet Guild Inc. Newsletter
Good H	Good Housekeeping
Good Sp	Good Speech (London)
Gr Teach	Grade Teacher, see Pop Educr
Grand R Mir	Grand Rapids Mirror Newspaper (Michigan)
Grapev	Grapevine Telegraph, also Grapevine
Graphic Arts	Graphic Arts Monthly
Graphis	Graphische Revue Osterreichs (Vienna, 1899)
Guide	Puppeteer's Library Guide by J. Francis Crothers
Harpers	Harper's Magazine (Harper's Monthly is same) London & NYC but there is slight variation sometimes in vol, no or page so both should be checked if not found in one. I have indicated when the source was clear.
Harpers Baz	Harper's Bazaar (This is not the same as just Harpers)
Harpers M	Harper's Weekly, see Harpers
Harpers W	Harper's Weekly, see Harpers
Harvard Ed R	Harvard Educational Review
Harvard Lib Bull	Harvard Library Bulletin
Hi F Childr	Highlights for Children, see Childr Act
Hi Fi and A	High Fidelity and Audio
Hi Points	High Points, see Bulletin of High Points, this is just a little different.
Hisp	Hispania (Witchita State Univ. Kansas, 1918-)
Hisp R	Hispania Review (Univ. Of Pennsylvania, 1933)
Hist Eng Pupp	
Thea	The History of the English Puppet Theatre by George Speaight, London: Harrap, 1955, 1st printing.
Hobbies W	Hobbies Weekly
Homecr	Homecraft Magazine
House B	House Beautiful
House & G	House and Garden
House W	Household Words (London, 1850)
Houst Tex Ch	The Houston Texas Chronicle Newspaper
Ill Ed	Illinois Education (Mount Morris, Ill: Illinois Education Association)

Illus	Illustration (London, NYC, Paris, <u>see also</u> L'Illustration and France Illustrated
Illus Lon N	The Illustrated London News, <u>see also</u> Illustrated News & just London News
Illus N	Illustrated News (a very early American publication)
Illus W	The Illustrated World, <u>see</u> New W Illus
(Illus,L')	
(L'Illus)	L'Illustration, see under L'Illus also Petite L'Illus
Illus Thea	see L'Illustration Theatracle
Indus Arts	Industrial Arts
Indus Arts M	Industrial Arts Magazine became Industrial Arts, 1920
Indus Arts and Voc Ed	Industrial Arts and Vocational Education
Instit	Institute (adjective usually follows, many versions
Instr	The Instructor
Integ Handw	Integrated Handwork
Intern Arch Fur Ethnegr	International Archives for Ethnography (Germany)
Intern Bur Ed Bull	International Bureau of Education Bulletin
Intern Ed R Cinemat	International Educational Review Cinemat or Review of Educational Cinematography
Intern J Relig Ed	International Journal of Religious Education
Intern M	International Monthly (1850)
Intern Mus	International Musician
Intern Q	International Quarterly (18?)
Intern Revu of Ed Cinem	International Review of Educational Cinematography <u>see</u> Intern Ed R Cinemat probably same, with little change by the source in title, but I have kept it as it was in the source.
Intern S	International Studio, see Conno
Intern Yrb Pupp	see Pupp (Puppetry) <u>It is</u> the International Yearbook of Puppetry by Paul Mc-pharlin, published in American. <u>see also</u> "Periodicals" under Puppetry: U.S.A. Do not confuse with British, Yearbook of Puppetry.
J Abner S Psych	Journal of Abnormal and Social Psychology (Washington)

J Ad Ed	Journal of Adult Education
J Am Folklore	Journal of American Folklore, <u>see</u> Folklore
J Child Psychol Psychiat	Journal of Child Psychology and Psychiatry
J Clin Psychol	Journal of Clinical Psychology
J D(d) Clin	Journal (De) Clinique Et De Therapeuti que Infantile (Paris)
J Des Deb	Journal Des Debates (Toronto)
J Ed	Journal of Education
J Excep Ch	Journal of Exceptional Children (Battle Creek, Michigan)
J Fulklore Inst	Journal of the Fulklore Institute (Netherlands) <u>see</u> Folklore
J Genet Psychol	Journal of Genetic Psychology, <u>see</u> Ped Sem
J Pediatrics	Journal of Pediatrics
J Project Techn	Journal of Projective Techniques (Glendale, Calif, 1956)
J Polyn Soc	Journal of the Polynesian Society
J Siam S	Journal of the Siam Society
J Univ Ann	Journal De L'University Des Annuales
Jr League Mag	Junior Leagues of America Inc. Magazine. I prefer to use Jr. for this magazine as I use that abbreviation for the Org.
Jun A & A	Junior Arts and Activities
Jun Lang A	Junior Language and Arts
Jun Lib	Junior Libraries, <u>see</u> The Library Journal
Jun S Hi Sch C H	Junior Senior High School Clearing House
Juv	Juvenile Magazine
Kindg & Fstg	Kindergarten and First Grade, became American Childhood
Kindg Pri	Kindergarten Primary Magazine, was just Kindergarten, but also had other subtitles
Ladies HJ	Ladies Home Journal
Leisure	Leisure Time, this may be earlier or later name for just Leisure
Lib J	Library Journal
Life Let	Life and Letters Today, or Life and Letters (English 1928)
L'Illus	L'Illustration (France)
L'Illus Thea	L'Illustration Theatracle (France)
Lippincott M	Lippincotts Magazine
Lit D	Literary Digest
Lit W	Literary World

Littel's Liv Age	Littel's Living Age, or Living Age
Little Thea M	see Drama League Monthly. Little Theatre Magazine
Little Thea N	Little Theatre News, see Drama League monthly
Liv A	Living Age, also called Little's Living Age
Lond N	The Illustrated London News, sometimes called just London News
Lond Mer	London Mercury (England)
Lond S	London Studio (England 1931-39)
Los A C P.G. Newsl	Los Angeles County Puppet League Newsletter, became Puppet Life, see Pupp Life as majority of my material comes after the new name was used, for this printing
McC Dec A	McCalls Decorative Arts
McCalls	McCall Magazine
Mans	Mans Magazine
Marionette	The Marionette Magazine, or Tonight at 8:30, The Marionette (Italy, 1918-1919)
Mary Psy Q	Maryland Psychiatric Quarterly (Baltimore)
Math Teach	Mathematics Teacher
Mech Ill	Mechanic's Illustrated
Mental Hyg	Mental Hygiene
Mercure Des Fr	Mercure Des France
Met Mus Bull	Metropolitan Music Bulletin
Mid Sch	Midland Schools
Milgate F	Milgate Foundation Publication
Minn J Ed	Minnesota Journal of Education
Miss R Wor	Missionary Review of World (Early NYC 1905)
Mlle	Mademoiselle
Model Am	Modeling for Amateurs
Mod Ed	Modern Education (Cleveland, 1928)
Mod Hosp	The Modern Hospital
Mod Lang F	Modern Language Forum
Mod Lang J	Modern Language Journal, formerly Mod Lang R
Mod Lang N	Modern Language Notes
Mod Lang Q	Modern Language Quarterly
Mod Lang R	Modern Language Review see Mod Lang J
Mod Mus	Modern Music (League of Composers Inc)
Mod Mus In	Modern Music Index
Mod Mus R	Modern Music Review
Mon R	Monthly Review (England)
Motion P M	Motion Picture Magazine

Movie Makers	Movie Makers Magazine
Moving P W	Moving Picture World
Mus J	Music Journal
Mus and M	Music and Musicians
Mus C M	Music Clubs Magazine
Mus Ed J	Music Educators Journal
Mus Cour	Musical Courier
Mus Q	Musical Quarterly

Nation & Anth	Nation and the Antheneum (1840)
Nat Assn Wom De & Wom De & Couns J	National Association of Womens Deans and Counselors Journal
Nat Bd of R.M.	National Board of Review of Motion Pictures
Nat Ed Assn J	National Education Association Journal
Nat El Prin	National Elementary Principal
Nat Geog	National Geographic Magazine (America)
Nat Parent Teach	National Parent Teacher, continued as just P.T.A. Magazine so I use that title.
National W	National Weekly, see Colliers
Nations Scho	The Nation's Schools (American)
Nebr Ed J	Nebraska Educational Journal
New Eng	New Englander, 1843
New Eng Mag	New England Magazine, 1905, formerly New Englander
N E Pupp G Newsl	New England Puppetry Guild Newsletter, became Control Stick which I use, Con Stick being the name of it when majority of my material was located. However some earlier items may be located.
N Repub	New Republic
N Statesm	New Statesman (England)
N Statesm and Nat	New Statesman and Nation, a later combination of New Statesman
News R	News Record (London)
Newsl	A Newsletter Periodical of the Puppet Group named in title
Newsweek	Newsweek
New Thea	New Theatre (London, see also Theatre)
New W Illus	New World Illustrated (Canada, Toronto & Montreal, 1939). The Montreal issue is often entirely in French.
N Y Am	New York American

29

N Y Eve S	New York Evening Sun
N Y Her	New York Herald, merged with New York Tribune, became New York Herald Tribune
N Y Her Trib	New York Herald Tribune
N Y Her Trib W Bk Revu	New York Herald Weekly Book Review
N Y Pupp G Newsl	See G N Y Pupp G Newsl
N Y Times	New York Times Newspaper
N Y Times Bk Revu	New York Times Book Review
N Y Times Mag	New York Times Magazine Section
N Y Tribune Mag	New York Tribune Magazine Section
N Y Tribune	New York Tribune Newspaper
Norm Inst & Pri Pl	Normal Instructor and Primary Plans
Norm Sch Inst & Pri Pl	Normal School Instructor and Primary Plans, this was formerly the Norm Inst & Pri Pl
Occups	Occupations
Occup Therapy	Occupational Therapy, became Am J of Occup Therapy
Occup Th & R	Occupational Therapy and Rehabilitation
Oeuvres D'A	Oeuveres D'Arte (French)
Oeuvres M	Oeuvres Music (French)
Ohio Sch	Ohio Schools
On the D	On the Dial Magazine
Opera and Con	Opera and Concerts
Opera N	Opera News
Out M	The Outing Magazine (NYC 1905)
Outl	The Outlook
Parks & Rec	Parks and Recreation, see Recreation
Parents M	Parent's Magazine
Parents M B H	Parents Magazine and Better Homemaker
P.T.A. Mag	The P.T.A. Magazine
Paster B	Paster Bonus (German)
Ped Sem	Pedagogical Seminary and Journal of Genetic Psychology. see J Genet Psychol, new name for it.
Penn Gazette	The Pennsylvania Gazette
Penn Monthly	Pennsylvania Monthly (Philadelphia, 1870-1881)
Penny M	Penny Magazine (London, 1832-1845)
Personality	Personality

Petit L'Illus	La Petit Illustration. In NYC Publ Lib.
Phil Publ Led	Philadelphia Public Ledger Newspaper
Philol Q	Philological Quarterly
Photop M	Photoplay Magazine
Pict Ed M	Pictorial Education Magazine (London)
Platoon Sch	Playtoon School
Play Bk	The Play Book (Madison, Wis, short lived)
Playb	Playbill
Playgr	Playground and Recreation, became Recreation, then Leisure, then Parks and Recreation
Plays	Plays for Young People (Boston: Plays Inc)
Players	Players Magazine
Pop Educ	Popular Education
Pop Educr	Popular Educator
Pop Educr and Prim Ed	Popular Educator and Primary Education
Pop Home Cr M	Popular Homecraft Magazine
Pop Mech	Popular Mechanics
Pop Sci	Popular Science
Pract Hom Econ	Practical Home Economics
Pract Mec	Practical Mechanics
Pract TV	Practical Television
Prim Ed	Primary Education (Boston)
Prof Hob	Profitable Hobbies
Prog Ed	Progressive Education
Prog Ed Bull	Progressive Education Bulletin
Psych Monog	Psychological Monographs, General and Applied
Publ H N	· Public Health Nursing (Madison, Wisc., 1913)
Publ Sch J	Public School Journal (San Francisco)
Das Puppensp	Das Puppenspieler (German)
Das Puppenth	Das Puppentheater (German)
Der Puppensp	Der Puppenspieler (German)
Der Puppenth	Der Puppentheater (German). It woula be wise to see also: Puppet "Periodical" Section on all Puppet Magazines as they are quite confusing in titles, dates, etc.
Pupp	Puppetry (America) This takes in several slightly different titled periodicals by Paul McPharlin, see also: "Periodical" Section. But Mr. McPharlin seemed to to call them all by this name in his Puppet Theatre In America. New York: Harpers, 1939. (Puppetry, An International Yearbook, The International

	Yearbook of Puppetry, beginning 1930-1948.
Pupp Bull	Puppetry Bulletin (America)
Pupp HandB	Puppetry Handbook, Puppetry Imprints see Pupp Imp
Pupp Imp	Puppetry Imprints, see also "Periodical" Section
Pupp J	The Puppetry Journal (American) The main periodical of puppetry in America. Copies in NN. See also "Periodical" Section.
Pupp Life	Puppet Life, was Los Angeles County Puppet Guild Newsletter
Pupp Master	The Puppet Master (England 1943-), not to be confused with the Hungarian Puppet Master
Pupp Post	The Puppet Post (English). Many copies are in NN.
Pupp of Am Direct	The Puppeteers of America Membership Directory. A yearly publication, from Pupp Journal Office. See also "Periodical" Section. There are other Directories for many puppet organizations but I always indicate the group name when using them.
Pupp Talk	Puppet Talk, was San Diego Puppet Guild Newsletter
Pupp Thea Am	The Puppet Theatre in America by Paul McPharlin, New York: Harpers, 1949 edition. A new revised edition has just been made by Marjorie Batchelder McPharlin, Boston: Plays, 1969; has a supplement Puppets in America Since 1948 by Mrs. McPharlin but the abbreviation for this later edition would be different. See Pupp Thea Am Rev and see Pupp Thea Am Sup
Pupp Thea Am Rev	Puppet Theatre in America by Paul McPharlin, revised edition by M. B. McPharlin, 1969
Pupp Thea Am Sup	Puppet Theatre in America by Paul McPharlin, revised edition with supplement by Marjorie Batchelder McPharlin, Boston: Plays, 1969. Item is in the supplement section.

Pupp Thea Mod World
        The Puppet Theatre of the Modern World.
        Boston: Plays, 1967, compiled by the
        World UNIMA Organizations, ed by
        M. Niculesco. See also "Czechoslovakia"
Pupp Yrb   The Puppet Yearbook (England) c 1950-1960
Puppeteer's Newsl The Puppeteer's Newsletter of Saint Louis
        Mo. Puppet Guild See Newsl.

Q J of M   Quarterly Journal of The Mask, See Mask
Q J of A of Th Quarterly Journal of The Art of the
        Theatre, See Mask
Q J Speech Ed Quarterly Journal of Speech, became
        Education in 1927
Q V Rept   Quaker Village Report, The Philadelphia
        Puppet Guild Newsl, or often called
        just Report, Check on this in "Periodical"
        Section. Sources use several titles.

Read Dig   Readers Digest
Recre   Recreation, see Playground and Recreation,
        Leisure, then became Parks and
        Recreation
Redb   The Redbook
Relig Ed   Religious Education
Rev Brit   Revue Britannique (France)
Rev Des D M   Revue Des Deux Mendes (France)
R of Revus   Review of Reviews (NYC, 1805),
        continues beyond 1950 s
Rev Sept   Revue Septentrionale (Paris)

Safety Ed   Safety Education
Salem N   Salem, Ohio, News; a newspaper
Sales Mang   Sales Management
Saint Nic   The Saint Nicholas Magazine
San Fra D Eve
    Bull   San Francisco Daily Evening Bulletin,
        sometimes given just San Fr Bulletin
(San Fr Bulletin) See San Fra D Eve Bull
San Fra Chron San Francisco Chronicle Newspaper
San Fra Pupp G
    Newsl
    (SFBAPG Newsl)
        San Francisco Bay Puppetry Guild News-
        letter, which often is cited as SFBAPG
        Newsletter: San Francisco Bay Area
        Puppet Guild Newsletter
Sat Eve Post   Saturday Evening Post

Sat N	Saturday Night
Sat R	Saturday Review
Sat R Lit	Saturday Review of Literature (London)
Sec Ed	Secondary Education
Sch & Com	School and Community
Sch & H	School and Home
Sch Activ	School Activities
Sch Arts	School Arts Magazine
Sch Lib J	School Library Journal
Sch Life	School Life
Schol	Scholastic Magazine
Sci & Inv	Science and Invention
Sci & Mech	Science and Mechanics
Sci Am	Scientific American
Sci Am Sup	Scientific American Supplement
Scrib	Scribner's
Scrib C	Scribner's Century
Sharpe's Lon J	Sharpe's London Journal
Sharpe's Lon Mag	Sharpe's London Magazine
Sierra Ed N	Sierra Educational News
Sight and S	Sight and Sound (London)
Soc M P Eng J	Society of Moving Picture and Television Engineers Journal
Soc Studies	Social Studies
Sold Han M	Soldiers Hand Manual, an irregularly published booklet
Spect	The Spectator
Sp Mono	Speech Monographs
Strand	The Strand Magazine (London)
Studio	Studio Magazine
Studio Imp	Studio Imprints
Sunset	Sunset Magazine (America, west coast area)
T. C. P. Note	Twin City Puppeteers Notebook (see "Periodical" Section)
Teacher J of N C	Teachers Journal of Northern California See Publ Sch J
Tex Outl	Texas Outlook
Theatre	The Theatre
Thea & School	Theatre and School
Thea Arts	Theatre Arts
Thea G M	Theatre Guild Magazine (NYC 1923-39) then called Stage
Thea J	Theatre Journal (Los Angeles)
Thea NBk	Theatre Notebook
Thea R	Theatre Review (N.J. 1940)

Thea W	Theatre World
Thea & Mus N	Theatrical and Musical News
Time	Time Magazine (American) <u>See</u> Times Educ
Times Educ	Times Educational (London)
The Times	The Times Newspaper (London)
The Times Educ Sup	The Times Educational Supplement (London)
The Times Lit Sup	The Times Literary Supplement (London)
Train Sch Bull	Training School Bulletin
Travel	Travel Magazine
TV G	Television Guide Today
TV Mag	T. V. Magazine
T V Guide	Television Guide
T V Guide M	Television Guide Magazine
UNIMA-U. S. A. Newsl	UNIMA International Org. Newsletter for U. S. A.
Univ Hi Sch J	University High School Journal
Univ of Calif Chron	University of California Chronicle
Univ Ottawa R	University of Ottawa Review
Van F	Vanity Fair
Va Gaz	Virginia Gazette (American, 1776). Some copies at Trinity College Lib, Hartford, Conn.
Va J Ed	Virginia Journal of Education
Va Med Mo	Virginia Medical Monthly
Vogue F	Vogue Fashions
Vogue P Bk	Vogue Pattern Book
Volta R	Volta Review
Week R	Weekly Review (London)
West A	Western Arts (Western Arts Assn. Bulletin)
West Monatsh	Westermans Monatschefte
West Speech	Western Speech (Western Assn of Teachers of Speech, Los Angeles)
Westminister J	Westminster Journal (London)
Wis Lib Bull	Wisconsin Library Bulletin
Wil Lib Bull	Wilson's Library Bulletin
Woman H Comp	Woman's Home Companion
World Ch	World Children
World's F	The World's Fair Magazine of different countries where a World's Fair was held, will have adjective or country

World's Fair	World's Fair Magazine (London) with puppet column
World Outl	The World Outlook
World R	World Review
World Tel	World Telegram
World Thea	The World Theatre
World Trav	The World Traveler, see Mentor
Young C	The Young Citizen
Younst V	The Youngstown, Ohio, Vindicator Newspaper
Z Psycho Med	
Psychol	Zeitschrift Fur Psychotherapie Und Medizinische Psychologie (Germany)

Sources Consulted

I have not examined every item in the Guide. Many different people have contributed to this great collection of
material and many, many sources and libraries have assisted
me in the gathering of articles and books and small items.
I have attempted to acknowledge these people. I trust I
have not omitted anyone; if I have I thank them now and will
be glad to mention their name in future volumes and supplements if I am notified.

This section includes the sources that I have used in
all the volumes, to date, but it is constantly being enlarged.

> Note: In this Section only when a date is given thus:
> (1908-1960) it means it has been indexed between
> those dates. It does not mean that the Source
> stopped publication at the last date.
>
> If no date is given, that means that the source
> has been checked as completely as possible.

American Bibliography. Vol 12: by Charles Evans,
  Worcester, Mass: American Antiquarian Society, 1959.
  (1629-1820)

In rare book section of Chapin Lib. at Williams College,
Williamstown, Mass.

American Book Publishing Record. (1960), New York:
  Bowker, 1967.

American Catalogue of Books. by F. Leypoldt, New York:
  Publishers Weekly (1901-1910).

A. L. A. Catalogue. ed by American Lib. Assn. Chicago:
  American Lib. Assn. (1929-1970).

Annual Mag. Subject Index 1900-1941. ed by various editors,
    Boston: Boston Bk. 1941.

This became the Dramatic Index in 1941 and continues by
    that name, as far as 1962, but I found no copies after
    that, so it is checked (1900-1962).

Annals of Opera 1547-1940. by A. Lowenberg Keffer, London:
    Heffer, 1943.

Art of the Puppet, The. by Bill Baird, New York:
    MacMillan, 1965.

Art Index. ed by J. & M. Furlong, New York: Wilson
    (1900-1970).

"Asian Studies; Bibliography of" by H. P. Linton and others
    in Journal of Asian Studies Magazine, 1957-1959, p. 780.

Basic Reference Guide. ed by Winchell.   Chicago:
    American Lib. Assn. (1900-1947).

Bibliographies which are listed in the "Bibliographic" Section
    of this particular Guide which are so indicated with the
    word "indexed".

Bibliography of British Dramatic Periodicals. by Carl J.
    Stratman, London: n publ, 1720-1960.

Bibliography of Costume. ed by M. Miler, New York: Wilson,
    1939.

Bibliography of Speech Education. ed by L. Thonsen and
    E. Fatherson, New York: Wilson, 1939.

Bibliotheca Americana. by O. A. Roorbach (1820-1852).
    New York: Author, 1852.

Checked for first works published in America and the
    first one recorded was 1821, "Pug's Visit to Punch," in
    city of Philadelphia. See also: "Punch and Judy" section.

Bibliographic Catalogue Francais. Paris: Circle De La
    Libre (1935-1968). n. author indicated.

Books Abroad Magazine. Norman, Okla: Univ. of Oklahoma,
    (1927-1968).

Books In Print. New York: Bowker, only (1960-1967) n. author indicated.

British Books In Print. London: Whitaker (1965-1969). See Five Year Cumulative Book List. An Index to the Publishers Trade List Annual.

British Humanities Index. London: Lib. Assn. (1962-67) but this was formerly British Technology Cataloge and was joined by Subject Index to Periodicals which was covered much farther back. See that title.

British Information Service Library. Miss Ruth Isaacs, in NYC.

(British) Educational Puppet Assn Library List. London: E. P. A. , 1969.

British Museum Catalogue. ed by various editors, London: Clowes (1908-1970) and ed by various editors, National British Museum Press.

British National Bibliography, London: Council of British Nat. Bibliog. Ltd. (1950-1969).

British Technology Catalogue. London: London Lib. Assn. From start to 1962, then see British Humanities Index.

Bulletin of Bibliographies and Dramatic Index. New York: Wilson (1933-1962). See Dramatic Bibliography; See Dramatic Index.

Canadian Periodical Index (& Documentary Films). Ottawa: Canadian Library Assn. 1928-1932.

This was a Mimeo publication that I saw and seemed to be interrupted several times.

Card Index Files of all the Libraries and Institutions mentioned in the Preface of this Guide were checked and indexed except for exhaustion of their material on Puppet Plays, Theatres and Ventriloquism except the Yale, Harvard, and Boston City, Libraries which will be covered completely after the publication of Volume I.

Catalogue Géneral de la Libraire Francais. by D. O. Lorenz, Paris: Lib Ancienne Hornoré Champion (1840-1925).

Catalogue Général Des Livres Imprimes De La Bibliotheque
Nationale. Paris: Nationale Imprimerie (1886-1968) n.
author indicated.

Catholic Periodical Index. n. author, New York: Wilson,
from (1930-1969).

Catholic Literature: Guide to. Detroit: Romig, (1888-1962).

Discontinued search as it seemed to have very little
material.

Childhood, American Magazine. (From 1950-69).

Childhood Education Magazine (1961-69).

Chilaren s Catalogue. by S. Andrews, D. Cook, & A. Cowing,
New York: Wilson, 1941 ed and 1951 ed.

These editions were called the "6th" and "8th" but were the
only editions I saw in my research.

Complete Art Reference Catalogue. Boston: Soule Art Co.,
1902 (n author).

Costume Index. ed by I. Monroe and D. Cook, New York:
Wilson, 1937.

Craft Horizons Magazine. From 1959 to date.

Cumulative Book Index. ed by various persons. Minneapolis:
Wilson (1910-1969). See U. S. Catalogue of Books.

Deutsches Bucherverzeichnis. Leipzig. Borfenvereins,
1927-68. n. a. dates from 1911-1968.

Dictionary of Puppetry. by A. R. Philpott, London:
Macdonald, 1969.

Dissertations and Abstracts from 1950 to date.

Drama Magazine. The puppet column work from (1950-1956)
was indexed for me by its author, Jero Magon. The
work by J. J. Hayes in this magazine is not checked
completely.

Dramatic Bibliography. ed by B. Baker, New York: Wilson, 1933-1941. See Dramatic Index; See Bulletin of Bibliography and Dramatic Index.

Dramatic Index. ed by B. Baker, New York: Wilson (1941-1953). See Dramatic Bibliography; See Bulletin of Bibliography and Dramatic Index, which seems to be the last of the three titles for this group of 3 publications.

Doctoral Dissertations Accepted by American Universities. New York: Wilson (1933-1938) and (1954-1957).

There are not very many dissertations on puppets and because of richer fields of research I did not search further.

Doctor's Dissertations, American. ed by D. B. Gilchrist and others, New York: Wilson, back to 1912 from 1934. See Index to American Doctoral Dissertations.

Early American Children's Books from 1682. by A. W. Rosenbach, Portland: Southworth, 1933.

Educational Film Guide. New York, Wilson (1953-1969).

Elementary English Review Magazine. From 1960-1967.

Educational Puppetry Association. (London) Much personally sent by A. R. Philpott, editor of their publication Puppet Post and their files and private listings.

Educational Index. ed by D. R. Carpenter, New York: Wilson (1929-1970)

Essay and General Index. ed by various editors, New York: Wilson (1900-1962).

Federal Theater Bibliographies on Puppets. See also: "Bibliographies" Section and "Federal Theatres" in "Recreation" Section.

Fiction Catalogue. by D. Cook and E. Fidell, New York: Wilson (1941-1946) and then (1951-1965).

Fifty Years of German Drama. by J. Hopkins, n. 1: John Hopkins Press, 1941.

Five Year Cumulative Booklist. (British) London: Whitaker,
1930-1962. See Subject Guide to Books in Print. (eng)
This was a bibliography from 1880 to 1930.

Grade Teacher Magazine. (1960-1969)

Guide to the Performing Arts. (Index) by S. Y. Belknap,
Metuchen, N. J.: Scarecrow, 1960. This index covers
from 1957-1960.

Guide to Free Films 1961.

Guide to the Musical Arts. by S. Y. Belknap, Metuchen,
N. J.: Scarecrow, 1956. This covers from 1953-1956.

Guide to Lists of Master's Theses. by Dorothy M. Black,
Chicago: American Lib. Assn. 1965.

Guide to Bibliographies of Theses. U. S. & Canada. by T. H.
Palfrey and H. E. Coleman, Chicago: American Lib.
Assn. 1936, 1940.

Handbook on Soviet Drama. by H. W. L. Dana, New York:
American Russian Institute 1938.

Handicrafts. See Index to Handicrafts.

Hinrichs' Bucherkatalog. Leipzig: Hinrich (1886-1912).
Exceptionally good German source book.

History of the English Puppet Theatre. by George Speaight,
London: Harrap, k 955 Hobbies Magazine. (1957-1969)

How-to-do-it Books (A Selected Bibliographic Guide). by
R. E. Kingery, New York: Bowker, 1954, and 3rd
revised ed, 1963.

Index to American Doctoral Dissertations. Ann Arbor:
University Microfilms Dept. , University of Michigan
(1955-1962). See Microfilm Abstracts.

This sort of thing should be done for all Universities
and Colleges which are indicated as having any puppet work.
See also: "Colleges" Section. Few Master's Theses and Dissertations are given in the regular sources under title of
"Puppetry". This is because the wording of the titles of most
such works indicate other than Dramatic, or Art or Puppet
Department work as the most direct subject matter concerned,

thus they are extremely difficult to sift out of Educational, Therapy, etc. works.

Index to Handicrafts, Model Making & Workshop Projects. by E. Lovell & H. Hall, Boston: Flaxon, 1936; supplements of 1948, 1950.

The supplements by A. Winslow & A. Turner (1950-1961).

Index to Plays. See Plays Index.

Index to Plays in Collection. by J. H. Ottemiller, 2nd ed. Washington, D. C.: Scarecrow Press, 1951. (This publishing company is now at Metuchen, New Jersey).

Instructor, The. Magazine indexed for (1960-1969).

International Index to Periodicals. ed by various editors, New York: Wilson (1916-1969). Name was changed to Social Sciences & Humanities Index. from 1966- .

Jr. League Catalogue of Puppet & Marionette Work. New York: Assn. of the Jr. Leagues of America, Inc. 1963 ed. , and Supplement. 1968. No author is listed. This is mostly concerned with plays.

Kasyer's Bucher-Lexikon. 1841-1910.

Leipzig: Herm Tauchnitz, yrly. under Kasperl Marionette Puppen

Library of Congress Catalogue Index. (Subject Titles) of Puppetry, Shadows, Marionettes and Punch; (1950-1969)

The Catalogue Index is not subject-indexed before this time and is almost impossible to investigate. However, I looked under authors who wrote many puppet books for additional material by them.

Mask Magazine. Volumes 5, 5, 6 are indexed.

National Education Association Journal. (1957-1969)

Nepal Bibliography. by H. B. Wood, Eugene, Oregon: American Nepal Ed. Foundation, 1959. (An educational adventure by the Educational Advisor to His Majesty's Governor of Nepal, 1953-1959). This being near Tibet and concerned with the arts of this country I found a few very old items.

New York Times Index. ed by that paper, New York: N Y
Times (1913-1969) and Micro-Films of actual papers
which had questionable material was further researched.

Opera News Magazine (1959-1962).
This will be exhausted for the "Musical" Section of
Volume III of this Guide.

Puppet Files on Clippings, etc. In all Libraries mentioned
in Preface except Yale, Harvard, and Boston City Lib.

Philippine Islands: A Catalogue of Printed Materials Relating to, compiled by D. V. Welsh, Chicago: Newberry
Library, 1959.

This is only to be found at that library, it was
mimeographed,dates from (1519-1900).

Play Index. comp. by I. T. E. Firkins, Bronx: Wilson, 1927,
and supplement of 1937.

This dates from (1800-1927, then 1927-1927) compiled by
D. H. West and D. M. Peake: Wilson, 1952.

This dates from (1949-1952) compiled by E. A. Fidell
and D. M. Peake: Wilson 1960.

This dates from (1953-1960).

Puppet Theatre in America--1524-1949. by Paul McPharlin,
New York: Harpers, 1949 (See Key No. 2).

Puppetry. (1930-1947) See "Periodicals" Section.

Puppet Master (England). Only scattered volumes because
not yet available but by publication of Vol. II, of Guide
many more will have been indexed (1950-1955) and
beginning (1969 to date).

Puppet Theatre of the Modern World. comp. by "UNIMA",
Boston: Plays, 1965. See (Key No. 2).

Puppetry Journal. ed. by Vivian Michael, See also "Periodical Section. Indexed from start to 1969.

Many of the earlier Grapevine and Grapevine Telegraph
(branches of this Journal) and many of the different
Guilds, of the "Puppeteers of America" group, Newsletters

have been indexed. Not exhausted in any sense of the
word.

Private and Personal letters and contacts: From and with
master puppeteers and amateur puppeteers, librarians,
therapists, Drs. and teachers, social workers and
psychological workers, ministers and playground directors.
I thank them all for even the few bits of information
which they gave. They are too numerous to list except
for the large lists.

Reader's Guide & Pool's Index to Periodicals. New York:
Wilson 1802-1970.

Pool's being the early name for The Reader's Guide.

Reader's Guide to Prose Fiction. by Elbert Lenrow, New
New York: Appleton, 1940.

Reference Catalogue of Current Literature (British) London:
London: Whitaker, 1940-1962.

School Arts. Magazine 1960-1970.

School Life. Magazine (1918-1950).

Social Sciences & Humanities Index. ed by various editors,
New York: Wilson, 1966 to date. Formerly called
International Index to Periodicals. See that name.

Speech Index. ed by R. B. Sutton, New York: Wilson,
1935-1955. Supplements No. 1 and No. 2 bringing it up
to 1961.

Speech Monographs, Index. ed by C. Simons, Ann Arbor:
University of Michigan (1936-1947). Located at University
of Connecticut (at Storrs) Library.

Speech Therapy Magazine (1935-1941) London:

This is a publication of the British Society of Speech
Therapists, with Sir I. Pittman and Son as publishers.
I believe it is still active. I will attempt to exhaust it
For Volume II of this Guide.

Subject Guide to Books in Print. (England) London: Whitaker,
See Reference Catalog of:

Subject Guide to United States Government Publications. by
H. S. Hirshberg & C. H. Melinat, Chicago: American
Lib. Assn. (1947-1967)

Subject Collections. by Lee Ash, New York: Bowker, 1958
and Supplement, 1961-1967.

Subject Guide to Books in Print. (American) ed by S. L.
Brakken, New York: Bowker (1957-1968)

Subject Readings: Library of Congress. ed by M. V. Quat-
tlebraum, Washington: Lib. of Congress, 1957.

Subject Index of Books to 1880. by R. A. Peddie, New
Series A-Z, London: Grafton, 1948.

This went back within the one book group by year but I
followed only back to 1933 as there was little material.

Subject Index of the Christian Science Monitor (1961-1967)
Boston: Ch Sci Mon, 1967.

Not available much before this time in this type of publication but much material can be sifted out with serious
research work previous to these years.

Subject Index to Periodicals, 1931-1965. (British) ed by
Lib. Assn., London: British Lib. Assn.

Theatre Magazine (England) (Ag. 1878-Jan 1879) Vol. 1.

This was a monthly review publication, found bound in
the Hartford, Connecticut City Library.

Theatre Arts. Magazine (1918-1967)

The Theatre Handbook. ed by Bernard Sobel, New York:
Crown, 1940.

Theatre and Allied Arts Index. by B. M. Baker, New York:
Wilson, 1952.

Thailand Bibliography. by J. Brown Mason and H. C. Parish,
Bibliographic Series No. 4, Gainesville, Fla.: Dept. of
Ref. and Bibliog., Univ. of Florida Libraries, 1958.

Theses Card Indexes and Files of Colleges and Universities
mentioned in Preface. Yale, Harvard, are not completed

by publication of Vol. I of the Guide, but I have had no
indication leading me to suspect material would be available at the two universities.

University of Connecticut Films Catalogue, 1962-63. Storrs,
  Conn.: Audio Visual Dept. 1963.

  Very difficult to sift out, but material is indicated as
  being rich if much research is done in all Film
  catalogues.

University of Connecticut Films for Teaching Catalogue.
  Storrs: Audio-Visual Dept. (1964-1967)

United States Catalogue of Books. ed by various persons, New
  York: Wilson (1905-1910). Then became Cumulative Book
  Index. (1910-1969)

United States Office of Education Bibliography of Research
  Studies in Education. Washington, D. C. by that office
  (1926-1937)

Union List of Serials. Bronx, New York: Wilson,.....
  nothing given.

Variety. Magazine. (1961-1962) done with careful research
  but the material, which is buried, but there, would take
  much research. Such other periodicals of this particular
  style, such as Cue, Players, World Theatre will bear
  deep research.

Vertical File Service Catalogue. ed by various persons, New
  New York: Wilson (1937-1947)

Medical Source Material*

American Journal of Orthopsychiatry. ed by L. G. Lowrey,
  Menosha, Wisconsin: Banter (1936-1962)

  Note: These periodicals were researched article by article
  for period indicated. The material is not given under
  "Puppetry Vocabulary Words", but it is there. It seems
  to be listed in most medical periodicals under such
  headings as those listed below.

  I have checked the enclosed material under all these
  ___ headings, article by article for years indicated.
*Additional Medical Source Material to be published in Vol. II.

Names used where Puppetry work existed:
Child Play
Doll Play
Recreation
Therapy
Children
Psychiatric Social Work
Speech Therapy
Structural Play
Psychodrama (very rich in material)
Therapeutic Play Techniques
Hobbies
Sociodrama (very rich in material)
Projective Techniques (rich in material)

Medical work or publications of articles by the following Doctors will probably be concerned with doll play or a form of puppet work in many cases. They of course have written on other subjects but have been much interested in this form of therapy. It is suggested research into their writings might be worth while.

Dr. H. R. Bender, much puppet work in the USA by:
Dr. Loretta Bender
Dr. Sylvia Cassell
Dr. J. H. Conn
Dr. E. Cheatle
Dr. A. D. Faber
Dr. David Levey
Dr. M. H. Pintler
Dr. R. R. Sears and Dr. P. S. Sears
Dr. J. C. Soloman
Dr. A. G. Woltman (In Eng.)
Dr. M. L. Hawkey

Chapter I: Historical Background of World Puppetry

A.   Bibliographies of Puppet Literature

"Adventures With Puppets Symposium, Bibliography," Prog Ed, 5:9-20, Jan.-Mr, 1928.

Ager, S.   Puppets of Time.   London, Lane, 1930, p. 16.

Anderson, Madge.   Heroes of the Puppet Stage.   New York, Harcourt, 1923. p. 415-20.

Association of Junior Leagues of America, Children's Theatre Dept. Catalogues. New York, Assn. of Jr. Leagues of Am. Inc. Puppet Plays Catalogue, Harvard Univ. Lib. 1946.

Baring, M.   Puppet Show of Memory.   London, Heinemann, 1922.   Bibliog. at end.

Batchelder, Marjorie.   The Puppet Theatre Handbook.   New York, Harper, 1947.   p 261-79.

---Rod Puppets and the Human Theater.   Columbus, Ohio State Univ. Press, 1947.   Bibliog. at end.

---and Vivian Michael.   Hand-and-Rod Puppets.   Columbus, Ohio State Univ. Press, 1947.   Bibliog. at end.

Becker, May L.   "The Reader's Guide,"   Sat R Lit, 7:933, Je 27, 1931.

---"The Reader's Guide,"   Sat R Lit, 9:494, Mr 18, 1933.

---"The Reader's Guide,"   Sat R Lit, 9:667, Je 24, 1933.

Besely, Jindrick.   Prirucka Ceskehe Leutkare.   Prague, Hlvata, 1914. p. 27-53.

Boehn, Max von.   Puppen-Spiele.   trans. by Josephine Nicoll, , London, Harrap, 1932.   Very extensive and valuable bibliog. at end.

Brennan, Dorothy (comp).   Puppets and Mask-Theatre Technique, No. 33.   U. S. Fed. Thea. Project, Nat. Serv. Bur. Public., Thea. Technique--U. S. Fed. Works Agency, W. P. A., New York; Fed. Thea. Projects, Dec., 1937. At Oberlin Univ. Lib and in NN.

Bunin, Louis.   "The New Russian Puppet Theatre Films," New Thea, 2:20-21, D, 1935. Bibliog. of non-commercial film producing org.

Burke, Isabel M. "Puppets and Puppetry," Wil Lib Bull,
10:639-40, Je, 1936. Intern. bibliog.
Carolyn, Rose. (comp). A Bibliography of Marionette Plays.
2nd ed. U. S. Fed. Thea. Project, No. 12. Mimeo., Bur.
of Research and Public., U. S. Fed. Works Agency,
W. P. A., New York: Fed. Thea. Projects, D, 1937, 52
plays.
   At Document Room, Deering Lib. Northwestern Univ.
and in NN. It has comments, notes and synopses.
---Same as above but with a different heading on the title
page and an earlier date is filed under the "Government
Works" rather than "Puppets" in NN under: United States
Works Project Administration Dept. Federal Theatre Projects Office: A Bibliography of Marionette Plays. Comp.
by R. Carolyn, U. S. Fed. Thea. Project No. 12, Mimeo.,
Nat. Play Bur., Dist. of Columbia Project. W. P. A.,
New York: Fed. Thea. Projects, 1936.
---Puppets, Masks and Shadows. U. S. Fed. Thea. Pro-
ject, Mimeo., Bur. of Research and Public., U. S. Fed.
Works Agency, W. P. A., New York: Fed. Thea. Projects,
1936. A Dept. of Playgrounds of Dist. of Columbia Pro-
ject. at NN.
Cavalle, A. S. "The Puppetry Collection of Paul McPharlin
in the Detroit Institute of Art Museum," Pupp J, 4(4):
7-10, 20, 1935.
Chambers, Sir E. K. The Medieval Stage. Vol. II, London,
Oxford, 1903. Extensive puppet bibliog. at end.
Chicago Park District Bibliography on Simple Puppets. ed,
Chicago Parks Dept. Theatre Division, Chicago: Parks
Dept. Sept., 1938.
Clark, B. H. Study of Modern Drama. New York, Apple-
ton, 1925. Bibliog. at end.
(Clipping File Bibliography) New York Public Library The-
atre Subject Headings. Boston: Hall, 1960.
Coleman, Henry E. Marionettes and Puppets. Urbana,
Library School., Univ. of Illinois, D 20, 1934. (Mimeo.)
At Deering Lib., Northwestern Univ. in "Puppet File."
---A Bibliography on Pantomime: Punch and Judy, Shadows,
Marionettes or Puppet Shows. N 12, 1926. (Mimeo.)
At Deering Lib., Northwestern Univ., in "Puppet File."
Craig, Gordon. "The Mask Puppet Index," Marionette 1
(4):31, Ap 1918.
---"The Complete Mask Puppet Index," Marionette 1(5):
91-93, My, 1918. Bibliog. of all puppet articles in nine
issues of The Mask Magazine.
   Also in "Puppeteers Library," Thea Arts, 12:527-28,
Jl, 1928.
Crothers, J. Frances. Puppeteer's Bibliographic Handbook.

Unpublished Master's essay. Evanston, Northwestern Univ., Deering Lib. 1942.
Detroit Inst. of Art Ref. Lib. File on Puppets. Detroit, Detroit Museum of Art, 1950-
    The Puppet Library is considered the "Nat. Center of American Puppet Information." It is more often referred to as, "The Paul McPharlin Memorial Puppet Library and Collection." The collection was donated by Mr. McPharlin, by will, and contains most of his private library and writings, many of which are quite rare. Some things remain in Mrs. McPharlin's personal library. This collection was indexed for this book, in its original condition previous to removal to Detroit.
Dunn, Louise. see W. H. Mills.

Era Almanack. Published by Era Magazine London, issued irregularly, 1838-1939. In NN.

Far Eastern Bibliography. comp. by G. E. Gaskill and J. J. Nolde, Ithaca: Cornell Univ. Press, 1951.
Fatherson, F. See L. Thonssen

Federal Theatre Puppet Project-Marionette Group. U. S. Fed. Thea. Project, Mimeo., Bur. of Research and Public., U. S. Fed. Works Agency, W. P. A., Mr. Robert Warfield, Supervisor. Published at 1500 Eye St., NW, Washington, D. C. : Fed. Thea. Projects, 1937.
    Ten pages of plays are included in this general bibliog.
Fletcher, Ian K. "Puppet Bibliography Check List of Books," Bk Coll Q, 12:22-31, 1933.
Follansbee, F. Puppet Show. Philadelphia, Dorrance, 1932.
Gaskill, G. E. See Far Eastern Bibliography.

Gervais, André C. Marionnettes et Marionnetistees de France. Paris, Berdas, 1947, bibliog. at end.
"Greek, Roman and Shakespearian era of bibliographical puppet material," in G. Speaight, Hist. Eng. Pupp. Thea. p. 273-82.
Hasty, C. G. "Puppets and Marionettes." Cue, 10:33-36 My, 1931.
Heller, O. "Puppet Bibliography," in Washington Univ. Studies, Social and Philosophical Sciences. NS, No. 2. St. Louis, Washington Univ, 1931, p. 122-50, 155-72.
Inverarity, R. B. A Manual of Puppetry. Portland, Binford, 1938, p. 215-80.

"Javanese Shadow Material in England, a Bibliography,"
Mans, S, 1957, p. 131-33.
Jacob, George. Erwahnungen des Schattentheaters in der
Welt Litteratur. 3rd ed., Berlin, Mayer, 1906. Bibliog.
dates from 11th Century.
---Bibliographie über das Schattentheater. Erlanger, Ger-
many, Junge and Sohn, 1902.
---Geschichte des Schattentheaters im Morgen und Abend-
land. Hanover, Lafaire, 1925. Bibliog. at end.
Jeanne, Paul. Bibliographie des Marionettes. Paris,
Lévy, 1926.
Joseph, Helen Haiman. Book of Marionettes. rev. ed.,
New York, Viking, 1931. p. 192-202.
Kredel, F. Dolls and Puppets of the 18th Century. Lex-
ington, Gravesend, 1958. Bibliog. at end.
Leslie, D. Puppets Parade. London, Lane, 1932.

Library Association. "Puppet Bibliography," County Li-
brary's Section on Modern Drama. London, The Library
Assoc., 1939. p. 51-53 [sic]
McDonough, F. D. "List of Books for Puppeteers," El
Eng Rev, 9:250-51, D, 1932.
McPharlin, Paul. "Producers in American Puppetry-1930,"
Pupp, 13-14: 1942-43.
---Puppets in America, 1739 to Today. Birmingham, Pup-
petry Imprints, 1936.
---"Puppet Chronicles, 1916-1941." Players, 18:22-23,
Jan, 1941.
---The Puppet Theatre in America, 1524-Now. New York,
Harper, 1949, p. 396-483.
---Repertory of Marionette Plays. New York, Viking,
1929. see also "Plays" sec. for other bibliog. of plays.
Martinovitch, Nicholas N. The Turkish Theatre. New York,
Theatre Arts, 1933, p 125.
Meilink, Wm. Bibliographie von het poppenspel. Uitgave 'Ned-
erlandse Vereniging voor het Poppenspel,' Amsterdam 1965.
Mills, Winifred H. and Louise Dunn. Marionettes, Masks
and Shadows. New York, Doubleday, 1928. p. 241-62.
National Recreation Association. Bibliography on Mario-
nettes in Recreation Work. New York, Nat. Rec. Assn., 1937.
Nicoll, Josephine. see Max von Boehn.

Nikolais, Alwin T. (comp) Index to Puppetry, 1910-1938.
ed. for the Parks Dept., Hartford, Conn., as a W. P. A.
Project. Rec. Div. Hartford Parks Dept., 1938.
(mimeo.)
    Also published as Connecticut Index to Puppetry, 1910-

1938. Comp by A. Nikolais. U. S. Fed. Thea. Project, Mimeo. , Bur. of Research and Public. , Hartford, Conn. Parks Project, U. S. Fed. Works Agency, W. P. A. , New York: Fed. Thea. Projects, 1938.

Nolde, J. J. see Far Eastern Bibliography.

Park, F. "Puppeteers Library," Thea Arts, 12:527-28, Jl, 1928.

Peixette, E. C. "Marionettes and Puppet Shows, Past and Present," Scrib. 33:341-48, Mr, 1903.

Philpott, A. R. Dictionary of Puppetry, London, Macdonald, 1969.

Pischel, Richard. Home of the Puppet Play. trans. , M. C. Tawney. London, Luzac, 1902. (From an address. Wittenberg: Friedrichs Univ. Hall, Jl 2, 1900.)

Proctor, Romain. "Notes on the Proctor Puppet Library," Players, 34(3):51, D, 1957.

Ransome, Grace. "Punch and Judy's Ancestry," Thea and Sch, 7:9-12, D, 1928.

---Puppets For Amateurs. Hayward, Calif, Author, 1930. p. 26-39. Mimeo. at NN.

---(comp) Puppets and Shadows, A Bibliography. Boston, Faxon, 1931.

Reisdorf, Helen L. (comp) Marionettes and Puppets--A Bibliography. ed. for the Detroit (Michigan) Pub. Lib. (Mimeo.) Detroit, Pub. Lib. , 1929.

Robinson, Francis. "The Paul McPharlin Book Collection," Pupp J, 4(1):23-24, 1952.

Sanford, A. "A List of Books about Marionettes," Lib J, 54:909, N 1, 1929.

Schmidt, Dr. Hugo F. Aleriei Kasparstüke. Eine Bibliographie des Handpuppentheaters. Leipzig, 1929.

Sibbald, R. S. "Some Books about the Marionette." Unpublished Ph. D. dissertation. Philadelphia, Univ. of Pennsylvania, 1936.

---Marionettes in the North of France. New York, Oxford, 1936. Bibliog. at end.

--- "Marionettes in the North of France." Philadelphia, Univ. of Pennsylvania, 1934.

Simon's Directory of Theatrical Materials, Services & Information. 3rd ed. rev. ; 1963-1965. New York, Package Publicity Service, 1965. p. 105-06. A list of manufacturers of puppets in the U. S. A.

Speaight, George. The History of the English Puppet Theatre. London, Harrap, 1955, p. 272-312.
    This sig. m includes a list of "Puppet Showmen in England, 1600-1914" p. 313-24. and "Plays Performed by Puppets in England," p. 324-43.

Stead, P. J. Mr. Punch. London, Evans Bros. , 1950.

Stephens, T. E. "A Bibliography of Puppetry," Unpublished Master's dissertation. Seattle, Univ. of Washington, c 1940.

Terwilliger, George (ed.) 101 Selected Plays for a Puppet Theatre. Publ. No. 44 U. S. Fed. Thea. Project. Comp. by Community Serv. Dept., Supervisor, I. A. Rubenstein. New York, Fed. Thea. Projects, Ag, 1938. Mimeo.

Thonssen, L. and F. Fatherson (ed.) "Puppets" in their Bibliography of Speech Education, 1900-39. New York, Wilson, 1939, p. 352-66.

U. S. Library of Congress, Division of Bibliographies. The Division of Bibliography Checklist on Marionettes and Puppets. No. 940. Washington, D. C., Gov. Print. Off., Ag. 25, 1925.

Warsage, Rodolphe de. Histoire du Celebre Theatre Liegoeis de Marionnetees. Bruxelles, G. Vanoest, 1905, p. 18-21. A list of French magazine articles.

West, W. see A. E. Wilson

Whanslaw, H. W. A Bench Book of Puppetry. London, Heinemann, 1949.

---A Second Bench Book of Puppetry. London, Heinemann, 1957.

Wilkinson, Walter. Puppets Through America. London, G. Bles, 1938. Bibliog. at end.

Wilson, A. E. and W. West. Penny Plain, Two Pence Colored. New York, Macmillan, 1932, p. 114-16. Concerned with English "Toy Theatres and Prints."

Zwickley, Fern. List of Puppet Books. Ashville, Puppetry Journal. Mimeo.

B. General History of Puppets of All Kinds

* * *

The items that follow on this page are "notices" of very early puppet shows in America, hinting at first dates of such published material.

There will be no section on "Notices-Shows-Billings, or Advertisements" of, or by, companies in this bibliography except for this page, which is considered as a "sample page."

Although puppets are mentioned as early as 1524 the earliest American item found that was purely about puppetry was published in 1709. The notices are:

1. "...puppets are playing on Barbadoes Island and Leward Island..." quoted from J. Oldmixon, British Empire in America. Vol. II, London, 1709, p 127-28.
2. An anonymous article in Pupp J, 16(6):25, M, 1965, suggests that, "This following item may have been America's first published advertisement. 'Pantomime, 1739, by the Henry Holden puppets is to be in Queen Heads Tavern...'"
3. According to America's outstanding puppet historian, Paul McPharlin, in his history, Pupp. Thea. Am., p. 41; the first record he found of a puppet show was in the Boston Chronicle, (Mr 14, 1768). "Show at the sign of the Coach and Horses."
4. "Williamsburg Show by P. Gardiner," Va. Gaz., Ap. 13, 1769.
5. "Perspective Theater," Pennsylvania Journal, My 12, 1773.
6. "Ricketts Amphitheatre and Shades," New York Minerva, My 12, and Je 21, 1795.
7. "Genety's Show of 350 Chinese Shades," New York Gazette, Jan. 21, 1796.
8. "Circus Garden Theater, T. White Puppeteer," New York Her, Jl 1, and 2, 1796.

9. "Italian Fantoccini at Peale's Museum, New York City,"
    Commercial Advertiser of New York City, S 25, 1837
    and same item and public. for the date of O 14, 1837.
10. "Fantoccinis," Phil Publ. Led, Feb. 23, 1846 same
    title, same public. Mr. 5, 1846.
11. "Fantoccini Show," San Fra. D Eve Bull, Je 29, 1857.

12. "German Puppet Shows in New York City," Staatz-
    Zeitung, Mr. 16, 1873.
13. "German Puppet Show," Long Island Star, Ap 4, 1879.

* * *

Addison, Joseph. "The Puppet Show," a Latin poem in his
    book, Musarum Anglicanarum Analecta. Vol. II, London,
    no publ., 1699. Trans. in G. Speaight's, Hist. Eng.
    Pupp. Thea. p 88-90.
        Important to see "No. 37-Note," p 284 in Hist. Eng.
    Pupp Thea. concerning the many trans. and ed. of this
    item which is historically of great import.
Alber, Maurice, pseud. Theatre de la Foire. Paris, no
    publ., 1900.
Alden, C. S. See Ben Jonson.

Alexandre, Arsène. See A. Tavernier.

"Alfred Lunt presents--Penny Plain-Tupence Colored," Thea.
    Arts, 31:48-49, Jan, 1947.
Allen, Arthur B. Puppetry and Puppet Plays. London,
    Allman, 1937.
Andersen (Hans Christian)--Puppet Showman, ed. by Paul
    McPharlin, N. Y., Blue Ox, 1941. Rev. trom trans. by H.
    W. Duiken, 1851.
Anderson, D. "The Jewell Mannikins--Very Early Ameri-
    can Marionettes," Pupp J, 12(1):3-4, 1960.
Anderson, Gayle M. "Puppets and the Commedia Dell
    'Arte," Pupp J, 17(2):6-8, 1965.
Anderson, Madge. The Heroes of the Puppet Stage. New
    York, Harcourt, 1923.
Apuleius. De Mundo II, 351 ... about 100 A. D... [sic] No
    translator listed but liberal translation of material on this
    topic is made in Speaight's, Hist. Eng. Pupp. Thea. p.
    25, 275 "No. 8 Note"
Archbold, G. "Puppetry Through the Ages," Design, 38:
    3-10, My, 1936.
---"Puppetry Through the Ages," in Book of Puppetry, ed.
    by F. Payant. Columbus, Design, 1936.

---"Notes on Puppets--Puppets in America," Four Arts, Jan-Mr. 1935.

Aronson, Boris. "Long Forgotten Magic Lantern," Interiors, 108:84-95, D, 1946.

Athenaeus. The Deinosophists. I. 1-19E [sic] No translator listed but liberal translation of material on this topic is made in Speaight's, Hist. Eng. Pupp. Thea., p 25, "No-5 Note" p 275.

Austin, G. L. "Common Man in English Drama of the 18th Century." Unpublished Master's essay. Kent, O., Kent State Univ., 1947.

Aveline, C. "Marionettes de Shakespeare et Vraies Marionettes," L'Europe Nouvelle, 16:182, F, 1925.

Avery, V. "Music History for the Marionette Theater," Pupp J, 2:2-6, 1950.

Babington, John. Pyrotechnia. London, no publ., 1635.
     In British Museum. Early publication concerning the "Castle-type" puppet stages used in Eng. Item referred to in Pupp, 14:62, 1945.

Baird, Bill. The Art of the Puppet. New York, Macmillan, 1965.
     Early Greek, Roman and Indian puppetry is well illus. Sig. m. for 20th century history.

Baker, D. E., I. Reed and S. Jones. Biographia Dramatica. Rev. ed. London, Longman's, 192. passim.

Barnum, P. T. Struggles and Triumphs. Vol. I, New York, Macmillan, 1930. p 195.

Baskerville, C. R. The Elizabethan Jig. Chicago, Univ. of Chicago Press, 1929. passim.

Batchelder, Marjorie. "Our American Puppet Theater," Pupp J, 18(2):3-5, 1966.

---"Rod Puppets and the Human Theatre," Unpublished Ph. D. dissertation. Columbus, Ohio State Univ., 1942. Revu. of "Rod Puppets and the Human Theatre Dissertation," by H. R. Walley, Pupp, 18:7, My, 1947.

---Rod Puppets and the Human Theatre. Grad. School Monograph Contribution in Fine Arts No 3. Columbus, Ohio State Univ. Press, 1947.
     Revu of Rod Puppets and the Human Theatre. N Y Her Trib W Bk Revu, Feb, 1947. p 10.
     Revu of Rod Puppets and the Human Theatre. Wis Lib Bull, 43:51, Mr 1947.
     Revu of Rod Puppets and the Human Theatre, by Paul McPharlin, Thea Arts, 31:70 Ag, 1947.
     Revu of Rod Puppets and the Human Theatre, San Fra Chron, Ap 13, 1947. 11 w, p 20.

---Puppetry, a Backward Glance and a Forward Look,"

Pupp J, 20(2):11-15, 1968.

See also V. Michael.

Bates, Walter. "The Prisoner Puppeteer," in The Mysterious Stranger, or Memoirs of Henry More Smith. New Haven, Yale Univ. Press, 1817.

Baumgardner, Ernestine. "Life of the People as Reflected in the Comic Drama of the Times." An Honor's dissertation. Kent, O., Kent State Univ., 1940, passim.

Beaumont, Cyril W. "The Marionettes." Studio, 1: Ap-May, 1919. A special number on puppets.

---The Marionettes. A Studio Imprint. New York, Viking, 1919.

---History of Harlequin. London, Beaumont, 1926. p 133-47; rev. ed., New York, Blom, 1967.

---"Puppets and the Puppet Stage." Studio, 124, Winter 1938. A Special Number on Puppets, ed by C. G. Holme.

---Puppets and the Puppet Stage. New York, Viking, 1938. rev. ed 1958.

Revu. of Puppets and the Puppet Stage, by C. R. C., Conno, 103:115, Feb. 1939.

Revu. of Puppets and the Puppet Stage, by Walter Crane, Thea Arts, 23:231, Mr 2, 1939.

---Puppets and Puppetry. New York, Viking, 1958.

Beckmann, Johann. A History of Inventions and Discoveries. trans. by W. Johnson. Vol. III., London, Walker, 1814. passim.

First edition London, 1797 in British Museum. Very sig. m. because of mention of Father Lupi's notations on the history of puppetry.

See also Father Antonio M. Lupi.

Bernard, John. Retrospection of America, 1797-1811. New York, Harper, 1887. p 52, and passim. in Brit. Museum.

---Retrospection of the Stage. London, R. Bentley, 1830. passim.

Bicknel, Frank. See Frances B. Carpenter

Bieber, Margaret. "History of the Greek and Roman Theatre-Masks to Mimes and Punch," Unpublished Master's dissertation. Princeton, Princeton Univ., 1939, illus.

Bingham, Jane. "History of Marionettes," Leisure, 4:35-37, My 1937.

Blattner, Gera. "Report on a French Puppet Theatre, 1939-'48 and Art Researches of this Experimental Puppet Theatre," Pupp 7:47, 1936.

Bleton, Auguste. See M. Duplateau.

Blickle, Peg. "Puppeteers of America--History," Pupp J, 5(1):3-6, 1953.
---"General Puppet History," Pupp J, 5(3):3-5, 25-26, 1953.
Boehn, Max von. Puppen-Spiele. 2 Vols., Munich, Bruckmann, 1929.
---Dolls and Puppets. trans. by J. Nicoll into 1 Vol. London, Westerman, 1930, rev., London, Harrap, 1932; New York, McKay, 1932.
Revu. Puppen-Spiele, Thea Arts, 14:532, Je 1930.

Revu. Dolls and Puppets, Pupp, 3:101-02. 1932.
Revu. Dolls and Puppets, by M. B. Wilson, Carnegie Mag, 31:352-53, D, 1957.
---Dolls and Puppets. rev. ed., trans. by J. Nicoll. New York, Branford, c 1960 and New York, Cooper, 1967.
    Quite a few changes from the first issue of Puppen-Spiele. This is very important history and the different editions give added information of importance.
Bostick, W. A. Puppets, Past and Present. Detroit, Detroit Institute of Art, Jl, 1962, illus.
Boswell, Eleanore. The Restoration Court Stage, 1660-1702. Cambridge, Harvard Univ. Press, c 1932, passim.
Revu of The Restoration Court Stage. Pupp, 3:105, 1932.
---"The Puppet Theatre," Studio, 133:176, Je, 1947.
Boulton, W. B. The Amusements of Old London. London, Nimmo, 1901, passim.
Bowie, A. G. "Story of Punch and Judy," Theatre, 3:17-24, Jan 1, 1884.
Bragdon, Claude F. "Mickey Mouse and What He Means," Scrib, 96:40-43, Jl, 1934.
    Note: This will be only item on "Animated Cartoons" as this is not true puppet form when done in the non-stop-action method.
Brammal, E. "Puppet Panorama," Studio, 154:106-09, O, 1957.
Braybrooke, Lord. See S. Pepys.

Brennan, Dorothy. Puppets and Masks--Theatre Techniques, No. 3. U. S. Fed. Thea. Project, Mimeo. Public. No. 331, Nat. Serv. Bur. U. S. Fed. Works Agency, W. P. A., New York, Fed. Thea. Projects, D, 1937.
Broman, Nellie E. "Historical Sketches," Pupp, 8:75, 1937.
---"Historical Sketches," Pupp, 9:73, 1938.
Bromley, Bob. "Grand Old Lady of Puppetry--Early Calif." Pupp Life, Aug, 1968. p. 7-8.

Brooks, G. S. "Memoiries of Marionettes," Cent, 111: 576-83, Mr 1926.

Brooks, Van Wyck. The Flowering of New England. New York, Dutton, 1936, p. 310-34. The John L. Motley puppets of early Am.

Brown, E. H. "Puppet People; Women, First National Exposition," Independent Woman, 18:66, Mr, 1939.

Brown, Forman G. Punch's Progress. New York, Macmillan, 1936. History of his Co., "Yale Puppeteers."
Revu. of Punch's Progress. Thea Arts, 20:567, Jl, 1936.

Brown, J. MacMillan. The Riddle of the Pacific. Boston, Small, 1925, p. 142. Puppetry of Easter Island.

Bufano, Remo. The Show Book of Remo Bufano. New York, Macmillan, 1929.
Revu. of the Show Book of Remo Bufano. by Carl Craer, Thea Arts, 14:317-18, Ap 1930.

---"Puppets of Sicily, a History," Thea G M, 7:28-31 S, 1930.

---"Marionettes Make A New Entrance," Pupp, 2:22-24, 1931.

---Remo Bufano's Book of Puppetry, ed. by Arthur Richmond, New York, Macmillan, 1950, p 1-10.

---Be a Puppet Showman. New York, Century, 1933.

Burger, J. "New Light on Old Mr. Puppet," Sch Arts, 57:31-33, Jan, 1958.

Burke, Isabel M. "Puppets And Puppetry," Wil Lib Bul, 10:639-40, Je, 1936. Bibliog.

Burnet, T. and G. Duckett. Second Tale of a Tub, or History of Robert Powell Puppet Showman of England. London, no publ., 1715.
In British Museum; a satire on "Scouting publications" of Sir Powell about puppetry.

Bussell, Jan. The Puppet Theater. London, Faber, 1946.
Revu of the Puppet Theatre. Studio, 133:176, Je, 1947.

---The Model Theater. London, Dobson, 1948. Sig. m. on the Paper-puppet types of Eng.

---Puppets And I. London, Faber, 1950.

---Puppet's Progress. London, Faber, 1953. Autobiography.

---Through Wooden Eyes. London, Faber, 1956.
Revu of Through Wooden Eyes, Players, 34:105, D, 1957.

Cain, Alice. see M. E. Flexner.

Calhoun, Lucy. "Another Venture in Puppets," Drama, 11: 7-9, O, 1920.

Calthrop, A. "An Evening with Italian Marionettes,"
Theatre, 1:244-48, My 1, 1884.
Calvi, E. "Marionettes of Rome," Bellman, Jan. 20, 1917,
p 69-71.
Camparden, Emile. Spectacle de la Foire, 1877. Paris,
Berger, 1877. 2 vols.
Carlton, Helen. "Puppet Show at Cooper Union," N Y Her
Tribune, Sun., N 27, 1949.
Carmet, Carl. "Puppetry 1931," Thea Arts, 16:129-36,
Feb, 1932.
Carpenter, Francis B.   Six Months at The White House.
(Frank Bicknell)   New York, Hurd & Houghton, 1867.
In British Museum.
Chambers, E. K. The Medieval Stage. Vol. II, London.
Oxford, 1903, passim.
Chambers, Robert (ed). The Book of Days. London, Cham-
bers, 1863, passim, revised several times. In British
Museum; very sig. m. scattered through these listings.
Charles, William. see "Punch" Section. One of the earlier
puppet books in Am.
Chesnais, Jacques. Histoire Génerale des Marionettes.
Paris, Bordas, 1947. In Harvard Univ. Lib.
Chiesa, Carroll, Della. Puppet Parade. London, Long-
man's, 1932.
Child, T. "A Christmas Mystery in the 15th Century,"
Harpers, 78:59-77, D, 1888. Valuable illus (Use of pup-
pets in "mystery" productions was indicated, see "Punch"
Section under "Harlequinate."
Clark, D. F. see M. E. Flexner
Clipping File. In NN - Theatre Research Room,
"History-Wartime" puppets.
Collings, E. "Marionette Revival," Cath Sch J, 36:8-12,
Jan, 1936.
Conniff, J. C. G. "The Ancient Art of Puppetry," Columbia,
34:6-7, D, 1954.
Craig, Edward Gordon. "History of Marionette Stage,"
Marionette, 1:55-57, Mr. 1918.
---"A Brief History of Puppetry," Marionette, 1:20-23,
Ap, 1918.
---"History of Puppetry," Marionette, 1:152-54, Je, 1918.
---"Brief History of Puppetry," Marionette, 1:171-74, D,
1918.
---Theatre Advancing. Boston, Little, 1919. Chapter,
"Gentlemen, The Marionette."
see also: The Marionette Mag. or Tonight At 8:30;
sometimes it goes by the full name of Marionettes, To-
night at 8:30. (Sources use all three names.) There is

61

only one year of this 1918-1919. Craig was the editor and wrote many anon. articles for it. Available at NN on micro-film.

---"Le Theatre des Marionettes," Arts, My 10, 1946, p 1.

Daniels, George (ed). Puppetry Clipping Collection on 18th Century Puppetry. Cambridge, Harvard Univ. Lib., n. d. This includes program collections and material on puppet companies.

Day, Clarence. "No Movies Then," New Yorker, O 31, 1936, p 22.

DeCasseres, Benjamin. "Renaissance of Puppetry, or Broadway Up to Date," Arts and D, 38:56, Feb, 1933.

Derrigni, P. "History of Puppets," Mask, 6:205-16, Jan, 1914.

Dickens, Charles. American Notes. London, Nonesuch, 1938, p 84. Sig. m. of NYC. puppets, c 1842.

Dilley, Perry. "Deaves Manikins, Touring from 1883-1919," Pupp, 4:39-44, 1933.

Dime Museum Puppets. see "Exhibits and Museums" Section.

Don Quixote, Comical History of. see D'Urfey.

Draper, George. "Back To The Beginning," Brit Pupp Thea, 3(3):2, 1952.

Duckett, G. see T. Burnet

Dudevant, Jean. see George Sand

Duiken, H. W. see Hans C. Andersen

Dumont, Jean. Les Soupirs de la Grand Bretaigne. London, no publ. 1713, passim. In British Museum.

Duncan, W. M. The Puppets of Father Bouvard. London, Melrose, 1948, 1950. In British Museum.

Duplateau, M. (Auguste Bleton). Véridique Histoire De L'Académie de Gourguillen. Lyons, 1898, passim, and 1918. In British Museum.

Duranty, L. E. E. Theatre des Marionettes du Jardin des Tuilieries. Paris, Carpentier, 1863, illus.

---Théâtre des Marionettes. Paris, Carpentier, 1880.

D'Urfey, Tom. Comical History of Don Quixote. (Master Peter's Puppet Show, within the story) Act III, Scene 2, and Act IV, Scene 2. London, 1695.
see G. Speaight's, Hist Eng. Pupp. Thea. p 86-88 sig. m. since this is the basis of Defall's Puppet opera.
see D. Hussey
see also: "Music" Section, under "Don Quixote" "Master

Pedro's Puppet Show," "DeFalla's Opera" and "Master
   Peter's Puppet Opera."
"Eighteenth Century Automata," Harper's Baz, 74:74-75,
   Mr 15, 1940, illus. Automata's are not true puppets but
   are included to a limited degree in the bibliography.
Elliot, E. C. A History of Variety-Vaudeville in Seattle.
   Publications in Drama, No. 1. Seattle, Univ. of Washing-
   ton Press, 1944, p 71.
Elson, John. The Wits, or Sport Upon Sport. Ithaca, Cor-
   nell Univ. Press, 1932 passim.
   "A Revue of, The Wits, or Sport Upon Sport," Anon.
   Pupp, 3:105, 1932.
Encyclopedia Britannica. see Helen H. Joseph

"Expense Account, 1734, of A Young Lady At School," Pupp,
   4:4-5, 1933.
Ferrigui, P. C. see P. C. Fertigni

Fertigni, P. C. (Yorick).   "La Storia dei Burattini." Flor-
   also spelled (Ferrigui)   ence, Fieramosca Newspaper
                              Co. 1884.
---La Storia dei Burattini. Firenze (Italy), R. Bemperad,
   1902. In NN.
---"Notes Upon Ancient Puppets," Mask, 4:301-08, Ap, 1912.
---"History of Puppets," Mask, 5:111-40, O 12, 1912.
---"History of Puppets," Mask, 6:205-16, Jan, 1914.
   Revu. of La Storia Dei Burattini. by Gordon Craig,
   Marionette, 1(8):346, S, 1918.
Films, History of. see "Film" section

Fischer, Mrs R. "Story Book Puppeteers," Carnegie Mag,
   22:84-85, O, 1948.
Fisher, Douglas. Wooden Stars. London, Boardman, 1947.
   Photographic history of Waldo Lanchester's puppets, showing history of stages in England.
Flexner, M. E. , Alice Caine, and D. F. Clark. Hand Puppets: A Practical Manual for Teachers and Children.
   New York, French, 1935. Sample entry, all such books
   have very brief but often times valuable historical chapters. see the section of type interested in.
Folklore Fellowship. "The Folklore Academy Monograph on
   the parallel to Punch in other Countries," Brit Pupp Thea,
   1(4):9, 1950.
Fournier, Édouard. Histoire des Jouets et des Jeux d'Enfants. Paris, Dentu, 1889.
Freedly, G. see R. Gilder

Frost, T. Old Showmen and the Old London Fairs. London, no publ., 1874. passim.

Furst, A. "Notes on the History of Marionettes," Mask, 2:72-76, O, 1909.

Gauchat, Pierre. Marionettes-1949. Zurich, E. Rentsch, 1950. A collector's item. at Mme S. Z.

Gervais, André C. Marionettes et Marionnettistes de France. Paris, Bordas, 1947. Revu. of Marionettes et Marionnettistes de France. by Paul Morharlin, Thea Arts, 31:70, Ag, 1947. The bibliog. is discussed here.

Gilbert, Douglas. American Vaudeville. New York, Dover, n.d. passim, (see, Walter Deaves in this book.)

Gilder, R. and G. Freedly. Theatre Collections in Libraries and Museums, an International Handbook. New York, Theatre Arts, 1936.

Gillespie, E. D. A Book of Remembrance. Philadelphia, Lippincott, 1901, p 61.

Gleason, A. H. "Last Stand of the Marionette, Salvadore L'Cascio's Sicilian Theatre, New York City," Colliers, 44:16, O 23, 1909; continued in D 2, 1909, p 15.

Goethe, Johann von. see Paul McPharlin's Pupp. Thea. Am. p 321.

Goralik, Mordecai. New Theatres For Old. New York, French, 1940 and New York, Dobson, 1948, p 528-29.

---"Young America," Arts, p. 29-32, Jan 1926.

Greenwood, I. J. The Circus, Origin and Growth Prior to 1835. 2nd ed. New York, Hobby, 1962, p 135.

Gregerevius, Ferd. "Roman Marionettes," Marionette, 1(12):184-94, D, 1918.

Gregg, Harold. Art for the Schools of America. Scranton, Haddon, 1947, p 155-62. An International Text Book; sample of small to large amounts of puppet history in art text books.

Gregg, W. W. see W. Shakespeare.

Gröber, K. Children's Toys of Bygone Days. New York, Stokes, 1928, passim.

Guiette, Robert. Marionettes de Tradition Populaire. Brussels, Editions du Cercle D'Art, 1950.

Gustafason, G. "Suzari Marionettes," Design, 47:6, D, 1945.

Hagemann, Carl. Die Spiele der Vulker. Berlin, Mayer, 1912. Important history used by first Intern. puppet historian Max von Bohen.

Haines, Elizabeth. "Something about Marionettes and their

64

History," Recre, 29:192-93, Jl, 1935.
Harnell, Phyllis. The Oxford Companion to the Theatre.
London, Oxford, 1951. "Puppets," p 646-49; "Marion-
ettes," p 154; "Puppets in Education," p 647.
Hartman, E. A History of the Puppet Theatre. New York,
Obolensky, c 1962.
Hayes, J. J. "Totmes III," Drama, 16:59, N, 1925.
---"Puppets," Drama, 19:14, O, 1928.
---"About Puppeteers," Drama, 19:81, D, 1928.
---"Puppets," Drama, 19:236, My, 1929.
---"Puppets In San Francisco," Drama, 20:48, O, 1929.
Hayman, Sylvia. "The Age of the Puppet," Guardian, 16:
8, Feb, 1962.

Heinlein, R. A. Puppet Masters. New York, Doubleday,
1949.
Herbert, Sir Henry. "A Letter About 1669 Puppet Troubles,"
Marionette, 1:321-22, O, 1918.
"Historians and Collectors," Pupp J, 12(3):26, 1960.

Hogarth, Ann. Look at Puppets. London, Hamilton, 1960.
---Little Muffin Book Series. London, Brackman, 1954-1955.
Primarily for Eng. history.
Hogarth, W. see his paintings, "Southwark Fair," 1733
(copy in G. Speaight's, Hist. Eng. Pupp. Thea. p 177.
---see also: Sixty Masterpieces. Painters Series, New
York, Stokes, 1910. Another field of puppet research
which often helps the historian. This is offered as a
sample of a different type of recorded history on puppetry.
Just about our only, and first method of tracing the very
early recorded puppet drama in any country.
see: Hist. Eng. Pupp. Thea. p 179 and 184 for paintings
by Thomas Rowlandson, 1785 and R. Cruikshank, 1825
concerning puppetry.
Holden, Thomas. Children's Variety Entertainment. London,
1880. Verses by E. Wells illustrating period
performance. Another field of puppet research, especially from children's poetry of the early 1800's.
Holme, C. G. see C. W. Beaumont.

Holzknecht, Karl J. "Puppet Plays in Shakespeare's Time,"
Pupp, 4:36-39, 1933.
see also: "Motions in Shakepeare's Time," Anon. Times
Lit Sup, Ja 29, 1920.
Hone, W. Ancient Mysteries. London, 1823.
Chapter on "Early English Show."
---The Everyday Book. London, 1825, passim.

Revu. of Everyday Book. Anon. , Mask, 5:141-42, O, 1912.

Horace. Satires. 2nd Vol. written 30 B.C. , p 82. No translation listed but a liberal translation of material on this topic is made in Speaight's, Hist. Eng. Pupp. Thea. p 25 and p 275.

Hughes, Glenn. Story of the Theatre. New York, French, 1928, p 100-01 and p 283-84.

---Discusses Gordon Craig and his Marionette Mag.
see also: G. Sand.

Hussey, D. "Master Peter's Puppet Show," Sat R, 38: 443-44, N, 1924.

Indian, American. see "Intern." Section, in "United States of America."

Inverarity, R. Bruce. A Manual of Puppetry. Portland, Binfords, 1938. Early Indian puppetry discussed.
Revu. of Manual of Puppetry. by W. Crane, Thea Arts, 23:230, Mr, 1939.

Jacob, George. Geschichte des Schattentheaters im Morgen- und Abendland. Hanover, Lafaire, 1925.

James, M. R. (ed) The Romance of Alexander. ed by Lambert Le Tort, London, Oxford, 1933. Available at Bodleian Lib. Eng. and a copy of one of the very impor- tant illustrations appears in Speaight's Hist. Eng. Pupp. Thea., p 30, with notes regarding this rare bk. on p 276.

Jeanne, Paul. "The Revival of Primitive Marionettes," Pupp, 3:12-14, 1932.

Johnes, R. B. "A Manual of Puppetry." Unpub. Master's dissertation, Iowa City, Iowa Univ. , 1931.

Johnson, W. See J. Beckmann

Jones, S. see D. E. Baker

Jonson, Ben. Bartholomew Fair. London, D. Midwinter, 1614, passim, Rev. ed. 1739.
see also: "Bartholomew Fair-up-to-date," Pupp Master, 3(4):111-14, 1950, by G. Speaight.
see also: Sharpe's Lon Mag, 14:107-14, 171-78, 203-08, 1851.
see also: Bartholomew Fair. ed by E. M. Waith, New Haven, Yale, 1964.
see also: Bartholomew Fair. ed by C. S. Alden, New Haven, Yale, 1904.
see also: E. Pollock
see also: W. J. Lawrence
---Discoveries. London, no publ. , c 1600, passim

Joseph, Helen Haiman. Book of Marionettes. New York, Huebsch, 1920. One of the first American histories of puppets.
Revu. of Book of Marionettes. Anon. Thea Arts, 4:256-57, Jl, 1920.
---"History and Development of Puppets," Encyclopedia Britannica. Vol. 13, p 5884-6671.
---Book of Marionettes. rev. ed. New York, Viking, 1929.
Revu. of Book of Marionettes. by C. Cramer, Thea Arts, 14:357, Ap, 1930.
---Book of Marionettes. rev. ed. London, Allen, 1931.
Jurkowski, Henryk, M. Niculescu and H. Siegel "International Artistic Festvals and Meetings," in Pupp. Th. Med. World, p 52-55.
Kellogg, M. J. "History of Puppets in England," Unpublished Master's dissertation, Madison, Univ. of Wisc., 1937.
Kennard, J. S. Masks and Marionettes. New York, Macmillan, 1935.
Kerchever, Edmund. Medieval Stage. Vol. II. London, Oxford, 1903, p 406+.
King, G. G. Comedies and Legends for Marionettes and Theatres for Boys and Girls. New York, Macmillan, 1904.
Koehler, J. M. "Letter on Puppet Revival," NY Times, Je 25, 1922, Sect. VI, 1:6
Kredel, F. Dolls and Puppets of the 18th Century. Lexington, Gravesend, 1958.
Kure, B. Historical Development of the Marionette Theatre in Japan. New York, Columbia Univ. Press, 1920.
Lago, Roberto. Mexican Folk Puppets, Traditional and Modern. Birmingham, Pupp. Imprint Series, P. McPharlin Co., 1941. In NYC Pub. Lib. and McPharlin Coll.
Lano, David. A Wandering Showman I. East Lansing, Michigan State Univ. Press, 1957. Early Am. puppetry.
Revu. of A Wandering Showman I. Pupp J, 9(6):27, 1958.
Lawrence, G. "Puppetry 1940 and Paul McPharlin," Thea Arts, 25:319, Ap, 1941.
Lawrence, W. J. "Elizabethan Motions," Times Lit Sup, Jan 29, 1920, p 66, columns 1-3.
Leach, H. S. see W. Shakespeare

LeTorte, L. see M. R. James

Levin, Meyer. "New Laurels Grace the Puppet's Brow, NY Times, My 3, 1931, Sect. V, p 10.
Levinson, A. "Le Grande Saison des Marionettes," L'Art Vivant, 6:118-20, Feb, 1930.

Lindsay, Frank W. "Dramatic Parody by Marionettes in the 18th Century Paris." Unpub. Ph. D. dissertation, New York, Columbia Univ., 1945.
---Dramatic Parody by Marionettes in the 18th Century Paris. New York, King's Crown, 1946. Bibliog at end.
Revu. of Dramatic Parody by Marionettes . . . by H. D. Lanchester, Med Lang N, 61:486-88, N, 1946.
Lindsay, Hugh. History-1859. Macungie, Pa., Knauss, 1883. German puppetry in Pennsylvania, from the vaudeville stage. In Harvard Lib.
Logan, Olive. Before the Footlights and Behind the Scenes. New York, Parmalee, 1870, passim.
Luitjens, H. L. (Mrs.) "The Contribution of Puppetry to the Art Life in Los Angeles, California." Unpub. Master's dissertation, Los Angeles, Univ. of Southern California, 1943.
Lupi, Father Antonio M. Storia Litteraria della Sicilia. Vol. I, Rome, c 1720, passim. Earliest attempt to record history of puppets in antiquity.
---Dissertazioni. (Marionettes of the Ancients) Le Journal Etranger, Jan 1757.
Revu. of Dissertazioni. Marionette, 1(5):155-62, Je, 1918.
Revu. of Dissertazioni. "History of Puppets. A Critical Review," by G. Craig, Marionette, 1(12):171, D, 1918.
Luttrell, N. A Brief Historical Relation of State Affairs. London, Oxford, 1857, passim. Powell puppet Co. and Queen Ann's Indian Chiefs performance in 1710.
McCabe, Lida R. "The Marionette Revival," Theatre, 4 (5), N, 1920.
MacClaran, M. Jean. "The Revival of Puppetry in America." Unpublished Master's dissertation, Evanston, Northwestern Univ., 1931.
MacGowan, Kenneth. Footlights Across America. New York, Harcourt, 1929. passim.
McIsaac, F. J. Tony Sarg Marionette Book. New York, Heubsch, 1921 and rev. ed., New York, Viking, 1940.
McKechnie, Samuel. Popular Entertainments Through the Ages. London, Stokes, 1932. Chapter on 1650 puppets and passim.
McPharlin, Marjorie Batchelder. see M. Batchelder.

McPharlin, Paul. Exhibition of Puppets and Marionettes. Chicago, Marshall Field Dept. Store, 1933. 23 pages of historical material concerned with this special exhibit. In McPharlin Coll.
---Puppets in America, 1739 to Today. Detroit, Hastings, 1936, and Birmingham, Puppetry Imprint, 1836. In Mc

Pharlin Coll.
Revu. of Puppets in America, 1739 to Today, Pupp Bull,
9:81, 1938.
---"Puppets in American Life, 1524-1915." Unpublished
Master's of Arts dissertation, Detroit, Wayne Univ.
Teacher's Coll. In McPharlin Coll.
---"Aesthetics of the Puppet Revival." Unpublished Master's
of Science dissertation, Detroit, Wayne Univ. Teacher's
Coll. 1938.
---Puppet Art Today. Birmingham, P. McPharlin Co.,
c 1938. In McPharlin Coll. with note that limited copies
were made. Discusses 60 famous puppeteers. Collectors
item. see: Pupp Bull, 9:75, 1938.
---"Das Jahr des Puppenspiels in Amerika," trans. by W.
Meyer, Theater der Welt, 2:8-14, 1938.
---"Puppets in American Life." Unpublished Ph. D. disser-
tation, E. Lansing, Michigan State Univ., 1940.
---"Puppets in Review, 1940," Thea Arts, 25:319, Ap,
1941.
---"Quarter Century of Puppets," Thea Arts, 25:532-36,
Je, 1941.
---"Puppet Chronicles, 1916-1941," Players, 18:22-23, Jan,
1942.
---Puppet Theatre in America, 1524 to Now. New York,
Harpers, 1949. Most outstanding American history. This
book is now in the process of revision by Marjorie Batch-
elder McPharlin. But references herein refer to the 1949
edition.
    Many little known historical puppet articles, books, and
"Punch and Judy" chapbooks written, or collected by Mr.
McPharlin are part of an 800 book collection willed to the
Detroit Museum of Art Puppet Library, called "The Mc
Pharlin Collection." Some of the items remain in the personal library of Mrs. Paul McPharlin.
Magazin Pittoresque. Paris: about 1883, and Irr Public
(Magasin Pittoresque) 1884-to date. Early French artistic magazine, often using pictorial puppet, guignol, mario-
nette material. In Harvard Univ. Lib., Yale Univ. Lib.
and Hartford Sem. Lib.
Magnin, Charles. "Histoire des Marionettes en Europe
depuis L'Antiguité jusqua nos Jours," La Rev des D M,
(n. d. 1848)
    This is first appearance of the rare European history
of puppets, as a series of articles during the year 1848.
More exact information not yet available.
---"Puppets in England," Anon. trans., Sharpe's Lon J, 14:
107-14, 171-78, 203-08, Jl-D, 1851. This is very im-

portant and the only (only partial) Eng. trans. we have of his History of Marionettes . . . Rather difficult to find this issue of Sharpe's Lon J. Available in Trinity Coll. Lib. (Watkinson Room), Hartford. The book followed the series of articles.
see: Ben Jonson,
see: Wm. Shakespeare
---Historie des Marionettes en Europe depuis l'Antiguité jusqua nos Jours. Paris, Lévy, 1852 and a rev. ed., Paris, Lévy, 1862. In NN, the first real European history of puppetry. No counterpart in English, much space given to Spain and Mexico.
Magon, Jero. "Golden Jubilee: American Puppet Revival, 1915-Upward Trends," Pupp J, 17(2):9-11, 196.
Maindron, Ernest. Marionettes et Guignols. Paris, Juven, 1900. Very rare book, available at Mme. S. Z.
Malik, Jan. "Traditions and the Present Day," see: Pupp Thea Mod World, p 7-14.
---Puppetry in Czechoslovakia. London or Prague, Orbis, 1948.
Mankenburg, K. and A. Taylor. "Puppeteering in Hawaii," Players, 18:19, Mr, 1942.
"Marionettes in Vaudeville," Pupp, 6:13, 1935.

"Marionettes Stage a Comeback," Buick Magazine, Jan, 1938.

Matthews, James Brander. "Paradox of the Puppet: An Extinct Amusement Born Anew," Curr Op, 56:28-29, Jan, 1914.
---"Forerunner of the Movies," Century, 87:916-24, Ap, 1914.
---"Puppet Shows, Old and New," Bookman, 40:379-88, D, 1914.
---A Book About the Theatre. New York, Scribners, 1916, p 287-302.
Meyer, W. see: P. McPharlin.

Michael, Vivian. "Historians and Collectors," Pupp J, 12(4): 27, 1961.
---"Bill Baird's Marionettes-(Historical)," Pupp J, 15(3): 9-10, 1963.
---"The Puppeteers of America--History," Pupp J, 13(5): 2-3, 1962. Publications and festival history for the organization of "Puppeteers of America."
---"Tatterman Marionette Theater (Historical)," Pupp J, 18 (2):6-8, 1966. This theatre attempted the first adult puppet drama in America.

--- and Marjorie Batchelder. Hand and Red Puppets. Columbus, Ohio State Univ. Press, 1947, Applied Art Series No. 1. passim.

Milhouse, Katherine. Herodia. The Beautiful Puppet. New York, Scribners, 1942. More fiction, yet historical in nature. See also: Altoona, Pennsylvania Tribune, (Je 17, 1943) for information on "Herodia," a child labor case of an 1870 puppet show in U. S. A.

Murray, Margaret. The God of the Witches. Castle Hedingham, Essex, Eng., A. Tiranti, Daimond Press, 1962.

Netze, Hans. Das Suddeutsche Wander Marionettentheater. Munich, 1938.

Neuville, L. Histoire Anecdotique des Marionettes Modernes. Paris, Mendel, 1892.

New International Encyclopedia. Vol. 19, New York, Funk, 1927, p 378.

Nichols, Dean G. "Pioneer Theatres of Denver." Unpublished Master's dissertation. Ann Arbor, Univ. of Michigan, 1938.

Nichols, E. K. "Puppet History and Use in Schools." Unpublished Master's dissertation. Los Angeles, Univ. of Southern California, 1932.

Nicoll, Allardyce. Masks, Mimes and Miracles. New York, Cooper, 1931, passim.

Nicoll, J. see Max von Boehn

Niculescu, Margaret (ed). Puppet Theatres of the Modern World. trans. by Ewald Osers and Elizabeth Strick. Boston, Plays, 1967.

Obry, Olga. "Tradition Revived in Brazil," Brit Pupp Thea, 1(4):25, 1950.

Odell, G. C. D. Annals of the New York Stage. 15 Vols. New York, Columbia Univ., 1949, passim.

Oden, G. "Remo Bufano, Puppet Showman, (History)," Detroit Inst Bull, 39(1):17-19, 1959.

---"Victorian Hand Puppet Theatre added to the McPharlin Collection," Detroit Inst Bull, 35(4):97-8, 1955.

O'Donnol, S. "Historians, and Collectors; The Brander Matthews' Collection at Columbia Univ. in Low Lib. (NYC)," Pupp J, 12(5):12-13, 1961.

"Old Puppet Playbills," Pupp, 7:127, 1936.

"Oldest Working Marionette," Pupp J, 13(6):21, 1962.

"Origins of Puppetry," Lit D, 122:24, 26, 28, O 17, 1936.

Osérs, Ewald. see M. Niculescu

Parker, W. L. see S. Pepys.

Patten, William. "Puppets," N Y Times, My 4, 1913,
Sect. V, 5:1.
Patterson, Adia. "The Puppets are Coming to Town,"
Theater, 26:138-39, S, 1917.
Payant, Felix (ed). A Book of Puppetry. Columbus, Design,
1936, illus.
"Pedigree of Puppets," House W, (London, 1850-59) 4:438,
1854.
Peixotte, E. C. "Marionette and Puppet Shows, Past and
Present," Scrib, 33:341-48, Mr, 1903.
Pepys, Samuel. Diary. 4 vols. ed. by Lord Braybrooke,
London, Dent, 1854. Available Pepysian Lib. Magdalene
Coll., Cambridge, Eng. See dates of My 26, 1662, S 4,
1663, S 21, 1688.
---Diary. 4 vols. ed. by Willis L. Parker, New York,
Grosset, 1936. Chapter VI, see, Introduction and Part 1,
Plays, "Droll Puppet Plays."
---Everybody's Pepys. ed by O. F. Marshead, London,
Harrap, 1926.
Philo (The Greek). On the Creation. XL, Athens, about
1, A. D. passim, no trans. listed but material on this
topic, trans. liberally in G. Speaight's Hist. Eng. Pupp.
Thea., p 25, "Note 7" p 275.
Philpott, A. R. Puppet Diary. London, Ed. Pupp. Insti-
tute, 1950.
See L. V. Wall
---Dictionary of Puppetry. London: Macdonald, 1969.
---Modern Puppetry. Boston, Plays, 1966.
Pischel, Richard. Home of the Puppet Play. trans. by M.
C. Tawney, London, Luzac, 1902.
---Der Heimat des Puppenspiels. Stamberg: Haller, 1900.
See also "Dutch" and "German" sections.
Pollock, E. "Puppets in the Plays of Ben Johnson." Un-
published Master's dissertation, Brookings, S. Dakota,
Univ. of So. Dakota, 1936.
"Popular Puppets," Chambers Edinburgh Journal, 27:123,
1871.
Powell, G. M. "Martin Powell, The Puppet Showman,"
No. 506, Sp Mono, 2: 1931-34.
---Martin Powell, The Puppet Showman. Los Angeles,
Univ. of Southern Calif. Press, 1933. This author is not
the same as the very early English puppet master of the
same name.
Prescott, H. F. M. (trans). Flamenca. London, 1930. The
original was written in the 13th Century. See also G.
Speaight's Hist. Eng. Pupp. Thea. p 29 and 275 for trans.

of poem from this book.

Proctor, Romain. "Twenty-five Golden Years," Pupp J, 12(2):3-7, 1960.

---"Twenty-five Golden Years," Pupp J, 12(3):7-11, 1960.

"Punch's Co. Performs 'Babes in the Wood' - An "Optick Tragedy" of the Mineature Stage," New York Journal, S 19, 1749.

Punchinello. (Pseud.). "Dog Gets Puppet At Southwark Fair," Va Gaz, D 22, 1738.

"Puppet Advertisements for Punch," Pupp, 6:27, 1935. Tells of such advertisements in 1739.

"Puppeteers Plan a Comeback," Life, 3:72, Jl 19, 1937.

Puppet Playbills Collection. Cambridge, Mass., Harvard Theatre Lib.

"Puppet Plays in Shakespeare's Time," Pupp, 4:36-39, 1933.

"Puppetry Year in the U.S.A.," see every issue of the yearly Pupp, 1930-48.

"Puppet Show History Comment," N Y Times, Je 22, 1955, 28:4.

"Puppet Shows in England, 1600-1914," List of; in G. Speaight's Hist. Eng. Pupp. Thea. p 313-43.

"Puppets Through the Ages," Design, 33(1), My, 1936.

"Puppets and Puppeteering," Mentor, 9:35-36, Ap, 1921.

"Puppets Are Stealing the Show," Read Dig, 28:43-45, Jan, 1936.

Quinn, D. M. "History of Puppetry." Unpublished Master's dissertation, Stanford, Stanford Univ., 1930.

---"History of Puppetry," No. 528, Sp Mono, 2, 1931-34.

Rabe, J. E. Kasper Putschennlle, Historisches über die Handpuppen und althamburgische Kasperszenen. Hamburg, Boysen, 1924.

Raebaam, Edith M. "Puppets: Their History and Use in the Field of Creative Dramatics." Unpublished Master's dissertation, Berkeley, Univ. of California at Berkeley, 1935.

Ransome, Grace G. Puppets and Shadows. Boston, Faxon, 1931, passim.

Reed, I. see D. E. Baker

"Return of the Marionettes," Curr Op, 58:209-10, Mr, 1913.

"Revival of the Puppet," Curr Op, 61:28-29, Jl, 1916.

Richmond, A. see: Remo Bufano

Ridgeway, W. Dramas and Dramatic Dances of Non Europe-
and Races in Special Reference to Origin of Greek Tragedy. London, Cambridge, 1915 and again 1918.
See also: Marionette, 1(4):30, Ap, 1918.
Rose, A. The Boy Showman. New York, Dutton, 1928.

Rosenfeld, Sybil. Strolling Players and Drama in the Provinces. New York, Macmillan, 1940. 18th Century English puppetry.
Sand, George (Pseud). (Jean Dudevant, Barrone Dudevant)
Homme de Neige. Paris, Lèvy, 1859.
See also: B. Baird's Art of the Puppet, p 144, 152 for
illus. of Maurice Sand's puppet theatre.
Sand, Maurice. History of Harlequinade. Philadelphia, Lippincott, 1915. rev. ed. , London, Lippincott, 1955.
---Le Théâtre Des Marionettes. Paris, Lévy, 1890. This
original version of Plays For Marionettes, has fourteen
plays and an introduction by George Sand.
---Plays For Marionettes. trans. by Babette and Glen
Huges. New York, French; New York, Macmillan, 1931.
    This trans. of the work which has quite an introduction
by George, written for her son, M. Sand's marionette
theatre; has only 5 plays but quite a lot of history. The
original book called Le Théâtre des Marionettes, is by
Maurice Sand.
Sarg, Tony. "Movies on Strings," Photop M, 21:36, 114,
D, 1921. History of Chinese puppets in France.
---"Revival of the Puppet Play in America," Thea Arts, 12:
467-75, Jl, 1928.
Schell, Sherrill. "Czech Puppets with a History," Shadow-
land Magazine, Jan. 1923.
Schoberlin, M. From Candles to Footlights. Denver, Old
West, 1941, passim.
Schumann, Peter. "Puppets Who Protest--on the Streets of
New York," Pupp Life, Aug. , 1968, p 10-11.
Shakespeare, W. Shakespeare Folios and Forgeries. ed by
R. M. Smith and H. S. Leach, Lehigh Univ. , 1927. In Packer
Linderman Mem. Lib. , Lehigh Univ. & British Mus. Lib.
---See: First Folio of Plays, London, 1623, passim. ed
by Sir W. W. Greg, London, Oxford, 1955.
    In these plays Shakespeare often refers to "motions"
(meaning puppets) and "puppets," using the Punch charac-
ter as his clown or fool; going so far as to have him with
hunch-back and large nose.
See also: Sharpe's Lon Mag, 14:107-14, 171-178, 203-208,
1851.

See also   Pupp, 4:36-39, 1933.

Shepard, R. F.   "Obratsov and the Bill Bairds', Pupp J,
15(3):3-4, 1963.
Shoemaker, Henry.   Altoona, Pa.   Tribune, Feb. 4, 1943,
his column and in Altoona, Pa.   Tribune, My 6, 1943.
Sibbald, Reginald.   "Marionettes in the North of France."
Unpublished Ph. D. dissertation.   Phila., Univ. of Penn-
sylvania, 1935.
---Marionettes in the North of France.   New York, Oxford,
1936.
Skinner, R. D.   "Théâtre dei Piccoli," Commonweal, 17:
301, Jan 11, 1933.
Smith, R. M.   See W. Shakespeare.

Soifer, M. K.   With Puppets, Mimes and Shadows.   New
York, Furrow, 1939.
Speaight, George.   Juvenile Drama: History of the English
Toy Theatre.   London, Harrap, 1946.
---"Reconstruction of R. Powells English Puppet Theatre,"
Pupp, 15: 1944.
---The History of the English Puppet Theatre.   London,
Harrap, 1955.
---History of the English Toy Theatre.   London, Degraff,
1955.
Stage, The.   London: 1900- See "Puppet Column" by many
different authors for many years, date of first puppet
column not known.
Stahl, L.   Pepy's Puppet Plays.   Minneapolis, Dennison,
1950.
"Stamps, Puppet on,"   Puppet Teaching News Bulletin.   New
York, Fed. Thea. Projects Public W. P. A. Project, (5):
3, Ap, 1938 and Nov 13, 1937.
Stead, Philip John.   Mr. Punch.   London, Evans, 1950.
Stevenson, Robert Louis.   "A Penny Plain, Two pence Col-
oured," in his Memories and Portraits.   London, Chatto,
1887.
---Penny Plain, Twopence Coloured.   London, Pollock, 1948,
and London, Thule, 1949.
Stoddard, Ann.   "The Renaissance of the Puppet Play,"
Century, 96:173-86, Je, 1918.
---"Tony Sarg," Mentor, 38: 1933.
---"Tony Sarg," Pupp J, 17(2):3-6, 1965.
"Story of the Theatre 5," Pict Ed, Feb, 1947.

Strick, Elizabeth.   See   M. Niculescu

Symonds, J. A. Shakespear's Predecessors. London,
    Smith-Elder, 1884.
Tavernier, A. and A. Alexandre. Le Guignol Des Champs-
    Elysées, Paris, Delagrave, 1889.
Taylor, A. See: E. Mankenburg.

Teall, Gardner. "Punch and Judy Shows," Theatre, 8:240-
    42, S, 1908. See also: "Punch and Judy" Section.
Trentleman, Alvina. "History of Puppets," El Eng Rev, 9:
    251-55, D, 1932.
Trollope, Frances. Domestic Manners of the Americans.
    2 Vols., London, Whittaker, 1832, passim. Rev. ed.,
    2 Vols., New York, Vintage, 1949, p 175 and passim.
    Revu. and summary of Domestic Manners of Americans.
    (1st ed.) Mon R 1(4):540-66, Ap, 1832.
Tyson, G. M. "History of Oriental Puppets." Unpublished
    Master's dissertation. Los Angeles, Univ. of Southern
    California, 1932.
---"History of Oriental Puppetry," No. 487, Sp Mono,
    1931-34.
Verdelis, N. M. "Private House Discovery at Mycenae; A
    Puppet," Archaeology, 14(1):12-15, 1961.
Vizetelly, Bros. (ed). The Puppet Showman Album. London,
    Vizetelly, 1849.
"Vogue for Puppet Plays," Pop Educ, 42:266-67, Jan, 1925.

Von Boehn, Max. See: Boehn, Max von

Waith, E. M. See: Ben Jonson

Walkley, A. B. More Prejudice. London, Heineman, 1923,
    passim.
Wall, L. V., G. A. White, and A. R. Philpot. The Puppet
    Book. Boston, Plays, c 1966.
Walters, F. G. "Marionette Memoirs," Gentleman's Maga-
    zine, New Series, London, 41:578, D, 1868.
Ward, Edward (Ned). "Puppets at Bartholomew Fair This
    Year," London Spy, 1699 Part VII; and Part XI in 1700.
    No other dates or pages listed at source, but see G.
    Speaight's, Hist. Eng. Pupp. Thea. p 85 for partial quote
    of this article.
Warsage, Rodolphe. Histoire du Célèbre, Théâtre Liége de
    Marionettes. Brussels, Van Oest, 1905.
Weaver, R. T. See: "Film" Section

Wells, E. See: Thomas Holden

West, W. See A. E. Wilson

Westwood, J. O. "Notice of a Medieval Mimic Entertaine-
ment-puppets," Archaeological Journal. England, 5:198,
S, 1848.
Whanslaw, H. W. Everybody's Theatre. Redhill, Surrey,
W-Gardner, 1923. Model Theatre Series.
---Everybody's Marionette Book. Redhill, Surrey, W-Gardner,
1935 and rev. ed. 1948.
---Specialized Puppetry. Redhill, Surrey, W-Gardner, 1939.
Model Theatre Series.
---Bench Book of Puppetry-compiled. London, Heineman,
1961. This is a rev. ed. of his two other Bench Books.
See "Bibliography" section.
White, G. A. See L. V. Wall

Wiksell, Jean Starr. "Puppetry in the Junior Leagues of
America," Pupp J, 2(5):8-9, 1951. Historically impor-
tant in development of therapeutic puppetry.
See also: "Jr. Leagues" in the "Organization" section.
---"Puppetry in the South and Southwest," Players, 13:19,
N, 1936.
Wilder, G. "Puppetry in a New Age," Recre, 30:207-08,
Jl, 1936.
Wilkinson, Walter. "Puppet Revival," Chi Sci Mon W,
Mr 25, 1936, p 8 of Mag. section.
---A Sussex Peep-Show. rev. ed. New York, Stokes, 1933.
---Puppets Through America. New York, Stokes 1937.
rev. ed. London, Bles, 1938, rev. ed. 1940.
---"A History of Puppets in Europe," Pupp Master, 5(4):
7-10, 1957.
Williams, E. C. "Puppets to Marionettes," Jr. League Mag,
19:56, Mr, 1933.
Williamson, Hamilton. "Old China Comes to Broadway,"
Motion P M, 22:36-37, 88-89, N, 1921.
Williamson, S. L. "The Historical Background of Puppetry,"
Thea and Sch, 14:18-23, Mr, 1936.
Wilson, A. E. and W. West. Penny Plain, Two-Pence
Colored. New York, Macmillan, 1932. Term used for
Eng. "Toy Theatre" - "Paper-puppet Theatre" - "Juvenile
Drama," with puppets.
Wilson, Winifred G. "Europe, Puppet Shows in Last World
War and This," World R, My, 1941, p 45-49.
---"Theatre in the Trenches," 1917-198, Life Let, 24:80-84,
Jan, 1940.
Wood, R. K. "Puppets and Puppeteering," Mentor, 9:35-
36, Ap, 1921.

World's Fair, The. London: "The Puppet Column," weekly
publication, 1800-to date. By diff. authors; puppetry a-
round the world items. Concerned with all aspects of the
puppetry booths, shows, etc.
Wright, John F. The Puppet Book. (Home Craft Series)
London, Bennett, 1950.
---My Puppetry. London, Sylvan, D 7, 1951.
---Your Puppetry. No. 11 (Home Craft Series) London,
Bennett, 1952.
Wyatt, E. V. "Teatre dei Piccoli," Cath W, 136:719-20,
Mr, 1933.
Xenophon, ---- Symposium. Athens: c 420 B. C. , p 4, 55.
No trans. listed but brief trans. relating in G. Speaight,
Hist. Eng. Pupp. Thea., p 24, 26, 275. Mentions Syra-
cusian puppet showman with his "Neurospastes," stringed
puppet, "keree," glove puppet.
Yates, Helen E. "Revival of Interest in Puppets and Mario-
nettes," Leisure, 3:12-14, 60, D, 1936.
"Yorick" (pseud). See P. C. Fertigni
--- "History of Puppetry in England," Mask, 6:215-216, 1913.

Zeigler, Francis J. "Puppets, Ancient and Modern,"
Harpers, 96:5, D, 1897.
Zweers, John U. (ed). History of Puppetry. Los Angeles,
County Museum, 1959.
---"Puppeteer's Odyssey," Pupp J, 12(5B):3-6, Ap, 1961.
Relating to American Collections.

C. Punch and Judy

It would be almost impossible for the historical student to study the history of "Mr. Punch" or "Mr. John Pickle-Herring" of Anglo-Saxon fame, without a few hints as to where to start tracking down this worldwide character, with his many, many changes of name.

The man, the clown, the wit, the human personality reacting to life, is the dramatic character we are talking about in this part of puppet history. Around the world "Mr. Punch" is always of the people not of the aristocracy. He may enter into the latter group, in their drama in the 17th and 18th century puppetry or stage, but he is still not "of them."

I have attempted to suggest, in the following list, places for further study of him, through these many names and a brief note about them. This may help to clear up, in the minds of the average puppeteer, which articles he should investigate for his particular need, especially when searching into foreign language material in other sections of the Guide.

Most outstanding in false conceptions about "Punch and Judy" drama is the idea that it has always been a glove-type booth. This was not true until around 1800. This means that we must consider early marionette as well as glove-type articles when tracing Mr. Punch. Sometimes he becomes a rod or shadow-type in the East. This, to say nothing of different spellings of his National names, helps toward the confusion of the student and the bibliographic material. Let us begin our list with a brief definition, then, of the true, "Mr. Punch" and his wife "Joan" or "Judy." See Pupp. Master 7(1):18-20, 1962, illus. of Punch around the world by Waldo Lanchester.

"Punch" - (John Pickle-Herring)

The loveable, rogue, clown, wit, character in puppet drama who belongs only to England. He grew up and out of the nature, ways, and drama of that country. He suggested

in nature, wit, and dialogue the Italian "Pulcinella" puppet
character and the French "Polichinelle" puppet character.
He differed from them in his costume, booth, shape, and
face and the characters of his production. "Joan" was his
wife; she became "Judy" in 1818 when he went into the
streets from the theaters. He was a marionette in the 17th
and 18th century English society puppet drama but the same
character, occasionally was found in a glove puppet-booth, as
hero, at the Fairs of the day; the streets and beach resorts
knew him well. By 1800 he was out of strings and consist-
ently a glove-booth hero of the people, as always. Bibliographic material, thus far, could be string, mechanical; now
it should settle into hand puppet. The change was, when a
string puppet, he came into plays; but when a hand puppet,
the people came into talk to him as the main figure. He
seldom used a human voice at any period; a reed in operator's mouth gave nasal twang which needed interpreting.
Has Hump, hook-chin and nose and cap, checkered booth;
dog often found with him in booth. He uses eleven characters in plot, one woman, three animals. In 18th century
England there was a loose union of about 16 Punch men;
today almost 100 are active in park, beach, resorts, and
Fairs but not on the street. They combine magic with show
when giving performances for parties.

Articles which have the name "Punch" or "Judy" in
their title, or relate to their production will be found only
in this section; they will not be repeated in "Hand," "Marionette," or other sections unless they are under the foreign
countries which are named in this list under the names given
here. Many of the foreign items are cross referenced into
this section, but the majority of this research is yet to be
done and will be in a future supplement of international material.

"Neurospastos" 500 B. C. Greece and Sicily:
   The Greeks used this to describe a string type puppet having the manners, behavior, wit, roughness, and talk of
   the common people. He appeared at banquets, feasts,
   etc. He was probably one of the first "Punch" character
   type puppets. He did not belong in drama or on the stage.
"Koree" 500 B. C. Greek
   Seems to have been a long sleeve with a figure on the end
   which probably was a type of glove-booth puppet. He also was purely "of the people" not the stage or theater.
   He was rough, raw, and bawdy.
Burattini 1583 Italy

The glove-puppet, booth-puppet, but not particularly "Punch" character or drama. Found all over southern Europe by this name, wandered up into Central and Northern Europe. Used a "castello" or castle form of booth. The Minstrels used him and he could be called anything. He was most often rough, told news, sang songs, drama, etc. Name was used several centuries; sometimes still used for glove-booth.

"Pulcinella." "Arlichino" (in the villages only) Italy.
The Italian character puppet resembling "Punch" of England. He is dressed in white, with a half-black mask if he is in true production. He came to England and France with the famous Italian puppet trouper, Piccini. He has a slight hump, patchwork clothes with bells, hook nose, but not hook chin. The Booth is not checkered, nor the hat the same as "Punch." Often the watcher hesitates to make distinction between him and "Punch" because their actions, wit, character are so much alike. It does not have the same cast in the production, and seldom the live dog, but is still slap-bang, glove-street-booth action. He uses the "Piretta" mouth squeaker and "castello" booth as early burattini, and must be interpreted by someone outside the booth. Sometimes we still see strings on him in the streets. Early in the 17th and 18th century, especially in England, he was a fancy string of large size, doing drama. He wandered all over Europe in all kinds of theatres but his name gradually disappeared, through changes in the different countries; but without much change in his type of part and character.

"Polichinelle" or "Pollicinella," "Polichinello," "Polichinelli," "Punchanello," "Punchinello," France.
The Puppet hero, "Punch" type character of the French street and often the courts and high society in 17th and 18th century France. He became as large as four or five feet tall, and was often made of wax, wires, string and highly mechanized parts which made him almost human. He did opera and drama at times so he was not always "of the people" as "Punch" was, but he was always a witty rogue; he was a clown with a hump and slight hook on his nose and usually far more handsome of face. In the 19th century, he derived more of "Mr. Punch's" English ways and manners, and became a full glove-puppet, booth man of the park, fair, and street. He uses a cat rather than a live dog; he is seldom seen in his own drama now. His hat is different from Punch. He was seldom a string after the middle of the 18th century. He wandered over Europe but disappeared in name into the character of

"Guignol" in France and "Don Christobal" of Spain and
far southern France's "Christovita." His booth was called
the "castellet."

"Guignol" - France (from Lyons)
    The popular, loveable, simple, amusing hero of the 20th
century French parks and their puppet booths. He took
the name and part away from "Polichinelle" but kept his
Punch-like character, wit, rough, slap-stick ways "of the
people" around the beginning of the 19th century. He may
be Hand, String, or Rod, depending on his location in
France or western European countries, but is usually a
glove-puppet. He often resembles "Punch" in hump, hook-
nose, but not in clothing as it is plain color, tricorner
hat, pigtail hair arrangement, and a cat. He plays different dramas, not just Punch plot but is usually classed
with "Punch" and "Judy" in our thoughts.

"Christovita" - "Don Christóbal," Northern Spain and Spain.
    The hero character who took over the part played by poor
"Punchinello" of French fame. He is a pure Punch-like
character and is usually found as a glove-puppet in his
"castillo" booth at Fairs, on the streets or in parks of
Spain, Spanish-Italy, or Spanish-France sections. He
took over his braggart, witty, slap-stick dramatic role in
the 19th century but differs in cast, costume, exact looks
and booth. He still uses whistle, has a twangy, hard to
understand voice, but may have different story plots.

Kobalds, Tattermans - Germany, Austria, Central Europe.
    These were the names of the type of puppets which the
very early central European puppet-minstrels popped out
of their magic bags to tell the news, bawdy, swaggering
tales and drama of Medieval time. They may have been
string, hand, or jiggling, but held the jester's part, usually swashbuckling like "Punch." No hero's name comes
down to us from this period.

"Hansworst," also "Kasperl," "Pickleharing," "Kasperl-
Larifari," "Kaspar", "Kaspar," "Hartenstein" Theater,
"Hohnsteiner" Theater, "Kašpárek," "Polizinell," "Meister
Hammerlin" - Germany, Austria, Central Europe.
    "Hansworst" is the name of the traditional German clown,
while "Kasperl" is the name of his puppet counterpart or
Punch-like character. These names of the people's hero
come from the 16th, 17th, 18th and 19th century. "Hansworst" was in the early Dr. Faust productions but was,
in time, expelled to the puppet booth where his name was
stolen away by "Kasperl" or "Kašpárak" in Austria and
Czechoslovakia.

"Kasperl" is the name used for the puppet hero of the German "Punch" drama play. He is the fellow who stole the title from the title "Polichinelle" and "Pulcinella" from the glove-booth traveling shows. In early times he might be string, but still that same rough, braggard, slap-stick, squeaking voiced tramp. He does bear a resemblance to "Punch" in looks and costume. He is usually more round-faced and clownish. These were different productions, different casts and an outline of drama; certainly not regular Punch plots. He was found on live stage as the Jester with slight variations in name. He, as a Punch-type glove puppet, will bear careful research because he was so often a marionette in 19th century literature. In the 20th century the names "Kaspar" or "Kasperl" was used in the glove puppet theater and now it is called "Hortenstein" or "Horensteiner."

The famous German playwright, Franz Pocci, used the name "Kasperl-Larifari" for the jester character in his plays for marionettes, not hand puppets; and other authors did not mean string if they used this name. The character was a Punch-like puppet in manners, entrances, wit and attitude, but certainly not in plot.
"Kašpárek" or "Pimperle"
"Kašpárek" is the clever little Austrian wit and the modern descendent of "Hansworst" from the Dr. Faust drama. He is much more refined and less of "Punch's" type. See Goethe's "Dr. Faust" in the Music, and German Sections. Sometimes Glove, now seldom found in booth of street or fair.
"Jan Klaasen" - Holland - also "Klaasen," was the hero character of the "Punch and Judy" form of drama in Holland from the 18th to the late 19th century. Usually glove puppet but could be string in 17th and 18th century. Took over name from the "Polichinelle" and "Pulcinella" traveling shows, becoming glove puppet from need of production cast and trouping.
"Pimperle" or "Kašpárek" - Bohemia, Czechoslovakia, etc. He took the name from "Polichinelle" and "Pulcinella" shows around early 20th and late 19th centuries. He disappeared in the first years after the second World War. He was revived in 1950's but "Pimperle" name is gone again, in the main, since Professor Skupa.
"Hurvínek and Papa Spejbl."
Now, since Professor Skupa's puppet work, 1892-1957 we are seeing a different type, not "Punch" character or drama but still a witty, puppet of the common people in the clown-like; sly, intelligent, sometimes dangerous charac-

ter of the naughty little "Hurvínek" and his befuddled, wise, old-fashioned papa, "Father Spejbl." They came in the 1900's and flourished happily in the Park, and Fair, but are not hand; they are usually string. Do not confuse with the glove "Punch" character.

"Hans Joggeli" - Switzerland.
Name for the "Punch" like hero of the people, usually hand puppet.

"Mester Jakel" or "Meistr Jacel" - Denmark.
Name for the "Punch" like hero of the people, usually hand puppet.

"Tchantches" - Belgium.
Name for the "Punch" like hero of the people, usually hand puppet.

"Vanka Rutyutyu" - Ukrainian.
Name for the "Punch" like hero of the people, usually hand puppet.

"Vasilache" or "Valicke" - Rumanian.
Name for the "Punch" like hero of the people, usually hand puppet.

"Pencho" - Bulgarian.
Name for the "Punch" like hero of the people, usually hand puppet.

"Paprika Jancsi" or "Vitez Laszlo" - Hungarian.
Name for "Punch" like hero of the people, usually hand puppet.

"Petroushka" or "Petroushka Farnos," or "Krasny Nos" (Red Nose) or "Samovaror" or "Peter Ivonovich Uksukov" - Russia and East Europe, 18th and 19th Century.
The lovable, rough and tumble, clown-like hero character resembling English "Punch" a great deal. He was the actor for the Fairs; live sometimes, but usually in the puppet booth, string or glove type show. He was often made more pathetic than "Mr. Punch." See the Ballet of that name and the "Music" Section. He stole the part of "Polichinelle" and "Pulcinella." Not too much resemblance to Punch character but still thought of in the same family group because of manners and wit. Ivan Zaitsev should be studied as he was outstanding with this character puppet. Samuil Marshak has short plays about him. He left puppetry around 1917, but may still be found in rural Fair.

"Katchel Pehlavan" - Persia.
The bawdy, puppet drama character like "Punch," usually hand puppet.

"Palwan-Katchal" (Giant Bald-Head)

"Karapet" - Armenian, Persian.
   Punch like character of the people.
"Semar" - Indonesia.
   The name for the "Punch" like hero of the people, usual-
   ly a type of glove puppet.
"Vidushaka" - India.
   The name for the "Punch" like hero of the common
   people; usually a type of glove puppet but now as common
   as the rod and shadow puppet of that country.
"Karankioses" - Greek and Turkish.
   Today's double for "Mr. Punch;" usually hand puppet but
   sometimes found in the shadow drama plays.
"Karagoz" or Karaghevz" or "Karoghioz" (Black Eye), or
"Semar" - Java Shadow - Far East, Turkish, etc.
   He is usually a shadow rather than glove and we do not
   seem to class him with "Punch and Judy" type of drama
   and yet his character is most certainly the same and he
   was certainly around much earlier in the theater world
   than "Mr. Punch." He is a braggard, bawdy, rough, wit,
   slap-sticking his way through his production and throwing
   in "ad lib" comments as our "Mr. Punch" did and does.

   The word "Swazzle" means the "Squeaker voice."
The instrument held in the mouth by Italian, French, English,
and practically all international "Punch" type players over
the world. Articles with that word would be in this section.

   Do not confuse the word "Galanty Show," or "La
Planchette" with glove puppets shows, "Punch" type shows,
or "Hand shows." See "Toy Theater" and "String" Sections.
Neither should the word "Rastaxii" be confused with this section but under "Jiggling" or "String."

Glossary of Punch words:
      Professor - The Punch showman
      to reign - perform undisturbed
      barrows - rough, tough gang of boys on street
      snowing - lots of money, good collection
      the bottle - the collection, to collect donations
      Pitch - the performing sight, to actually perform
      Roundings - the draperies
      to drop - to donate
      Nark - complain to police
      Busker - street performer

Punch and Judy Material

Note: Many of the early Punch and Judy Chapbooks and like short material gave no publishers and much early English puppet material is found to be likewise rather vague on statistical information. I have attempted to locate these out of print articles and books. Many articles which sound like Punch and Judy material turn out to be about the periodical "Punch" which derived its name, its witty, sarcastic ways and its drawings from our dramatic actor. Again we remind the reader it was impossible to scan every item. There is a little Punch and Judy work in "Plays" Section, and a small amount under "Hand and Glove" but the majority is here, or in the "International" Section under the name of each country.

Abbot, C. S. (ed). Recollections of a California Pioneer. New York, Abbot, 1917, p 114.
Abeckett, Arthur W. The Abecketts of "Punch." Westminster, Constable, 1903.
Aiken, Conrad P. Punch: The Immortal Liar. New York, Knopf, 1921.
---"Punch, a poem," Thea Arts, 8:651, O, 1924.
---"Punch, a poem," Thea Arts, 12:464, Jl, 1928.

Aldine Publ. Co. (ed). Punch and Judy, Tales for Little People. London, Aldine, n. d. In McPharlin Coll.
Allen, A. B. "Punch and Judy Dialogue," in his Model Theatre. Redhill, Surrey, Wells, G. D. , 1950.
Allen, G. and Unwin (ed). Tragical Comedy of Punch and Judy. London, G. Allen, 1928. In British Museum.
Amusing Punch and Judy Theatre. Bavaria, c 1880. In Mc Pharlin Coll.
Anderson, Doug. Punch and Judy. Record Catalogue, RHLP 1010. Ashville, Puppetry Journal Public. , 1959.
---See also G. W. Dougherty.

"Are We Forgetting Punch and Judy?" R of Revus, 49:102, Jan, 1914.
Arndt, F. "Kaspertheater ist auch Hausmusik," Hausmusik, 16:70-74, My-Je, 1952.
"Australian Punch," All Yr R, 9:610, 1863. Probably writ-

ten by Charles Dickens, the editor and describing clever, witty, satiric, likeness of material in this periodical to our actor.

Bachut, J. Guignol Congresisse. Lyons, Unima Org. , 1911.

Bacon, Peggy. "Puppet Show of R. Patterson, Punch Man," Stage, 12(2):68, Je, 1935. More for "Variety" Section material.

Baird, Bill. The Art of the Puppet. New York, Macmillan, 1966. "Percy Press, King of English Punch Men," p17; "Petrouchka," p 71, 106; "Karaghioz" p 78; "Mr. Punch" p 71, 88-114; "Polichinelle" p 99, 103; "Hanswurst" p 71; "Guignol" p 102; "Kasparek" p 75.
There is much more scattered material on this subject, check index. Excellent color illus.

Baker, F. Playing With Punch. London, T. V. Boardman, 1948.

---Comical Tragedy of Punch and Judy. London, T. V. Boardman, 1944.

Baretti, Joseph. Tolondron: Speech to John Bowle About "Don Quixote," London, 1786. Comments upon Punch and "Master Peter's Puppet Show." In British Museum.

Baring, Hon. Maurice. (The first 2 are rare items and are found in McPharlin Coll.)

---Punch and Judy and Other Essays. New York, Doubleday, 1925 and Heineman, 1925.

---Punch and Judy, Covet Garden. London, 1881.

---"Punch and Judy" in his Lost Lectures. London, n. d. , p 208-227. In British Museum.

---"Punch and Judy," Lond Mer, 6(33):270-81, Jl, 1922.

---"Punch and Judy," Lond Mer, 6(33):272-Script, Jl, 1922.

---"Punch and Judy," Liv A, 314:452-55, Ag, 1922.

Barnum, P. T. Struggles and Triumphs. Vol I, New York, Macmillan, 1930, p 195 and passim.

Baumann, Hans. Caspar and His Friends. trans. by Joyce Emerson, London, Phoenix, 1967.

Beard, E. "Guignol and the Butterflies," Brit Pupp Thea, 3(5):4, 1952.

Beard, L. "New Year's Punch and Judy Shows," Delin, 65:109-11, Jan, 1905.

Bechdolt, J. E. "Punch and Judy," in his Modern Handy Book for Boys. New York, Greenberg, 1958, p 325-39.

Beck, E. "Punch and Judy" Register (Frankfort, Pennsylvania) My, 1896, p 128.

Beer, L. Punch and Judy. Boston, Humphries, 1962.

---See F. G. Pocci

Bell, George and Sons (ed). Punch and Judy. London, G. Bell, 1881.

Bellow, Frank. The Art of Amusing. New York, Calton, 1866, Chapter 2. Material about the "Squeaker" and the "Swazzel."

Bennett, Charles H. The Wonderful Drama of Punch and Judy. London, H. Ingram, 1854, 1919. In British Museum and McPharlin Coll.

Beresford, J. D. "The Philosophy of Mr. Punch," Lond Mer, 6(33): Jl, 1922.

Besissieur, F. Théâtre de Guignol. Paris, Lévy, 1887.

Bideaus, Suzanne. Guignol en Famille. Lille, Demailly, 1948. Two volumes in one. In NN.

Biographia, by Dramaticus. See Dramaticus.

Blackmantle, Barnard. "Punch and Judy" in his English Spy. Vol II, London, 1825-26. illus by R. Cruikshank. In British Museum.

Blickle, Peg. "It's news to me--Punch in England today," Pupp J, 9(6):27, My 1958.

Bloch, Edward. The Edward Bloch Kasperl Theatre. Berlin, Bloch, c 1928.

Boecklin, Von B. Kasperl. Munich, Collowey, n. d. Not located, but it is listed as "very important" in Max Von Bohen's, Dolls and Puppets. See also: "German" Section for books of this title.

Bonus, A. Kasperl. Munich, Calloway, n. d. Listed in Max von Boehn's, Dolls and Puppets.

Boough, Robert Barnabas (pseud). See C. H. Bennett.

Bougersdickinus (pseud). "Punch and Judy," European Mag., 1: new series, no 2, Ap, 1953.

Bowie, A. G. "Story of Punch and Judy," Theatre, new series (3):17-24, Jan, 1884.

Bragalia, A. G. Pulcinella, Rome, G. Casini, 1953, p 523.

Broadway Booklets (ed). Tragical Comedy of Punch and Judy. New York, Broadway Booklets, 1904-1905. In British Museum.

Brown, F. K. "The Merry Play of Punch and Judy," Playgr, 15(4):251-58, Jul, 1921.

Brown, Forman G. Punch's Progress. New York, Macmillan, 1936. Mainly about "Yale Puppeteers Group."

---"Putting Punch and Judy into Life," Playgr, 15(4):249-51, Jl, 1921.

Brown, Margaret W. Punch and Judy. New York, W. R. Scott, 1940. In McPharlin Coll. and NN.

Byron, Lord. "Triumphant Punch," (a poem) in his collec-

tion, The Works of Lord Byron; His Letters of Life. 14
vols. London, Murray, 1832. Called also "Sonnet a
Polichinello". In British Museum.
Calthrop, Dion C. Punch and Judy, A Corner in the History
of Entertainment. London, Dulau, 1926. In McPharlin
Coll.
Cambridge, W. "Life and Character of Harry Rowe--Punch
and Judy Man," Old Moore's Almanac. London and New
York, T. Roberts, 1894. In British Museum.
Carr, J. See "Fiction" Section.

Carroll, L. "Punch and Judy Abroad--Russian Puppet Show,"
Newsweek, 29:78, Je 23, 1947.
Chamfleury, J. Les Bons Contes Font Les Bons Amis.
Paris, Truchy, 1888. In McPharlin Coll.
Chancel, Jules. Le Coffre Fort de Polichinelle. Paris,
Delagrave, 1903. In Montreal Univ. Lib.
Chapbooks, English. (in this bibliog.) These are Punch and
Judy booklets, paper bound, and usually undated, without
authors, and seem to have been written and/or ed. by
publishers around the period 1835-1850. They are listed
here by those publishers and many can be found in Mc
Pharlin Coll. and many more in the British Museum Li-
brary.
Charles, William (ed). Pugs Visit to Mr. Punch. Phila-
delphia, Morgan, 1821, first printed 1810 by "Mr. W.
Charles and Son" [sic]. In Chapin Lib. at Williams Coll.
Lib., Williamstown, Mass.
   It was printed again in 1815 by Morgan, and the 1821
printing was "with wrappers" and says that "It is the first
colored illustration in a child's book in America." It was
one of the first published on puppets in America. Col-
lector's item.
Clark, H. G. (ed). The Little Showman. London, H. G.
Clark, 1864. Pamphlets on Punch and Judy, Marionettes
and Model Theatres. In McPharlin Coll.
Cleland, J. R. "Some Notes on the Punch Play," Pupp
Master, 2(3):65-68, 1948.
Clerke, E. M. "Punch and Judy and Pulcinella," Cornhill
Mag, London, 44:182, 1860-1861.
---Punch and Judy. London, 1863. A penny-Chapbook, in
McPharlin Coll.
---"Punch and Pulcinella." Electic Mag, (Am) 97:558-63,
O 1881. In Harvard Univ. Lib.
Clinch & Rimbault (ed). Sche and Its Associations. London,
Clinch, 1895, passim. In British Museum. One of very
important Punch men of England, Jobson,___, is particu-

larly noted, playing around 1759 at Canterbury in "Faust"
and "Caeser theme plots" with Punch.
---See also G. Speaight's, His. Eng. Pupp. Thea. p 157-
159.
Clipping File on Puppets. NN, Research Theatre Room,
"Punch and Judy."
Codman, John. "Prof." "The Famous Codmans," Pupp
Master, 7(1):29-30, 1962. Son of Richard Codman, their
Punch booth in Lime St. London, is over 100 years old.
Codman, Richard. "Prof." "Death of a Famous Punch Man and
His Work," Pupp Master, 3(6):199-200, 1951. With modern
Punch Booth at Colwyn Bay, Eng. See local papers for items
concerning shows.
Cole, Nacy. "Guignol." Unpublished Master's dissertation,
Stanford, Stanford Univ., Spring 1958.
---"Salute Guignol," Pupp J, 11(2):13, 14, 27, 28, 1952.
Coleman, Henry E. A Bibliography on Pantomime: Punch
and Judy, Shadows, Marionettes or Puppet Shows. (Mimeo)
N 12, 1926. In Deering Lib., "Puppet File," North-
western Univ.
Coleman, S. J. The Story of Punch and Judy. London, R.
A. Publishing Co., 1946 (another source said Allman
Publ.)
Collier, John Payne. (All of these articles and items can be
found in the British Museum Lib.)
---The Collier-Cruikshank Punch and Judy. London, Prow-
ett, 1828 and 1832, 1844. "Text from Piccini's," this
version uses Father Lupi's citations in historical part,
first editions.
In McPharlin Coll. See also Baird's, Art of the Puppet,
p 90.
---Collier-Cruikshank Punch and Judy. London, Lacy, 1859.
4th ed. Gives history material in this version.
---Punch's Real History, printed for Thomas Tegg. London,
Collier, 1844. Printed again 2nd and 3d ed. London,
Spearight, 1856. In McPharlin Coll.
---The Collier-Cruikshank Punch and Judy. London, Bell-
Daldy, 1870, "color illus." 5th ed. In McPharlin Coll.
---An Old Man's Diary. "Punch's Franks Script." London,
1871-72, p 77, Vol. IV. This script was used in 1822-23
according to the Diary. This item is in McPharlin Coll.
---The Collier Cruikshank Punch and Judy. rev. ed. with
color, London, Bell-Daldy, 1873 and 1881.
---See also: Morning Chronicle (S 22, 1813) issues, his
puppet column. (Not in British Museum Coll. of Collier's
work.
A London Newspaper. I was not able to check just how

long he wrote for the paper.

---<u>Punch and Judy With Foreword by Tony Sarg</u>." Rev. ed.
of the original <u>Collier-Cruikshank Punch and Judy</u>." London, Rimington and Hooper, 1929.
 This version has a bibliographical note by Ann L. Haight. In McPharlin Coll. (Not in British Museum.)
Revu. of <u>Punch and Judy with Foreword by Tony Sarg.</u> by Carl Cramer, <u>Thea Arts,</u> 14:358, Ap 1930.

---"Sonnet to Punch," <u>Pupp Master,</u> 7(1):13, 1962. This article says that the "Poem attributed to Lord Byron is falsely attributed to him and is by Collier." (Not in British Museum.)

Collier, J. P. and G. Cruikshank. <u>Punch and Judy</u>. (Centennial ed.) London, Rimington, 1949. This has 28 illus. by Cruikshank and a dialogue of the Piccini show. With introduction by Tony Sarg.
 <u>See also</u> Cruikshank. G.

Collings, Sam. "Italian Punch Show." (A Painting) London, Carington Bowles, n. d.
 <u>See also</u> Bill Baird's, <u>Art of the Puppet</u> for other famous paintings by B. R. Haydon, 1829 and Hogarth, p 94-100.
 Study of paintings made of street scenes around this period will give much information on dates, types, locations, booths, "Professors" etc.

Collins, A. F. "How to Give a Punch and Judy Show" in his <u>Making Things For Fun</u>. New York, Appleton, 1934, p 208-13.

Conant, S. S. "The Story of Punch and Judy--the Collier Cruikshank Play," <u>Harpers,</u> 70(252)830-48, My, 1871.
 Gives the script and many good illus.

Conrad, J. "Punch Was a Gentleman," <u>Pupp J,</u> 14(4&5): 3, 1943.

Cordier, A. and Hadol. <u>See</u> Hadol and A. Cordier.

<u>Cosmotama Amusant</u> (Cosmorama Ausant). Paris, Librairie France Hollandaise, c 1375. In McPharlin Coll.

Croce, Benedetto. <u>Pulcinella e il Personaggio del Napoletano in Commedia</u>. Rome, 1899. In McPharlin Coll.

Croft, John. <u>Memoirs of Harry Rowe, Punch Man of England</u>. London, c 1800.
 <u>See</u> W. Cambridge.

Crowther, A. "I'll Take the High Road With Punch and Judy," <u>Pupp Master,</u> 2(4):110-11, 1948.

Cruikshank, George. Note: ...All of these editions are slightly different and of value, as those given under Collier, J. P. These are listed under Cruikshank's name in

British Museum Catalogue. (art work only)
---Punch and Judy. London, Scott, T. , 1870.
---Punch and Judy. London, Cowes, 1880.
---Polichinelle. Paris, 1836. (See O. and T. de Penöet.)
  Illus. for this book.
---"Lamentable Tragedy of Punch and Judy," Bookman,
  38:367-74, D, 1913.
---Punch and Judy. ed by J. P. Collier, New York, Double-
  day, 1930. (Rimington also given as publ. 1929.)
  Revu. of the Rimington ed. of Punch and Judy. by C.
  Cramer, Thea Arts, 14:359, Ap, 1930.
  See also J. P. Collier.
  See also R. McLean
Cruikshank, Isaac. "Punch's Puppet Show," (A Painting).
  London, Laurie and Whittle Co. , 1795. This painting was
  published and sold in a little booklet as well as in large
  prints.
Cruikshank, Robert. This artist illustrated many French
  books around 1811 and it is sometimes hard to tell which
  illustrations are by him and which are by George or Isaac.
Damon, S. Foster. A New Punch and Judy. Barre, Mass. ,
  Barre Gaz. 1957. In NN. It includes a bibliog.
Darton & Son (ed). Histories of Punch and Judy and Jenny
  Wren. London, Darton, n. d. A "Chapbook" in McPhar-
  lin Coll.
Das Kaspertheater des Leipzig Dürerbonde. Leipzig, 1927
  to 1930. A series of Kasperl plays, published between
  these dates.
Dean & Son (ed). Royal Moveable Punch and Judy. London,
  Dean, c 1885. A "Chapbook" in McPharlin Coll.
---Mr. Punch and Judy in Verse. London, Dean, 1864, illus.
  In British Museum and McPharlin Coll.
DeHempsey, Sydney. How to do Punch and Judy. London,
  Andrews, 1889. In McPharlin Coll.
Depare, Abel. Men Ami Pelichinelle. Paris, Levy, c 1887.
Desnoyers, F. Le Théâtre De Polichinelle. Paris, Poulet,
  1861.
De Tanneguy. See O. Pënhoet.
Dickens, Charles. Old Curiosity Shop. London, W. Collins,
  1937. Chapters 16, 17, 18.
---(ed). "Old Curiousity Shop." (An essay) in All Yr R,
  London, 1841.
---"Punch a Modern Frankenstein" All Yr R, 21:200-203,
  Jan 30, 1869.
Disher, M. W. Clowns and Pantomimes. London, Constable,
  1925, p 342 and passim. Sig. m. on early Punchinello
  and Punch work in Europe.

Dog Toby. See: Punch and Judy and Their Little Dog Toby.
anon.
See Sergeant Bell and His Raree-Show. anon.
See Peter Parley's Annuals. anon.
See Rachel Field
See also Paul McPharlin's, Pupp. Thea. Am. p 146.
Domon, M. "Polichinello," Pupp Master, 2(2):40-41, 1948.
Dougherty, G. W. (ed). Punchum Puppet Comic Books.
New York, Dougherty, 1946.
See also: Dough Anderson. In McPharlin Coll.
Dramaticus, (pseud). Biographia. London, 1782, also rev.
ed. 1816.
Listing of dramatic personalities, good on "Punch
Men." In British Museum.
---The Stage As It Is. London, 1847. Dramatic work of
England. In British Museum.
Ducharte, P. L. The Italian Comedy. trans. by R. Weaver,
London, Harrap, 1929.
Duranty, Louis E. Théâtre des Marionettes du Jardin des
Tuileries. Paris, Carpentier, 1880. Concerning the
string version of Polichinello in France. Dedicated to
George Sands and Maurice Sands with note on puppets by
them.
Duve, H. "Die Wiedererweckung des Kasper Theaters,"
Westerm. Monatsh, 143:601-08, Feb, 1928.
"Early 'Judy' and 'Joan' and Washington Irving," Pupp, 17:
86, 1946.
"Early Punch and Judy Man," Pupp, 3:33, 1932.
Material concerned with Mr. Bellenfant.
See also: Paul McPharlin's, Pupp. Thea. Am, p 402.
Eckereley, Peter. "Three Hundred Years of Mr. Punch,"
Guardian, 31:6, Mr, 1962.
"Educational Value of Punch and Judy," Christian Cent, 64:
1200-01, O 8, 1947.
Emberley, Edward. Punch and Judy, A Play for Puppets,
Boston, Little
Emerson, Joyce. See Hans Baumann.

Ernsting, Norman. "Modern Old World Punch and Judy
Showmen," Pupp J, 17(4):14, 16, 23, Jan 1966. illus.
Evans Brothers (ed). Mr Punch. London, Evans, 1950.

"F. A." (pseud). "Punch and Judy Modernized," Liv A,
280:183-84, Jan 17, 1914.
Feasey, Lynette. Old English at Play. London, Harrap,
1944.
Feuillet, Octave. Vie de Polichinello et ses Nombreuse
Adventures. Paris, Hetzel, 1846.

---The Story of Mr Punch. 1st ed. trans. by J. Hetzel, New York, Dutton, 1929. In McPharlin Coll.

---Life and Adventures of Punchinello. 1st ed., trans. (by author) O. Feuillet, New York, Appleton, 1847; 2nd ed., London, Oxford, 1856.

---Punch: His Life and Adventures. trans. by Paul Mc Pharlin, New York, Didier, 1946.

Revu. of Punch: His Life and Adventures, by P. Mc Pharlin, Pupp, 17:82, 1946.

Field, Rachel. Little Dog Toby. New York, Macmillan, 1938.

"First Punch Man in U.S.A.--1866," Frankfort, Pennsylvania, Register, May, 1896.

See Paul McPharlin's Pupp. Thea. Am., p 128.

Fisher & Bros. (ed). Punch and Judy, No 9. Philadelphia, Fisher. n.d. In McPharlin Coll.

Fisher, D. C. Handbook of Fist Puppets. New York, Stokes, 1935. Has much Punch and Judy material, which is quite often true of Hand or Glove puppet books. That section might lead to more information on Punch.

Foa, Eugénie (pseud). (E. A. Gradis) Memoires d'un Polichinelle. Brussels, 1838 and 1840.

Franklin, M. J. "Guignol," Plume et Encre, 7:8-10, Ap, 1940.

French or Foreign Punch Material. See also "International" Section. Using the names for Punch given in the Introduction to this Section one may locate additional material under different countries.

Frost, T. Old Showmen and Old London Fairs. London, 1874.

---Lives of the Conjurors. London, 1876, passim.
    These two books give sig. m. and tell of the combination, still used, of Punch and Judy with a magic show. Both are in the British Museum.

Fryer, W. de B. "Punch and the Puppets," All Yr R, 27: 517, Ap 27, 1872.

Fyleman, Rose (ed). Punch and Judy. London, Saunders, 1944, and London, Methuen, 1945. In McPharlin Coll.

Gable, J. H. See O. Feuillet.

Gate, E. M. Punch and Robinetta. New Haven, Yale Univ. Press, 1923; London, Oxford, 1924.

Giant-Schaefer, G. A. Punch and Judy (Operetta) Chicago, Hoffman, 1940.

Gibbs Co. (ed). Punch and Judy Chapbook. London, Gibbs, n. d. From the Gibb's, Good Child's Picture Library Series. In McPharlin Coll.

Gilmore, Margaret. Trying Toby and the Punch and Judy Show. Philadelphia, McKay, n. d. In McPharlin Coll.

94

Graham, Martha. "Punch and Judy's Dance," Mus Cour, 124:15, S, 1941.

Grandgent, C. H. Punch and Judy, The Tragical Comedy. Cambridge, Washbourne, 1925; rev. 2nd ed., London, G. Allen, 1928.

Green, Evelyn C. Guignol et ses Amis. New York, Holt, 1966.

Gringoire, Matthieu. See G. Cruikshank.

"Guignol A Paris," L'Illus, 88:pt 2, 438-39, Jl, 1930.

"Guignol Théâtre de Paris," Pupp, 9: 1938.

Guildhall Library, England. Has Punch and Judy collections: The Osborne Collection (Gr 5. 1. 16): The Kremble Collection (A. 6. 6.) Bartholomew Fair Collection (Gr 2. 1. 7.) [sic]
   The markings within parentheses are those used in the Library Collections.

Hadol and A. Cordier. Histoire de Polischinel: Les Alphabets Amusants. London, Darton, 1863. Paris: Au Journal Amusant, Henri Plon, 1863-1865. In McPharlin Coll. and in British Museum.

Haguenthal, ___ (ed). Memoires De Polichinelle. Paris, Happy Hours Co. (A. Point & A. Moussott) 1870 [sic]
   A group of Lithographs in McPharlin Coll.

Haight, A. L. Punch and Judy. New York, Rimington, 1929.

Hambling, Arthur. Punch and Judy. London, 1938. Mc Pharlin Collection.

Hammond, E. The Victorian Child. London, Oxford, n. d. In British Museum.
See also: Pupp J, 12(1):29, 1960.

Happy Hours Co. (ed). Punch and Judy: Acting Drama No 98 (In three acts). Paris, A. Point, n. d. In McPharlin Coll.

"Harlequinade or Popular Puppets" Chambers J, 27-28:(164), 123-125, Feb 21, 1857.
See also: T. Child in "History" Section, sig. short history, French, refering to mystery play use of Punch and Judy.

Harnell, Phyllis. "Punch and Judy," Oxford Companion to the Theatre. London, Oxford, 1951, p 643-46.
   Mentions that the Strand Theatre of London was called "Punch's Playhouse."

Harvard Univ. Lib. Has large collection of Punch and Judy Play Bills, many old chapbooks and much material on Punch and Judy.

Hatten. J. "Punch," American, 9:204, 1888-1889. In Phila-
delphia Free Lib.
Haut-Coeur et Gayet. ed, Polichinelle Instituteur. Paris,
Haut-Coeur, 1824.
Hayden, Benjamin. "A Painting of Punch." (Cover) M. D.
(Magazine for Dr's) D, 1966.
Hayes, J. J. Punch and Judy. No 5. in Add-A Puppet Play
Series, Birmingham, Mich., McPharlin, 1931 and New
York, French 1931.
Hazlitt, William. "Punch and the Puppet Show," in his
Lectures on Leading English Comic Writers. New York,
Dutton, 1910.
    Also in the Everyman's Library Series, 2nd ed., Lon-
don, Oxford, 1920. In British Museum.
Hempsey, S. de. How to do Punch and Judy. London, And-
rews, 1939.
Herald Traveler News Magazine. Boston, 1943 and also
records of "The Bostonian Society," found in the old State
House in Boston, will give rare puppet show hiring ma-
terial for Boston Common. Example F. Martin and R.
Geddis in summer of 1943.
Hetzel, J. See O. Feuillet

Hillman, ___ ed, Punch and Judy Comics: No 6. Chicago,
Hillman Periodicals. Jan, 1946.
Hodges, ___ (ed). Downfall of Punch. London, Hodges,
Pitt's Wholesale Toy Warehouse, n. d. In McPharlin Coll.,
Broadside verses by Punch himself.
Höffman, "Prof." (A. J. Lewis). Drawing Room Amusements.
Routledge, c 1879. Somewhat incomplete booklet with Punch
and Judy Fantocci, etc. In McPharlin Coll, and British
Museum.
Höflings Kasperl Theater. Berlin, 1929-1930. Series of
plays published between these dates.
Hogarth, William. See many of his paintings, especially
"Southwark Fair" 1733 in Masterpieces, (60) Painters Se-
ries, New York, Stokes, 1910.
    See also B. Baird, Art of the Puppet, p 101.
    See also Hogarth, by Charles Lewis Hind, New York,
Stokes, 1910.
Hone, William. Everyday Book. Vol. III, London, Ward,
1826, 1831, 1888. In British Museum.
Hope, Ascott R. The Adventures of Punch. London, Black,
1905.
Houseworth, D. "Toy Punch and Judy Show," Pop Sci, 117:
91, D, 1930.
Howard, Sidney Coe. "Paradox of the Puppet--An Extinct

Amusement Born Anew, Punch Most Immortal Character,"
Curr Op, 60:28-29, Jl 1916.
---"Tony Sarg and Others," Boston Transcript, Spring, 1916.
Under...H. T. Parker's "Scrapbooks of Dramatic Criti-
cism in Boston Transcript-1904 to 1924" In Harvard Univ.
Lib.
Howard, T. E. "Punch Pottary--Secondary Puppet Collec-
tion," Pupp Master, 9(3):8-9, 1936.
Hubbard, O. B. History of O. B. Hubbard's Celebrated Lon-
don Punch and Judy in United States and England. Law-
rence, Mass., 1874. In Harvard Lib.
Humbug'em, Rev. J. (pseud). Punch and Judy, A Whimsi-
cally Queer Tragically Operatical Comedy With Cruikshank
Designs. New York, Elton, n. d. In McPharlin Coll.
Hutton, Clarkee. Punch and Judy, an Acting Book With
Drawings. New York, n. d. In McPharlin Coll.
Hyman, E. Punch and Judy. London, Constable, 1930.

Illman & Son (ed). The Variety Book for Children. Phila-
delphia, Illman, c 1825, passim. In McPharlin Coll.
"Immortal Punchinello With His Play," Pupp Master, 4(2):
33-37, 1952.
"India's Punch and Judy," All Yr R, 7:462, Jl, 1862.
One of those deceiving titles, concerned with the periodical, but of value to puppeteer for background and com-
parison to Punch character. Article probably by editor,
Charles Dickens.
Irish Punch Shows. see "Smock Alley Theatre" Dublin Evening Mail, O 17, 1908. Director: Mr. Stretch, James
Harrey. Material found on either name might be of help.
see also G. Speaight's, Hist. Eng. Pupp. Thea., p 124,
127, 290.
see also Dublin Puppet Theater called "Patagonian Theater," in London 1776-81 (Check local papers.) Director
Kane O'Hara.
Irvine, J. "Widow Polichinelle: Our first Tragedienne Addresses her Audience," Lippencott M, 91:231-32, Feb,
1913.
Irving, Washington. The Sketch Book. 2nd ed., ed. by E.
E. Wentworth, New York, Allyn and Bacon, 1820.; rev.
ed. New York, Macmillan, 1929.
Jack Pudding (pseud). The name of the person who went a-
head of the Punch and Judy shows with a trumpet, to gather in the crowds. Material might be found under this
title.
Jardiel, P. "Le Folklore Lyonnais, et Mieux le Guignol
Lyonnais," in Academie des Sciences, Lettre et Arts

97

d'Arras. Memoires, Lyons, Arras, 1933. Folklore
Punch and Judy of France.
Jesson, W. H. Punch and Judy. N. 1, 1932. Tells of de-
cline from 19th century and then revival. In Detroit Mu-
seum Lib.
John, D. Punch and Judy: St. George and the Dragon
Plays. Puffin Series, London, Penguin Bks, 1966.
Johnson, W. S. J. (ed). Punch's Nursery Rhymes. London,
Johnson, W. , n. d. - c 1830. In McPharlin Coll.
Jonson, Ben. Bartholomew Fair. ed. by E. M. Waith, New
Haven, Yale Univ. Press, 1963.
Jordan, Nina R. "Finger-Puppet Punch and Judy Show,"
The Home Toy Shop. New York, Harcourt, 1941, p 216-
23.
Judd, W. J. The Tragical Acts or Comical Tragedy of
Punch and Judy. New York, Happy Hours, 1869. In Mc
Pharlin Coll.
Kahn, G. (ed). Polichinelle de Guignol Précede D'une Étude.
Paris, Kahn, 1906.
Kasparspiele, Kleine. Leipzig, Hasse, 1930.

Kasperl Theater. Kasperl Theater Plays. Prague, Hasse,
1851. Leipzig, 1850 and 1922. (In British Museum.)
Berlin, Ullestein, 1929-1931.
A series of plays published between these dates.
Kemp, Tom. "Prof." "One Bottle for Mr Punch," Pupp
Master, 2(4):108-110, 1948.
"Bottle" means collection in the Punch terminology.
This modern Professor has booth at Brighton, Eng. Lo-
cal papers would give added information as he has been
at a regular beach booth many summers.
---"Mr. Punch Reigns Again," Pupp Master, 7(1):16-17,
1962. Very sig. m. in this article.
Kierman, Irma. "Punch and Judy," Pupp, 13:8, 1942.
Kimberley, Edward. Punch and Judy. Ashville, Puppetry
Journal Public. , n. d.
King, S. (ed). Punch and Judy With Illustrations designed
by George Cruikshank. New York, King, 1828. In Mc
Pharlin Coll.
Koller, Hans. Spela Kaspertheater. Stockholm, Viking,
1956.
Laskey, D. E. "The Punch and Judy Man," Pupp P,
Autumn, 1954, p 12. Concerned with 20th century work.
Laurence, G. Gilbert Laurence's Original Punch and Judy
Puppet Show. New York, Laurence Enterprises, 1943.
Lawrence, W. J. "Immortal Mr. Punch," The Times, Jan.
22, 1921 Puppetry Column.

--- "Immortal Mr. Punch," Liv A, 308:(3994) Jan 22, 1921.

Leech, M. T. "Punch and Judy; Drama," Plays, 26:91-98, N, 1966.
Leipsic, F. V. Punch's Merry Franks. 2nd ed. London, W. Tegg, n. d. - c 1840's; also London, Myers, c 1842. In McPharlin Coll.
Lennep, William Van. "The Earliest Known English Playbill," Harvard Lib Bull, 1(3):352-355, Autumn 1947. Mentions John Harris Tower Hall, 1721.
Leoncavallo, Ruggiero. Pagliacchi. (Punchinello) trans. H. G. Chapman, Boston, Schirmer, 1907. This is the famous musical number but Punchinello is the basis.
Lettre de Polichinelle a Jules Mazarin. Paris, 1649.

List, Arzubide G. Punch Beats the Devil. trans. Philip Stevenson, New York, Author, 1936 (Typescript). In NN. A Mexican Punch and Judy Show.
Lodwig, David. "Bochumer, Germany's Figurentheater- woche," Pupp J, 18(5):31-33, 1967. 20th century Punch and Judy players from Germany and Switzerland.
London Town, Pictures and Verses, Including Punch and Judy Show. London, Marcus Ward, 1883. In McPharlin Coll.
"London's Early Punch Men and a Pleasure Garden Theater," Pupp, 11:56, 1940.
Lyser, J. P. Bildergallerie Zu Polichinell: Stuttgart, Von Paulnoff, 1865.
McKenchnie, Samuel. Popular Entertainments Through the Ages. London, Low, 1931.
McLean, Ruari. George Cruikshank, His Life and Work as an Illustrator. (part 2) New York, Pellegrini, 1948.
McLendon, E. "Punch and Judy," Instr, 66:41, D, 1956.

McManaway, Dr. J. G. "Puppet Playbills, 1690-1710." Washington, D. C. , at the Folger Shakespeare Lib. , c 1960.
McPharlin, Paul. "The Collier-Cruikshank Punch and Judy Book" Colophan, new series 1:(3) 371-87, Feb-Je, 1936.
---The Collier-Cruikshank Punch and Judy Book Thea Arts, 14:357-58, Ap, 1930.
---Punch: His Life and Adventures. trans. P. McPharlin, see O. Feuillet.
---"Mrs. Punch's Name," Pupp, 13:4-5, 1942.

---Puppet Theatre in America 1524 to Now. New York, Harper, 1949, p 116-155. Much Punch material scattered under many headings through the book.

--- <u>see</u> "Pulcinella," p 116 and "Punchinello," p 26, 38, 116, 118, 129 in <u>Pupp. Thea Am.</u>
--- (ed). <u>Tragical Comedy of Punch and Judy</u> by J. P. Collier, Now Edited With an Introduction by Paul McPharlin. New York, Limited Editions Club, 1937. In Deering Lib., Northwestern Univ.
<u>Magic Punch and Judy Show.</u> New York, Lou Tannen Magic House, 1950. Punch and Judy Show Kit. Originally published London, 1862. In the British Museum.
Malik, Jan. "Traditions and the Present Day," <u>Pupp. Thea. Mod. World</u>, p 10-11, 19. Speaks about "Petroushka."
Marks, O. L. (ed). <u>The Serio-Comic Drama of Punch and Judy.</u> London, Marks, 1891. A chapbook in the Mc Pharlin Coll.
Marspen Series (ed). <u>Punch and Judy.</u> London, Marspen Series Toy Books, No. 3, n. d. In McPharlin Coll.
Marten, D. (ed). <u>Punch's Pleasantries.</u> London, D. Marten, c 1870. In McPharlin Coll.
Martini, Ella. <u>Kasperle-Bastelbuch; Eine Anleitung Sur Herstellong Von Handpuppen Aus Verschiedenema.</u> n. 1., n. d.
Matthews, Brander. <u>Punch and Judy. No 3.</u> of Puppet Plays and Pamphlets. Worchester, Malvern, n. d. In McPharlin Coll.
---"Excerpts--(about Punch and Judy)," <u>Am Rev of Rev,</u> Jan, 1914, p 102.
---"Punch and Judy Excerpts," <u>Bookman,</u> 38:367-74, D, 1913.

---"Most Immoral Character--Punch," <u>Curr Op,</u> 56:28, Jan, 1914.
---"Lamentable Tragedy of Punch and Judy," in his <u>Book About the Theater.</u> New York, Scribner's, 1916, p 271-86.
Maxwell, J. R. <u>Punch and the Puppets.</u> London, 1865.

Mayhew, Henry. <u>London Labour and the London Poor.</u> Vol. 3, London, c 1850. In British Museum.
---<u>London Labour and the London Poor.</u> rev. ed., London, Kimber, 1951. In British Museum.
---<u>London's Underworld.</u> ed. by P. Quennell. New York, Kimber, 1950. In British Museum.
---<u>Mayhew's London.</u> ed. by P. Quennell. New York, Kimber, 1950. In British Museum.
---<u>Mayhew's Characters.</u> ed. by P. Quennell. New York, Kimber, 1951. In British Museum.
<u>See also.</u> Mr. Punch. by P. J. Stead.
Michael, Vivian. "George Larson, Punch and Judy Man,"

Pupp J, 5(1):11, 1953.
---"The Punch and Judy Man," Pupp J, 15(5):4-5, 1964.

Miller, Thomas. Picturesque Sketches of London Past and
   Present. London, 1851-1854--(In National Illustrated
   Library) In British Museum.
   see also: Pupp Master, 4(3): 1950.
Monsell, J. R. Polichinelle. New York, Oxford, 1930.
Revu. Polichinelle. by Carl Cramer. Thea Arts, 14:
   357-58, Ap, 1930.
Morice, Gerald. "England's Modern Punch and Judy Show
   Still Strong," Pupp, 11:33, 1940.
---"Bygone Punch and Puppet Shows," Pupp Master, 3(4):
   115-19, 1950.
---"Round the Resorts," World's Fair, N 1, 1952, in his
   "Puppet Column," n. p.   He continued this title in his
   "Puppet Column" in World's Fair from around 1950-1966,
   N 29, 1952; N 21, 1953; O 24, 1953; N 13, 1954; O 30,
   1954, etc.
Morley, Henry. Memoirs of Bartholomew's Fair. London,
   1859. In Chandos Lib., England.
Mourquet, Laurent. "Originator of Character Guignol,"
   Pupp J, 10(5):3-5, 1959.
"Mr. Punch or the Drama at the Street Corner," Chambers
   J. (Edinburgh) 59:75, 1882 (4th series, no 19).
"Name of Punch and Judy and Its Meaning," Marionette, 1
   (3):89-90, My, 1918.
Neal & MacKenzie (ed).   The Tragical Comedy of Punch and
   Judy.   Philadelphia, Neale, 1828.   In McPharlin Coll.
"New York City Exhibit depicts history of puppet King,
   Punch," N Y Times, Ap 6, 1951, 28:1.
Nette, Papa de.   Le Théâtre de Polichinelle.   Paris, Li-
   brairies-Impremeries Reunies, n. d.   In McPharlin Coll.
Newnes, George (ed).   Punch and Judy Children's Annual.
   London, Newnes Periodicals, 1931.   In British Museum.
Nisbet, ___ (ed).   Punch and Judy.   London, Nisbet, 1901.

Oldham, Arthur.   Mr. Punch.   Chicago, Sadler Wells, 1946.
Revu. of Mr. Punch.   Anon, Pupp, 17:56, 1946.
Oliver and Tannequy de Penhoet.   (ed)   see Penhoet, O & T.

Owl, The.   see   C. H. Bennet

Oxberry, William and Mrs. eds.   Dramatic Biography and
   Histronic Anecdotes.   Vol. 5, London, Oxberry Public.
   1825-1826.   In the British Museum.
---Literary Speculum.   London, Oxberry, 1821.

See also   British Museum Catalogue. Vol 41, p 518-19.
"Periodical Publications, Dramatic." (Ann Arbor, J. W.
Edwards, 1946 ed.)
Papernose Woodensconce see: C. H. Bennett.

Papyrus et Marine.   Punch et Judy.   Celebre Drame Guig-
nolesque Anglais.   Pour la Premiere Fois Adapte en
France.   Paris, 1903.
Parks, A. (ed).   History of Punch and Judy.   Finsbury, Eng. ,
Park, 1847.   In McPharlin Coll.
---Parks Punch and Judy.   Finsbury, Park, 1847.   In Mc
Pharlin Coll.
Parry, G. H.   "Prof. R. Codman Gets New Punch and Judy
Booth From the City of Liverpool," Pupp, 1:31-32, 1930.
Paul, H. (ed).   The Serio-Comic Drama of Punch and Judy.
Spitalfield, Eng. , H. Paul, c 1840.   In McPharlin Coll.
Peepshow Pictures, Pop-up Type.   (Ernest Nister) New
York, Dutton, n. d.   In McPharlin Coll.
Penhöet, Olivier and Tannequy de.   Polichinelle.   Paris,
Penhoet, 1835.
Bureaux de L'histoire Pittoresque D'Angleterre.   S. Fau-
bourg Montmarte.
---et Cruikshank.   Polichinelle.   (Drame) Paris, Penhoet,
1836.   In British Museum.
Pennington, J.   "Origin of Punch and Judy," Mentor, 12:
47-48, D, 1924.
Pepys, Samuel.   see "History" Section
see also: Pupp Master, 7(1):12, 1962.
Percival, R.   "Punch and Judy Return to South Africa,"
World's Fair, Jan 20, 1940 "Puppet Column."
"Percy," Prof. (Percy Press).   "20th Century" "Punch King
of England.
see   Bill Baird's, Art of the Puppet, p 17.
see   G. Speaight's Hist. Eng. Pupp. Thea. , p 217.
Has permanent theatre at the Festival Pleasure Gar-
dens.   London, Eng.   Local papers and World's Fair
"Puppet Columns" should be studied.
Peter Parley's Annals.   Anon. , London, c 1883.   In Mc
Pharlin Coll.
Petite, J. M.   "Guignols et Marionnettes" in his Suite du
Repertoire du Théâtre.   Paris, Joel, 1822 and 1826, p
117-281.   In Oberlin Univ. Lib.
Phillips, Jane.   "The Professors--Hard Working Showmen,"
Pupp Master, 7(1):14-15, 1962.
---"The Punch Tercentenary Celebrations and Shows in Eng-
land," Pupp Master, 7(1):22-23, 1962.
Phillips, M. D.   Punch and Judy Drawings.   Chicago, 1937.

These are available only on special request at the Mc
Pharlin Coll.

Pierce, L. F. "Punch and Judy Up To Date," World Today,
20:352-55, Mr, 1911.

Pocci, Franz Graf. Kasperltheatre. Berlin, Ullestein, 1920.
8 fascicules, pièces par le Comte Pocci. In NN.

---Kasper, The Portrait Painter. trans, 1. Beer, Boston,
Humphris, 1961.

---Lustique Kasperlkomodien. Lipzig, Insel, 19--
Mit sechs Holzschnitten nach zeichnugen des Dichters.
(Kasperl Larifari).
see also: "German" section.

Polichinelle. Paris, n. d. Available at Mme S. Z. Le
Théâtre de Polichinelle par le Papa de Nénette.

Politicks in Minerature. London, printed for J. Macbell,
O 30, 1741 and N 6, 1941 [sic]. In McPharlin Coll.
Title page reads as above.

---"Politicks in Minerature," Westminster J, Mr 20, 1741,
p 2.

Pope, Jessie. Punch and Judy. Rainbow Series, No. 1,
London, Ward, 1933.

"Powell at Punch's Theater," Pupp, 17:61, 62, 1946.

Preston, E. E. Punchinello Puppet Plays. Framingham,
Dennison, 1936.

Priestley, J. B. (Peter Goldsmith) pseud. "Mr. Punch," in
his The Balconniny. London, Harper, 1931, p 16-22.
In Harvard Univ. Lib.

---"Mr. Punch," Sat R, 146:176-78, Ag 11, 1928. (London
Issue).

Priestly, Harold E. Six Little Punch Plays. London, Paxton, 1956.

Proctor, E. and Romain. "Puppets Old and Puppets New,"
Pupp J, 5:10-12, 21-22, N, 1953. Mrs. Romain Proc-
tor collects "Punch" material and has a good lib. See:
Puppeteers of America Directory. In NN.

"Pulcinella--The Punch Ballet," Pupp Master, 7(1):12, 1962.

"Punch," Pupp, 6:80, 1935.

"Punch and Judy," Mon R, London, 115(31):368-79, Mr,
1828. Sig. m.

"Punch and Judy," Fraser's, 3:350, 1824.

Punch and Judy. ed. by Chambers, London, Chambers
Journal Co., 1832. In McPharlin Coll.

"Punch and Judy," Marionette, 1(4):126-27, Jan, 1918.

"Punch and Judy," Nation, London, 33:13-14, Ap 7, 1923.

Punch and Judy. Boston, Little, c 1962, illus. by E. Emberly.

Punch and Judy. London, Longman, 1962. Book Series, ed by Longman.

Punch and Judy. Boston, Humphries, c 1962. Silver Series, of Puppet Plays.

Punch and Judy: A Serio-Comical Tragedy in Three Acts. London, 1861. In British Museum.

Punch and Judy and Their Little Dog Toby. London, Moveable Edition, Epworth, 1861. Verse form, in British Museum.

Punch and Judy Alphabet, in Verse. London, Ward, 1880. Color illus. In British Museum.

"Punch and Judy Banks," Pupp J, 13(3):30, 1961.

Punch and Judy Books. London, Oxford, 1931. 4 Vols.

Punch and Judy Box. see: Punch and Judy Books.

"Punch and Judy in Australia," All Yr R, 9:610, 1863. This is more about Punch periodical work than puppets.

Punch and Judy, Periodical, London, 1869-1870. In the British Museum, several of these.

Punch and Judy in Animal Land. London, Epworth, 1938.

Punch and Judy Picture Book With Plates. London and New York, 1873. In the British Museum.

"Punch and Judy Pictures," Holly Leaves (Eng.), D, 1965. 5 pages.

Punch and Judy, Record. New York, Twinkle Records Tw-10, n. d. The complete story, 33-1/3 rpm. See "Music" Section this title.

"Punch and Judy Revival," Ch Sci Mon, Eastern, Jl 1, 1964, p 2, col. 1.

"Punch and Polichinello," Marionette, 1(3):88-9, My, 1918.

Punch and Puppets. British Standard Hand Books, No 38. London, I. & R. Maxwell, 1883. In British Museum.

"Punch at Brooklyn Terrace Gardens," Brooklyn Daily Eagle, Jl 8, 1873, p 15.

"Punch at Dime Museum," Brooklyn Daily Eagle, Mr 1 and Feb 23, 1879.

"Punch at New Gardens in Bowery," Odell, 9:448, Ag, 1874.

"Punch at Spectaculum," N Y Am, D 22, 1828. n. p.

"Punch at the Fair," Va Gaz, D 22, 1738. n. p. are given
in this periodical.

"Punch Has No Feeling," Marionette, 1(3):88-89, My, 1918.

"Punchiana Exhibits," Pupp Master, 7(1):26, 1962.

"Punch in America," Pupp, 1:17, 1930, ...a brief listing
from 1747.

Punch in Camera-Land. New York, Pitman, 1948.

Punchinello's Picture Book. London, Routledge, 1882.

Punchinello. London and New York. A satirical periodical
like Punch and Puppet Show periodicals. Some copies
may be found in British Museum and in Harvard Univ.
Lib.

"Punch, on Coney Island," Harpers W, Ag 10, 1878, p 631.

"Punch, or The London Charivari," Pupp Master, 7(1):12,
1962. Concerned with Punch the actor and the publication called Punch.

"Punch Prospers Under President Hayes," - 1866. Pupp, 6
80, 1935.

"Punch Show," N Y Her Tribune, D 19, 1861.

"Punch, The Immortal Puppet," Craft Horiz, 11(2):16-17,
1951.

"Punch's Address on His Master's Recent Imprisonment,"
Marionette, 1:281-83, N, 1918.

Punch's Comic Broad Sheet. London, 1854. In British Museum.

Punch's Illustrated Comic Gallery. London, 1854. In British Museum.

Punch's Magnetic Table-moving, Grin-producing, Side-split-
ting Sheet of Fun. London, 1854. In British Museum.

"Punch's Pedigree," Brit. Pupp Thea, 1(5):29, 1950.

Punch's Pocket Book. London, n. d. In British Museum.

Punch's Politicks in Several Dialogues Between Him and His
Acquaintances. London, 1762. In British Museum.

"Punch's Props," Pupp, 6:29, 1935.

Puppet Show, The. London, Mr, 1848, Vol. 1. Early Eng.
satiric periodical. British Museum and Harvard Univ.

Lib. a few copies, good Punch illus.
Quennell, Peter (ed). Selections from "London Labor and London Poor." by Henry Mayhew. London, Kimber, 1851.
---Mayhew's London. London, Kimber, 1951. see H. Mayhew. Both in British Museum.
Rabe, J. E. Kasper Putschennele. Hamburg, Quickborn, 1924.
Racca, Carlo. (Akkar) Burattini E Marionette. Torino, Paravia, 1921.
Ralph, James (A. Primcock). The Touchstone. London, 1728, 2nd printing, passim.
---The Taste of the Town or Guide to All Public Diversions. London, printed and published by the Book Sellers of London. In British Museum and Harvard Univ. Lib.
Ransome, Grace G. "Punch and Judy's Ancestry," Thea and Sch, 7:9-12, D, 1928.
Rémond, Jules. Polichinelle. Paris, 1838. G. Cruikshank illus.
Richmond, E. T. Punch and Judy: A Tragical Drama in One Act for Toys. New York, French, c 1904.
Ringelnatz, J. Kasperle Verse. Berlin, 1954.

Roberts, Cecil. "Il Pulcinella, an Italian Exploration," Liv A, 17:313, 151-54, Ap 15, 1922.
Rogers, I. F. "Punch and Judy on a South African Beach," Pupp P, Spring 1951, p 11-12.
Romand, Alexandre. Manuscript, 1388 and 1344 - in Bodleian Lib. Oxford, Eng. See also J. O. Westwood this section.
Rose, Arthur. The Boy Showman and Entertainer. New York, Dutton, 1926, p 1-35, 115-41. In McPharlin Coll.
Rose, E. J. Punch and Judy Carry On. London, Faber, 1963.
Rosenberg, J. N. Punchinello, A Ballet. Chicago, Argus Bk, 1923. In McPharlin Coll.
Rosenfeld, Sybil. Strolling Players and Drama in the Provinces, 1660-1765. Cambridge, Cambridge Univ. Press, 1939, passim.
Routledge and Sons (ed). Every Little Boy's Book. London, Routledge, c 1875. Incomplete, extracted form in the McPharlin Coll.
---Punch and Judy in Eight Acts. London, Routledge, 1866.

Rowlandson, Thomas. A Painting, "George III and Queen Charlotte" - 1785, Pupp Master, 3:(7)--1951.
Russell, Ernest. "The Most Popular Play in the World,"

Out M, 51:463-79, Jan, 1908.
Ryan, Kate. "Old Boston Museum Days." New York, Thea
Arts, 1915, p 10.
Sargeant Bell and His Raree-Show. London, Tegg, 1839.
Concerned with Dog Toby. In McPharlin Coll.
Sayer, Robert. Harlequinade. No 13, from the "Turn-Up
Set" London, Mr 23, 1772, passim.
---Punch's Puppet Show. No 14, from the "Turn-Up Set"
London, Ap, 1772. In British Museum.
Schetty, Madeline. "Impressions of 'Guignol' in Lyons,"
Pupp, 17:49-50, 1946.
Schick, Joseph S. The Early Theatre of Eastern Iowa.
Chicago, Univ. of Chicago Press, 1939, p 273.
Schmidt, Dr. Hugo. Allerlei Kasparstücke. Leipzig, 1929.

"Seven Years With Punch and Judy," Pupp, 8: n.p., 1937.

Smith, Albert. Comic Tales and Sketches. London, Bently,
1852, p 19.
Smith, Horace. "Stanzas to Punchinello," New Monthly,
10: n.p, 1824. In McPharlin Coll.
---"Stanzas to Punchinello," Pupp Master, old series, 1947.
In McPharlin Coll.
Smith, Mathew H. Sunshine and Shadow in New York. Hart-
ford, and Boston, 1868, p 440. In British Museum.
Smith, "Prof." The Book of Punch and Judy. London, c
1926.
"Smithsonian Institute Punch Indian Card-Punch Sells Cigars,"
Pupp, 13:64, 1942.
See also Pupp J, 18(3):38, 1966.
Somers, P. H. "Punch and Judy Sticks," Sch Arts, 52:314,
My 1953.
Speaight, George. "Devil in the Puppet Punch Show," Pupp,
11, 1940.
---Juvenile Drama. History of Toy Theatre. London, Har-
rap, 1947. passim.
---Studies in English Theatrical History. London, Society
of Research, 1952, passim.
---"Payne Collier and Punch and Judy," Notes and Queries,
1:1, 1954.
---The History of the English Puppet Theatre. London,
Harrap, 1955.
---"Mr Punch--An Editorial," Theatre Notebook, 1962.
See: Pupp Master, 7(1):8-9, 1962.
---"Evolution of (Punch) Drama," Pupp Master, 7(1):27-28,
1962.
---"Tercentenary Mr Punch-1662-1962," Pupp Master, 7(1):
1, 1962.

Staddon, Bert. "Prof. B. Staddon and Punch," Brit Pupp
Thea, 3(5):2, 1952.
Stanyon, Ellis. "Punch and Judy in Magic," Magic, 5:no 5
(Feb, 1905); 5:no 6 (Mr 1905): 5:no 7(Ap 1905); 5:no 8
(My 1905); 5:no9 (Je 1905).
Stead, P. J. Mr Punch. London, Evans, 1950.
see H. Mayhew. In NN.
Revu. Mr Punch by Jan Bussell, Pupp Master, 3(6):201-
03, 1951.
Stevenson, Philip. See A. G. List

Steward, M. Land of Punch and Judy. London, Revell,
1922.
Stone, Wilbur M. "Punch, Prince of Rogues," American
Collector, O, 1938, p 12-14.
Stonier, G. W. "Punch Over Hamstead," N Statesm, 44:
132, Aug. 2, 1952.
Story, Alfred T. From Punch to Padan Aram, or Thoughts
by a Rambling Philosopher. London, Stock, 1892, passim.
In McPharlin Coll.
---"Punch and Judy," Strand, S-O, 1895, p 462-71.

Swift, Jonathan. Mad Mollinix and Timothy. London, 1728,
passim. In British Museum.
Symonds, E. M. "Prototypes of Punch," Cornhill, London,
71(24):305-13, Mr, 1895. New Series.
Teall, Gardner. "Punch and Judy Shows," Theatre, 8:240-
42, S, 1908.
Tearle, P. Punch and Judy Puppets. Leicester, Dryad,
1957 and 1966.
Tegg, Thomas (ed). Sargeant Bell and His Raree Show.
London, Tegg, 1839. In McPharlin Coll.
Tertulias de la Infancia. El Teatro de Guignol. Paris,
Libreria Nachette 1879. In McPharlin Coll.
"Tercentenary of Mr Punch-Issue" Entire issue of Pupp
Master 7(1); 1962.
Tesorek, A. Kasperl Sucht Den Weibnachtemahn. Vienna,
Jahrbuch, 1927.
Tesknovitser, Orest and Igor Eremin. Petroushka Theater.
Leningrad and Moscow, Orbis, 1865.
The Punch and Judy Man. Film Association, British Picture
Corp., London, 1963-1964. Biography of puppet "Prof."
Joe Hastings of Eng.
see also Pupp J, 15(5):14, 16, 18, 1964.
Thorndike, R. and R. Arkell. Tragedy of Mr Punch: With
an Essay of Introduction by Max Beerbohm. London,
Duckworth, 1923; also London, Liveright, 1924.

Tickner, P. F. Story of Punch and Judy. 1937.

Tour in England, Ireland, etc. by a German Prince. (Sir
    Puecklen-Musken) Philadelphia, Casey, Lea and Blanch-
    ard, 1833. In McPharlin Coll.
Tozer, H. V. "Putxinel-Lis," (Catalan for Pulcinello),
    Pupp Master, 2(2):41-49, 1948.
"The True Story of Punch and Judy," in The Magic Picture
    Book. London, A. N. Myers Co., c 1830. In the Mc
    Pharlin Coll.
Turner & Fisher (ed). Serio-Comic Story of Punch and
    Judy. Philadelphia, Turner, 1840. In McPharlin Coll.
Verhoeven, Jan J. Kuskenfeest hij Jan Klaassen. Lier, J.
    Van Incorp, 1953.
Wallis, E. (ed). Punch and Judy, A Comical Tale. Lon-
    don, Wallis, c 1830. In McPharlin Coll.
Ward, Lock and Tyler (ed). Punch and Judy With Colored
    Illustrations. London, Ward, 1806. In British Museum.
Ward, Thomas A. M. Punch and Judy. Janesville, Wis.,
    Veeder & Leonard, 1874. In McPharlin Coll. and British
    Museum.
Weaver, R. see P. L. Ducharte

Webb, Aileen. "The Fabulous Punch." Pupp J, 2:(5)7,
    1951.
Wehnert, E. H. Great Fun for Our Little Friends. London,
    1862, p 35. In British Museum.
West, M. P. Punch and Judy Away. London, Longmans,
    1969.
Westwood, J. O. "Notice of a Medieval-Mimic Entertain-
    ment Resembling Punch and Judy," (Roman) Archeologi-
    cal Journal 5:198-200, Sept, 1848.
    see also: Romand Alexandre
Wheatley, H. B. Notes on the Life of John Payne Collier.
    London, 1884. In British Museum.
    see also J. P. Collier, this section.
Whitechurch. "Mr. Puch, Material From 1662-1962," Pupp
    Master, 7:(1), 1962.
Wilkinson, Walter. Vagabonds and Puppets. London, Bles,
    1930; and New York, Stokes, 1931.
---How to Give a Puppet Show: Leaflet No. 50. London,
    Dryad, n.d. (Dryad Handicraft Series). In McPharlin
    Coll.
---Peep Show. London, Bles, 1932.
---"My First Punch and Judy Puppet Show," Pupp, 13-14:
    22-23, 1942-1943.
Wilshaw, Judith. Punch and Judy. London, Raphel Tuck,

n. d. (but c 1938). In McPharlin Coll.

Wilson, E. "Notes From a European Diary," New Yorker, 42:57-58, My 28, 1966. Punch and Judy and Pulcinella.

Wilson, N. S. Punch and Judy. London, French, 1934.

World's Fair, The. "Puppet Column," Lancashire, Eng. Weekly periodical that gives much material on Punch show and performers all around Eng. and the Island. Different authors as it has been active since about 1900.

D - International Material

Introduction

The Section is arranged by the countries in which, or about which, the article is written. When the article is not limited to one national but seems international it is placed in the first part under the heading International. American material has been listed by states. I know there should be much more given under these States but time did not permit individual research for each, except as they came to my attention in the general research work for the Guide. American Indian material is rare and is given in the American Section in alphabetical order under the heading Indian instead of under each state.

Much of the foreign material has been cross-indexed into other appropriate places but this material is still not covered exhuastively. Furthermore, there will be mistakes in this foreign material because different sources give different spellings and titles for the same book.

McGill University Library, in Montreal, has a very, very large French puppet collection. The New York Public Library has a large German collection of puppet material. All puppet material has been transferred from the Central New York Public Library to "The Museum and Library of Performing Arts" at Lincoln Center, in New York City, so wherever the note says "In N. Y. Pub. Lib." the material will probably be in this new Branch library.

D. 1 - International

Anderson, Madge. The Heroes of the Puppet Stage. New York, Harcourt, 1924.
Andrews, A. K. "Puppets Abroad," Pupp J, 18(4):16-17, 1967.
"Around the Puppet World," Pupp, 14: n.p, 1943.

111

Avery, Verna. "Music for the Marionette Theatre; Its History and Use," Pupp J, 2(3):2-6, 1950.
see also "Music" Section.
Baird, Bill. The Art of the Puppet. New York, Macmillan, 1966.
---"Baird to Tour Under State Dept. Auspices," N Y Times, D 9, 1960, 21:1. Anon. interview.
---"Bairds to Tour Asia," N Y Times, D 26, 1960, 45:2. Anon. interview.
---"Report on World Tour of Asia by Baird's Puppets," N Y Times, My 5, 1962, 18:2.
---"Bairds Representing U. S. ," Pupp J, 16(2):10, 1964. This trip was for C. B. S. Broadcasting Co.
see also A. R. Philpott
Barbuta, M. see A. R. Philpott

Batchelder, Marjorie. (Mrs. Paul McPharlin) Rod Puppets and the Human Theatre. Columbus, Ohio State Univ. Press, 1942.
Benegal, Dom. Puppet Theatre Around the World. New Delhi, Bharatiya, Natya Sangh Organization, 1961.
see also "Periodicals" Section, this group.
Blickle, Peg. "It's News to Me," Pupp J, 9(6):27, 1958.

Brinbaum, A. "Puppets for Goodwill," Gr Teach, O, 1946, p 42-44.
Broman, Nelle E. "International Themes," Pupp Bull, 8: 75, 1937.
Burknolder, M. "Link of U. N. Friends Through Puppets," Am Childh, 34:29-31, S, 1948.
Bussell, Jan. "European Puppet Week," Pupp Master, 5(5): 10-14, 1957.
---"UNIMA Meeting in Prague," Pupp Master, 5(8):14-15, 1958.
---"Bucharest Report," Pupp Master, 5(9):3-4, 6, 1958.

Calendar of Puppet Festivals-1963 Bulletin No 5 Prague, Secretary General's Office of UNIMA Organization, 1963. irregular.
see also Pupp J, 14(6):13, 19, 1963.
Carr, J. "International Puppet Tour," Pupp Master, 2(6): 144, 1954.
Coleman, S. J. (ed). Puppets of Many Races. London, Folklore Academy, 1957. In Harvard Univ. Lib.
Copfermann, E. see A. R. Philpott

Detroit Museum of Art Bulletin. Between Museum office quarterly. This publication has much material about the international puppet shows that appear at the puppet theatre in this museum because it is the center for visiting foreign troups, in America. Charles Elam, ed. 1960's published q.

Edwards, Julia. "From Sweden to Turkey With Puppets," Brit Pupp Thea, 1(5):4, 1950. Directing and writing on the "Marshall Plan Explanation Program."
see also "Plays" Section Walter Lucas, "The Village of Europe."

"Even puppets meet in International Conventions," N Y Times, S 22, 1929, 9:

"Expeditional Alexandre " N Y Pupp G Newsl 2(6):1, 7, 1965. The International traveling unit from France of Philippe Gentry and Yves Brunier. See also "France," and "Theatres" Section.

Falkenstein, Mollie. "Europe by Volkswagon," Pupp J, 15 (2):9-11, 22, 23, 1963.

---"Molly Reports," Pupp J, 16(4):11-12, 13, 1965.

---Puppets International. Ashville, Puppetry Journal Public, 1966. Names and addresses of puppeteers around the world.

---"UNIMA News," Pupp J, 19(1):41-42, 1967. Became continuous item to 1970, following M. Batchelder McPharlin's columns of "International Reports." As Secretary General in U. S. A. of UNIMA she handles all international puppet information.

--- (ed.). Souvenir Pictorial Calendar of Puppets and Puppeteers. Los Angeles, M. Falkenstein, 1968. The 1968-1969 issue is the first of these and it is published in Aug. instead of Jan. For the American chapter of "International UNIMA." Comments with photographs.

---(ed). UNIMA-U. S. A. Newsletter, 1:2, Je 1968. First issue of this publication giving "Impressions of England's International Colwyn Bay Festival of 1968."

"Foreign Puppeteers," Puppeteers of America Membership Directory. Ashville, Puppetry Journal Public, yearly since 1961. In NN.

Forster, John. Life and Times of Oliver Goldsmith. Vol 2, Bk 4, Chapter 14, London, Bradbury & Evans, 1854, Chapman & Hall, 1871, Hutchinson, 1903. In British Museum.
Title is sometimes given as Life and Adventures of Oliver Goldsmith.
see also "England" under J. Forster.

Genty, Philippe. "Los Angeles Entertains French "Expeditions Alexandre" International Puppet Theatre of Paris," Pupp J, 15(5):28-31, 1965. See also "Expeditions Alexandre."

"Giant Puppets For Barong Landog," Thea Arts, 20:604,
Aug, 1936.
Giddings, June. "Around the Puppet World," Pupp, 5:15-17,
1934.
Gilmore, Spence. "Our Neighbors Abroad," Pupp J, 4(4):
20-21, 1953.
---"Abroad With the Gilmores," Pupp J, 4(3):22-24, 1952.

Guignol Fait La Guerre. Paris, 1919 - see also "France,"
H. Blondeau
Hainaux, R. see A. R. Philpott

Head, Cedric. "Rebuttal from Cedric-Historical," Pupp J,
15(3):27-28, 1963.
Hoffmansthal, Hö Von. "Prologue for a Marionette The-
atre," International, 10:103-104, Ap, 1916.
International Puppet Calendar. see: Calendar
see also Mollie Falkenstein
Inverarity, Bruce. "International Puppetry," International
Folk-Art Museum Bulletins, Santa Fe, Museum, n.d.
Johnson, Peggy. "Daniel Llords' International Puppet The-
atre," St. Louis Dispatch Everyday Mag, Feb 21, 1968,
p 1F-4F
"Leige Marionette Congress, Papers and Proceedings,"
Pupp J, 13(3):3, 1961.
    This was also published under title, Leige Marionette
Congress, by the Commission of Folklore de la Saison,
Muse de La Vie Wallone, Rue Fer Oristee, 136 Liege,
Belgium, Liegeoise of 1958, 1958-59.
    A copy is in the library of Dan Keller, 1062 Miller
Dr, Davis, Calif. (in 1962)
Lincoln Center Branch of NYC Pub. Lib. The Research
Dept. of the "Museum and Library of the Performing
Arts" has a large collection of International puppet materi-
al in books, periodicals, clippings and playbills. It also
sponsors international and national puppet productions vis-
iting the city.
Llords, Daniel. "Cannery Row Theater to Tour to Arctic
Circle," Monterey Peninsula Herald, (Monterey, Calif.)
N 5, 1960, p 14, in "Peninsula Notebook Column."
Articles about Llords, include:
---"Llords International" puppet productions: (International
Concert Theatre-adult) performing only for City Symphony
Groups, Universities and with Concert Orchestras.
---'Llords to Braunschweig Festival," Carmel Pine Cone,
My 31, 1962, in the "Music on the Peninsula" column.
---"Daniel Llords with Bunraku from Japan," Los Angeles
---By "International Notebook." Regular feature Pupp. J.
1970.

---"With Strings Attached-World Tour by Daniel Llords,"
Philippine Times, Mirror Section, D 7, 1963, p 22.
This was the first of five world tours to date.
---"First World Touring Puppet Symphonic Master," Flotter-
transport, (publ. by Volkswagon, 6 times a year, in Eng-
lish, German, and French), Jan, 1964 issue. In NN.
---"Acteurs San Touwtjes," Margreit, Weekbeau, Mr, 1964,
p 123-25. The Braunschwieg Festival of 1963-64.
---"Teatro Dos Nil Cordelinbas," Seala International, 7:45,
Jl, 1963. Published in French, German, English, Fin-
nish, Portugese, and concerned with "Braunschweiger
woche des Internationalen Puppenspiels of 1963. Same
title: Scala International, D, 1963, p 47.
Lodwig, David. "Review of The International Festival at
Bochumer, Germany; the Figuren Theater Woche," Pupp J,
18(5):31-33, 1967.
Lucas, Walter. "Erpinotto and the Economic Recovery Pro-
gram Administration," Pupp J, 3(2):9, 1951.
See also "Plays" Section under "Operation Bambi"
MacDonald, C. M. "Impressions of Warsaw Convention,"
Pupp Master, 7(2):16-17, D, 1962. illus.
McFadden, Lee. "Around the World Puppet Show," see
Dallas, Texas local papers of 1957-1958.
McGill Univ. Library, Montreal, Canada. Unusually large
French puppet section.
McKay, Ken. "Sidelights from Canadian Festival-Interna-
tionals," Pupp J, 19(1):36-37, 1967.
McPharlin, Marjorie Batchelder. "Bucharest Fstival Pic-
tures," Pupp J, 11(1):12, 19, 1959.
---"International Festival by Countries," Part 1, Pupp J,
10(2):8-12, 1958; Part 2, Pupp J, 10(3):11-14, 1958;
Part 3, Pupp J, 10(4):9-11, 1959; Part 4, Pupp J, 10(5):
9-11, 1959.
---"International "UNIMA" News-Festivals," Pupp J, 14(2):
8-9, 1962.
---"International "UNIMA" News," Pupp J, 14(3):5-7, 1962.
---"International "UNIMA" News-Interpretations of a play,"
Pupp J, 14(4&5):6-8, 18, 1963.
---"On Tour-American Specialist for International Educational
Exchange Service of the U. S. Dept. of State," Pupp J, 12
(1):22-23, 1960.
---"Second International Festival-Bucharest," Part 1, Pupp J,
13(2):3-6, 1961; Part 2, Pupp J, 13(6):7-10, 1961.
---"Trip Abroad," Pupp J, 12(5a):31, 1961.

McPharlin, Paul. "The Puppet World, 1942-43," Pupp, 13-
14:3, 1942-1943.

---Puppet Theatre in America. New York, Harper, 1949, p 440-456. Relates to Central America and South America.

Malik, Dr. Jan. "Festival (at Bucharest) Pros and Cons," Pupp J, 17(4):3-6, 1966.

---"Review of 'Large' International Festivals," Pupp J, 17 (4):10-11, 1966.

May, E. C. "Puppet Shows Around the World," Travel, 65: 13-17, 47 Jl. 1935.

Meharg, Frances. "Festival of Traditional Puppetry, Liege, Belgium, 1958-'59," Pupp J, 10(6):22-23, 1959.

Michael, Vivian. "Bill and Cora Baird, Cultural Exchange Program," Pupp J, 17(3):14, 1965.

Mick, H. L. "Puppets Here, There and Everywhere," Drama, 13:96, D, 1922.

Munoz, P. "Drama in Miniature," Americas, 6:13-16, Ap 1954.

Niculescu, Margareta. "International Festival 1958," Pupp J, 11(1):11, 1959.

--- ed. Modern Puppet Theatre of the World. Berlin, UNIMA Organization, Kunst und Gesellschaft, 1965.
    Copyright by Henschelverlag, First English trans. by E. Osers & E. Strick, London, Harrap, 1967. Printed in E. Germany, by Fortschritt, Erfurt, 1966.

---Puppet Theatre of the Modern World. Boston, Plays, 1967. This is the same book as the one above, with a slightly different title. Full names of translators given as Edwald Osers and Elizabeth Strick.
    Most sig. m. and unusual illus. are given, with articles by outstanding international puppet masters and directors of large puppet theatres around the world. It is often referred to in this Guide as Pupp Th Mod World.

Revu. of Puppet Theatre of the Modern World, Anon., Pupp J, 16(4):11, 1965.

Revu. of Puppet Theatre of the Modern World. Anon., Pupp J, 18(5):37-38, 1967.

Peterson, A. E. "The Bath Assembly of European Puppeteers," Pupp Master, 2(3):87-88, 1948.

Phemister, Pippa. "The Multi-Racial Puppets," New Society, 18:24-25, Mr, 1965.

Philpott, A. R., B. Baird, E. Copperman, M. Barbuta and R. Hainaux. "Present Day Puppetry by International Puppeteers," World Thea, 15(2):102-34, 1966.

"Popular Puppets in Europe," N Y Times, S 22, 1919 V p 9.

Procter, Ellen and Romaine. "From Abroad," Pupp J, 10 (6):21-22, 1959.

---"International Puppetry," Pupp J, 12(2):12, 1960.

---"Puppetry-Worldwide; Report of UNIMA Festival," Pupp J, 10(2):5-7, 1958.

---"Puppets Old and Puppets New, Tour of Europe," Pupp J, 5:10-12, 21, N, 1953.
---"Report on UNIMA," Pupp J, 12(1):10-11, 21-22, 1960.

"Puppet Styles-Moscow to Seattle," Thea Arts, 18:919-25, D, 1934.
Puppetry, 9: 1938. ed. by Paul McPharlin, "A Tour of European Puppet Theaters," is title of this issue of the periodical.
"Puppets of All Nations," Blackwood's, ... Edinburgh, 75: 392, Ap, 1854.
"Puppets Outside Europe," World Thea, 14:448-95, S, 1965.

Putz, F. "A letter from Fred Putz," Pupp J, 9(1):6-7, 1957.
Raines, L. "The World Stage," Players, 10:9, Ja-Feb, 1943.
Ransome, G. G. see: "Bibliographies," Section.

La Scala International, Jl, 1963, "International Puppets."

"The Simplest Form of International Entertainment," Colliers, 46:1023, O, 1922.
Somerville, C. C. "International Puppet Festival," Pupp Master, 7(2):13-14, D, 1962.
Speaight, George. "International Relations in the Puppet Theatre," World Thea, 8:53-55, Spring, 1959.
---"Puppets Over Europe," Twentieth Century, 170:59-64, Jl, 1961.
---"UNIMA News," Pupp Master, 9(4):16-17, D, 1968... A history.
"UNIMA Organization News," Pupp, 1: 1930, and every year till 1949.
"University of Richmond, Virginia has Caroline S. Lutz's World Puppet Collection," Pupp J, 11(2):34, 1959, item only.
Wallace, Al. "Summer in Europe," Pupp J, 9(5):25-28, 1958.
Wiksell, Jean Starr. "Puppet Theatre in Europe," Players, 16:22-23, Mr, 1940.
Wilson, Winifred. "Europe, puppet shows in the last war and in the present," World R, 41:45-48, My 1941.
"World and the Theatre," Thea Arts, 17:89, Feb, 1933.

World Theatre, 15(1), 1966. Entire issue is on puppetry, with vol. 15(2):146-50, 1966 on "International Festival."
"World Theatre, The Great." Thea Arts 12:455-64, 1928.

Young, Rod. "International News Notes," Pupp J, 10(2):33-
34, 1958.
---"News from Abroad," Pupp J, 10(5):33, 1959.
---"News from Abroad," Pupp J, 11(1):28, 1959.

D. 2 - Puppetry in the United States of America

Note: Questions concerning American puppetry may
be addressed to the National Secretary of The Puppeteers of America, Inc., Mrs. Olga Stevens, P.O.
Box 1061, Ojai, Calif., 93023. Purchase of Puppetry
Journal Publications may be addressed to Mrs. Vivian
Michael, 5013 South Union St., Ashville, Ohio. Questions about Guilds, Regional Directors, etc., may be
addressed to Mrs. Olga Stevens. Mrs. Molly P. Falkenstein, Sec. General of The American Chapter of International Marionette Organization "UNIMA," 132 Chiquita
St., Laguna Beach, Calif. 92651, would answer International questions.

General

"American Regional Guilds," Pupp J, 17(2):31-32, 1965.

"Arizona-Pacific Southwest Region," Pupp J, 15(4):26-28,
1964.
"Chicago World's Fair Puppets," Pupp, 2:13, 1931; Pupp,
3:10, 1932; Pupp, 4:5, 1933; Pupp, 5:34, 1934.
Other "World's Fair" puppet material will be located
by state or country.
Festivals of America. See "Organizations" under "Puppeteers of America."
See "Festivals" Section
Guilds of America. (The official chartered guilds of "Puppeteers of America, Inc.") The Pupp J issues have much
material about guilds which I have not listed. It is sug-
gested that the interested reader see issues for that Region
or Guild, or contact Regional Directors. NYC Pub. Lib.
has a very large collection of Pupp J issues and direc-
tories.
No. 1. Quaker Village Puppeteers, 1940, Pennsylvania.
No. 2. Columbus Guild of Puppetry, 1940, Ohio (inactive)
No. 3. Houston Guild of Puppetry, 1956, Texas (inactive)
No. 4. Los Angeles County Guild of Puppetry, 1957, Calif.
No. 5. San Diego County Guild of Puppetry, 1958, Calif.
No. 6. Detroit Pupeteens Guild, 1960, Michigan (inactive)

No. 7. San Francisco Bay Area Puppeteers Guild, 1960, Calif.

No. 8. Rocky Mountain Guild of Puppetry, 1961, Colo. See No. 23.

No. 9. New England Guild of Puppetry, 1961, Mass. and New Hampshire.

No. 10. Chicagoland Puppetry Guild, 1961, Illinois.

No. 11. Seattle Guild of Puppetry, 1961, Washington state.

No. 12. Orange County Guild of Puppetry, 1961, Calif. (inactive)

No. 13. Phoenix Guild of Puppetry, 1961, Arizona.

No. 14. Twin City Puppeteers, 1962, Minnesota.

No. 15. Empire Guild of Puppetry, 1962, Calif.

No. 16. Detroit Puppeteers Guild, 1963, Michigan.

No. 17. Puppet Guild of St. Louis, 1963, Missouri.

No. 18. National Capital Puppetry Guild, 1964, Virginia and Washington, D. C.

No. 19. Puppetry Guild of Greater Miami, 1965, Florida.

No. 20. Puppetry Guild of Greater New York, 1965, New York State.

No. 21. The Puppet Guild of Long Island, 1966, New York State.

No. 22. The Red River Guild of Puppetry, 1966, Canada (Manitoba)

No. 23. The Mile High Puppeteers Guild, 1968, Denver, Colorado

"Increasing Popularity in U. S. of Puppetry," N Y Times, N 18, 1928, IX, 11:3.

Lano, David. Wandering Showman. E. Lansing, Michigan State Univ. Press, 1957.

Latshaw, George. "Festival Performances," Pupp J, 12(3): 24-25, 1960.

see also "Festival" Section under "Puppeteers of America.

McPharlin, Paul. The Puppet Theatre in America. New York, Harper, 1949.

see also The "Historical" Section, this name in particular but many other American historical articles and books will be found there.

see also The "Punch and Judy" Section, this name in particular.

"Marionettes in Museums of the United States," Pupp 1:23-28, 1930.

"Notice to all Guilds of America," Pupp J, 15(4):31, 1964.

"Pacific Coast Regional Area Material," Pupp J, 12(5B):26-27, Ap, 1961.

From Pupp J, 16(5):28, 1965, most Regions began to send
in material, some but not all of these reports are given
in The Guide. They continue to date.
"Pacific Coast Festival," Pupp J, 14(4&5):31-34, 1963.

Puppeteers. see Puppeteers of America Membership Directories. Ashville, O., Puppetry Journal Public., yearly.
Puppeteers of America, Inc. see "Organizations" Section.

"Puppeteers of the Southland; Uncle Sam's Puppets," Thea
Jour, Los Angeles, 1: Ag, 1936.
Puppetry Journal, The. see: "Periodical Publications" Sec-
tions. This is the main publication of the Puppeteers of
America. Other publications are mentioned under each
state.
see also: Puppetry, Grapevine, Grapevine Telegraph, all
are early official publications of the "Puppeteers of Amer-
ica."
Regional Puppet Divisions: the present directors of these
regions are found on the back of Pupp J issues.
Northeast Regional Division: Conn., Del., Maine., Md.,
Mass., N.H., N.J., N.Y., Pa., R.I., Vt., Wash.,D.C.
Southeast Regional Division: Ala., Ark., Fla., Ga., Ky.,
La., Miss., N.C., S.C., Tenn., Va., W.Va.
Eastern Canada Regional Division: N. Brunswick, New-
foundland, Nova Scotia, Ontario, Quebec.
Great Lakes Regional Division: Ill., Ind., Mich., Ohio,
Wis.
Great Plains Regional Division: Colo., Iowa, Kan., Mani-
toba, Minn., Mo., Neb.,N. Dak., Saskatchewan, S. Dak.,Wyo.
Southwest Regional Division: N. Mex., Okla., Republic
of Mexico, Tex.
Pacific Regional Division: Alaska, Alberta, British Colum-
bia, Idaho, Mont., Ore., Wash.
Pacific Southwest Regional Division: Ariz., Calif., Ha-
waii, Nevada, Utah.
"Regional Ramblings," Pupp J, 14(4&5):14-17, 1963.

Rice, Lanette. "Regional Ramblings," Pupp J, 20(1):26-27,
1968, and continuous every issue to date.
Sarg, Tony. "Revival of Puppet Play in America," Thea
Arts, 12:467-75, 1925.
Schools and Universities of Puppetry and Courses of Puppetry
in America. See "Universities and Colleges" Section.
Smith, C. "Turnabout Movies and Theatre," Pupp J, 7(5):
8-9, 1956.
"Southwest Region," Pupp J, 15(3):30-31, 1963.

Sweers, J. "Puppet Regions of America," Pupp J, 14(3):
11, 23-26, 1962.
see also: Zweers, J. Both spellings are used (it is the
same person.
"United States of America Puppetry," Pupp Th Mod World.
p 227 and illus. no. 186, 187, 188, 189, 190.
U. S. A. Federal Theatre Projects on Puppets in America.
See also: "Recreational" Section under "Federal Theatre"
and "Organizations" under W. P. A.
Wiksell, Jean S. see also: "History" Section.

Wilkinson, W. Puppets Through America. London, Bles,
1938.
Zweers, John. "From the West Coast," Pupp J, 11(5):29-
30, 1960; 11(6):27-29, 1960.
---"Los Angeles Guild," Pupp J, 15(4):27-28, 1964.
---"Pacific Southwest Convention," Pupp J, 15(6):29-30, 1964.

By States (Including the American Indian)

Note: If a Guild or group or organization is given
for a State it is recommended that the "Organizations"
Section be consulted under that name. If a periodical
or publication is given consult "Periodicals" Section,
likewise with theatres, consult "Theatres of America" Section. If any puppeteers are known they will
be named and the words See Directory, meaning they
are in the Puppeteers of America Directory, Regional
Division, refers to National Puppet Org.

Alabama - No Guild, no periodical. Southeast Regional Div.
Puppeteers, See Directory, yearly
Birmingham Jr. League Puppet Group
Mobile Jr. League Puppet Group
Montgomery Playhouse Group
Alaska - No Guild, no periodical. Pacific Regional Div..
Puppeteers, See Directory, yearly
Sometimes Pacific Northwest Regional puppet material
will have material about Alaska.
See also: American Indian
Arizona - Phoenix Guild of Puppetry, org. 1961, No. 13 of
"Pupp of Am." periodical is Punch Line, Pacific
Southwest Regional Div.
Puppeteers, See Directory, yearly
Phoenix Jr. League Puppet Group
Tucson Jr. League Puppet Group

121

California - "Carmel, Calif. Guild of Puppetry, organized,"
    Pupp J, 11(6):27-28, 1960. No periodical located.
    Empire Guild of Puppetry, org. 1962, No. 15 of "Pupp
    of Am. ," no periodical.
    Long Beach California Jr. League Puppet Group
    Los Angeles County Guild of Puppetry, org. 1975, No.
    4 of "Pupp of Am. ," Periodical is Puppet Life.
    Los Angeles Jr. League Puppet Group
    Orange County Guild of Puppetry, org. 1961, No. 12
    of "Pupp of Am. ," (inactive). Had a Newsletter.
    Pacific Southwest Regional Div. Puppeteers, See Di-
    rectory, yearly.
    San Diego County Guild of Puppetry, org. 1958, No. 5
    of "Pupp of Am. ," periodical is Puppetalk.
    San Francisco Bay Area Puppeteers Guild, org. 1960,
    No. 7 of "Pupp of Am. ," periodical is SFBAPG
    Newsletter.
Bromley, Bob. "Tony Urbano, Universal Studio Puppet
    Man," Pupp Life, S, 1968, p11-12, 20-22.
"Children's Fairyland, Theatre, In Oakland," Pupp J, 8
    (4):28, 1957.
    See also "Theatre" Section, under America
Club Guignol, Hollywood, U. S. A. , org. 1930
Dilley, Perry. "Daniel Meader of California, 1856-1929,"
    Pupp 1: 1930, p 18-20.
Hayes, J. J. "San Francisco Puppets," Drama, 19(5):148,
    Feb. 1928.
Hurdy Gurdy Marionette Club, Berkeley. org. 1947.
Jerome, L. B. "Marionettes of Little Sicily in Old San
    Francisco Quarter," New Eng. Mag, 41:745, Feb 1910.
Lano, David. A Wandering Showman. E. Lansing, Mich.
    State Univ., 1957
"Los Angeles Area and the Bay Area, Padre Puppet The-
    atre," Pupp J, 11(1):29-30, 1959.
"Los Angeles Guild Workshop," Pupp J, 8(4): Jan, 1957;
    9(6):9-10, 1958; 11(1):29, 1959; 14(2):26, 1962; 14(3):
    26, 1962.
"San Francisco, Blanding Sloan's Puppet Theatre," Pupp
    1:33-35, 1930; Pupp Life, Sept. 1968, p 19-20.
"San Francisco Marionettes," Drama, 20:48, N 1929.
Santa Monica Recreation Puppeteers Club, org. c 1954.
Scattergood Y. M. C. A. Puppetry Club, Pasadena, org.
    c 1950. Periodical was Puppet Club News.
Stevens, Olga. "The Lowdown from Ojai, Calif." Pupp
    Life, every issue starting 1967.

see   Sunset in "Periodicals and Publications" Section

Turnabout Puppet Theater, Pasadena, had periodical called
The Puppet Show for its patrons.

see also "Theatres" - American
Colorado - Rocky Mountain Guild of Puppetry, org. 1961,
No. 8 of "Pupp of Am.," no periodical.
Great Plains Regional Div.
Puppeteers, See Directory, yearly
Colorado Springs Jr. League Puppet Group
Denver Jr. League Puppet Group
Denver - Mile High Puppetry Guild No. 23 - "Pupp of
Am." Group, org. 1968, no periodical.
"Moppets and Puppets Exhibition, Denver Art Museum,"
Pupp J, 2(3):25, 26, 29, 1950.
Connecticut - no Guild, See: New England Guild, No. 9 of
"Pupp of Am."
Northeast Regional Div.
Puppeteers, See Directory, yearly
Bridgeport Jr. League Puppet Group
Greenwich Jr. League Puppet Group
Hartford Jr. League Puppet Group
Delaware - No Guild. Northeast Regional Div.
Puppeteers, See Directory, yearly
Dist. of Columbia - National Capital Puppetry Guild, org.
1964, No. 18 of "Pupp of Am." Periodical is
D. C. Puppetimes, published every 2 months, former-
ly a Newsletter.
Northeast Regional Div.
Puppeteers, See Directory, yearly
Washington Jr. League of Puppeteers group
Florida - The Puppet Guild of Greater Miami, org. 1965,
No. 19 of "Pupp of Am." Publication is Newsletter
of Puppet Guild of Greater Miami - no other name
located.
Southeast Regional Div.
Puppeteers, see Directory, yearly
Ft. Lauderdale Jr. League Puppet Group
Jacksonville Jr. League Puppet Group
St. Petersburg Jr. League Puppet Group
Tampa Jr. League Puppet Group
Georgia - No Guild. See Southeast Regional Div.
Puppeteers, see Directory, Yearly
Atlanta Jr. League Puppet Group
Hawaii - See Pacific Southwest Regional Div.
Puppeteers, see Directory, yearly
"Hula Kii" is name for puppets here, meaning Dance
images.

Hawaii
"Berta Metzer in Honolulu Theater," Pupp J, 16(6):30,
1965.
Brown, J. MacMillan. Riddle of the Pacific. London,
T. F. Unwin, 1926, p 142-45.
Revu. of Riddle of the Pacific. Anon. Pupp, 11:40,
1940.
Cowan, James. Journal of Polynesian Society, Je 1921.
Emerson, Dr. Unwritten Literature of Hawaii. c 1940's.
Revu. of Unwritten Literature of Hawaii. Anon.
Pupp, 11:40, 1940.
Mankenberg, K. and A. Taylor. "Puppeteering in Ha-
waii," Players, 18:19-26, Mr 1942.
Mills, Bob. "T. V. work in Hawaii," Pupp J, 8(6):12,
14, 1957. Working with puppets in television from
1954-1957 in Hawaii. see local papers and publica-
tions.
Taylor, A. see K. Mankenberg.
Idaho - No Guild. See Pacific Regional Div.
Boise Jr. League Puppet Group
Illinois - Chicagoland Puppetry Guild, org. 1961, No. 9 of
"Pupp of Am.," periodical is Puppet Patter. See
also Newsletter of Chicagoland Puppeteers.
Cellar Playhouse Group, org. c 1939 or Cellar Players
Chicago Jr. League Puppet Group
Chicago Marionette Guild, org. 1930
Chicago Northside Puppeteers, org. c 1934
Chicago Southside Puppeteers, org. c 1934
Decatur Marionette Guild, org. c 1936
Evanston Jr. League Puppet Group
Evanston Marionette Fellowship, org. 1949
Good Teeth Council Puppets, org. 1947
Midwestern Puppeteers, org. 1939 or "SPAC" Strings
was their periodical.
Peoria Jr. League Puppet Group
Puppet Tree see "Periodicals and Publications" Sec-
tion. Puppeteers, See Directory, yearly.
Society of Puppetry and Allied Crafts, org. 1947
Southern Illinois Puppet Center Group, org. 1939
Springfield Jr. League Puppet Group
see "Recreation" Section, and "Theatres" -American
see "W. P. A." in "Organization" Section and Federal
Theatre Project in "Recreation" Section.
Pierce, L. F. "A Successful Show in Chicago," Theatre,
24:152-53, S 1916.
Weed, I. "Puppet Plays for Children in Chicago,"
Century, 91:717-25, 1916.

Indian

Baird, Bill. The Art of the Puppet. New York, Macmillan, 1965, p 250. Lists many ref.

Becker, G. Museum of American Indian Catalogue.
New York, Heye Foundation, No 1, 8928 and No 8,
2606. In Museum of American Indian Lib. NYC.

---"Marionettes of the American Indian," Pupp, 1:13-16,
1930. The Nishka, Taimshian Tribes of British
Columbia discussed.

Bielensteain, Mrs. K. "Marionette Show Tells Indian
Story," Calgary Herald, (Edmonton, Canada) Ag 23,
1967, p 24.

---"Walking Buffalo's Headdress," The Globe and Mail,
(Toronto) c to the Fall of 1967.

---"Walking Buffalo's Headdress," by E. Reading, in
Ottawa Journal (as dictated by Mrs. Bielenstein) Ag
1967.

---"Puppets Tell Indian Story," Kelowna Daily Courier,
Ag 19, 1967.

Bogs, Franz. (Boas, Franz.) "Puppetry and Secret
Masking Societies of North West Coast of North America," Annual Report of the U. S. Museums-1895. Washington, D. C. , Govt. Prtg. office, 1897. In Lib. of
Congress.

---Primitive Art. New York, Capitol, 1951, passim.

Curtis, E. S. North American Indian. Cambridge, Mass. ,
Univ. Press, 1907, 1930, passim, in vols. 9-20.

Dunn, J. H. "Puppets of the Skeena," Can Geog J (Ottawa) 47(6):248-52, D 1953.

Fawcett, C. H. "American Indian Dolls of the 1880's,"
Hobbies, 66(3):36, My 1961.

Fewkes, Jessie W. "Hopi Puppct Katchinas," Twenty-
first Annual Report of the Bur. of American Ethnology.
Washington, D. C. , Bur. of Am. Ethnology, n. d. In
Lib. of Congress.

---"A Theatrical Performance at Walpi Tribe-1899, Hopi
Indians," Proceedings of the Washington Academy of
Science, 2: n.d. , p 606ff. In Lib. of Congress.

Horrwitz, E. P. (or) Herrwitz. Indian Theater. no publ. ,
no date, Chapter 13.

Inverarity, R. B. "North West Indian and Asiatic Puppets,"
Pupp, 4:27-30, 1933.

---Manual of Puppetry. Porland, Binford, 1938, and New
York, W. Morrow, 1938.

--- Summary of Manual of Puppetry. (Pamphlet). Ashville,
Puppetry Journal Public, 1939. See Pupp Bull, 1938-
39, p 69. In NN; also Folklore Museum, Santa Fe,
New Mexico.

Indian (cont.)
--- Moveable Masks and Figures of the North Pacific
    Coast Indians-Pamphlet No 89039. Bloomfield Hills,
    Michigan, Cranbrook Inst. of Science, 1941. In U. S.
    National Museum, Wash. , D. C. , also Folklore Museum,
    Santa Fe.
---Art of the Northwest Coast Indians. Berkeley, Univ.
    of Calif. Press, 1950. In Folklore Museum, Santa Fe.
Leeper, Vera. "Indian Projects in New Mexico," Pupp
    Life 12(4&5):6-8, Jan. & Feb. , 1968. Traveling to
    Indian settlement schools with puppet teaching course,
    for the Bur. of Indian Affairs in 1967.
---"Indian Project," Pupp Life, 12(8):5-7, My 1968.
---"Puppetry With the Indians," Pupp J, 19(5):18-20, 1968.
McPharlin, Paul. Puppets in America 1739-1936. New
    York, Hastings, 1936.
---Puppet Theatre in America. New York, Harper, 1949,
    p 10, 12, 13 and passim.
    See also: "History" Section this name.
Malm, S. M. "Indian Marionettes at Haskell Institute,"
    Sch Arts, 36:171-81, N 1936.
---"Haskell Institute, Indian Marionettes," Players, 16:
    19, D 1939.
    See also: Pupp Thea Am by Paul McPharlin, p 441.
Mantell, __. "American Indian Marionettes," Pupp, 7:7
    1936.
Museum Bulletins and Catalogues.
    Milwaukee Public Museum Catalogue. No 17373, Mil-
        waukee, Museum Press, n. d. p 4615
        The Kwakiuti Tribe of Northwest Coast.
    Natural History Catalogue, Chicago, Natural History
        Museum Press, n. d.
    Provincial Museum Bulletin. Victoria, British Colum-
        bia, Museum Press, n. d.
    Royal Ontario Museum of Archeology Catalogue, Toron-
        to, Museum Press, n. d.
Savage, G. "Puppetry in the Northwest," Players, 13:36
    S-O, 1937.
Indiana-- No Guild, but uses Chicagoland Puppetry Guild No.
    10. No periodical. Great Lakes Regional Div.
    Puppeteers, see Directory, yearly
    Fort Wayne Jr. League Puppet Group
    Indianapolis Jr. League Puppet Group
Community Puppet Theatre and Workshop, The U. S. A.
    org. 1949, Indianapolis
Cole Marionette Theatre, Lake Village, Indiana and Palos
    Park, Ill.

Iowa - No Guild. No periodical. Great Plains Regional
    Div.   Puppeteers, see Directory, yearly
  Cedar Rapids Jr. League Puppet Group
  Des Moines Jr. League Puppet Group
  Friendly House Marionette Club, org. 1936, Davenport
  Pasek, Cepha. "Puppets in Northwest Iowa," Players,
    17:2708, Jan 1941.
  Schick, Joseph S. The Early Theatre in Eastern Iowa.
    Chicago, Univ. of Chicago Press, 1939, p 230.
Kansas - No Guild, or periodical. Great Plains Regional
    Div.
  Wichita Jr. League Puppet Group
Kentucky - No Guild or periodical. Southeast Regional Div.
    Puppeteers, see Directory, yearly
  Lexington Jr. League Puppet Group
Louisiana - No Guild or periodical. Southeast Regional Div.
    Puppeteers, see Directory, yearly
  New Orleans Jr. League Puppet Group
  Shreveport Jr. League Puppet Group
Maine - No Guild or periodical. Northeast Regional Div.
    Puppeteer, see Directory, yearly
Maryland - No Guild or periodical. Northeast Regional Div.
    Puppeteers, see Directory, yearly
  Baltimore Jr. League of Puppetry
Massachusetts - New England Guild of Puppetry, org. 1961,
    No. 9 of "Pupp of Am." Northeast Regional Div.
    Puppeteers, see Directory, yearly
  Periodical is The Control Stick
  Boston Area Guild of Puppetry (see New England Guild)
    sometimes called by this name.
  "Puppet Theatre for Children, Boston," Ch Sci Mon, Feb.
    16, 1939. Eastern, n. p.
Michigan - Detroit Puppeteers Guild, org. 1963. No. 16 of
    "Pupp of Am." Puppeteers, see Directory, yearly
    Great Lakes Regional Div.
  Periodical is Detroit Guild Gazette, Detroit Newsletter
  Detroit Marionette Fellowship, org. c 1929
  Detroit Puppet Guild, org. 1930. Periodical was
    Grapevine Telegraph, Grapevine
  Detroit, Marionette Fellowship of America, org. 1937
    Periodical, used Puppetry
  Detroit Puppeteens Guild, org. 1960, (inactive) No. 6
    of "Pupp of Am."
  Duluth Jr. League Puppet Group
  Flint Jr. League Puppet Group
  Lansing Jr. League Puppet Group
  See "Theatres" Section

Minnesota - Twin City Puppeteer Guild, org. 1962, No. 14
of "Pupp of Am." Periodical is T. C. P. Notebook.
Great Plains Regional Div. Puppeteers, see Directory,
yearly
Minneapolis Jr. League Puppet Group
Twin City Puppeteers, org. previous to 1945, became
the present Guild No. 14, periodical was Twin City
Puppeteers Notebook.
Mississippi - No Guild or periodical. Southeast Regional
Div. Puppeteers, see Directory for 1962, 1965,
1966.
Jackson Jr. League Puppet Group
Missouri - St. Louis Puppet Guild, org. 1963, No. 17 of
"Pupp of Am." Periodical is St. Louis Guild News-
letter.
Great Plains Regional Div. Puppeteers, see Directory,
yearly
The Saint Louis Puppet Guild, org. in 1940's, and be-
came the present Guild No. 17. Its periodical was
called Puppeteers Newsletter.
St. Louis Jr. League Guild of Puppetry
Mendham, Nellie. "Puppet Project at Peoples Art Center,
St. Louis," Players, 21:18, O 1944.
Montana - No Guild or periodical. Pacific Regional Div.
Puppeteers, see Directory, 1962, 1965, 1967.
Butte Jr. League Puppet Guild
Great Falls Jr. League Puppet Group
Wiksell, Jean S. "Great Falls, Montana, Has a Mario-
nette Project," Players, 21:26, Ap 1945.
Nebraska - No Guild or periodical. Great Plains Regional
Div. Puppeteers, see Directory, yearly
Lincoln Jr. League Puppet Group
Omaha Jr. League Puppet Group
Lincoln City Library Puppet Club, org. 1948

New Hampshire - New England Guild of Puppetry, org. 1961,
No. 9 of "Pupp of Am.," periodical is called Control Stick, formerly, Newsletter of New England
Guild.
Northeast Regional Div. Puppeteers, see Directory,
yearly.
New Jersey - See the New York Puppetry Guild No. 20 and
the Puppet Guild of Long Island, No. 21 of "Pupp
of Am." Periodical used is Greater New York Puppetry Guild Newsletter and Newsletter of Puppet
Guild of Long Island.

Northeast Regional Div. Puppeteers, see Directory, yearly
Englewood Jr. League Puppet Group
Durham Jr. League Puppet Group
Plainfield Jr. League Puppet Group
New Jersey Public School Marionette Guild, Newark, org. c 1930
Marionette Guild of Plainfield, New Jersey, org. 1940
Puppet Associates Group, org. Great Neck, Long Island, and New Jersey has many members. 1960
See also "Community" Recreation Div., West Orange, Essex County, New Jersey. Much puppetry done there by community.
See also "W. P. A." in "Organization" Section.
New Mexico - See the Phoenix Guild of Puppetry, No. 13. No periodical or groups located. Southwest Regional Div. Puppeteers, see Directory, yearly.
"Folk Art Foundation-G. Baumanns are back to world of puppets," Pupp J, 10(6):9-10, May 1959.
"South and Southwest Puppetry," Players, 13:19, N-D, 1936, by J. S. Wiksell.
New York - Puppetry Guild of Greater New York, Inc., org. 1966. No. 20 of "Pupp of Am." Northeast Regional Div. Periodical is Puppet Guild of Greater New York Newsletter or Newsletter of Greater New York Guild of Puppeteers; Greater New York Puppet Guild Newsletter - all were used, diff. times.
Puppeteers see Directory, yearly
Binghamton Jr. League Puppet Group
Brooklyn Jr. League Puppet Group
See Players and Puppets periodical for all Jr. League Groups
New York City Jr. League Puppet Group
See "Recreational" Div. under "Parks" in particular.
"Theatres" - American Section
"Federal Theatres" - "Recreation" Section
"W. P. A." in "Organization" Section
International Marionette Laboratory, org. 1929, NYC
Marionette Guild of New York City, org. before 1930
Marionette Repertory Theatre Group, org. before 1931
Marionette Society, org. 1913-1914 - or New York Marionette Society
New York City Dept. of Parks Puppet Group, org. c 1930. Sometimes called The Marionette Circus Group. Has "Swedish Cottage Puppet Theatre," Central Park.
Producers Workshop Group-Branch of Guild No. 20 of

129

New York (cont.)
Greater New York Guild, org. 1967.
"A Marionette Theater in New York," Cent, 63:677-82,
1902.
"An Italian Marionette Theater in Brooklyn," Phil Publ
Led, Ap 19, 1890. See "Italian" Section, by S. Culin.
"An Italian Marionette Theater, New York," J Am Folk-
lore, 3: Ap 1890. See S. Culin.
"Corner of Sicily in New York," Travel, 67:26-29, My
1936.
Canfield, M. C. "Reflections on Tony Sarg's Marionettes
in New York," Van F, Ap 1923.
Culin, S. "Brooklyn Marionette Theatre," J Am Folklore,
3:155-57, Ap 1890. This is the first mention of pub-
lished material in Poole's Readers Guide, 1892-1896.
Dembitz, Lea Wallace. "Isolationism is out," Pupp J,
14(4&5):34-36, 1963.
"DeSoto Motor Corporation Gives Puppet Show," N Y Times,
Jan 7, 1934.
Dwiggins, W. A. "Drawings in a Corner Stone." New
York, American Institute of Graphic Arts, in NN.
Frame, V. "Marionette Show of Little Italy in the
Bowery," Theatre, Jl 1906, p 175-76.
Frank Leslie's Illustrated Newspaper. New York City, O
25, 1890, p 199.
Hayes, J. J. "Puppetry Column" Drama, 19:14, O 1928.
This column continued for some time.
"Marionettes from Halk Street Theater," Graphic, 117:17,
Jl 2, 1936.
Nichols, F. H. "Marionette Theatre in New York," Cent,
63:677-82, Mr 1902.
---Same article in Curr Lit, 32:455-57, Ap 1902.
See also: "Punch and Judy" Section, as much is men-
tioned concerning early NYC puppetry and around the
state of New York.
Puppetry Guild of Long Island, org. 1967. No. 21 of
"Pupp of Am." Periodical, Newsletter of Puppet Guild
of Long Island.
"Puppet Shows must be Licensed," N Y Code of Ordinances.
NYC 1936, Chap 3, Article 3, Sect. 60-62.
Puppet Teaching. See "Periodicals" Section
"Smallest Theatre in the world," N Y Tribune Mag, Jan
27, 1924, p 5.
Stevens, Martin. See his regular column, "Under the
Bridge" in Pupp J.
Tichenor, George. "Marionette Furioso - Papa Manteo,"
Thea Arts 13:913-19, D 1929.

North Carolina - No Guild or publication. Southeast Region-
al Div. Puppeteers, see Directory, yearly
Ashville Jr. League Puppet Group
Charlotte Jr. League Puppet Group
Durham Jr. League Puppet Group
High Points Jr. League Puppet Group
Raleigh Jr. League Puppet Group
Winston-Salem Jr. League Puppet Group
"Mint Museum of Charlotte, N. C. has new puppet the-
atre," Pupp J, 19(4):24, 1968.
Ohio - Columbus Guild of Puppetry, org. 1940. No. 2 of
"Pupp of Am." No periodical. Puppeteers, see
Directory, yearly
Uses Puppetry Journal when needed. Published
for many years from Ashville, Ohio, by Vivian
Michael, pres. of the Columbus Guild (when active).
Great Lakes Regional Div.
Akron Jr. League Puppet Group
Cleveland Jr. League Puppet Group
Cincinnati Jr. League Puppet Group
Toledo Jr. League Puppet Group
Canton Jr. League Puppet Group
Alma Puppet Theatre, Cain Park, Cleveland Heights
"Cain Park Puppet Theatre, Cleveland Heights," Players,
D 1947, p 1.
Cleveland Playhouse Puppet Theatre, see "Community Rec-
reation" Div. and "Theatres"
See Tatterman Marionettes, Cleveland, "Puppeteer" Sec-
tion, as they had large theatre in Cleveland in 1936,
then moved to Oxford, O. See Pupp Thea Am,
p 471-72.
See Federal Theatre, Cincinnati in "Recreation" Section.
Oklahoma - No Guild or periodical. Southwest Regional Div.
Puppeteers, see Directory, yearly.
Oklahoma City Jr. League Puppet Group
Tulsa Jr. League Puppet Group
Puppeteens, The, org. 1948, Oklahoma City - became
Detroit Puppeteen Guild, No. 6 of "Pupp of Am."
(inactive)
Vagabond Puppeteers, Fed. Thea. , org. 1937
Federal Theatre of Oklahoma Puppet Group, org. 1937
in Oklahoma City and throughout state. Publication
was Tanglestrings Talk. Published 6 scripts - see
"Recreation" Section - Federal Theatres
Oregon - No Guild or periodical. Pacific Regional Div.
Puppeteers, see Directory, yearly
See the Seattle Guild, No. 11 of "Pupp of Am."

Oregon - (cont.)
    Portland Jr. League Puppet Group
Pennsylvania - Quaker Village Puppeteers Guild, org. 1940.
    No. 1 of "Pupp of Am." Northeast Regional Div.
    Puppeteers, see Directory, yearly
    Periodical is Quaker Village Report, or Report;
        sometimes Quaker Village Puppeteers Report.
    Lancaster Jr. League Puppet Group
    Lancaster Marionette Group, org. c 1940
    Marionette Guild of Philadelphia, org. 1925
    The Puppet periodical from Pittsburgh, Carnegie Insti-
        tute
    "Arts and Crafts Puppet Show Center," Pittsburgh Press,
        D 25, 1949.
    "Perspective Theater or Italian Fantoccini," Pennsylvania
        Journal, My 13, 1773
        Show from Europe by Sleur Mercier and Mr. Bessiz,
        using the words "Perspective" and "Fantoccini" for
        first time in America in regard to puppets; used for
        next 100 years.
    See also: "Community Recreation" Section, Harrisburg
    "Quaker Village Puppeteers," Pupp J, 17(6):10, 1966.
Rhode Island - No Guild or periodical. Northeast Regional
        Div. Puppeteers, see Directory, since 1965 only.
South Carolina - No Guild or periodical. Southeast Regional
        Div. Puppeteers, see Directory, yearly
    Columbia Jr. League Puppet Group
    Greenville Jr. League Puppet Group
    Spartanburg Jr. League Puppet Group
South and North Dakota - No Guild, organization or periodi-
        cal. Great Plains Regional Div. Puppeteers, see
        Directory, yearly
Tennessee - No Guild or periodical. Southeast Regional Div.
        Puppeteers, see Directory, yearly
    Chattanooga Jr. League Puppet Group
    Knoxville Jr. League Puppet Group
    Memphis Jr. League Puppet Group
    Memphis Tenn. Puppet Guild, not a "Pupp of Am."
        Guild, mentioned in articles without any ref. as to
        when org. or other information.
    Braun, P. "Marionettes in the Tennessee Mountains,"
        Pupp, 2:25-26, 1931.
Texas - Houston Guild of Puppetry, org. 1956, No. 3 of
        "Pupp of Am." Southwest Regional Div. Puppeteers
        see Directory, yearly; (inactive). Periodical is a
        Newsletter (title unknown)
    Corpus Christi Jr. League Puppet Group

132

Dallas Jr. League Puppet Group
Ft. Worth Jr. League Puppeteers
Galveston Jr. League of Puppets
Lubbock Jr. League Puppet Group
Midland Jr. League of Puppeteers
Pettey, Emma. "Trail of the Long-Nosed Princess-
    Puppets in Texas" Drama, 18:206-07, 1928.
See also Texas local papers about "The Hemisfair-
    World's Fair," of 1968-69, many very large puppet
    theaters active.
Krofft Puppet Theatres at "Six Flags Park," very large
    and very active during 1968-70. See local papers
    and other material concerning this fair and this park.
Utah - No Guild or periodical. Pacific Southwest Regional
    Div. Puppeteers, see Directory, yearly
Ogden Jr. League Puppet Group
Salt Lake City Jr. League Puppeteers
Pioneer Craft House Puppet Theatre and Educational
    Group org. 1963. See "Organization" Section in Salt
    Lake City
"Pioneer Craft House Puppet Association," Pupp J, 19(5):
    9-11, 1968.
Lindsay, John Shanks. Mormons and the Theatre. Salt
    Lake City, Century, 1905, p 134.
Vermont - No Guild or periodical. New England Guild of
    Puppetry. No. 9 of "Pupp of Am." Periodical is
    Control Stick. Northeast Regional Div. Puppeteers,
    see Directory, yearly
Virginia - National Capitol Puppetry Guild, org. 1964, No.
    18 of "Pupp of Am.," Southeast Regional Div. Pup-
    peteers, see Directory, yearly. Periodical is
    Newsletter of National Capitol Puppetry Guild.
See Richmond Univ., Richmond, Va., in "College"
    Section. See also: "Theaters," "Recreation"
Washington - Seattle Guild of Puppetry, org. 1961. No. 11
    of "Pupp of Am." Pacific Regional Div. Puppeteers
    See Directory, yearly. Periodical is called Puppet
    Tales which was also the publication of earlier group.

Seattle Jr. League Puppet Group
Spokane Jr. League Puppet Group
Tacoma Jr. League Puppetry Group
See "Universities" Section, "Recreation" Section
"Northwest Drama Conference," Pupp J, 15(4):26, 1964
"Puppetry in Spokane, Washington," Playg, 24:24, O 1930
Northwest Drama Conference," Seattle Times, Mr 29, 1964

133

West Virginia - No Guild or periodical. Southeast Regional
       Div. Puppeteers, see Directory, yearly
       Charleston Jr. League Puppet Group
       Huntington Jr. League Puppeteers
       Wheeling Jr. League Puppeteers
Wisconsin - No Guild or periodical. Great Lakes Regional
       Div. Puppeteers, see Directory, yearly
       Milwaukee Jr. League Puppet Group
       Polish Student's Puppet Club, org. c 1940's
       See: Univ. of Wisconsin in "Universities" Section
Wyoming - No Guild or periodical. Great Plains Regional
       Div. Puppeteers, see Directory in 1962, none
       given since.

          D. 3 - World Puppetry, Alphabetically Arranged
                        by Country

       Note: This portion of the Bibliography will give the
       reader a start for further work in many countries.
       It is hoped that errors will be corrected and forward-
       ed for a future supplement. Reference is often made
       to UNIMA's, Puppet Theatre of the Modern World,
       Boston: Plays, 1967 which is shortened to Pupp Th
       Mod World.

                    Africa and South Africa

Beach, Marion. "South African Puppetry," Pupp, 13-14:39,
       1942-1943.
Chesnais, J. "African Puppets," World Thea, 14:448-50,
       S 1965.
Latimer, Norah. "In a South African School, Johannesburg,"
       Brit Pupp Thea, 1(4):7, 1950.
Levy, J. Langley. "South African Punch and Judy," Pupp,
       12:39-40, 1941.
Lyonese Society. In Morocco, see "Organization" Section.

Pupp, Michael. "Toe Puppets from Africa," G N Y Pupp G
       Newsl, 6(4):8, 1969.
Rogers, Mrs. Iris. "Durban South Africa, Puppetry," Brit
       Pupp Thea, 1(5):10, 1950. Concerned with Punch and
       Judy work there.
Stewart, J. "Puppets in Africa," Midwest, Chicago Sun
       Times Mag., D 9, 1962.
"South African Puppetry," Brit Pupp Thea, 2(1):15, 1951.

Talbet, P. A. "African Savages and Their Magical Plays,"
Strand, 49:691-96, Je 1915.
Trentman, Charles. In his puppet column, London's Stage
and Television Today, O 22, 1964, p 7. Telling a little
about Betty Coleman, in Southern Rhodesia television
puppet work.
Wright, John. "Puppetry in Capetown, South Africa," Pupp
Post, Winter 1951-1952, p 4.

Albania

Craytor, Hallie L. "Marionetting from the Classroom to
Albania," El Eng Rev, 9:258-59, D 1932.

America, Central and South

General

"Central American puppets," Pupp J, 16(5):31, 1965.

Holmes, Kathleen. "Construction and Use of Marionettes,
Particularly in Reference to the Spanish American Ele-
mentary School Children." Unpublished Master's disser-
tation, Austin, Texas Univ., 1938.
O'Hara, H. "Puppets Can Teach Health Education in El
Salvador." Americas, 2:20-22, D 1950.

Argentina

Acuña, Juan E. Teatro De Titeres. Buenos Aires, Editori-
al Futuro, 1960. In NN.
Aqular, Don Pedro. See Paul McPharlin's, Pupp Thea Am,
p 77.
"A Decree-Concerning The Puppet Theatre Buenos Aires
Maguina Real," Buenos Aires, My 17, 1759. See Paul
McPharlin's, Pupp Thea Am, p 77, 257. This explains
the puppet shows in Buenos Aires in English translation,
the decree was by Don Floremio, a Moreyra Lt. General
and Governor.
Bagalio, Alfredo S. El Teatre De Titeres En La Escuela.
Buenos Aires, Kapelusz 2nd ed., 1944 (Puppet plays).
In NN. This book gives historical organization, etc. of
puppetry in Argentina.
---Acuarelas De Germén Gelpi. (2ed) Buenos Aires, Kape-
lusz, 1944. In NN.
Bastian, Don. Puppeteer playing in Buenos Aires in 1910.
An article in a local paper by Alfredo Dolver concerning
him was printed that year. Source did not give name of

Argentina (cont.)
paper. See Paul McPharlin's, Pupp Thea Am, p 259, 299.
Bernardo, Mano. Teatro de Títeres. Buenos Aires, Na-
tional Culture Institute, 1946. In Library of Congress.
---Títeres de Quante. Santa Fe, Dept. of Extension, Univ.
de la Universidad National del Litoral, 1959.
---Títeres: Magia Del Teatro. Buenos Aires, Ediciones
Culturales Argentints, Ministry of Educ. and Justice,
1963. In Lib of Congress.
---"The Puppet Theatre in Argentina," Pupp J, 14(6):19-20,
1963.
Bianber Masa, Nora. (pseud). Títeres Para Ninos. Buenos
Aires, Ediciones T. L. A. T. 1947, [sic] In Lib. of Con-
gress.
Brunclik, Milos. See Paul McPharlin's, Pupp Thea Am,
p 405.
Bufano, Airel. See Pupp Th of Mod World, p 227.

Butler, Horacio. See Paul McPharlin's, Pupp Thea Am,
p 467.
Canone, Vito. See Paul McPharlin's, Pupp Thea Am, p 299,
408. Working with rod and paladin puppets in Buenos
Aires from 1900-1910. See local papers those years.
Coronado, Martin. See Paul McPharlin's, Pupp Thea Am,
p 257.
Cossettini, Leticia and Olga. El Nino Y Su Expreion. n. 1,
c 1948.
DeBuckley, Mrs. Magdalena. Director of "La Curtina The-
atre" for 15 years and at the "Mane Bernardo-Sarah Bi-
anchi" puppet theatre.
Dolver, Alfredo. (pseud.). See also, Ramos, Juan.
See Paul McPharlin's Pupp Thea Am, p 299, 350.
Fridman, Liber. Puppeteer working with hand puppets in
Argentina around 1936, in the rural back countries by
canoe. See Paul McPharlin's Pupp Thea Am, p 350.
Gutmur, W. "Orlando Furioso at Manteos Theater," Thea
G M, 7:31-32, S 1930.
See also G. Tichenor
Hermitte, A. See A. Dolver
Lira Galero, Elsa. Titererías. Montevideo, Impr. Pan-
Americana, 1961. In Lib. of Congress.
McPharlin, M. Batchelder. "Mrs. Magdalena de Buckley...
of Argentina," Pupp J, 14(6):19, 20, 1943.
See also her collection of material on puppeteers of the
world in the back of Paul McPharlin's, Pupp Thea Am.
Manteo, Agrippino. (The Father). The famous "Papa Man-
teo" of New York City puppetry theater lived and played in

Argentina in 1896-1912. Son, Michael Manteo worked with him, in Buenos Aires.
See Bill Baird's, The Art of the Puppet, New York, Macmillan, 1965, p 118-29.
See W. Gutmur; and New York City in "America" Section
See G. Tichenor
See "Italy"
See Paul McPharlin's Pupp Thea Am, p 258, 298, 302
Manteo, Ritz. "Papa Manteo's Marionettes," Pupp, 8:8, 1937.
Marionetas. Dóminicana: Claudad Trujillo, Editora Libreria, 1958. (Author not given.)
Moneo Sanz, C. Titirilandia. Títeres Del Triángulo. Buenos Aires, M. Zeff, 1953.
Moreyra, A. "A Document of Complaint Against Puppet Shows in Montevideo, Argentina, Aug. 7, 1795." Buenos Aires, Govt. Archives, 1795.
See Paul McPharlin's Pupp Thea Am, p 77.
The author was the Governor, Don Florencio, a Lt. General.
"National Puppet Theatre," National Institute for Theatrical Studies, Bulletins. Buenos Aires, Govt. Press, yr.
Ramos, Juan Pedro (pseud). (J. Villafane.) Also occasionally used his friend's pseud. of Alfredo Dolver. See A. Hermitte.
See J. Villafane
Richardson, Ruth. Florencio Sanchez and the Argentine Theatre. New York, Instito De Los Espanosen les Ested of Unidos, 1933, p 32-34.
Information about puppets in Montevideo previous to 1800.
Sanchez Rego, Maria D. C. Títeres, En La Actividad Escolar. Buenos Aires, Editorial Ciordia, 1960. In NN.
Schell, Maria. Titeres, Sombras Y Marionetas. Buenos Aires, Casilla-Correocentral, 1947. In NN.
Somma, Luis Mario. Obras Para Títeres. Montevideo, 1961. In Lib. of Congress.
Tichenor, G. "Marionette Furioso: A Marionette Show in the House of Agrippina Manteo in New York," Thea Arts, 13:913-19, D 1929.
---"The Longest Show in the World," Thea G M 7:31-32, S 1930.
Villafane, Javier. (Used name of Juan Pedro Ramos, and Alfred Dolver.)
---Teatro De Títeres, La Andariega. 1st ed. Buenos Aires, Francisco A. Colombo Co. 1936, rev. 1943, same Co. In NN.

Argentina (cont.)
---Los Ninos-y Los Titeres. Buenos Aires, Colombo, 1938,
rev. 1944. (printed in Buenos Aires, "El Anteo" - In NN.
---"Argentina Puppet News," Pupp, 13:34, 1942.
--- See Pupp Thea Mod World, p 227 and Illus No. 194.
See Paul McPharlin's Pupp Thea Am, p 350-51, 366, 475-
76

Other Countries

Arabia

Jacob, G.   See "Shadow Puppets" Section
Littman, E.   "Ein Arabische Karagöz-Spiel," Zeitschrift Der
Deutschen Morgenlandischen Geseilschaft, 44: 1900.
---Arabische Schattenspiele.   Berlin, 1901.
See also: Egypt

Armenia

Note: Mostly shadow puppet work, check material under
Turkey and Iran.   Part of this country is now under the
Soviet Union, so Russian material could also be investi-
gated.

Asia

"Puppets Outside Europe," World Thea, 14:448-494, S 1965.
Discusses many countries and has a good bibliog.
Puppet Theatre in Asia. Ceylon: Dept. of Cultural Affairs,
1969. By Prof. Tilakasiri. For India, Ceylon and Indo-
nesia and Japan.
Scott, A. C.   "Asian Travelogue," World Thea, 14:448-454,
S 1965.

Australia

Australian Puppeteer, The.   The only puppet periodical I
have located in this country although probably more exist
because of the many English members mentioned in the
British puppet pulications. See "Periodicals" Section.
Ehmer, Bernard.   "Puppeteer Producer," Pupp J, 17(5):16,
19, 1966.
Harry, M.   Proved Popular Puppet Plays: Australian. Vic-

toria, Temperance Committee, Presbyterian Church.
In NN.
Hetherington, N. "Puppets in Australia," Pupp Master, 4
(6):278-80, 1956.
---"Melbourne Teachers College," Brit Pupp Thea, 2(1):15,
1951.
"Marionette Theater of Australia," Pupp J, 17(2):34, 1965.
The Australian Elizabethan Theater, sponsored by the
Trust and Arts Council of Australia, called the "Tin-
tookies."
Mulgrive, G. "Puppets Take Their Degrees," Sch Arts, 47:
314-15, My 1948.
National Fitness Youth Theatre.   Victoria, Australia,
has a branch puppet group.
Puppet Guild of Australia. See "Organizations" Section.

Puppeteers. Many are mentioned in British puppet publications and occasionally in Puppeteers of America Directories. In NN.
"Puppetry in Australia," Brit Pupp Thea, 2(1):15, 1951.

"Puppets in Australia," Pupp, 13:35, 1942.

"Puppets, Punch and Judy in Australia," All Yr R, 9:610,
1863.
Stevens, Martin. See his column, "Under the Bridge" a
letter from H. Griffin, Pupp J, 15(6):32-33, 1964.
---Short notes only but may be of value; Pupp J, 16(5):30,
1965; See "Rev. Roger Green," Pupp J, 19(5):30, 1968.
"Tintookies" - Tour of Australian States," Pupp J, 17(5):35,
1966. Discusses very briefly the work of Peter Scriven,
1956.

Austria

Aicher, Anton. See Paul McPharlin's, Pupp Thea Am, p
322 (1912, Salzburg).
Aicher, Hermann. "Salzburg Marionettes in U. S. A. ,"
Pupp J, 3(2):8, 1951.
---"The Dying Swan," Brit Pupp Thea, 1(5):7, 1950.
He is the director of the Salzburg Marionette Group but
does not write for publication much himself. A great deal
is written about him.
"Austria, International Puppetry," Pupp, 6:65, 76-7, 1935.
---Pupp, 8:33, 1937.
---Pupp J, 2(6):28-29, 1951.

Austria (cont.)
"Austria, The International Festival," Pupp J, 10(2):9, S
1958.
Australian Puppeteer, The. See issues c to World War II,
some material about Richard Teschner of Austria given
as he moved there for the war years. Further investigation and information was not possible at this time.
Baird, Bill. The Art of the Puppet. New York, Macmillan,
1965, p 161-67, 168.
Bayer, Jerome. "Richard Teschner's Work," Pupp, 3:57,
1933.
B. O. (pseud). "Richard Teschner," Die Graphischen Künste,
41: 1918.
Bramall, E. "Puppets in Salzburg, Austria," Pupp Master,
2(5):159-62, 1949.
De Curson, H. "Les Marionettes de Salzbourg et le Directeur de Théâtre, Mozart," J Des Dep, 40(1):377-78,
Mr 3, 1953.
De Munoz, P. See P. Munoz

De Pange, J. See J. Pange

Dumesuil, R. "Mozart et les Marionettes de Salzbourg,"
Mercure Des Fr. 242:701, Mr 15, 1933.
Eisler, M. "Richard Teschner," Dekorat Kunst, 24: 1921.

Gazda, E. "Teschner's World of Puppets," Studio, 142:
110-11, O 1951.
Gugitz, Gustav. Der Weiland Kasperl. Vienna, Jahrbuch,
1920.
---"Regesten zur Geschichten des Mechanischen Theaters in
Wien," Gesellschaft Fur Wiener Theaterforschung Wien,
Jahrbuch 1954, p 69-79.
Hadamowsky, F. Richard Teschner und sein Figurenspiegel,
die Geschichte Eines Puppentheaters. Vienna, Wancura
Co. , 1956. In NN.
harriet, (pseud). "Salzburg at Town Hall, New York City,"
Pupp J, 16(4):4-5, 14, 17-18, 1965.
---"Salzburg in New York," G N Y Pupp G Newsl, 2(2):3,
1965.
Houville, G. "Le Théâtre de Marionettes du Luxombourg,"
Rev des D M, Series 8:464-65, Jl 15, 1934.
Joseph, Heln H. "The Figure Theatre of Richard Teschner,"
Thea Arts, 7:264, 296-301, 303, 307, O 1923. illus.
Kraus, Gottfried. The Salzburg Marionette Theatre. trans
Jane Tyson. Salzburg, House of Verlag Publ. , 1968.
A Revu of Salzburg Marionette Theatre, Anon. Pupp

Master, New Series, no. 3, 1968, p 22.
Krotsche, F. Kunstler-Marionetten Theater; Bildhauer
Professor Aichera, Salzburg. Salzburg, A. Polst, 1926.
Lefftz, J. "Puppenspeal in Altern Strassburg," Elsassland,
1929, p 233-37, 273-76.
Levetus, A. S. "Miniature Plays and Marionettes in Vienna,"
Creat A, 4:433-35, Je, 1929.
McPharlin, Paul. "Anton Aicher's Marionette Theatre in
Salzburg," Drama, 19:202-04, Ap, 1929.
---Puppet Theatre in America. New York, Harpers, 1949,
p 322.
Melling, J. K. "Vienna-Puppets," Pupp Master, 6(8):21-22,
1958.
Meyer, Rosalind. "Travel Notes in Austria," Pupp, 7:464-
65, 1936.
Munoz, P. de "Miniature Opera from Salzburg Marionette
Theatre," Etude, 75:14-15, Ap 1957.
Pange, J. de "Marionetten de Salzbourg á Paris," J des
Dep, 40:337, Feb 24, 1933.
Puhonny, Ivo. "Marionette-Philosophy," (Quotations from
Him) in Bill Baird's, Art of the Puppet, p 168.
Resatz, Gustav. Kasperl-Geheimnisse. Hornhauer, Wien:
Fährmann, 1944.
"Richard Teschner's Figuren Spiegel Theatre," Thea Arts,
12:491-95, Jl 1928.
"Salzburgs appearing in U. S. A.," Pupp J, 17(2):13, 1965.

"Salzburg Marionettes," Pupp J, 10(1):29, Jl 1958.

"Salzburg Marionettes," at Brooklyn Academy of Music,"
N Y Times, 32:4, O 11, 1954.
"Salzburg Marionettes, Don Giovani," N Y Times, 17:3, D
30, 1965.
"Salzburg Marionettes-Marionettes with Music, Town Hall,"
N Y Times Mag, D 13, 1964, p 126-27.
"Salzburg Marionettes, Puppets from overseas," Newsweek,
38:88, O 15, 1951.
"Salzburg Marionette Theatre-illustrations," see Pupp Th
Mod World, p 221 and illus. no 66, 67.
"Salzburg Marionette Theatre Tours in U. S.," N Y Times,
D 5, 1952, 22:2; D 22, 1952, 21:3; D 29, 1953, 7:8;
Ag 26, 1951, 60:5; Jl 29, 1951, II 7:2; D 24, 1966, 9:3.
Whenever the company returns to the United States the
Times gives it good space. It usually plays in New York
City around Christmas.
"Salzburg Marionettes Christmas Show in New York," N Y
Times, D 26, 1953, 11:6.

Austria (cont.)
"Salzburg Opera Guild," Time, 30:65, N 15, 1937.

"Salzbourg Puppets," International Index to Periodicals.
    New York, H.W. Wilson, 1931-34, p 194.
"Salzburg, The Wee Folk from," Ch Sci Mon, (Eastern),
    D 23, 1964, p 2-3. Usually this publication carries
    something about the Salzburg puppets when they return
    each year.
Stevenson, F. "Miraculous Marionettes-Salzburg's famed
    troup tours the U.S.A.," Opera N, 30:26-28, Mr 5, 1966.
Teschner, Richard. Theatre of the Pigmes. Vienna, Wan-
    cura, 1804.
---Und Sein Figurenspiegel. Vienna, Wancura, n.d.
See Thea and School, Ap 1933, p 8.
See "Teatro del Mio Cuore," by Amico, Senario, (Milano)
    N 1937, p 523-25.
See A. S. Levetus
See Pupp Thea Mod World, p 221 and illus. no. 65, 68.
Austrian National Library has his puppet collection now
and material would be found there.
See F. Hadamowsky
    The "Farsenklauier," or fusion of music and color was
first done by him and his puppet clow at the organ.
See Bill Baird's, Art of the Puppet, p 167.
Troyon, P. "Les Marionettes de Salzbourg à Paris," Rev
    des D M, 14:series 8, Mr 1933, p 198-202
Wismantel, Prof. Leo. "Austria's Puppeteer," Pupp J,
    2(6):28-29, 1951.
Young, G. Gordon. "Anton Aicher and His Salzburg Mario-
    nettes," Drama, 16:59, N 1925.

Bali

See also   Java, Indonesia, and "Shadow" Section
Avery, Verna. "Music for the Marionette Theatre-Balanese
    Puppet Show," Pupp J, 2(3):3, 1950.
Baird, Bill. The Art of the Puppet. New York, Macmillan,
    1965, p 54, 56-61.
Covarrubias, Miguel. "The Theatre in Bali," Thea Arts,
    20:574-658, Ag 1936.
---"The Classic Drama-Wayang Wong," Thea Arts, 20:634-
    37, Ag 1936.
---"The Shadow Play in Bali and Java," Thea Arts, 20:629-
    35, Ag 1936.
Damais, L. C. "Shadow Theatre in Java and Bali," World

142

Thea, 14:450-95, S 1965.
Wagner, F. A. The Art of Indonesia. (And the Island Group).
New York, Greystone, 1967.

Belgium

See also   Flemish.

Note: Most familiar and popular character is called
"Tchantches" in puppetry and is probably a good deal
like "Punch" character of England. Some French material may discuss puppets under that name, for this
country. See "Publications" and "Organizations" Sections as there are aseveral given. It is a popular
place for International puppet meetings, see also
"Festivals" Section.

"Belgian Jubilee Festival of the Theatre 'Hoppla Internation-
al', 1955 Mechelen, Belgium," Pupp J, 17(4):4, 1966.
"Belgian Puppetry," Brit Pupp Thea, 1(5):7, 1950; Pupp, 6:
65, 1935; 8:33, 1937; 12:36, 1941.
"Bolomes" These will be the puppets at Liege, Belgium, of
lighter weight than the heavier Rod puppets usually used
there. Any articles under this title would concern Belgian
puppetry of the rod variety.
Bockwoldt, Henry. "Henry Bockwoldt Writes About Belgium,"
Grapev, D 1948, p 8.
Bulthuis, R. J. Puppen, Schimmen, Marionetten ...
Maastricht, Leiter-Nypels, 1954.
Camerlynck, Gerald. "Pat Puppenspel," Pupp J, 1(4):21,
1950. This is an Antwerp (Belgium) Puppetry Co. and
Theatre.
Colombier, H. Le Bandeau D'Illusion. Brussels, 1900.

Contryn, Jozef. "International News," Pupp J, 2(3):24-25,
1950.
Cuwaert, Floris. De drij Vagebonden. (Comic puppet plays
in Flemish). Antwerp, De Magneet, 1948. In NN.
David, E. Étude Picards Sur Lafleur. Amiens, Jeunet,
1896.
---Les Théâtres Populaires à Amiens. Amiens, Invert,
1906.
---Vieilles Rederies, Amiens, Jeunet, 1920.
DeKayser, Paul. see Dr. Paul Keyser

Eggermont, J. Puppenspiel. Leuven, S. V. De Pojl, 1944.
In NN.

Belgium (cont.)
"Franchonnet Theater," Pupp Thea Mod World, p 219. Illus.
No 28.
Feller, Jules. "Le Bethléem Verviétois," Société Verrié-
toise Dârchaéologie et d'Histoire Vervierg. Bulletin,
Verviers, Vol. 2, 1900, p 1-60. A history of the an-
cient Nativity plays of Belgium, some of which had me-
chanical puppet-like figures, and some that were done with
puppets. In NN (42nd St. card catalog.)
Fisher, D. C. "Vive Guignol!" Schol, 24:80-9, Ap 7, 1934.

Flament, Julien. Les Marionnettes de Belgique. Bruxelles,
1937. This is a program brochure and would be found in
puppet files of Belgian puppet organizations.
Ghelderode M. Le Mystere de la Passion de Notre Seig-
neur Jésus avéc tous les Personnages pour les Théâtres
de Marionettes. Brussels, 1905.
Giradot, Mme. Théâtre et Marionnettes pour les Petits.
Paris, n. d. In British Museum.
Guiette, Robert. Marionettes de Tradition Populair, Brus-
sels, Cercle d'Art, 1950. In NN, good illus.
Revu. of Marionettes de Tradition Popular, Anon. Brit
Pupp Thea, 3(4):4, N 1952.
Heuseux, Lucette. A surrealist Belgian puppeteer who vis-
ited the U. S. A. and Eng., 1950.
Hevvel, G. Van de. "Marionette Play in the Low Country,
Belgium," Unpublished thesis, Liege, Belgium Univ.,
1949 or 1950. Philology Dept. Pupp J 2(3):25, 1950.
Houville, G. D. "Le Theatre des Marionettes du Luxom-
bourgh," Rev des D. M, Series 8:464-65, Jl 15, 1934.
Jean, Yvonne. Marionettes Populares. Rio De Janeiro,
Ministry of Education and Cultural Service of Documents,
1955.
Jeanne, Paul. "Belgian Puppetry," Pupp, 12:36-38, 1941.
---De Poesjenellenkelder. (Th. De La Marionettes D'Anvers)
Paris, 1934. In NN.
Keyser, Dr. Paul de. Has published studies in Belgian
puppetry but unable to locate.
Kiek, Rober. "Antwerp Revives Puppetry," Holiday, 4:17,
Mr 1949.
---"International News," Pupp J, 2(1):21, 1950.
---"Armand Deschamps, Dean of Belgian Puppetry," Holiday,
4:18-20, 1949.
Lampo, Hubert. "Het Beste Theater Van Antwerp," Het
Toneel Jaarg, 81(4):87-90, 1960.
Landsman, Leo. Het Puppentheatre Van Sergei Obraztsov Te
Moskow. Antwerpen, Boekuil En Karveel Uitgaven, 1947.

Levin, M. "Liege, Marionnette Congress-1930," Thea Arts, 15:140-53, Feb, 1931.

Maeterlinck, M. Alladine Et Palomides.. Avec Trois Petits Dramas Pour Marionettes. Brussels, 1894. In British Museum.

Meharas, Frances. "Festival of Traditional Puppetry, Liege, Belgium, 1958," Pupp J, 10(6):22-23, 1959.

Michael, Vivian. "Belgium Conference," Pupp J, 10(1):26-27, 1958.

Olbrechts, F. M. See "France"

Organizations. See "Organizations" Section

Periodicals. See "Periodicals" Section

Pischel, R. Die Heimat Des Puppenspiels. A published address at Friedrichs Univ., Halle-Wittenberg in 1900. Trans. by Mrs. R. N. Vyvyan, London, Luzzo, 1902, under title Home of the Puppet Play. In NN. "Puppetry in Belgium," Brit Pupp Thea, 3(3):5, 1952.

Schuyster, Jan de. De Antwerpshe Poesje; Zija Geschiedenis En Eijn Speelteksten, Door Jan De Schuyter. Antwerp, De Sikkel, 1943. Revu. of "De Antwerpshc Poesje . . .," Anon, Brussels Museum Royal Bulletin, 18: Jan, 1946. In NN and at Univ. of Calif., Los Angeles, Puppet Dept. "Tchantches Statue in Leige," Pupp, 7:65, 1936.

"Toone Theater-Brussels," See: Pupp Thea Mod World, p 219 and Illus. No. 26 and No. 27.

Trentman, Charles. See: His "Puppet Column," Stage and Television Today. London, O 22, 1964, p 7.
    J. Contryn, Director of "Popla Puppet Theater" in Mechelen, Belgium is discussed.

Vandenbroucke, J. Het Puppenspel in De Netherlanden. Antwerp, De Nederlandsche Bookhandel, 1946. In NN, a history of Belgium, Flanders puppets.

Verhoeven, Jan J. Koekenfeest Bij Jan Klaasen. Lier, J. vn In, 1953. In NN, Flemish puppet plays.

---Het Gestolen Varken; Een Corspronkelijke Spel Voor De Puppenkast. Lier, J. Van In, 1953.

Vyvyan, Mrs. R. N. See R. Pischel.

Warsage, R. de. "Belgian Puppetry," Pupp, 2:28-30, 1931.

---Pupp, 3:11, 57-58, 1932; 5:30, 1934; 7:65, 75-76, 1936.

---Histerie Du Celebre Theatre Llegois De Marionettes. Brussells, G. Vancest, 1905. In McPharlin Coll., has bibliog.

Belgium (cont.)
---Au Royaume Des Marionnettes À Liège. Liège, La Muse
1903.

Bohemia ... See Czechoslovakia

Bolivia, South America

Gamble, James. "Titeras En Bolivia," Pupp J, 10(3):26-
27, 1958.
Garavaglia, F. and Aida were puppeteers of Bolivia, 1944.

McPharlin, Paul. Puppet Theatre of America. New York,
Harper, 1949, p 284.
Mahlmann, L. "The El Chasky Puppet Theatre, La Paz,
Bolivia," Pupp J, 17(3):6, 1965.

Brazil

"Mamalenao" means puppetry in Brazil. Pernambuco
State has much glove puppetry in Cherroso. Local
papers may give material.

Bastian, Don. Played in Sao Paolo, Brazil, in 1898 with
his very famous wife Dona Carolina Bastian. See local
papers.
Bernardo, M. Teatro de Titeres. Buenos Aires, National
Cultural Institute, 1945. In Lib. of Congress.
"Brazilian Society of Puppeteers," Pupp Thea Mod World, p
227 and Illus No. 193.
"Brazil's Achille Greco," Pupp 5:36, 1934. In Rio and
Rome in 1900-1934.
"Brazil's Puppets," Pupp, 15:35, 1944.

Jones, H. F. Castellinaria, and other Sicilian Diversions.
London, Fiefield, 1911, p 93, passim.
McPharlin, Paul. Pupp Thea in America. New York,
Harpers, 1949, p 299.
    Tells about São Paulo, 1896 puppeteer and San Carlos
Theatre in 1910. See also "Puppeteer Section"
It lists many from Brazil.
Obry, Olga. "Tradion Revived in Brazil," Brit Pupp Thea,
1(4):25, 1950.
---"Progression in Puppetry in Brazil," Brit Pupp Thea,
1(6):28, 1950.
---"Rod Puppet Theater 'Gibi' in Brazil," O Globo (Rio news-
paper).
---"Haps and Mishaps of Brazilian Puppets," World Thea,

146

14:455-60, S 1965.
"Panameous Puppet Theater," see Paul McPharlin's, Pupp Thea Am, p 452-62. Director was Carol Rosecrans Woods, 1942-43, for the Dept. of Education. Students might investigate the Departmental Records for further material.

Yvonne, Jean. Marionettes Populares. Rio de Janeiro, Ministerio da Educakao e Cultura, Service de Documentacao, 1955.

Bulgaria

Baird, Bill. The Art of Puppetry. New York, Macmillan, 1965, passim.

"Bulgaria." International news notes, Pupp J, 2(1):30, 1950.

---International news notes, Brit Pupp Thea, 1(2) 1950.

"Bulgarian Simplicity at International Festival," Pupp J, 13 (3):8-9, 1961.

"Central Puppet Theatre of Sofia, Bulgaria," Pupp J, 15(1): 27, 1963.

---Pupp Th Mod World, p 226, Illus No 174 and 180.

Falkenstein, Mollie. "The Central Puppet Theatre of Sofia," Pupp J, 17(3):6, 1965.

Gerdjikov, Stantscho. "A New Art is Born," Puppet Theatre of the Modern World, Boston, Plays, 1967. (Published under the sponsorship of UNIMA) p 45.

---"Bulgarian Childrens Puppet Theatre," Pupp J, 13(6):3-4, 1962.

McPharlin, M. Batchelder. "State Theatre from Varna, Bulgaria," Pupp J, 10( ):3, 12, 1958.

---"International Festival, Bulgaria" Pupp J, 10(2):29, 1958.

"Municipal Puppet Theatre, Sofia," see Pupp Thea Mod World, p 226 and Illus No 176.

"Plovdiv Puppet Theatre," See Pupp Thea Mod World, p 226, and Illus. No. 177.

"Puppets at Bulgarian Exhibition," Pupp Master, 3(2):65-66, 1950.

"State Puppet Theatre, Burgas," see Pupp Thea Mod World, p 226, and Illus. No 175.

"Touring Puppet Theatre of Sofia," see Pupp Thea Mod World, p 226, and Illus. No 178.

"Varna Puppet Theatre, Varna," see Pupp Thea Mod World, p 226, and Illus. No 179.

Burma

Note: See also "Indonesia" and "Shadow" Sections as these overlap. "Katputles Katamasha" means "Marionette Performance" so material may be sought under this title as well as regular puppet vocabulary. Some string puppets are used, but mainly shadow work and rods are used. See also "India."

Baird, Bill. The Art of the Puppet. New York, Macmillan, 1965, p 46-61 and passim.
Boehn, Max von. Dolls and Puppets. New York, McKay, p 387-90.
Brown, Maurice. "I Remember," Asia, D 1910.
---"I Remember Burma," Pupp, 8:33, 1937.

"Burmese Puppetry," Pupp 9:33-35, 1938.

Clark, B. H. "Burmese Puppets in New York," Drama 16: 289, My 1926.
Hackett, W. D. "Puppets in Burma Today at the Festival," Pupp 10:40, 1939.
Hagemann, Carl. Die Spiele der Völker. Berlin, Schuster, 1912 and 1919. In British Museum.
Hürlimann, Martin. "Burmanisches Puppenspiel," Atlantis, Zurich, Jahrg. 7, 1935, p 73-77.
Maindron, Ernest. "Marionettes et Guignol," see also "France."
Oman, John C. Cults, Customs, and Superstitions of India. London, Unwin, 1908, p 195 and passim.
Ridgeway, Sir William. Dramas and Dramatic Dances of Non European Races. New York, Macmillan, 1915.
---"Puppet Plays of Burma" in his Puppet Play and Hindu Drama. London, Cambridge Univ. Press, n. d.
---Java Puppet and Shadow Plays. no publ., n. d.

Canada

Note: The libraries of Montreal, Quebec, Ottawa, and the University libraries of Ottawa and McGill were quite well explored. A good French puppet section is at McGill. Many Guilds of puppetry and Junior Leagues are active, especially around Toronto and Montreal. See "England" and English puppet periodicals as they write much about Canada. "Puppeteers of America" Guilds are also located here and Regional Districts include parts of Canada.

Bielenstein, Karin. Calendar of Indian Tribe Puppets. Edmond, Alberta, Commercial Printers, 1967.
---Canadian Indian Music on Tape. Edmonton, author, 1967. See Puppeteers of America Membership Directory, 1967 or 1968 for address.
---"Indian Puppets," Town Talk (Edmonton, Ap 1967), sponsored Allied Arts Council.
---Program of Teachers Association of Edmonton. Edmonton, Teachers Assoc., 1967.
---"Puppetry for Indian Education and Pleasure," Edmonton Journal, Ap 1961.
---"Talk at Librarian Convention." a leaflet (typed) on file with librarian of Edmonton Pub Lib with date May 1967. See also "American Indian" Section; K. Bielenstein.
Brown, G. M. "Puppeteer," Atlantic Advocate, Univ. Press of New Brunswick, 53:26-28, 30-31, Mr 1963.
"Canada's Puppetry," Pupp 7:65, 1936.
---Brit Pupp Thea, 1(5):10, 1950.

Conway, John. "Regional Activities in Canada, Pupp J, 2 (3):26, 28, 1950.
Crawford, K. N. "DaSilva Puppets of England and Canada-Indian Play" in his booklet, International Festival Report 1968. London, British Pupp & Model Thea Guild, Oct. 1968. In NN.
Cross, J. M. "Huron Legend Performance by London Marionettes," Sat N, Toronto, 63:18, Ag 28, 1948.
"Daddy Marseille's Puppet Theatre-Quebec," see P. A. Gaspe's, Memoires, p 544 (this country).
Dunn, J. "Puppets of the Skeena," Can Geog J, 47:248-52, 1953.
Eaton, Dr. John. "Wolfville, Nova Scotia Puppets," Brit Pupp Thea, 1(5):10, 1950.
Films. See "Film" Section.

Gaspe, Philippe A. Memoires, Quebec, N. S. Hardy, 2d ed. 1885, p 544 and passim. Ottawa, 1st ed. 1866.
Guilds of Canada. "Eastern Ontario Guild of Puppeteers."
--- "Ontario Puppet Association Guild"
--- "Ontario South Western Puppet Guild"
--- "Red River Guild." Winnipeg, No 22 of the "Puppeteers of America" org., started 1965. See Pupp J, back cover, any issue for address and president. See Puppeteers of America Membership Directory, yearly.
--- "Toronto Guild of Puppeteers"
See also "Organizations" Section
Junior League Groups doing puppet work. See also "Organization" Section.

Canada (cont.)
    Hamilton Jr. League Puppet Club
    Montreal Jr. League Puppet Group
    Ottawa Jr. League Puppeteers
    Vancouver Jr. League Puppet Group
    Winnepeg Jr. League Puppeteers
Keogh's, The. "Cabout, Toronto Puppet Co. ," Brit Pupp
    Thea, 2(1):15, 1951. Active from 1930-1951.
McGregor, M. "John Conway, Puppeteer," Canadian Hobby-
    craft, 6:8-9, Feb 1962.
McPharlin, Paul. Puppet Theatre of America. New York,
    Harpers, 1949, p 79-85, 259.
"Marionettes for Adults," Star-Phoenix, (Saskatoon, Saskatche-
    wan) O 21, 1967, p 24.
    Demonstrations of Creative Art by the American mario-
    nette company of Daniel Llords, called "Llord's Interna-
    tional," working only with symphony orchestras and at
    universities.
Massicotte, E. Z. "Les Marionettes Au Canada," Bulletin
    des Recherches Historiques, 28:12-13, 338, 1922 (Quebec)
Merten, G. "Puppets in Canada," Food for Thought,/ 18:
    295-97, Mr 1958.
---Pupp Thea Mod World, p 226, and Illus. No 184 and No 185.
"Montreal Parks," Pupp J, 12(3):34, 1960.

Murdoch, Beamish. History of Nova Scotia. Vol. 3, Hali-
    fax, J. Barnes, 1867, p 350.
"Naxnax Puppets," Pupp 6:65, 1935. Indian puppets of Can-
    ada.
Oldmixon, John. The British Empire in America. Vol. 2,
    London, 1708. In British Museum.
"Ontario Has Seventeen Puppet Theaters," Pupp J, 17(3):33,
    1965.
Osborne, J. "Canada's Historical Record of Puppetry,"
    Pupp, 6:33, 1935.
---"Enter Canadian Puppet," Curtain Call, 6:35-36, Je 1935.
Osborne, R. F. "Canada's Puppets," Pupp, 11:33, 1941;
    6:65-67, 1935.
---"Canada's Western, Most Active in Puppetry," Pupp, 9:
    17-18, 1938.
---"Canadian Puppetry-Hamilton, Quebec," Pupp, 14:35-36,
    1943.
---"Hamilton, Ontario Puppet Conference," Pupp, 10:35,
    1939.
---"Puppetry in Canada," Pupp, 8:33-34, 1937; 11:33, 1940.
"Our Visitors from Canada," Pupp J, 5(1):26-27, 1953.

"Peppy Puppeteers Co. ," Grapev, Je 1949, p 11-12.

Periodicals.　There are several in Canada, see "Periodical"
　　Section.
Puppeteers.　See Paul McPharlin's, Pupp Thea Am. in
　　"Puppeteer Index"
　　See British Puppet and Model Thea Club Directory, yearly
　　See American Directory, yearly
　　A few are listed in "Puppeteer" Section
Roy, Pierre-Georges.　Archives De La Province De Quebec.
　　Quebec, P. J. Roy, 1917.　In British Museum.
Rowland, Clara.　"Llord's International Delights Adults,"
　　The Tribune, Winnipeg, Saskatchewan, O 17, 1967, p 15.
"Royal Ontario Museum of Archeology has Primitive Puppet,"
　　Pupp J, 2(3):26-28, 1950.
Russell, Ernest.　"The Most Popular Show in the World,"
　　Out M, 3:473, 1908.
Stewart, Doug.　"Canada's Centennial Year," Pupp J, 18(1):
　　25-26, 1966.
Television.　See "Television" Section

"Toronto Guild of Puppetry's 'Puss in Boots,'" Pupp J, 19
　　(1):14, 1967.
"Waterloo University Has International Convention of Puppe-
　　teers of America-1967," Pupp J, 20(1), 1968 - most of
　　the issue.

Ceylon

Tilakasiri, Prof.　Puppet Theatre in Asia.　Ceylon, Dept.
　　of Cultural Affairs, 1969.

Chile

Alexandri,　See Paul McPharlin's Pupp Thea Am, p 257.
　　A founder of Chilean puppetry.
Arago, Jacques.　"Chilean Success Story of 1840," Deux
　　Oceans. Paris.　(Deu Monde - another title, same book.)
　　In British Museum.
Brunet, Marta.　"Writer of Chilean Revival of Puppetry,
　　1939," Pupp, 11:35, 1940.
Lano, Alberto and Oliver.　Working in Chile and South Amer-
　　ica 1894-1897.　See Paul McPharlin's Pupp Thea Am,
　　"Puppeteer's Index."
Llados, Luis.　"Puppetry in Chile," Pupp, 17:53, 1946.

Machucas, Francisco.　Escenas Historico-Militares Coquim-

Chile (cont.)
  babas. Valparaiso, 1938, p 204-205.
Salas, Eugenio Pereira. "Chilean Puppetry," Pupp, 11:33,
  1940; 15:34, 1944.

China and Formosa

Note: Quite often the public is led to believe that only
shadow work is done in China and Formosa, this is not
true. The strung and perfected marionette, and the
rod puppet have been used from early times, although
not as much written material is available about them as
there is about the shadow puppets. The tiny, interesting hand or, almost finger, puppet has been on the
streets and in the villages in one-man booths, for centuries; but little material has been located in printed
form about them. Mr. Bill Baird's book is one of the
few with information on the finger puppet of China, and
the UNIMA book, Puppet Theatre of the Modern World
has illustrations of China's puppet work.

"Kui-lui" is the name of the early marionette or rod
puppet so search should be made under that name, while
"Pu-Tai-Hi" was the early sock-like hand puppet. There
is no counterpart for the "Punch" type character. The
"squeaker" is used but articles that mention it do not
necessarily deal with Punch and Judy-type puppet work.
Puppet drama is generally of a classic, historic nature
in all fields, although some modern propaganda material is used to teach the peasant-farmer. Formosa puppetry resembles the old patterns, with much shadow
work. Shadow work of the highest order is found in
the far back country of Cheng Tu, in Szechwan Province
and near the coast. See also "Oriental," and "Shadow"
Sections.

Arlingon, L. C. Chinese Drama: From the Earliest Times
  Until Today. Shanghai, Kelly, 1930. In the Dramatic
  Museum at Columbia Univ., N.Y.
Baird, Bill. The Art of the Puppet. New York, Macmillan,
  1965, p 132-37.
Batchelder, Marjorie. "Chinese Production at International
  Festival," Pupp J, 13:20, 1961.
---Rod Puppets and the Human Theater. Columbus, O.,
  Ohio State Univ. Press, 1947. Grad. Sch. Monograph in
  Fine Arts No. 3.
Benton, Pauline. "Cantonese Rod Puppets, Pupp, 11:7,
  1940.

--"China's Puppetry," Pupp, 7:65, 1936.
See this name "Puppeteers" Section, as any material a-
bout her work will concern Chinese shadow work and her
outstanding "Red Gate Shadow Players Company."
Blackham, Olive. Shadow Puppets. London, Rockliff, 1960,
p 3-18.
Breton, J. B. J. de la Marinière. China. Vol 3 and 4, London, Stockdale, 1812, p 127-33.
Buss, Kate. The Chinese Drama. New York, Cape and
Smith, 1930.
Crothers, J. Frances. "Ancient China's Ballads and Shadow
Puppets," Apograph material, W. Hartford, Conn., au-
thor, 1966.
--- "The ancient mission college at Cheng-Tu and its rela-
tion to the shadow plays of the streets of the "Old City
of Cheng Tu," Apograph material, W. Hartford, Conn.,
author, 1967.
---"The Chinese Shadow Puppets of Cheng-Tu," Apograph
material. W. Hartford, Conn., author, 1967.
"Daminf District Puppet and Shadow Theatre," see Pupp
Thea Mod World, p 228 and Illus. No 222 and No 223.
Falkenstein, Mollie. "Puppets and Shadow Theatre of Hunan,
China," Pupp J, 17(3):5, 8, 1965.
See "Hunan Province Puppet and Shadow Theatre."
"Formosa Puppetry," Pupp, 10:35, 1939; 15:64, 1944.

Grube, W., E. Krebs and B. Laufer. Chinesische Schatten-
spiele. Munich, Bayer, 1915. In the Chicago Museum
Lib (Chicago Field Museum of Natural History).
Halde, Jean Baptiste. Description...de L'Empire De La
China. Paris, La Haye, 1736, p 96-97 of Vol. 2. In
British Museum.
Huana, Ming. "Marionettes," Pupp, 8:8, 1937. This is a
poem written 618-905 A.D. giving proof of the string pup-
pets existence at least that early in China. Search in the
beautiful poems of early China may bring out more rare
historical material about puppets.
"Hunan Province Puppet and Shadow Theatre," See Pupp Thea
Mod World, p 228, and Illus. No 216 and No 217, No 218
and No 219.
Jacob, George. Schattenschnitte Aus Nordchina. Berlin,
1923. In British Museum.
---"Chinesische Schattenschnitte," Cicerone, 15:22, 1923.
---Das Chinesische Schattentheater. Stuttgard, Kohlhammer
1933. In British Museum.
Kincaid, Zoë. "Artists of the Ningyo Stage," Asia, 38:341-
45, Je 1938.

China and Formosa (cont.)
Krebs, E. See W. Grube

Lagarde, E. Ombres Chinoise, Guignols et Marionettes. Paris, Michel, 1900.
Laufer, Berthold. See also W. Grube
---Oriental Theatricals. Chicago, Field Museum of Natural History, 1923.
Lee, H. M. "Aug. 25, 1931 in Hong Kong's Puppet World," Pupp, 12:18-19, 1941.
Lutz, Caroline. "Chinese Puppets at the University of Va., Richmond." Players, 17:29, My 1941.
M., The Soul of China. New York, Stokes, 1925, Chap. 1.
MacDermott, J. T. See S. Obraztozov.

McPharlin, Marjorie B. "China at Festival," Pupp J, 13(3): 8, 1961.
McPharlin, Paul. A Repertory of Marionette Plays. New York, Viking, 1929. A trans. of the Chinese shadow play "The Drum Dance."
---"The Chinese Puppet Man," Pupp 1:37-42, 1930.
---Puppet Theatre in America. New York, Harpers, 1940, p 68, 110, 271, 289.
Maindron, Ernest. "Marionettes and Guignols," see "France," this name.
March, Benjamin. "A Chinese Rod Puppet Man," Pupp 1: 37-42, 1930.
---"Chinese Puppetry," Pupp, 2:65-71, 1931.
---Chinese Shadow-figure Plays and Their Making. Birmingham, Mich., Puppetry Imprints, 1938. In McPharlin Coll.
Mariniere, J. B. de la. See also J. B. Breton
---China: Its Costume, Arts and Manufactures. 6 Vol. London, Stockdale, 1812 to 1813. Trans. from French ed. Paris, c 18.. Vol. 2 of the 2d ed. which has four volumes within two books has about 160 pages on puppets.
Meader, Deborah. "Revival of the Art of the Chinese Shadow Theatre," Sch Arts, 38:85, N 1938.
Michael, Vivian. "Puppets in Guerrilla Training-China," Pupp J, 17(3):12, 1965.
Miller, R. A. See S. Saito

Obraztonov, Sergei. The Chinese Puppet Theater. London, Faber, 1961. Trans. J. T. MacDermott. A very unusual book with good bibliog. by the famous Russian puppeteer and director.

"Peking Puppet Theatre," see Pupp Thea Mod World, p 228 Illus. No 220.

Press, A. "Puppet Show Tells Chinese Kids How to Fight," Ashville, N. Carolina Times, O 28, 1965.

"Puppets of China," Pupp, 8:8, 1937.

Quennell, Peter. A Superficial Journey Through Tokyo and Peking. London, Faber, 1932. A chapter called "The Puppet Theater," and passim.

Rhein, J. "Mededeeling omtrent de Chineesche Puppenkast," Intern Arch Fur Ethnogr 2: 1869.

Ridgeway, William (Sir). Dramas and Dramatic Dances of Non European Races. London, Cambridge Univ. Press, 1915 and New York, Macmillan, 1915, passim.

Saitó, Seijiro and R. A. Miller. Masterpieces of Japanese Puppetry. Rutland, Vt., Tuttle. In NN.

Schlegel, G. Chinesische Brauch und Spiele in Europe. Dusseldorf, Jena, 1869.

Shadow Plays of Peking. Peking, People's Art Publishing Co., 1954. Text is in Chinese but many illus. make it of interest and value to average reader. Available at Distributors Collet's Chinese Bk Shop, London. "Shadow" Section of this Bibliography.

"Szechwan Puppet Theatre," Pupp Thea Mod World, p 228 and Illus. No 221.
See also J. F. Crothers.

Wimsatt, Genevieve. Chinese Shadow Shows. Cambridge, Mass., Harvard Univ. Press, 1936. In NN.

---"Curious Puppet Shows of China," Travel, 46:24-35, 46, D 1925.

---Griffin in China. London, Funk, 1927. Chap. 3.

"Work of Helen T. Tacchi," Brit Pupp Thea, 2(1):15, 1951.

Cuba and West Indies

Camps, D. "Puppets in Cuba," World Thea, 14:454-58, S 1965.

"Instituto Cubano De Arte E Industria Cinema," (ICAIC) Havana. See also Pupp Thea Mod World, p 227, and Illus. No 192.

Jurado, Carlos. Construya Un Teatro De Titeres. Santiago de Cuba, Univ. de Oriente, 1961 passim.

"National Puppet Theatre, Havana," See Pupp Thea Mod World, p 227, and Illus. No 191.

Tyson, G. M. "History of Oriental Puppetry." Unpublished

Cuba and West Indies (cont.)
Master's dissertation. Los Angeles, Univ. of Southern
California, 1932, passim.

Czechoslovakia
Estonia and Bohemia

"Alhambra Theatre-Prague," Pupp Thea Mod World, p 224, and
Illus. No 124.
"Amalgamated Factory Puppet Club-Bystřice, near Benešov,"
Pupp Thea Mod World, p 224, and Illus. No 124.
Augusta, Oldvich. Kazvistěd. Prague, Orbis, 1964. In Lib.
of Congress.
Baird, Bill. The Art of the Puppet. New York, Macmillan,
1965, p 250-51, passim.
Bartoš, Jaroslav. Material About Jan Malik and Others.
Prague, 1955. In L. C.
---Loutkars Ka Kronika. Prague, Orbis, 1963. In NN.
Bednar, Kamil. Puppets and Fairy Tales. trans. C. Cas-
lavsky, Prague [SNTL], 1958. In Harvard Univ. Lib.
Benešová, Marie. Oa Spaličau Ke Snu Noci Svatojanské.
Prague, Orbis, 1961.
Boček, Jarsolav. Artist and Puppeteer-Jiri Trinka. Prague,
Artia, 1963. Eng. trans by T. Gottheiner.
---"Czechoslovakian Puppet Films," Graphis, 16:416-21, S
1960.
---Works of Jiri Trinka. Prague, Artia, 1965. Trans. T.
Gottheiner. In L. C.
Bockwoldt, Henry. "Henri writes from Czech." Grapev,
D 1948, p 18. Director of the "Muchon," Czechoslovakian
puppet theater tells of 1200 puppet theatres, at that time,
in the country.
Brdecka, Jiri. "Jiri Trinka-Master Film Craftsman,"
Graphis, 17:390-97, S 1961.
Brunclik, Milos. See Czechoslovakian Periodicals in the
"Periodical" Section.
Bussell, Jan. "Jiri Trinka Puppet Films," Pupp Master,
5(8):20, 1958.
---"Prof. Skupa Dies," Pupp Master, 5(4):21, 1957.
---"Puppets in Czechoslovakia," Pupp Master, 2(1):28-31,
1948.
Căslavsky, C. See K. Bednar

"Central Puppet Theatre-Prague," Pupp Thea Mod World, p
224, and Illus. No 117, No 129, No 131 and No 132.
"City Gives Puppet Show-Prague," N Y Times, Jan 13, 1939,
III, 3:4.

"Czech. Change because of dismemberment of the Republic," Pupp 9:18, 1938.
"Czech. Puppetry," Pupp, 6:67, 1935.
Czechoslovakian Puppetry Films Catalogue. Prague, Consulate General's Office. Irr. publications beginning 1952, puppetry items in the Bulletin of the Czech. Nationalized Films. Available in NYC office of the Consulate. The English version available in NN. See "Film" Section.
"District Puppet Theatre, Ostrava," See Pupp Thea Mod World, p 224, and Illus. No 121.
Dvŏrak, Jan. Zahrajte si Divadélko. Prague, Orbis, 1956.

Fedotov, A. Anatomie Loutky. Prague, Orbis, 1953.

Festivals. They hold a great many national and international meetings and festivals throughout the country. See "Festivals and Exhibits" Section and periodicals of this country.
---"International Festival of Amateur Puppet Theaters at Karlovy Vary, Czech." Pupp J, 17(4):4, 1966.
"Films, Czechoslovakian puppets," Art Kino, no. 9, S 1952.

Fishcherova, Marianna. "A Short History of Puppetry in Czechoslovakia," Pupp Post, Spring, 1946, p 10-11.
Flanagan, Hallie. "Puppets in Prague," Thea Arts, 11:359-62, My-Ap, 1927. The Realm Puppet Theatre is discussed.
"German and Czechoslovakian Puppetry and Prof. Skupa," Brit Pupp Thea, 1(4):13, 1950.
---Brit Pupp Thea, 1(5):6, 1950.
Goldreich, B. See Dr. Jan Malik

"Hand, The New Czech. Puppet Film," N Y Times, S 20, 1966, s9:1; My 20, 1962, II 7:6.
Handler, J. "New Turn for Tiny Film Puppet Troupe," N Y Times, My 20, 1962, 11, 7:6.
Hansmann, L. "Ein Sommernachtstraum Ein Puppenfilm Von Jiri Tinka," Gebrauchs, 31:2-7, My 1960. This is in English, Spanish and French.
Herick, E. Folk-Toys les Jouets populaires. Prague, Orbis, n. d. Available Corner Bk Store, NYC.
"History of Puppetry in Czechoslovakia," Pupp, 4:62-66, 1933.
Hošek, Otakar. Náš Soubor. Prague, Stáni Pedagogiché Nakl, 1958.

Czechoslovakia (cont.)
Hrbkova, Sarka B. "Czechoslovak Puppet Shows," Thea Arts, 7:69-73, Jan 1923.
Isaieff, K. "Puppets in Eastern Europe," Pupp J, 4(4):7-8, 1953. Trans. by Basil Milovsoroff.
Jirásek, Alois. Pan Johannes; Pohádková Hra Ve Čtyřech Obrazech Dramaturická, Uprava Jan Malik. Prague, Uměni Lido, 1950. Concerned with his popular play "Mr Johannes."
Jirásek, František. Stauka, Osuetleal, A Režie Loutkovébo Divadla. Prague, Villimek, c 1934, Kc 25, 25 7 32 [sic] Revu. of the above Pupp, 5, 1934, p 101.
---Lautkářova Priročka. Prague, Vilimek, c 1934, Kc 25, 25 & 32 [sic]. A puppeteers guide for furniture and properties, can be understood from illus.
---Odhalena Tajemstri Loutek. Prague, Vilimek, c 1934 Kc 25, 25 & 32, [sic]. Puppet costume and mysteris and tricks are discussed. Illus. can be understood. Revu. Pupp, 5:101, 1934.
Kainar, J. Sceňování Na Loutkovém Diradie. Prague, Vilimek, 1935.
---Zlatovláska. Prague, Orbis, 1953. In L. C.
Kalmet, Leo & B. Rosenvald. "Estonian Puppetry," Pupp, 8, 34-35, 1937.
Kasperltheater. Prague, "Ombres" Haase, 1922.
Kolár, Erik Dr. The Puppet Theater in Czechoslovakia. Prague, Orbis, 1955.
See also Pupp J 71(5):3-7, 1956. In L. C.
---Puppetry in Czechoslovakia. Trans into English by R. S. Samsourova. Prague, Orbis, 1957. Well illus.
Kopecky, M. See Dr. E. Kolar

Krapf, P. "Cinema Block-Head; A Czech." N Y Times Mag, D 14, 1947, 32.
McPharlin, Marjorie B. "International Festival-Prague," Pupp J, 10(20:9, 1958.
---"Solo Recitals-Sdenek Rajfanda of Czechoslovakia," Pupp J, 10(3):13, 1958.
See also. "International" - General, Section, this name as many of the festivals discussed are at Prague.
McPharlin, Paul. "Puppets High in Czechoslovakians Favor," Ch Sci Mon, Ag 11, 1938.
Machon, Josef. See also "Music" Section, this name.
Mahlmann, L. "Puppet Theater of Ostrava, Czech." Pupp J, 17(3):7, 1965. The "Black Theatre" work, which is often spoken of, and the rod puppet work are explained.

Malik, Dr. Jan. Actor with Puppets. trans. S. V. Obrazsov, Prague, Orbis, 1946.
---"Ceskoslovensky," Universal Newspaper, Bucharest, N 22, 1936 and My 16, 1937.
---"Czech. Gynastic Association of "Sokol" Sponsors Puppetry," Pupp, 6: 1935.
---"Czech. Puppet Organizations," Pupp, 8:34-35, 1937.
---"Czech. Puppetry in War Time," Pupp, 17:54, 1946.
---"Czech. Puppetry Story," Pupp, 7:66-69, 1936.
---Loutkarstvi V Ceskoslovensky. Prague, Ministerstro Informact, Orbis, 1948. In L. C.
---Národni Umělec Josef Skupa. Prague, Státní Nakl, Krásné Literatura Uměni Lido, 1962. In L. C.
See also: Baird, Art of the Puppet, p 250.
Marionettes Et Guignols En Tcheceslavagues. ed, Henri Vesely, Prague, L'Institute Masaryk, 1930 and 1948. (For the Populaire Education Org. of Prague.) In NN.
Meyer, Rosalind. "Travel Note-Czechoslovakia," Pupp, 7: 77, 1936. (item only).
"Midsummer Nights Dream" Film shown in New York, N Y Times, D 19, 1961, 39:1.
Milovsoroff, B. See E. Tsaieff.

"North Bohemian Puppet Theatre-Liberec," see Pupp Thea Mod World, p 224, and Illus. No 123, and No 125.
Novák, Ladislav. Mate; Kopesky. Prague, Orbis, 1946. In NN.
"Outline of Puppet Organization in Czech." Pupp, 5:30, 1934. Sig. m. as it has table and summary of theaters and organizations, etc.
Paomátce Matěje Kopeckého, Mikoláše Aise A Bedřicha Smetany. Prague, Masaryk Instit.
Pilcher, V. "In the Land of the Puppet People," Graphic, 10:916, D 16, 1922.
Pojar, Břetislav. "Director of Second Prague Studio for Puppet Films," Pupp J, 10(1):29, 1958.
Powell, V. M. Riše Loutek. Prague, Orbis, c 1930.
Revu. of Riše Loutek. by V. M. Powell, Thea Arts, 14:875-83, O 1930. This revu. gives unusual amount of material, trans. a great deal into English.
"Puppenspieler Pfingstfest in Prague," Das Puppenth, 3:129-38, 1929.
"Puppet Contests in Czechoslovakia," Pupp, 3:17, 1932.

"Puppet Ensemble of the Czech. Red Cross, Prague," see, Pupp Thea Mod World, p 223, and Illus. No 114.
Puppet Festival Week is held yearly in the town of Chrudim,

Czechoslovakia (cont.)
  Eastern Bohemia; where a "Theatre Harvest" contest is given.
"Puppet's World Theatre," - Prague, See Pupp Thea Mod World, p 224, and Illus. No 119 and No 120.
"Radost, Brno Puppet Theatre," Brno, See Pupp Thea Mod World, p 224, and Illus. No 122.
Rao, Prasana. "Puppetry in Czechoslovakia," Natya, New Delhi, 4(3):27-31, Autumn 1960.
  Records of Scripts for Czechoslovakian puppets are available from the Library of Czechoslovakian Puppetry, in Prague; but are sometimes hard to get through customs. Check with Czech Consulate in NYC and see "Gramophone Records" in Jan Malik, Puppetry in Czechoslovakia.
Rosenvald, B. See L. Kalmet.

Schell, Sherril. "Czech. Puppets With a History," Shadowland Mag, Jan, 1923.
---"J. Trncka, Czech. Puppet Maker, N Y Times, II 7:6, My 20, 1966.
Sirky,   Maňáskové Aktovky Pro Dospělě I Proděti. Prague, Osvěta, 1952. In L. C.
Skupa, Prof. J. "Spejbl And Hurvinek," Pupp J, 19(1):19-20, 1967. These are the two puppet characters Mr. Skupa created before World War I for propaganda use. They are still being used. He wrote very little but is much written about. Founded first professional Puppet Theatre in the new Czech. Republic. See Bill Baird, Art of the Puppet, p 170-712.
Smetara, Bedřich. Czech. Composer who wrote two overtures to puppet plays between 1824-1844.
Snyder, Don. "J. Trncka, Czech. Puppet Film Maker," Newsday, Long Island, My 12, 1966.
"South Bohemian Puppet Theatre, Ceske Budejovice," See Pupp Thea of Mod World, p 224, and Illus. No 127.
"Spejbl And Hurvinek Theatre-Prague," Pupp Thea of Mod World, p 224, and Illus. No 115 and No 116. This theatre is often said to be the "Satire and Humor Theatre" or "S & H Theatre." Any material with these names refers to the work of Prof. Skupa's characters and the theatre named for them.
"State Puppet Theatre-Bratislava," see Pupp Thea of Mod World, p 224, and Illus. No 128.
Sucharda, Vojtech. See Bill Baird, Art of the Puppet, p 172.
  See also material written about the "Library Theater" which he established in 1928, at Prague. Unusual stage with bridge and lighting.

Trncka, Jiří (Trinka) Ein Sommernachtstraum. Mit Bildern
Aus Dem Gleichnanigen Ubersetzung Von A. W. Schlegel.
---William Shakespeare, 1564-1616. Puppenfilm, Prague,
Artia, 1960. In LC.
See also "Film" Section, other films he has made.
See Bill Baird's, Art of the Puppet, p 209.
Name is found spelled both ways.
Tvrdek, F. Osvetlěnf a Zruk ns Loutkovém Jevišti. Prague,
Orbis, 1954. In LC.
UNIMA Organization. The Puppet Theatre of the Modern
World. ed. by Editorial Board of Union Internationale Des
Marionnettes under the chairmanship of Margareta Nicul-
escu. Trans. by Ewald Osers and Elizabeth Strick. Bos-
ton, Plays, 1967. First ed. Berlin, Kunst, 1965 and
London, Harrap, 1967.
See also "Organizations" and "Periodicals" Sections.
Vesely, Dr. Jindrick. Prirucka Ceskehe Leutkare. Prague,
A. Hlavata, c 1914.
---"Czech. Puppetry" Pupp, 2:30, 1931.
---Exlibris Marionett III. Prague, 1933. In McPharlin Coll.
--- Puppetry Before The Great War, Today and Tomorrow.
Prague, Orbis, 1939.
See also Marionnettes et Guignol... etc. ;
and Pupp, 5:102, 1934
Vodickova, Dr. E. See Pupp J, 17(1):2, 1966. Has much
published in the periodical Loutkar and other Czech. pub-
lications about puppetry, which will be listed in the supple-
ment, no English or French translations located. He is
an historian of puppet work at the Academy of Music and
Drama, in Prague.
"West Bohcmian Puppet Theatre-Karlovy-Vary (Karlsbad)."
Pupp Th Mod World, p 224 and Illus. No. 130
Wilkinson, W. "Czech. Puppetry," Pupp 6:67, 1935.

Denmark

Note: Material may be located under the title, "Illuminated
Theater," this is somewhat like the English "Paper
Theater" or English "Model Theatre" puppet work.

Andersen, Hans Christian. Puppet Showman. ed. by Paul
McPharlin, New York, Blue Ox, 1941.
Revised from trans. of H. W. Dujeken, 1851. In McPhar-
lin Coll.
---See also Paul McPharlin's Pupp Thea Am. , p. 312.

Clark, H. G. See W. Röhler.
161

Denmark (cont.)
"Copenhagen," Thea Arts, 13:626, Ag, 1929. - illus. of
   "Tivoli Theater" in Pleasure gardens.
Dvjeken, H. W. See Hans C. Andersen.
Green, L. and C. H. Green. Aladdin. Copenhagen, V.
   Prior, 1927, trans. from Danish, in NN.
Ibsen, Henrick. See Paul McPharlin's, Pupp Th Am. , p 312

"Illuminated Theater," Pupp J, 16(4):12, 1965

Jacobsen, A. See, L. Green.

Lewington, H. E. See T. Storm.

"Marionettes-Special Art On Increased Popularity," N Y
   Times, VI 1:6, Jl 9, 1922.
Mendham, Nellie. "It's Fun To Visit Puppeteers," Pupp J.
   8(6):9-10, 1957.
Röhler, W. "Puppet Theatre in Denmark," Pupp Master
   5(2):15, 1956
Schulze, K. See T. Storm

"Screweyes," Grapev, Feb. 1949, p 3

Shanafelt, Marjorie. "Here and There-Denmark With Mar-
   jorie," Pupp J, 3(4):2-4, 1952.
Storm, Theodor. Pole Puppenspäler. Leipzig, Insel-Bücherei,
   1919. In British Museum.
--- Puppeteer Paul. London, Harrap, 1933. (Der Puppen-
   spieler). In British Museum.
--- Puppeteer Paul, adapted by K. Schulze and H. E. Lewing-
   ton, London, Harrap, 1933.
   This is a book of fiction based on the authors boyhood
   memory of a Danish puppeteer with a theatre at Militia
   House.
Winther, Christian. En Student Ogen Jomfru. Copenhagen,
   C. G. Iversen, 1852. In NN.

               Dominican Republic. See also Africa

Marionetas. Liberia, Dominicana, Ciudad Trujillo, 1958.
   In LC.

               Egypt. See also Arabia

Ali El Rai, Dr. Pupp J, 13(3):7, 1961.

                         162

"Cairo Puppet Theatre," Pupp Th Mod World, p. 227, and Illus. Nos. 202, 203.
"Das Arabische Schattentheater in Ägypten," Blätter für Jugendspielscharen und Puppenspieler. 1:1, 1924.
"Das Islamische Schattentheater in Agypten," Orientalisches Archive, 3:103-08, 1913.
"Das Krokodilspiel; Ein Ägyptisches Schattenspiel," Nachrichten der Göttinger Gesellschaft der Wissenschaften, Phil-Hist Klasse 1915
"Egyptian Puppets," Pupp, 12:32-33, 1941

Falkenstein, Mollie. "The Cairo Puppet Theatre, United Arab Republic of Egypt," Pupp J, 17(3):3, 1965
Foyne, Vera. "Dancing Dolls of Destiny," Ch Sci Mon, 1948-1950. In the clipping file at Deering Lib. Northwestern Univ., Evanston, Ill.
Gad, L. F. "Puppet Theatre in Cairo," World Thea, 14:453-57, S 1965.
Horowitz, J. See F. Kern

Kahle, Paul. Der Lechtturm Von Alexandria. -ein Arabisches Schattenspiel, trans. by W. Kohlhammer. Stuttgart, 1934.
---Revu of Der Lechtturn von Alexandris. Anon, Pupp, 5: 95-96, 1934.
---"Islamische Schattenspielfiguren aus Ägypten," Der Islam, 1:264-299, 1910; 2:143-95, 1911.
--- Zur Geschichte des Arabischen Shattentheater in Ägypten. Leipzig, 1909.
"Kelmis," An early puppeteer who built a puppet theatre in Egypt which is believed to be the oldest in the world. See V. Foyne's article, "Dancing Dolls of Destiny."
Kern, F. "Das Ägyptische Schattentheater," in J. Horowitz's, Spuren Griechischer Mimen im Orient. Brenn, 1905.
Kohlhammer, W. See P. E. Kahle.
"Marktszene aus einem Ägyptischen Schattenspiel," Zeitschrift für Assyriologie, 27, 1912.
Shadow work. See also "Shadow" Section and some material might be found in Turkish material.

El Salvador and Central America

O'Hara, N. "Puppets can Teach Health Education," Americas, 2:20-22, D 1950.

Estonia

"Estonian Puppetry," Pupp J, 13(3):8, 1961.

England (Great Britain)

Note: All types of puppetry are found in England. The "Model Theatre" is not considered puppetry by some, yet the English consider it so and it is included in this book. Again, the "Toy Theater," the "Galanty Show" (1900 Flat Puppets), "Automats" (1889, Barry Gray), the "Optick" (1738-'49) and the "Jumping Jack Puppet Strowlers" (15th century) called "Pantins," are all included in this book. "String and Wire Marionettes" started 1573 in England. The first true English puppeteer may have been a "Captain Pod," in 1599, other puppeteers were mostly touring Europeans.

Adams, Moiley, (ed.) Boys' Own Book of Indoor Games and Recreation. London, Religious Tract Society, 1912, passim. This is typical of many such game books prepared in England with chapters on the different types of puppetry.

A. E. P. (pseud.) "The End of a Quest-Early English Puppeteer Work," Pupp Master, 2(3):69-73, 1948.

Ainsworth, R. Puppet Plays. London, Heinemann, 1955. 2 v.

Allen, A. B. Choral Speaking and Bible. London, Allman, 1950.

---Model Theatre. London, Wells, 1950.

---Puppetry and Puppet Plays. London, Allman, 1938, rev. ed. 1950.

---Puppetry for Beginners. London, Model Theatre Society, 1947. Wells, 1947. The "Model Theatre" or "Paper Theatre" Section would be almost entirely of English origin.

---Religious Drama for (Puppet and) Amateur Players. London, Faber, 1958.
See also "Plays" section, this name.

Aveline, C. "Marionettes de Shakespeare et Vraies Marionettes," L'Europe Nouvelle, 16:182, Feb 25, 1933

Ayer, A. M. Make and Manipulate Marionette and Puppet Secrets. A Series. London, Looker.

---Make Stick and Glove Puppets. London, Looker.

---Paint and Dress a Marionette. London, Looker.

Baird, Bill. The Art of the Puppet. New York, Macmillan, 1965, passim.

Barish, J. A. "Bartholomew Fair and Its Puppets," Mod Lang Q, 20:3-17, Mr 1959, bibliog.

Beard, E. B. Adventure With Puppets. London, Oxford Press, 1951.

Beaumont, Cyril W. Puppets and Puppetry. London, Studio, 1958.

Beecham, H. A. "A Hanging Puppet in Combe, North Oxfordshire," Folklore, S. 1956, p 159-61.

Bell, John. "Clunn Lewis and His Puppets, a Link With Old English Puppetry," Mask, 5:221-225, 1912.

Beresford, M. See "Education" Section, General.

Binyon, Helen. Puppetry Today: Designing and Making. New York, Watson, 1966.

---Modern Puppetry. London, Studio.

Birrell, F. "Puppets, The Tempest and Mr. Fagan," Nation (London) 33:310-12, Je 2, 1923.

Blackham, Olive. Puppets Into Actors. London, Rockcliff, 1948.

---Shadow Puppets. London, Rockcliff, 1960, p 95-115

Blake, Francis (pseud.) The Comedy of Marionettes. Chorley, Lancashire, Universal, 1917. In Harvard Univ. Lib.

Blanchard, C. W. Suitcase Puppet Theatre. London, Devereaux, 1946.

Bodor, John. See also "Hand Puppet" Section.

"Boom in London Performances Expected, Due to George VI Coronation," N Y Times, 4:10, Feb 28, 1937.

Boynton, Hilary. "The Prospice Puppet Theatre-College of Education Work," Pupp Master, 9(3):15-19, 1968.

Boy's Own Paper. Published, London, between 1889 and 1890 had puppet material. Especially Vol. 12, on "English Shadows."

Bramal, Eric. Expert Puppet Technique. London, Faber, 1963. Boston, Plays, 1966.

--- "Harlequin Puppet Theatre"-Colwyn Bay, Eng. Pupp Th Mod World, p 219 and Illus No. 8.

--- Making a Start With Marionettes. London, Bell, 1960.

--- "Puppet Panorama," Studio, O. 1957, p. 106-09, illus.

--- Puppet Plays and Playwriting. London, Bell, 1961. See also English Puppet Periodicals as he has written a great deal.

Bult, S. "Louisa Pollok and Penny Plain Theater," Pupp Master, 5(6):15-16, 1957.

Bundall, John. "The John Bundall Puppet Theatre," Pupp Th Mod World. p 219 and Illus Nos. 9 and 11.

Bussell, Jan. Art of Television. London, Faber, 1952.

---"The Art of the Puppet Theatre With Reference to England" Pupp Th Mod World, p 38-40; see p 219 for illus.

--- and A. Mills. (A. Hogarth or Mrs. A. Bussell), Blue Muffin Books. London, Univ. of London Press, 1952.

England (cont.)
--- Look at Puppets. London, Hamilton, 1960
--- Marionettes: How to Make Them. Ditchling, Sussex, Pepler, 1934.
--- Meet Muffin the Mule. London, Univ. of London Press, 1954.
--- Model Theatre. London, Dobson, 1948.
--- Muffin and Louise. London, Brockhampton, 1954.
--- Muffin and Peregrine. London, Brockhampton, 1954.
--- Muffin Climbs High. London, Brockhampton, 1955.
--- Muffin Sings a Song. London, Brockhampton, 1955.
--- Muffin's Birthday. London, Brockhampton, 1954.
--- Muffin's Thinking Cap. London, Brockhampton, 1955.
--- (ed.) Plays for Puppets. London, Faber, 1951.
--- Puppet Theatre. New York, Binny, 1946.
--- Puppets and I. London, Faber, 1950.
--- Puppets Progress. London, Faber, 1953.
--- Through Wooden Eyes. London, Faber, 1956.
    See also "Muffin" in "Television" section, and "Plays"
    section, "Supply" section.
Butler, Samuel. Remains. London (2 vols.) Tonson, 1759,
    p 233-66 in Vol 1; and p 264-65 in vol. 2.
Carroll, Lewis. In Paul McPharlin's, Pupp Thea Am. p 312.

"Christmas Puppetry in London, " Brit Pupp Thea, 3(5):9,
    1952.
Clark, M. "England and North Wales, " Rod Young's Column,
    (items). . "Mailbox, " Pupp J 10(2):31-4, 1958.
Cochrane, Louise. The Puppet Book of Play Ideas and
    Things to Do. London, Chatto, 1962.
Coleman, E. J. "Troubadour Puppet Theater." See
    Pupp Th Mod World, p 219 and Illus No. 4.
Coleman, Stanley J. (ed.) Puppets of Many Races. Douglas,
    Isle-of-Man, Folklore Academy, 1957 (typewritten)
Cook, Olive. See "Shadow" and "Film" Sections.

Craig, Gordon. "Puppet World Theatre, " Thea Arts, 12:
    457-61, 1928.
Crawford, K. N. "Barry Smith's Show, " Pupp J, 20(3):27,
    1968.
--- "Clifford Helps Miniature Theatre, " Pupp J, 20(3):27,
    1968.
--- International Festival Report 1968. London, Brit. Pupp
    and Model Thea Guild, 1968. In NN.
--- "Prof. Press, Punch Show, " Pupp J, 20(3):28, 1968.
Cross, J. M. "Huron Legend, " Sat N 63:18, Ag 28, 1948.
    Cox, J. C. See J. Strutt.
Davis, Colin. See "Plays" and "Production" Sections.

Dobson, Austin. Sidewalk Studies. London, Chatto, 1903, passim.
Dramatic Register. London. Excellent source material on puppet performances from early years.
Draper, G. Marionettes. London, Arnold, 1953.

Early, A. K. English Dolls, Effigies and Puppets. London, Batsford, 1955.
Revu of English Dolls... Pupp Master, 3(8):249, 1955.
Revu of English Dolls... Mus J, 55:298-99, Feb. 1956.
Educational Puppetry Association, British. The Complete Puppetry. London, Faber, 1956. Selected and ed. by L. V. Wall.
--- The Puppet Book. Boston, Plays, 1965. Rev. and ed. by A. R. Philpott, 1965.
See also This name in "Organizations" and "Education" Sections.
Ellis, C. L. See British Puppet Theatre periodical as he was editor for several years. See Vol 1, no. 6, 1950. In NN.
"England" clipping file. In NN - Research Theater Room - "Marionette Clippings."
"English Puppeteers," Pupp, 12:36-37, 1941
"English Puppetry," Pupp 3:12-13, 1932; 4:58, 1933; 5:32-33, 1934; 5:52-53, 1934; 6:67-70, 1935.

"English Puppetry," Pupp, 9:18, 1938; 15:36-39, 1944.

"English Puppetry in 1946," Pupp, 17:54-56, 1946.

"English Summer Schools," Pupp, 12:37, 1941.

"Expansion, (The Prospects of) for English Puppets," Times, Je 19, 1966, p 13.
Evec, J. Puppet Craft Books, Series, London, Müller, 1952.
--- Puppetry. London, Müller, 1952. In LC.
--- Puppetry, ed. by W. A. Foyle, London, 1951 (Foyle Handbook Series)
Fagan, J. B. "Tempest at the Scala Theatre; a reply." Nation, London, Je 9, 1823, p 334.
See also F. Birrell
Fallkenstein, Mollie. "Impressions of Colwyn Bay International Festival -UNIMA," UNIMA, U. S. A. Newsl., Je 1968, p 1-3.
Fawdry, R. C. "Benjamin Pollock's Theatres," Pupp Master, 4(2):238, 1955.
Festivals, English. See "Festival" Section, and Pupp J,

England (cont.)
17(4):4-10, 1966. "International Festival at North Wales"
and the "Festival of English Professionals and Amateurs."
Field, Joan. See "Plays" Section

Films, English. See "Films" Section

Fisher, Douglas. Wooden Stars. London, Boardman, 1947.

Forester, C. S. Marionettes at Home. London, Joseph,
1936.
Forster, J. Life and Times of Oliver Goldsmith. Vol 12,
Bk 4, Ch 14, London, Ward, 1888, "Puppets of Drury
Lane and Elsewhere."
Fraser, Peter. Introducing Puppetry. London, Batsford,
1968.
French, Susan. Presenting Marionettes. New York, Rein-
hold, 1964.
"Galanty Show, A" G. Speaight's, Hist Eng Pupp Thea, p 22.

Gilbert, Ella. Three Puppet Plays. London, Novello, 1960.

Goaman, M. Judy and Andrew's Puppet Book. London,
Faber, 1952.
Granger, Martin. "Phoebe and Geronimo," Pupp Th Mod
World, p 219 and Illus No. 14.
Green, Dana S. Masks and Puppets. London, Studio, 1942.
--- Puppet Making. London, Studio, 1938, Hours of Leisure
Series.
Harding, D. P. Glove Puppetry. London, Blackwell, 1938.

Hecht, E. Marionette Stage. New York, Macmillan, 1945.
--- Marionettes. London, Macmillan, 1945.

Henry, Nancy. Plays for Puppets, a series. London, Philip,
1957.
--- Poor Pierott: Puppet Plays. London, Gryphon, 1955.
--- Rag, Tag and Bob-Tail and Their Puppets. London, Gry-
phon, 1951.
See also "Plays" Section
Herrick, Jane. "Puppets in the British Isles," Pupp J, 17
(3):9-10, 1965.
Hogarth, Ann (Mrs. Jan Bussell). See J. Bussell

"Hogarth Puppet Theatre of London," See Pupp Th Mod
World, p 219, Illus No. 7
Hone, W. Ancient Mysteries of W. Hone. London, W.

168

Hone, 1823 passim and a Chap. on puppets.
--- "Early English Puppet Show: An Extract From Hone's
Book," Mask, 5:141-43, O 1912.
Howard, V. (Linwood) See also "Plays" Section.

Humphreys, W. G. and J. P. Parry. Puppet Plays. London,
Blackie, 1952.
Hussey, D. "English and German Puppet Theatres," Spect,
153:924, D 14, 1934.
Hutchings, Margaret. Glove Toys. London, Studio, 1958.

"In England, History of the Puppet Show," Anon. trans.,
Sharp's Lon Mag, 14:107-114, 1851, p 171-178 and p 203-
208. In Watkinson Lib., Trinity College, Hartford.
The use of puppets by Dr. Ben Jonson and Shakespeare,
among others, exact references given. See also "History"
Section from C. Magnin's, French Puppet History.
Jackson, Charles Vivian. Puppetcraft Made Easy. Exeter,
Wheaton, 1957.
Jagendorf, Moritz. First Book of Puppets. London, Ward,
1964, 1st ed. New York, Watts, 1952.
--- Penny Puppets. Penny Theatre, Penny Plays. New York,
Bobbs, 1941. Boston, Plays, 1966, rev. ed.
--- Puppets for Beginners. London, Watts, 1952. Boston,
Plays, 1966.
Johnson, Ben. See also "History" Section, valuable ma-
terial.
See C. Magnin and E. Pollock.
Johnson, D. "The Puppet Show," Fortnightly Rev, London
134, S 1930, p 378-80
Jones, J. M. See "Hand and Glove" Section

Joseph, Helen H. "Pastorial Puppets in England," Thea
Arts, 13, Ag 1929, p 579-81.
Kellogg, Marie J. "History of Puppetry in England from the
beginning to the middle of the 18th century." Master's
dissertation, Madison, Univ. of Wisc., 1937.
"Lanchester Marionettes," Illus Lon N, 223:991, D 12, 1953.

"Lanchester Marionettes-Stratford, Eng.," Pupp Th
World, p 219 and Illus No. 6.
Lanchester, Waldo S. "Buckingham Palace Puppets," Pupp,
10:8, 1939.
---"English Puppetry," Pupp, 13-14:26-27, 1942.
---"English Puppets," Pupp, 2:31-32, 1931.
--- Hand Puppets and String Puppets. London, Dryad, 1948,
Leichester, Dryad, 1957.

England (cont.)
--- See also English puppet periodicals. He wrote short
articles for them.
Lano, David. Wandering Showman. East Lansing, Mich.
State Univ. Press, 1957, passim on Canada and England.
"Leichester Puppets 1619, 1626" Pupp, 7:77, 1936.

Ledwig, David. "Pantopuck, The Puppetman," (of England)
Pupp J, 10(1):7-9, 1958.
Lewis, Clunn. "Middleton-Oldest English Puppeteer Living,
1892-1968," Pupp Master, 9(3):13, 1968.
"Little Angel Theatre-London," Pupp Th Mod World, p 229
Illus No. 2, No. 12 and No. 12, and "Theatre" Sections
of this bibliography.
--- Ch Sci Mon, (Eastern), Jan 24, 1964, p 4, col. 1.

McCrea, Lilian. Puppets and Puppet Plays. London, Oxford
Press, 1949.
--- Twelve Puppet Plays. London, Pittman, 1963.
See also "Plays" Section.
MacDermott, J. T. See "Russia" under S. V. Obraztsov.
McIsaac, F. J. Marionettes and How to Make Them. Buck-
inghamshire, St. Paul, 1923.
McMahon, J. Making and Playing Marionettes. London,
Harrap, 1957.
MacNamara, D. Puppetry. London, Arco, 1965.

McPharlin, Marjorie Batchelder. "British, News Abroad,"
Pupp J, 1(2):7, 1949.
--- "British Films," Brit Pupp Thea, 1(1): D 1950.
--- "British Foreign News," Pupp J, 1(5):20, 1950.
--- "International Festival," Pupp J, 1(2):7, 1949.
McPharlin, Paul. Puppet Theatre in America. New York,
Harpers, 1949. passim.
Magnin, Charles. "Puppets in England," Sharpes' Lon J,
14:107-114, 171-78, 203-08, 1851. The only trans. into
English we have and it is only a small portion of his His-
torie des Marionettes En Europe. Paris, Levy, 1852.
Published previous to book. Very sig. m.
Mahlmann, Lewis. "Pantopuck and Violet," Pupp J, 17(3):
6, 1965.
Malcolm, Isobel M. Puppetry for the Mentally Handicapped.
London, Nat. Assoc. for Mentally Handicapped, 1959.
"Marionettes in Scala Theatre," Spec, 130:886, My 26, 1923.

Marks, Hayward. "Growth of English Puppetry," Pupp 8:35-
36, 1937.

170

--- "English Educational Puppetry," Pupp, 10:35-36, 1939.
Marriott, E. "Liverpool Puppetry," Mask, 5:234-36, 237-47, 1912-'13.
Marsh, W. A. Glove Plays and Patterns. London, Harrap, 1955.
Mayhew, Henry. London Labour and the London Poor. See "History" Section.
Mendham, Nellie. "It's Fun to Visit Puppeteers," Pupp J, 8(6):9-10, 1957.
Mills, A. See Ann Hogarth.

Model Theatres, Paper Theatres and Like. See "Model" Theatre Section.
See also Model Theatre Series. London, Wells, 1951. 7 vols.
Morice, Gerald. "Activities of British Puppet Guild," Drama 17:44, D 1938.
--- "English Puppetry," Pupp 7:67-70, 1936.
--- "English Puppetry in 1939," Pupp, 10:36, 1939.
--- "Punch, Puppetry," his regular column in World's Fair beginning near 1937.
--- "Puppets of the English Past," Pupp Master 3(3):89-93, 1950.
--- "Television and Punch in English Puppetry," Pupp, 11: 33-34, 1940.
See also "Punch & Judy" Section
Morley, Henry. Memoirs of Bartholomew's Fair. London, 1859. passim. In Chandos Lib., England.
Morton, Brenda. See "Hand Puppet" Section.

"Mr. Punch or the Drama at the Street Corner," Chambers J, (Edinburgh) 59:75, 1882 (4th Series, No. 19)
Mulholland, John. Practical Puppetry. London, Arco, 1962.

Music. See "Music" Section

Newnes, George (ed.) Punch and Judy Children's Annual. London, News Periodical, 1931. In British Museum.
Nicol, W. Puppetry. London, Oxford Univ. Press, 1963, Illus.
Nisbet, -- (ed.) Punch and Judy. London, Nisbet, 1901.

Organizations. See "Organizations" Section.

"Pantopuck" (pseud.) See A. R. Philpott.

Park, A. (ed.) History of Punch and Judy. Finsbury, Park, 1847. In McPharlin Coll.

England (cont.)
--- Parks Punch and Judy. Finsbury, Park, 1848. In Mc Pharlin Coll.
Parker, Jack. Practical Puppetry. London, Jenkins, 1961. In NN.
Parry, G. H. "Prof. R. Codman Gets New Punch and Judy Booth From the City of Liverpool," Pupp 1:31-32, 1930.
Parry, J. P. See W. G. Humphreys.

Pepys, Samuel. See "History" Section.

Periodicals. See "Periodicals" Section.

"Percy Press Punch and Judy Booth," Pupp Th Mod World, p 219 and Illus No. 1.
Peterson, A. E. "Pilgrimage to Pollock's Show," Pupp Master, 3(2):46-49, 1950 (Anon)
--- "Shakespeare vs. Shaw," Pupp Master, 2(8):237-39, 1949 (Anon)
--- See also Puppet Master (England) 1948-50 as he was editor of the periodical during this time.
Philpott, Alexis R. (Pantopuck) Modern Puppetry. London, Joseph, 1966.
--- The Puppet Book. London, Faber, 1965, for the Educ. Puppet Assoc. of England.
--- Puppet Diary. London, Educ. Pupp Inst., 1950.
--- Puppets. London, Muller, 1966.
--- See also "Education" and "Plays" Section.

Philpott, E. See "Plays" Section.

Philpott, Violet. "The Violet Philpott Puppet Theatre," Pupp Th Mod World, p 219, and Illus No. 3.
See also "Theatres" Section, England.
Picard, L. B. Les Marionettes. London, Methuen, 1925.

Pollock, E. "Puppets in the Plays of Ben Johnson," unpublished Master's Dissertation, Brookings, Univ. of So. Dakota, 1936.
Poulter, M. R. "Editorial on Plays and Drama for the Puppet," Pupp Post, Summer, 1950, p 3.
Powell, Martin. "Martin Powell, The Puppet Showman," No. 506, Sp Mono, 2: 1931-34, by G. M. Powell.
--- Martin Powell, The Puppet Showman, Los Angeles, Univ. of Southern California Press, 1933, by G. M. Powell.
---"Powell at Punch's Theater," Pupp, 17:61, 63, 1946.
--- G. Speaight's, Hist Eng Pupp Thea, p 92-106 and passim.

Pringle, G. "A Young Puppeteer," Can H J, 36:56, D 1939.

Punch and Judy. See "Punch and Judy" Section

Puppet Secrets Series. Dorset, Eng., Looker, 1957. Author
    unknown.
"Puppet Show in England," Penny Mag, 14:114, 142,

Puppet Tales. London, W. Collins, 1957. author unknown.

Puppets. London, Evans, 1947. Activity Readers Series.
    Author unknown.
Reiniger, Lottie. "Film as Ballet," Life and Let, 14:157-
    63, Spring 1936.
--- "The Happy Prince Film," Pupp Th Mod World, p 219,
    and Illus No. 13
--- "Moving Silhouettes," Film A, 3(8):14-18, 1936.
--- --- "Sissors Make Films," Sight and S, 5:13-15, Spring
    1936.
    See also "Shadows" and "Film" Sections.
    See also Megroz, in "Shadow" Section.
"Revival of Puppetry in England" Illus Lon N, Mr 6, 1909,
    p 357.
Ridge, A. Puppet Plays for Children. London, Faber, 1953.

Robinson, S. and P. Exploring Puppetry. London, Cowell,
    1967.
Rose, A. Boy Snowman & Entertainor, London, Routledge,
    1926. In NN.
Rose, E. J. See "Punch and Judy" Section.

"Royal Marionette Theatre," Pupp, 7:78-79, 1936.

Saunders, E. F. Four Puppet Plays. London, Pitman, 1957.
--- Puppetry in Schools. London, Pitman, 1951.
Scaping, M. Toy Theatre. London, Premier, 1967.

Scott, Sir Walter. The Bride of Lammermoor. London,
    Chap. 1 of the 1818 ed. The preliminary chap. of the
    1832 ed. In British Museum.
Seager, D. W. Glove Puppetry. London, Macmillan, 1950.

Serjeant, F. I. Simple Puppets for Children. London, Pit-
    man, 1957
Shakespeare, William. See also "Marionettes, William
    Shakespeare," Clipping File of NN. See also "History"
    Section - very important.

England (cont.)

Sherson, Erroll. London's Lost Theatre of the 19th Century. London, Lane, 1926 "Lost Theatres of Toyland." Last 2 chapters in the book.

Showmen's Year Book. ed. by Thomas Murphy, London, World's Fair Press, (Brit. Showmen's Guild). Lists plays in which puppeteers work.

Slade, R. You Can Make a String Puppet. London, Faber, 1957.

Snook, Barbara. Puppets. London, Batsford, 1965.

Somers, P. H. "Hand Puppets from England," Sch Arts, 49: 126, D 1949.

--- "The Massacre of Pollock's Penny Plain," Pupp Master, 5(2):13, 1956.

Somerville, G. L. "Found--A Genuine Puppeteer-England," Pupp J, 11(1):9-10, 1959.

Speaight, George. History of the English Puppet Theater. London, Harrap, 1955; New York, J. de Graff, 1955. Very unusual and sig. book, especially the extensive bibliographic "Notes" at the end, and table of "English Puppeteers." Corresponds to Paul McPharlin's American history.

--- Revue of History of the English Puppet Theatre. Pupp Master, 3(9):257, 1955, by H. A.

--- Juvenile Drama, The History of the English Toy (Model) Theatre. London, MacDonald, 1945; rev. ed. London, Studio Vista, 1969.

--- "Puppets in the Festival Gardens at Battersea." Pupp Master, 3(6):185, 1951.

  Note: He has written much which is scattered throughout the Bibliography. See also English Puppet periodicals.

Stevens, Martin. "England," in his regular column, "Under the Bridge," Pupp J, 14(2):31, 1962. Also many other items in this column.

Stevenson, Robert Louis. "A Penny Plain, Twopence Coloured," in his Memories and Portraits. London, Chatto, 1887.

  See also Paul McPharlin's Pupp Th Am. p 312

Stockwell, Alan. Puppetry. London, Collins, 1966.

Stonier, G.W. "In a London Park," TV Show. N Statesm and Nat (London) 28:103, Ag 12, 1944.

Stratford-On-Avon Puppet Center. "The Puppet Center Theater," G N Y Pupp G Newsl 3(2):2, 1965.

Strutt, Joseph. Sport's and Pastimes of the People of England. London, Reeves, 1830, new ed. , London, Methuen, 1903. Telling of Fantoccini puppets and very early English puppetry. Later edition enlarged by J. C. Cox.

Television. See "Television" Section

Tearle, P. Felt Glove Puppets. London, Dryad, 1957.

"Tom Brown Theatre-1682, England," Pupp, 11:40, 1940.

Tuttle, Florence P. Puppets and Puppet Plays. Mankato,
Minn., Creative Educ. Society, 1962, passim.
Union Internationale De Marionettes. ed., Puppet Theatre of
the Modern World. comp. by M. Niculescu, trans., E.
Osers and E. Strick, London, Harrap, 1967.
Most unusually illustrated puppet history showing all different forms of puppetry in many, many countries. Short
articles by the leaders of outstanding puppet theaters and
listing of personnel in many of the shows. Shows are illustrated on separate pages.
"Victorian English Puppet Theatre," Pupp, 17:32-34, 1946.

Wall, L. V. and G. H. White (ed.) The Complete Puppet
Book. London, Faber, 1956.
Warsage, V. C. "Puppets in England," Pupp J, 16(4):23-24,
1965.
Whanslaw, H. W. Animal Puppetry. London, Wells, 1948.
--- Bankside Book of Puppetry. London, Wells, 1935; Second
ed. London, Wells 1948. Third ed., London, Heineman,
1952.
--- Bench Book of Puppetry. London, Wells, 1957, Rev. ed.
London, Heineman, 1961.
--- Bible Puppetry. Wallington, Surrey, Religious Educ. Co.,
1944; rev. ed. 1958.
--- Book of Marionette Plays. London, Wells, 1950 (Model
Thea Series)
--- Everybody's Marionette Book. London, Wells, 1923.
--- Everybody's Theater. London, Wells, 1923 and rev.
1948.
--- "The Famous Old Clowes Excelsior Marionettes-1873"
Pupp Master 4(1):20-22, 1952.
--- Making Bible Models (Puppets) Wallington, Surrey, Re-
ligious Educ. Co., 1942, rev. ed. 1962.
--- Marionettes and Rod Puppets. Wallington; Surrey, Re-
ligious Educ. Co., 1953 (Handicraft and Activity Book Se-
ries)
--- More Bible Models. Wallington, Surrey, Religious Educ.
Co., 1949. rev. ed 1961.
--- Puppetry for School and Home. London, Nelson, 1936.
--- "Puppets of the Past," Pupp Master, 2, Jl 1950.
--- Second Bench Book of Puppetry. London, Wells, 1957.

England (cont.)
--- Shadow Play. London, Wells, 1950 (Model Thea Series)
--- and V. Hotchkiss. Specialized Puppetry. London, Wells,
1939 (Model Thea Series) 1948.
--- Twelve Puppet Plays. Wallington, Religious Educ. Co.,
1957.
White, G. H. See L. V. Wall.

Wilkinson, Roy. Festival and Puppet Plays. Leads, Arnold,
1958.
Wilkinson, Walter. "English Puppets," Pupp Bull, 1938, p
71-72
--- "In the Beginning," (of English Puppetry) Pupp Master,
5(4):7-10, 1957.
--- Peep Shows in 1927 England. London, Bles, 1927, 1931,
1947.
--- Puppets in Lancashire. New York, Stoakes, 1932;
London, Bles, 1936.
--- Puppets in Sussex. London, Bles, 1933.
--- Puppets in Wales, London, Bles, 1948.
--- Puppets in Yorkshire. New York, Stoakes, 1931; Lon-
don, Bles, 1931.
--- Puppets into Scotland. London, Melrose, 1935.
--- Puppets Through America. London, Bles, 1938.
--- A Sussex Peep Show. New/ York, Stokes, 1933.
--- Vagabonds and Puppets. London, Bles, 2nd ed., 1930-
'31.
Note: All are found at McGill Univ. Lib. and NN; and
all are reviewed by M. L. Becker in Sat R Lit, 9:494,
Mr 18, 1933.
Wright, John F. Your Puppetry. London, Sylvan, 1951.
Yorick (pseud.) (P. C. Ferrigui, or Fertigni "History of
Puppetry in England," Mask 6:205-16, 1913.

Estonia, See Czechoslovakia

Finland

Anniki, Sundquist. "Visiting Finland Puppeteer," Pupp J,
S 1953, p 12, 14.
"Helsinki Dock Theater - (Helsingin Nukketeattern)." Pupp Th
Mod World, p 220, and Illus Nos. 40, 41, 42.
"Invisible Hand." Contemporary Films Inc., Pupp J, 20(2):
29-30, 1968. Embassy of Finland, Wash. D. C.

Flemish, See also Belgium

Baird, Bill. The Art of the Puppet. New York, Macmillan, 1965, p 250.

"Belgium." Grapev, Je 1949, p 10. (Mr. Deschamps Antwerp Show.)

Warsage, Rudolphe de. Historie du Celebre Theatre Liegeois de Marionettes. Bruxelles, Vanoest, 1905.

France

Achard, M. "Guignol." Annales Politiques et Litteraires. April, 1926.

Alber, Maurice. See Albert, Maurice

Albert Birot, P. Barbe-Bleue. Paris, 1926.
--- Matoum et Tréyibar ou Historie Édifiante Et Récréative du Vrai et du Faux Pôele. Paris, 1919.

Albert, Maurice. "Naissance et Vel des Marionettes." La Nature 61: pt 1 (Apr 1, 1933) p 322; 61: pt 1 (Apr 15, 1933) p 371; 61: pt 1 (May 15, 1933) p 467; 61: pt 1 (June 15, 1933) p 563; 61: pt 2 (O, 1933) p 323: (Oct 15, 1933) p 369; 61: pt 2 (D 15, 1933) p 563; 62: pt 2 (Ag 15, 1934) p 180; 64: pt 2 (D 1, 1936) p 514-515.

--- "Les Ombres d'Chinoise." La Nature 62: pt 1 (Jan 1, 1934) p 36; 62: pt 1 (Feb. 15, 1934) p 180; 64: pt 2 (July, 1, 1936) p 34-35.

--- "Les Ombres d'Ombres." La Nature 63: pt 1(N 1, 1935) p 422.

--- "Les Ombres Vivantes." La Nature 65: pt 1 (Jan 1, 1937) p 34.

--- "Les Théâtres d'Ombres." La Nature 65: pt 1 (June 15, 1937) p 573-74. 65: pt 2 (D 1, 1937) p 530; 66: pt 1 (Dec 1, 1937) p 88; 66: pt 2 (Jan 15, 1938) p 281; 66: pt 2 (Feb 1, 1938) p 217; 66: pt 2 (Ap 1, 1938) p 371.

--- Les Théâtres d'Ombres Chinoise. Paris, Mazo, 1896. In NN.

--- Les Théâtres de la Foire, 1600-1789. Paris, Hachett, 1900. 12 vols.

--- "Théâtres de Marionettes." La Nature 63: pt 1 (My 1, 1935) p 418.

--- Théâtres des Boulevards, 1789-1843. Paris, Lécene, 1902. 12 vols.

Alexandre, Arsène. See A Tavernier.

Allemagne, Henri-Rene. Les Jouets à la Worlds Fair, 1904. À Saint Louis. Paris, L'Auteur, 1908. In NN.

France (cont.)
--- Sports et Jeu D'Adresse. Paris, Hachette, c 1913, and
   Zurich, Rentsch, 1923, 1926. In British Museum.
--- Histoire des Jouets des Enfants. Paris, Grasset, c 1916

Allos, -- "Le Cycle de Charlemagne," Figaro, Jan 21, 1923.

Amieu, A. Cent Ans Aprés. Lyons, 1904.

André, C. G. Marionettes et Marionnettistes de France.
   Bordas, 1947. Bibliography.
André, M. E. Les Tribulations de Duroquet. Lyon, Lord-
   anchet, 1882. In Harvard Univ. Lib.
Anet, C. "Les Marionettes de Mme. Forain," Le Théâtre,
   My, 1908.
"Arc en Ciel Puppet Theatre," Pupp Th Mod World, p 219
   and Illus No. 25
"Artistes in Little," Graphic, 121:345, S 1, 1920.

Auburn, B. See D. Bonnaud

Auguier, Philippe. "Le Petit Theatre," L'Illus, No. 2555
   Feb 13, 1892, p 140-141.
Aurey, Mlle B and Mme J. Ainsi Font Les Marionnettes.
   Paris, Nathan, 1930. In Harvard Univ.
Aveline, C. "Marionettes De Shakespeare Et Vrains Mario-
   nettes," L'Europe Nouvelle, 16:182, Feb 25, 1933.
Avril, A. Saltimbanqueset Marionettes. Paris, Lévy, 1867.

Bachaumont, Louis. Memoires Secrets. Paris, A. Delahaye,
   1859, London, Adamson, 1777-1789; Paris, Brisot-Thir-
   ars, 1830. In Bibliotheque National, Paris.
Bachut, J. Guignol Congress. Lyons, UNIMA Org. 1911
--- See Dr. Gros

Baird, Bill. The Art of the Puppet. New York, Macmillan,
   1965, p 250.
Barbaret, V. Lesage et le Théâtre de la Foire. Dijen:
   L'Auteur, 1888. In Bibliotheque Nationale, Paris.
Baril, Gédeon. La Fleur, Garcon Apothicaire. Amiens,
   Impr. De Jeunet, 1901.
Baring, Maurice. Les Marionettes Du Souvenir. Trans. by
   Tanette Prigent Paris, De Flore, c 1948
--- The Puppet Show of Memory. trans. by Tanette Prigent,
   Paris, De Flore, c 1948. In Montreal City Lib.
Batcave, L. Les Petits Comediens du Roi au Bois de
   Boulogne. Paris, Schemit, 1908.

Baty, Gaston. "Marionettes," Le Théâtre, Jl, 1937.
--- Guignol. Paris, Bloud & Gay, 1934. In British Museum
and also in Mme S. Zlatin Bk Store, (See Key No 1)
--- "La Grande Parade Des Marionettes," L'Illus, No 4950
Jan 15, 1938, p 68-70.
--- & R. Chavance Trois Petits Tours et Puis S'en Vont-
1800-1890. Paris, O. Lieutier, 1943. In NN.
--- Le Montreur de Marionettes Paris. Paris, Coutan
1946. In British Museum.
--- "Parisian Puppetry," Pupp 17:34-36, 1946.
--- Historire, des Marionettes. 1st ed. Paris, Univ. of
France, 1959. In NN.
--- Le Théâtre Joly. Paris, Coutan, 1937. In British Mu-
seum.
Beard, E. "Guignol and the Butterflies," Brit Pupp Thea,
3(5):4, 1952.
Beaulieu, H. Les Théâtres D'Boulevard du Crime. Paris,
Daragon, 1905.
Beissieur, Ferdinand. Théâtre De Guignol. Paris, Théâtrale
(Lib.) 1887. At Yale Univ. Lib.
Bellec, Hilaire. "Marionettes," Outl., London, Je 16, 1923.

Beranger, P. (pseud.) (Collin De Plancy). "Negroes and the
Puppet Show," Oeuvres, Plancy, Society de St. Victor,
1840.
--- See also Pupp, 13-14:63, 1942. This is an unusual poem.

Bernard, Laure. Théâtre de Marionnettes. Paris, Didier,
1837. In NN. Good bibliography.
Bernardelli, F. "Per Un Teatro Di Marionettc," Nuova
Antologia, Ap, 1922.
Bernet, Henri. Guignol À Peyrebeille. Paris, Edit du
Piglannier, 1939
Bertrand, V. Les Silhouettes Animées À La Main. Paris,
Mendel, 1892.
Bideaux, Suzanne. Guignol en Famille. Lille, Demdilly,
1948. In Harvard Univ. Lib.
Bidon, H. "Les Petits Comédiens de Bois," J Des Déb,
37: pt 1, Jan 3, 1930.
--- Guignol en Société. Lille, Editions S. P. E. D. , 1953[sic]
In Harvard Univ. Lib.
Bistan, Claque. Guignol Au Maroc. Saint Etienne, Pensée.

Blackham, Olive. Shadow Puppets. London, Rockcliff, 1960,
p 65-86. Uses "Chat Noir" as the title for French Shadow work in addition to "Ombres Chinoise."
Blanc, Louis-Etienne. Les Canettes de Jirome Rouquet Dit
Tampio. Lyons, Mera, 1862. 2nd ed. 1875.

France (cont.)
Bleton, Auguste. See also Regular histories.
He also wrote many puppet history notes in his books a-
bout Lyon.
Blondeau, H. and V. Buteaux. Guignol S'en va-t-en Querre.
Paris, Eichler, 1915.
Bockwoldt, Henri. "Henri Bockwaldt writes," Grapev, D 1948,
p 8
Bodart-Timal, C. "Les Marionnettes À Roubaix," Rev Sept,
Feb. and Oct 1929
Boehn, Max von. Dolls and Puppets. trans by J. Nicoll,
New York, McKay, 1932 passim and see bibliog.
Bonaventure, Batant. Le Bottier de Saint Georges. Lyons,
1898
Bonnaissies, J. Les Spectacles Forains et la Comedie
Francaise. Paris, Dentu, 1875.
Bonnaud, Dominique. Pierret Pornographe. Paris, 1902.
--- Le Sacre de Clemenceau. Voy, Courteline, 1907,
passim.
--- Ulysse À Montmartre. Voy, Courteline, 1910
--- & B. Aubrun. Marionettes, Jeux D'Enfants. Paris,
Editions Du Scarabée, 1962. In NN.
Bonnefon, Paul. "Un Chapitre De L'Histore Des Marion-
nettes," L'Artiste, 1883.
Bordat, Dennis. Les Marionettes. Paris, Editions du
Scarabée, 1949.
--- & F. Boucret. Les Théâtre De'Ombres. Histoire et
Techniques. Paris, L'Arche, 1956.
Boucher, Maurice. Trois Mystères de Noel. Paris,
Charpentier, 1855. In Yale Univ. Lib.
--- Legende Biblique. Paris, E. Flammarion, 1890.
Boucret, F. See D. Bordat

Bouvier, Bernard. Maro-Mennier Et Geneve. Geneve, Im-
primerie Centrale, 1930
--- "An Théâtre De Marionettes A Roubaix," Rev Sept ,
O 1929.
Brazier, N. Chronique des Petits Théâtres du Paris De-
pouis Lour Creation Jusqu'a Ce Jour. 2 Vols. Paris,
Allardin, 1937.
Brun, Pierre. Pupazzi Et Statuettes, Etudes Sur Le Dix-
hitieme Siecle. Paris, Cornely, 1908.
See also W. Saroyan
Budry, Maurice. Trois Petits Tours, Pour Les Marionettes.
Lousanne, Payatard, 1932.
Bugnard, C. L'Ecole Des Menageres. Lyons, Mera, 1925.

Buteaux, V. See E. Blandeau

Cadilac, P. E. "Guignol à Paris," L'Illus, 175:-176: No 4457; pt 2 Jl 1930, p 438-39
--- "Guignol En Naut Cour," L'Illus, 179-180: Jan 16, 1932, p 91.
Cahuet, A. "Le Théâtre D'Ombres dans l'historire Montmartroise," L'Illus, No 4954 Feb 12, 1938 p 188.
Campardon, Emile. Les Spectacles de la Forie. 2 Vols. Paris, Berger, 1877.
Campbell, H. "With Certain Parisian Marionettes," Lit W, Boston, 19: 1888, p 249.
Canard, G. and A. Duroquet, G. Coquard. Mémoires De L'Académie Du Gourguillon. Lyons, A. Storck, 1887.
Canfield, D. "Vive Guignol..." Schol, Ap 1934, p 8-9, 15-16, 32
Capon, Alphonso. Flanders En Fête. Lille, J. Tallandier, 1925.
--- Pouvre Artiste. Lille, Tallandier, 1909
--- Marie-Claire. Lille, Tallandier, 1896, puppetry in North of France.
--- Recits Du Nord. Lille, Tallandier, 1912.
--- Petit Francois. Lille, Tallandier, 1908. Recitations of North French puppets.
Caron, Charles. Un Siècle de Théâtre de Cabotins à Amiens. Amiens, 1925.
Cassira, Henri. "Les Curiosites Cinematographiques-un film joué par des poupees," L'Illus, 161:542, My 26, 1923.
Castor, Père. Cinderella; Sleeping Beauty; Aesop's Fables; Folk Songs. Paris, Flammarion, 1950-1960.
Catalogue: La Marionnette en France et à L'Étranger. Paris, City of Paris Museum Calliera, Je-O 1939.
Chaipus, A. and E. Gelis. Le Monde Des Automates. Paris, 1928.
Chambers, E. K. The Medieval Stage. Vol. II, London, Oxford, 1903.
Champfleury, Le Musee Secret de la Caricature. Paris, Dentu, 1888.
"Champs Elysee" See "Film Revu" by Alfred Wallace, Pupp J, 10(5):3-5, 1959.
Chancel, Jules. Le Coffre-Fort de Polichnelle. Paris, Delagrave, 1903.
Chavance, R. See G. Baty.

Chereau, The Widow. Le Grande Charlatau. Paris, Author, 1810.

France (cont.)
Chesnais, Jacques.   Chés Histoires D'Lafleur.   Amiens,
     1906.
--- Comediens, De Bois.   Paris, Eclaireurs de France.
--- Histoire Generale des Marionettes.   Paris, Bordas, 1947.
     In NN.
--- Marionnettes à Gaine, à Fils, à Tringle, à Clavier, etc.
     Courbevoie (Seine): Les Editions "La Flamma," 1936[sic]
     In NN.
--- Revu of Marionnettes à Gaine...etc., Anon, Thea Arts,
     Feb 1937.
Chezel, F.   Pirrot-Barnum.   Paris, 1902.

Claqueret, I.   Chantecoine, du la Folie de Guignol.   Lyons,
     1910.
Claretie, L.   Lesage Romancier, D'Apres De Nouveaux Docu-
     ments.   Paris, Colin, 1890, passim
--- Histoire Des Théâtres Societe.   Paris, Molière, 1906,
     passim
"Claude and Daniel Bazilier Marionettes,"   Pupp Th Mod
     World. p 219 and Illus No. 21
Cole, Nancy.   Guignol.   A thesis, Stanford, Stanford Univ.,
     Spring 1958.
--- Revue of "Guignol" called "Salute Guignol," Pupp J, 11
     (2):14, 24, 27-28, 1959
"Compagnie André Tahon, Paris,"   Pupp Th Mod World,
     p 219, Illus No. 19
"Compagnie Jean-Loup Temporal-Paris,"   Pupp Th Mod
     World, p 219, and Illus No. 16
"Compagnie Yves Joly-Paris,"   Pupp Th Mod World,
     p 219, Illus No. 15
Constans, A.   See G. L. Roesbroecke

Conti, Henry.   Guignol.   Paris, Charpentier, 1897

Coquard, Galome. (A. Storck, pseud.)   Association Des Anciens
     Eleves Du Lycee De Lyon.   Lyon, Storck, 1887
     (Deux Artistes, Laurent Jessenand, Henri Deslisle)
     See also G. Canard
Correra, L. C."Il Prespe à Napoli," L'Arte, 1899, p 218

Croziere, A.   Le Vrai Théâtre Guignol.   Paris, Nathan, 1897

Cruishank, G.   See O. Penhoet

Cuisinier, J.   Le Théâtre D'Ombres à Kelantan.   2nd ed.,
     Paris, Gallimara, 1957.   In Yale Univ. Lib.

Curzon, M. De. "Les Marionetten de Salzbourg et le Directeur de Théâtre de Mozart," J Des Deb 40: pt 1, Mr 3, 1933, p 377

D'Angel, A. and L. Dor. Histoire des Santons. Paris, nd

Darthenay, L. Le Theâtre Des Pepits. Paris, Tresse, 1898
--- Coguelin Cadet, Le Guignol Des Salons. Paris, Plon, 1888

D'Auriac, E. Theâtre de la Foire avec un Essai Historique sur les Spectacles Forains. Paris, Carnier, 1878

Dausey, H. Le Patois Picard et Lafleur. Amiens, Invert, 1877 and Jeunet

David, Édouard. Étude Picard sur Lafleur. Amiens, Jeunet, 1896. sig m.
--- Lafleur, Ou La Valet Picard. Amiens, Jeunet, 1901
--- Lafleur En Service. Amiens, Jeunet, 1901
--- El Naissanche ed L'Einfant Jesus. Abbeville, Author, 1906
--- Chés Histoires D'Lafleur. Amiens, Jeunet, 1906
--- Les Théâtres Populaires à Amiens. Lafleur est-il Picards. Amiens, Invert, 1906 (Brochure)
--- Vicilles Réderies. Amiens, Jeunet, 1920
--- Ch'vieux Lafleur. Amiens, Jeunet, 1926
--- Los Compagnons de Lafleur et Sandrine. Paris, 1927

Davis, Richard H. About Paris. New York, Harper, 1895. Chapter on "Chat Noir Cabaret" Shadow puppets. See also Paul McPharlin's, Pupp Thea Am. p 288-89

De Fontenello, J. See Julia Fontenello

De Graffigny, H. de See H. Graffigny

De Kleist, Henri. See Henri Kleist

De Lafarge, D. La Vie et les Oeuvres de Palissot, 1730-1814. Paris, Hachett, 1912

Dellanoy, L. "Les Marionnettes Lille quelques autres," Les Amis de Lille, N 15, 1930
--- "Les Marionnettes Lilleises et quelques autres," Les Amis de Lille, D 1, 1929; D 1-15, 1931; and Jan 1, 1931.
--- "La Psychologie des Marionnettes et les Marionettes dans la Litterature," Les Amis de Lille, O 15, 1932 and N 1, 1932.

France (cont.)

Delaunay, Émile. Guignol du Grand Cerole. Aix-les Baines, Gérente, 1912

Delmotte, A. "Les Marionnettes de Lille," Revu Sept, Feb, 1929, p 59.

Delvau, A. Le Théâtre Erotique Francais Sous Le Bas-Empire. Paris, Pincebourse, 1867

De Manne, . Feu Seraphin 1776-1870. Lyon, Scheuring, 1875, 334 p. very Sig. m.

DeMont, Alfred. La Littérature Patoise Artésienne. Paris, Kleinman, c 1905.

De Neuville, L. See Lemercier De Nouville, Louis

De Plancy, Collin. See P. Beranger

Desarthis, Lucien. "French Puppetry in 1940," Pupp 11:34-35, 1940

"Desarthis (Robert). Théâtre de Jardin du Luxembourg-Paris,"   Pupp Th Mod World, p 219 and Illus No. 18.

Desnoirestrerres, G. La Comedie Satirique Au Dix Nuitieme Spiecle. Paris, Perrin, 1885

Desnoyers, Ferdinand. Le Théâtre de Polichinella. Paris, Poulet, 1864

Desrousseaux, Alexandre. Moeurs populaires de la Flandre Francaise. 2 vols. Lille, Quarre, 1889

Des Tilleuis, A. Les Naruibettes de Seraphin. Paris, 1874.

Desverndy, Felix. Laurent Mourguet Et Quignol. Lyons, Desverndy, 1912

Detchevérry, . Histoire Des Théâtres De Boreaux. Bordeaux, Dielmas, 1860. passim

De Visan, T. See T. Visan

De Wailly, Paul. See Paul Wailly.

De Warsage, R. See Rodelphe Warsage

Donde, M. M. "Marionettes in the Time of Shakespeare," Univ of Calif Chron, Jl 1923   French overtone.
--- The Pie and the Tart. London, Appleton, 1925
--- "Reflexions sur le Théâtre des Marionettes," French Review, 11:371-77, Mr 1938; bibliog, p 372
--- The Donkey. New York, Appleton, 1925

Donnay, M. Ailleurs. Paris, Grasset, 1891
--- Autour Du Chat Noir. Paris, Grasset, 1916
--- Phryne. Paris, Grasset, 1891. passim

Dor, L. See A. D'Angel

D'Orneval, . See Lesage

Doyen, E. Les Marionettes Amoureuses. Paris, Huré.

Drack, M. Le Théâtre de la Foire. Paris, Didot, 1889

Ducret. Cetienne. Marionnettes. Paris, Barnemann, 1923
History and plays of the Guignol Theatre, including string
Punch.
Ducret, Étienne. Le Théâtre de Guignol. Lyons, Barne-
mann, 1914
Dudevant, Jean F. M. A. See Maurice Sand

Dumesnil, R. "Mozart et les Marionettes de Salzbourg,"
Mercure de France, (Séries Moderne) 242:701-02, Mr 15
1933.
Duplateau, Mami (See also Auguste Bleton) Véridique His-
toire De L'Académie Du Gourguillon. Lyons, Morgin,
1898. In NN.
Duranty, Louis E. Edmond. Théâtre Des Marionettes Du
Jardin Des Tuileries. Paris, Dubvisson, 1863. Rev. ed.
Paris, Charpentier, 1880. In NN.
Durocher, Leon. La Marche Au Soleil. Paris, Dupret,
1899
Duroquet, A. See G. Canard

Eggermont, J. Les Marionnettes. Bruxelles, Sagitta, 1945

Escudier, G. Les Saltimbanques. (A Marionette Show)
Paris, Lévy, 1854
Eudel, Paul. Les Ombres Chinoises De Mon Père. Paris,
Rouveyre, 1885. In Montreal Univ. Lib. See"Shadow Sec-
tion"
Evelyn, John. "In Paris, 1644-1651," Pupp, 7:78, 1936
--- An extract from Evelyn's Diary, Vol. 1, London, 1906,
p 86, March 1st
Everden, M. "We Meet 'Guignol,' Noted Parisian," Carnegie
Mag, 26:330-32, D 1952
"Expedition Alexandre Puppet Theatre Group," from Paris, in
Los Angeles," Pupp J, 16(5):29-31, 1965
Falkenstein, Mollie. "The Giles et ses Marionnettes à Paris,"
Pupp J, 17(3):3, 1965
--- "The Martin-Marine Co. Paris," Pupp J, 17(3):6, 1965

185

France (cont.)

Ferny, Jacques. Le Secret du Manifestant. Paris, Fromont, 1893

Fertigni, P. A. See Yorick, P. C.

"Festival, June 1950, in France," Brit Pupp Thea, 1(5):6, 1950

Feu Seraphin. See D. F. Seraphin

Feuillet, Octave (pseud.). Vie De Polichinelle Et Ses Nombreuses Adventures. Paris, Hachett, 1924, passim In NN.

Fontenello, Julia de. Manuel Complet Des Sorciers. Paris, 1831, passim

Fournier, Édouard. Histoire Des Jouets Et Des Jeux L'Enfants. Paris, Dentu, 1889

Foyne, Vera. "Dancing Dolls of Destiny," Chi Sci Mon, Boston. In "Clipping File for Puppets," Deering Lib. , Northwestern Univ.

Fragerelle, G. See H. Rivierc

Franc-Nehan, (De France). Marionettes Pour Tous: Ce Qu'l Faut Savoir. New York, Maxwell,

--- "La Mystique des Marionnettes," Nouvelles Litteraires, Feb 18, 1933

France, Anatole. Les Marionettes. 4 Vols in 2 vols, 5th ed. Paris, Lévy, 1891 to 1895. In Oberlin Univ. Lib.

--- "La Vie Littéraire," in Ouevres Completes. Paris, Lévy, 1926

--- Oeuvres Completes. Vol 6, "Les Marionnettes de M. Signoret."

--- Oeuvres Completes. Vol 7, "Hrotswitha Aux Marionnettes"

--- Oeuvres Completes. Vol 7, "M. Maurice Boucher et l'histoire de Tobie, Punch and Judy

France,Henry. Les Marionnettes Pour Tous. Paris, Editions De L'Ermite, 1949. In NN.

"France's Puppets," Pupp, 6:70, 1935

"France's Traveling Puppeteers," Mask, 6:181, 1914

Francois, Victor E. Two Deaf Men. (A Play for Hand Puppets.) trans. by Lisi Beer, Boston, Humphries, 1962. Silver Series

Franklin, Mayer J. "Guignol," Plume et Encre, 7:8-10, Ap 1940

"French in North America," See Paul McPharlin's Pupp Thea Am. p 79-85. Material from 1755-1838

"French Puppeteers in Congress," Drama, 16:150, Jl 1938

"French Puppetry," Pupp, 13-14:37, 1942 & '43

"French Puppetry in 1938," Pupp 9:19, 1938

"French Terminology in Puppetry," Pupp J, 17(5):3-5, 1966
(by Andre Tahon)
"French Shows," See Rod Young's column "Mailbox,"
Pupp J, 10(2):33-34, 1958
Les Freres Parfaict. Memoires Pour Servir A L'Histoire
Des Spectactles De La Faire. Paris, Brissan, 1743,
passim
Gaebler, E. T. ed. Marionetten Kunst und Kunstler. Ber-
lin, Gaebler, 1926, passim. In NN.
Gambee, Budd. "Visit with the French Guignol," Pupp J,
6(4):3-6, 1954
Gandon, Y. "Les Commédiens de Bois," France Illus, 349:
604, Je 2, 1952
Gardnier, Jacques. Bibliographie Ferains D'Hier et D'Aujour
'd Hui, Paris, Gardier, 19?
Gaudefrey, L. Ech Mariage D'Laflcur. Amiens, Jeunet,
1907
Gautier, Theophile. "Les Marionettes," in his Souvenirs de
Theatre D'Art et de Critique. Paris, Charpentier, 1883
Gelis, E. See A. Chaipris

Gervais, André C. Marionnettes et Marionnettistes de
France. Bordas 1947. Good bibliog. In NN.
--- Revu of Marionnettes et Marionnettistes by Paul Mc
Pharlin, Thea Arts 30:70, Ag 1947
Gessler, Elizabeth F. Guignol à L'École. Paris, Gessler,
1937. In Oberlin Univ. Lib.
--- See also "Plays" Section

Ghislain Cloquet, Lafollye. "Paris-Capitole of the Marion-
nettes," Mode Illustre, D 1946, p 35-38
Gignoux, Hubert. "Marionettes; et L'Education," Cahiers
D'Art Dramatique, Jan 1948, p 37-40
Girardot, Mme. Théâtre et Marionnettes Pour Les Petits.
Paris, Nathan, 1907
Godart, Justin. Guignol et L'Esprit Lyonnais, Par Justin
Godart. Lyon, Rey, Revue D'Histoire De Lyon, 1912
In NN.
Goffic, Charles H. Le. Les Metiers Pittoresques. Paris,
Fontemoina. passim
--- "Le Petit-Théâtre des Marionnettes," Revue Encyclo-
pedique, Je 15, 1894

France (cont.)
   See Le Goffic, Charles Henri
Goldsmith, J. E. "French Pieces for Puppets by Nancy
   Henry," Pupp Bull, 9: 1938
--- See also Nancy Henry "Plays" Section

Gouriet, J. B. Personnage Celebre Dans Les Rues De Paris.
   Paris, Lerouge, 1811. 2 vol. passim.
Graffigny, H. de. Construction du Théâtre Guignol. Paris,
   Guyot, 1911
--- Le Théâtre à la Maison. Paris, Guyot, 1914
--- "Theatres of France," Pupp, 4:59-60, 1933

Graffigny, Mme F. Letters to M. Deveaux. Paris, Guyot,
   1783, on, D 11, 16, 17
"Grand Guignol about to be demolished," N Y Times, Ap 4,
   1929, III 3:8
Grimm, N. Ombres L'Heureuse Pêches, Paris, LeJay, 1770
--- Correspondence Litteraire. Vol 2, Paris, Garnier, 177-
   p 400
Gross, Dr. (Joanny Bachut) Pourquoi Aimons-Nous Guignol?
   Lyons, 1909. In NN.
Gubalke, L. "Marionettentheater," Vom Fels Zum Meer,
   No 17, 1905.
Guequen, P. "La Chapelle de Ronchamp Vue par Veronique
   Filozof," Aujourd'hui, 5:50, Feb 1960
Guiette, Robert. Marionettes de Tradition Populaires.
   Brussels, Editions du Cercle D'Art, 1950
Guignol. Lyon: Society de le Amis de Guignol, 1927
   Notes et Documents Pour Serviv à L'Histoire des Amis
   de Guignol, Le Mardi Gras.
"Guignol À Paris," L'Illus, 88: pt 2, Jl 1930, p438-39
"Guignol en Houte Cour" L'Illus, No. 4637, Jan 16, 1932,
   p 91
Guignol Lyonnais. Lyon, Scheuring. Available at Mme. S. Z.

Guignol (Théâtre de). 2 Vols. Lyon, Society de les amis
   de Guignol, 1929. Available at Mme. S. Z.
Guignol (Théâtre Classique de). Paris, 1922

Guignol (Théâtre Lyonnais de). 2 Vols. Lyon, Scheuring,
   1865 and 1869
"Guignol Théâtre of Paris," Pupp, 9: 1938

Guignol, P. Bonnardel. Théâtre Saynètes et récits par
   Chafron Fils de la rue Ferrachat, Reveu de Guignol.
   Lyon, Berneuxet, Cumin, 1886

Guitry, Sacha. Champs Elysee. A French film about puppeteers. See also "Film" Section.
--- "Birth of Guignol," in her If Memory Serves. New York, Doubleday, 1936
--- See Pupp J, 10(5):3-5, 1959

Halevy, Ludovic. Karikari. Paris, Lévy, 1892

Harry Perrault, M. See H. Perrault, name used both ways.

Hawkins, F. French Stage in the 18th Century. London, Chapman, 1888, passim
Hellain, J. ("Babenne," pseud.) "Marionettes in Amiens," La Vaolette, 1910
Hermant, Abel. La Marinette Flammarion. Paris, Flammanon, c 1926. In Montreal City Lib.
Heulhard, A. Jean. Monnet, Vie Et Adventures D'Un Entrepreneur De Spectacles Au Dixhitieme Siecle Avec Un Appendice Sur L'Opera Comique De 1752-1758. Paris, Lemerre, 1884
--- La Foire de Saint-Laurent. Paris Lemerre, 1878, passim
Himer, Kurt. Prinz Drosselbart. (Fécrie pour marionnettes) Leipzig, Lehmann, 1925
--- Till Eulenspicgel. (Piece pour marionnettes) Leipzig, Lehmann, 1925
--- & C. Teumer. Das Tapfere Schneiderlein. (Piece pour jeux d'ombres) Leipzig, Lehmann, 1926
Hirn, Irje, Y. Les Jeux D'Énfants. Paris, Stock, 1926. In NN.
Hirsch, P. "Un Peintre de Flandre; Albert Dequêne," Mercure de Flandre, Je-Jl, 1931
Horowicz, B. "Une page de L'Histoire de France Sous le Ciel De Sisile: ces Marionettes de P. B. Horowics," Rev des D M, 22, series 8, Jl 15, 1934, p 464-65
Horst, Adrian Van der. Orlando Furioso. Boston, Humphries, 1964
Hovaroff, A. Théâtres des Pantagonia du Carré Marigny. Paris, Michel.
Huges, B. and G. See M. Sand

Images D'Epinal. See Olive Blackham's Shadow Puppets. London, Rockliff, 1960, p 72. Sheets of French, black shadow figures like Seraphin's shadow puppets.
Jacob, P. Recueil de Farces, seties et morâlîtes. Paris, Michel, 1897 passim. Often times puppets were included in this type of miracle show. Investigation into miracle show material might bring to light valuable items.

France (cont.)
Jacobus, Marion. "Puppets at Parisian Fairs, 1649-1742,"
Ed Thea J, 18(2):110-12, My 1966. With bibliog. and
footnotes.
Jacquier, L. La Politique de Guignol, Gnafron et Eie.
Lyon, Scheuring, 1876
Jacquin, Joseph. La Prise de Pekin. Paris, Hatchett,
1903
--- Ame De Poupée. Voy, Davin, 1904
--- See also "Plays" Section

Jarry, Alfred. Ubu sur la Butte. Paris, Sansot, 1906

Jasseron, Louis. La Querelle de Guignol. Lyon, Storck,
1936. Lyon, Edition De La République, 1937. Available
at Mme S. Z.
Jeanne, Paul. Bibliographie des Marionettes. Paris, Lévy,
1926. In NN.
--- "France, Revival of Primitive Marionnettes," Pupp,
3:12-14, 1932
--- "France and the War Years," Pupp, 17:56, 1946
--- "French Exhibition, Paris," Pupp, 8:36, 1937
--- "French Puppetry," Pupp, 2:32-33, 1931; 7: 1936.
--- "French Puppetry in Wartime," Pupp, 15:37-38, 1944
--- "The Galliera Museum Collection," Pupp, 10:36-37, 1939
--- "Les Marionnettes à Anvers," Rev Sept., Feb 1929
--- "Les Marionnettes de Roubaix," Paris, Rosati, Feb 28,
1930. McPharlin Coll.
--- Orlando Furioso. Paris, 1930 (Adapted from A Van
Der Horst)
--- De Poesjenellenkelder. Paris, Là Concorde, 1934.
Also saw this as a Puppetry Imprint, unnumbered in Mc
Pharlin Collection. But it is not one of the usually
sighted 12, so may have been only a few copies, especial-
ly printed. Birmingham, Mich., Puppetry Imprints, prob-
ably c 1934. Available at Mme S. Z.
---"Puppetry of France," Pupp, 5:33-34, 1934
--- Les Théâtre D'Ombres à Montmartre de 1887-1923.
Paris, 1923 and 1937. In British Museum and NN.
Joly, Yves. "Hand-Ballet," Life, D 15, 1952, p 58-60, illus.
--- "The Hand Ballet Theatre," Pupp J, 3(4):19, 1952
--- "The Joly Company, Paris," Pupp J, 17(3):4, 1965
--- "Kukla's Trip to Paris and Hand Ballet," Pupp J, 3(2):
7-8, 1951
--- "Voila," Pupp Th Mod World, p 43, 219 and Illus
No. 15
See also F. Raphard
Jouvre, R. "Les Marionettes aux Noctambules," Études,

260:387-89, Mr 1949

Julien, A. <u>Les Grandes Nuits De Sceaux.</u> Paris, Baurer,
1876

Kahn, Gledl. <u>Polichinelle...Brecede D'Une Étude.</u> Paris,
Kah, 1906 [sic] In NN.

<u>Kaspertheatre.</u> Prague, Haase, 1919. Une collection de
jeux allemands pour marionnettes avec les omcres.
Available at Mme S. Z.

Kleist, Henri de. <u>Les Marionnettes.</u> Paris, "G. L. M."
publishers, 1947. In Montreal City Lib.

Koenig, Marie. <u>Le Menage De La Poupée.</u> Paris, Nathan,
1900.

--- <u>Poupées Et Légendes De France.</u> Paris, Lévy, 1900
Available at Mme S. Z.

Kori, T. <u>See</u> P. Morand

Kreymborg, A. "French Plays," in his <u>Puppet Plays.</u> New
York, French, 1916

"Lafays, Georges; Puppet Theatre of Paris," <u>Pupp Th</u>
<u>Mod World</u>, p 219

"Lafleur, means Rod Puppets from Amiens, France," <u>Pupp,</u>
10:56, 1939

Lagarde, E. <u>Ombres Chinoises, Guignol, et Marionnettes.</u>
Paris, Michel, 1900. In NN.

Laglaizc, J.-B. <u>Panins et Marionnettes.</u> Paris, Flammarion. Available at Mme S. Z.

Larcher, A. "Un Rol de Féerie, Ladislas Starevitch,
(Marionettes dans le film songe d'une nuit d'été) <u>France</u>
<u>Illus</u>, 5:114-15, Jan 29, 1949

Le Bolzer, Guy. <u>La Marionette.</u> Paris, Lafoye, 1958 and
Joly

Leclerq, P. Théâtres des Nabots; les Marionnettes De
Mae Forain," <u>Le Théâtre</u>, Mr 1906

LeGrand, -Chabrier. "La Marionette et la Danse," <u>Illus,</u>
189:558, D 15, 1934

Le Goffic, Charles H. <u>See</u> Charles H. Goffic

Lemaitre, J. <u>Impressions de Théâtre.</u> Paris, Lévy, 1888-
1889, vol. 5, p 263; vol. 6, p 375

Lemercier de Neuville, Louis. "Dossier de. Copie de
critiques, manuscrites ou coupures de presse, sur toute
l'oeuvre de L. de N. Cahier in-8". Paris, Bornemann,
given c 1897. Available at Mme S. Z.

    Une lettre manuscrite de Darthenay à Lemercier où
il est question d'une collaboration avec Lemercier; "Nous
ferons ensemble des choses merveilleuses"- Curieux dossier.

France (cont.)
--- Histoire Anecdetique des Marionettes Modernes. Paris,
Lévy, 1892 and 1897
--- Histoire Des Marionettes Modernes. Paris, Lévy, 1892
--- Nouveau Theatre De Guignol. Paris, Bornemann, 1898
--- Nouveau Theatre des Pupazzi. Paris, Hilaire, 1882
--- Paris Pattin. (Deuxième Séries Des Pupazzi) Paris,
Flammarion, 1868, well illus.
--- Les Pupazzi. (Inédits) Paris, Flammarion, 1903
--- Les Pupazzi Au Chalet. Vichy, Dentu, 1865
--- Les Pupazzi De L'Enfance. Paris, Delagrave, 1881
--- Les Pupazzi Noirs: Ombres Animees. Paris, Mendel,
1896
--- Souvenirs D'un Montreur De Marionnettes. Paris, Bauche
1911. Available at Mme S. Z. Avec le répertoire complet
du théâtre des Pupazzi 1863-1893.
--- Théâtre De Marionnettes à L'Usage Des Enfants. Paris,
Delagrave, 1904.
--- Le Théâtre Des Pupazzi (texts) Lyons, 1876

Lesage et D'Orneval Le Théâtre De La Poire Ou L'Opera
Comique. Paris, Gandoein 1737. 10 vol. passim
See also Lintilhac, E.
Le Semanier, "Pupazzi," Illus, 87: pt 2, D 28, 1929 p
820
Levinson, A. Le Théâtre des Marionettes. Paris, Lévy,
1890
Revu of Le Theatre des Marionettes, Marionette, 1:317-
18, O 1918
--- "Unima," L'Art Vivant, Nov 1929

Lindsay, F. W. "Dramatic Parody by Marionettes in 18th
Century Paris." Unpublished Ph. D. dissertation, New
York, Columbia Univ., 1945. Unusual bibliog.
--- Dramatic Parody by Marionettes in 18th Century Paris.
New York, King's Crown, 1946
Lintilhac, E. Lesage. Paris, Hachett, 1893

Little, L. See E. Merten

Lunel, E. Le Théâtre et la Revolution. Paris, Dragon,
1910, passim.
Lyonnais, Theatre de Guignol. Lyon, A. Waltener, 1890.
Anc^{ne} Librairie Mera-Mlle Vve Monavon [sic] In NN.
See also Guignol items.
Lyonnet, Henry. Dictionnaire des Comediens Francais:
Biographie, Bibliographie, Iconographic. 2 Vols, Paris,
Jorel, 1904, passim

McCloud, N. C. "A Doll Play in a Doll Setting," Mentor, 15:46-47, Jan 1928.
McGregor, Della. "Puppetry Abroad," (France) Pupp J, 19 (5):14-15, 1968. Luxemborg Gardens Marionette Theatre
McIntyre, Milton. "Parisian Puppet Theatre," Sci Am Sup, 54: O 18, 1902, p 22404
McPharlin, Marjorie B. "International Festival," Pupp J, 10(2):10, 1958
See also "Plays", "Rods," and "International Div." Sections.
--- Rod Puppets and the Human Theatre. Columbus, Ohio State Univ. Press, 1947
McPharlin, Paul. "Puppet Shows in Paris Parks," Ch Sci Mon. Ap 18, 1939, p 5
--- Puppet Theatre in America. New York, Harper, 1949
Maeterlinck, Maurice. See "Plays" Section.
See also "History" Section
Magnin, Charles M. Histoire des Marionnettes en Europe. (Depuis L'Antiquité Jusqu'a Nos Jours) Paris, Lévy, 1851 and 1862
Revu of Histoire des Marionnettes... Anon. Rev Des D M 1878.
--- Les Origines du Théâtre Moderne. Paris, Lévy, 1838, passim
--- "Puppets in England-C. Magnin" anon. trans., Sharp's Lon J, 14:107-114, 171-178 and 203-208, 1851. Watkinson Memorial Lib., Trinity College, Hartford, Conn.
     This is the only English translation we have and gives valuable material on Shakespeare and Jonson's puppetry.
Maindron, Ernest. Marionnettes et Guignols. Paris, Juven, 1900-01. In NN.
Manne, -- (de). Feu Séraphin. Lyon, Scheuring, 1875. Available at Mme S. Z.
Marc-Monnier. Théâtre de Marionnettes. Geneve, Richard, 1871. Available at Mme S. Z.
Marcel, Father. See J. Temperal

Marinier, Gerrard. La Marionnette. St. Mande (Seine) Editions de La Tourelle, 1953, with bibliog. p. 63. In LC.
Marionneau, Charles. Victor Louis, Architecte du Théâtre de Boreaux, 1731-1800. Bordeaux, Imprimerie G. Gouncuilhou, 1881. In NN.
"Marionnettes du Manigole-Paris," Pupp Th Mod World, p 219.
Marionnettes; Les Classiques du Gourguillon. Lyon, Théâtre à Lyon sur Rhosne. (With Preface by Claudius Canard) Available at Mme S. Z.

France (cont.)

Marionettes To-Night at 8:30. See also "Periodical" Section. Microfilm in NN.

Marquis, Raoul. Le Théâtre Guignol. Paris, Lesort, 1929. In Oberlin Univ. Lib.

Matthews, B. The Theatres of Paris. London, Low, 1880. In Brander Mathews Dramatic Museum Lib. , Columbia Univ.

--- "Puppet Shows, Old and New," Bookman, D 1914.

--- "Puppets in 19th Century Paris," Pupp 2:57-58, 1931.

Maurepas, Jean F. Recueils dit de Maurepas; de Chansons et de Vers Satiriques. 6 vols, Leyte, 1865. Collection of songs and satirical verse mentioning puppets of Paris. In Montreal Univ. Lib.

Maurey, Mas. "Les Marionnettes Picardes," Rev Sept, Ap 1928, p 71.

See also O. Lorenz's Catalogue Géneral, Vol. XIX, 1900-05, p 271, for his plays. He was Director General of "Grand Guignol Théâtre," Paris.

Maurice, Arnaud. See Maurice Sand

Maz, G. Le Sarsifi Petafine. Lyons, Desvernay, 1886

Mazauric, L. "Les Theatre populaires de Marionettes au Musee des Arts et Traditions Populaires," Mercure Des Fr, 316:516-18, N 1952

Meharg, F. "Glimpse of Old World Puppetry, Paris and Lyons," Pupp J, 5(4):22, 1954

Melling, J. K. "Paris Puppets," Pupp Master, 5(8):22, 1958

Memoires de L'Académis du Gourguillon. Lyon, Rhosne, 1887. Chex l'Imprimeur Juré de L'Académie, sous l'Enseigne de la Cigogne. Available at Mme S. Z.

Mera-Mlle V^{ve}Monavan. See Lyonnais, Théâtre de Guignol.

Merten, E. and L. Little. "The French Guignol," at 1959 Festival, Pupp J, 11(2):13, 1959

Métivet, Lucien and Jane Vieu. Aladdin. Paris, Flammarion 1904. Ombres Chinoises, available at Mme S. Z. with music.

Migneaus J. & Simon, . Marionnettes: Comment Los Fabriquer. Paris,

Migneaux, Marie. Marionettes. Paris, Editions Fleurus, 1951. In NN.

Mignon, Paul L. and Jean Mohr. J'Aimes Les Marionnettes. Lausanne, Éditions Rencontre, 1962.

Miomandre, Francis de. "Un Moliere en miniature, le Theatre des Marionnettes de Duranty," Revue, Paris,

1917, p 71-82
Mirecourt, E. De.   See   O. Feuillet

Miyajima, Tsnnao.   Contribution À L'Étude Du Théâtre De
 Poupées.   Paris, Univ. De France Press, 1928
--- Theatre de Poupees, Histoire.   Paris, Univ. De France
 Press, 1926
Mohr, Jean.   See P. L'Mignon

Monnier, Marc.   See Marc-Monnier

Morand, P. & T. Kori.   Trans., "L'Incantations; Drama
 pour Marionnettes," Rev Des D M, series 8, 31:588, 598,
 Feb 1, 1936
Mourguet, Laurent & Felix Desvernay.   Laurènt Mourguet et
 Guignol.   Lyon, Desvernay, 1912
Naugaret, J. B.   Almanach Forain.   Paris, Guillot, 1771,
 1775, 1786, passim
Neophebus, Dr.   See   Charles Nodier

Neuvecelle, Jean.   "Lettre de Rome," Le Magasin du Spec-
 tacle.   5:147-152, Ap-Dec 1946.
Nodier, Charles (pseud.) for Dr. Neophebus.   Nouveilles.
 Paris, Charpentier, 1871
--- Article on Puppets and Marionettes," La Revue de Paris,
 O 1842.
--- "Les Marionnettes," La Revue de Paris, N 1842; My
 My 1843.
Nouveau Recueil De Pieces De Guignol.   Lyon, P Masson,
 1925
Olbrechts, F. M.   Le Théâtre Javanais; Les Marionettes.
 Brussels, A Bulletin from the Royal Musees D'Art et
 Histoire, Vol 14(53):81-88, Jl 1932
"Old French Hand Puppets," La France Mag, D 1919

Onofrio, J. B.   Essai D'Un Glossaire des Patois du Lyonnais, Forez et Beaujelais.   Lyons, Scheuring, 1864
--- Théâtre Lyonnais de Guignol.   Lyon, Lardanchet, 1909.

Organizations.   See "Organizations" Section

Pange, J. de "Marionettes de Salzbourg à Paris," J Dés
 Deb, 40: pt 1, Feb 24, 1933, p 337-38
Parfaict, Les Freres.   Mémoires Pour Servir à L'Historie
 Des Spectacles De La Foire, Par Un Acteur Forain.
 Paris, Briasson, 1743, passim
Penöet, Oliver et Cruishank.   Polichinelle.   Paris, Drame,
 1836.   Available at Mme S. Z.

195

France (cont.)
Pepler, H. D. C.   Le Boeuf Et L'Âne Et Deux Autres Pieces
    Pour Marionettes.   Ditchling, S. Dominic, 1930
--- "Les Marionnettes," in Picard's, Théâtre Choisi.
    Paris, Lemerre, 1881, p 229-318
Péricaud, Lewis.   Théâtre des Petits Comediens de S. A. S.
    Monseigneur Le Comte De Beaujoliais.   Paris, Jorel,
    1909
--- Le Theéâtre des Funambules.   Paris, Sapin, 1897. In
    NN.
Periodicals   See "Periodical" Section

Perrault, Harry Myriam.   Au Pays Du Marionites et Des
    Druses.   Paris, Terrie, 1930. In NN.
Petit Repertoire de Guignol.   Nice.

Petite, J. M.   Guignols et Marionnettes, Leur Histoire.
    Paris, Joel, 1911
"Les Théâtre des Marionettes des Piccoli De V. Podrecca
    au Théâtre des Champs Elysees."   Toute La Danse et La
    Musique, No 69, Jan 1958, p 23.
Philippon, E.   La Bernarda Buyandiri.   Lyons, Scheuring,
    1885
Picard, L. B.   "Les Marionettes" in his Suite Du Reper-
    toire Du Théâtre.   Paris, Laplace et Sanchez, 1822-1826,
    p 117-281.   At Oberlin Univ. Lib.
    See also   H. Pepler
Polichinelle, Le Theatre de.   (Par Le Papa de Nénette)
    Paris.   At Mme S. Z.
Pougin, A.   Dictionnaire Historique et Pitteresque du Thé-
    atre.   Paris, Firmin-Didot, 1885
    See   sections on Marionnettes, Guignol, and Polichinelle.
    In Montreal Univ. Lib.
Punch and Judy.   See "Punch and Judy" Section

"Puppet Show at Paris Exposition,"   Sci Am, 83:299, N 10,
    1900
"Puppet Warfare in France,"   Lit D, 51:1172, N 20, 1915.

"Puppetry course to be given, France,"   Brit Pupp Thea,
    2(1):15, 1951
"Puppetry in France,"   Pupp 2:57, 32, 1931; 3:12-14, 1932;
    4:59, 1933; 6:70, 1935; Grapev, Je 1949, p 10, 19; Thea
    Arts, 33: 1949.
"Puppetry in Paris,"   Pupp, 7:70-71, 79, 1936
"Puppets in Paris Theatres,"   Brit Pupp and M Thea G Newsl,
    143:3, 1968

R. N. (pseud.) "Les Marionnettes à travers les âges,"
Rev Brit, 1899

Rabe, J. E. Kasper Putschenelle. Hamburg, Quickborn,
1924, passim

Raphard, Francis. "Yves Joly and his Hand Ballet Puppets
of France," Brit Pupp Thea, 1(6):26, 1950

Revue Septentrionale. See Rosati. (Bulletin des Rosati)

Richard, Leopold. Manuscript Letters to R. Sibbald, Puppeteer. For Ag 4, 1931; My 18, 1932, and Feb 11, 1933.
In Puppet File Folder, Deering Lib. , Northwestern Univ.
at Evanston.

Rictor, Léon, E. E. Lyon (Vol. 2) Guignol et les Canuts
Lyonnais. Paris, P. Roger, 1931. At Mme S. Z.

Riviere, Claude. "Lyons, The Cradle of Guignol," In
Puppet File Folder. Deering Lib. , Northwestern Univ. ,
at Evanston.
See also Studio, 15: 1899.

Riviere, Henri & G. Frageralle, (ed.) Album Du Chat Noir.
Paris, Plon, 1886.

--- Clairs De Lune. Paris, Lévy, 1897

--- L'Enfant Prodique. Paris, Nourrity, 1894. At Mme
S. Z.

--- Le Juif Errant. Paris, Frageralle, 1898. At Mme
S. Z.

--- La Marche À L'Etoile. Paris, Lévy, 1890. At Mme
S. Z.

--- La Tentation de Saint Antoine. Paris, E. Plon, 1888,
(Ombres Chinoises) and Nourrity Co. At Mme S. Z.
See also "Plays" Section

Roesbreeck, G. L. & A. Constans. Polichinelle Comte De
Paonfier. Paris, Champion, 1924

Rosati, Bulletin des. "Rosati Marionnettes Picardes,
Marionnettes dans le nord, Les Sociétés Rosatiques,
Marionnettes de Liège, etc." Revue Sept, (Bulletin des
Rosati) No 3, 1928, No 10 bis, Supplement À Décembre
1931, No 1, Janvier, 1931. Les 3 Nos in 8 brocure. At
Mme S. Z.

Rousseau, Jean J. See P. McPharlin's, Pupp Th Am, p.
312

Rousset, Pierre. Les Marionnettes Lyonaise. 2 Vols, Lyon,
Diszin, 1886. At Mme S. Z.

--- Parodies de Guignol. Paris, Chaney, 1911

Salme, Dieudenné. Li Houle. Liege, Vaillant-Carmanne,
1888. At Mme S. Z.

Sand, A. "Les Marionnettes de Nghant," Annuales Poli-
tiquest et Litteraires, 81:480-81, O 28, 1923

France (cont.)

Sand, George (pseud.) Dernieres Pages. Paris, Lévy, c
1870's, passim
See also B. Baird's, Art of the Puppet, p 13, 103, 149,
150-52

Sand, Maurice (pseud.) (Maurice Arnauld-Jean Francois Dudevant).
History of the Harlequinade. 2 v. London, Secker, 1915
--- Jouets et Mystères. Paris, Les Editions du Scarabée,
1954. In NN
--- Masques et Bouffand. Vol. 1, Paris, Lévy, 1860, p 134,
148-52. This may be the French edition of the first book
given here.
--- Plays for Marionettes. trans. Babette and G. Huges, New
York, French, 1931; London, Benn, 1931.
--- See also B. Baird's, Art of the Puppet, p 144, 149,
150-52
--- Le Theatre des Marionnettes. Paris, Lévy, 1890

Sarg, Tony. "French Movies on Strings," Photop M 21:
36, 144, D 1921

Saroyan, William. Marionettes Humaines. trans. , Yvonne
Brun, Geneve, Jeheber, 1947. In Montreal City Lib.

Sarrazin, J. Souvenirs de Montmarte et du Quartier Latin.
Paris, Sarrazin, 1895, passim

Schetty, Madline. "Impressions of Guignol in Lyons," Pupp
17:49-50, 1946

Schürmann-Linder, H. "Das Puppenspiel in Paris," Das
Puppenth, 3:168-72, 1929

Seraphin, Domunique F. Histoire de ce Spectacle Depus
Son Origine Jusgu'A Sa Disparition, 1776-1870. Lyons,
Scheuring, 1875. In NN.
--- Théâtre de Seraphin, ou les Ombres Chinoises Dia-
logues. Paris, 1816. In British Museum.
--- Le Théâtre Feu Seraphin, Depuis Son Origine Jusqu'A
Sa Disparition. Paris, 1875
See also "Father Seraphin," British Museum General
Catalogue, Vol 219, 1964; and "Shadow" Section, O. Black-
man.

Sibbald, R. S. "Marionettes in the North of France." Unpublished Ph. D. dissertation, Philadelphia, Univ. of Pennsylvania, 1934.
--- Marionettes in the North of France. London, Oxford,
1936

"Soldier Shows of France, Crimean Campaign," L'Illus, D
15, 1855. See also Pupp 12:25, 1941

Somm, H. La Berline De L'Émigré Ou Jannais Trop Tard
Pour Bien Faire. Paris, Lévy, 1885

"Story of Caran D'Ache," Studio, 13: 1898

"Story of French Puppetry and Louis Lemercier de Neu-
ville," N Y Post, Jl 4, 1873
Sturges, K. "Guignol banned in Paris," Harpers Baz, 59:
Je 1925
--- "Guignol goes to Sea," Harpers Baz, 59:92-93, My 1925
Tahon, Andre. "French Terminology in Puppetry," Pupp J,
17(5):3-5, 1966.
Tairig, Jules. Binettes Lyonnaises. Lyon, Georg, 1897
An extremely rare item; comment from Mme S. Z. :
"Aventures et tribulations de Mme Durand, oncierge, et
de Mme Lafont, Ganuse au Gourguillon. Dialogues,
Scênes comiques et amusantes en langage populaire lyon-
nais. Revue paraissant le 10 et le 25 de chaque mois.
Juin 25, 1896-10, April, 1897; 20 livraisons in 12 carré."
--- Nos Grande Hommes Peints en Vers, Silhouettes Lyon-
naise. Lyon, Georg, 1886
Tavernier, Adolphe and A. Alexandre. Le Guignol des
Champs Elysées. Paris, Delagrave, 1889. At Mme S. Z.
"Temperal Jean and Father Marcel." Pupp Th Mod World,
p 219 and Illus No. 12.
Teumer, C. See K. Himer

"Les Théatre des Marionettes des Piccoli De V. Podrecca au
Théâtre des Champs Elysees." Toute La Danse et La
Musique, No 69, Jan 1958, p 23.
Tillstrome, Burr. "Kukla and Ollie return from France,"
Pupp J, 3(2):7-8, 10, 26, 1951
Timal, Charles B. "Les Marionnettes à Roubaix," Rev Sept,
Feb 1929
"Tournaire, Georges and Robert Gouge Marionettes-Paris,"
Pupp Th of Mod World, p 219 and Illus No. 20
Troydon, P. "Les Marionettes De Salzbourg à Paris," Rev
Des D M, 14(8):198-202 Mr 1, 1933
UNIMA France Marionnettes - Institut Pédagogique National,
29 Rue D'Uim, Paris 5e, UNIMA - France, 228 Boule-
vard Raspail, Paris 14e
Vachit, Ad. Glossaire des Gones de Lyon. Lyon, Storck,
1907. At Mme S. Z.
Valentine, Denis. Pour Jouer Guignol. Paris, Editions,
"Magic," 192?. In NN.
Van Der Horst See Horst

Vanier, Leon. Théâtre des Ombres Parisienne. Paris,
Lévy, 1893. "Programme géneraldes représentations don-
nées à L'Exposition de Chicago."
Vermerel, Jean. Quelgue Petits Théâtre Lyonnais des XVIII
et XIX Century. Lyon, Cumin, 1918.

France (cont.)
Véron, P. Les Marionettes à Paris. Paris, Lévy, 1875

Vieu, Jane. See L. Metivet

Visan, Tancrède De. Le Guignol Lyonnais, Par Tancrède
de Visan. Paris, Bloud, 1910. At NN.
Voltaire, Francois. Calendrier Historique des Spectacles
de Paris. Paris, Lambert, 1751, passim
--- "Puppet et Marionettes," Dictionnaire des Théâtre de
Paris. Paris, Librairie des Bibliophiles, 1766, in 3rd
vol.
--- Le Monds Dramatique, Histoire des Théâtres Anciens
et Modernes. Paris, Garnier, 1837, passim.
Vuillernoz, E. "Les Picceli à Paris," L'Illus, 87: pt 1
Jan 5, 1929, p 18-19
Wailly, Paul De. "About Puppets," Revue Du Nord. Jl 1,
1896
Wallace, Al. "Guignol Immortal," Pupp J, 10(5):3-4, 1959

Warsage, Rodolphe De. (pseud., E. Schoenbroedt)
--- Conte Fol! Comédie En Vers. Verviers, Willems, 1905
--- Cypris. Roman de Femme. Charleroi, Hubert, 1905
--- Le Histoire Célèbre Théâtre Liègenois de Marionnets;
Étude de Folklorique Histoire. 12 Vols, Bruxelles, Van
Oest, 1905. Sometimes cited as Étude sur un Phénom-
òne Folklorique Unique et Curieux Prepre au Pays de
Liège. Liège or Bruxelles, Van Oest, 1905
--- Marguerite. Liège, Faust, 1897
--- Au Royaume des Marionnettes. Liège, Faust, 1899
--- Au Royaumme des Marionnettes; Histoire du Célèbre
Liegons De Marionnettes. Liege, La Musées, 1903. In
NN.
--- Le Théâtre en Miniature. Ostende, Bouchery, 1904
Wiksell, Jean. "Summer travel notes on Paris," Pupp,
10:39, 1939
Wolff, Pierre. "Guignols et Pantins," J Univ Ann, Ag 15,
1911
--- "Les Marionettes," L'Illus, c1910, but also as a book
Les Marionettes. Paris, Lévy, 1910. In Montreal City
Lib.
--- "Parisian Puppet Theatre," Sci Am Sup, 54:22404, O 18
1902.
Yorick, P. F. (pseud.) "Puppetry in France up to Voltaire,
1649-1743," Mask, 7(1):26-28, 1914. Says that "Brische
or Briocci" were very early names for puppets.
Young, Rod. "French Shows," Pupp J, 10(2):33-34 (item

only), 1958
Young, S. G. "Guignol Marionettes," Lippencott M, 24:186-
95, 1879
"Youth Theatre-Amiens (Somme)," Pupp Th Mod World, p
219, and Illus. No. 22

Germany - West & East

Note: West and East German authors and articles are combined under this because they were started together in
1947. Publishers, dates and locations were most difficult to obtain and it is hoped help on this will arrive from
Germany, upon publication of what I was able to locate.
The most common reference was the one selected and this
is a limited list.

German authors are found throughout the book, especially in "Shadow" Music," "Film," "History" and "Hand
Puppet" sections. The "Punch and Judy" section will have a
great many items. Punch names in German material are
given below in case the student might wish to look further for
material under those titles.

Puppenspel. ... Pennsylvania German Dutch language
Kobolk Wichetel... Dattermann, Tattermann... 13th Cen-
tury puppets that move.
"Himmelreich" ... Kingdom of Heaven, religious puppet
show of the 15th Century, usually hand puppets.
"Polizinell" ... Punch hand puppets of 16th Century.
"Meister Hammerlin" ... 17th Century Punch character
of the street booth
"Kleinhempel" ... Character dolls which we do not in-
clude in a puppet category
"Docke, Mima, Tocha" ... See also "Punch and Judy"
Introductory material for additional common names.

Arndt, Friedrich. Das Handpuppenspiel. Berlin,
--- "Die Hohnsteiner Theater-Ger Fed. Republic," Pupp Th
Mod World, p 221, and Illus No 50, 52
Auflage, Z. Das Puppenbuch. Berlin, 1921

Baird, Bill. The Art of the Puppet. New York, Macmillan,
1965, passim
Bannenberg, Alfredo. Eintrit Frei; Reisen Und Abenteur eines
Puppenspielers. Berlin, Neues, Leben, 1958.
In Harvard Univ Lib.

Germany (cont.)
Baumann, Hans. Kasperle Hat Viele Freunde. Reutlingen,
Ensslin, Laiblin, 1965
--- Caspar and His Friends (10 Puppet Plays), trans.
Joyce Emerson, London, Phoenix House, 1967
Beckert, Peter. See "State Puppet Theatre at Dresden."

Beckwoldt, H. "German Puppetry," Pupp J, 2(1):20-21,
1950
Benda, John. Puppenspiele, Hamburgh, Janssen, 1904. In
Yale Univ. Lib.
Benkert, Katharina. See "State Puppet Theatre-Dresden."

Berliner, R. Denkmaler der Krippenkunst. Augsburg,
Filser, 1926
Biel, W. ed., Vom Puppen-Und Laienspiel. Berlin,
Deutscher Kunsterverlag 1927
Bielschowsky, A. Das Schwiegerlingsche Puppenspiel vom
Doktor Faust. Berlin, Briegg, 1882
See also "Plays" Section, "Individual Div." under "Faust"
for other items on this play by different authors.
Bittner, K. "Beiträge zur Geschichte des Volksschauspiels
Vom Doktor Faust," Prager Deutsche Studien, No 27:
1922
Blachetta, Walther. Blachetta Spiele und Andere. Leip-
zig, Strauch, 1930. In NN.
Blümner, H. "Fahrendes Volk|im Altertum," Sitzungsber-
ichtelder K. Bayerischen Akademie der Wissenschaften.
Munich, phil-hist, Klasse, vi, 1918
Boehn, Max von. Dolls and Puppets. trans. by J. Nicoll
into 1 Vol. London, Westerman, 1930; rev. London,
Harrap 1932; and New York, McKay, 1932.
--- Puppenspiele. 2 Vols., München, Bruckmann, 1929
See also "History" Section for revus and later editions.
Bohatta, H. "Das Javanische Drama-Shadows," Miteilung-
en der Anthropol, Geselleschaft zu Wien. 1905.
Bonesky, Richard. Das Puppenspiel vom Dr. Faust. Dres-
den, Alicke, 1905. In NN.
Bonneschky, Guido. (trans.) "Dr. Faust,""Four acts, pub-
lished for the first time (from the) original manuscript
by Wilhelm Hamm, 1850," in Von Boehn's, Dolls and
Puppets, 1932 ed., p 453-79.
Bottcher, A. "Vom Ausdruck des Kindes belm Handpuppen-
spiel," Blätter für Laien-und Jugendspieler, 1:3, 1925
Braun, Paul. See Material on "Munich Artists Puppet
Theatre," Munich, as he was director there 1910, for
several years.

202

"Braunschweig Marionette Theatre Performs in New York,"
N Y Times, D 24, 1957 11:6.
See also Pupp J, 11(1):12, 14-15, Ag 1959, illus.
Group is from West Germany.
Brehn, W. Das Spiel Mid Den Handpuppen. Düsseldorf,
Pädagog. 1931.
Bross, Fritz-H. See "Stuttgart Theater"

Brumme, M. A. Das Kleine Theater. Esslingen, Schreiber,
1926
Brux, G. "Die Theatergeschichtliche Bedeutung des Marion-
ettenspiels," Jugendpflege, 3:1, 1925.
Buch, Joseph and A. Lehmann. Das Puppentheater. Vol.
1-4, Leipzig, Schwartz, 1923-31
Bullett, G. W. "Marionettes in Munich Germany," Sat R,
148:665-66, D 7, 1929
Buschmeyer, Dr. Lothar. Die Aesthetischen Wirkungen des
Puppenspiels. Oppein, C. J. Puhl, 1931. In Harvard
Univ. Lib.
--- Die Kunst des Puppenspiels. Erfurt, Bochum, 1931.
In Harvard Univ. Lib., 10 pages of bibliog. and many
illustrations.
Carlyle, Thomas. See J. W. Goethe

Caspar in Der Windmühle, Oder Allzugut Ist Liederlich;
Ein Lust- und Schaudspiel. Für Das Puppentheater. Leip-
zig, Geisler, 1858. In Harvard Univ. Lib.
"College for Art Education Marionette Stage-Berlin," (Fed.
Republic) Pupp Th Mod World, p 220, 221 and Illus No.
49, No. 50 and No. 52
"Continual Appeal of Marionettes," J. Expr, 3:31-36, Mr
1929
Crawford, K. L. "Die Hohensteiner, Hand Puppets of Ger-
many," Pupp J, 20(3):27, 1968
Das Fidele. (Kartoffel Theater) Mühlhausen, 1912. At
Corner Book Shop, NYC.
Deering, O. "Poccis Beziehungen zum Marionetten The-
ater," Magdeburgische Zeitung, 1903.
"DEFA Cartoon Film Studio-Dresden," See Carl Schröeder
(German Democratic Republic)
See also "Film" Section
Demmeni, Y. S. Puppen auf der Bühne. Berlin, Henschel,
1951. In NN.
Dennewitz, O. "Das Puppenspiel," Volksbühnenwarte,
Berlin, Jahrg 19, and Nr 9, 1938, p 4-6
"Der Dertsche Bund für Puppenspiele," (In English) no
trans. given, Pupp 2:33-34, 1931

Germany (cont.)
Der Puppenspieler (Puppen Spieler) See also "Periodical"
 Section
De Zotce, Berryl. See H. Von Kleist

Diamond, W. See A. Schnitzler

Dietrich, E. Unser Kasperletheater; ein Bastelbuch. Stuttgart, Körner, 1948 and Zeichnugen, Munz, 1946. In NN.
Dill, Susanne. Finger-und Schattenspiele. Heidelberg,
 Kemper, 1958
Dorst, Tankred. (ed.) Auf Kleiner Buhne. Müchen, Juventa, 1959. In NN.
--- Geheimnis der Marionette. Müchen, Rinn, 1957. In
 NN.
Drexler, I. and D. Hansmann. "Puppenspiel," Westerm
 Monatsh, 165:385-88, Jan 1939
Drobisch, Theodor. Der Schornsteinfeger; Oder Ehrlich
 Währt Am Längstein. Leipzig, Geisler, 1853. In NN.
Dube, H. "Die Wiedererweckung des Kasper Theaters,"
 Westerm Monatsh, 155:601-08, Feb 1928.
Dulberg, F. See "Shadow" Section
 See also "Austria" for some German material.
Ehrhardt, G. Das Puppenspiel vom Dr. Faust. Dresden,
 Alicke, 1905.
Ehlert, E. See G. Hirsch

Eichler, Dr. F. Das Wesen des Handpuppen-und Marionnettenspiels. Emsdetten, Lechte, 1937 and 2nd ed, 1949.
 In NN and available at Mme S. Z.
Eickemeyer, Max. Das Kindertheater. Esslingen, Schreiber, 1919; also Munich, 1919. In NN. This seems to
 be a "Lighting Plan Book" with very good illustrations.
Engel, C. and L. Dietrich. Deutsche Puppenkomödien.
 12 Vols. Oldenburgh, Schwartz, 1875 and 1879; and
 Leipzig, 1906, Schulzesche heft-buchunglung.
Engleman, T. "Märchen-Puppenfilme," Westerm Monatsh,
 166:270-71, Jan 1940.
F. H. K. (pseud.) See "Shadow" Section

Fadrus, Viktor. Puppen-und Kasperlspiele. Vienna, Jugend, 1946. In NN.
Falkenstein, Mollie. "Deutches Institute for Puppenspiele,
 Bocum, E. Germany," (In English) Pupp J, 17(3):8, 1965.
Fall, Leo. Das Puppenmodel. New York, J.W. Stern,
 c 1910. In NN.
Fassel, A. See Max Singer

Faustus, Dr. Johannes; A Puppet Play Now First Done
in English in Four Acts. London, Nutt, 1893 in NN
See also G. Bonneschky; "Plays" under "Faust"
Fertigni, P. C. See "Yorick"
Films, German. See also "Film" Section. Many shadow
films under the name of Lottie Reininger, among others.
Finckh-Haelssig, M. Puppenschneiderei. Ravensburg,
O'Maier, 1928, Habbel, 1928.
Flögel, K. F. Geschichte des Grotesk Komischen. Leip-
zig, Werl, 1862 and rev. ed. Münich, M. Bauer, 1914.
In NN.
Franck, P. Puppenspiele. Berlin, Deutscher, 1931;
Stamberg, Haller, 1931
Freisse, E. "German Puppet Theatre" Play Bk, D 1913,
p 20-23.
Freytag, Rudolf. Der Regensburger Kasperl. Rlgensburg,
Habbel, 1948
Gaebler, E. T. "Marionetten," Kunst und Kürstler. Berlin,
1826.
"Gay, Fritz, Shadow Theatre in Dresden," Pupp Th Mod
World, p 222 and Illus Nos. 84, 85.
Gehlen, M. E. "Die Reichpuppen Bühne spielt das Märchen
Gevatter Todd," Neue Jugend, Ap 12, 1936, p 572-73.
In Hartford, Conn. City Lib.
Gcissler, H. W. Der Puppenspieler, Roman Murnau.
München, Lux, 1949, 426 p.
See also K. J. Simrock
"Gerhard's Marionnetes-Schwäbish Hall, (Fed. Republic)"
Pupp Th Mod World, p 221, and Illus No 54
"German Festival of the Federal Republic," - Woche Inter-
nationalen Puppenspiels of 1957, Pupp J, 17(4):4, 10,
1966.
See also The local German papers for the Festivals at
Braunschweig, Germany in 1957, 1960, 1963, 1966.
"Bochumer Internationale Verstellungsreihe Meister des
Puppenspiels." This festival is held annually from 1958
to date at Bochum, Germany.
"The Jubilee Festspielwoche of the Theatre, Die Holz-
keppe," held in 1964.
"UNIMA 19th Congress and 14th and 15th Regular Ses-
sion of the Puppet Presidium," held in Munich, June 1-
9, 1966.
See also "Festival" Section
"German Hartenstein (later Hohnsteiner) Glove Puppet The-
ater," Pupp Th Mod World, p 11, 220, 221, and Illus Nos
49, 50, 52. See also Max Jacob
"German Puppetry," Pupp, 10:37-39, 1939

Germany (cont.)
"German-Wendish Marionette Theatre-Bautzen,"
Pupp Th Mod World, p 222, and Illus No. 74
Glanz, L.   Das Puppenspiel und sein Publikum, Von Dr.
Luzia Glanz.   Berlin, Junker, 1941. In NN.
Goethe, Johann Wolfgang Von.   Wilhelm Meister's Lehrjahre.
2 Vols. , Berlin, 1795.
--- Wilhelm Meister's Lehrjahre.   2 Vols. , Berlin, trans.
by Thomas Carlyle, New York, Scribners, 1824.   Six
chapters on puppet theatre.
See also Paul McPharlin Pupp Th Am, p 312 and his
index.
--- Wilhelm Meister's Lehrjahre. 2 Vols. New York, Dut-
ton, Everyman's Library Series, 19, translation in NN.
Göhler, C.   "Vom Kasperletheater," Kunstwart, 1908.

Grágger, R.   "Deutsche Puppenspiele aus Ungarn," (Gypsy)
Archiv für das Studium der neuren Sprachen und Litera-
turen.   80:3-4, 1925
Grässe, R.   "Zur Geschichte des Puppenspiels und der
Automaten, in Romberg," Geschichte des Wissenschaften
im 19. 1856
Gröber, Karl.   Kinderspielzeug aus Alter Zeit, Eine Ge-
schichte des Spielzeugs, Von Karl Gröber.   Berlin,
Deutscher Kunstverlag, 1928
Gropius, W. and Laszlo Moholy-Nagy.   Die Bühne in Bau-
haus.   Munich, Boyer, 1924.
Grumbine, Dr. E.   "Stories of Old Stumpstown," (German
puppetry in Fredericksburg, U.S.A. , 1840's), Lebanon
County Historical Society Mag, 5(5).   In Philadelphia
City Publ. Lib.
Guthmann, H.   "Nationaltheater Des Kindlichen Menschen,"
Westerm Monatsh, 160:349-52, Je 1936
Haefker, H.   "Vom Kasperletheater.   Ein Stück Kultur-
geschichte," Der Thürmer 8: 1905
Hagemann, C.   Die Spiele der Völker, Berlin, Mayer,
1912
Hager, G.   Die Weihnachtskrippe.   Munich, Gesellsch, 1902
Munich, Kunst, 1902.
Hamilton, Clayton.   "Where Puppets Outplay Players,"
Vogue, 44:39, Jl 1, 1914
Hamm, Wilhelm.   See G. Bonneschky

Hampe, T.   Die Fahrenden Leute in der Deutschen Vergangen-
heit.   Leipzig, 1902.
"Hand Puppets of M. Pokerny," Der Kunsthammer, Feb
1936, p 19

"Hansjürgen Fettig Experimental Theatre-Stuttgart," -
Fed. Republic. Pupp Th Mod World, p 221 and
Illus No. 56
Hansman, D. See I. Drexler

Hansman, G. C. Schattenspiel aus Szetschwan. München,
Ehrenwirth, 1964. In NN.
"Hartenstein Theatre - or Hohsteiner Theatre" Official
hand puppet national theatre of Germany, under the lead-
ership of Max Jacop, originally. See Max Jacop
Hayes, J. J. "German Marionette Books," Drama, 19(3):
8, D 1928
---"Leipziger Puppenspiele" Drama, 19(8):236, My 1929
Hempel, O. Das Dresden Kasperle. Leipzig, Strauch,
1931
Hirsch, G. "A Master Marionette Man - E. Ehlert,"
Harpers W, 62:475-76, Ap 29, 1916
--- "Puppet Performances in Germany," Harpers W 62:
478, Ap 1916
Höfling (Val.) (pseud.) (ed.) Der Spielführer durch die
Laienspiele des val Höffinger. München, Höfling, 1952.
This was a regular company for publishing, but is con-
fusing when found with such a title.
Holthof, L. "Die Uberreste des Goetheschen Puppenthe-
aters und deren Geschichte," Freies Deutsche Hoch-
schrift. 1882.
See also J. Goethe
Hundt, P. Deutsche Märchenspiele. Oldenburg, Hinkel,
1922. Available at Mme S. Z.
Hussey, D. "English and German Puppet Theatres," Spect,
153:924, D 14, 1934
--- Ein Puppenheim. Berlin, Fischer, 1901. In Harvard
Univ. Lib.
Ibsen, Henrik. Bibliothek der Gesamt-Literatur. Halle,
(a.d.s) O. Hendel, 1892. "Ein Puppenheim," 82 p.
"Iwowski Berlin Theatre," Pupp Th Mod World, p 221-2 and
Illus Nos. 73, 80.
See also "Films" Section
Jacob, Georg. Arabische Schattenspiele...Mit Anhängen
Von Dr. G. Jacob. Berlin, Mayer, 1901. Bibliog. Br. M.
--- Erwähnungen des Schattentheaters in der Welt-Litera-
tur. Berlin, Müller, 1901
--- Geschichte des Shatten-Theatre im Morgen-Und Aben-
land. Hanover, Lafaire, 1925
--- Karagöz-Komödien. Berlin, Müller, 1899
--- "Neue Studien über das Chinesische Schattentheater auf
Grund der Neuerwerbungen in Offenbach und Hamburg,

Germany (cont.)
  Kiel, 1933 (Typewritten), British Museum.
--- Das Schattentheater. Berlin, Mayer, 1901 and 1907.
  In NN.
--- Das Schattentheater Innerhalb Des Indischen Kultur-
  kreises. Stuttgart, Kohlhammer, 1931. In British
  Museum.
Jacob, Max. Freundeskreis des Hohnsteiner Puppenspiele.
  Kassel, Bärenreiter, 1958. In NN
--- "Folk Kasperl National Theatre, Hartenstein or Hohn-
  steiner Theatre-Berlin-Fed. Republic" Pupp The
  Mod World, p 220-21 and Illus Nos. 49, 50 and 52.
--- Puppenspiele (Hohnsteiner Theatre) Leipzig, Ritter
  Elfenbein. At Mme S. Z.
--- "Union International Des Marionettes, UNIMA Organiza-
  tion and its work. Germany and the World," Pupp Th
  Mod World, p 49-52, see also p 11-12.
Jensen, Dr. Hans. Vulgargriechische Schattenspieltexte.
  Berlin, Wissenschaften, 1954. In NN.
Jhering, H. "Marionettentheater," Schaubuhne, 4: p 5

Joseph, Helen H. The Puppets of Brann and Puhoeny,"
  Thea Arts, 8:565-71, illus., Ag 1924
--- trans. of "The Physiognomy of the Marionette" by Ivo
  Puhonny, Thea Arts, 12:507-14, Jl 1928
Jügel, Carl. Das Puppehaus. Frankfurt, Für Den Ver-
  fasser, 1857
Jürgens, G. "Aus Kaspars Bunstem Reich," Westerm
  Monatsh, 163:205-08, N 1937
Just, Herbert (ed.) Puppenspieler. Kassel, Bärenreiter,
  1958
"Kasper" See also "Punch and Judy" Section

"Kasper, Tod und Teufel in Banne des Handpuppen Theatres," Illustrierte Zeitung, Leipzig, No. 4904, Mr 9,
  1934
Kasperle (Das Dresdener). Available Mme S. Z. (No 482)

Kasperltheatre. Leipzig, 1919-1920. "Une collection de
  jeux allemands pour marionnettes aussi la main." Available Mme S. Z.
Keller, Therese. Der Musikalische Bär; Vier Kasper-
  stücke Mit Anleitungen Und Hinweisen Für Die Spieler.
  Bern, Haupt, 1960. In Ohio State Univ. Lib.
"Die Klappe" - The Alfred Köhler Puppets at Göttingen,"
  Pupp Th Mod World, p 221 and Illus No. 59. This is in
  the Fed. Republic of Germany.

Kleist, Heinrich Von. "A Marionette Theatre," Thea Arts, 12:476-84, Jl 1928
--- "The Puppet Theatre," in his, Works. Berlin, Breslau, c 1910
--- "Puppets and Dancers," trans. by Beryl De Zocte, in Ballet, London, 2:42-49, Je 1946.
--- Über Das Marionnettentheatre. Jena, Weimar, Lichfenstein, 1920. Rare, original copy at Mme S. Z.
--- Uber Das Marionnettentheater. Leipzig, Insel-verlag, 1935 and Jena, Lichfenstein, 1935. In NN.
Köhler, A. See "Die Klappe"

Köhler, W. "Kleines Haustheater," Westerm Monatsh, 169: 237-40, Jan 1941
Kola, Richard. Puppentragödie. n. 1., Rikola-Verlag, 1923. In NN.
Kollmann, A. Deutsche Puppenspiele. Berlin, Mayer, 1891, and Leipzig, Grunow, 1891.
Kommerell, M. "Terzinen an die Nacht," Neue Rundschau, 50: pt 2 N 1939, p 374-84
--- "Kasperle wird Einsiedler," Neue Rundschau, 51: pt 1 Jan 1940, p 7-21
--- Kasperle-Spiele für grosse Leute. Krefeld, Scherpe, 1948. In NN.
Krafft, Ludwig. München und das Puppenspiel. Münich, Juventa, Höfling, 1961
Kralik, R. and S. Winter. Deutsche Puppenspiele. Vienna, Konegen, 1885. Plays are included.
"Kramer, Harry; Mechanical Theatre, Berlin-Paris," Pupp Th Mod World, p 221 and Illus No. 58 (Fed. Republic)
Kraus, A. V. Das Böhmische Puppenspiel vom Docktor Faust. Berlin, Breslau, 1891
Krause, Käthe. Das Grosse Puppenspiel. Heidelberg, Vowinckel, 1951. Available at Corner Bk Store, NYC.
Küpper, Gustav. Aktualitat im Puppenspiel, Eine Stoff-und Motivgeschichtliche Untersuchung. Emsdetten, Lechte, 1965
Landau, Georgi. See "State Puppet Theatre-Dresden."

Landsmann, Leo. Het Puppentheater Von Sergei Obraztsev Te Moskow. Antwerp, Karveel Uitgaren, 1947. In NN.
Laube, G. and G. Lesemann. Schwarzweisskunst In Der Hillfschule, Schattenspiele. nach Märchen und Verwandten Stoffen. Halle, O. Hendel, 1929.
Lefftz, J. "Puppenspeel im Alten Strassburg," Elsassland, 1929, p 233-37, 273-76

209

Germany (cont.)

Legband, P. "Die Renaissance Der Marionette," Literarisches Eco, 9: p 248

Lehmann, A. "Das Deutsche Puppenspiele," Die Vierte Wand, 1927, p 19
See also J. Buch

Leibrandt, Reinhard. "Wie der Teufel das Lautenspiel Lernte; ein Handpuppenspiel," Das Puppensp, 1953
--- Wie der Teufel das Lautenspiel Lernte; ein Handpuppenspiel. Weinheim, Deutscher Lainespielverlag, 1952

Leibrecht, G. P. J. "Gesichtspunkte zu einer Geschichte Des Puppenspiels," Das Literavische Eco, 23: 1920
--- Über Puppenspiel und Ihre Pflege. Innsbruck, 1921
--- Zeugnisse und Nachweise zur Geschichte des Puppenspiels In Deutschland. Freiburg, Diss, 1919; Leipzig, Borna, 1919.

Leisegang, H. W. "Marionettenspiel Als Künstler, Zeitausdruck," Das Neue Reich, 11: 1929.

Lenau, Nicolaus. Lenaus Werke. Vol 2, Berlin und Stuttgart, Spemann, 1802, p 31-45, rev. ed. 1850. In Oberlin Univ. Lib.
This is a poem play about "Die Marionetten."

Leonhard, P. R. See M. Ressel

Lesemann, G. See G. Laube

Leuchs, Fritz A. H. The Early German Theatre in New York. New York, 1928

Lindemann, R. "Das Kasperltheater Von Maz Pokorny," Dekorative Kunst, Jahrg 23, 1929, p 269-72

Linder, H. See Schürmann

Lindsay, Hugh. History of Life and Travels and Incidents of Col. Hugh Lindsay, The Celebrated Comedian. 1st ed., Pennsylvania, 1859, 1883

Link, Otto. "German National Society of Socialists in Puppetry," Pupp, 6:70-71, 1935
--- "International Festival in East and West Germany," Pupp J, 10(2):10, 1958

Littmann, E. "Das Malerspiel, ein Schattenspiel aus Aleppo, Nach Einer Armenischtürkischen Handschrift," Sitzungsberichte Der Heidelberger Akademie Der Wissenschaften, phil. Hist, Klasse, 8: 1918.

Llords, Daniel. "In Memory of Max Jacops, President of UNIMA," Pupp J, 19(5):3-4, 1968

Lodwig, David. "Bochumer Figurentheatrewache," (Bochum, Germany) Pupp J, 18(5):31-33, 1967

Loewel, C. Der Puppenspieler. München, Höfling, 1912.

"Losses and Gains in German Puppets," Pupp 9:19-20, 1938
Lux, J. A. "Geschichte und Ästhefik des Puppenspiels," Kind und Kunst, 1906.
--- "Poccis Kasperlkomödien und die Marionettentheater," Allgemeine Zeitung, No. 36 (Munich) 1909
"Luxembourg Theatre of Marionetes," Rev Des D M, Jl 15, 1943
Mackenbeau, Theodore. See "Film" Section

McPharlin, Marjorie Batchelder. See "International Festivals" Section
--- "Marionette Theater of Braunschweig," Pupp J, 9(5): 7-10, 1958
McPharlin, Paul. Puppet Theatre in America. New York, Harpers, 1949, p 312, 320, 322 passim
Maeterlinck, M. See "Music" Section

Mahlmann, Lewis. "The Puppet Theatre of Dresden, East Germany," Pupp J 17(3):4, 1965
Mahlmann, S. A. Marionetten-Theater oder Sammlung Lustiger und Kurzweiliger Actionen für Kleine und Grosse Puppen. Leipzig, Schwarts, 1806; In British Museum.
"Marionettes in Munich," Graphic, 103:189, Feb 12, 1921

Martini, Ella and Fritz. Kasperle-Bastelbuch. Ravensburg, O'Maier, 1951
Mayer, F. A. "Beitrag zur Kenntnis des Puppentheaters," Euphorion, 7, 1900
Meharg, F. "Glimpse of Old World Puppetry," Lubeck, Munich and Bavaria, Pupp J, 6(4):22-23, 1954
Meholy-Nagy, Laszlo. See W. Gropius

Meier-Graefe and E. Klossowski. Orlando und Angelica. Berlin, Cassirer, 1912. Available at Mme S. Z.
Meilink, W. Handbook voor de Poppenspeler. Purmerend, J. Muusses, 1952. In NN.
Mell, Max. Das Apostelspiel, Von Max Mell. Wien, Amandus-Edition, 1947. In NN
Melling, J. K. "Karl Funck's Theatre, Cologne," Pupp Master 5(8):21, 1958
Mentzel, E. Das Peppenspiel vom Erzzauberer, Dr. Johann Faust. Frankfurt am Main, Der Verfasser, 1900
Merck, H. Die Kunst der Marionette. Hamburg, Toth, 1948. In NN.
Mirbit, Rudolf, (ed.) Schulbühnen und Puppenspiel. Berlin, Rembrandt, 1958

Germany (cont.)
Moltke, Marlanna Von. "McPharlin's Imprints into German," Pupp, 4: 1933 p 32
--- "German Puppetry," Pupp 7: 1936, p 71-73. Sig. m.
--- "German Puppetry," Pupp 12: 1941, p 37-38
Morin, Edgar. Der Mensch und das Kino. Stuttgart, Kiett, 1958
Mueller, (Schauspiel Von Hans) pseud. Die Puppenschule. Berlin, 1908.
Mueller, Walter. Ombres, Tischlein, Deck Dich, Als Schattenspiel. Leipzig, ... Available at Mme S. Z.
Mühlmann, J. "Alpenländische Weihnachtskrippen," Kunst und Kunsthandwork, 23: 1920
"Municipal Puppet Theatre, Karl-Mark-Stadt, Ruth Fisher Puppets-Germ. Democratic Republic," Pupp Th Mod World, p 222, and Illus No 72
"Municipal Puppet Theatre-Magdeburg, Hans Haupt Puppets-Germ. Democratic Republic," Pupp Th Mod World, p222, and Illus Nos 76, 77
Naumann, H. "Studien über das puppenspiel," Zeitschrift Für Deutsche Bildung, 1929, p 1-14
Netze, Hans. Das Süddeutsche Wander-Marionettentheater. Munich, 1938
New York Staats-Zeitung. An early New York newspaper. It lists much German puppet material in the early 1850's, in and around NYC. In NN.
Nicoll, J. See Max Von Boehn

Niessen, C. (or Karl) Das alte Kölner Hänneschen-Theater; ein Gabe für Freude Rheinischer Volkskunst. Koln, Gehly, 1927. In NN., historical and critical.
--- Das Rheinische Puppenspiel. Bonn, Röhrscheid, 1928. A well illustrated, rare book, available at Mme S. Z. It is about Vittorio Podrecca.
Noeth, O. "Die Grazer Puppenspiele," Das Puppenth, 1: 129-35, 1923-24
Obraztsov, Sergi V. Mein Beruf. Berlin, Henschel, 1952
"Oestreich-Chnesurge Puppet Theatre at Gera-Germ. Democratic Republic," Pupp Th Mod World, p 222 and Illus No. 75
Organizations of Germany. See "Organization" Section

"Otto Grotswohl Works Puppet Group-Bohlen-Germ. Democratic Republic," Pupp Th Mod World, p 222 and Illus No. 83
Pewny, Gustav. Zwei Dramen. (Puppenspiele In Drei Akten) Zürich, Amalthea, 1929. In Harvard Univ. Lib.

Pinner, E. See L. Pritzel

Pischel, Richard. The Home of the Puppet Play. trans.
M. C. Tawney, 1902. London, Luzac, 1902.
--- Schattenspiele. Berlin, Reimer, 1902
"Pity the Puppets in East Germany." Time 57:32 Jan 29,
1951; Pupp J 2(6):11, 1951
Pocci, Frantz Graf Von. Heitere Lieder Kasperliaden und
Schattenspiele. Munich, Etzold, 1908
--- Kasperltheatre. Berlin, Ullstein, 1920. In NN.
--- Lustige Kasperlkomödien. Leipzig, Insel-verlag, 19?
In LC.
--- Lustiges Komödienbüchlein. Munich, O. Galler, 1893,
1895
--- Puppenspiele. Munich, Müller, 1909
--- Puppentheater. Münich, Hyperion, 1910
--- See also "Plays" Section
Pritzel, Lotte and E. Pinner. Puppenbuch. No 1. Available
at Corner Bk Store, NYC
Prüfer, C. "Das Schifferspiel," Beiträge zur Kenntnis des
Orients, ii (1906) p 154-169 [sic]
Puppen und Kindertheater. Leipzig, Geisler, 188-. In
Harvard Univ. Lib.
Puppen und Puppenspiele. 2 Vols., ed. F. Bruckmann,
A. G., 1929. In NN. Bibliog at end of each volume.
Das Puppenbuch. Berlin, Reiss, 1921. In NN. A bk of
plays. No author.
Das Puppentheater-Modellierbuch. Berlin, Reiss, 1927.
In NN.
Das Puppentheater. See also "Periodical Section. Several
German publications are given. This particular one was
absorbed by Di Puppenspieler. in 1931
"Puppet Literature in Germany," Pupp Post, Sp 1951, p 8-9
"Puppets in Germany," Brit Pupp Thea, 1(5):7, 1950
"Puppets in Germany," Pupp 5: 1934, p 35
Purschke, Hans Richard. A. B. C. Des Handpuppenspiele
Rotenburg an der Fulda. Weinheim, Deutscher Laienspiel,
1951
--- Das Allerzierlischste Theater. Munich, Heimeran, 1969.
History of 49 countries, and puppets.
---Libenswerte Puppenwelt. Hamburg, Von Schröder, 1962;
New York, Hafner, 1962.
--- Puppenspiel In Deutschland. Därmstädt, Neue Darm-
städter Verlagsanstalt, 1957
--- The Puppet Theatre in Germany. trans. W. Moss, Ga-
shet & Co. Langen, Gashet, and Därmstädt verlagsanstalt,
1957. This is a sig work.
Rabe, J. E. Kasper Putschelle. Hamburg, Beysen, 1912

213

Germany (cont.)
339 p. 2nd ed. Hamburg, Baysen, 1924, 269 p. In NN.
Rachel, J. See H. J. Simrock

Rapp, E. Die Marionettes in der Deutschen Dichtung.
Leipzig, Lehmann, 1924
Rehm or (Rehn), Hermann S. Das Buch der Marionetten.
Berlin, Frensdorff, 1865 and rev. ed. 1905. In NN.
Reich, H. Der Mimus. Berlin, Weidmann, 1903, passim

Reininger, Lottie. "Scissors Make Film," Sight and Sound,
5: London, Spring 1936, p 13-15
See also "Film" Section, and "England" Division
Reiss, E. (Reis). Das Puppenbuch. Berlin, Springer, 1921
In NN and Weidner Lib. at Harvard Univ.
--- Die Handpuppen. Junge Welt, Oplanden, Rhode Co.
1950 [sic] In Harvard Univ Lib.
Ressel, M. and P. R. Leonhard. 10 Lustige Stüeke Für
Das Kasperle Theater. Mülhaussen, 1931
Rilke, Rainer Maria. Puppen. Munich, Hyperion-verlag,
1921, Leipzig, Poeschel, 1914. In NN. Unusual illus.
by Lotte Pritzel.
Ringelnatz, Joachim. Kasperle Verse. Berlin, Hennsel,
1954
Riedelsheimer, A. Die Geschichte Des J. Schmid'schen
Marionettentheaters in Müenchen Von Der Gründung 1858
Bis zum Heutigen Tage, Von A Riedelsheimer. Munich,
schönen, 1906. In NN.
Röhler, Walter. 'From the Continent," Brit Pupp Thea, 1
(5):6, 1950
--- Grosse Liebe Zu Kleinen Theatern (Paper Theater)
Hamburg, Von Schröder, 1963. In NN.
--- "War Puppetry," Pupp, 11: 1940 p 34-35
Roser, Albrecht. "Albrecht Roser's Marionettes-Stuttgart,"
Pupp Th Mod World, p 220 and Illus Nos. 43, 44
--- "Puppenspieler-Stuttgart, Germany", Pupp J, 11(1):20-21
1959
---"West German Expo. '67, Canada, " Pupp J, 19(1):36, 1967
Schede, Wolfgang Martin. Das Puppenspiel. Rotenburg an
der Fulda, Deutscher Lalenspiel-Verlag, 1949.
(No.1 thru No. 20) In NN
Schepelmann-Reider, E. Lustige Kasperlstücke für jung und
alt. Ravensburg, O'Maier, 1955. In LC
Schimmrich, Richard. Das Hohnsteiner Handpuppenspiel.
Jena, Diederichs, 1937. In NN
Schink, J. F. Marionettentheater. Wien, Berlin, Wei-
mar, 1778. In British Museum.
Schmid, Dr. Hugo F. (Schmidt) Alerlei Kasparstuecke.

Leipzig, Insel, 1929 at Mme S. Z. Early bibliog., rare
and unusual bk.
--- Anleitung Zur Selbst Anfertigung Eines Kasper Theaters.
Esslingen, Schreiber,... At Mme S. Z. This is a con-
struction bk with understandable illus.
Schmid, Joseph (Papa Schmid). See Bill Baird's, Art of
the Puppet, p 153, 171, 175.
Schmidt, W. "Heron Von Alexandria," (Puppets in Ger-
many) Neue Jahrbücher für das Klassische Altertum, 2:
1899.
Schnitzler, A. Gesammelte Werke Von A Schnitzler.
Berlin, Fischer, 1912 Abteilung 1-2.
--- Marionetten. Berlin, Fischer, 1906
--- Der Puppenspieler. New York, Lust, 1929
Schott, G. Die Puppenspiele des Grafen. Frankfort-A-
Main, Verfasser, 1911
Schreiber, L. "Iva Puhony-Marionetten und Plakate für
das Marionetten Theatre," (English and German Texts)
Gebrauchsgraph, 12: Mr 1935, p 40-47
Schreibers Kinder Theatre. (Théâtre D'Enfants) 35 numbers,
Esslingen Schreiber is publ. et Muenchen. At Mme S. Z.
Schröder, Carl (Shroder) Director of Cartoon Film Studio
in Dresden, called "DEFA Films," in Germ. Democratic
Republic. See also "Film" Section
--- "Between Yesterday and Tomorrow," Pupp Th Mod
World, p 44-46
--- "Puppets from Carl Schroder's Puppet Films," Pupp Th
Mod World, p 220, 221 and Illus Nos. 69, 79, 82 and 86.
Schulenburg, W. Von. "Von der nationalen Mission des
Puppentheaters," Das Echo, 19: 1917
Schultze, Herman. Das spiel Vom Klugen und Tapferen
Schneiderlein. Ein Handpuppenspiel in Fünf Scenen. Leip-
zig, Strauch, 194?
Schürmann and H. Linder. "Vom Wachsen des Puppen-
spiels," Heimblätter, 6: 1929 p 272-77
Schwabach, E. E. Das Puppenspiel. Leipzig, Wolff, 1917

"Schwartz, Harold; Stage and Puppets at Essen," Pupp Th
Mod World, p 220 and Illus No. 55
Shadow work of Germany. See also "Shadow" Section

"Shows in Germany," Sat R, 59: p 340

Siegel, Harro. "Puppetry and Its Significance in Cultural
Life," Pupp J, 2(5):23, 1951
--- "Actor and Puppeteer," Pupp Th Mod World, p
21
--- "The Harro Siegel Marionette Theatre, Brunswick,"

215

Germany (cont.)
Pupp Th Mod World, p 220, and Illus Nos 46, 47
Simrock, K. J. Der Puppenspieler, ed. by J. Raclel, Berlin, Schöningh, 1927
--- "Puppenspiele," in H. W. Geissler's edition of Gestaltungen des Faust. Vol. 1 Munich, Barcus, 1929
Singer, Max and A. Fassel. Kasperl Ist Wieder Da. Berlin, 1946
Smith, William O. Fifty Years of Rhyming. Punksutawney, Pa. , 1932
Stadler, Dr. E. ed. , Theater der Welt. Zürich, 1955, passim. Available at Corner Bk Store, NYC
Stanhope, A. "A Marionette Theatre in Munich," Theatre, 47: Mr 1928, p 43-60
"State College of Visual Arts, Marionettes Studio of Kassel, Germany," Pupp Th Mod World, p 221, Illus No 51
"State Puppet Theatre-Dresden, Peter Beckert Puppets," Pupp Th Mod World, p 222, Illus Nos 70, 81
"State Puppet Theatre-Dresden, Georg Landau Puppets," Pupp Th Mod World, p 222, Illus No 71
"State Puppet Theatre Dresden, Katherina Ben Kert Puppets," Pupp Th Mod World, p 222, Illus No 78
Stölting, W. Van den Fisher un seine Fro. Niederdeutsches Handpuppenspiel. Leipzig, Stravech, 19?
Storm, T. Puppenspieler. London, Harrap, 1938
"Studio G 12, Brunswick, Gottlieb Mordmüller puppets," Pupp Th Mod World, p 221, Illus No 57
"Stuttgart Marionette Theatre, Fritz H. Bross Puppets," Pupp Th Mod World, p 220, Illus No 48
"Stuttgart Youth Puppet Stage Centre, Anni Weigand Puppets," Pupp Th Mod World, p 220, Illus No 45
"Surviving the War Years in Germany," Pupp, 17: 1946 p65

Sylvester, Ernest Von. Das Puppenspiel. Leipzig, Wolff, 1917. In Harvard Univ. Lib.
Szerelmes, Richard. Spielt Kasperltheater. Wien, Österrichischer Bundesverlag, 1949. In NN.
Tawney, M. C. See R. Pischel

Tesorek, A. Kasperl Sucht Den Weibuschtemahn. Vienna, Jahrbuch, 1927
Thalmann, M. "Puppenspiele," Westerm Monatsh, 165: Jan 1939, p 385-88
--- "Weltanschauung im Puppenspiele vom Docktor Faust," Modern Language Association of American Publications, 52: S 1937, p 675-81
Thiel, Reinold E. See also "Film" Section

216

--- Puppen und Zeichenfilm. Berlin, Rembrandt, 1960

"Tin Puppets made in Germany," Ed Screen, Jan 1933, p
26
"Toy Booth, German," Toledo Museum of Art Bulletin,
Toledo, O. , c 1940's
Trümper, Herbert (ed.) Handbuch der Kunst und Werker-
ziehung. Bd 2. T. 2. [sic] In NN.
--- Schulbunne und Puppenspiel. Berlin, Rembrandt, 1958.
In NN.
Vom Puppen-und Laienspiel. ed. W. Biel, Berlin,
Deutscher Kunstverlag, 1927.
"Von" names will all be found under the family name.

Von Boehn, Max. See Max Boehn

"Wartime Puppetry in Germany, under Goebels," Pupp,
15: 1944 p 38
Weaver, Randolph T. "Prince Achmed" and other Silhou-
ette Films," Thea Arts Mo. , 15: Je 1931, p 505-08
Weismantel, Leo. Buch der Krippen. Augsburgh, A.
Böhm, 1888 and rev ed 1930. A book of "Christmas
Cribs" or playlets, with a good bibliog.
--- Das Werkbuch der Puppenspiele. Frankfort au Main,
Bühnervolfsbundes, 1924. In NN
Wiksell, Jean Star. "Summer Travel in Aachen, Germany,"
Pupp, 10: 1939, p 140
Winter, S. See R. Kralik

Winzer, Richard. "Puppetry in Germany since World War
II," Pupp J, 2(6):28-29, 1951
--- "International News, Prof. H. Siegell's Lecture," Pupp
J, 2(5):23, 1951
Wolf, G. J. "Marionette Theatre Münchner Künstler," Die
Kunst, 15: Jl 10, ?, p 54-61
Yorick (pseud.) (P. S. Fertigni) "History of German Pup-
petry," Mask, 6: 1913, p 297-305
Zellner, H. "Vom Puppentheater zum Heimkino; mit aqua
rellierten Weinachtserinnerungen Von G. G. Kobbe,"
Westerm Monatsh, 147: D 1929, p 601-08
Zotce, Beryl de. See H. Von Kleist

Note: Greek theatre or puppetry is usually of the "shadow" family, but figures are not as delicate as those of the French. The main character in their productions is called "Karagiozis" or "Karagheuz." He is a good deal like "Punch" in nature and action, sometimes has strong physical resemblance in the shadow figure. There are no entries indicating a hand puppet, however, the very early Greek puppets were called, "neurospastios," from the word "neuron" meaning string... so marionettes may be found in some early studies and once in a while in modern Greek puppetry.

There are currently a few Greek puppet shows in America but they are rare and little is written about them. Chicago seems to be rather active at times. Much investigation is needed for this section and the supplement will need help from Greek puppeteers. See also "Shadow" Section.

"Athens Puppet Theatre, The Helene Theochari-Peraki Puppets," Pupp Th Mod World, p 226, and Illus Nos 182-3
Baird, Bill. The Art of the Puppet. New York, Macmillan, 1965, p 250, passim.
Ballamos, William. "Greek Shadow Play, Chicago," Pupp 9: 1938
Blackham, Olive. Shadow Puppets. London, Rockcliff, 1960, p 59-65
Caimi, Giulio. Karaghiozi. Athens, Hellinikes Technes, 1935. In NN
Cook, Alan. "Mrs. Helen Theocharis Perakis Puppet Troup," Pupp J 17(4):9, 1966
D'Agostino, C. "Karaquez," Mercure De Fr, 284:121-32, My 15, 1938
Drakoulalos, Bill. "Greek Shadow Shows in Chicago," Chicago Daily News, 1926 (all year)
Flanagan, Hallie. "Karagiozis in Athens," Pupp 5:68-70, 1934
Foyne, Vera. "Dancing Dolls of Destiny," Ch Sci Mon (between 1947-50). In "Puppet Clipping File," Deering Ref. Lib. , Northwestern Univ. Campus, Evanston.
Gautier, Theophile. Constantinople. Paris, Lévy 1854. Passim Greek material.
"Greek Karagiozis Puppets," Nat Geog, Jl 1963, p 124-5

"Greek Play," Pupp 2:43, 1931

"Greek Puppet Show," All Yr R, 74:206, Mr 3, 1894

"Greek Shadow Plays," Sphere, London, O 1934, p 20

"Greek Shadow Theatre in Chicago," Chicago Daily News,
  Ag 29, 1942 p 10
Illyne, Catherine. "Athens, Theatre of Shadows," Lond S,
  9:79-83, Feb, 1935
McDougall, A. R. "An Athenian Shadow Show," Thea Arts,
  17:387-93, My 1933
McPharlin, Paul. Puppet Theatre in America. New York,
  Harpers, 1949, p 289-92
Magnin, Charles. Histoire des Marionettes en Europe.
  Paris, Lévy, 1852, passim
Meharg, F. "Festival of Traditional Puppetry-Liege, Bel-
  gium (Greek Show)" Pupp J, 10(6):22-23, 1959
Paraskevaides, Stratos. "Greek Puppetry," Pupp, 17:
  66, 1946
Prou, V. "Les Théâtre d'automates En Grèce," Mem-
  oires Presentes...A L'Academie, I, ix, 1884
--- See also Max Von Boehn, Dolls and Puppets. London,
  Harrap, 1932, p 500
Rinvolucri, Mario. See E. Spatharis

Roussel, Louis. Karagheuz ou le Théâtre d'Ombres à
  Athens. 2 Vols. Athens, Raftanis, 1921
Spatharis, E. Sotiris. Behind the White Screen. trans.
  Mario Rinvolucri, London, London Magazine Editions
  Publishing Co. , 1968
--- "Satire in the Karaghiozis Shadow Theatre," World
  Thea, 8(4):339-41, 1960
Speaight, George. History of the English Puppet Theatre.
  London, Harrap, 1955, p 12-13, 23-27, 273-275

Ghana, See also Africa

"Jan Bussell established native puppet group for Ghana
  Art Council State Puppet Theater," Brit Pupp and M
  Thea Newsl, No 73, My 1962 p 2

Guatemala, See also South America

López, Marilena. Teatro De Titeres. Guatemala, 1959.
  In NN.
Mills, Winifred. "Remarks About Guatemala, in 'Screw-
  eyes' " Grapev, Feb 1949, p 4

Holland

Note: Some material may be found overlapped with Germany, Belgium or Flemish items. There is material to be found for this country as it is rich in puppetry and popular for international gatherings. See also "Films" and "Conventions" Sections.

Arnold, Frank. Maskers En Marionetten. (In Dutch) 195? Zaandijk, Toneelfonds, J. Heijnis Tsz. In LC.

"Die Blauwe Souyte Puppet Theatre-Maastricht," Pupp Th Mod World, p 220, and Illus Nos 34, 35

Bulthuis, Rico Johann. De Kleine Comedie, Eeen Puppenlandse Geschjedenis. S-Gravenhage; D. de Jong, 1945

--- Het Moderne Poppenspel. Amsterdam, Heijnis, 1961. A good bibliog., p 158-64. In NN.

--- Poppen, Schimmen, Marionetten. Maastricht, Leiter-Nypels, 1954.

Coenen, Joop. Shadows. (In Dutch) Gravenhage; Sint Joris, 1952

Dassen, Picke. See "Die Blauwe Scuyte Puppet Theatre."

Doering, O. "Poccis Bezleungen zum Marionnettentheater," Magdeburgische Zeitung, 1903

Eggermont, J. Puppenspiel. Leuven, S.V. De Pojl, 1944. In NN

Engel, K. and A. Tille. Deutsche Puppenkomödien. Oldenburg, Hinkel, 1879

Gordon, . Knowing the Netherlands. New York, American, 1940, p 43-55

Groenewold, Hip-Katwijk. "Dutch Puppetry," Pupp, 5: 35, 1934; 8:36, 1937; 9:20, 1938; 15:38, 1944

--- "Dutch Puppets in Wartime," Pupp, 11:35, 1940

--- "Holland's Puppetry," Pupp, 13-14:37-38, 1943

--- "Puppetry in Holland," Pupp, 4:60, 1933

--- "Puppets of Holland," Pupp, 17: 66, 1946   (concerned with the "occupation" years.)

"Kluysken, B. Puppet Show Farewell," Saskatoon Star, Phoenix, c 1958-59

See also Pupp J, 10(6):7-8, 1959, concerning this article.

Kollman, A. see Germany

Krali, K.R. see Germany

Lehmann, A. see Germany

Leibrecht, G.P.J. see Germany

McPharlin, Marjorie B. "International Festival," Pupp J, 10(2):10, 1958

Meltz, Hy. See G. Van Deth

Merlijin Puppet Theatre, at Haarlem," Pupp Th Mod World, p 220 and Illus No. 32

Murray, M. I.   Poppeteater.   Ses Poppespele Met Inleiding
   Kaapstad, H. A. U. M. , 1962. In NN.   Some Dutch in
   Africa.
Pereodicals, Dutch. See "Periodical" Section

Pischel, Richard.   Die Heimat Puppenspiels.   Berlin,
   Rektoratsreden, Hallesche, 1901
Pletinchx, Karl.   See "Film-General" Section

Puppenspiele. (Deutsche). Leipzig, Public Par L'Institut
   National Pour Les Marionettes.   5 Fascicules: 1, 2, 3, 4
   et 7"   At Mme S. Z.
"Puppet Booth at Delft, Holland, " Pupp,   17:46, 1946

"Puppetry in Holland, " Pupp,   6:67-68, 1935

"Puppetry in the Netherlands and Belgium, "   Brit Pupp Thea,
   1(5):7, 1950
Rodenko, Paul.   Harten Twee, Harten Drie, Een Toneelspel;
   Een Poppenspel.   Den Hague, B. Bakker, 1963
Schuyter, J. de   De Antwerpsche Poesje: zijn geschiedenis
   en zijn speeltenksten.   Antwerp, c 1946
--- Revu of De Antwerpsche Poesje... Anon, Brussels
   Museum Royal Bulletin, series 3, 18: Jan 1946, p 83-
   84
Slagt-Prins, M.   Een Eigen Puppenkast.   Zutphen, Thieme,
   1956.   Texten en beschrijving door M. Slagt-Prins en
   theatre Slaght.
Tussenbroek, Harry Van.   De Togepaste Kunsten In Nether-
   lands.   Rotterdam, 1905
--- Poppen En Marionetten.   Amsterdam, LanKamp, 1950
   In NN.
Vandenbroucke, J.   Het Poppenspiel in de Nederlanden.
   Antwerp, Nederlandsche Boekhandel, 1946.   In LC
Van Deth, Guido and Felicia.   "Slides of Netherland Pup-
   pets. "   The Hague, Author, 1968
   See also Pupp J, 20(2):6, 1968, for an article about the
   "Slides of Netherland Puppets. "   Article is by Hy Meltz.

Hungary

Note: In this country the word "Bábjátekos" means Puppet
   Theatre, and "Fogantyus Bubok" means "Handle puppets"
   or rod puppets.   The National Puppet Theatre at Budapest, the most important center, is sometimes called
   "State Theatre of Budapest, " without the addition of the
   word "Puppet. "   There will be some confusion of materi-

221

Hungary (cont.)
al sighted, at times, as coming from Puppet Master.
This is the name of their official publication but it is
also the name of England's publication (See "Periodical"
Section). I have written the full name out when I think
the source means the Hungarian publication, Pupp Master being used for the English publication. The coverage
of Hungarian material herein is very slight.

Amaral, L. "Hungarian Puppet shows," Pupp Post, Autumn
1954, p 13
Arany, Janos. A Fulemile (Babokat Tervezte Es Kezzitet-
te Girardi Korhel). 2 Klad, Budapest, Kepzőmüveszetti
Alap Kiadovallatta, 1959. In NN.
Babszinpad. Budapest, Dendolat. In LC

Baird, Bill. The Art of the Puppet. New York, Macmil-
lan, 1965, p 250 for index, passim
Boyce, R. "Hungarian Puppetry," Pupp Master, 3(1):
1950 (possibly Puppet Master (Hungary)
"Debrecen Marionette Students Theatre," Pupp Th Mod
World, p 224, and Illus No 150
"Festivals" Pupp J, 17(4):10, 1966. See also "Festivals"
Section
Holzbérlin, Fritz. Pupp J, 8(6):27, 1957, item only

"Hungarian Puppets," Pupp, 7:76-77, 1936 "Travel
Notes"
"Hungarian Television Puppets," Pupp Th Mod World, p 224
and Illus No 144
"International News," Pupp J, 2(1):20-21, 1950
Magyarsag Neprajza. Vol. 2:411 and Vol 3:257
Mahlmann, Lewis. "National Puppet Theatre of Budapest,"
Pupp J, 17(3):5, 1965
Meyer, Rosalind. "Travel Notes in Hungary," Pupp 7:1936
"Napsugár Puppet Theatre at Békésczaba," Pupp Th Mod
World, p 224
"A Nation's Spirit Kept Alive by Puppets," N Y Times, O 21,
1928, 20:40
"National Puppet Theatre at Budapest, Puppets," Pupp Th
Mod World, p 225 and Illus Nos 133-149
See also Brit Pupp and M Thea G Newsl, No 145, 1968, p 6
for an item.

Népmüvészeti Intézet. A Bábjátszás Magyarországon. (The
Puppetry of Lajos). Budapest, 1955. In NN

"Puppet Theatre at Cultural Center, Municipality of Pest,"
Pupp Th Mod World, p 224, and Illus No 145
"State Puppet Theatre of Budapest," Pupp J, 15(1):27, 1963

Szilágyi, Dezsö. "The Modern Puppet Stage and its Audience," Pupp Th Mod World. p 35-36.
--- Bábjáték Az Iskolában Es Az Óvodában Irták, Szilágyi Dezsö es Meszáros Vincéne. Budapest, Muvelt Nep, 1954. In NN.
Viski, Charles. "Marionnettes Hongroises," Nouvelle Revue De Hongrie. Budapest, Feb 1935, p 148-155

India

Note: In India the strongest field of puppetry is the "Pavai-koothu" and "Tholubomalatta" shadow work, which is somewhat like the Indonesian "Wayang" shadow work. It is a very, very old art and it uses beautifully cut out and painted rod puppets. One must know the special vocabulary when reading books on India's drama or confusion is certain.

Some of these terms are: "Putliwala" or puppeteer of wood marionettes or rods, he is much respected as he tells religious and historic tales. It is "Viduska," who is the puppet "Punch" character of India that we find in the Calcutta street booths, although he is more of a clownish, classical, character than the European common-man character. South India uses string puppets called "Yakshaghana" and "Pavakai." Malabar, India, has the "Andhra shadows" and "Karntaka shadows." The "Rajasthani" is a newer large marionette with dramas called "Heer Ranja" and "Amar Singh." The "Kathputlis" are the two string marionettes of Rajasthan, India.

The "Samavakara" is the main play for shadows and runs about eleven hours. The "Ramayana" and the "Mahabharata" and the "Panji" are other traditional war-like dramas with rod and shadows. "Bomalattam" are older rod and string marionettes from southern India near Madras.

Music is inseperable from Indian puppet drama and the dance form is likewise very closely interwoven with puppet work. Material in both of those sections of this bibliography should be investigated.

India (cont.)

There are over 200 "Rajasthan" puppeteer families in Delhi alone, and the government is making great strides to revive the ancient art so that it can be used as a means of instruction. The Lok Kala Mandal Theatre in Udaipur, India does a great deal of puppet drama and is very willing to assist in research work.

There are many other important words but these will serve as a start for the interested reader.

"Andhra Shadow puppets in Madras, India Area," Pupp J, 17(1):9-10, 1966.
See also Any material about the Darpan Drama School, Ahmedabad, India. Work by Mrs. Meher Contractor and sister.
Baird, Bill. The Art of the Puppet. New York, Macmillan, 1965, p 64-55 and passim. Sig. m. which is well illus.
"Bharatiya Natya Sangh Indian Arts Organization," Pupp J, 13(3):28-29, 1961. This group works with puppets and is located at 34 New Central Market, New Delhi. Willing to help research work.
Bibliography on Puppets. New Delhi, National Institute of Audio Visual Education, c 1965.
    Marjorie Batchelder McPharlin helped to compile this work while she was in India on a Fullbright Grant assisting in organizing puppet work.
Blackham, Olive. Shadow Puppets. London, Rockcliffe, 1960, passim
Contractor, Mrs. Meger. A Guide to Puppetry and Creative Drama. New Delhi, (Gov't.) 1966
--- "India's puppets," Pupp Master, 5(9):11-12, 1956
--- "India's puppets," Pupp Master, 5(10):10-11, 1958
--- "Shadow puppets," Pupp J, 17(1):10, 1966
--- "Puppetry in India," Marg. (India), S-O, 1968 - the entire issue. This is published by TATA Enterprises, in Bombay and this special issue is available from them.
See also Pupp Life, O 1968, p 13-15; San Fran Bay Pupp G Newsl, O 1968, p 2
Coomaraswamy, Dr. A. "Notes on Indian Dramatic Techniques and Puppets," Mask 6:109-128, 1913
"Darpan Drama School of Ahmedabad, Shadows by Meher Rustom Contractor," Pupp Th Mod World, p 227, and Illus Nos 204-207

Deri, Shrimati. Village Theatres of India. Kahmir, c 1938-39.
Doran, J. See J. A. Dubois

Duarte, Adrian. "India's puppetry," Pupp, 12: 1941
---"The Maewari Marionette Man," Times of India Annual, 1943. See also issues of this Annual 1940 and 1941.
--- "Provincial Puppetry," Pupp, 11:66, 1940; 17:67, 1946.

Dubois, J. A. and J. Doran. "Marionettes in India 1806, through Western Eyes," Pupp 10:40, 1939
Dutt, Suresh. "Calcutta Children's Theatre Puppet Unit," Pupp J, 17(1):10, 1966
Falkenstein, Mollie. "Puppet and Shadow Theatre of Bhartiya, Lok Kala Mandal, Udaipur, India," Pupp J, 17(3): 7, 1965
"Festival of Puppetry-All India, Calcutta, Jan. 1, 1966," Pupp J, 17(4):34, 1966, item
Foulds, Mrs. J. (Maude MacCarthy). "India's Puppets," Pupp, 7:73, 1936
Foyne, Vera. "Dancing Dolls of Destiny," Ch Sci Mon, Clipping, undated, in Deering Lib., Northwestern Univ., Evanston, Puppet File, Research Room (bet. the years 1947-1950).
Gupta, Kedar, N. Education Through Marionettes. Calcutta and New York, Macmillan, 1937
--- "Education Through Marionettes," Marg, c 1936
This was a series of articles carried in eight issues of this periodical during this year. Is reported to have appeared in several others.
--- "India's Educational Puppetry," Pupp, 7:73-4, 1936;
--- "People's Puppet Theatre needs Reviving," Pupp, 10: 37, 1939
--- "Puppetry in India," Pupp, 8:36-37, 1937
--- "Puppets in Revival, India," Pupp, 6:72-74, 1935
The Rajputana Region.
Hagemann, Carl. Die Spiel der Volker. Berlin, Mayer, 1912.
"India's Puppetry." The entire issue of Marg, Bombay, S-O 1968
Jacop, G. and Hans Jensen. Das Indische Schatten-Theatre. Stuttgart, Kohlhammer, 1931
See also "Germany" this name.
Jensen, Hans. See G. Jacop

Kamaladevi Chattopadhyay, Mrs. Pupp J, 14(6):19, 1963
National Chairman of "All India Handicrafts Board" and Vice Chairman for Dance, Drama Music Folk Theatre

225

India (cont.)
  at Bombay.
Keith, A. B. The Sanskrit Drama. New York, Oxford
  Univ. Press, 1924
"Literacy Village Grant," Pupp J, 19(2):33, 1967, item

Llord, Daniel. "Puppets in India," Pupp J, 16(2):7-8, 1954
  See also this name in "Music" Section
Lucknow Literacy House, Workshop for Puppetry, Udaipur,
  India and The Lok Kala Mandal (Folk Art Institute)
  See M. B. McPharlin's articles below.
MacCarthy, M. See J. Foulds

MacDonell, A. A. History of Sanskrit Literature. New
  York, Appleton, 1900, p 290-98, p 302-17
McPharlin, Marjorie Batchelder. Bibliography on Puppets.
  New Delhi, For National Institute of Audio Visual Educa-
  tion of India, c 1965.
--- "India" Pupp J, 14(6):19, 1963
--- "India's Puppetry," Pupp J, 16(4):14-15, 1965
--- "Mrs. Meher Contractor," Pupp J, 20(2):27, 1968
--- "Puppets in India," Pupp J, 15(4):9-11, 1964
--- Rod Puppets and the Human Theatre. Columbus, Ohio
  State Univ. Press, 1947, passim
--- See also "History" Section and "Rod" Section for her
  other books which will have scattered material on shadow
  and rod India's work.
--- See also "International" general section for her articles
  as many will have passim material on India. Such as,
  Pupp J, 15(5):7-9, 1964 and Pupp J, 17(1):2-11, 39,
  1966.
    She assisted in the compilation of this list while work-
  ing in India on puppet assignment.
Murdeshvar, B. G. "Chitrakathis, the Showmen of Deccan,
  India," Pupp, 15: 1944.
--- "Picture Showmen of the Deccan, India," Times of India
  Annual, Bombay, 1940
Pischel, Richard. Die Heimat des Puppenspiels. Halle,
  O. Hendel, 1900
--- Home of the Puppet Play-India. trans. M. C. Tawney,
  London, Luzac, 1902
--- "Rural India's Traditional Puppets," Asia, D 1946 p
  562. Also published as a separate form by this publica-
  tion, 1946.
Popo, Omar. Pupp Life, O 1968, p 5. Teaching for
  American Society for Eastern Arts in California in sum-
  mer 1969. See O. Stevens

Puppet Organizations and Periodicals of India: See
  "Organizations" and "Periodicals" Sections
Ridgeway, William Sir. Dramas and Dramatic Dances of
  Non-European Races. London, Cambridge Univ. Press,
  1915
Samar, Derilal. A Puppet and Puppet Plays Book. (In
  Indian lang.) In LC.
Schuyler, Montgomery. Bibliography of Sanskrit Plays and
  Drama. New York, Columbia Univ. Press, 1906, passim
Scott-Kemball, J. "The Kelantan Wayang Siam Shadow Pup-
  pets... India and Southeast Asia," Man, My 1959, p 27-28
Speaight, G. S. "A Puppet Show in Colombo, Ceylon,"
  Pupp, 15:56, 1944
Stevens, Olga. "Oriental Puppetry for 1969 Summer,
  Berkeley, Calif.," Pupp Life, O 1968, p 5
Tawney, M. C. See R. Pischel

"Third Indian Festival by Indian Puppet Theater, Sitladevi
  Industrial Estate, Sitladevi Temple, Bombay," Pupp J,
  16(3):28, 1964
Tilakasiris, Prof. Puppetry in Asia. Ceylon, Dept. of
  Cultural Affairs, 1969

Indian - General

American Indian... See "America," alphabetical order
  "Indian"
Eskimo Indian... See "Canada"

Other Indian Tribes... Listed under the country in which
  that tribe is or was commonly located, such as Mexico,
  Panama, South America, etc.

Indonesia - See also "Java," "Oriental," etc.

Note: Most of work is Shadow and is scattered through
  articles and books when being written about. Very little
  was found about "Puppetry in Indonesia," as such.

Baird, Bill. The Art of the Puppet. New York, Macmillan,
  1965, p 55-60, and passim
Gulik, R. "Dostersche Shimmen," Elsevier's Geillustreera
  Maandschrift, (Amsterdam) 82: 1931, p 94-110 and p
  153-163
Keep, A. A. See F. A. Wagner

Indonesia (cont.)
Rassers, W. H. Panji, The Culture Hero. The Hague,
   M. Nijhoff, 1958. In NN.
Tedjohadisumarte, R. "Wayang Plays" in "Plays" Section

Tilakasiri, Prof. Puppet Theatre in Asia. Ceylon, Dept.
   of Cultural Affairs, 1969
Van Weeran, Griek, H. "Indonesian Art: Batik and Puppetry of East Indis, " Design, 50:10-11, My 1949
Wayang-Golek Performance; Pupp Th Mod World, p 228,
   and Illus Nos 224-228
Wagner, Fritz A. Indonesia, The Art of an Island Group.
   New York, Crown, 1959 and rev. ed. New York, Greystone, 1967. The Greystone edition was trans. by A. A.
   Keep and discusses Java and Bali, on p 115-119, 128-43,
   and 144-73.

Iran

"Iranian Marionettes, " Pupp Th Mod World, p 227 and Illus
   No 200
Mitcoff, Elena. "A Persian Puppet Master, " Pupp 4:52-56,
   1933
--- "Work of Sufi Hussain Kashifi, " Pupp, 8: 1937, p 40
"Notes on Persian and Easter Island Puppets in 1823, "
   Mask, 5:157-58, O 1912
"Pahlevan Kachal, " (Pulchinello) Pupp Th Mod World, p
   227, and Illus No 199
"Puppetry in Persia, " Pupp, 4: 1933. Short anon. article.

Quseley, Sir William. "Puppet Show at Tabriz, Persia, "
   in his Travels in Various Countries of the East. Vol. 3.
   London, Rockwell, 1819 and 1823. p 404-05.

Ireland

Note: There are several companies and active theatres but
   little is written about it in general books and material
   available in the U. S. A.

Boyne, Patricia and John. Irish Independent. There is a
   weekly puppet feature in this publication, covering a
   third of a page. This is referred to in Brit Pupp Thea,
   1(5):7, 1950.
"Dublin, Ireland's Puppets of 1775, " Pupp, 7:78, 1936

"Dublin Marionette Group," Brit Pupp Thea, 1(4):10, 1950

"Dublin Puppets," Irish Times, Mr 1950

"Eire," Pupp, 13-14:36, 1942.

Herrick, Jane. "Puppets in the British Isles, Ireland's
 only puppeteer Eugene Lambert does TV in 1965."
 Pupp J, 17(3):9-10, 1965
"Ireland's Puppetry," Pupp, 15:36, 1944

Kelley, Michael. Reminiscences of Michael Kelley. Vol I.
 London, 1826, p 5
 Revu of Reminiscences of Michael Kelley, Pupp, 7:78,
 1936
O'Leary, Siobhan. "An Irish Caterpillar," Pupp Post,
 Spring 1954, p 14
"Puppetry," Belfast Ireland, Telegraph, Jan 13, 1941

"Puppetry in Ireland," Pupp, 12:38, 1941
Worth, Frank, "My Puppets in Ireland," Pupp 9:20-21, 1938

Israel - See also "Palestine"

Ben-Shaldom, David. "Bubstron Puppet Theatre at Givath
 Haim, Israel, Pupp J, 6:19, 23, 1954.
--- "From Givat Haim, Israel," Pupp J, 4(5):10, 16, 1953
"Bubatron Puppet Theatre, Kibbutz of Givat-Chaim," Pupp
 Th Mod World, p 227 and Illus. No. 196, 197
"Israel Puppets- A Grossman's Work," Brit Pupp Thea, 2
 (1):15, 1951
"Modjacot Shpulsyiddish Marionettes," Thea Arts, 10:383-84,
 1936
 See also "B-Gay Puppeteers" and Ann Cohen, U.S.A. -
 "Theatre" Section, "Plays" Section, Jewish Plays and
 much American Jewish community work.

Italy - See also "Sicily"

Note: Italy is most intersting for its unusual rod puppet of
 giant size. They are wonderfully balanced "warrior" puppets telling the story of Charlemagne. Any articles a-
 bout "Orlando Furioso" will usually be about puppets in
 this epic. Sicilian marionettes also use this epic. "Orlando," like "Punch" and "Kasperle" has given his name
 to a particular style of puppet and production. These

229

Italy (cont.)

large marionette-rod puppets require a very strong man
to manoeuvre them in bloody battles. They are found in
Italy, Sicily, Belgium, Argentina and New York. The
most famous family working them was and still is "Papa
Manteo's" family group, now of America. See also
"Argentina." The "Teatro Mazzini Cantania" deals with
this type puppet.

Other names to watch for in Italian research would be
"Pupazzi" Rod-"Paladin," Rod-"Burattini," String-
"Fantoocihi" and "Bamboochi," the 15th and 16th century
string puppets. Puppet history in Italy goes far back of
1 A.D. "The Fantoccini" lasted 100 years and was well
known in the 18th century. The very first puppet show-
man we have any record of was a Roman. See G.
Speaight's, History of English Puppet Theatre, London,
Harrap, 1955, Chapter 1, and D. Salme in the "French"
Division.

See also "Punch and Judy" Section introduction as
they still have a form of this in Pincio Park and in
Gianicolo Park as well as in the little villages. There
is only one main marionette theatre in Rome, today, it
is "Teatro Pantheon."

Adami, Giuseppe. Batocchie E Caviochio. Milano, Casa
Editrice Italia, 1920. In NN
"Adamo, Frank-Royal Marionette Man of Milan," Pupp J,
6:21, 1954
Agate, J. "Roman Marionnetes at New Scala Theatre,
London," R of Revus, 67:391-96, Ap 1923
Allacci, Leone. Drammaturgia. Rome, Vatican Library,
under Alessandro VII. It has some material on puppetry.
He was a librarian in the Vatican. In Vatican library.
Amicis, E. D. "A Celebrated Little Theatre of Torino,
Italy," Marionette, 1:237-50, Feb. 1918. These
are the Eurico Luigi Lupi Marionnets.
Baird, Bill. "Orlando Furioso." The Art of the Puppets.
New York, Macmillan, 1965, p 116-130 and passim.
Barberi, A. P. Burattini o Burattini. Bologna, Italy, Zani-
chelli, 1923. In Yale Univ. Lib.
--- Revu of Burattini o Burattini. Anon, Pupp, 12:4-6,
1941
Batchelder, Marjorie. trans. "A Bolognese Puppet Man,
1806-1872, Filippo Coccoli," Pupp 11: 1940
--- Rod Puppets and the Human Theatre. Columbus, Ohio
State Press, 1947, passim.

Beltrami, A.   Fantocci Alla Ribalta; Commedie Per Burat-
tini.   Milan, Ditta S. Majocchi, 1935. In Harvard Univ.
Lib.
Bernardelli, F.   "Per un Teatro di Marionette," Nuova
Antologia, series 6, 217:272-77, Ap 1, 1922
Bragaglia, A. G.   La Maschera Mobile... Foligno.   Rome,
Camitelli, 1926
--- Pulcinella.   Rome, Casini, 1953.   In NN.   Good bibli-
og. on p 523-97
Bufano, Remo.   "Marionettes March Once More," N Y Eve
S, Mr 9, 1917, p 10
--- "Puppets of Sicily and Italy," Thea G M   7:28, 31, S
1930.   See also "Puppeteer" Section this name.
"I Burattini Della Famiglia Ferrari-Theatre of Parma,"
Pupp Th Mod World, p 221 and Illus No. 60
Caldo, Joseffi.   "The Old Puppet Show is to be restored
to favor," N Y Times Mag, My 4, 1913, p 5
Calthrop, A.   "An Evening with Marionettes in Venice,"
Theatre, 3:245-48, My 1, 1884
Calvi, E.   "Marionettes of Rome,"   Bellman, 22:69-71,
Jan 20, 1917
Cardano, Gerolamo.   De Subtilate Rerum.   Bk XVIII, Rome,
1551, passim
Chiappini, F.   "Gaetanaccio, memorie per servire alla
storia dei burattini," Il Volgo Di Roma. Vol I, Rome,
1890, p 7-33.   In NN
Cimatti, Leone.   "The Children's Theatre in Italy," Intern
Ed R Cinemat, Rome,   2:420-34, 1950
Coppula, M.   Teatro dei Burattini.   Rome, Menaglia,
c 1930's
Correra, L.   D Presepe A Napoli.   Rome, L'Arte, 1899

Craig, Gordon.   "Burattini at Bologna," Graphic, London,
106:988, D 30, 1923
See also all issues of his periodical, Marionettes Tonight at 8:30, published for one year, 1918. This was
written while he was in Italy and would have much ma-
terial.   On microfilm in NN, almost entire year.
See also Other "Theatre" books written by him as he
will be constantly mentioning puppetry, for it was one of
his important hobbies.   His material while editor of
Pupp Master should be checked for Italian material.
See also "Publications" Section, this periodical.
Cuccoli, Angelo.   Il Dottore Innamorato... Teatro Di Angelo
Cuccoli No 8, Bologna, Libraria "Ancora," 1938
--- Teatro (Per Burattini) Di Angelo Cuccoli. No. 7.
Bologna, Libreria "Ancora," 1939

Italy (cont.)
--- --- No. 5. Bologna, Libraria "Ancora," 1939
--- --- No. 3. Bologna, Libraria "Ancora," 1939
--- --- No. 15. Bologna, Libraria "Ancora," 1939
--- --- No. 17. Bologna, Libraria "Ancora," 1939
This entire series in NN.
--- Teatro (Per Burattini) Di Angelo Cuccoli. No. 9.
Bologna, Libraria "Ancora," 1938
--- --- No. 10. Bologna, Libraria "Ancora," 1938
--- --- No. 13. Bologna, Libraria "Ancora," 1938
All in NN.
Culin, Stewart. "Italian Marionette Theatre,"J. Am. Folk-
lore, 3:155-57, Ap 1890
--- "An Italian Marionette Theatre in Brooklyn," Phil Publ
Led, Ap 19, 1890
"DePero, Signor; His Italian toys called Marionettes,"
Marionette, 1(6):196-97, 1918
Dickens, Charles. "Pictures from Italy," Marionette,
1(8):229-32, Feb 1918
Dilley, P. "Burattini, Marionettes that are not mechani-
cal," Drama, O-D, 1923, p 12-15, 101-103
Duchartre, Pierre L. Italian Comedy. trans. R. T. Weav-
er, London, Harrap, 1929, Chap 11
Faniculli, G. Il teatro di Takiû. Milan,

Ferrigini, Pietro. "History of Puppets," Mask 4:301-08, Ap
1, 1911, 5:111-40, O 12, 1912; 6:205-16, Jan 1914

--- (Yorick, pseud.) La Storia Dei Burattini. Florence,
Bemporad, 1912 first published 1884, Florence, (Tip.
Editrice del Fieramosca) Rev. ed. 1902 by Fieramosca.
In NN.
--- Vent'Anni Al Teatro. Vol. 1. "La Storia dei Burattini,"
Florence, Editrice Del Fieramosca, 1884
Festival   See also "Festival" Section

Films   See also "Films" Section

Fool, Tom (pseud.) "Burattini, Balogna" Marionette, 1(4):
98-104, Jan 1918
Foyne, Vera. "Dancing Dolls of Destiny," Ch Sci Mon, A
slipping, undated, in Puppetry clipping Files at Deering
Lib. , Northwestern Univ. , Evanston (between 1942-1950)
Frame, V. "Marionette shows of Little Italy," Theatre
6:175-76, Jl 1906
Gandolfi, G. Burattini Di Guerra. Italy, c 1940

Revu of Burattini di Guerra. Pupp, 12: 1941, p 4-6
Gentile, A. V. Burattini Interessanti. Milan, 1925
--- Teatrino Per Bamine E Faniculetti. Milan, 1922
--- Teatro Per Faniculli E Faniculle. Milan, 1925
Glackens, W. "Italian Rod Puppet Master Papa Pietro's
  Paladin Puppet Plays," Scrib, Ag 1899, p 173
Gleason, A. H. "S. Lo Cassio's Italian Paladin Puppet
  Show in New York," Collier's, O 23, 1909, p 16
Golding, Louis. "Marionettes in Palermo," Apollo, London,
  2: p 169-73
Goldoni, Carlo. "Goldoni's Glove and Rod Puppets of
  Florence," Pupp, 15:56-57, 1944
Graves, C. "Marionettes in Naples," Pupp Master 3(10):
  265, 1955
Gregorovius, F. "Roman Marionettes," Marionette 1:
  84-94, D 1918
Gutman, Walter. "Orlando Furioso at Manteo's Theater,"
  Thea G M, 7:31-32, S 1930
Head, Cedric. "Paladin Puppets," Pupp 1(5):4, 1950

Holroyd, M. "Marionette Theatre in Italy," Nation & The
  Atheneum. London, 31:821, S 23, 1922
Howells, W. D. "Venice in 1862," Venetian Life. Chap 5.

Irwin, Elizabeth. "Where the players are Marionettes,
  Italian Puppets of New York," Craftsman, S 1907, p 677-
  79
"Italian Rod Puppets," N Y Times, O 20, 1895

"Italy," Pupp, 17:67, 1946, item only

"Italy's Hand Puppet War," Pupp 15:38, 1944

Jal, A. "Marionettes in Italy," Marionette, 1:374-77,
  Ag 1918
James, R. H. "Puppets in Palermo," Pupp Master, 4(4):
  262-63, 1955
Jerome, Lucy B. "Italian Puppet in California Puppet
  Show," New Eng Mag, Feb 1910, p 745
Jones, H. F. Castellinaria. London, 1911, p 93 and passim

Joseph, Helen H. "Romische Marionetten," Das Puppenth,
  1:177-81, 1924
Keller, A. I. "Paladin Puppets from Southern Italy,"
  Cent, Mr 1902, p 677
Kennard, J. S. "Italian Marionette Theatre History," in his
  Masks and Marionettes, New York, Macmillan, 1935
  in Boston Pub. Lib.

Italy (cont.)
Kick, Robert. "Paladins in Belgium," in "International News," Pupp J 2(1):21, 1950
King, H. B. "Marionettes at the Teatro Gerolamo," Thea Arts, 31:35-37, Jan 1947
La Rosa, F. S. "Vertichio and Nofvio," Pupp 2:52, 1931

Le Semainier. "Pupazzi," L'Illus, 87:pt 2, 820, D 28, 1929
Lee, V. Studies in the 18th Century in Italy. 1880, passim

Lees, D. N. "Puppetry in Florence," Pupp 3:15-16, 1932

Levinson, A. "A propos de Poupees. Le Théâtre dei Piccoli De Podrecca," Art Vivant, Paris, 5:49, 1929
Lewisohn, L. "Puppet show from the Teatro dei Piccoli," Nation, 117:331, S 26, 1923
Leydi, Roberto. Marionette E Burattini. Milan, 1958

Lieb, E. K. "Italian Enigma," Hobbies, 50:26, Jan 1946

Li Gotti, Ettore. Il Teatro Dei Pupi. Florence, Sansoni, 1957. In NN. Bibliog p 173-78.
"Lilliputian Variety Show: Podrecca's Piccoli Theater," Illus Lon N, 224:23, Jan 2, 1954
Lo Presti, Salvatore. I Pupi: Vagabondaggi Siciliani. Catania, Studio Editoriale Moderno, 1927. In NN
Lorenzini, Paolo. ... Don Florindo Ha Vinto Un Terno Secco. Firenze, "Deposito Edizioni" 1933
Ludington, L. A. "Teatro dei Piccoli," Pupp J, 15(3):11-13, 1963
Lyonnet, Henry. Pulcinella and Company. (Le Théâtre Napolitain) Paris, Société D'Editions Littéraires et Artistiques, 1901. In NN.
Maccioni, Signor. "Thirty years of puppets lost in flood of Milan," Pupp J, 19(2):26-27, 1967
Mackay, C. B. "Children's Plays in Italy," Drama, 18: 15-16, O 1927.
McPharlin, Paul. Puppet Theatre in America. New York, Harpers, 1949, passim
Maes, Constantino. Curiosita Romane. Rome, 1885.

Malamani, Vittorio. "Marionettes and Burattini in Venice, 18th Century," Marionette, 1:346-56, S 1918
--- "Il Teatro Drammatico le Marionette e i burattini a Venezia Nel Secola," Nuova Antologia, (lxvii, lxviii)
Manning, H. J. "Mr. Fagan's Roman Marionette Theatre in England," Mask, 9:41, 1923; 10:39, 1924

Manteo, Michael and Agrippino.   See Bill Baird, Art of
   the Puppet.   New York, Macmillan, 1965, p 125-29
   See also "Argentina" Division
"Marionettes at Milano," Marionette, 1:376-77, Ag 1918

"Marionettes at Venice," Marionette, 1:378, Ag 1918

"Marionette shows of Little Italy," Theatre, 6:175, Jl 1906

Marta, G. "Una Tradizione Che Si Rinnova; La Marionette
   De Podrecca," Empolum Instituto Italiano D'Arti Gratiche
   Bergano, 72:241-47, O 1930
Meadmore, W. S. "Behind the scenes with Italian Mario-
   nettes," Windsor, 71:235-40 (London) Jan 1930
Mejer-Graefe, Julias. Orlando Furioso. Berlin, Cassirer,
   1867, 1912 and 1935
Melling, J. K. "Milan Puppets," Pupp Master 5(8):22, 1958

Meltzerm, Charles H. "Dr. Podrecca's Italian Marionette
   Theatre," Theatre, 38:24-25, 48, O 1923
Menghini, M. "Il Teatro Dei Burattini; Tradizioni Cavel-
   leresche Romane," La Cultura Moderna, 1911, p 39-42,
   110-111
Morice, Gerald. "Opera dei Pupi," (In film form also)
   "Pupp Master, 3(4):124-28, 1950
"Multum in Parvo," Art Digest, 8:25, My 1934

Nascimboni, G. "Le Commedie D'un Burattinaio Celebre,"
   Il Marzocco, 15:9
Nathan, G. I. "Vittorio Podrecca's Theatre of the Piccoli,"
   Time 35:49, 1940; and Newsweek, 15:44-45, Ap 1, 1940
Nichols, F. H. "Italian Marionette Theatre in New York,"
   Century Illustrated Monthly 58(5):677-82, Mr 1902
Niessen, G. "Teatro Dei Piccoli," Die Verte Wand, 1927,
   p 18
Novelli, Enrico. Il Teatro dei Burattini. Rome, Scotti,
   1906 and 1925. In NN.
   Revu of Il Teatro dei Burattini. Anon, Pupp, 3:16, 1932
"Opera Dei Burattini-Theatre in Rome of Maria Signorelli,"
   Pupp Th Mod World, p 221 and Illus No 61.
Organizations. See also "Organization" Section

"Orlando Furioso." See A. Manteo

"Paladin Puppet Collector - Grace Weil, in Conn., U.S.A.,"
   Pupp J, 12(5B):4, 1961
Paltinieri, R. Il Teatro Dei Piccoli. Milan, Casa Editrice
   Italia, 1925. Texts of the Podrecca Theatre.

Italy (cont.)
Pandolfini, B. A. Puppets in Bologna Italy. Bologna,
Zanichelli, 1923. In NN.
Periodicals. See "Periodical" Section

Petito, Antonio. Conno Sterico Romantice Sulla Origine
Della Mascheia Del Pulcinella. Naples, Tipografia
Editrice Ferdinando Bideri, 1928. In Oberlin Univ. Lib.,
Oberlin, Ohio
Petrai, Giuseppe. "Italian Roman Marionettes of Filippo
Teoli," Marionette, 1:255-86, N 1918
--- Maschere E Burattini. Rome, 1885
--- La Spirito Delle Maschere. Torino, 1901
--- Revu of La Spirito Delle Maschere. Anon, Marionette,
1:284, N 1918
Picco, F. "La Scartafaccio di un Burattinaio," Bulletino
Storico Piacentino, 1: 1907
"Piccoli Puppets on T. V." Hartford, Conn. Hartford
Courant, TV Weekly Section, D 30, 1962, p 3.
See also Pupp J, 15(3):11-13, 1963
"Pinnochio Defeats Communism," Pupp J, 4(4):19-20, 1953

Podrecca, Vittorio. "Exposing our human foibles," Lit D,
115:15, Feb 25, 1935
--- "Teatro dei Piccoli," Thea Arts, 7:295, O 1923
--- "Le Théâtre Des Marionettes," Cahiers Du L'Etcile,
Paris, 1929, année 2, p 232-35
See also Max Von Boehn, Dolls and Puppets. London,
Harrap, 1932, p 424-26
"Podrecca's Lilliputian Variety Show," Illus Lon N, 224:23,
Jan 2, 1954
Poignant, Roslyn. "Paladinis, Puppets and Painted Carts in
Sicily," Geographical Mag, London, 34(6):337-53, O 1961
Pullen, E. J. "At the Opera Di Li Pupi," Atlantic M, 73:
797-802, Je 1894
"Puppets in Italy," Pupp, 4:10, 1933; 5:36, 1934.

Quadrio, Francesco Saverio. Storia E Ragione D'Orgnipoe-
sia. Vol. III, pt 2. Milan, 1744; & Torino, Paravia,
1922, p 245-48. Partial trans. in G. Speaight History
of English Puppet Theatre, London, Harrap, 1955, p 36,
and is sig. m. In NN.
Racca, Carlo. Burattini E Marionette. Torino, Paravia,
1922 and a 2nd ed. 1925. In NN.
Ragus-Molerti, G. "Una sacra rappresentazione in un teatro di Marionette," Psiche, XIII, 3 [sic]
Randell, W. L. "Puppetry," Sat R, 135:563-67, Ap 28,
1923

--- The Roman Marionettes at the New Scala Theatre,"
R of Revus, London, 67:391-96 Ap 1923. Concerning V.
Podrecca's work.
Ricci, C. "I Burattini in Bologna," La Lettura, III, 11 [sic]
--- "Italy, The Burattini of Bologna," Marionette, 1:121,
142, 162, Je 1918; 1:166, D 1918.
Rosa, Frank S. "Vertichio and Nofrio," Pupp 2:52-54, 1931

Rota, A. "Marionette Veniziane," Emporium, Bergamo, 63:
361-73, 1926
Rousseau, Victor. "A Puppet Play which lasts two months,"
Harpers W, 52:15-16, O 3, 1906
Signorelli, Maria. I Burattinaio Perfetto. Rome, Avio, 1955.
In NN. Good bibliog p 51-52
--- "Puppets and Marionettes in Italy today," World Thea,
11:181-84, Summer 1962
--- "The Vitality of a Tradition," Pupp Th Mod World,
p 30-31. Author is director of one of the few "modern"
Italian puppet theaters in Rome, today.
Smith, W. "Rome plays with Puppets," Children's Royal,
Winter, 1921-'22
Sommers, A. E. "Smallest Theatre in the World," Frank
Leslie's Illustrated Newspaper, O 25, 1890, p 199
Speaight, George. "Italian Fantocchi and Opera, in England,"
p 129-42, in his History of the English Puppet Theatre.
--- "Italian Puppets," in his History of the English Puppet
Theatre. London, Harrap, 1955, p 35-40, passim
--- "Powell and Italian Opera," p 73-91, in his History of the
English Puppet Theatre.
--- "The Puppet Theatre of Cardinal Ottoboni," Theatre Re-
search, (Recherches Théâtrates), Rome, Vol 1(2):5-10,
Je 1958. In NN
Sperry, Margaret. "Pasquale Provenzano's Rod Puppets,"
N Y Tribune Mag Sect, Jan 27, 1924, p 5
Stendhal, "Puppets of Rome," Marionette, 1:287, N 1918
Stone, W. M. "Work of Italian Rod Puppet Master Comardo,"
Pupp, 9:23, 1938
Story, W. "Puppets of Rome," Mask, 5:326, Ap 1913
--- "Roman Puppetry," Mask, 4:323-26, 373, 1912
--- "Roman Puppets," Mask, 5:234, Jan 1913
"Teaching History, by Palidin Puppets," Kindg Pri, D 1908,
p 91
"Theatre dei Cuticchio and Son in Palermo," Pupp Th Mod
World, p. 221.
"Theatre dei Piccoli in America," Pupp 3: 1933
---N. Y. Times Mr 1940 22:2
"Theatre in Venice, 18th Century," Nuova Antologia, Mr 1897
Tichenor, G. "Marionette Furioso: A Marionette show in the

Italy (cont.)
    House of Agrippina Manteo, New York,"Thea Arts, 13:
        913-19, D 1929
Toldo, P. "Nella Baracca dei Burattini," Giornale Stori-
    codella Letterature Italiana, LI, 1908 [sic]
"Toy Paladin's in war-Pulcinella Booth," Pupp, 15:31, 1944

Trewin, J. C. "Continental Tour of Podrecca's Piccoli
    Theatre-London," Illus Lon N, 237:162, Jl 23, 1960
Uccello, Antonio. L'Opera Dei Pupi Nel Siracusano; Ri-
    cerche - Contributi," Archivio Storico Siracusano, Sira-
    cusa, 1962, Anno 7, p 119-137 [Sic]
Valle-Inclán, Ramón Del. Tablado de Marionetas. Madrid,
    Impranta Ribadeneyra, 1930. In Oberlin Univ.,Lib., Ober-
    lin, O.
    See also "Spain" Division as there may be some overlap-
    ping of material by other authors.
"Venetian Marionettes," Mask, 10:72, 1925

"Venetian Marionettes," (Frontispieces-1772) Mask, 6: 1913

Veni-Vedi. "Podre Coa's Piccoli Theatre," Pupp Master,
    3(6):232, 1955
Volpi, Luigi. "Il Teatro Di Gioppino," Rivista di Bergamo
    (Bergamo) 1932, Anno 11, p 253-58
Walpole, H. "Signo Podrecca's Piccoli," Spect, 152:882,
    Je 8, 1934
Weitenkamf, Dr. Frank. Manhattan Kaleidoscope. New York,
    p 226
Wells, F. C., Jr. "Marionettes; Quaint Folk," World Outl,
    3:21, O 1917
Wheddon, Bronx. "An invasion of the Salici Puppets,"
    Pupp Thea, (England)](5):19, 1950
Whipple, L. "Italy sends us Marionettes of Rome Buffano,"
    Survey, 58:43-44, Ap 1, 1927
Yambo,   . Il Teatro dei Burattini. Milan, Casa Editrice
    Italia, 1925
Yorick, P. F. (pseud.) "History of Puppets," Mask, 6:129-
    33, 297-305, 1913
--- "Italian Puppetry," Mask, 6:17-32, 1913
--- "Italian Puppets," Mask, 5:248-66, 308-12, 1912
    See also Ferrigini
Young, S. "Good Hope Notes; The Piccoli Theatre," N Repub,
    73:295, Jan 25, 1933

Note: Puppets are often referred to as "dolls" instead of puppets in this country, but do not confuse them with the "doll" that is generally meant by this term in other countries. The puppet theatre may be called, "Doll Theatre," "Bunraku," "Bunraku-za Theatra," "Ningyo Stage" or any of the following names, all of which should be investigated for overlap of material:

"Bunraku" - 3.5 ft. to 4 ft. rod puppet, most important puppet style, needing two hooded assistants besides the main operator, who works in plain sight of audience.

"Bunraku-za" - Remaining puppet theatre of 20th century, at Osaka, Japan.

"Ho-Ayatsuri" - String type of marionette.

"Jōruri" - Puppet Play Reciter, also name of an early theatre which came into the old drama at end of the 16th century and was quite strong around 1610. A reciter of script.

"Kabuki" - Live actors, "Kaboki" - puppet actors.

"Kugutsu" - very, very early puppets, 1000 A.D. of the traveling puppet turners, "Kugutsu-mawashi."

"Kami-Shibai" - a paper doll show, but not real puppet, could be Japanese version of the English "Paper Theater" or "Penny plain, Two Pence colored" type puppet work.

"Kuruma Ningyo" - rare wheel puppets of the 19th century.

"Ningyo-Shibai" - puppets and marionettes, of very simple construction and usually with musical work.

"Osaka Theatre" - The 1955 main puppet theatre, more or less hand and rod style at Osaka, Japan.

"Origami puppet" - The art of Japanese paper folding, but with the word "puppet" added it means a manipulation figure, probably used with the "Kami-Shibai" theatres.

"Puk Theatre" - Marionette and Hand puppet theatre of 1923 and revived today, director being Taji Kawajiri.

Japan (cont.)

"Samisen" - a helping player to puppets main operator.

    The scholar will have to go back to early feudal times
for the start of Japan's puppetry of hand, string and rod
styles. The "Golden Age" of puppetry in Japan was 1710-
1760 in Old Tokyo. The revival began with 1872 and continued into the 19th century. Intensive study of these periods
and study of the 10th century A.D. under the word "Kugutsu,"
a wandering low-class player for fishermen and farmers will
be necessary. This minstrel-like puppeteer kept puppetry a-
live until the 16th century when it became the traditional musical puppetry called, "Ningyo Joruri." Valuable puppet material will be found in ancient poems, paintings, and carv-
ings as often as in written works. The following is a very
limited list.

Alcott, Henry. "Modern Puppetry in Japan," Pupp J, 15(6):
    12-13, 1964
Amaral, L. "Japanese Puppets," Pupp Master, 5(4):13-17,
    1957
"Automatic Puppets Made by Japanese," N Y Times, Mr 23,
    1930, 5:23
Avery, Verna. "Music for the Marionette Theatre-Japan,"
    Pupp J, 2(3):2-4, 1950
"Awaji Island Traditional Puppet Group, The Awaji-Ningyo-
    Za," Pupp Th Mod World, p 228 and Illus No. 231
    See B. Baird
Baird, Bill. The Art of the Puppet. New York, Macmillan,
    1965, p 132, 135-39, and 140, 250 under "Bunraku".
    Well illustrated material.
Batchelder, Marjorie. See also "Rod Puppets" Section
    There will be passim material in her writings concerning
    rod puppet work.
Bénazet, Alexander. Les Marionettes, Le Théâtre Au Japan.
    Paris, Le Roux-at-the-Sourbonne, 1901
Berge, Ted (Jack). "Puppetry in Japan," Pupp J, 3(3):10-11,
    1951
Berthelson, Larry. "Review of the Bunraku Puppet Theatre,"
    G N Y Pupp G Newsl., 3(3&4):6, 1966
"A Brief Report on Japan's Television Puppet Use," Time,
    1953, c Jan-Feb. issue.
"Bunraku Company on British T.V.," Brit Pupp and M Thea
    G Newsl, 147:3-4, Jl-Ag 1968
"Bunraku-Doll Theater, Seattle World's Fair," Pupp J, 14(2):
    3-4, 1962

"Bunraku-National Theatre," Brit Pupp and M Thea G Newsl, 143:2, 1968. (Historical material from Stanislavsky's My Life in Art.)

"Bunraku Theatre in America," Newsweek, Mr 28, 1966 p 88 --- Pupp J, 17(4):29, 1966; 17(6):34, 1966.

"Bunraku-Za" Pupp, 3: 1932

"Bunraku-Za Mask," Pupp Th Mod World, p 228 and Illus No. 232

Chatani, Hanjirō. A Book on Puppets (In Japanese) In LC

Cheney, Sheldon. Japanese and Javanese Puppets-The Theater. London, Longmans, 1929 and rev. ed. London, Tudor, 1949

Chikamatsu Monzayemon. Masterpieces of Chikamatsu, The Japanese Shakespeare. trans. A. Miyamori and revised by R. Nichols in Nichols, Japanese Drama. New York, Dutton, 1926. In Boston Pub. Lib.
--- Masterpieces of Chikamatsu. trans. Miyamori and revised by K. Paul, London, Trench, Trubner. In Northwestern Univ., Deering Lib., Evanston and Oberlin Univ. Lib., Oberlin, O.
--- --- trans. by Donald Keene, London, Taylor's Foreign publ., 1951.

Cochrane, M. L. "The Japanese Doll Theater, Bunraku-za," Travel, 41:16-17, 36, S 1923

Craig, Gordon. "Japanese Marionettes," Mask, 7:104-07, My 1915

Denison, H. L. "Classic Puppets of Japan," Pupp J, 5(2): 9-11, 19, 21, 1953

Dunn, C. J. "The Early Japanese Puppet Drama." Unpublished thesis, London, Univ. of London, 1965 with bibliog p 149-151
--- The Early Japanese Puppet Drama. London, Luzac, 1966. In NN, and Mystic, Conn., L. Verry, 1966

"Doll Theatre Masters, New York Debut of Japanese Bunraku Puppet Theatre," Newsweek, 67:88, Mr 28, 1966

"Doll Theatres of Old Japan," Mask, 12:104-06, Jl 1927

Drummond, K. R. "Bunraku-za," Pupp Post, Spring 1951, p 4-5

Elliott, Archie. "My Visit To (The Master Puppeteer) Takeda," Pupp J, 17(5):7-9, 1966

Fleming, T. R. "Japanese Drama," Drama, 20:15-16, O 1929

Gakuya Zuya. Marionette 1:118, 125, Jan 1918. The original was published in Osaka, c 1800.

Japan (cont.)
Gidayu, Nempyō Hensankai.   A Book on Puppets (In Japanese)
    See, Lib. of Congress Subject Catalogue 3:256, 1963.
    In Calif. Univ. , East Asiatic Lib.
Gowen, H. H.   "The Old Drama in New Japan, " Drama,
    14(6):207-10, Mr-Ap 1924
Haar, Frances.   Japanese Theatre in Highlight. c 1954
    Rutland, Vt. , Tuttle, 1952, 1954
Hagemann, Carl.   Die Spiele Der Völker. Berlin, Fischer,
    1912 and 1921
Harnoll, Phyllis.   The Oxford Companion to the Theatre.
    New York, Oxford Univ. Press, 1951, p 411-15
Hiroichi, Y.   See S. Seijiro
Hirokawa, Kiyoshi.   A Puppet Book (In Japanese) in LC
    Subject Catalogue 1965
Hironaga, Shuzaburo.   Bunraku: An Introduction to the Japa-
    nese Puppet Theatre.   Rutland, Vt. , Tuttle, 1959
--- Bunraku, Japan's Unique Puppet Theater.   Tokyo, Tokyo
    News Service Ltd. , c 1959. In NN.rev. ed. 1964, Boston
    Pub. Lib.
    Revu of Bunraku, Japan's Unique Puppet Theater.   by M.
    B. McPharlin, Pupp J, 16(5):26, 1965
"Historians and Collectors in America, " Pupp J, 12(3):26,
    1960
"A History of Puppets in Japan, " Mask, 6:217-20, Jan 1914

"Hitomi-Za" - Television puppet film of 1963-'64, " Pupp
    Th Mod World, p 228, and Illus No 234
    "The Little Samurai Kagomara. "
Hughes, Glenn.   "The Rise of Doll Play, " - Story of the
    Theatre. New York, French, 1928, p 20-24
Hunda, Isou.   Origami, How To Make the Japanese Art of
    Paper Folding. New York, McDowell, 1959, passim
Inverarity, R. B.   "Indian and Asiatic Puppets, Japanese, "
    Pupp, 4:27-30, 1933
Ishiwari, Matsutara.   "Puppet Play in Osaka, " Travel in Ja-
    pan, 2(1): Spring 1936
--- Japanese Puppets.   Tokyo, Japanese Tourist Bureau
    Publication, c 1936
    Revu of his, Japanese Puppets.   Anon. , Travel in Japan,
    23(8): Aug.
"Japan's Puppets. " Deering Lib. , Northwestern Univ. , Evan-
    ston, "Puppet Clipping File. " Many undated, unheaded
    articles about Japan.
"Japanese Legend of Origin of Puppetry, " Japan Advertiser,
    N 22, 1936, p 9
"Japanese Puppet Show in New York, Kami-Shibai, " N Y

Times, My 10, 1959 VI 50:3
"Japanese Puppet Theatre," Marionette, 1:118, 125, 127,
   Jan 1918
"Japanese Puppetry," Pupp, 1:30-32, 1930

"Japanese Puppets," Mask, 10:20, 1924; Pupp, 5:36, 1934

"Japanese Working Drawings for A Puppet Man," Marionette,
   1(5):5-8, 1918; 1:175-76, 182-83, 197, D 1918; 1:207-208,
   223, Jan, 1919; 1:233-34, 257, Feb 1919.
Jiro Nan-e (Kyoto-Fu). "Puppets," Pupp 4:60-61, 1933

Joly, N. J. Random Notes... On Early Forms of Theatre in
   Japan.
"Kabuki" See Z. Kincaid

"Kami-Shibgi Theaters, Japan," Pupp, 17:67, 1946

Kanagawa, Bunrau. A Puppet Book (In Japanese). See
   LC Subject Catalogue, 3:378, 1965
Katsumata, Senkichiro. See Waseda Eisaku

Kawajiri, Taiji. "Puppetry in Japan," Pupp Th Mod World,
   p 41-42. He is director of the famous modern puppet
   theatre, "The Pux" in Tokyo.
Keene, Donald. Battles of Coxinga. (Cambridge Oriental
   Series No. 4) London, Univ. of Cambridge Press, 1956.
--- Bunraku: The Art of the Japanese Theatre. 1st ed.
   Tokyo, Kodansha Intern, 1965, and Rutland, Vt., Japan
   Publications, 1965. In NN. Good bibliog, p 279-80
   Revu of Bunraku: The Art of the Japanese Theatre.
   N Y Times, S 19, 1965, 7:7
Kincaid, Zoe (Zal). "Artists of the Ningyo Stage," Asia,
   38:341-45, Je 1938
--- "Japanese Doll-Drama, A Form of Marionette Show,"
   Illus Lon N, 179:1056-058, D 26, 1931
--- Kabuki-The Popular Stage of Japan. London, Macmillan,
   1923 and 1925, Chap. 16.
--- "The Puppets in Japan," Thea Arts, 13:207-10, Mr 1929
--- "With the Puppet Players of Japan," Japan, (San Fran)
   15:5-8, Jl 1926. In NN.
Kirstein, Lincoln. Bunraku. New York, Dunetz & Levett,
   1966. In LC
Kōri, Torahiko. "Kanawa: The Incantation." A Marionette
   Play With Comments. London, Gowans, 1918
--- "Kanawa: The Incantation" in C. M. Martin's, Fifty One-
   Act Plays. London, 1934, p 853-64

Japan (cont.)
Kure, B.   Historical Development of the Marionette Theatre
in Japan.   New York, Columbia Univ. Press.
"Legend of Puppetry, " Pupp, 12:21, 1941

Leiter, Samuel L.   "Authentic Kabuki, American Style, "
Theatre Crafts, S-O, 1968
Lep, H. M.   "September 1931, Osaka and Japan's Puppetry
to November 1931, " Pupp, 12:19-22, 1941
Lombard, F. A.   Outline History of Japanese Drama.   Bos-
ton, Houghton, 1929, passim
McGee, Betty.   "The Japanese Puppet Theatre, " Ed Thea J,
Columbia, Mr 1951, p 44-48
McPharlin, Marjorie B.   See   S. Hironaga

"Manai-Za (Oita Pre, Kyushu) - The Great Puppeteer With
Puppets, "   See   Pupp Th Mod World, p 228 and Illus No.
230
March, B.   "Bunraku-za Japanese Puppet Theatre, " Pupp,
3:60-64, 1932
Marin, C. M.   See   T. Kōri

"Masks of Asani-Gennojyo-za (Tokushima Pre, Shikoku), "
Pupp Th Mod World, p 228, and Illus No 229
Maurenbrecher, E. W.   De Panakawan-figuren in de Cheri-
bonsche Wajang Ojawa; Jogjakarta, Indon, Tijdschrift Van
Het Java-Institute, 1939, Joarg. 19, p 187-90.   In NN.
Maybon, Albert.   The Marionettes; Le Théâtre Japonais.
Paris, Laurens, 1925
Michael, Vivian.   "The Bunraku Theater, " Pupp J, 18(2):8-
9, 1966
Miller, Roy A.   See   S. Onishi
--- See Saito Seijīro
--- trans. by Seijiro. Masterpieces of Japanese Puppets.   Rut-
land, Vt. , Tuttle, c 1959
Miyajima, Tsunso.   Théâtre Japanais de Poupées; (Contribu-
tion à l'Etude du Théâtre Japanais de Poupée. Paris,
En Vente aux Presses Univ. De France, 1928 and 1931
In NN and McGill Univ. Lib (Canada)
---"Puppetry of Japan. " Pupp, 2:34-36, 1931
Miyake, S.   "Training for Bunraku, " World Thea, 14:477-
79, S 1965
Miyamori, Asatario.   Masterpieces of Chikamatsu.   trans.
K. Paul, London, Trench, c 1920.   Trans. again and rev.
by R. Nichols, New York, Dutton, c 1927
Available, Northwestern Univ. Deering Lib. and McGill
Univ. Lib. , Canada, Oberlin Univ. Lib. , Ohio.

--- Tales from Old Japanese Drama. New York, Putnam, 1912
"Mokuba-Za Puppet Theatre in Tokyo,"   Pupp Th Mod World, p 228 and Illus No. 238
Monzaemom, Chikamatsu. See Chikamatsu

Mori, Shinroku. A Puppet Book. (In Japanese) In LC Subject Catalogue 1966
Munsterberg, Oscar. "Japanese Marionette Plays and the Modern Stage," Marionette, 1:143-50, Je 1918
--- "Japanese Marionettes," Marionette, 1:229, Feb 1918

Nan-é, Jiro. "Japan," Pupp 5:36, 1934
--- "Japan's Puppetry," Pupp 4:60, 74, 1933
Nathan, J. "World's most expressive puppets-Japanese Bunraku," N Y Times Mag, Mr 13, 1966, p 34-35; Mr 16, 1966, 50:1; Mr 18, 1966, 35:1
Neil, S. "Puppets of Japan-Bunraku Theatres," Hobbies, 54:42, Ag 1949
Nichols, Robert. See A. Miyameri and Chikamatsu Monza-emom
"Ningy Joruri Bunraku-za," Pupp J, 16(5):26, 1965
The official puppet company of Japan since 1964 with the-atres in Osaka and Tokyo. New theatre, built in 1955 under Director Kyokai, seating 1000.
Noguchi, Yone. "Japanese Puppet Theatre," Arts and D, 13:328, O 1920
Oguri, Masaye. "Puppet Plays at St. Juke's Medical Center, Japan," Japan Christian Quarterly, 9(2): Spring 1934
Onishi, Shigetaka, and T. Yoshinaga. Bunraku-Za. Osaka, Tokyo, Kōdansha, 1959
See also R. A. Miller
Origami, How to Make. See I. Hunda

"Osaka Japan's Puppet Theatre-Bunraku," Thea Arts, 43(2): 16, Feb 1959
"Osaka, Japanese Puppet Theatre," N Y Times, My 1, 1960, 131:1
"Osaka Puppets Make a Visit," San Fran D Eve Bull, Feb 13, 1928
Paul, K. See A. Miyameri and Chikamatsu Monzaemom

Piper, Maria. Das Japanische Theater. Frankfurt, 1937. In British Museum.
--- Die Schaukunst Der Japaner. Berlin, 1927. In British Museum.
"PUK Theatre, Tokyo, (La Pupu Klube)", See Bill Baird The Art of the Puppet, p 140. Started by Toji Kawajiri,

Japan (cont.)
   revived under Taki Kawajiri
   See also Pupp Th Mod World, p 228, and Illus Nos 236-37
Puppeteers of Japan. See Puppeteers of America, Member-
   ship Directory. Ashville, O. , Puppetry J. , 1960
"Puppets in Japan," Tokyo Times, Jan 16, 1963
   Concerning the Takeda family, working in television pup-
   petry.
"Puppets in Japan," Thea Arts, 13:207-10, Mr 1929
--- Mask, 6:216-20, Jan 1913
Quennell, P. "Bunraku-za Puppet Theatre," N Statesman
   Nat, 2:167-68, Ag 8, 1931
Ridgeway, William (Sir) Dramas and Dramatic Dances of
   Non-European Races. New York, Macmillan, 1915
Rodriguez, P. "The Bunraku visits Los Angeles," Pupp J,
   14(2):4-5, 1962
Roger, D. "Japanese Wheel Puppets," Pupp 7:113-25, 1936

Ross, Peter. "Japan's Puppetry," Pupp, 17:67, 1946
--- "Japanese Theater of Paper-Kami-Shibai," Theatre Annu-
   al 1946, referred to in Pupp, 17:67, 1946
--- "War and the Japanese Theatre," Theatre Annual, NYC,
   1945, p 7-8
"Saibota Ninygyo-za, (Kochi Pre, Shikoka-Traditional Rod
   Puppets),"   Pupp Th Mod World, p 228 and Illus No.
   233
Saito, Sejiro. Kashira. (In Japanese)   LC Subject cata-
   logue, 3:378, 1965
Seijiro, Saito, Y. Hiroichi and Y. Tahao. ed. Masterpieces
   of Japanese Puppetry. Comment in English, adapted by
   R. A. Miller, Rutland, Vt. , Tuttle, 1958
Scott, A. C. The Puppet Theatre of Japan. Rutland, Vt. ,
   Tuttle, 1963
   Revu of The Puppet Theatre of Japan. by V. Michael,
   Pupp J, 15(4):32, 1964
   Revu of The Puppet Theatre of Japan, by M. B. McPhar-
   lin, Pupp J, 16(5):25, 1965
Shinkokai, K. B. La Poupée Japonaise. Tokyo, 1940

Sykes, J. "Japanese Puppets," Pupp Master, 5(9):22-23,
   1958
Tadafusa, Ōe. (1040-1111 A. D.) Kairaishi-Ki. Tokyo
   Chronicle of puppeteers, called "puppet turners."
Tahao, Yoshinaga. See S. Saito.

"Takeda-Ninguyze Theatre-Hand Puppets, Tokyo,"
   Pupp Th Mod World, p 228, and Illus No. 235
   Puppeteer is Kinasuke Takeda, but these are not at all

like western hand puppet mitten.
See also Pupp Life, S 1968, p 3 and Pupp J, 20(2&3):
16, 1968, illus.
"Take-meta-za Theatre, Osaka, Japan," Pupp J, 6(2):9-11,
1954. Director is Gidayu Takemoto.
Temko, F. "Origami Puppets," Gr Teach, 79:63, N 1961

Tenberge, Jacobus. "The Japanese Puppet Theatre," Pupp J,
3(3):2-3, 1951
Torahiko, Terada. The Living Puppets. New York, Japa-
nese Inst. In NN.
"Toyotake-za Theatre at Osaka, Rival of Tokyo's Theatre,"
Pupp J, 6(2):10, 1954. Called the "Literary Pleasure
Theatre."
Tilakasiris, Prof. Puppet Theatre in Asia. London, Dept.
of Cultural Affairs, 1964
Tyson, G. M. "History of Oriental Puppetry." Unpublished
Masters dissertation, Los Angeles, Univ. of Southern
Calif., 1932
Uchiyama, K. "Japanese Puppets," Pupp 5:36, 1934
--- "Puppets," Pupp, 4:30-32, 1933

Ueda, Makoto. "Japanese Theater," Ed Thea J, My 1960;
repeated in Pupp J, 12(1):28-29, 1960
"Uremura, Bunraku-Ken Theatre," since 1909, Pupp J, 6(2):
11, 1954
Utsusmi, Shigetaro. A Puppet Book. (In Japanese) In LC
Subject Catalogue, 1955
Vokoyama, Tadashi. A Puppet Book. (In Japanese) In LC
Subject Catalogue, 1964

Wallace, Lea. "East is West and West is East," Pupp J,
4(3):21, 1952
---"Reception for Bunraku players," N Y Pupp G Newsl.,
3(3&3):4-5, 1966. In NN

Waseda, E. "Japanese Puppet Plays," Tourist, Tokyo,
Ag, S. N. D. and Feb 1930-'31 issues.
--- Gleams from Japan. Tokyo, Japanese Tourist Bureau,
1937. In NN.
Watanbe, Yoshio. Bunraku-Za. Tokyo, Japan Photo Serv.,
1939. In NN.
Werntz, C. N. "Marionette Theatre of Japan," Our World,
5:58-59, Ap 1924
Yasuji, Wakatsuki. Study of the Puppet Jeruri. Tokyo

Yomiuri, Shimu. Tokyo, Newspaper giving much puppet information.
Yoshinaga, Takao. See S. Onishi

Java, See also "Oriental"

Note: Much of this material will be found under "Shadow,"
"Rod" and some in "Marionette" Section. The main puppet work is done with the first two forms. Many authors
treat Indonesia, Bali, Siam and other eastern countries
together in articles and books.

Books concerned with religious activities will have some
information as the priest is very often the puppeteer, because the legend has it that puppets took the place of Gods
on earth at one time. Only men see colored puppets,
women can see only the "Shadows" of the Gods. The religious belief that a real magic transpires between puppet
and audience and God is strong, so great beauty in carv-
ing, piercing, painting, and manipulating to music is de-
manded in this dramatic art. Puppet history goes back
1000 A. D. or earlier. Words to watch are:

Wjang-Kelitik - marionette type puppet not like western style.

Wayang-Gedog and Wayang-Purwa, Beber, Kerutjil - new
and old types of true shadow puppets

Wajang-puppen, Golek - popular hand puppet and rod type
puppet

Wayang Kulit - true shadows of leather from India

Wayang-Golèk - true rod style puppet, in round and having
form

Gunungan - leaf shape "tree of life" which opens performance.

Gamelan - orchestra, required, usually metallophones, Da-
lang-priest puppeteer
Wayang -Topeng - human actors.

"A. B. C." (pseud.) "Marionettes of Java," Marionette, Mr
1918, p 404-05
--- "On the Marionette Theatre in Java - The Wayang purwa
Shadow Theatre," Marionette, 1:209-22, Jl, 1918.
Avery, Verna. "Music for the Marionette Stage," Pupp J,
2(3):3, 1950
Baird, Bill. The Art of the Puppet. New York, Macmillan,
1965, p 56-61, passim
Banner, Hubert. "Java Is Shadow-Shows and the Kawi-
Epics," Lond Mer, Ag 1927 and My 16, 1928

Batchelder, Marjorie. Rod Puppets and the Human Theatre. Columbus, Ohio, Ohio State Univ. Press, 1947, Graduate School Monographs. Contribution in Fine Arts No 3. See also "Rod" Section and M. F. Verneuil

Blackham, Olive. Shadow Puppets. London, Rockcliff, 1960, p 18-42

Block and Coomaraswamy. "Javanese Theatre," Asia, Jl 1929

Cabaton, Antoine. Java, Sumatra and Other Islands. London, Leipsic, 1911

Cheney, Sheldon. Japanese and Javanese Puppets. London, Longmans, 1929 and London, Tudor, 1949

Commission for Popular Literature. ed. Vokslectuur. -Javanese Wayang Figures. Welstevreden, Indonesian Printing Office, 1919. In NN

Craig, Gordon. "Javanese Marionettes or Wayang Figures," Mask, 6:283-85, Ap 14, 1913

Cuisinier, Jeanne. Le Théâtre D'Ombres à Kelanton. Paris, Gallimard, 1957

Damais, L. C. "Shadow Theatre in Java and Bali," World Thea, 14:448-94, S 1965

"F. H. K." (pseud.) See "Shadow" Section

Foyne, Vera. "Dancing Dolls of Destiny," Ch Sci Mon, clipping undated (bet. 1947-50) in "Puppet File," Deering Lib., Northwestern Univ. Sig. m. but without date or page note.

Goldmann, Wilhelm. ed., Javanische Schattenspiele. Leipzig, Goldmann.

Gronemann, J. "Das Meisseln der Ledernen Wajang-Puppen der Javaner in der Vorstenlanden," Intern Arc Für Ethnog, 21: 1913

Guest, L. P. "Javanese Rod Puppets." Pop Sci, 33:65, S 1938

Gulik, R. H. Von. See "Indonesia"

Hall, M. P. "Java's Dancing Shadows," Overland Monthly, Jl 1928

Hardjewirogo, R. Sedjarah Wajang Purwa. Djakarta, Balai Pustaka, 1949. In LC

--- Sedjarah Wajang Purwa. Djakarta, 1952

Hazeu, G. A. J. "Eine Wajang-Beber-Verstellung in Jogjokarta," Intern Arc Für Ethnogr, 16: 1904

Heine, C. See "Shadows" Section

Helsdingen, R. "The Javanese Theater: Wayank-purwa and Wayang-gedog," Royal Asiatic Society, Straits Branch, Journal. (Singapore) 65:19-28, 1913

249

Java (cont.)
Holt, C. See P. Mangkunagore

Hover, Dr. Otto. "Javanese Shadow Stage," Lond Mer,
    Jan 1928
--- Javanische Schattenspiele. Leipzig, Goldmann, 1923.
    In NN.
Huges, Glenn. The Rise of Doll Play-Story of the Theatre.
    New York, French, 1928, p 20-24
Jacop, Georg See "Shadow" Section

Java and Madura, ed. by Javanese Foreign Office, New York,
    Historical Section Javanese Foreign Office, Handbook No
    82, p 24-29.
"Java's Puppets," Discovery, 18:184, Je 1937

"Javanese Marionette Play in Cleveland," Design, 38:36, Je
    1936
"Javanese Marionettes," Mask, 6:283-85, Ap 194; Marionette,
    1(3):32, Mr 1918; 1(4):Frontispiece, Ap 1918; 1(I):100 and
    Tailpiece; 1(7):Frontispiece, Jl 1818)
"Javanese Masks and Puppets," Coronet, 2:99-100, Jl 1934

"Javanese Puppets," Man, Jl 1939

"Javanese Topeng Dalang," Illus Lon N, 139:594, O 14, 1911

Jones, J. M. F. (Mrs.) "The Wayank Kulit of Java and Bali
    with particular reference to study material in England,"
    Man, S 1957, p 131-33
Journal of the Royal Asiatic Society. D 1936, p 287 -
    See A. Rentse
Juynboll, H. H. Het Javaansche Tooneel, Deer Dr. H. H. Ju-
    ynboll, Baarn, Drukkerij, 1915 (Serie 2, no 2) In NN
--- Wayank Kĕlitik Oder kĕrutjii. Baarn, Drukkeri, c 1915
    In NN
--- --- Intern Arch Für Ethnogr, 13:4-17, 97-119, 1900
Katachulam, C. Von See: C. Von Katachulam

Kats, J. Het Javaanische Tooneel, Door J. Kats. Weltevre-
    den, Commissie Voor De Volkslectuur, 1923. In NN
--- Programme of the Wayang-Wang for the Sultan. Welte-
    vreden, Koliff, 1923. In NN
Kunst, J. "Een En Ander Over De Javaansche Wajang,"
    Koloniaal Instituut, Amsterdam. (Modeeling, Amsterdam)
    53:1-12, 1940. In NN. Good illus. and bibliog.
La Valette, J. "Drama and Dancing in Java," Indonesian

Arts and Letters. London, 7:134-39, 1933
Lee, H. M. "Batavia, Java's Rural Shadow Show (Ag 2, 1931)" Pupp 12:18-19, 1941
Leebèr, J. A. Javaansche Shaduwbeelden. Amsterdam, Het Instuut, 1908
London Mercury. (Ag 1927) and (Oct 1932)

Maindron, Ernest. Marionettes Et Guignols. Paris, Juven c 1900. In McGill Univ. Lib., Canada.
Mangkunagere VII, Prince. On the Wayang Kulit-Purwa and Its Symbolic and Its Mystical Elements. trans., C. Holt. Ithaca, Cornell Univ., Far East Dept., 1957
Mechejen, C. Puppetry of Java. 2 Vols. (In Dutch) Gravenhage, Nijhoff, 1884 and Leiden, Brill, 1882. In NN.
--- and W. Bruning. Puppetry of Java (In Dutch) Batavia, 1879. In NN.
Mellema, R. L. Wayang Puppets, No. 48. Amsterdam, Royal Topical Institute, Dept. of Cultural and Physical Anthropology, 1954. Available at Corner Book Store, in NYC
Moons-Zorab, M. V. "Bimba and His Kin," Slvyter's Monthly (Datavia) 3:270-74, 1922. This is first Batavian periodical mentioned; investigation of it might bring more material.
Oberschall, M. de B. "Marionettes of Java," Beaux-Arts, 9:16, Mr 25, 1932. See Education Section
Oemartoo, Mr. See "Mills College," 1969

Olbrechts, F. M. Le Theatre Javanais: Les Marionettes Brussels. Brussels, Musees Royaux D'Art et Histoire, Bulletin No. 53, Vol 4, Jl 1932
"Origin of the Wayang Theatre," Royal Asiatic Society of Great Britain and Ireland, Journal. (Malayan Branch, Singapore. London, Je 1947, p 12-15. In NN
"Puppet Dolls-West Javanese Puppet Show," Hobbies, 57:53, Feb 1953
"Puppet Types in Java," Pupp, 6:113-17, 1935

"Puppets New in Java," Science, 6:251-52, S 1885

Raffles, Sir Thomas S. History of Java. London, Black, 1817, and London, Murray, 1830, p 374-78
Rehm, Hermann S. Das Buch Der Marionetten. Berlin, Frensdorf, 1905
--- First Book on Shadow Theatre of Java-The Wayang-Purwa. Berlin, Allgenmeiner Verein für Deutsche Literatur
--- Revu of Book on Shadow Theatre, Marionette, 1:54, Mr 1918

Java (cont.)

Rentse, A. "The Kelantan Shadow Play (Wayank Kulit),"
Royal Asiatic Society of Great Britain and Ireland, Journal... (Malayan Branch, Singapore Journal) London, D
1936, p 284-301

Ridgeway, William Sir. Dramas and Dramatic Dances of
Non-European Races. New York, Macmillan, 1915

Schüller, Sepp. "Das Javanische Wajang-Schattenspiel,"
Atlantis, Zürich, 7:78-80, 1935

Serrurier, L. De Wayang-Purwa. London, Brill, 1896. In
NN.

Shawn, Ted. "Puppet Play of Java," Gods Who Dance.
New York, Dutton, 1929

Siswoharsolo, See also "Wayang Plays" in "Plays" Section.

Soemosapoetro, R. See also "Plays" Section, under "Wayang Plays."

Stewart, M. A. Boys and Girls of the Orient. St. Louis,
Webster, 1946, p 203-05

Stewitts, J. J. "Java, The Home of Orchestral Drama,"
Thea Arts, 13:187-191, Mr 1929

Stutterheim, U. F. Cultuurges Chiedenis Van Java in Beeld.
Weltevreden, Java Institute, 1926. In NN.

Subandric, Dr. H. "The Shadow Play in Java," Pupp Master,
3(1):27-31, 1950. Sig. m. personalized with detail on
music.

Tace, . ed. De Wajangvorhalen; Van Pålå-Sårå (Javanese
Puppet Plays) Gravenhage, Nijhoff, 1869

Tedjohadisumarto, R. See "Plays" Section, under "Wayang
Plays"

"Theatre in Java," Illus Lon N, 134:383, Mr 13, 1909

Verneuil, M. P. "Javanese Theaters, Wayangs," Art and D,
45:119-28, Mr 1924. Trans, M. Batchelder in Pupp c
1924

Von Katachulam, G. "Javanese Theatre," Theatre, Banga-
lore, 1:13-19, 1931

Wagner, F. A. The Art of Indonesia-The Island Group of
Java, Bali. New York, Greystone, 1967. Unusually good
illus. and material.

"Wajang, Javanese Puppet-Shadow Picture Show," South Sea
Association Bulletin. Tokyo, Feb 1941, p 35-43

Wayang and Education. A periodical published by Indonesian
Embassy, 1958, passim material on puppetry.

Wignjowirjanta, Pedalangan Djangkep Sedalu Muput. Sala,
Keluraga Suebarno, 1964

Korea

Note: Puppetry in this country is 2,000 years old, with a
strong period from 900 A.D. to 1400 A.D. The name to
watch for is "Kokdoo Kakshi," this is a musical, satiric,
puppet show from 1392 to 1910. At that date it was
stopped by the Japanese, but is springing up again. It is
something of the order of the satiric "Punch" of England.
Rods and Marionettes are used. In Seoul the main puppet
center is called "Ko Kyu Whan," local papers will have
material about it.

"D. P. R. K. Government Puppet Group," Pupp J, 10(1):3, 1958

"Ko Kyu Whan Puppet Center, Seoul," is located at 13 Pan
8 Tong, San 6, Po Kwang Dong, Yong-Sana Ku, Seoul,
Korea. The director invites questions for material about
Korean puppetry.
"Korean Puppetry," Pupp J, 10(1):4-6, 1958

Metzger, Berta. Organized puppet groups in Korea in 1940.

Michael, Vivian. "Letter From Korea," Pupp J, 15(5):35,
1964
Whan, Ko Kyu. "Puppetry in Korea," Pupp J, 17(4):11-12,
1966

Labrador

"Animal Rescue League in Labrador Uses Marionettes,"
Bost Eve Trans, 27: Jl 1933
Phillips, B. Maude. "Labrador learns through puppets,"
Pupp, 11:6, 1940

Lebanon

Beirut College for Women. Beirut, Lebanon, Care of the
Education Dept., P. O. Box 235, does puppetry program
work.

Malaysia - See also Indonesia

Note: This material overlaps with "Bali, Java and Oriental"
divisions. The "Shadow" and "Rod" Sections will be helpful as much of their work is in these two forms. Shad-

Malaysia (cont.)
    ows are called, "Wayank Kulit," while their 18th century
    Rod and String puppets were called "Munoco Titers."
    See also "Shadows" under Mel Helstein.

Baird, Bill. The Art of the Puppet. New York, Macmillan,
    1965, p 250
Harnell, Phyllis. "Malaya," Oxford Companion to the The-
    atre. London, Oxford, p 727-28
"Helen T. Tacchi's Work in Malaya," Brit Pupp Thea, 2(1):
    15, 1951
"Malaya Shadows-A Brief Note," Pupp, 17:67, 1946

"Malay Shadows," Nat Geo, Nov 1963, p 746

Rohman, N. K. Abdul. One of their great Shadow workers,
    at Univ. of Calif. at Los Angeles, 1969.

Mexico

Note: Mexico has done a great deal with educational puppets
    and the Government Educational Dept. can furnish infor-
    mation as to articles, puppeteers and locations in which
    to investigate.

    Mexico City has a, "Calle De Fenere" (Street of Pup-
    pet Shows) which will be spoken of quite often in the local
    papers. The word to watch for will be "Titeres," their
    word for puppets. They use all forms but do little Shad-
    ow work. See also "Spain."

Acevedo Escobedo, A. Ya Viene Gargonio Espaarza. Mex-
    ico City, 1944. In NN. History and plays and puppetry
    work under R. Lago.
Altimirano, Maestro. "Puppet Article," La Republican.
    See Pupp Th Am, by Paul McPharlin, p 245
    This article speaks of "Teatre Del Seminaro," in 1880
    and about the Aranda Brothers group.
Avila, F. A. Pupp J, 18(5):44, 1967, item only about his
    work with puppets for "Institute Jalisicense De Ballas
    Artes" at Guadalujara, Mexico.
Ayala, Siska. "About Teatre De Las Artes," Pupp, 12:39
    1941.
Baird, Bill. The Art of the Puppet. New York, Macmillan,
    1965, p 26, 240, 245

Batchelder, Marjorie. "Mexican Puppetry," Players, 21:24, Jan 1945
Beloff, Angelina. "Mexican Puppetry Articles," (a series) Chapulin Mag, 1942, published by Secretary of Public Education, Mexico City.
--- Munecas Animados, Historia. Mexico City, Secretary of Public Education, 1945. In NN and Harvard Univ. Lib.
Berg, Harriet. "People," Grapev, Feb 1949, p 5

Campos, Armando de Maria-y. "Mexican Puppet Plays of I. T. Orellana and A. M. Orellana," Pupp 13:32-33, 1942
--- "Mexican Puppetry," El Nacional, (newspaper of Mexico City) 1940, a series of articles. See also Pupp, 11:36, 1940.
--- Presencias De Teatre. Mexico City, 1929
--- El Teatre Mexicano De Munecos. Mexico City, Orellana, 1941. Available at Corner Book Store, NYC.
Campos, Reuben M. El Folklore Literarie De Mexico. Mexico City. Secretary of Public Education, 1929, p 211-216, 257-85.
Castro, Hector. Mexican Children and Toys. (puppet work) trans. Ruth Paye, Mexico City. Fischgrund, 1949

Coe, A. M. "Notes on Puppetry in Mexico," Hispania (Monasha, Wis.) 28:199-207, My 1945. In NN
Comino, . "Mexico's means of spreading mass education," Time, 44:84, D 25, 1944
Cordry, Donald. "The Aranda Puppets in Mexico City," Pupp, 17:27, 1946
--- "Mexican Diary," Pupp, 7:20-22, 1936
Cueto, A. Mexican Folk Puppets. Detroit, Puppetry Imprints, 1941. In McPharlin Collection.
--- "Origin and History of Puppetry in Mexico," Sch Arts, 47:311-13, My 1948
--- "Puppet Theatre in Mexico," World Thea, 14:458-94, S 1965.
--- "Titeres Populaires Mexicano," Pupp, 11: 1940
Diaz, Bernal. 16th Century Spanish author. He mentioned puppetry in Mexico with Indian tribes. See Paul McPharlin Pupp Th Am, p 9.
Education work. See also "Education" Section

Escobedo, Antonio Acevedo. I Ya Viene Gorgonio Esparza, Mexico City, (Sobretire del Annuarie de la Sociedad Folklorica de Mexico) IV, 1944 [sic]
Films. See "Film" Section

Garcia, Icazbalceta J. See J. G. Icazbalceta

Mexico (cont.)
Guillermo, Prieto. Memorias. Mexico City.

Holmes, Kathleen. "Construction and use of Marionettes-
Spanish American Children." Unpublished Master's disser-
tation, Austin, Univ. of Texas, 1938
--- "Mexican children taught puppetry in a Texas school,"
Pupp 11:25-31, 1940
Icazbalceta, Jaaquip Garcia. Los Coloquies De Gonzales
Eslavia. Mexico City, 1877. In British Museum.
Lago, Roberto. Director of "Teatre Rin Tin," in 1934,
Mexico City.
--- "Government Supported Puppetry," Pupp, 11:35-36, 1940
--- "The Institute of Fine Arts, Mexico," Brit Pupp Thea,
1(4):4, 1950
--- "Mexican Folk Puppets," Pupp, 13-14:38, 1942-43.
--- Mexican Folk Puppets, Traditional and Modern. Detroit,
Puppetry Imprints, 1941.
--- "Mexican Puppetry has had a bad year," Pupp, 12:38-
39, 1941
--- "Mexican Puppets, Roberto Lago Writes," Grapev, N
1948, p 11-12, and Ap 1949, p 16-17
--- "R. Lago with Visual Aids Dept. of Mexican Govern-
ment." Pupp J, 14(4&5):28, 1963
--- "Titeres Populares Mexicanos," Cuadernos Ameri-
canoes, Mexico 31(1):191-97, 1947
---- "Tour of the U.S.A., Pupp, 15:39, 1944
Lauterer, Arch. "Humanettes in Mexico," Thea Arts, 20:
247, Ap 1936
Lawrence, Gilbert. "Mexico's Fighting Puppets," New
Masses, N 21, 1944, p 30
Leeper, Vera. "Helping Lago in Mexico," Pupp J, 11(5):
23, 1960
List, Arzubide, G. See "Punch and Judy" Section

McPharlin, Paul. Puppet Theatre in America 1524 to Now.
New York, Harpers, 1949. See "Index," has much ma-
terial on Mexico and its puppeteers, p 69, 221, 239, 317-
18, 241-43 particularly good.
--- Repertory of Marionette Plays. New York, Harpers,
1929, p 22
Magmin, Charles. Historie des Marionnettes in Europe.
Paris, Lévy, 1852, 1862. Unusually good material about
Mexico.
"Marionettes in Mexico," Pupp, 3:27, 1932

Maximilian, Emperor. See also Paul McPharlin's, Pupp
Th Am, p 241-43

"Mexican Puppetry," Pupp, 9:61, 1938; 17:67-68, 1946.

"Mexico's Puppets," Pupp, 17:46, 1946

Michael, Vivian. "El Teatra Nahucil," (Mexico Puppet The-
ater), Pupp J, 14(3):12-14, D 1962.
National Mexican Convention of Educational Puppetry, Mexico
City. Pupp, 11:36, 1940
Organized by Head of Theater Section, Armando De
Marja Y Campos at the Palace of Fine Arts. Other such
conventions have been held regularly.
"National Puppet Theatre," Pupp, 11:35, 1940. Organized
under R. Lago and R. De Cueto, 1934, and still under
their leadership in 1940.
Oppenheim, Beatrice. "Good Neighbor Puppets Teach Mexi-
can Farmer," Ch Sci W, D 1943, p 10-11.
Orallana, Idlefense. See A. Campos

Organizations. See "Organizations" Section

Parsons, Lewis. "A Visitor in Mexico," Pupp J, 5(5):3-6,
1954.
Payo, Ruth (or Poyo) See H. Castro

Pietro, G. "Function Estraordinaria..." in his Memorias.
Mexico City.
Poore, Charles. "Dramatic Puppet Activity in Mexico,"
Ch Sci Mon, O 4, 1941, p 14
Puppeteers of Mexico. See Puppeteers of America Direc-
tory. Ashville, O., (yearly) Puppetry Journal Publica-
tion.
"Puppet Pedagogy; Comino, Mexico's most popular puppet,"
Time, 44:84, D 25, 1944
"Puppets of Mexico," Pupp, 10:38, 1939

Pusada, Jose G. Published puppet plays and material in
Mexico City 1864-1916. See also Pal McPharlin's,
Pupp Th Am, p 253
Ramirez, Gilberto. Directed Hand Puppet Group work for
Municipal Dept. of the Federal District of Mexico in 1942.
See also Federal publications for that year, Mexican
Govt. Printing Offices.
Sahaqun, Fray Bernardo De. Historia De las Cosas De La
Nueva Espana. Mexico City.
A facsimile of manuscript, Mexico City National Lib.
between 1905-1938, telling about Telteo Medicine Man
puppetry in Mexico at Tianquiztli.
Smith, Susan (Mrs.) Made in Mexico. New York, Knopf,

Mexico (cont.)
1930, passim
Stevens, Olga. "Mexico sans puppet shows," Pupp J, 18(4): 31-32, 1967
Teatro-Mexicano De Munecos, 25 Piezas De Teatro Guignol. ed., A. and M. Campos, Mexico City, Mexican Dept. of Fine Arts, Ediciones Encuadernables De El Nationale, 1941.
A technical history of puppets and theaters and puppeteers. Other sources indicate this was also published by Orellana, 1941.
See also A. and Maria Campos
Usigli, Rodolfo. Mexico En Al Teatro. Mexico, 1932, p 75 In British Museum.
Vela, Argueles. Introduccion.. Del Teatro De Munecos Guignol. Mexico City, 1936, passim and p 3
Wiksell, Jean Starr. "Mexican Puppetry," Players, 21:24, Jan 1945

Mongolia, See also China, Russia

McPharlin, M. B. "Theatre Festival, International," (Rods) Pupp J, 10(2):10, 1958
"Theatre of Ulan-Bator, Mongolian Peoples' Republic," World Th, 8(1):53, Spring 1959

Netherlands, See Holland

New Zealand
See also Australia, England

Boyce, Raymond and Geraldine. "Work in Australia," 1956. Pupp J, 16(4):10, 14, 16, 1965
Burtons, The. "Puppets," Pupp J, 17(2):24, 1965

"From Overseas," Brit Pupp and M Thea G Newsl, No. 150, 2, 1968
"Goodwin Marionette Theatre in New Zealand," Pupp, 17:68, 1946
Morice, G. "Puppet Column," World's Fair (London), N 23, 1946
"Mrs N. Reid of Yarraville, West State, New Zealand Writes," Brit Pupp Thea, 1(5):10, 1950
"New Zealand Puppetry," Pupp, 13-14:38, 1942-43

"Puppet Films Being Made," Brit Pupp Thea, 2(1):15, 1951

Stevens, Olga. "New Zealand Puppeteers," Pupp J, 16(4): 10-11, 1965

Wilkinson, Winifred. "Puppets as Pioneers in New Zealand," Pupp, 13-14:23, 1942-'43

Nigeria, See also Africa

Berry, Eric. "Puppets in Northern Nigeria," N Y Her Mag Section, Je 28, 1925

"Puppets in Northern Nigeria, British West Africa," Pupp, 5: 39-40, 1934

Norway

"Bernard Lewis," Brit Pupp and M Thea G Newsl, No. 150, N 1968

Blckastad, Miloda. Skodespel For Bern. Oslo, Dreyer, 1949

Kaprino, Yvo (Ivo). See also Puppet Theatre in Russia. Moscow, Gov't Theatre Bureau, 1966, p 21. In NN.

Morice, G. "Puppetry Notes," World's Fair, London, Jl 6, 1946

"Scandinavian Puppet Congress Opening," (Oct. 26 and 27, 1968), Brit Pupp and M Thea G Newsl, No. 150:2, N 1968

"Oslo Puppet Theatre, The Törbjorn Egher Puppets," Pupp The Mod World, p 220, and Illus No 37

"War Puppetry in Norway," Pupp, 17:68, 1946

Oriental Puppets

See also: Siam, Java, Bali, Indonesia, China, Japan, etc., as the material overlaps in most articles and books about these countries.

Barany, M. de (Oberschall). "Les Marionettes Wayan Au Musee D'Extreme Orient de Budapest," Les Gazette des Beaux Art, 10:16, Mr 1932

Brown, J. M. The Riddle of the Pacific. Boston, Small, 1925, p 142. Concerned with Easter Island puppets.

Cowan, James. "Maori Tribe Dances," J Polyn Soc, Je 1921

Cowan, H. W. Asia. Boston, Little, 1929

Oriental (cont.)
Grube, W. & B. Laufer. Chineseische Schattenspiele.
Munich, Der Königlich, 1915. In British Museum.
Jacob, G. "Schatten und Puppentheater im Orient," Der
Buhnenvolksbund, 2: 1926
King, H. B. "Marionetti Alla Milanese; Teatro Gerolamo,"
Thea Arts, 31:35-37, Jan 1947
Laufer, Bertheld. Oriental Theatricals. passim
See W. Grube
Markley, Rachel. "Glimpse of puppets and plays in the
Orient," Thea and Sch, 10:19-21, D 1931
"Oriental Puppets in America," Pupp, 12:54, 1941. Material
on 1853 to 1927.
"Oriental Puppets-Portsmouth Plaza, San Francisco," Alta
California, S 2, 1853
Ouseley, W. "Notes on Eastern Puppets," Mask, 5:157-58,
O 1912.
Rosse, Hermann. "Sketches of Oriental Theatres," Thea
Arts, Jan 1919, p 38
Stoughton, Dusty. "Even on the Islands," Pupp J, 6(2):4-5,
1954
Tyson, G. M. "A History of Oriental Puppets." Unpub-
lished Master's dissertation, Los Angeles, Univ. of South-
ern California, 1932

Pakistan, See India

    Has 6 foot rod puppets in the central part of the coun-
try. Shadows of skin material used in educational and religious puppetry, see Pupp J, 16(5):30, 1965.

Palestine, See also Israel

"Drama of the Crucifixion-Jerusalem," Pupp 6:76-77, 1935

"Oelverg's Puppet Show," Pupp, 17:46, 1946

The Modjacet Schpoel Yiddish Marionettes," Thea Arts, 10:
383-84, Je 1926.
"Palestine Puppetry," Pupp, 13-14:39, 1942-'43. Work of
Dr. Paul Lowery.

Persia, See Iran

Note: The word "Munecos" means puppets, puppetry seems to have been active as early as 1597. The listing below is very incomplete.

Allyen, Juan De (Father). Poem on the Festival. Canto III, Folio 69, Lima, Peru, 1630.

Bravo, Silvestre. "Document of Je 1, 1783 to Don Ambrosie Cordany Pontero," Lima, Government Files, Documents, Mr 12, 1787. Author was in charge of theaters in Lima and forbade puppet shows.

Covarubias, Manuel M. Diccionarie Teatral Del Peru. Lima, 1905, passim. Puppets in a theatre in Barbones Quarter of Lima in 1828.

Dunbar, T. E. "Titeres Y Titeres en La Lima de Finas del Sigle XVIII," Tres, Lima, Mr 20, 1941, p 18 and Je 10, 1941, p 18-25. Periodical in NN.

Egana, Jose Maria De. "A Document" - Unpublished paper of Feb 27, 1787 to the Supt. General of Peru, concerning Puppet Theatre work in the Dramatic Coliseum on Mr 17, 1787. Lima, Government Document Files, 1787.

--- "Amateur Puppet Group of Peru," Pupp 11:37-38, 1940

Gálvez, José. "Puppets of Yore in Peru," Turismo, Jan 1938

--- Vna Lima que se Va. Lima, 1921 (First Series). Ciudad de los Aeges del Peru, Editorial Euforion, several series. In Brown Univ. Lib.

Hermeisilla, Solari. Longtime puppeteer of Lima, doing some television work. See Pupp J, 19(3):37, 1967.

Hermandoz, Jusepe. Puppeteer at Pero's, "Castle of Marvels," in Lima, 1597.

Lemaitre, V. A. "Puppets of Peru," Pupp, 11:17-18, 1940

McPharlin, Paul. Puppet Theatre in America, 1524 to 1948. New York. Harper, 1949, p 74-76, 255-257, passim.

Poland

Note: Much of the puppetry takes place at Christmas time. Recently, the government has taken a strong interest in puppets and given much assistance to puppetry. There are 24 nationally supported puppet theatres, with 1500 workers.

The word, "Kuklelek" is one to watch for. People with puppet masks, and acting as puppets are very popular.

Poland (cont.)
Christmas puppetry has a special title, "Scopki" (manger).
Quite modern techniques are used and unusual rod puppet
and experimental work is done.

"Ateneum State Puppet Theatre," Pupp Th Mod World,
p 223 and Illus No. 93
Baird, Bill. The Art of the Puppet. New York, Macmillan,
1965, passim. p. 251
"BAJ State Puppet Theatre-Warsaw," Pupp Th Mod World,
p 223. These are the puppets of Stanczak in a production
by Kopalko, and Illus No 92.
Baran, Stefan. "Polish Puppets, rods in England," Brit
Pupp & M Thea G Newsl, No. 143, p 1, 1968
Bramall, Eric. "Visit to Poland," Pupp Master, 7(2):22-24,
D 1962
Crawford, K. N. "Arlekin" Pupp J, 20(3):28, 1968
--- "State Theatre, 'Arlekin', Lodz, Poland," International
Puppetry Festival Report, 1968. London, British Puppet
and Model Theatre Guild Office, 1968. In NN.
Dalgliesh, Alice. "Puppets," Christmas. New York, Scrib-
ner, 1934, p 212-24
Falkenstein, Mollie. "The Marcinek Theater, Poznan, Po-
land," Pupp J, 17(3):7, 1965
--- "The Miniature Theatre, Gdánsk," Pupp J, 17(3):8, 1965
Festivals of Poland. See "International" and "Festival"
Sections
Films. See "Film" Section

"Groteska Theatre at Cracow (with masks and puppets),"
Pupp J, 15(1):26, 1963
--- See also Pupp Th Mod World, p 222, 223. Puppets are
by L. Miniticz.
"Gulliver State Puppet Theater, Warsaw," Pupp Th Mod
World, p 223 and Illus Nos 87, 98
Harper, Wilhelmina. Merry Christmas to You. New York,
Dutton, 1935, p 40-53
Hartwig, Myszkowski. "Laika Theatre of Warsaw in Guignol
Difficulties," World Thea, 8(1):54, 1959. A Spring issue.
Jarecka, L. L. "Poland Builds Palaces for Christmas: The
"Szopka" Christmas Puppet Play and Creche," Craft Horiz,
11:10-13, N 1951
Jurkowski, H. "The Eternal Conflict," Pupp Th Mod World,
Boston, Plays, 1967, p 25-27. (ed. by UNIMA)
--- "Polish Puppet Theatre," Pupp Master, 7(2):8-9D 1962
--- "Puppet Theatre in Poland," World Thea, 6(2):133-138,
1957.

--- See J. Sztavdynger
--- See also Le Theatre En Pologne
Kelley, Eric P. Christmas Nightingale. New York, Mac-
    millan, 1932, p 33-48
Kownackiei, Marji. Teatrzyk Kuklelek. Warsaw, Naszej,
    1935
    Revu of Teatrzyk Kuklelek. Anon, Pupp, 8:71, 1937
"Lalka Theatre (State)- Warsaw," Pupp Th Mod World, p 223
    Puppets are by A. Kilian, and Illus Nos 89, 91, 97
--- See also Pupp J, 16(1):31, 1964. Puppets are by Jan
    Welkowski
Le Theatre En Pologne. A monthly publication carrying
    many puppet articles.
L/owski, Stanis/aw. Teatr Kuke/ek; Podrecznik Praktycsny.
    Warsaw, "Sztuka" 1949. In NN.
McPharlin, Marjorie B. "International Festival," Pupp J,
    10(2):10-11, 1958
--- "Two State Theatres from Poland," Pupp J, 10(3):25-26,
    1958.
McPharlin, Paul. Most of the anon. articles from Pupp, on
    these foreign countries are probably by him as he traveled
    a great deal and was editor of the publication.
"Marcinek Theater, Poznan," Pupp Th Mod World, p 222,
    223. Puppets by L. Serafinowicz and J. Berdyszak.
--- Pupp J, 17(3):7, 1965
Meyer, Rosalind. "Travel Note in Poland," Pupp, 7:77,
    1936, item only
Minkiewicz, J. See "Film" Section, General articles.

"Minatura State Puppet Theatre at Gdánsk," Pupp Th Mod
    World, p 223
--- Pupp J, 17(3):8, 1965
Molïke, Marianna Von. trans. History of Polish Puppetry
    1739-1936. by Dr. Jan Sztaudynger. 1937
    Revu of History of Polish Puppetry, Pupp 8:37-38, 1937
Morice, Gerald. "A Tribute to the Polish Puppet Theatre,"
    Pupp Master, 7(2):18, D 1962
"Opole District, State Puppet Theatre,"   Pupp Th Mod
    World, p 222 and Illus No. 90. Puppets of Z. Smandzik.
Organizations. See "Organization" Section

Periodicals. See "Periodical" Section

"Polish Puppetry," Pupp, 6:74, 1935

"Princess and the Dragon, A Puppet Film," Pupp J, 1(3):4,
    1949

Poland (cont.)
Proctor, Rumain. "Report on UNIMA-Section on Lalks
Theatre of Varsovie, Poland," Pupp J, 11(2):5-6, 1959
"Puppets of Poland," Pupp, 8: 1937

Reinfuss, Roman. Szopki Krakowskie. Prasa, W. Krakowie,
1958. In LC.
Schildenfeld, L. de. "The Designer Wyspignski Influenced by
Szepká Puppet Show," Pupp, 9:24, 1938
--- "Puppets Influence Designer," Mask, 11:27, 1918

Strzelecki, Zenobios. Polska Plastyka Teatralna. Warsaw,
c 1965.
Szokás, O. "Szopka Z Sieteszy W Powiecie Przoworskim,"
Polska Sztuka Tudowa, Warsaw, 1949, 3(11-12):326-36.
[Sic] In NN.
--- Theatre Lagek. New York, Capelia Corp., Polish Arts
and Crafts.
Sztaudynger, Dr. Jan. "History of Polish Puppetry," Pupp,
8:37-38, 1937; 9:71, 1938.
--- History of Polish Puppetry, 1739-1936. trans. by M.
Moltke, Warsaw, c 1937.
--- Marionetki. Warsaw, Lwow, c 1948.
--- "Das Polnische Marionettenwesen Im Jahre, 1937,"
Theater Der Welt, Amsterdam, Jahrg 2, 1938, p 29-34.
--- "Puppetry in Poland," Pupp, 17:68, 1946
--- & K. Kurkowski. Od Szopki De Teatru Lalek. Lodz,
Poland, 1961.
Zawacki, Edmund J. "Polish Legend in Wisconsin," Pupp,
13-14:7, 1942-'43.

Puerto Rico

"Puerto Rico Dept. of Ed. Organizing 'Minitheatre Infantil
Rural' - George Latshaw to help," Pupp J, 19(3):27, 1967,
item only.
See also UNIMA - U. S. A. Puppet Calender, 1968, Feb.
page available, Puppetry Journal Publication, Ashville, O.

Portugal

"Braca-Flor Theatre, Lisbon-Puppets by Lilia Da Fanseca,"
Pupp Th Mod World, p 221, and Illus No 64

Rumania

Note: Many International Festivals of puppetry are held in
Bucharest. There is a very modern and experimental
trend and approach toward plays, films, television and
variety acts.

Their puppet is called, "Va Silache" and we find puppetry strong in 18th and 19th century theatre. Check
"Festivals" "Organizations" and "Periodicals" in addition
to "Films" and "Television" Sections. They like to work
with rods and marionettes.

Alecsandri, Vasile. A writer of classical comedies who in-
cludes puppets in his plays. Investigation of his work is
advised.
Baird, Bill. The Art of the Puppet. New York, Macmillan,
1965, passim
"Brasov Puppet Theatre, Puppets by Maria Dimitresou,"
Pupp Th Mod World, p 225-26
"Cluj Puppet Theatre," Pupp Th Mod World, p 226, and
Illus No 166
Conachi, Costache. 19th Century poet who wrote many pup-
pet plays.
"Craiova Puppet Theater," Pupp Th Mod World, p 225, and
Illus No 155
Falkenstein, Mollie. "Bucharest," Pupp J, 17(4):6-10, 1965.
Puppet theatre of Alva Lulia.
--- "The Bucharest Festival Report," Pupp J, 17(3):3, 1965
--- "International Festival of Puppet Theatres to be every
five years," Pupp J, 17(4):4, 1965. Have been held
1958, 1960, 1965.
Hanganul, Ion. Famous 19th Century puppeteer, early part
of century.
"Jassy Puppet Theatre-Rodica Scraba and A Groapă Puppets,"
Pupp Th Mod World, p 226, and Illus No 156
Kogălniceanu, Mihail de. Esquisse Sur L'Histoire, Les
Moeurs et la Lanque des Cigans. Berlin, 1837. In
British Museum.
Revu of Esquise Sur... des Cigans. Anon, Pupp, 1939, p56.
Kughes, B. "Rumanian Puppets," Pupp Master, 4(7):285-87,
1956
Link, O. "Das Puppentheater in Rümänien," Das Puppenth,
3:173-76, 1929
McPharlin, Marjorie B. "International Festival," Pupp J,
10(2):8-9, 1958. Date for festival was May 15, June 1,
1958. Bucharest papers will list much material at that
time.

265

Rumania (cont.)
--- "International News," Pupp J, 16(2):11-12, 1964
--- "Second International Festival," Pupp J, 13(2):3-6, 1960
--- "State Theatre From Cluj, Roumania," Pupp J, 10(3): 11-12, 1958
--- "Tandarica Theatre, Bucharest," Pupp J, 10(3):12-13, 1958
See also her name in "Rod" Section as her books and articles on these puppets will give passim material.
Mahlmann, L. "The Craiova Theater," "The Rod Puppet Theatre of Timrsoara," "The Tandarcia Theatre, Bucharest," and "The Oradea Theatre," Pupp J, 17(3):4-8, 1965
--- "The Puppet Theatre of Cluj," Pupp J, 17(3):4, 1965
Malik, Jan (Dr.) "Roumanian Puppetry," Pupp, 10:38, 1939

Mora, Vera. "Puppets in Rumania," Pupp, 3:16, 1932
--- "Rumania," Pupp, 5:37, 1934
--- "Roumanian Puppetry," Pupp, 4:62-63, 1933
Natasi, Prof. T. A well known Roumanian puppet master spoken of in the article by V. Mora, Pupp 4:62-63, 1933
Niculescu, Margareta. "International First Puppet Theatre Festival," Pupp J, 11(1): 1959.
--- "Puppet Theatre in Rumania," Pupp J, 9(5):6-7, 1958
--- Puppet Theatre of the Modern World. trans. by E. Osers, and E. Strick, for the UNIMA Organization. Boston, Plays, 1967. In NN.
--- "Rumanian Puppets," World Thea, 13:223-30, Autumn 1964.
"Oradea Puppet Theatre," Pupp Th Mod World, p 226, and Illus No 173
Osers, E. See M. Niculescu

"Puppets in Rumania," Pupp, 6:65, 75, 1935

"Rod Puppets in Gangster Film Parody," World Thea, 8(1): 53, Spring 1959
"Roumanian Puppetry," Pupp, 2:36, 1931

Sarñean, L. "Les Marionettes En Roumanie Et En Turqure," Revue De Traditions, 16: p 409-19
"State Puppet Theatre of Crajova," World Thea, 8(1):55, 1959
Strick, E. See M. Niculescu

"Tandarica Theatre, The Five Fingered Hand," Players, 35(4):77, Jan 1959

See also Pupp Th Mod World, p 225-26, and Illus Nos
157-158, 161, 164-172
"Le Théâtre Tandarica De Bucharest," Spectacles 3:64, D
1958
Victoriei, Calea. "Second International Festival," Pupp J,
11(5):12-13, 1960

Russia

The Union of Soviet Socialist Republics (USSR)

Note: Articles concerning all of the Republics are listed together in a single alphabet.

Russia has 57 theaters in the largest Soviet Republic
and 27 in smaller Republics but this number increases
constantly. Intense work has been going on for twenty to
thirty years and the literature will be great in quantity
and quality, prolific in the native language from around
1936, but rich from 1922.

From 400 to 1000 shows a year are given by the State
Theatres, many for adults only. "Bertep" is the Christ-
mas puppet play and "Petroushka" was their popular
"Punch" character for many years.

Agnenko, A. The Soviet Puppet. (Sovetski Petrushka). Mos-
cow, 1927.
Albu, Erna. "Puppets and Cigarettes," Pupp J, 15(6):25-27,
1964. Also tells a little of Rumanian work.
Alferov, A. A Book on Puppets. Moscow, 1895. Title in
Russina, in British Museum.
Baird, Bill. The Art of the Puppet. New York, Macmillan,
1965, passim
Barchash, I. Teatr. Moscow, 1945, p 64-76. Under title
of "Koroly-Cleny."
Baryshau, H. I. A Book on Puppetry. (In Russian) See
LC Catalogue, Bk Subjects, 1962, p 64.
Beauplan, R. de. "Les Poupees Animees de Ladislas Stare-
vitch," L'Illus (Petite) No 472, Mr 22, 1930, p 22-24.
Bertram, N. D. "Das Puppentheater in der Sowjet Union,"
Das Puppenth, 3:161-68, 1929
Bockwoldt, Henry. "News From H. Bockwoldt," Grapev,
Feb 1949, p 10
Boehn, Max Von. Dolls and Puppets. London, Harrap,
1932, passim
Bogatyrev, P. G. Russian Puppet Folk Plays. Moscow, 1896.
In NN.

Russia (cont.)

Bogomazov, S. "Moscow children welcome guest shadow
puppeteer," Brit Pupp Thea, 3(4):5, 1952
"Bolshoi Theatre in Leningrad, Korolev Puppeteer Producer,"
    Pupp The Mod World, p 223 and Illus Nos. 110, 112,
    113
Bower, F. "Puppet Theatre From Moscow," Thea Arts,
    47:245, O 1963
Bunin, Louis. "The New Russian Puppet Theatre Film,"
    New Thea, 2:20-21, D 1935. A review of the great pup-
    pet film, "Gulliver" with a bibliog of the non-commercial
    producing organizations. See also "Film" Section this
    title.
Carlson, Barbara. "Moscow spectacular--a puppet play
    Strictly Adult," Hartford Courant, 261:1, S 18, 1967
Carmer, Carl. "Puppetry 1931," Thea Arts, 16:135-36, Feb
    1932
Carroll, L. "Punch and Judy Abroad-Russia," Newsw, 29:
    78, Je 23, 1947
Chowl, Hay. "Mickey's Rival," Close Up, 6:493-95, Je 1930

Clurman, N. H. "Obraztšev's Puppet Theatre," Nation, 197:
    268, O 26, 1963
"Comment on S. V. Obraztšov's Puppet Theatre in Moscow,"
    N Y Times, Je 12, 1956, 39:1
Dana, H. Handbook on Soviet Drama. New York, Ameri-
    can Russian Institute, 1938. In NN.
Demmeni, E. S. Kukli Na Stzene. Moscow, 1949. In LC.
--- and Y. Gaush. Samedeiny Teatr Petrushka, (The Ama-
    teur Theater of Puppets). Leningrad, 1931.
"Director Sergi Obraztsov, State Puppet Theatre," Pupp J,
    6: 1951; 6:10, 1955.
Dreiden, S. D. "Puppet Theatre in Soviet Russia," Studio,
    131:79-84, Mr 1946
--- A Puppet Book, 1959 (In Russian) In LC.
Effiosa, N. E. See V. V. Kallasha

Efimova, Nina (Iakovlevan Simonovich). Adventures of a
    Russian Puppet Theatre, (1877) trans. E. Y. Mitcoff,
    Birmingham, Mich., Puppetry Imprints, 1935. At Mc
    Pharlin Coll. (See Key No. 1)
--- Adventures of a Russian Puppet Theatre. trans. E. Y.
    Mitcoff. Toronto, Hastings House, 1945. In NN.
--- Revu of Adventures of a Russian Puppet Theatre. Anon.
    Pupp, 6:131, 1935
--- Revu of Adventures of a Russian Puppet Theatre. Anon,
    Pupp, 7:151, 1936

--- Revue of Adventures of a Russian Puppet Theatre.
    Anon, Thea Arts, 20:243, Mr 1936
--- "Notes on Hand Puppets," trans. by E. Y. Mitcoff,
    Pupp 1:55-58, 1930
--- Zapiske Petrushetchnika. Moscow, De L'Etat, 1925
"Estonian Puppet Theatre at Tallin," Pupp Th of Mod World,
    p 223, and Illus No 109
Falkenstein, Mollie. "Central Puppet Theatre, Obraztŝev,"
    Pupp J, 17(3):8, 1965
Fedotov, A. "Amateur Puppetry Groups," Pupp, 11:37-38,
    1940
--- Anatomie Teatrainoi Kukli. Moscow, 1944
    Revu of Anatomie Teatrainoi Kukli, Pupp, 17:81, 1946
--- A Puppet Book (In Russian) 1953. In LC '50 & '64 and NN.
--- "Puppet Theater," Thea W, London, 50(355):38-40, Ag
    1954.
--- "Russia's Puppets in War Time Moscow," Pupp, 15:
    37-38, 1944
"Figures From N. Russia's Samoied," Marionette, 1:22-27,
    Ap 1918
Films. See "Film" Section

Fletcher, J. "Russian Puppets," Pupp Master, 5(6):8 1957

Fox, Eleanor. See S. Obraztŝev

Getoomob, A. A Puppet Book. (In Russian) 1950. Available
    from Four Continents Bk Shop, NYC.
"Gorky Doll Theatre Is Important In Moscow," G N Y Pupp
    G Newsl, 3(2):2, 1965. In NN.
"harriet" (pseud.) "An Unusual Concert," Pupp J, 15(3):6-
    9, 1963
Inckepckan, T. A Puppet Book (In Russian) 1950. In LC.

Jackson, Stella. See S. Obraztŝev

"Kalinin Puppet Theatre, puppets of I. Bayarsky,"
    Pupp Th Mod World, p 223 and Illus No. 101
Kallasha, V. V. and N. E. Effiesa. History of the Russian
    Puppet Theatre. Moscow, 1914
Karamanenko, T. N. A Puppet Book. (In Russian) 1955. In
    LC and NN.
"Kharkov Puppet Theatre at Kharkee," Pupp Th Mod World,
    p 223. Puppets of E. Chegov and E. Goumenuke, Illus 103
Kiprensky, A. "Moscow Central Puppet Theatre," Thea W,
    41:19, N 1945
Kolosova, S. A Puppet Book (In Russian,) 1957. In LC.

Russia (cont.)
Korolov, M. M. "A Producer's Reflections on the Roles of the Actor and the Designer," Pupp Th Mod World, p 33-55. By the director of the Bolshoi Puppet Theatre in Leningrad.
Kownackiei, Marji. Teatyzk Kuliekek. (Naszej Ksieqarni) Warsaw, 1935.
Landsman, Leo. Het Poppentheater Van Sergei Obraztsev Te Moskou. Antwerp, Bookuil En Karveel, 1947. In NN.
"Latvian Puppet Theatre, At Riga," Pupp Th Mod World, p 223, and Illus Nos 105-106
--- Pupp J, 16(2):11-12, 1964
"Leningrad Puppet Theatre, Eugene Demeni," (Demmeni) Pupp Th Mod World, p 223, and Illus No 112
Levin, Mark. "Moscow-Obraztsev's Central Puppet Theatre," Moscow News, My 22, 1946, p 4
Lozowick, Louis. "Alexandra Exter's Marionettes," Thea Arts, 12:514-19, 461, Jl 1928
--- "Puppets," Soviet Russia Today, Ap 1936, p 12, 23, illus
MacDermott, J. T. See S. V. Obraztsov

McPharlin, Marjorie B. "International Festival," Pupp J, 10(2):11-12, 1958
--- "Leningrad Puppet Theatre," Pupp J, 13(2): 1960
--- "Solo Recitals, S. Obraztsov," Pupp J, 10(3):13, 1958. Musical satires.
Mahlmann, L. "Central Puppet Theatre of Moscow," Pupp J, 17(3):7, 1965
Marionette Theatre of Leningrad, for the Young Spectator. Leningrad, State, 1934
"Marionettes in Moscow," Ch Sci Mon Mag, Feb 26, 1936, p 14.
Milovsoroff, . "Russian Doll Theatre, Pupp, 8:106, 1936.

Mitcoff, Elena. "Puppetry of Russia," Pupp, 2:37-43, 1931
--- "Puppets," Pupp, 6:75, 1935
--- "Russian Puppetry," Pupp, 7:74-75, 1936
--- "Russian Puppets," Pupp 5:37, 1934
See N. Eflmova
"Moscow Central Puppet Theatre Producing Political Plays," Newsweek, 33:41 My 23, 1949
"Moscow Shadow Theatre of Em. May and N. Tslikov," Pupp Th Mod World, p 223
"Moscow State Puppet Theater," Brit Pupp Thea, 1(4):13-14, 1950
"Moscow State Central Puppet Theatre," Pupp J, 16(2):11-12, 1964

Pupp Th Mod World, p 223-4, and Illus Nos 100, 102, 104,
107-08
Mulholland, John. Pratical Puppetry, New York, Aico, 1962
Obraztsov, Sergei V. Actor With Puppets. Moscow, 1940.
--- A Book on Puppetry. (In Russian) Moscow, 1938. In NN.
--- The Chinese Puppet Theatre. trans. by J. T. MacDer-
mott. London, Faber, 1961. Originally publ. Moscow,
State Art Publ. House, 1957. Boston, plays 1963.
--- "From Moscow to New York," Pupp J, 14(4&5):4-6,
1963
--- Mein Beruf. Berlin, Henschelverlag, 1950 and 1952.
In NN.
--- --- (In Russian) In LC.
--- Il Mestiere Di Burattinaio. Bari, Italy, Laterza, 1956
--- Mon Métier. Moscow, Editions en Langues Estrangères,
c 1950.
--- My Profession. Trans. by R. Parker and V. Scott,
Moscow, Foreign Languages Publ. House, 1957. In NN.
---"My Work in Russian Puppetry at Central Puppet Theatre
in Moscow," Pupp, 10:38, 1939
--- "Obraztsov and the Bairds," Pupp J, 15(3):3-5, 1963
--- "Obraztsov Puppets; Moscow Magic," Newsweek, 62:77,
O 14, 1963
--- "Pantopuck," Pupp Post, London, Spring 1954, p 6-8
--- "Puppet Theatre in Moscow," Thea Arts, 31:70-73, 1947
--- "Puppetry," USSR, Issues No. 1, 2, 3, Cultural Informa-
tion Publication, c 1944-45
--- "Puppets," Soviet Life Today, Mr 1965
--- Puppets and the Puppet Theatre. Trans. by E. Fox and
S. Jackson. London, Society for Cultural Publications,
1954. In NN.
---"Russian Puppetry," Pupp, 13-14:30, 1942
Organizations. See "Organizations" Section

Osborne, R. F. "Travel Notes," Pupp, 7:76, 1936

"Overseas News," Brit Pupp Thea, 2(1):15, 1951

Parker, Ralph. See S. Obraztsov

Periodicals. See "Periodical" Section

"Pity the Puppets," Pupp J, 2(6):11, 1951

Prideaux, T. "Will it go on Broadway?-The Obraztsov's
Puppet Show," Life, 55:9, S 13, 1963
"Project Puppets, Soviet Made," Best E Trans, 18: Ap
1932

Russia (cont.)
"Punch and Judy Show-Russia's Moscow Art Theatre," N Y
   Times, Ag 28, 1925 8:2
Puppet Theatre in USSR.   An anon. general information
   pamphlet, Moscow: Presidium of International Union of
   Puppeteers, Je 1964. In English. In NN.
"Puppetry Shows for Children Should Avoid Horror," World's
   Fair, Jl 11, 1964, p 50.
"Puppets in Germany, The Russian Zone," Pupp J, 2(6):28-
   29, 1951
Roux, Edmonde C.   "Notes on Moscow," Vogue, Jl 15, 1947

"Russia's Puppets," Grapev, 47:4, S 1947

"Russian Puppet Theater," Sat R, 14:22, Jl 25, 1936

"Russian Puppetry These Days," Pupp J, 6(4):30, 1954

"Russian Puppets of the London Casino," Illus Lon N, 225:
   75, Jl 10, 1954
Scott, Valentia. See S. Obraztsov

Shpet, L. G. "Russia, Puppet Theatre and its audience,"
   Pupp J, 19(1):10-11, 1967
"Siberian Puppet Theatre meets in Kemerovo," Pupp Th in
   USSR, p 20
Simonovich, I. See N. Efimova

Smirnova, Natalina. The Soviet Puppet Theatre (Several
   Vol.) Vol. 1, Moscow, Publishing House of the Academy
   of Sciences, 1963. In NN. Good bibliog, but in Russian.
Soloviova, I. "Sergei Obraztsov-Central Puppet Theatre of
   Russia," Pupp J, 9(5):3-7, 1958
"Soviet Puppet Theatre," Anglo-Soviet Journal, O 1937, p 8-
   9.
"Soviet Puppets on Broadway," Ch Sci Mon, (Eastern, West-
   ern), O 5, 1963, col 4, p 6
Starevich, L. See "Film" Section

"State Central Puppet Theatre of Moscow," Pupp J, 19(1):
   20, 23, 24, 1967
--- Pupp, 17:68, 1946
The State Theatre of the Children, Book. Moscow, State
   Dept. , 1934. In NN.
Stevens, Martin. "Obraztsov Invitation to New York City,"
   Pupp J, 15(2):29, 1963, item
"Swift's Classical Hero," Gulliver, in Soviet Puppet State,"
   Newsweek, 6:53, N 9, 1935. See also "Film Section this
   title.

Tearp, . A Book on Puppetry. (In Russian) 1955. In LC.

Thornton, R. "Famous Soviet Puppeteer Touring Britain,"
Pupp Master, (New Series) 1(10):89.
Tsulukidze, T. A Book on Puppetry. (In Russian) 1957.
In LC.
Verkhovski, Naum N. ed. A Book on Puppetry. (In Russian)
c 1934. In NN.
--- "Puppet Theatres," Young Spectators, Leningrad, 1934.
"What Makes Ivan Laugh?" N Y Times Mag, Sun., Jan 31,
1960

Scotland, See also England

Dervang Mulls Puppet Theatre," Brit Pupp and M Thea G
Newsl, No 146, Je 1968
Lee, Miles. Puppet Theater Production and Manipulation.
New York, London, Fabers, 1958
Revu of Puppet Theater Productions and Manipulation.
Anon, Pupp Master, 5(9):13-14, 1958
"More News From Scotland," Brit Pupp and M Thea G Newsl,
No. 146, June 1968
Proctor, E. and Romaine. "Puppets Old and New," Pupp J,
5(3):22, 1953. About the Edinburgh Festival of that year.
"Scottish Puppeteers," Pupp Master, 4(2):244, 1955

Wilkinson, Walter. Puppets in Scotland. London, Bles,
1927 and 1947
--- "Scotland's Puppets," Pupp, 6:131, 1935
Willings, J. A. "Puppet Opera An Experiment in Edinburgh,"
Opera, (London) 5:94-97, Feb 1954.

Siam

Note: Shadow work is the main interest. See also "Shadows," "Thailand," "Oriental," etc. Sections.

Blackham, Olive. Shadow Puppets. London, Rockcliff,
1960, p 18-42.
Graham, W. A. Siamese Shadow Play-Siam. 2d ed. London,
Moring, 1912.
Harnell, Phyllis. "Siam," The Oxford Companion to the
Theatre. London, Oxford, 1951, p 1509-1510
Hartlaub, G. F. "Siamesiche Schattenspiele," Die Woche,
28:28, 1925

273

Siam (cont.)
Müiler, F. W. K. See "Shadow" Section

Nicholas, R. "Le Théâtre D'Ombres au Siam, " J Siam S,
   1927, p 37-52
Scintilla, A. "Das Theater in Siam, " Scene, Berlin,
   Jahrg 22:38-44, 1930
"Siamese Nang, " This is the title of their puppet shadow
   drama.
"Wayeng-Kulit, " Shadow puppets using Ramayanna, the nine-
   day cycle of plays.

Sicily, See also Italy

Note: This country uses the Paladin rod puppets which are
   also called "Catalan" puppets. There was much activity
   in Palermo around 1966. "Magatelli" was the typical
   15th century string-to-leg marionette, and they were highly developed mechanically. These puppets smoked, fought,
   blew trumpets, prepared meals, etc. See also "Rod"
   and "Marionette" Sections.

Baird, Bill. The Art of the Puppet. New York, Macmillan,
   1965, passim
Ballantyne, E. "Sicilian Puppet-Shows, " Theatre, Feb 1893

Boehn, Max Von. Dolls and Puppets. London, Harrap,
   1932, passim
Brenner, Anita. "Corner of Sicily in New York, " Travel,
   67:26-29, My 1936
Bufano, Remo. "The Puppets of Sicily, " Thea G M 7:28-
   31, S 1930
--- "The Vanishing Sicilian Theatre, " Pupp J, 6(3):3-4, 1954
Cavazza, Elizabeth. "At the 'Opera Dili Pupi' in Palermo,
   Sicily, " Atlantic M, 73:797-802, Je 1894
Cocchira, Giuseppe. L'Arte Del Papolo Siciliano. Milano,
   Flaccovio, passim.
--- Il Folklore Siciliano. Vol. 1 & 2. Palermo, Flaccovio,
   1928 and Milano, 1929, passim. In NN.
--- Pitrè, La Sicilia. E Il Folklore. Firenze, Sansoni,
   1951, passim
Crouse, E. B. "Dedication at Stoney Creek, Conn. of Si-
   cilian Puppet Theatre-Manteo Family, " Pupp J, 15(2):3-
   4, 1963
   See also "Argentina" Manteo family; "Italy" Manteo
   family; Bill Baird, "Manteo family"

Dilla, G. P. "An Incident in the Marionette Theatre in Palermo, Sicily," Dalhouse R, 20:353-56, O 1940.

--- "Sicilian Marionettes," Dalhouse R, Canada 20:353-56, O 1940

Dodd, Lee W. "Two Knights of Sicily," Sat R, 6:1014, My 3, 1940

Emerson, Isabel. "Sicilian Marionettes," Contemp R, London, 137:369-72, Mr 1930

Fulchignoni, E. "Le Marionette in Sicilia," Scenario, Milano, Anne 8, 1939, p 426-29

Golding, L. Sicilian Noon. Palermo, Chatto, 1925, passim

L'Gotti, Ettore. Il Teatro Dei Pupi. Firenze, Sansoni, 1957. In NN. Bibliog p 173-78

Guercio, W. Sicily, The Guardian of the Mediterranian. London, Faber, 1938, passim

Gutman, Walter. "Longest Show on Earth," Thea G M, 7:31-32, S 1930

Horowicz, P. B. See "Une Page De L'Historie..."

"How Sicilian Marionettes are worked," Pupp, 2: 1931.

Jackson, Mrs. E. A Student in Sicily. New York, Dodd-Mead, 1926, p 228-41

Jacops, E. R. "The Puppet Theatre of Sicily," Ed Thea J, 6(1):12, 14, Mr 6, 1954

Jerome, L. B. "Marionettes of Little Sicily," N Eng Mag, 41:745-50, Feb 1910

Jones, Henry F. Castellinaria and Other Sicilian Diversions. London, Fiefield, 1911, passim

--- Diversions in Sicily. London, Rivers, 1909, and London, Fiefield, 1920, passim

Kubly, Herbert. "Easter in Sicily," Pupp J, 11(6):3-5, 1960

McPharlin, Paul. The Puppet Theatre in America. New York, Harper, 1949, p. 258, 293, 298, 299, 387. Concerning the "Manteo family."

Macri, Cavalier and Salvatore. "Macri Puppet Theatre, Acireale, Sicily," Pupp J, 15(2):4-5, 1963

"Manteo's Sicilian Theatre, Brooklyn, New York," Pupp J, 15(2):6, 1963

Maraini, F. "Temples and Marionettes in Sicily," Geographical Mag, O 1949.

Michael, Vivian. "The Sicilian Theatre," Pupp J, 15(2):4-7, 1963. Mentions the "Macri-Weil Sicilian Theatre."

Milano, P. "L'Opera dei pupi in Sicily," Pupp, 5:40-43, 1934

Morice, Gerald. "Punch and Pars Column," World's Fair, London, O 24, 1964

Poignant, Roslyn. "Paladins, Puppets and Painted Carts in Sicily," Geographical Mag, 34:353-57 O, 1961

Sicily (cont.)
Rosa, Frank S. (La) "Vertichio and Noffio, Comic Sicilian
Puppets," Pupp 2:52-54, 1931
Sicilia Magazine. No 5, 1954; No 25, p 12-32, 1960
Tozer, H. V. Catalan Puppetry. Ashville, O. , Puppetry
Journal Publ.
--- "Putxinel-Lis (Pulcinello)" Pupp Master 2(2):41-49,
1948
Trentman, Charles. "Puppet Column," London Stage and
Television Today, O 22, 1964 p 7
Tweedle, Mrs. Alec. Sunny Sicily. London, 1904

"Une Page De L'Histoire De France Sous Le Ciel De Sicile;
Les Marionettes De P. B. Horowicz," L'Illus, 6:89, Jl
22, 1950
Vergani, Orio. Coleri Di Sicila. N. L: Edizioni Radio
Italiana, 1953, passim. In NN.

Spain

Note: "Titere" means puppet in this country; "Paladin" and
"Catalan" are rod puppets.

"Pito" is the mouthpiece to change the voice of the
"Punch" type hand puppeteer who roams the Spanish
countryside and Fairs.

Bagaho, Alfredo S. El Teatre De Titeres En La Escuela.
Buenos Aires, Kapelusz, 1945. In Harvard Univ. Lib.
"Barcelona Marionette Theatre, Puppets by H. V. Tozer,"
Pupp Th Mod World, p 221, and Illus No 63
Benitez, J. R. El Mundo De Los Titeres. New York, 1931

Bernardo, Mano. Titere: Magia Del Teatro. 1964.
--- Titeres De Guantes. Santa Fe, Dept. of Extension,
Univ. Naticonal Del Litoral, 1959. In LC.
Boehn, Max Von. Dolls and Puppets. London, Harrap,
1932
Canfield, D. and D. C. Fisher. "Basque Puppets," N Y
Times Bk Revu, O 11, 1931
--- "Spain's Puppeteers and Theaters," Pupp, 12:40, 1941

Cerda, G. H. Teatro De Guignol. Caracas, Ministry of
Education, Dept. of Public, 1965. In LC
Cervantes, M. De (Saavedra) Don Quixote. About the opera
by M. Defalla. Madrid, c1605, 1615, in Brit. Museum

The puppet show within this opera called "Master Peter's Puppet Show." Much material on this in "Music" Section, and "Ballet" Section.

George Speaight, in his History of the English Puppet Theatre, p 86, indicated Tom D'Urfrey as perhaps an early author of a "Don Quixote" version by saying, "Tom D'Urfrey introduced the puppet play into the third part of his Comical History of Don Quixote, 1695, Act III, Scene II and Act IV."

Covarrubias, M. Treasury of the Castilian Language. Madrid, c 1920's under the words, "Titero, Titere."

Crouse, E. "Madrid Marionettes Capture Capital," Pupp J, 17(6):4-5, 1966. DeFalla's opera "Don Quixote" under Master Manuel Merone.

"Dido" (Ezequiel Vigue)-Spain's Di Do," Pupp J, 11(1):12-13, illus

--- Pupp J, 11(5):14-15, 1960

Escobedo, A. A. Ya Viene Georgonio Esparza. Madrid, c 1947

Revu of Ya Viene Gorgonio Esparza. by W. K. Jones, Poet Lore, 53:376 Winter 1947

Fanciulli, G. Il Teatro Di Takiu. Milan,

Fisher, D. C. "Vive Guignol, Story of the Basque People," Schol, 24:8-9, Ap 7, 1934

--- "In Memory of 'Dido' the Great Puppeteer, E. Vigue," Pupp J, 12(4):31, 1961

Gasch, Sebastian. Titeres Y Manionetas. Barcelona, Argos, 1949. In NN. This is first book of its kind on contemporary puppets of Spain.

Revu of Titeres Y Manionetas, Anon., Pupp Master, 3(3):98-99, 1950

Keller, D. S. "Historical Notes on Spanish Puppetry," Hispania, 42:205-9, My 1959

--- "Seven Rare Catalan Puppet Plays of Spanish Puppet Work," Pupp J, 9(6):3-4, 1958

--- "Theatre of Dido at a Spanish Fair," Pupp J, 3-6, 23-25, 1960

Lira Gaiero, Elsa. Titerías. Montevideo, Impressions Pan Americana, 1961. In LC.

McPharlin, Paul. Puppet Theatre in America. New York, Harpers, 1949.

The author takes up Spanish puppetry in America and hints of it in Europe by centuries; sig. m. See following pages and passim material, p 6, 69, 71, 77, 79, 201, 239-61, 271, 302.

Spain (cont.)
Martinez, O. A. Teatro De Marionetas. Madrid, Impressi-
en de "Alrededer Del Mundo," 1920. In NN.
Millá, Luis. "Plays of the Spanish Showman Dido," Pupp
J, 11(4):3-7, 1960
--- Six Hand Puppet Plays for Catalan Puppets. Barce-
lona, c 1936 Liberia Milla, Imp. R. Plana, 1934
Munger, M. P. and A. L. Elder. El Libro De Les Titeres.
Barcelona, Juventud, imp. R. Plana 1944-45.
Piedrabuena, Antolines. Carnestolendas De Zaragosa.
Spain, 1961
"Puppet Theatre in Barcelona," Pupp, 3:19-26, 1932

"Puppets in Spain," Pupp, 8:38, 1937

Racca, Carlo. Burattini E Marionette. Spain, 18__

Reller, Daniel. "Historical notes on Spanish puppetry,"
Hispania, My 1959
Rusiñoly, S. "Catalan Puppet Plays," Drama, 8(25):90-
116, 1917
Santos, Francisco. Arc De Noc. Zargoza, 1697

Shergold, N. D. See J. E. Varey

Somma, Luis Mario. Titeres Y Pantomima. Montevideo,
1963
"Spain's Puppets in Photos," Pupp, 17:47, 1946

"Spanish Puppetry," Pupp, 7:75-76, 1936

"Spanish Puppets in New Orleans," Pupp, 3:27, 1932

Speaight, George. "International News," Pupp J, 2(2):19,
1950. Sub-title "Gibralter."
Tozer, H. V. "Barcelona Puppetry," Pupp, 5:37-8, 1934
--- Catalan Puppetry. Mimeo-Monograph, Ashville, O.;
Puppetry Journal Publ., c 1944. Available for loan from
Los Angeles County Guild of Puppetry Library, Write,
Pupp Life Publication.
--- "Catalan Puppets," Pupp, 3:24, 25, 26, 1932
--- "Dido-Life of Ezequiel Vigues, Master Puppeteer of
Spain," Pupp J, 6(6):4-7, 1955
--- "Evolution of a Repertoire in Barcelona," Pupp Master,
5(1):18-20, 1956
--- "My Autobiography," Pupp J, 4(5):3-5, 1953
--- "Puppets of Barcelona," Pupp, 6:75-6, 1935
--- "Spain Loses Great Puppeteer," Pupp, 9:20, 1938

--- "Spain's Civil War Puppetry," Pupp 10:38, 1939
--- "Spain's Puppetry in War," Pupp, 15:40, 1944
--- "Spain's Puppets," Pupp, 13-14:39-40, 1942
--- "Spanish Puppeteers," Pupp J, 2(2):19, 1950
--- "Spanish Puppeteers," Pupp, 17:70, 1946
Valle Inclan, Ramandel. Tabado De Marionnettas. Madrid,
Imprenta Ribadeneyra, 1930. In Oberlin Univ. Lib.
Varey, J. E. Historia de los Titeres En Espana. Madrid,
Revistia De Occidente, 1957. In NN.
--- Minor Forms of Spanish Drama With Special Reference
to Puppets. Cambridge, Cambridge Univ. Press, 1949
See also Pupp J, 12(3): 1950 in "Under the Bridge."
(Col.) He was director of Merlin Marionette Co.
--- "Puppets in Spain Today," Pupp Master, 3(2):49-52,
1950
--- Titeres, Marionetas y otras Diversiones Populares de
1958-1959. Madrid, Institute De Estudios Madrilenos,
1959. In LC
Revu of Historia de los Titeres En Espana. by N. D.
Shergold, Mod Lang R, 53:601, O 1958. Bibliog. p 417-
439
Williams, R. H. "Seventeenth Century Spanish Puppets,"
Pupp, 11: 1940
Yorick, (pseud.) "Puppets in Spain," Mask, 6:129-32, 1913

Sweden

Crouse, Elisabeth. "Stockholm Marionettes," Pupp J, 16
(2):29, 1964
Hammar, T. See Y. Hirn

Hirn, Yrjö. Les Jeux D'Enfants. trans. into French by
T. Hammar, Paris, Hammar, 1926
--- Barnlek, Nå Gra Kapitel Om Visor, Danser Och Små
Teatrar. Stockholm, Wahström, 1916. In NN.
Les Jeux D'Enfants Stockholm, och Widstrand.
Koller, Hans. Spela Kaspertheater. Stockholm, Viking,
1956
Lagerlöf, Selma. Dockteaterspel. Malmö, Allhems, 1959

Mahlmann, L. "The Marionette Theater of Stockholm,"
Pupp J, 17(3):9, 1965
"Michael Meschke Marionette Theatre-Stockholm," See
Pupp Th Mod World, p 228 and Illus Nos. 38, 39
Morice, G. "From Viggbyholm-Sweden," Brit Pupp Thea,
1(5):7-8, 1950

279

Sweden (cont.)
"Stockholm Marionette Theatre of Fantasy, Production of
'Three Penny Opera'," N Y Times, O 28, 1966, 33:1
--- "of 'Wizard of Oz' at Hunter College on D 26-31, 1966,"
N Y Times, D 27, 1966, 49:1
"Swedish Model Theatre," Brit Pupp Thea, 1(4):13, 1950

Switzerland

Note: The "Punch" character beloved by everyone is called,
"Chasper" in this country and is found in many of their
productions. Little shadow work is done but they have
several theaters of very delicate and high quality construction of marionettes, rod and hand puppets. There
is a high standard of intricate mechanism to many of
their puppets and many dolls are so mechanized that it
might be wise to call them "automats" or mechanical
puppets.

Altherr, Alfred. "Zurich," Pupp, 2:42, 1931
--- Marionetten. Zürich, Rentsch, 1926
and Erlenbach, 1936. In Yale Univ. Lib.
Revu of Marionetten. Erlenbuch, by J. J. Hayes, Drama,
19:81, D 1928
"Ambrosius Mumm Marionettenbuhne Theatre." No written
material found as yet. Peter W. Loosli, puppeteer.
"Ascona Marionetten Theater," at Basel, Switzerland. No
written material found as yet, except See J. K. Melling.
Balmer, H. Mein Gemüsetheater. Bern, 1928. Con-
cerned with vegetable puppets, unusual material.
"Basel Marionette Theater," Brit Pupp Thea, 1(6):26, 1950

Basler Puppenspiel. De Waelburgh, Blaricum, 1926. In
NN, Swiss German Puppet Plays.
Boehn, Max Von. Dolls and Puppets. Trans. by J. Ni-
coll, London, Harrap, 1932.
Budry, Maurice. Trois Petits Tours Les Marionettes.
Lausanne, Payot and Cie, 1932. In NN.
Buhrmann, Max. Das Farbige Schattenspiel. Berne,
Haupt, 1955.
Gauchat, Pierre. Marionetten. Vol 1, Zürich, Rentsch,
1949. In NN.
--- "Puppet Theatre in Zurich," in his, Theater Der Welt.
Amsterdam, Jager, 1938, Vol 2, p 34-36
--- "They Have No Home," Brit Pupp Thea, 1(5):12, 1950
"In Switzerland, A Trio of Proficient Puppeteers," Sunset,
117:10 S 1956.

Keller, Therese. Das Kasperspiel. Bern, Haupt, 1954
In NN.

--- "Puppets at Festival," Pupp J, 15(1):26, 1963
Köelner, Richard. Marionette, Belauscht Von Richard
Köelner, Basel, Basler Mario. Th, 1954, in NN.
Ludwig, David. "Bochumer Germany Figurentheaterwoche,"
Pupp J, 18(5):31-33, 1967. This Swiss article is about
the Punch and Judy operator Theresa Keller.
McPharlin, Paul. Puppet Theater in America. New York,
Harpers, 1949, p 322, item only.
Melling, J. K. "Jakob Flach's Theater at Ascona, Switz-
erland," Pupp Master, 5(6):17, 1957
Michael, Vivian. "From Abroad-Ueli Balmer, Switzer-
land," Pupp J, 11(5):14, 1950. This article lists many
theatres and puppeteers.
Moynier, Marcelle. "Puppetry in Switzerland," Pupp, 11:
39, 1940
--- "Switzerland's Geneva Marionette Co." Pupp, 12:40,
1941
Nicoll, J. See Max Von Boehn

"Puppin in Switzerland," Pupp, 4:62, 1933

Scherrer, H. Inhaber Und Leiter.. Hermann Scherrer's St.
Gallen Theatre. St. Gallen, Buchdr Zollikofer, 1934.
In NN.
Stössel, Rudolf. Schnitzt, Malt Und Spielt Kasperli. Zurich,
Pro Juventute, 194?. In NN.
"Switzerland," Pupp, 5:36-44, 1934

Therese Keller's Theater-Munsing (Kanton Bern), Pupp Th
Mod World, p 220, and Illus No 31
"Ueli Balmer's Theater," Pupp J, 11(5):14, 1959

Wittiche, E. "Fahpende Puppenspieler," Schweizer, Archv.
Für Volkskunde, 1929, p 54-61
Wittkop-Ménardeau, Gabrielle. Von Puppen Und Marionetten:
Kleine Kulturgeschichte Für Sammler Und Liebhaber.
Zurich, Classen, 1962
"Young Swiss Puppeteers," Ch Sci Mon, Eastern, S 16,
1965, p 17: col 2
"Zürcher Marionetten Theater at Zürich With Fred Schneck-
enburger," Pupp Th Mod World, p 220, Illus Nos 29, 30
"Zürich-April 28th," Pupp, 9:37, 1938

Zürich, Kunstgewerbemuseum. Zürfcher Poppenspiele.
Zürich, Helmshaus, 1963

Switzerland (cont.)
"Zürich puppets," Pupp 2:17, 1932

Thailand, Siam

Note: The Shadow play is called "Nang" in this country.

Bridhyakorn, H. H. Prince D. K. Bidyalabah (Royalty). Sia-
mese Theatre. Bangkok, Siam Comm. Press, 1934. The
Thailand Culture Series No. 12. Natl. Culture Inst., Fine
Arts Dept. 1962 and in New Series, No. 3, 6, 7.
Dhaninivat, Prince (D. Sonakul) The Nang. Bangkok,
Siam Comm. Press, 1954(?) Thailand Culture Series.
National Cultural Institute.
Kahsalak, Nagyai. The Arts of Thai Picture Play: Sil-
houettes of the Shadow Play. Bangkok.
"Thailand." Geographical Mag, London, S 1946

"Puppets." Jour. of the Siamese Society, 21: pt 1, 1927, p
37-52; 37: pt 1, 1947, p 30-31
"Puppets." Man, May 1959

"Puppets of Siam," Mask, 6(2): 1914

Wagner, F. A. The Art of Indonesia. (And the Island
Group). New York, Greystone, 1967, passim

Turkey

Note: The "Shadow" Section will have much overlap on this
country and the material about "Karogöz" or "Karagheuz"
(Black Eye.). This is the favorite puppet clown, resembling the "Punch" character. This was a very common form in the 14th and 15th centuries. It declined
in the 16th and 17th centuries, and has almost vanished
now. Revived a little in the 19th century but by 1950
had begun steep decline.

Agastine, C. D. "Karagheuz," Mercure De France, 284:
121-32, My 15, ?
Anderson, Madge. Heroes of the Puppet Stage. New York,
Harcourt, 1923, passim.
Avery, Verna. "Music for the Marionette Theatre." Pupp J,
2(3):3, 1950
Baird, Bill. The Art of the Puppet. New York, Macmillan,
1965. Sig. m. in chapter called "A Turkish Delight."

Blackham, Olive. Shadow Puppets. London, Rockcliff,
1960, p 42-59
Boehn, Max Von. Dolls and Puppets. Trans. by J. Nicoll.
London, Harrap, 1932
Dumanil, Talat. "Marionnettes in Gulhane Park, Ishtan-
bule," Pupp J, 17(4):9, 1966
Flanagan, Hallie. "Turkish Shadow Hero," Pupp 3:55-56,
1933
--- "Le Théâter De Karagheuz," L'Amoar De L'Art, 16:
102-03, Mr 1935
Gamble, M. and J. "Karagöz," Pupp J, 16(5):4-5, 1965

Gautier, Theophile. Constantinople. Paris, Levy, 1854,
passim
--- "Karagheuz, Turkish Shadow Hero," Part 2, Marion-
ette, 1:253-56, Feb 1918
Gordlevsky, V. Iz Nastcyashchage I Proshlage Maddahov V
Turcii. St. Petersburg,"Mir" Islama, 1912
Horn, P. "Das Türkische Schattenspiele," Altgemeine
Zeitung, 112: 1900.
Jacob, G. Geschichte Des Schattentheaters Im Morgen Und
Abendland. Hannover, Morgen, 1925 and Stuttgart, Kohl-
hammer, 1933. In British Museum.
    Available at Corner Bk Store, NYC. This is his most
complete and main history of East and West shadow work,
with complete bibliog from 11th century.
--- Türische Volkslitteratur. Berlin, 1901. In British
Museum. Schattentheater work. Corner Bk Store, NYC
has copies.
--- Vorträge Türkischer Meddahs. (Mimischer Erzählungs-
kunstler) Berlin, Turkische Bibliothex, Band I, 1904[sic]
See also "Shadow" Section
Kahle, Paul. Der Leuchtturm Van Alexandria Ein Arabis-
ches Schattenspiel Aus Dem Mittelalterlichen Agyten.
Stuttgart, Kohlhaman, 1930.
"Karagöz," National Geographic, S 1957

"Karagheuz, Islam, 1:264-299, 1910; Islam 2:143-195,
1911.
Kilner, M. "Turkish Shadows," Pupp Master, 4(1):17, 1952

Kucuk, Ali. "The Master Punch Operator of Turkey,"
Pupp J, 16(5):4-5, 1965
Kúnes, Ignaz. Das Tukkische Volksschauspiel-Orza Ojnu.
Leipzig, 1908
--- "Türische Puppentheater," Ethnologische Mitteilungen
Aus Ungarn, 2: 1889

Turkey (cont.)
--- "Uper Türische Schattenspieler," Ungarische Revue,
    7: 1887
McDougall, A. R.   "An Athenian Shadow Show," Thea Arts,
    17:387-93, My 1933.   Also speaks of Turkey
Maindron, Ernest.   Marionettes et Guignols.   Paris, Juven,
    c 1900.   In NN.
Martinovitch, N. N.   Turetskiy Teatr Karagöz.   St. Peters-
    burgh, "Mir" Islama, 1910.
---"The Turkish Puppet Theatre," Thea Arts, 18:54, Feb
    1934
--- The Turkish Theatre.   New York, Theater Arts, 1953.
    In Oberlin Univ Lib. , and Ottawa Univ Lib.
Nerval, Gerald de.   Voyage En Orient.   Vol 2, Paris,
    Charpentier, 1851, p 198-212
Nicholl, J.   See Max Von Boehn

Nuzhet, Selim.   Turk Temasasi.   Meddah-Karagöz-Orta
    Oyunu.   Ishtanbul, 1930.   In NN.
Ritter, Hellmut.   Karagöz.   Turkishe Schattenspiele.   Han-
    nover, Lafaire, 1924
--- Karagöz Turkishe Schattenspiele.   Ishtanbul, Druckerei-
    Universum (Bibliotheca Islamica 13) 1933, and Ishtanbul:
    Devlet Matbassi, 1932.
--- and Steiner Wiesbaden.   Karagöz Turkishe Schattenspiele.
    Orient-.   Hannover, Lafaire, 1953
Saussey, Edouard.   "Une Farce De Karaghuerz En Dialecte
    De Damas," Bulletin D'Etudes Orientales, 7-8:5-38,
    1937-38
"Shadow Karagöz," Marionette, 1(7): 1918; 1(8): 1918.

"Shadows of Turkey," Pupp, 2: 1931; 5: 1934; 8: 1937.

Siyavusgil, Sabriesat.   Karagöz.   Ishtabul, Drukkerij, 1951
    and Turkish Press & Tourist Dept. , Ankara, Turkey 1955.
Spies, Otto.   Turkisches Puppentheater.   West Emsdetten,
    Lechte, 1959.   In NN.
Thalasso, Adolphe.   Moliere Théâtre Turquie.   Paris,
    Tiesse, 188.   Available at Mme S. Z.
--- "Le Théâtre Turc," La Revue Theatrale, 1904.
--- "Le Théâtre Turc Contemporain," Revue Encyclopedique
    Larousse, 1899.
"Turkish Shadows" Sphere, Oct 1934; Studio, Feb 1935;
    Thea Arts, My 1933.
Whanslaw, H.   See "Plays" Section, under division on
    Shadow plays.

United States of America, See America

United States of Soviet Russia, See Russia

Vietnam

"Hoang Luân Puppets From a Higher Elementary School,"
Pupp Th Mod World, p 228, and Illus No 208
Tuy, Le Vinh. "Vietnam's Terrestial and Aquatic Puppets,"
World Thea, 14:490-94 S 1965
"Vietnam Central Marionette Theatre-Hanoi," Puppet Th Mod
World, p 228, and Illus No 209-214

Venezuela

"Visiting in Venezuela," Grapev, Je 1949 p 2
The Wallace puppets playing there.

Wales

Note: Some material may be found in the "English" Division and under the following theatres in "Theatre" Section, Harlequin, Caricature Theatre.

Brown, Betty. "Jane Phillips, "Pilgrim's Progress,"
UNIMA, U. S. A. Newsl, Je 1968, p 29
--- "Pilgrim's Progress-The Caricature Theatre of Wales,"
Pupp Life, S 1968, p 3
Clark, M. "England and North Wales," in Rod Young's
column, "Mailbox," Pupp J, 10(2):31, 34, 1958, items
only
Crawford, K. N. "The Caricature Theatre of Cardiff,
Wales," Pupp J, 20(2):26, 1968
--- Colwyn Bay International Festival Report-1968. London,
British Puppet and Model Theatre Guild Office, 1968.
In NN.
--- The Eric Marionettes of Colwyn Bay, Wales, Pupp J,
20(2):27, 1968
--- "Harlequin Theatre," Pupp J, 20(2):28, 1968
--- "UNIMA's Pilgrims Progress, Giant Rods," Pupp J,
20(2):34, 1968
"Eric Bramall's Theater at Colwyn Bay, North Wales,
Harlequin," Pupp J, 10(2):33, 1958, item only. Located

Wales (cont.)
at Rho-On-Sea. This was first puppet theatre in Wales.
See also "Found a Genuine Puppeteer," Pupp J, 11(1):
9-10, 1959
Perrottest, Edna L. "Village Puppetry," Pupp, 11:36, 1940
--- "Wentworth N. S. Wales Puppetry," Pupp 12:39, 1941
Proctor, E. and R. "Puppets Old and New- N. Wales,"
Pupp J, 5(3):11, 1953
Rees, Jack and Doreen. "Puppeteers of Wales," Pupp
Master, 3(3):94-95, 1950
Wilkinson, W. Puppetry in Wales. London, Bles, 1948

Yugoslavia

"Ali Baba and the Forty Thieves Production,"   Pupp
Th Mod World, p 225 and Illus No 151
Play be Zvenko Agbaba and A. Augustinčic. Production
by Berislav Brajković.
Baird, Bill. The Art of the Puppet. New York, Macmil-
lan, 1965, p 250
"Bráikerić, Berislav Puppets," Pupp Th Mod World, p 251,
and Illus No 151
"Festetic, Zerka," Pupp Th Mod World, p 251, and Illus
No 153
Festivals. Pupp J, 17(4):10, 1966. Concerned with Chil-
dren's Festival, July 1, 1966 at Sibenik.
Howard, T. E. "A Puppet Theatre in Belgrade," Pupp
Master, 9(4):18-19, D 1968
"Jugoslavia Refugee Camp Puppets," Pupp, 15:39, 1944

"Jugoslavian Puppetry," Pupp, 4:61, 1933

"The Little Dog and the Little Cat Production," Pupp Th
Mod World, p 225, and Illus No 153
McPharlin, Marjorie. "The Puppet International Festival,"
Pupp J, 10(2):12, 1958
Mahlmann, L. "The Puppet Theater of Zagreb, Yugoslavia,"
Pupp J, 17(3):7, 1965. Rod puppet work.
"Marija Kulandžić puppets," Pupp Th Mod World, p 225
and Illus No 152
Marshall, Clader. The Star and The Sand.
Revue of Star and the Sand. Anon., Cornhill Mag,
Ap 1945.
"Pionir Marionette Theatre," Pupp Th Mod World, p 225
and Illus No 154
"Pionir Marionette Theatre at Split, The zvonko Kevać

Puppets," Pupp Th Mod World, p 251, and Illus No 154
"Puppets of Jugoslavia," Pupp, 5:30, 1934

Smasek, Emil. "The Puppet Play in Slovania," Pupp J,
4(2):3-6, 1952
"Tale of the Sea Production," Pupp Th Mod World, p 225
and Illus No 152
Zaconick, Dorothy. "Puppetry in Jugoslavia is growing,
and the work of Louis Karach," Pupp, 4:62, 1933

Chapter II

The Organizations, Guilds and Publications of Puppetry

A. World Organizations of Puppetry

Note: There are, of course, many more groups
than I have been able to gather material about for this publication. Much more material about those I have listed is a-
vailable.

It is hoped that the groups which are unlisted will
write to us so that later editions may include these and other
corrections.

The determining factor in listing was that group was
a "club" rather than a "company."

General

Clipping File. In the N Y Publ Lib. under "Organizations,"
"Associations," and "Theatres"
Hartman, John. "Non-Profit Puppetry Organizations-Taxable
Without A Charter," Pupp J, 19(2):23-24, 1967
Philpott, A. R. Dictionary of Puppetry. London, Madonald,
1969. Has a section on organizations.
Whanslaw, H. W. Second Bench Book of Puppetry. London,
Wells, 1957, p 218-20. Many organizations given.

World Organizations and Guilds
(alphabetically)

"Agrupacion De Marionetistas Amateurs Del Fomento De Las
Artes Decorations." or, "Marionetas, Ama," Spain.
Has other names with or without "Del Fad." Organ.
about 1946. Seemed to be the Marionette theater sec-
tion of "The Fomento de las Artes Decorativas" of
Barcelona.
Director: H. V. Tozer, Barcelona, group tours,

also plays at home theater in Fomento's Auditorium, Barcelona.
No periodical was located.
Pupp, 15:70, 1944; 17:71, 1946; 4(4):25, 1953
See also H. V. Tozer, "Acting and Manipulation" Section, "Marionette" Section

"American Educational Teachers Assn. , Puppetry Div. ," U. S. A.
    Organ. c to 1950's
    Director or Pres. was Bill Duncan around 1953
    Periodical not known
    Pupp J, 4(4):25, 1953

"American Puppet Arts Council," U. S. A.
    Organ. c 1963, New York City with grant from Population Council, New York City, non-profit group.
    Pres. Bill Baird
    "Other News" G N Y Pupp G Newsl, 8(1):5, O 1969

"Amis De Guignol," France
    Organ. 1922-1939. In Lyons, France, with a branch in Morocco, N. Spain, called "Lyonese Society."
    First Director or Pres. is not known.
    Periodicals: Bulletin Des Amis De Guignol; The Almanach De Marionette & Guignol; Bulletin Trimestriel.
    Pupp, 4:58, 1933; 5:34, 1934

"Amis De LaFleur," France
    Organ. in 1920's in Lyons, France, sponsored by Picardy Marionette Co.
    Director unknown but it was considered a very "scholarly group" by Mr. Paul McPharlin, suggesting adult type drama.
    Periodical not known.
    Pupp, 4:34, 1933

"Amis De La Marionette," France
    Organ. c. 1930's or earlier, in Paris at the Vaugirard Hall, doing unusual and outstanding work which was well publicized in French, and world periodicals.
    See also "French" Section
    No periodical was located.
    Pupp, 5:33, 1934

"Anglo-Australian Puppets Ltd. ," British
    Organ. c 1939, became "Puppet Theater Ltd." and

"Anglo-Australian Puppets Ltd.," Brit. (cont.)
then became "Educational Puppetry Institute" under
Mr. Bruno Tublin, 1949. See These names.
Not to be confused with "The British Educational
Puppetry Association." See "Long Arm of Coinci-
dence" by A. E. Peterson, Pupp Master, 3(1):12-14,
1950; and Pupp Master, 3(2):63, 1950
First Pres. was Bruno Tublin
Had a periodical by the name of Educational Puppetry
Institute.

"Antwerp Group, or Society, of Puppetry," Belgium
United with the "National Belgium Federation Org."
Organ. c 1947 in Antwerp Belgium.
Director or Pres. unknown.
No periodical known.
Pupp J, 2(3):24, 1950

"Association Des Marionettes," France
Organ. 1930's, Lyon, France
Director or Pres. unknown.
No periodical known.

"Australian Puppet Guild," Australia
Organ. c to 1940's in Melbourne, Australia
Pres. was W. D. Nicol who published a mimeo paper,
The Australian Puppeteer, 1949
"International News," Pupp J, 1(3):10, 1949

"Belgian National Fellowship," Belgium. (See "National
Belgium Federation")
Organ. 1930's, Now, "Flemish League for the Puppet
Theatre."
Director, or Pres. unknown.
Periodical was The Messenger.
Pupp, 3:57-58, 1933;
Pupp J, 2(3):24-25, 1950

"Birmingham Puppet Guild," England
Affiliated with "British Puppet and Model Theatre
Guild."
Organ. 1949 in Birmingham with 90 members. Holds
annual exhibitions in April, gives many shows at this
time. Has classes in puppetry with local education
authorities.
Pres. or Director unknown.
Periodical unknown.

"Birmingham Juvenile Dramatic Festival," Brit Pupp
Thea, 1(4):15, 1950
"No 8 of Puppeteer Profiles, Frank Worth," Brit
Pupp Thea, 1(6):6-4, 1950
Brit Pupp Thea, 2(1):2, 1951

"Boston Area Guild of Puppetry," U. S. A.
Now affiliated with "New England Guild of Puppetry,"
No 9 of "Puppeteers of America" since 1961
Organ. 1959-1960 in Boston area by Gordon Bennett.
Had first festival at Sturbridge, Mass., 1962
Pupp J, 14(2):28, 1962
Director or Pres. (first) not known.
Periodical now called Control Stick.

"Bristol Puppet Club," England
Organ. 1950 by Miss Beckenridge at Bristol, England
Has about 30 active members.   Teaching courses in
puppetry at Royal Fort.   Officers not known.
Periodical is Spotlight on Bristol.
Brit Pupp Thea, 1(4):10, 13, 28, 1950

"British Educational Puppetry Association," (E. P. A.), England.   (See "British Educ. Pupp. Institute.")
Organ. c 1943.   Seems to have grown out of the "British Puppet and Model Theatre Guild-School Section,
Manchester Div.," which began in 1938.   Group has
strong influence on British puppet world, especially
educationally.   It sponsors summer courses for teachers in London, and Oxford, and sometimes in Edinburgh.   Has many exhibits, festivals and publishes
pamphlets and guides and books on puppets. Interested
in therapy work.
Directors and Pres. were Percy Press, John Cox,
E. Davis, Bruno Tublin and A. R. Philpott and others.
Usually no director.
Periodicals have been varied, and irregular and at
times confusing.   First ones seem to have been a
Newsletter in the 1940's and Puppet Post.   But British
Puppet Theatre also appeared (See "British Educational Puppetry Institute") This older periodical was
named as that of another organization and is discussed
by A. E. Peterson in "Long Arm of Coincidence,"
Pupp Master, 3(2):63, 1950 and Pupp Master, 3(1):12-
14, 1950.   The N Y Publ Lib. has these early few
periodicals.
Publication of the E. P. A. Yearbooks was apt to get

291

"Brit. Educ. Puppetry Assn." (cont.)
readers of historical material confused with the early
Puppetry Yearbooks of Paul McPharlin, in America
(which are all referred to as just Puppetry in this
bibliography). Many of these may be found in N Y
Pub. Lib.
The group wrote and sponsored a "Guide" to puppets in educative work called Complete Puppet Book,
London, Faber, 1950 which was edited by L. V. Wall
and republished by Faber in 1956. It has lately been
enlarged, revised and re-edited by A. R. Philpott and
others (1965). See "English" Section, under A. R.
Philpott. Publication of 22 Instructional Leaflets,
London, British Education Association.
Present periodicals: E. P. A. "Spotlight," a news-
sheet, and Puppet Post. There has been no mention
of a yearbook for some time.
"Last Twenty-Five Years," by H. W. Whanslaw,
Pupp Master, 3(2):41-43, 1950. See also Dictionary
of Puppetry by A. R. Philpott, London, Macdonald,
1969.

"British Educational Puppetry Institute," England
Organ. of this group seems to have had several previous names. Some sources say it developed from a
branch of the "British Puppet Guild, North Section,"
into "British Puppet Guild, School Section, Manchester
Div. ," then into "Puppet Theatre Ltd. ," and thence into the group called "Educational Puppetry Institute," in
about August of 1942. This was a spur of "Educational Puppetry Association." (See this last mentioned
group.) The organization was dissolved because of
legal troubles, which explains confusion and short life
of the periodical published under "Institute."
Original Directors or Pres. not known.
Periodical was a Newsletter early in its history and
then British Puppet Theatre, which was the same name,
with only slight, if any, difference, as the periodical
used for a while by "British Puppet and Model Theatre
Guild." See article by A. E. Peterson, "Long Arm of
Coincidence," Pupp Master 3(1&2):63, 12-14, 1950.
Dictionary of Puppetry, London, Macdonald, 1969, by
A. R. Philpott.
Explains much of this confusion and also in many
organizations throughout the world.
Brit Pupp Thea, 1(4):11, 19, 1950; 3(3):7, 1950
Pupp Master, 3(2):41-43, 1950
"British Puppet Guild Activities," by Morice, G.

"British Puppet Guild," England
Name used by G. Morice and some other sources to
indicate either the educational or model theatre group,
whichever the author was concerned with in the articles.
This was not, I think, the name of an organization,
different and independent from other British groups
mentioned previously or immediately following this
item.
"British Puppet Guild Activities," G. Morice, Drama,
17:44, D 1938.

"British Puppet and Model Theatre Guild," England
Organ. 1925, and first called "British Model Theatre
Guild." May also have included the words "Toy Theatre" early in history of group. This is the professional and amateur group not entirely concerned with
educational puppetry. Has annual exhibits and sponsors international festivals with the "British UNIMA"
organization. Does a little publishing of exhibit catalogues.
Director or Pres. (early) Seymour Marks, Waldo
Lanchester, H. W. Whanslaw, Percy Press, George
Speaight, and other puppet masters who were often
editors of the periodical. Gordon Craig was in this
position for some time.
Periodicals have been interrupted, and are confusing in the matter of numbering, not name. For a
brief time it published under News and Notes, 'War-
Time' Bulletin or Newsletter, and the very confusing
British Puppet Theatre Limited-The Model Stage, of
which I found a few copies, in the N Y Publ Lib. The
famous dramatist and puppeteer, Gordon Craig, was
editor of Puppet Master in 1938, which may have been
the first issuing of this still continuing periodical of
the group.
The Puppet Master has been very irregular and
started a "New Series" every so often, with different
editors, type and size of publication. It continues today and is supposed to appear 4 times a year. The
group also has a British Puppet and Model Theatre
Guild Newsletter.
Pupp, 3:12, 1933 (gives early pointers on group)
Grapevine, Je 1949 p 10
"Twenty-Five Years," by H. Whanslaw (gives good
discussion) Pupp Master, 3(2):41-43, 1950

"British Puppet and Model Theatre Guild, " (cont.)
Pupp Thea Am., by Paul McPharlin, p 391 (gives
1949 version
Brit Pupp Thea, 1(5):24, 1950
Pupp Master, 4(2):240-41, 1955; 4(7):287, 1956
Illus Lon N, 225:799, N 6, 1954
Brit Pupp & M Thea G Newsl, 152:4, Jan 1969

"British Puppet Theatre Ltd. ," England
Organ. - details very uncertain.
If this was an authentic organization it organized late
in 1940's as a spur group.   Seems to have sponsored
the publication of "British Educational Puppetry Institute," called British Puppet Theatre Limited or just
British Puppet Theatre, 52 Bedford Row, London,
W. C. 1, 1950.   A few copies are in N Y Publ Lib.
with both titles.

"Burroughs Marionette Theatre Guild," U. S. A.
Organ. in Detroit, Mich. c 1930
Director or Pres. not known.
Periodical was The Puppeteer, monthly. Had at least
four issues.
Pupp, 2:122-124, 1931
Pupp J, 2(3):29, 1950

"Carmel California Guild of Puppetry," U. S. A.
Organ. 1960
Director or Pres. not known but one of the leading
groups in the organization is the "Red Gate Shadow
Players."   The only large and authentic Chinese
Shadow Group in America with a complete shadow
theatre trouping group.
Pupp 2:(1931) p 122-24
Pupp J, 11(6):27-28, 1960 and near issues

"Cellar Playhouse Group," U. S. A. (See "Midwestern Puppeteers")
Organ. c 1939 in Chicago with Romain Proctor as one
of the founders.   This was a short lived group which
combined with others in area.   It was sometimes
called, "Chicago North Side Puppeteers."
Director or Pres. was George Cole, and Romain
Proctor.
Periodical was a type of Newsletter.   Name not known.
Pupp, 10: 1939, and many issues in 1940's - short
items.

"Central International Pour L'Etude De La Marionette
Traditionelle." (C. I. P. E. M. A. T.) France
Organ. 1959 in Paris. Information might be gotten
from UNIMA France on this group.
Director, or Pres. unknown.
No periodical known.
Theatre Notebook, 14(3): Spring 1960
Pupp J, 11(2):33-34, 1959

"Ches Cabotans," France
Organ. 1920's at Amis, in Picardy
Director was Renes Villeret, and they gave produc-
tions in the old puppetry traditional way.
Periodical not known.
Pupp, 10:34, 1934

"Chicago Marionette Guild," U. S. A.
Organ. 1930 at Chicago. Did adult professional and
semi-professional shows with classic topics. They
divided into the "Chicago North Side" and the "Chicago
South Side" puppeteers around 1934. Originally were
about 20 members meeting in homes.
Director or Pres., not known.
Periodical was a very informal Newsnote.

"Chicago North Side Puppeteers," U. S. A. (See "Midwest-
ern Puppeteers")
Organ. c to 1934 as a branch of the "Chicago Mario-
nette Guild." Friendly rivalry with the "South Side"
group and inter-exchange of ideas and programs.
Director or Pres. was George Cole.
Periodical was a mimeo News Bulletin.
Pupp J, 1(2):16, 1949 and "Regional Activities."
Pupp J, 2(3):25, 26, 29, 1950

"Chicago South Side Puppeteers," U. S. A. (See "Midwestern
Puppeteers")
Organ. c to 1934 as a branch of the "Chicago Mario-
nette Guild." Friendly rivalry with "North Side"
group.
Director or Pres. was A. and I. Hoffman.
Periodical was Newsnote.

"Chicagoland Puppetry Guild," U. S. A. (See "Midwestern
Puppeteers")
Organ. 1961 as a regular Guild of the "Puppeteers of
America" with the Number 10. Information about its

"Chicagoland Puppetry Guild" (cont.)
    work will be found under "Guild" sections in Pupp J
    for many issues and under "America" Section in this
    bibliography.
    Director or Pres. was Mildred Gordon early in its
    history.
    Periodical is Puppet Patter
    Pupp J, 14(2):25, 1962

"CIPEMAT," France (See "UNIMA, France")

"Circle of German Shadow Players," Germany
    Organ. c 1949 in Hamburg under sponsorship of a large
    number of shadow puppeteers. Had about 40 members
    and first met in Barsbuettel, Germany. Very active
    and in later years quite experimental. Doing some
    film work.
    Director or Pres. was Mrs. Margaret Cordes.
    Periodical, Der Schattenbrief; original editor was M.
    Cordes.
    "International News" Pupp J 2(6):28-29, 1950
    Pupp Master, 3(4):124, 1950

"Club Guignol, The," U. S. A.
    Organ. about 1930 in Hollywood.
    N Y Times, Je 1, 1930, 8:4

"Columbus Guild of Puppetry," U. S. A.
    Organ. c 1940 in Columbus, O. Was called the "First
    Guild" in the "Puppeteers of America" group for many
    years but became inactive, and in 1965 seems to ap-
    pear on record in Pupp J as No. 2 Guild. Material
    will be found in early issues of Grapevine, Pupp, c
    1940's and Pupp J, 1950.
    Director or Pres. was Vivian Michael at first.
    Periodical not known.

"Community Puppet Theatre and Workshop," U. S. A.
    Organ. c 1935 in Indianapolis. Sometimes went by the
    name of "Indianapolis Community Puppet Theatre of
    Jr. Leagues." They met once a week with a paid pro-
    fessional instructor and performed at Art museums,
    parks, and recreational facilities. The Jr League Mag
    of these years should have more information.
    Director or Pres. was Jean Starr Wiksell.
    Periodical not known.
    Pupp J, 1(3):7, 1949

"Czechoslovakian Puppetry Commission Club," Czech.
Organ. c 1931 in Prage, "No 8 Theatre." Gradually
925 puppet theatres and groups banded together under
this commission with State support. There is a new
recognized Puppet School, or College, in Prague, from
this group. Publication of leaflets and information is
quite large. Many international festivals and exhibits
are sponsored. The "International Marionette Org. of
UNIMA" started from the interest of this group. Theatres and groups will also be found in "Theatre" Section.
Director or Pres. was Dr. Jan Malik and his leadership has lasted many years.
Periodical is Cesky Leutkar and Leutkeva Seena which
is richly illustrated and carries some English articles.
There are other periodicals; see also that section.
Pupp 5:30-32, 1934

"Dansk Modelteater-Samfund," Denmark
Organ. previous to the 1940's in Copenhagen. It is a
Model Theater organization of puppeteers in the main
sense of the word.
Director or Pres. was Sevend Lougreen
Periodical was called Suffloren
Pupp Master, 3(2):43, 1950

"Decatur Marionette Guild," U. S. A.
Organ. previous to 1937 in Decatur. Interested in
children's classical and musical productions.
Director or Pres. was George New.
Periodical not known.
Pupp Th Am., by Paul McPharlin, p 390-91, 449

"Detroit Marionette Fellowship," U. S. A. (See "Marionette
Fellowship")
Organ. 1929 with very loose grouping under Paul Mc
Pharlin.
Director or Pres. was Paul McPharlin, if officers
elected.
Periodical - uncertain.
Grapev, Ap 1949, p 6

"Detroit Puppet Guild," U. S. A. (See "Detroit Puppeteers
Guild No. 16")
Organ. early 1930's from "Detroit Marionette Fellowship," and others. Became a stronger group around
1940's and from it has come one of the largest organizations of puppeteers in the world called, "Puppeteers

"Detroit Puppet Guild," (cont.)
of America." This group became Guild No. 16 officially in 1963, although its members were consistent in moving out and forming earlier Guilds.
Director or Pres. - the first was Paul McPharlin but many well known puppeteers were early leaders.
Periodical was a Newsletter at first, then The Grapevine Telegraph became official communication, then Grapevine, again from the inclusion of "The Marionette Fellowship" Group. Puppetry Yearbook of America (which in this bibliography is indicated as just Puppetry) and today has its own Detroit Guild Gazette.
Grapev, Feb 1949, p 4.
Other issues of above mentioned periodicals c to 1930's-1950's should tell of early activities. (See "Detroit Guild No. 16")
Pupp J, 21(1):32, 1969
See Pupp J, "Regional and Guild" information in all issues.
See also "American" Div., "International" Section.

"Detroit Puppet Guild No. 16," U.S.A. (See "Detroit Puppet Guild")
Organ. 1963 in Detroit. Became very active after the Detroit Museum of Art was given the "McPharlin Library and Puppet Collection." Now helps to sponsor a National Puppet Theatre, in the Museum, for visiting puppet masters from this country and abroad. One of the most complete puppet theatres and libraries and museums is sponsored here.
Directors or Pres. will be given on back of Pupp J, issues.
Periodical is Detroit Guild Gazette or earlier, Detroit Guild Newsletter. Information in most all of the Pupp J. issues, under "Regional and Guild" headings.
See also "American" Div., "International" Section
"Under the Bridge," by M. Stevens, Pupp J, 2(1):22, 1950
Pupp J, 2(5):21, 1951, concerns early group
"Eleven Years Old Party," Pupp J, 9(1):29, 1957 - earlier group
"Review of Work by Members," Pupp J, 8(4):28, 1957
"Billy the Kid, Musical," Pupp J, 9(5):22-23, 1958
"Oedipus Rex Display at Institute," Pupp J, 10(1):27, 1958
Pupp J, 21(1):32, 1969

"Detroit Puppeteens Guild No. 6," U.S.A.
Organ. c 1960, joined "Puppeteers of America" group.
Branch of the Detroit Guild for the younger puppeteers.
Inactive now.
Director or Pres. not known.
Periodical was a Newsletter.

"Deutsche Buhne," Germany
Organ. c to 1934. Seems to have been directly connected with a National German Theatre which may be
same as "Deutscher Bund Fur Puppenspiel."
Director or Pres. not known, unless F. Wortelmann.
Periodical seems to be Deutsche Buhn after the Puppet
Theatre and may, under the Nazi control, have taken
the place of Die Puppenbuhne or Der Puppenspieler -
yet be the same periodical.

"Deutsche Puppen Theatre V," Germany
Organ. 1969 in West Germany at Bielefeld and very ac-
tive in experimental puppetry.
Director or Pres. is Herr Albrecht, of Stuttgart.
Periodical not known.
Brit Pupp & M Thea G Newsl. No 154, Mr 1969, p 3

"Deutscher Bund für Puppenspiel," Germany (See also
"Die Puppenspieler Guild")
Organ. c 1930-33, stopped and began again 1948-50 in
Bochum, Germany
Director, or Pres. and Editor was Fritz Wortelmann
Periodical - changed first part of name several times
and causes much confusion in "Periodical" Section, but
in the McPharlin Collection I found Vol. 1-3 called
Die Puppenbuhne. See also Der Puppentheater, Des
Puppenspieler and Des Puppenspiels, Mesiter, Die
Puppenspieler and Der Puppenspieler Und Monats
Hefte

"Deutsches Institut für Puppenspiel," Germany
This seems to be more of a school than a group or
club; but it sponsored a periodicale edited by Fritz
Wortelmann. Starting in 1959, the periodical was published irregularly out of W. Germany. (Some were published previous to 1949 and can be found in the McPharlin collection, as seen by the author of this bibliog.) It
was concerned only with work of Master puppeteers.
Periodical, Meister Des Puppenspiels - a few copies
are found in the McPharlin Collection and one or two
copies are in NY Publ. Lib. It seems to be a spe-

"Deutsches Institute Für Puppenspiel," (cont.)
cial edition, as a spur from the regular Der Puppenspieler.

"Dublin Marionette Group," Ireland
Organ. c 1930's at Dublin, with a theatre in the home
of the Director. Has about 20 members and does
adult and children's drama. This modern group may
have had its roots in the 1776 "Patagonian Theatre"
group from Dublin that was so successful in London.
See also G. Speaight's Hist Eng Pupp Th, p 117-120
Director or Pres. - Nelson Paine, Theatre at Dun
Laoghaire, Kinston
Periodical not known.
Pupp, 13:36, 1942

"Dutch Society of Puppet Players," Netherlands
Organ. - no published information was found about the
group itself, only remarks, very brief, concerning the
work. Future supplement will discuss it.
See also "Holland" in the "International" Section and
"Theatre" Section
Periodical not known.

"Eastern Ontario Guild of Puppeteers," Canada
Organ. - no information as yet except material mentioned in Pupp J, 9(1):30, 1957

"Educational Puppetry Association," (E. P. A.), England
(See British Educational Pupp. Assn.)
This appears occasionally without the word "British"
before it. But as far as we know the only Educational group of this type is in England.

"Empire Guild of Puppetry No. 15," U. S. A.
Organ. 1962 in Redlands, Calif. and joined the "Pup-
peteers of America." It does not report in the Jour-
nal very often and little information has been gathered
concerning it.
Pres. or Director was Jack Cox.
Periodical not known.
Pupp J, 14(2):27, 1962

"Evanston Marionette Fellowship," U. S. A.
Organ. previous to April 1949 in Evanston, Ill. and
quite active for sporatic periods, working with "Northwestern Univ. Children's Theatre" players and Jr.
Leage workers, as well as functioning as independent
group.

300

Director or Pres. not known.
Periodical not known.
Grapev, Ap 1949, p 6

"Federal Theatre Puppet Groups, The," U. S. A.
Organ. in many cities throughout the nation during the
Depression and subsidized by the Works Project Administration, Federal Theatre Div. These city groups
sponsored many large, outstanding puppet productions,
research articles and papers, exhibits and classes,
giving work to many puppeteers both professionals and
semi-professionals.
Directors and Pres. were such men as Paul McPharlin, Tony Sarg, Remo Bufano, David Lano and others.
Periodical was a Newsletter, and Instructional sheets
issued by the city of the group. Not one for the entire org.
See "W. P. A." this Section and "Federal Theatres" in
the "Recreation" Section. "Theatres, American" Section might also be helpful.

"Femento de los Artes Decoratives," Spain
Organ. c 1930 in Barcelona by strong, ambitious professional group of artistic and well trained puppeteers:
adult plays, very impressionistic. It became inactive
for lack of funds; with the "Society for the Promotion
of Decorative Arts."
Director or Pres. not known.
Periodical not known.
See "Agrupacion De Marionetistas..." as I think it may
have developed out of this earlier group.
Pupp, 5:37, 1934

"Friendly House Marionette Club," U. S. A.
Organ. 1936 in Davenport, Iowa, was connected with
"The Yankee Marionette Guild."
Director or Pres. was Orville W. Boeck.
Periodical not known.
Pupp Th Am, by Paul McPharlin, p 420

"Friend's Guild Marionettes," U. S. A.
Organ. 1938 at Univ. of Pennsylvania
Director or Pres. was E. D. W. Collins
No periodical.
Pupp Th Am, by Paul McPharlin, p 420

"Friends of French Speaking Marionettes," France. (See
"Les Amis de la Marionettes)

"German League of Puppeteers," (See "Puppenspieler Gilde")

"German Professional Puppeteers, Association of," Germany
(See groups listed under "Deutscher Bund...")
Organ. in 1940's but no clear information as to its
name. Gerald Morice tells of it in Pupp Master,
3(4):124, 1950

"German Shadow Players," Germany (See "Circle of German Shadow Players.")

"Good Teeth Council Puppet Group," U. S. A.
Organ. 1947 in Chicago. A traveling educational group
more club-like than a company, was made up of sev-
eral small, playing, companies who went to the schools
and parks with their message. Sponsored by firms
and health groups interested in good teeth.
No Director or Pres., as such.
Periodical was a brief Newsnote.
"Kitt-Kat Tales," Grapev, D 1948, p 30. I found
many very brief "mentions" of their work scattered
over the Mid-West, but no articles.
"Puppets on Tour for Dental Health Education" Players,
My 1959, p 186, article by M. White
See also "Educational" Section, "Health" Div.

Guilds of "The Puppeteers of America," U. S. A. (See
also "Puppeteers of America")
Organ. began in early 1940's. There are now 23
Guilds in the organization scattered throughout the
United States. They are gatherings of many smaller
clubs, many of which are mentioned in this Section.
Both professional and amateur puppeteers are in the
same guild. Companies, individuals and variety performers, work, learn and perform for festivals given
in their particular regions. One large National Convention is held yearly. See also "Festivals and Exhibits" Section.
Directors and Pres. and Regional Leaders can be
found listed on the back of Pupp J with their Guild or
Region.
Periodicals - these vary with the different Guilds but
many are discussed under "Regional" pages in the national organization's Pupp J. Most of their periodicals would be found in their local city library or in
N Y Publ. Lib.
See also "American Div.," "International" Section.

302

Note: They are not a recognized Guild of the National Group, unless they have an assigned number.

"Hamburg Puppet Guild, The," U. S. A.
Organ. previous to 1935, the group is at Hamburg, N. Y.
Director was Ken Worthy, of Buffalo, N. Y., also editor of paper.
Periodical was a pamphlet called Puppets, published 1935.
Published - A Handbook of Marionettes. Buffalo, Bacon and Vincent, 1935, ed. by Ken Worthy (In NN.)
Pupp Bulletin, 1938-39, p 68

"Houston, Texas Guild No. 3 of Puppetry," U. S. A.
Organ. 1956. The group is inactive at this time.
Director or Pres. was Rena Prim.
Periodical was a Newsletter.

"Hurdy Gurdy Marionette Club," U. S. A.
Organ. previous to 1948 in Berkeley, Calif.
Director or Pres. not known.
No periodical.
Grapev, N 1948, p 4

"Indianapolis Community Puppet Theaters of Jr. League Puppeteers," U. S. A. (See "Community Theatre and Workshop Club")

"International Marionette Laboratory Group," U. S. A.
Organ. 1929-31 in NYC, this group gave serious classical puppet productions, instructions and did experimental work under general direction of visiting "Master Puppeteers" and their director.
Director was Sue Hastings (in her studio); Pres. was Garrett Becker.
No periodical.
Pupp, 1:13, 1930
Pupp Th Am, by Paul McPharlin, p 207, under "Becker" and p. 402.

"Junior Leagues of America, Puppet Groups," U. S. A.
Organ. as a very loose unit within the parent organization of "Jr. Leagues of America," 1931-67; about 60 of 183 Jr. League Clubs had puppetry units working. They do invaluable work for and in children's therapy and recreational centers in addition to serious

"Jr. Leagues of America, Puppet Groups" (cont.)
adult work, working with musical groups to present
children's opera, "lead-in" shows and some have work-
shops.
Director or Pres. was Jean Starr Wiksell, but since
she left the New York office, the group has become
somewhat weaker as a functioning, united, publishing
group.
Periodical - usually in Jr. Leagues of America Mag
but I have found traces of a periodical called Players
and Puppets which seems to have been put out around
1931 (discontinued now) from the Jr. League office.
They also have a Catalogue of Puppet and Marionette
Plays. New York, Jr. League Office, 1963, and a
supplement. They published many articles through
Pupp J.
These groups will be given alphabetically. Some
clubs are probably missing, and many have much more
material published about them, so this should be considered just a start. "General Material" about the
club is given first.

General Material:
"Jr. League Theatre Conference," Pupp 4:5, 1933,
In Cleveland, O.
"News and Notes," by J. S. Wiksell, Players, 19:17,
O 1942 and same in Players, 25:42-43, N 1948
Pupp Th Am, by Paul McPharlin, 1949, p 389, 431-33
This is a very good write-up on the work done up
until 1949. Pupp Th Am has been revised (Boston:
Plays, 1969) and without doubt the new publication
will include valuable additional material on these
many Jr. League Puppet groups.
"Under the Bridge" pages by Martin Stevens, and other
authors, within Pupp J, every issue since 1949 -
usually has illustrations or short items.
Pupp J, 2(5):8-9, 1951; 13(2):30, 1961; 14(4):36, 1963
(article by N. Amsden); 15(1):34-35, 1963; 15(6):22-
24, 1964; 17(6):6, 1966 (article by Mary Jane Rid-
dicks)

U. S. A. Junior League Puppet Groups
(The majority are also listed in Pupp of America Directories)
Akron, O.   Pupp J, 14(6):28, 1963
Ashville, N. C.   Pupp J, 14(6):27, 1963; 15(6):27, 1964;
                   16(2):30, 1964; 18(4):36, 1967

Atlanta, Ga.	Pupp J, 15(6):27, 1964; 16(2):30, 1964; 18(2):27-28, 1966; 19(5):31, 1968 "Kay Ottley"
Baltimore, Md.	Pupp J, 18(4):37, 1967
Binghamton, N.Y.	Pupp J, 15(4):11-12, 1964
Birmingham, Ala.	Grapev, S 1948, p 29
Birmingham, Mich.	Pupp J, 16(5):27, 1965
Boise, Idaho	Pupp J, 14(3):26, 1962; 2(6):30, 1951
Bridgeport, Conn.	Pupp 5:79, 1934
Brooklyn, N.Y.	Grapev, Ap 1949, p 26
Butte, Mont.	"Puppets for Mental Therapy" Pupp J, 2(3):12-13, 22-24, 1950
Canton, Ohio	Pupp of Am Directory, 1967
Cedar Rapids, Iowa	Pupp J, 13(2):30, 1961
Charleston, W. Va.	Pupp of Am Directory, 1967, p 18
Charlotte, N.C.	Pupp J, 14(6):27, 1963
Chattanooga, Tenn.	Pupp J, 13(2):30, 1961; 15(4):12, 1964; 17(6):6, 1966; 18(2):19, 21, 1966
Cincinnati, O.	"Regional Activities" Pupp J, 2(3):25-6, 29, 1950; 16(5):27, 1965; 4(4):25, 1953
Cleveland, O.	Grapev, N 1948, p 5, by H. H. Joseph
Colorado Springs, Colo. (Organ. 1961)	Pupp J, 14(3):26, 1962
Columbia, S.C.	Grapev, Ap 1949, p 26
Columbus, Ga.	Pupp J, 18(2):28, 1966
Corpus Christi, Tex.	Pupp J, 17(6):6, 1966
Dallas, Tex.	Pupp J, 18(4):36, 1967; 11(1):28, 1959
Denver, Colo.	Pupp J, 14(4):18,21, 1963; 14(5):36, 1963; 17(6):6, 1966; 18(4):36, 1967
Des Moines, Iowa	Pupp J, 15(4):28, 1964
Detroit, Mich.	Pupp J, 14(6):28, 1963; 18(2):28, 1966
Duluth, Minn.	Pupp J, 14(6):28, 1963; 16(5):28, 1965
Durham, N.C.	Pupp J, 5(1):22,31,1953; 15(6):27,1964;

USA - Jr League Puppet Groups (cont.)

Durham, N. C. cont.　Pupp J, 16(2):30, 1964; 18(2):28, 1966

Englewood, N. J.　Grapev, Ap 1949, p 26

Evanston, Ill.　Pupp J, 5(1):11, 22, 1953; 14(6):28, 1963; 16(5):28, 1965; 18(4):36, 1967

Flint, Mich.　Pupp J, 14(6):28, 1963

Ft. Lauderdale, Fla.　Pupp J, 16(4):13, 1965

Ft. Wayne, Ind.　Pupp J, 16(5):28, 1965

Ft. Worth, Tex.　Pupp J, 14(4):18, 1963; 14(5):22, 1963; 15(4):12, 1964; 16(4):13, 1965; 17(6): 6, 1966

Galveston, Tex.　Pupp J, 17(6):6, 1966

Great Falls, Mont.　Grapev, S 1948, p 9

Greenville, S. C.　Pupp J, 15(6):28, 1964; 15(4):12, 1964; 16(2):30, 1964; 17(6):6, 1966; 18(4): 36, 1967 (Much occup. therapy work done by this group.)

Greenwich, Conn.　Pupp J, 10(5):30, 1959; 18(4):37, 1967

Hamilton, Canada　Pupp J, 17(3):25, 1965

Hartford, Conn.　"Millie Presents" and "Hector" Grapev, S 1948, p 19 by J. Houghmaster; Brit Pupp Th, 1(5):9-10, 1950 Pupp J, 1(1):4 (and photo sec.) 1950; 3(1):26, 1951; 5(1):23, 30-31, 1953; Grapev, Ap 1949, p 20 See Bibliographic Section, this name for a book.

High Point, N. C.　Pupp J, 18(4):36, 1967

Huntington, W. Va.　Grapev, Ap 1949, p 20; Pupp J, 17 (6):6, 1966

Indianapolis, Ind.　Pupp J, 1(3):7, 1949. Organ. 1935, by J. S. Wiksell. See "Community Puppet Theatre" this section.

Jackson, Miss.　Grapev, Je 1949, p 19

Jacksonville, Fla.　Grapev, Ap 1949, p 26; Pupp J, 3(1): 26, 1951; 15(6):27, 1964; 16(2):30, 1964; 17(3):25, 1965; 18(4):36, 1967

Knoxville, Tenn.　Pupp J 15(4):12, 1964

Lancaster, Pa.	Grapev, N 1948, p 22; Pupp, 3:46, 1933; Pupp J, 17(3):25, 1965; 18(4): 36, 1967
Lansing, Mich.	Pupp J, 2(6):31, 1951; 3(1):26, 1951; 11(6):34, 1960; 12(4):26, 1961; 14(6): 28, 1963
Lexington, Ky.	Pupp J, 14(6):27, 1963
Lincoln, Nebr.	Pupp J, 14(4&5):36, 1963
Long Beach, Calif.	Pupp J, 15(4):12, 1964
Los Angeles, Calif.	Pupp J, 2(4):22, 1951 (Much occup. therapy work.)
Lubbock, Tex.	Pupp J, 17(3):25, 1965; 18(4):36, 1967
Memphis, Tenn.	Pupp J, 13(2):30, 1961
Mexico City, Mex.	Pupp J, 14(3):26, D 1962
Midland, Tex.	Pupp J, 17(6):6, 1966
Minneapolis, Minn.	Pupp J, 14(6):28, 1963; 17(6):6, 1966
Milwaukee, Wisc.	Pupp J, 16(5):27, 1965; 18(2):28, 1966
Mobile, Ala.	Pupp J, 17(6):6, 1966; 18(5):23, 33, 1967 (Educ. therapy)
Montgomery, Ala.	Pupp J, 2(4):7, 16-17, 1951; 16(2):30, 1964; 18(2):28, 1966
New Orleans, La.	Grapev, D 1948, p 33 (Mrs. Louella Ray in charge; Ap 1949, p 19, 27; Pupp J, 3(1):26, 1951; 5(1):31, 1953; 10(3):5, 1958
New York, N.Y.	Pupp J, 15(4):12, 1964; G N Y Pupp Newsl, 8(1):5, O 1969
Ogden, Utah	Pupp J, 13(3):22, 1961; 14(3):26, 1962; 18(3):26, 17, 1966
Oklahoma City, Okla.	Grapev, Je 1949, p 19; Ap 1949, p 19; Pupp J, 1(5):10-11, 1950; 2(4):22, 1951; 3(2):10, 13, 1951; 13(3):22, 1961; 8(6):28, 1957; 16(2):22-23, 1964; 17(3):25, 1965. See local papers around dates of Je 22-26, 1948, as they did much work for "Pupp of Am. Convention" held there. They also do a great deal of occup. therapy work.

USA - Jr. League Puppet Groups (cont.)

Omaha, Nebr.	Pupp J, 13(3):23, 1961; 14(4&5):36, 1963; 16(4):13, 1965
Peoria, Ill.	Pupp J, 16(5):27, 1965
Plainfield, N. J.	Pupp J, 18(2):28, 1966
Portland, Ore.	Pupp J, 2(4):14, 1951; 4(3):10-14, 1952; 2(5):22, 1951; 2(6):26, 30, 1951; 13(3):22, 1963
Raleigh, N. C.	Pupp J, 5(1):18, 21, 22, 31, 1953; 17(6):6, 1966
St. Louis, Mo.	Pupp J, 13(2):30, 1961
St. Petersburg, Fla.	Grapev, Ap 1949, p 26
Salt Lake City, Utah	Pupp J, 13(3):24, 1961; 14(4&5):36, 1963; 20(4):25, 1969. Sponsoring "Puppeteers of America Convention."
Seattle, Wash.	Pupp J, 2(4):22, 1951; 2(3):25, 26, 29, 1951; 2(6):30, 1951; 3(2):10, 13, 1951; 18(3):23, 1961
Shreveport, La.	Pupp J, 17(6):6, 23, 1966
Spartansburg, S. C.	Pupp J, 15(6):27, 1964; 16(4):13, 1965
Spokane, Wash.	Pupp J, 17(6):6, 1966
Springfield, Ill.	Pupp J, 14(6):28, 1963; 9(5):30, 1958 16(5):27, 1965; 17(3):25, 1965
Tacoma, Wash.	Pupp J, 14(3):26, 1962; 14(4&5):36, 1963
Tampa, Fla. (Org. 1948)	Grapev, Ap 1949, p 26; Pupp J, 2(4): 22, 1951; 17(6):6, 1966
Toledo, Ohio	"Classes at Toledo Museum," by H. Bentley, Jr League Mag, 23:56-7, N 1936
Toronto, Canada	Pupp of Amer Directory, 1967 p 19
Tulsa, Okla.	Pupp J, 14(4&5):36, 1963
Tuscon, Ariz.	Pupp J, 14(3):26, 1962
Vancouver, Canada	Pupp J, 13(3):23, 1961
Washington, D. C.	Grapev, Feb 1949, p 17; S 1948, p 20; Pupp J, 18(2):28, 1966
Wheeling, W. Va.	Pupp J, 14(6):27, 1963

Wichita, Kan.   Grapev, Ap 1949, p 26; Pupp J, 13
                     (3):23, 1961; Pupp J, 17(3):25, 1965;
                     18(4):36, 1967

Winnepeg, Canada   Pupp J, 14(5):23, 1963; 16(5):27, 1965;
                     18(4):36, 1967

Winston-Salem, N. C. Pupp J, 14(6):27, 1963; 16(2):30, 1964;
                     18(4):37, 1967

"Junior Puppeteers," Los Angeles, U. S. A.
    Organ. 1968-69 in Los Angeles County Guild No 4" as
    a branch of that guild for its many younger members.
    Director or Pres. not known.
    Periodical was same as Parent Guild, Puppet Life,
    Ap 1969, p 13

"Kala Pathak Group," India
    Organ. by State Government of Madhya Pradesh c 1965.
    Director or Pres. not known.
    No periodical.

"Lancaster Marionette Group," U. S. A.
    Organ. c 1940 in Lancaster, Pa.
    Director or Pres. not known.
    No periodical.

"L. E. R. A. ," Lockheed Aircraft Puppet Group, U. S. A.
    Lockheed Aircraft Factory at Palo Alto, Calif. , Spon-
    sors group which organized c 1968 and is quite active.
    Has a brief newsletter.
    Pupp J, 21(1):23, 1969

"Lincoln City Library Puppet Club," U. S. A.
    Organ. in 1940's at Lincoln, Nebr.
    Director or Pres. not known.
    No periodical.
    Grapev, N 1948, p 5
    Pupp J, 9(6):9-10, 1958

"Long Island Puppet Guild No 21, The," U. S. A.
    Organ. 1966-67 at Great Neck, as a very progressive
    and active group of puppeteers, interested in satire
    shadow and hand productions, using much "Black Light"
    affects.   Doing Biblical shadow shows with great atten-
    tion to theatrical approaches.   Has very progressive
    yearly festival, about June.
    Director and Pres. Carol Fijan.

"Long Island Puppet Guild No 21," (cont.)
Periodical is a short Newsnote, and uses the "Greater
New York Guild," periodical a great deal.
"Festival" G N Y Pupp G Newsl, 5(5):5, 1968
Pupp J, 21(1):33, 1969

"Los Angeles Valley College Puppetry Club," U. S. A.
Organ. c 1967
Director, Betsy Brown
Publication, not known.
Pupp Life, S 1969, p 12
Pupp J, 21(2):10, 25, 1969

"Los Angeles County Guild of Puppetry, No 4," U. S. A.
(See "Junior Puppeteers") (This name changed May 1969,
to "Los Angeles Guild of Puppetry, No 4")
Organ. as Guild No. 4 in the "Puppeteers of America"
group in 1957 but was an individual group earlier.
This is a very active professional and semi-professional group, scattered geographically but close-knit. They
have instructional meetings, festivals, contests, exhibits and well-stocked "Walsworth Lending-Library,"
left to them by a member.
Director and Pres., Bob Bromley, "Genii" Wohler and
Gayle Schluter, among other well known puppeteers.
Periodical is Puppet Life which is quite professional
and well illustrated, growing out of a lengthy Newsletter.
Pupp J, 11(1):20; 11(5):29-30, 1960; 11(6):29, 1960;
14(2):26, 1962; 20(3):31-32, 1968; 21(1):32, 1969

"Lyonese Society," Morocco. (See "Amis De Guignol)

"Marionette Congress, The European," Europe
(See "UNIMA")
Organ. in 1930's under the sponsorship and guidance
of the Prague group of puppeteers, and the new
"UNIMA" organization of companies and puppeteers
festival. It meets at the "International UNIMA" festi-
vals in different parts of Europe; usually in Spring or
Fall.
Director or Pres. - changes occasionally, but I believe
it is the same as the Pres. of "UNIMA Intl." Dr. Jan
Malik has headed this group for many years.
Periodical - Uses the "UNIMA" periodicals throughout
Europe and other areas.
"The Marionette Congress Meets," Thea Arts, 15:140,

53, 140, Feb 1931. This was the meeting at Liege, Belgium.
See also "Festivals and Exhibits," Section and "International."

"Marionette Fellowship of America," U.S.A. (See also "Marionette Fellowship, Detroit")
Organ. 1931-35 in Detroit, but not with that city name in the title. Was to be like the European "UNIMA" group. They met at Artisian Guild Bldg., had classical and adult drama. Held first convention, 1936 in Detroit.
Director or Pres. was Paul McPharlin
Periodical was a type of Newsletter and Grapevine and they used Mr. McPharlin's, Puppetry Yearbook or Pupp.
See "Detroit Marionette Fellowship," "Detroit Puppet Guild" and "Detroit Puppeteers Guild No 16."
See also "Festivals and Exhibits," "Theaters" and "American" Sections and Divisions.
Grapev, Ap 1949, p 6
The group eventually became the founders of "Puppeteers of America" around 1937 and became affiliated with the European Group of "UNIMA." See "UNIMA, U.S.A." and Garret Becker was the American Sect. General of org.

Pupp Th Am., by Paul McPharlin, p 387-89
Sources and individuals, and early leaders of this group and the "Puppeteers of America" do not agree exactly on origins, dates, leaders and even the earliest name of periodicals. I have tried to clarify things a little but hope to be forgiven by those not in agreement.

"Marionette Fellowship of Detroit," U.S.A. (See "Marionette Fellowship of America")
Organ. shortly after 1930 in Detroit. Seems to have been more of a distinct group of Michigan puppeteers working out of Wayne Univ. Studio Theatre rather than those from other cities joining in later to form the "Marionette Fellowship of America." The group did very sophisticated productions. Paul McPharlin seems to indicate that it started out first under W. Herrschaft, dwindled down and then came back up with P. McPharlin's assistance going almost directly into "...America" group.
Directors and Pres. were then: W. Herrschaft, Paul

311

"Marionette Fellowship of Detroit" (cont.)
McPharlin. (Other important leaders who came later
were Fern Zwickley, Olga and Martin Stevens, Remo
Bufano, Edith Flack Ackley.)
Periodical seems to have been Pupp, Grapevine Tele-
graph, Grapevine.
Pupp Th Am, by Paul McPharlin, p 387-89
Pupp, 1:7, 1930
See "Detroit Guild" there are slight changes of name
This group may have continued side by side with the
enlarged "... American" group. Sources are not
clearly expressive. The "Detroit Guild" eventually
cleared this up by changing the name "Marionette Fellowship" to "Detroit Guild."

"Marionette Guild of Philadelphia," U. S. A.
Organ. 1925 in Philadelphia and interested in children's
production, meeting at The Delancy Place.
Director or Pres., Helen A. Smiley
Periodical not known.

"Marionette Guild of Plainfield, N. J.," U. S. A.
Organ. 1940 but had to become inactive during war
years, probably reorganized after. May have been
basis for strong clubs in Long Island and New Jersey
Guilds.
Director, Bruck Williams
Pupp Th Am, by Paul McPharlin, p 441, 480

"Marionette Guild of New York City," U. S. A. (See
"Greater New York Puppet Guild")
Organ. previous to 1930's in NYC. This group devel-
oped through various slight changes in name to the
very large, and active, present New York Guild.
Director or Pres., early in its history, included Jero
Magon, Dir., and Edith F. Ackley, G. Becker and B.
Fulton either as officers or early presidents.
"Puppet Photographs, International Collection" Thea
Arts, 14:312-21, Ap 1930
Periodical was Greater New York Puppet Guild News-
letter which has gradually developed into a profession-
al periodical rather than newsnotes. Still keeps
same name.
N Y Times, Ap 19, 1931, p 8; D 26, 1933 18:6
Pupp Th Am, by Paul McPharlin, p 440
See also "Marionette Repertory Theatre Group"

"Marionette Repertory Theatre Group," U. S. A.
    Organ. previous to 1931 in NYC. May have been
    branch of Guild.
    Director, or Pres. not known.
    Periodical - none.
    N Y Times, Ap 19, 1931, p 8

"Marionette Society, The," U. S. A.
    Organ. 1913 and lasted only until 1914 because of the
    war. It was organ. in NYC by the literary and the-
    atrical people for the preservation of "Paladin" type
    puppetry in NYC's Mulberry St. Theatre. Although
    shortlived it was very education minded.
    Director or Pres. - A NYC editor and educator, Wm.
    Patten.
    Periodical not known.
    "Old Puppet Show Restored," N Y Times, My 4, 1913

"Masaryk Puppetry Institute, The," Czechoslovakia
    Organ. in the 1920's as a sort of "Guild" from many
    clubs and having about 3, 200 puppeteers affiliated.
    It has become more of a teaching school than club.
    The Institute correlates and sponsors shows, festivals
    and work of the state-supported puppet theatres and
    groups.
    Director or Pres. was Dr. Jindřich Vesely near the
    start.
    Periodical seems to have been Cesky-Loutkar. It may
    also have been called Loutkova Scena or The Czech
    Puppeteer.
    Pupp, 1:91, 1930; 5:32, 1934
    Pupp J, 7(5):5, 1956
    Drama, 19(6):175, Mr 1929, old series
    See also "Theatres" and "Festivals" Sections as well
    as "International."

"Memphis Tennessee Puppet Guild," U. S. A.
    Organ. c 1960's in Memphis but not a guild within the
    "Puppeteers of America." No information except a
    mention of its existence.

"Miami, The Puppet Guild of Greater," U. S. A.
    Organ. as Guild No 19 of the "Puppeteers of Ameri-
    ca" group with headquarters at Miami Beach. It has
    become quite active and strong, with many profession-
    al troups and variety entertainers.
    Director and Pres. , for many years, was Jero Magon.
    Periodical is a Newsletter.

"Miami, The Puppet Guild of Greater," (cont.)
Pupp J, 21(2):35, 1969

"Midwestern Puppeteers, The," U.S.A. (See "Cellar Playhouse Group" or "Cellar Players")
Organ. 1939-1944 and began again in 1946-1951 at
Aurora, Ill., but met mainly in Chicago at the homes
of North or South Side Chicago puppeteer groups. It
Seems to have developed into a group called "S.P.A.C."
which was probably the group I have listed as "Society
of Puppetry and Allied Crafts." It also may have been
a basic group of "Southern Illinois Puppet-center
Group." About 40 members and guests met every two
months, very loosely knit as a formal group.
Director or Pres. - there were no officers, dues, or
regularly planned meetings. Romain Proctor, Ray
Fenton, leaders.
Periodical - none at first except a newsnote but this
became a mimeo periodical, Strings.
See also "Chicagoland Puppetry Guild," and early issues of Grapevine Telegraph and Grapev.
Brit Pupp Thea, 1(5):5, 1950
Chicago Tribune, Feb 19, 1950

"Mile-High Puppeteers," U.S.A.
Organ. c. 1968 as Guild No 23 of "Puppeteers of
America" group.
Director or Pres. Jean Fleck
Periodical - a Newsletter
Pupp J, 20(3):31, 1968; 20(5):32, 1968

"Montgomery Playhouse Group," U.S.A.
Organ. previous to 1950's in Montgomery, Ala. from
a Jr League Group of puppeteers. The group became
very active and gave many productions.
Director or Pres. not known.
No periodical.
Pupp J, 2(4):16-17, 1951

"Munich Artists Marionette Players in U.S.A."
Organ. in 1930's as a touring group out of NYC. Very
professional.
Director was Tony Sarg
Pupp J, 21(1):3-4, 1969

"National Belgium Federation of Puppeteers," Belgium
Organ. in 1947-1948 and then again in the 1950's.

Director or Pres. was first Armand Suls, Jan De
Schuyter and Jan Burugman
Periodical was a good one, Messenger (only 9 issues)
"Belgium Puppetry" by C. Jozef, Pupp J, 2(3):24,
1950
See also "International" and "Festivals" Sections
    They held conventions and started a "Puppet Acad-
emy" but suddenly went inactive. The foundation for
present Belgium "UNIMA" groups and International
Festivals often gather in this country. Future study
and information will show a strong organization today.
See also Het Poppenspiel, "Periodical" Section

"National Capital Puppet Guild," U. S. A.
    Organ. as Guild No 18 of "Puppeteers of America" in
    1964, but had previously been a club. It meets in
    homes and is becoming more active, especially since
    the Smithsonian Museum has opened a permanent pup-
    pet theatre under the direction of Bob Brown.
    Director or Pres. - earliest not known.
    Periodical is Newsletter of National Capital Puppetry
    Guild, changed to National Capitol Puppetry Guild News-
    letter, then D. C. Puppetimes
    Pupp J, 20(3):30, 1968
    D. C. Puppetimes, 1968, p 1
    National Capitol Puppetry Guild Newsletter, 1(3):2,
    1968

"National Syndicate of the Arts of the Marionette and of
    Animation in France"
    Organ.
    Pres., 1969, Lucien Caron
    See   UNIMA, U. S. A. Newsl, S 1969, p 3

"National Theatre of Puppet Arts," U. S. A. (See "Puppet
    Associates")
    Organ. Oct. 1, 1969, with "Repertory Puppet Theatre
    of Washington, D. C. - doing Greek to Modern drama
    Pres. Carol Fijan
    No periodical.
    "11th Hour News," G N Y Pupp G Newsl, 8(1):5,
    O 1969

"Nederlandse Vereniaing voor het Puppenspiel," Holland
    (Dutch Society of Puppet Players)
    Organ. shortly after the second World War, but prob-
    ably in existence previous to the war with slightly

"Nederlandse Vereniaing voor het Puppenspiel" (cont.)
   different name.
   Director or Pres. not known.
   Periodical not known.
   Brit Pupp & M Thea G Newsl, 154:2, Mr 1969 (Over-
   seas)
   See also "Holland," "International" Section

"New England Puppetry Institute, The," U.S.A.   (See
   "Boston Area Guild")
   Organ. 1937 in Boston.   Had a strong program for
   several years and from it has developed the "New Eng-
   land Guild of Puppetry No 9" of the "Puppeteers of
   America."   The "Boston Area Guild" probably devel-
   oped after the war from this meeting of earlier clubs
   and thence into "Guild No 9."
      This was more of a festival type of grouping, rather
   than regularly meeting club group.   Had quite a gather-
   ing in 1939.   Usually met in Fall.
   Director or Pres. - not known
   Periodical - none
   Pupp Th Am., by Paul McPharlin, p 418-420
   Pupp J, 3(2):24, 1952; 14(2): , 1962

"New England Guild of Puppetry, No 9," U.S.A.
   Organ. 1961 as part of "Puppeteers of America" group
   in Boston, from the "Boston Area Guild."
      Has a very widely scattered group of puppeteers, is
   active in educational work and semi-professional shows.
   Has good, small festival, see the one held at Stur-
   bridge, Mass., in 1962 under "Festivals" Section.
   Director or Pres.   Gordon Bennett and Edg. W. Rice
   were early leaders.
   Periodical was a Newsletter at first and this became
   Control Stick.   Much will be found in Pupp J issues.
   Pupp J, 14(3):11, 1962; 20(3):31, 1968

"New Jersey Public School Marionette Guild," U.S.A.
   Organ. c 1930's in Newark at Normal School
   Director or Pres. not known.
   No periodical.
   "Second Conference at State Normal School," Pupp,
   4:5, 1933

"New York City Dept. of Parks Puppet Group," U.S.A.
   Organ. c 1930's in NYC, and became very strong,
   especially during the depression period.

Out of it developed Federal Theatre puppet groups and the present "Guild No 20." It has now become more a part of the Park Recreation Dept. than a club, and yet maintains some of the flavor of the group. It sponsors very, very active educational work. Now has its own "Swedish Cottage" Theatre. Rod Young and several famous early NYC puppet masters have been very active in taking troups throughout city. They now have 85 different playing locations in the summer.
See also "Recreation," "Theatres" and "American" Sections. Sometimes called "The Marionette Circus." Directors - there have been many
Periodical - none
Pupp J, 4(4):25, 1953. The pages "Under the Bridge," of this periodical usually carried many items about the group, and does to date.
G N Y Pupp G Newsl, all issues carry much material about it.
New York newspapers are the main publicity outlet because of Parks connection. Many classes, etc.

"New York Marionette Society," U.S.A. (See "Marionette Guild of New York")
Organ. in spring of 1913 in NYC. This seems to be the same group but yet the items I have seen indicate it may have been slightly different grouping of puppeteers. Has now been gathered into "Guild No 20."
Director or Pres. not known.
Periodical not known.
N Y Times, My 4, 1913
Pupp Th Am, by Paul McPharlin, p 385

"New York Inc., Puppetry Guild of Greater," U.S.A.
Organ. 1966 as No. 20 Guild in NYC, under "Puppeteers of America" group, by several professional and non-professionals with educational puppeteers from the many small groups within area and city park department puppeteers.
This is a very active performing and study and social group. Usually acting as "American Hosts" to foreign groups, with receptions and exhibits of their work. Performing usually at the Museum Theatres or Lincoln Center Theatre. The Park Dept. "Swedish Cottage" has only its own performers, but includes some classes under Rod Young from this group.
Director or Pres., Rod Young, a strong early leader and editor of publication. Pres. at the time the group became Guild was Frank Paris.

"NY, Inc. , Puppetry Guild of Greater," (cont.)
Periodical - Greater N Y Guild of Puppetry Newsletter,
listing all important puppet productions in New York
State area, as well as the city, and TV work.
Pupp J, all issues under "Under the Bridge" pages for
many years previous to 1966 and to date.
Pupp J, 20(3):31, 1968
See also "Theatres" and "American" Sections

"North German Puppetry Union, The," Germany
Organ. before the 1949 years in Hamburg as part of
a "Trade Union of Arts and Crafts."
Director or Pres. - not known
Periodical not known.
Grapev, S 1948, p 29
"International News," Pupp J, 2(6):28-29, 1951

"Nos Marionettes," France
Organ. 1918-1926
Director or Pres. not known
Periodical was Artistique.

"Nottinghamshire Puppet Guild," England
Organ. 1940's in Nottinghamshire. Does much educa-
tional puppet work within schools. Has competitions
and helps with exhibits and festivals in England's two
leading puppet groups.
Director or Pres. not known.
No periodical - uses Pupp Post and Pupp Master
Brit Pupp Thea, 1(4):15, 1950

"Ontario Puppetry Association," Canada. (See "Southwestern
Puppet Guild")
Organ. 1957 at Waterloo, Ontario, Canada with the help
of the Drama Dept. at the Waterloo Univ. It is quite
active; brought the "Puppeteers of America" to the
Univ. for its 1967 yearly convention.
See also "Festivals" Section and "Puppeteers of Amer-
ica"
Director or Pres. was Ken Wyndham at time of Con-
vention. Early leaders not known.
Periodical - a type of Newsletter.
Pupp J, 10(1):6-7, 1958
Pupp J issues carry some items about Canada in "Un-
der the Bridge" pages.

"Orange County Guild of Puppetry," U. S. A.
Organ. 1961 as Guild No 12 of "Puppeteers of America" at Laguna Beach, Calif. Quite active and often acts as "West Coast Hosts" to foreign companies especially since Mrs. Mollie Falkenstein, Sect. General of "U. S. A. UNIMA," is one of the leading members of the group. Became inactive as a Guild in 1968, working with "Los Angeles Guild."
Director or Pres. was Mollie Falkenstein.
Periodical was a Newsletter.
Pupp J, 12(5):26-27, 1961; 11(6):27, 29, 1960
"Pacific Coast Regional News" speaks of club but not yet of Guild. Article by L. Connell.
Pupp J, 14(2):26, 1962
See also Laguna Beach newspapers of Feb 11, 1961, for material about a puppet conference and festival.

"Palo Alto, Calif. Puppet Club," U. S. A. (See "L. E. R. A.")
Organ. 1967 at Lockheed,Calif., for members who work in the Lockheed plant.
Director or Pres. was Mr. Godbury
No periodical.
Pupp Life, D 1968 p 33

"Pedagogie Working Club of Leer," Germany
Organ. in 1940's in Leer, with leading puppeteers of the factories of that city who were interested in educational type puppet work.
Director or Pres., was Walter Kipsch
Periodical was Rundbriefe with W. Kipsch as editor.
Pupp J, 2(5):23, 1951

"Phoenix Guild, No 13, of Puppetry," U. S. A.
Organ. 1959 as No 13 of "Puppeteers of America" but active as local group previous to this, in Phoenix.
Director or Pres. was Henry Alcott and Claire Radich.
Periodical was called Punch Line.
Pupp J, 14(2):26-27, 1962; 20(3):31, 1968
Pupp Life, D 1968, p 31

"Pioneer Craft House, Educational Puppetry Association," U. S. A.
Organ. in Salt Lake City, 1967, and has very active group. Is teaching extension work for the Univ. of Utah. Sponsored the National Festival in 1969. Has own building with theatre. They are interested in therapy work. Their work is quite professional.
Director or Pres., Mrs. Glenn Beeley, Nancy Giles, Julie Allen.

"Pioneer Craft House, E. P. A." (cont.)
Periodical not known
Pupp J, 19(5):9-11, 1968; 21(1):28-32, 1969 "Festival
at Salt Lake"
See also "Educational" Section

"Poland Ministry of Culture Puppet Dept.," Poland
Organ. c 1930 at Central Institute at Lodz
Director, Dr. Jan Sztaudynger
Periodical, Od Szepki De Testry Lajek
See also Teatry Lalek - this was probably the local
periodical as it was published in Lodz

"Polish Students' Puppet Club, The," U.S.A.
Organ. previous and c to 1940's in Wisconsin, at the
Univ. of Wisconsin, in Madison
Director or Pres. was E. Zawacki
Pupp Th Am, by Paul McPharlin, p 455
"Polish Legend in Wisconsin," by E. Zawacki, Pupp,
13:7, 1942

"Producers Workshop Group," U.S.A. (See "New York,
Inc. Puppetry Guild")
Organ. 1967 in NYC as a spur of the "New York
Guild" - particularly interested in experimental type of
puppetry; meeting in evenings for classes with Rod
Young, but not in any way competitive to the Guild
Director was Rod Young
Periodical - none; publishes through the "New York
Guild," periodical
See also Spring and Summer issues, 1967, of N Y G
of Pupp Newsl; especially 5(5):2, 3, 5, 6 of that publi-
cation.

"Die Puppenspieler Gilde," Germany (See "Deutscher Bund
Für...")
Organ. in 1940's at Bachum. This group has many
members from the central European puppetry area.
It might be compared with a Guild of the American
type. There are many smaller clubs within it which
must be covered in a supplement.
Material under "Theatres" Section, and "International" might well discuss some; and certainly German
periodicals provide this particular coverage.
Director or Pres. was Fritz Wortelmann who did much
organizing and editing of material.
Periodical had many slightly different titles, at different times or for different groups, I cannot be sure

which. The main one now is Der Puppenspieler. It
carries some English translations.
See periodicals listed under group called "Deutscher
Bund für..."
Pupp J, 2(1):20, 1950

"Puppenspiel Verband," Germany
Organ. Jan. 12, 1947 in Frankfort, but also meets at
Darmstadt, Germany.
Director or Pres. Hans Walter Wohmann
Periodical not known.

"Puppet Associates, The," U. S. A. (See "Puppet Guild of
Long Island")
Organ. 1960's more as a club-like group than a company and yet giving productions semi-professionally as
a company. Sponsors festivals, and was very instru-
mental in gathering the "Long Island Guild No 21" to-
gether. Group organized in New Jersey.
See "National Theatre of Puppet Arts"
This group is very much interested in educational
and therapy work. Very professional production work
from "live theatre" type of technical acting and stage
work. Uses "Black Light" and satire, hand and shadow work, religious productions a great deal.
Director - Carol Fijan
Periodical - uses Control Stick and Pupp J, and N Y
G of Pupp Newsl.
See also Local New Jersey newspapers c 1965-to date.
Pupp J, 19(1):16-17, 1967; 19(2):11, 16, 17, 1967

"Puppet Guild of Long Island," U. S. A. (See "Long Island
Puppet Guild")
Pupp J, 20(3):31, 1968

"Puppeteens, The," U. S. A.
Organ. 1948 in Oklahoma City at the National Convention as an outgrowth of the intense interest in young
puppeteers at this meeting. Many being of Detroit
Guild, the group eventually came mainly from that
area. It was officially organized as Guild No 6 of
"Puppeteers of America" in 1960. Irregular as an
active group. In 1969 several teenage puppet groups
were evident around the country, using the same or a
similar name.
Director or Pres. not known
Periodical - Had a Newsletter, The Puppeteer. May

321

"Puppeteens, The," (cont.)
>have done some publishing for this Guild in 1950's.
Do not confuse with Puppeteers Newsletter of St. Louis.
Grapev, S 1948, p 35; N 1948, p 14
See also early issues of Pupp J., short items.

"Puppeteers Club Association," U. S. A.
>Organ. 1969 in Cromwell, Conn.   Active in work with
hard of hearing.
Director of Pres. not known.
Periodical is P. C. A. Newsletter.   Editor was J. S
Miner, Jr.

"Puppeteers of America, The," U. S. A.   (See "Marionette
Fellowship" groups)
>Organ. 1937 in Cincinnati, Ohio but first discussed in
Detroit at the first national puppet conference.
See Pupp Th Am, by Paul McPharlin, p 387.
>The group has both professional and amateur puppe-
teers, and a few spur groups of teenagers at different
times.   It is composed, as of date, of 23 "Guilds,"
(see "American" Div., "International" Section).   These
Guillds being from all around the U. S. A. and having
"Regional Directors" both in Canada and the U. S. A.
>Information and addresses of officers for each year
are given on last page of Pupp J., every issue.
"National Convention" is usually held in summers at
invitation of any Guild or sponsoring group.   Most
Regions and Guilds holding small festivals during the
year.
>"The UNIMA, U. S. A." is not a part of the "Puppe-
teers of America" but works as a side-by-side group
of members who are interested in European puppet
work, it is not competitive.   (See this organization.)
Pres. was Paul McPharlin, although the first organization was directed by Martin and Olga Stevens.   Other
early leaders were: R. Bufano, E. F. Ackley, M.
Levin, P. Benton and Catherine and Val Smith.   V.
Michael was editor of news letter.
Periodical was, according to Mr. McPharlin, first the
Puppetry Yearbook (or Puppetry).   Mainly used after
the war, a bi-monthly news letter, The Grapevine
Telegraph, which became just Grapevine.   Puppet Bulle-
tin was a section of "Yearbook," for advertisement,
but is often quoted as a separate publication.
See also Puppetry Imprints.   These were all dropped
in 1949 for the now, inclusive, periodical, called

"Puppeteers of America," (cont.)
Puppetry Journal, coming out 6 times a year, starting
in Aug., after the National Convention.
P. of A. Membership Directory, yearly.
Publications: In 1969 Work Sheet Bulletins, a series
was published and from time to time the organization
has published mimeo booklets on different subjects for
its members. Plays and photographic booklets have
also been published. For all these, see inside back
cover or last sheet in any Pupp J. They are listed
in their respective sections by their authors in this
bibliography.

The Pupp J maintains a regulation publication department, at Ashville, Ohio, under the leadership of
Vivian Michael, editor-in-chief of the periodical from
1950-1969, except for about 1 year (1967-68).
Advisors: Different puppet masters and educational
leaders have been appointed as "Technical advisors
since the first organization." They are changed and
can be found listed on inside first pages of Pupp J
(each issue). They usually hold office for several
years, freely sending information to anyone.

General articles about the group: See also "Festi-
val" Section and "American" Div. in "International"
Section, "Periodicals" Section. Many different ones
by groups within the National organization.
"Text of Speeches at First American Puppetry Confer-
ence in Detroit, Pupp 7: 1936
Puppets in America, by Paul McPharlin, Birmingham,
Mich., Puppetry Imprints, 1936; Detroit, Hastings,
1937.
In McPharlin Collection
"Puppeteers of America," Thea Arts, 20:562, Jl 1936
"Report of Second Puppetry Conference," Pupp 8:
1937.
"Puppeteers of America Lending Library Books,"
Grapev, N 1948, p 2; O 1949, p 17-18
"What is Puppeteers of America? and What do They
Do?" by W. I. Duncan, Players, 26:66, D 1949
"Puppeteers of America," by W. H. Cleveland of the
George School, Pennsylvania, The Allied Youth, N
1948 or 1949
Puppet Theatre in America, by Paul McPharlin,
New York, Harper, 1949, p 387-89
"Members of Puppeteers of America to Date," Pupp J,
1(3):2, 18-24, 1949
Soon after this they began the regular separate pub-
lication of Puppeteers of America Membership Directory.

"Puppeteers of America," (cont.)
Ashville, O. , Pupp J. publications, yearly.
"The Story of Puppeteers of America," by K. Hough-
master, Players, 26:17-18, O 1949
"The Puppet World," by H. Hewes, Pupp J, 2(1):2-3,
1950
"You Should Know About 'P. of A.'," Pupp J, 2(3):27,
1950
"Puppet Shows 'boomed', by TV," Herald Journal,
Dayton, Je 26, 1951
"A New Year for the 'P. of A.'," by G. Merten,
Pupp J, 8(4):21-22, 1957
"Twenty-five Golden Years," Romain Proctor, Pupp J,
12(2):3-7, 1961.   Early leader within the
group.
"Regions of the 'P. of A.'," Pupp J, 12(4):4, 1961
"Incorporation of the 'P. of A.' Constitution, By-laws,
proposals, by W. Bauer, Pupp J, 12(5):16-19, 1961.
   Speaks of first Regional and District Divisions,
Guilds, and other groups.
"Regions of the Puppeteers of America," Pupp J, 12
(4):4, 1961
"Regional News From 'P. of A.' Guilds and Groups,"
Pupp J, 14(3):11, 23-26, 1962
Pupp J, 15(4):31, 1964
   This became a regular feature in almost all Pupp J
issues under the same title. I do not list all this, as
I feel it is so general and a reader can seek it out
easily in that periodical for the year desired.
See also "Regional Ramblings" Pupp J, 17(2):31-32,
1965, by L. Ludington. N Y Publ. Lib. has all issues,
as do many of the public libraries of large cities such
as Detroit, St. Louis, Los Angeles, Miami. Some
university libraries have been given sets and many now
subscribe both here and abroad.
"Official Announcement-All 'P. of A.'" Members to
belong to "UNIMA," N Y G Pupp Newsl, 6(2):1, D 1968
   This was an error and there was much controversy
about the connection of the two groups at this time. It
is discussed in many articles. (See also "Theory and
Critical" Section.) It is also discussed from the point
of view of "Puppeteers of America" in the Pupp J issues of 1969 and all puppet periodicals of that year.
See "UNIMA, U. S. A."
"P. of A." (Philanthropic) Work and Committees," by
Daniel Llords, Pres. Pupp J, 20(4): 1969
Pupp J, 21(1): 1969, supplement - entire issue

See also "History" Section. Most history sections or chapters in puppet books written since 1937, discuss this large organization.

"Puppetry Guild of Greater New York, " U. S. A.   (See "Greater New York Puppet Guild")

"Quaker Village Puppeteers, The, " U. S. A.
   Organ. 1940 in Philadelphia, it soon became Guild No 1 of "Puppeteers of America" taking the place of the inactive "Columbus Guild" which was first but moved down to No 2.
   Director or Pres. at beginning not known.
   Periodical was Quaker Village Puppeteer's Report, shortened often to just Report, sometimes just Q. V. R.
   "Twenty Year Flashback on History of Quaker Village Puppeteers, " Pupp J, 15(4):25, 1964.   In NYC Pub Lib.
   "Quaker Village Puppeteer Work, " Pupp J, 4(3):26-28 1952
   Pupp J, 14(2):24, 1962; 20(3):31, 1968

"Red River Guild of Puppetry, " Canada
   Organ. 1966-67 as Guild No 22 of "Puppeteers of America" but active earlier as private group.   This is the only Canadian Guild and probably members live both in U. S. A. and Canada.
   Director or Pres. was Lawrence Levson.
   Periodical not known.

"Rocky Mountain Guild of Puppetry, " U. S. A.   (See "Mile-High Puppeteers")
   Organ. 1961 as Guild No 8 of "Puppeteers of America" group at Denver, Colo.   Became inactive for a while.   A group calling itself "The Mile High Puppeteers" formed and some sources say it took the place of the "Rocky Mountain Guild" but both are listed as active again on the back cover of Pupp J, 21(1): 1969.
   Director or Pres. was Dale Chisman in 1962, and now that it is active again, Elton Norwood, 1969.
   Pupp J, 14(2):25, 1962; 20(3):31, 1968

"St. Louis, Puppet Guild of, " U. S. A.
   Organ. in 1940's in St. Louis, Mo. as Guild No 17 in the "Puppeteers of America" group in 1963.   A large, very active group, it has sponsored National Conventions; see also "Festival" Section and "American" in "International" Section.

325

"St. Louis, Puppet Guild of," (cont.)
Director, or Pres. when joining Guild was Claude
Dontag.
Periodical at first was called St. Louis Guild News-
letter or Newsletter of St. Louis Guild, became Pup-
peteers Newsletter. Don Avery as editor for long
period.
Grapev, 1947, p 11; S 1948, p 21.
Pupp J, 20(3):31, 1968; 21(1):33, 1969
Pupp, 13:6-7, 1942

"San Antonio Guild of Puppetry," U. S. A.
Organ. 1960's in San Antonio, Tex., private group.
Director or Pres. not known
Periodical not known.
Pupp J, 20(3):32, 1968

"San Diego County Guild of Puppetry," U. S. A.
Guild No 5 of "Puppeteers of America" group, organ.
c 1958 and very active, giving series of summer pro-
ductions at the Balboa Park since 1965.
Pres. or Director not known.
Periodical not known.
Pupp J, 21(2):33, 1969

"San Francisco-Oakland Bay Area Puppeteers Guild," U. S. A.
Organ. in 1950's and becoming Guild No 7 of "Puppeteers of America" in 1960, in San Francisco. This
is a very active group of professional and amateur
puppeteers; many doing much work with City Parks
Dept., universities and schools. Many are trouping
throughout the world.
Director or Pres. at time of joining as Guild was Patricia Lavin; Lewis Mahlmann has been among early
leaders and editors.
Periodical is San Francisco Bay Area Puppeteers Guild
Newsletter which is often shortened to just SFBAPG
Newsletter. Words "Bay Area" were not always in
title. Began early 1960.
Pupp J, 8(6):28, 1957; 9(5):12, 16, 20, 1958; 10(1):35,
11(1):29-30, 1959; 11(5):30, 1960; 12(1):26-27, 1960;
14(2):26, 1962; 21(1):32, 1969

"Santa Monica Recreation Puppeteers Club," U. S. A.
Organ. previous to 1956, Santa Monica, Calif. and
developed from Park and Recreation classes.
Director or Pres. not known.
Periodical - none. Pupp J, 8(6):28, 1957

"Scandinavian Puppetry Congress," Norway
Organ. 1960's but exact location not known. This is
a group which demands much more research within
these countries. It is of great importance, since so
little has been published about puppet groups in this
area of Europe. It met in Oslo, Norway, O 26-27, 1969.
Director or Pres. not known.
Periodical not known.
Brit Pupp & M Thea G Newsl, 150:2, N 1960

"Scattergood Y. M. C. A. Puppetry Club," U. S. A.
Organ. Pasadena, Calif. in the early 1950's.
Director or Pres. was John Sweers, editor of periodi-
cal.
Periodical was Puppet Club News
Pupp J, 5(6):30, 1954

"Seattle Guild of Puppetry, The," U. S. A.
Organ. previous to 1960's and became Guild No 11 of
"Puppeteers of America" group in 1961. This is a
very active and strong guild because of the great a-
mount of work done at the Univ. of Washington under
Aurora Valentinetti. It helped to bring foreign puppe-
teers to the World's Fair held there in 1967; sponsors
festivals, exhibits, classes and foreign programs on
puppet work.
Director or Pres. at time of joining as Guild was Lois
Ludington, early leaders were Bruce Inverarity, and
A. Valentinetti, among other well known puppeteers.
Periodical - Newsletter
Pupp J, 11(6):28, 1960; 14(2):25-26, 1962
See also "Festival" Section and "University" Section

"Society of the Marionette," Italy
Organ. 1912 in Florence, by Gordon Craig. It was
very short lived because of the war years but it was
an active classical group using the theatre magazine
Mask for some time.
Director was Gordon Craig.
Periodical for one year was published by G. Craig and
was a valuable and splendid publication called by several names: Marionettes Tonight at 8:30, Marionette
and Marionette Magazine but not, exactly, sponsored
by the group, as came later. N Y Pub Lib. has it on
microfilm. The originals were destroyed in the move
to Lincoln Center.
Pupp Th Am, by Paul McPharlin, p 387

"Society of the Marionette," Italy (cont.)
Mask, 5:144, 1912. Short items about the group will
be found in other 1912-1913 issues of Mask.

"Society of Puppetry and Allied Crafts, The," U.S.A.
(SPAC) (See "Midwestern Puppeteers," Chicago)
Organ. 1947-51 in Chicago, by spur group of "Puppeteers of America after the National Convention in St.
Louis of that year. "Midwestern Puppeteers" of North
and South Side of Chicago joined it temporarily but did
not drop "Puppeteers of America" membership. It
seems to have been short lived.
Professional members were not to hold any office,
thus many left, but about 100 stayed in this group for
some time. It met at Ogden Park, in Chicago.
Director or Pres. was George Cole and Mrs. Liten-
burger
Periodical was a News Letter
"A World Fair of Puppetry," The National Puppetry
Fair sponsored by SPAC," Chicago, Ill., June 24-27.
Batavia, Ill. News, c to May 29, 1950 an item by
E. Dickinson
Pupp J, 1(1):7, 1949; 1(3):10, 1949

"Southern Illinois Puppet Center Group, The," U.S.A.
(See "Midwestern Puppeteers")
Organ. c 1939-43 as a group somehow connected with
the Federal Theatre Puppet work being done in this
area. Very active in various Illinois cities and doing
much with hand puppets and marionettes.
Director or Pres. not known.

"Southwestern German Puppet-Playing and Research Group,"
Germany
Organ. in 1940's at Museum of Weimaron, "Goethe's
Puppet Stage and Theatre." It sponsors educational
shows and exhibits.
Director or Pres. not known.
Periodical not known.
"International News" Pupp J, 2(5):24, 1951

"Southwestern Ontario Puppetry Guild," Canada (See
"Ontario Puppetry Guild")

"Strength Thru Joy Puppet Club," Germany
Organ. for the youth working with puppets during the
Nazi period. It seems to have also been active around

1925 (or at least their periodical was active) for a group which became this under Nazis. It was active till at least 1939 under this name.
Director or Pres. not known.
Periodical during Nazi period was called Das Deutsche Puppenspiel, editor, originally was Dr. Alfred Lehman.
Pupp, 10:37, 1939; 11:35, 1940

"Le Théâtre Des Nations," France
Organ. 1922 as a united friendly group of puppeteers, Paris.
Director or Pres. was J. L. Temporal
No periodical.
Pupp J, 10(6):21-22, 1950

"Third Deutsche Institut für Puppenspiel Guild," Germany
Organ. in 1950's c to April 1959 in Bechom. There was a large meeting at the time. (Ap 24-30, 1959).
Director or Pres. not known.
Periodical not known.
Pupp J, 10(6):21-22, 1959

"Toronto Guild of Puppeteers," Canada
Organ. previous to 1940's in Toronto, not connected with U. S. A. Guilds.
A very large, active group. They sponsor festivals, exhibits, classes and shows and were most active in sponsoring a National Convention for "Puppeteers of America" held at Waterloo Univ., Ontario, in the summer of 1967.
Director or Pres. not known.
Periodical not known.
Pupp J, 9(1):30, 1957
See also "Festival" and "International" Sections

"Twin City Puppeteers, The," U. S. A.
Organ. previous to 1945 in Minneapolis and St. Paul, Minn. It became Guild No 14 of "Puppeteers of America" group in 1963.
A very strong, active group sponsoring festivals, exhibits and work-shops; meeting at homes. Sponsored a National Convention.
Director or Pres. was Lew Williams, and when it joined the P. of A., M. Samanisky
Periodical - Twin City Puppeteers Notebook or often this is shortened to TCP Notebook.
Grapev, S 1947, p 11; N 1948, p 4

329

"Twin City Puppeteers," (cont.)
"Regional Festival of Puppeteers," St. Paul newspapers
for July and Aug 1951
Pupp J, 2(3):25, 26, 29, 1950; 14(2):25, 1962; 20(3):30,
1968
See also "Festival" Section

"Tygerberg Marionette Theatre Group," South Africa
Organ. Nov. 1964
Director, Dan Kirchner
Periodical - Puppet News
Pupp Post, Spring 1969, p 20-21

"Union Corporative Et National Des Montreurs De Mario-
nettes," France
Organ. 1948-5?. The group did not survive long but
did French classical works by Moliere and by other
modern French poets who were among its founders.
Director was Hubert Gignoux
Periodical was Theatre De Marionettes Des Champ
Elyses. It was short lived but good.
Pupp J, 1(3):12, 1949

"UNIMA International" (Headquarters - Prague) See "UNIMA
U. S. A.," "UNIMA...etc."

"Union Internationale Des Marionettes Association," Europe
and World
See also all countries in "International" Section
Organ. 1927 in Baden-Baden, Germany by important
worldwide puppeteers at a convention-festival. Very
active until 1941 and inactive generally during war
years.
Started up again strong in 1945 to date. The original pattern for Paul McPharlin's plan for American
puppet group. Formally organ. in Prague, with Dr.
J. Malik as first Sect. General. Sponsors yearly exhibits and work shops. Has groups in other countries,
always with name "UNIMA" in title. Each country has
a Pres. and a Sect. General.
Director, Dr. Jan Malik; Pres. was Jindřich Vesely at
first. Prof. Skupra became pres. in 1957.
Pupp Master, 9(4):16-17, 1967 says it started in 1929,
reorganized in 1957, started up again after the war.
So again, dates are questioned by different authors.
See also Puppetry in Czechoslovakia by Dr. Erik Kolár,
Prague, Dept. of Fine Arts, Puppetry, c 1965.

Periodicals is Loutkar and Loutkora Scena which often
appear with slightly different titles. These may be
"UNIMA" periodicals of different groups in other
countries. Such as UNIMA France Marionettes, and
UNIMA U. S. A. Newsletter.
Publications. There are many small bulletins and
summary type articles of speeches made at festivals
that are published in Europe but seldom get to the
Americas. A Bibliography of Puppetry was published
in the 1950's for members only, by UNIMA Headquarters. in Prague.
Modern Puppet Theatre in the World, edited by a committee headed by Margareta Niculescu was published in
Berlin, Henschelverlag, 1966; and Kunst, of Berlin,
1966.
The Puppet Theatre of the Modern World, is the same
book (but published in England), London, Harrap, 1967;
(in America) Boston, Plays, 1967 and in 6 other countries the same year. Trans. by Edwald Osers and E.
Stick, for the English editions.
Pupp J, 16(4):11, 1965; 18(5):37-38, 1967
    Most issues of Pupp J have some mention of it un-
der many different headings.
    Many issues of Pupp from about 1945 to 1949 will
mention it under different headings.
Pupp Post and Pupp Master of England carry scattered
items.
Brit Pupp and M Thea G Newsl, 142:4, 5, 1968
See also "Festivals" and "International General" Sec-
tions.
"The Marionette Congress," Pupp 1:13, 1930
"The Marionette Congress at Liege-Sept 1930," by M.
    Levin, Thea Arts, 15:140-53, Feb 1931
"UNIMA," Pupp 4:56, 1933
"History of UNIMA," Pupp J, 1(3):12, 1949
"International News" (these were usually by M. McPhar-
    lin) Pupp J, 2(3):24, 1950
"Rebirth of UNIMA" Pupp J, 9(5):10, 1958, by R.
    Proctor; Pupp Master, 9(4):16-17, 1967, historical
    note on this. The Convention at Prague D 4-14,
    1957
"UNIMA Convention," Pupp J, 9(6):10, 1958
"Puppetry Worldwide," by R. Proctor, Pupp J, 10(2):
    3-5, 1958
"Dr. Malik and UNESCO, The Pres. of UNIMA Writes,"
    Pupp J, 11(5):11, 1959
"UNIMA," Theatre Notebook, 14(3):77, Spring 1960

"UNIMA Intl." (cont.)
  "International News" by M. McPharlin, Pupp J, 14(2):
    8-9, 1962, illus. p 12, 13
  --- by M. McPharlin, Pupp J, 15(3):26-27, 1963, this
    explains the organization well.
  The Art of the Puppet by Bill Baird, New York, Mac-
    millan, 1965, p 174, 175, 189, 193, 194, 205, 209
  "UNIMA Notes," by G. Speaight, Pupp Master, 9(4):
    16-17, D 1969
  "UNIMA Czech Puppeteers" In Crisis of 1967, and
    sig. m. on "UNIMA" History
  "To the 'P. of A.' Board on UNIMA, U.S.A. Contro-
    versy," Pupp Life, Mr 1969, p 1
  "Report on Final Status of UNIMA U.S.A." Pupp Life,
    S 1969, p 28-30. There was quite a lot of discus-
    sion about whether "UNIMA, U.S.A." should be a
    separate group, or should be made to be all under
    the membership of "Puppeteers of America," from
    1968-69 National Convention time. See also "Theory
    and Critical" Section and See "UNIMA, U.S.A."
  Controversery Letter on "UNIMA," from Prague, June
    1969, by Dr. Jan Malik. N Y Publ Lib. Puppet
    File; or Mrs. Mollie Falkenstein, Sect. Gen. of
    UNIMA U.S.A., 132 Chiquita, Laguna Beach, Calif.,
    92651
  "UNIMA-Ready for 1969," by R. Gilpin, Pupp J, 20(4):
    25, 1969

Sub Groups of "UNIMA"

"CIPEMAT" (pronounced Sip-E-Mah)
"Central International Pour L'Etude de la Marionette Tra-
    ditionelle," France
  Organ. previous to 1955, seems to be a sort of spur
    of the International "UNIMA." Active in Paris area,
    it has had a festival of puppet shows in Paris in 1959
    with many countries represented.
  Director or Pres. not known.
  Periodical not known.
  Pupp J, 11(2):5-10, 1959; 12(1):10-12, 21-22, 1960.
    I believe this group became "UNIMA France."

"UNIMA France," France
  Organ. c 1968 in Paris
  Directors: There is a comité: In 1968 the members
    were Rose-Marie Moudoues, Jacqueline Delassaire,
    André Verdun and several others.

Pres. was André Tahon, 1968.
Periodical was UNIMA France Marionnettes which
started 1968. Pupp J, 19(1):41, 1967

"UNIMA Great Britain," England (UNIMA United Kingdom)
Director or Pres, in 1968-69 was Jan Bussell. G.
Speaight was one of the early leaders in this group.
Periodical - none but uses Pupp Post and Pupp Master
Articles will be found in all British periodicals of
puppetry.
Pupp Master, 7(2):13-15, 1962
Pupp J, 20(2):30, 33-35, 1968

"UNIMA U. S. A." Americas
Organ. c 1966.
This group is not a part of "Puppeteers of America"
but was originally (1960-1966) a friendly side-by-side
group of those people interested particularly in International puppetry affairs. The group is not in any way
competitive. An effort was made to have all "Puppe-
teers of America" members automatically members of
this group in 1968, but this did not materialize.
Main work is keeping members informed of foreign
puppet festivals, advising, providing information, meets
usually at National Conventions or Regional Festivals.
Very loose organizational set-up.
Pres. - Bill Baird and Sect. General, Mrs. Mollie
Falkenstein.
Periodical - UNIMA U. S. A. Newsletter
Publication. A very unusual pictorial, Calender UNI-
MA 1968-1969. Laguna Beach, Calif., Mollie Falken-
stein, Aug. 1968
"UNIMA" (U. S. A. early Situation) by M. Batchelder
McPharlin, Pupp J, 15(2):20, 1963. Has 53 members
but not called "UNIMA, USA," just under "Interna-
tional" grouping.
"UNIMA Explained," by M. Batchelder McPharlin,
Pupp J, 15(3):26-27, 1963
"UNIMA Membership," Pupp J, 16(2):23, 1964
"A Mission For UNIMA, U. S. A. Representative,
Mollie," Pupp J, 16(3):30, 1964
"Mollie Falkenstein Reports, (for UNIMA)," Pupp J,
16(4):13, 1965
"UNIMA News," Pupp J, 17(2):13, 1965. The Salz-
burgh Marionette U. S. A. schedule.
"UNIMA International News," by Mollie Falkenstein,
Pupp J, 18(1):22-25, 1966. The organization for

"UNIMA, U. S. A." (cont.)
"UNIMA, U. S. A." at the San Diego Festival, officers, committee.
"UNIMA Photos," by Mollie Falkenstein, Pupp J, 18 (2):21, 1966
"UNIMA News," Pupp J, 19(1):41-42, 1967. The second Festival International at Colwyn Bay.
"UNIMA News," Pupp J, 19(3):6-8, 1967
"UNIMA, U. S. A.," by Mollie Falkenstein, Pupp J, 19(4):22-23, 1968
"UNIMA-Festivals Abroad," by Mollie Falkenstein, Pupp J, 19(5):26-29, 1968
"UNIMA-U. S. A. News," by Mollie Falkenstein, Pupp J, 20(2):30, 33-35, 1968
"UNIMA, U. S. A." (A new structure suggested), Pupp J, 20(4):8, 1969
"UNIMA Proposal for Settling Controversy," Pupp J, 20(5):4-6, 1969. This very disturbing controversy was discussed in many articles, in many periodicals of these dates. Pupp Life (of west coast) taking one side, that of the 1966 original plan, and Pupp J taking other viewpoint of "Puppeteers of America" group, (not entire organization necessarily). See "Theory and Critical" Section.
"Where Do We Go From Here?" Pupp J, 20(5):6, 1969
"UNIMA, U. S. A. Status Settled, Report From Prague," Pupp Life, S 1969, p 28-30.
"UNIMA in Prague-1969," Pupp J, 21(1):35, 1969 The articles suddenly become anonymous after controversy began. Some are indicated as being from Board of Trustees of "P. of A."
"UNIMA News (of International Election)," Pupp J, 21 (1):7, 1967 supplement. Here it is called only "American Section of UNIMA" instead of "UNIMA-U. S. A." Written from the negative viewpoint before National Convention.

"Vagabond Puppeteers," U. S. A.
Organ. c 1938 in Oklahoma City as group from the Federal Theatre.
Director, John W. Dunn, State Director
Periodical was Tanglestrings.
Publication of a mimeo. pamphlet, ed. by J. W. Dunn We Produce a Puppet Show, U. S. Fed. Thea. Project, Number M W p. v. 79; U. S. Fed. Works Agency (W. P. A.) Oklahoma City, Fed. Thea Projects, 1938. A group of six scripts located in NY Publ. Lib.

"Vancouver Guild of Puppetry," Canada
    Organ. c 1950's or earlier in Vancouver.   Quite active
    and sponsoring festivals, exhibits and workshops.
    Director or Pres. not known.
    Periodical not known.
    Pupp J, 20(4):37, 1969

"Ventriloquist Association, International," U. S. A.
    Organ. 1968 in NYC for worldwide membership on the
    same idea as "UNIMA International."
    Director or Pres. is Jerry Lane.
    Periodical.   This is a bi-monthly Newsletter, the ex-
    act name is not known.
    Con Stick, Mr 1969, p 3
        Its address is 99-05 Fifty Eighth Ave. , Rego Park,
    N. Y. , 11368

"Verband Deutscher Puppenspieler," Germany
    Organ. 1930's in Darmstadt, but became inactive dur-
    ing the war years and had its first convention since
    the war at Techlenburgh, Germany in 1948.   Another
    was held at Ahlsfeld, Germany.   Seems to be in Rus-
    sian zone.   Russian puppet periodicals may tell of it.
    Director or Pres. not known.
    Periodical - it has one but we do not have name.
    Pupp J, 2(5):23, 1951
    "Reorganization of Verband Deutscher Puppenspieler,"
    Pupp J, 2(6):28-29, 1951

"Woche Europaischen Puppenspiels," Germany
    Organ. 1940's.
        Is a member of the "Puppeteers of Europe" group.
    This may be another name for "UNIMA."
    Director or Pres. not known.
    Periodical not known.
    Pupp J, 9(1):6-7, 1957

"Works Progress Administration Puppet Groups, The," USA
    "W. P. A. Puppet Groups," "Federal Theatre Puppet Groups"
    Organ. c 1938 in all parts of the country as a means
    of giving employment to professional puppeteers who
    directed large, usually classic, productions in rebuilt
    theatres.   These groups were paid by the government
    from Federal Theatre Funds.
        Were very active and their technical productions
    were very good.   They encouraged puppetry in this
    country a great deal, as we find much more written
    at this time.

"W. P. A. Puppet Groups," U. S. A. (cont.)
   A director was appointed for each group, with one
over each state. Much publication of scripts, bibliographies, work sheets and teaching pamphlets. These
are usually found in the large city libraries, or university libraries, under "Government, Federal Theatre" and occasionally under "Puppetry." They will
very often differ in title for the same work, when it
has been reprinted in another city. See also "Recreation" Section under "Federal Theatre" Division.
   The groups broke up around 1941 and many became
Guilds and clubs already mentioned in this Section,
such as "Vagabond Puppeteers."
Director or Pres. This differed with each state and
with each city.
   Some of the State directors were Paul McPharlin,
Remo Bufano, Tony Sarg, George New, George Middle-
ton, Perry Dilley. Others may be located by research
in Pupp Th Am, by Paul McPharlin, (1949 ed.) in the
"Listing of Puppeteers" Section which was edited by M.
Batchelder McPharlin. The revised edition of this his-
tory may hold additional information. (Revised c 1969
by M. Batchelder McPharlin.)
Periodicals were local news sheets, if any.
Pupp Th Am., by Paul McPharlin, p 266, 369-72, 386
   See also the Index, p 506 for related projects.
Pupp, 4:39-45, 1933 by Perry Dilley
Pupp, 5:30-32, 1934, "Puppets by Public Welfare"
N Y Times, Jl 8, 1934, 2:3
N Y Times, Ag 18, 1935, 2:4
N Y Times, Jl 18, 1936, 18:34
Pupp, 6:6-8, 1935
Ch Sci M, Je 24, 1936, p 13, (the magazine). This is
   very sig. m.
Recreational Puppetry Bulletin, No 6, by D. Meader
   U. S. Fed Thea Project, Mimeo. Bur. of Research
   and Public Parks, U. S. Fed Works Agency; W. P. A.
   St. Paul, Minn., Fed Thea Projects, 1938
        Pupp Bull, 1938, p 71
N Y Times, Jl 3, 4, 1939, p 8 (for both days) "W. P. A.
   World's Fair Puppets."
Grapev, S 1948, p 29
See also "America" in "International" Section,
   "Theatres" and "Exhibits and Festivals" Section.
Most large city newspapers and many theatre periodi-
   cals of the years 1935-39 will have small items.

"Yankee Marionette Guild, The," U. S. A.
Organ. early 1930's in Davenport, Iowa, at Friendly House.
Director of Pres. not known.
Periodical not known.
Pupp Th Am, by Paul McPharlin, p 482

"Y. M. C. A. Puppet Club of Aurora," U. S. A.
Organ. in the 1960's at Aurora, Ill.
Director or Pres. not known.
Periodical - none.
Pupp J, 20(5):34, 1968

"Young Wives of Penrith Puppet Group," England
Organ. 1950 in Penrith for those particularly interested in amateur puppet shows.
Director or Pres. not known.
No periodical.
Brit Pupp Thea, 1(4):24, 1950

II-B.   Periodicals of the Puppet World

Note: The publications listed here are only a few of many that exist or have existed in the puppet world.

The New York Public Library, Puppet Center, which is now located at Lincoln Center Art Museum Theatre Library, has complete or partial sets of a great many of these periodicals and countries and groups are increasingly sending copies of their publications to this great center of puppet literature. The Detroit Museum of Art Library has the "McPharlin Library Collection of Puppet Literature" which includes copies of many of the French and German periodicals listed. McGill University and Toronto Public Library carry Canadian and French items. Most large city public libraries have copies of Guild Newsletters or puppet periodicals from their areas.

Foreign embassies are usually very willing to help the student obtain copies of publications from their respective countries. These offices may usually be found through their offices in the U. N. building in New York City or in Washington, D. C.

Puppet Periodicals

(Alphabetically arranged by title)

Almanach L'Des Marionnettes Et Guignol: France
The periodical of the French puppet group called, "La Société des Amis de Guignol." It started in 1922-39, Paris. The "McPharlin Collection" has copies. I have also seen a few copies in other libraries. It seems to have been interwoven with two other publications by the same group, or groups of almost the same name but from different places. Also in Harvard University Library.
See Bulletin Des Amis Des Guignol and Bulletin Trimestriel

Amateur Theatre: England
    A London theatre periodical which carried a "Puppet
Parade" monthly page by Gerald Morice for a long
time. He also wrote a regular column called "Punch
and Puppetry," for World's Fair (London) from 1937
to the 1970's.

Annals of the Poets: U. S. A.
    It appears with Vol. 16 on the cover in the "McPhar-
lin Collection" but I have not found other issues. Published by Hastings House in 1947, with Paul McPharlin
as editor, it seems like a special volume of the Puppetry Yearbook for 1946-47. In McPharlin Collection.

Artistique Revue des Marionettes et Guignols: France,
Imprimereie de l'Eclaireum
    The periodical of the puppet group called, "Nos Mario-
nettes," with Gaston Cony as editor. Started 1918-
1924 in Nice. There is a book called Nos Marionettes,
by Marcel Temporal which may be about this group.
The McPharlin Collection has all of the series except
Nos 1-2, 12, 45-46, 52 and 54. Then in the New Series Mr. McPharlin had all but 1, 4, 8 & 10 of 1923.
I have seen one other issue in 1926 so it must have
continued at least that long.

Arts in Philadelphia: U. S. A.
    Published in Philadelphia, had a puppetry page by Gil-
bert Lawrence in Vol 2, (Jan. 1940) p 27, which continued through at least that year then stopped. It may
have appeared in earlier issues.

Australian Puppeteer: Austraia
    The periodical of The Puppet Guild of Austrial. It is
mimeographed and the publisher was W. D. Nicol in
1949. It continues to be referred to in current British
puppet periodicals.
Grapev, 47:4, S 1947; Pupp J, 1(3):10, 1949

Balulal: Poland
    In N Y Publ. Libr., uncataloged but kept in a general
folder of "Marionette Periodicals."

La Baraque Foraine: France
    A French newspaper with puppet section from the 1950's
and 1960's, if not from much earlier. Published at
38 Rue De Dovai, Lille, France.

Bharatiya NATYA: India
> A theatre journal, quarterly, with much puppetry. It
> was of brief duration, published in New Delhi, 1961
> by the "Bharatiya NATYA."
> Pupp J, 13(3):28-29, 1961, mentioned in article by M.
> B. McPharlin.

British Puppet Theatre, The: England (See Puppet Post)
> The periodical of the short-lived English "spur" group
> called, "The British Educational Puppetry Institute."
> See also "Organizational" Section this name. From
> all indications the periodical stopped publication because
> of duplication of another British group's periodical
> name, and published material for its members in
> Puppet Post or in Puppet Master.
> See British Puppet Theatre Limited

British Puppet Theatre, The: England (See Puppet Post,
and Puppet Master)
> This appears to be the publication of the "Anglo-Aus-
> tralian Organization" and the "British Educational Pup-
> pet Association." See article "Long Arm of Coinci-
> dence" in Pupp Master, 3(1):12-14, 1950. But another
> source says that C. L. Ellis began its publication Dec.
> 1949 for the "English Puppet and Model Theatre Guild."
> Another date is given as July, 1951, when it was re-
> organized by George Draper as a "New Series" and ran
> until January 1953.

British Puppet Theatre Limited: England
> The few copies in the N Y Publ Library say this was
> published in London, by "British Puppet Theatre, Lim-
> ited, Organization" 1939-1940's. But this seems to be
> connected to the "Anglo-Australian" group and thus to
> the "British Educational Puppet Institute." The title of
> just "British Puppet Theatre" may be a shortened ver-
> sion of this full name in some source material.
> It is confused by some sources with the "British
> Puppet and Model Theatre Guild" periodical, but in-
> spected copies give no indication that it was connected
> with that group at any time. It seems to have begun
> c 1939 and published into the early 1940's, then stopped.
> In the spring of 1949 the "British Model Theatre Guild"
> began a "reorganized publication." (See Brit Pupp
> Thea, 1(5):20, 1950.) But indications are this was not
> at all a reorganization of the original British Puppet
> Theatre Limited.

See also
A. R. Philpott, Dictionary of Puppetry. London,
Macdonald, 1969
H. W. Whanslaw, Second Bench Book of Puppetry.
London, Wells, 1957

Bristol, Spotlight on: England
Sponsored by the "Bristol Puppet Club," in mimeo, it
started around 1950's. An educational club newsletter.
Brit Pupp Thea, 2(1):2, 1951

Bulletin Des Amis De Guignol: France (See also Bulletin-
Trimestriel)
Periodical of group called, "Amis De Guignol." Pub-
lished quarterly at least as early as 1931 in Lyons,
and seems to have followed the Bulletin-Trimestral, or
to have been a part of that publication.
See Almanach Des Marionette and Guignol
Pupp, 2:126, 1931

Bulletin-Trimestriel: France
Periodical of group called "Les Amis De Guignol."
Started 1926-1947 and the group had a second periodi-
cal, Bulletin Des Amis De Guignol. A few copies of
the Trimestriel are in the McPharlin Collection but the
Nov 1947 issue is not complete.

Cesky-Loutkár: Czechoslovakia (See Czech. Puppeteer)
Periodical of an early group that began in 1912-1924
in Germany and moved into Czechoslovakia in 1917
during or right after the war. Edited by Dr. J. Vesely, it closed about June 1939 and is often referred
to as Loutkar.
Pupp, 10:34, 1939
The use of the last name alone is confusing for students because "UNIMA International" Org. periodical is
also referred to in many sources as Loutkar. Dates
may help decide whether the article is from the early
Czech. group or from "UNIMA."
See Loutkova Scena and Loutkár.

Chapulin. La Revista Del Niño Mexicano: Mexico
A Mexican educational "comic" puppet book series
which Paul McPharlin considered "puppet-like" and
which was included in his library. It was published
by the Mexican Secretariat of Public Education (La
Secretaria de Educacio Publica) in the early 1940's.
The McPharlin Collection has Nos 1 to 5, 8-9, 1942-43.

Chapulin. La Revista Del Niño Mexicano (cont.)
The Education Dept. of Mexico has other recent puppet publications and periodicals which continue to date
but these have not been investigated.

Children's Theater Conference News-Letter: U. S. A.
A publication of the "American Educational Theater
Association," from 1959 to date. It contains some
puppet material, especially around convention times.

Control Stick, The: U. S. A.
Periodical of the "New England Guild of Puppetry-No 9"
of "Puppeteers of America" group. The editor from
1967 to date is L. S. Rice. It is a printed newsy letter from one to three pages in length.
Pupp J, 15(6):28, 1964; and 18(5):38, 1967

Curtain Call: Canada
A Canadian theatrical magazine which since at least
1935 has had a puppet page written by various important professional puppeteers. Rosalynde F. Osborne
was the first writer of the page and wrote of the 1st
Canadian Puppetry Convention at Hamilton in May 1939.

Czech. Puppeteer, The: Czechoslovakia See Cesky-Loutkár
and Loutkova Scena

D. C. Puppetimes: U. S. A. (See National Capitol Newsletter)

Das Deutsche Puppenspiel: Germany
Published in Leipzig, by "Strength through Joy Society
for Youth," for the groups working with puppets during
the Nazi period. Originally edited by Dr. Alfred Lehman in 1925; it continued at least until 1939.
Pupp, 10:37, 1939; 11:35, 1940

Das Deutsche Volkspiel: Germany
Edited by Hans Higgeman and published in Berlin during the war years. It may have continued for some
time after the war but only the D 1936-1938 issues are
in the McPharlin Collection.

Design Magazine, The: U. S. A.
This art publication had much puppetry information and
a special puppet number was reprinted as a book. That
was Vol. 38: no 1, 1936, and was called A Book of
Puppetry. Columbus, O., Design Publ. Co., 1936-37.

From the 1930's for some time, the puppet page was
done by Felix Payant.

Detroit News Letter or Detroit Guild Gazette: U. S. A.
Periodical of the "Detroit Puppeteers Guild, No 6" of
"Puppeteers of America" group.   Active at least as
early as 1949 with Jail Januzzi as publisher.   Dave
Gibson was editor in 1950.   In 1953 it was being edited
by Norma Appel.   Copies are in McPharlin Library.
Grapev, Feb 1949, p 4

Deutsche Buhne: Germany (See Die Puppenbuhne and Der
Puppenspieler)
Seems to be the name of a National German Theatre
and also its publication having much puppet material.
It may have taken the place of Die Puppenbuhne, (or
Der Puppenspieler) for a while.   But it was published
in Berlin as early as Jan. 1934 under this title.

Deutsche Kunst Und Dekoration: Germany
This magazine helped to stimulate German puppetry to
a very great extent by publishing much European puppetry material and many illustrations.   Several issues
in McPharlin Collection are dated before 1949.
Pupp Th Am, by Paul McPharlin, p 390

Educational Puppet Association Yearbook: England (E. P. A.
Yearbook)
Published for the "British Educational Puppetry Association" once a year since c 1944.   Started by Ellen M.
Marks.   Ref. to this British Educational Puppet Yearbook should be indicated by E. P. A. Yearbook.   Published by C. W. Baumont Co. , London.   Now discontinued - some copies in N Y Publ Lib.
Pupp J, 6(5):24, 1955; and Pupp, 15:36-37, 1944

E. P. A. "Spotlight:" England
A mimeo. news-sheet, eight or nine times a year, by
the "British Educational Puppetry Association."   It
gives advance information and news of exhibits, festivals, school productions and important educational bits
on puppets.

Era, The: England
"The columns of this publication over a period of some
50 years, (1900-1955) at least, disclose a mass of fas-
cinating detail... "G. Speaight, in his History of Eng-

343

Era, The: England (cont.)
lish Puppet Theatre.   London, Harrap, 1955, p 308-09.

Figurentheater: Germany
Sometimes shortened to just Figuren.   It is a contemporary publication at least from Oct 1948 since copies
around that date are in Harvard Univ. Library.   It is
issued quarterly, well illustrated.   Published by
Deutsches Inst.

Grapevine Telegraph: U.S.A. (See Grapevine) and (Puppetry: U.S.A.)
Mimeo paper of the "Midwestern Puppeteers of America" which was started as a bi-monthly news letter
c Nov 1936 to 1943.   May have been interrupted by the
war but continued shortly thereafter.   Seems to have
been about 44 volumes.   N Y Publ Lib. has Nov 1937
to 1947.
From a note in the McPharlin Collection it may have
originally begun within the St. Louis Guild and came
to Detroit later.   It was followed by just Grapevine,
Sept. 1948, then was absorbed into the Puppetry Journal.
Pupp, 8:71, 1937
Pupp J, 5(2):3, S1953; 2(3):4, 1953

Grapevine, The: U.S.A. (See Grapevine Telegraph
Puppetry and St. Louis Guild Newsletter)
Mimeo. paper which was the Grapevine Telegraph until
Sept. 1948.   This shortened name is a written note on
No. 44 of the N Y Publ Lib. copies.   It came out
quarterly with the first title, after being 'borrowed'
from St. Louis Puppet Guild, and the first issue under
this title in 1940's.   Sponsored by the new young official American puppeteer's organization of "Puppeteers
of America" group, with Marjorie Batchelder McPharlin
as editor until 1949.   It then became
Puppetry Journal for that same group, continuing under
the editorship of Vivian Michael.   The title Grapevine
then returned to St. Louis Guild for a short time.
The Grapevine Telegraph and Grapevine had a yearbook from 1936, published and edited by Paul McPharlin, out of Detroit.   It seems to have been his International Puppetry Yearbook which began c 1930 (without
a news letter).   See this publication... Sometimes
called Puppetry Magazine or just Puppetry.   G. Lat-

shaw was also active in these early periodicals of the
"Puppeteers of America" group.
Pupp Th Am, by Paul McPharlin, p 388
Pupp, 8:71, 1937; 18:2, 1947; and Pupp J, 6(5):3, 1955

Halequinade: N. Wales (Harlequinade)
    Both titles seem to appear in sources but I believe the
    second one of Harlequinade is correct. It was first
    published c 1966 and edited by Christopher Somerville,
    from the Laurels, 6 Woodlands Rd., Colwyn Bay, No.
    Wales. He was connected with the "Harlequinade
    Theatre" of that area. The issue seen in N Y Publ.
    Lib. had puppet articles but was not all puppetry.
    However, in Pupp Master, 9(1):25, 1967, it is de-
    clared a magazine for puppeteers.

Het Poppenspiel: Belgium
    Periodical first published in Bochelen, by L. Contryn
    as a mimeo. publication for Belgian puppeteers, c
    1947. After the war it was a printed periodical, pub-
    lished in Antwerp, in 1960's, and is still active.
        Sometimes it is referred to as The Marionette
    Theater, because there is an English summary transla-
    tion appearing at end of each issue. In this bibliogra-
    phy it will always appear as Het Poppenspiel, with a
    note if the article is in translated section. Because of
    this translated title, do not confuse with Marionetten
    Theatre, of Germany, or Gordon Craig's, Marionettes
    published only in 1918-1919.
        It is well illustrated and now contains serious medi-
    cal and educational, as well as entertainment material.
    Many copies may be found in the N Y Publ Lib.

International Yearbook of Puppetry: U. S. A. (Usually called
just Puppetry) (See Puppetry, Puppetry Magazine, Puppetry
Bulletin)
    Originally published and edited as a private publication
    by Paul McPharlin from 1930. In 1936-1949 it became
    the official yearly summary of "Puppeteers of Ameri-
    ca" group, still edited by Paul McPharlin. It was in-
    terrupted briefly in 1942 but resumed almost at once,
    being published, NY, Hastings House, 1944-49; still
    edited by Paul McPharlin. He refers to it in his book,
    Pupp Th Am as just "Puppetry" from the 1930 printing
    forward. I have followed his example giving it the ab-
    breviation of Pupp, 1: 1930. It was in regularly print-
    ed book form, with hard covers and illustrations. It
    gave a yearly summary of work in America and around

Intl. Yearbook of Puppetry (cont.)
the world from 1930 forward.
See Puppetry and Puppetry Magazine, for previous type
of issue.
See also Pupp Th Am, by Paul McPharlin, p 387-88
and index.

Sometimes incorrectly called Puppetry Yearbook
which was rightfully the title of "British Puppet and
Model Theatre Guild" summary of yearly work by their
group, see that title.

Easily confused with "British Educational Puppetry
Association's" yearly summary of work called British
Educational Puppetry Yearbook or just E. P. A. Year-
book, see this title.

Volumes from 1931-1941 had 26 "special copies"
printed as gifts with special extra illustrative material,
and clearly designated as "gift copy" inside the cover.
They are numbered 1-A to 26-Z. I have seen them
only in Mr. McPharlin's private collection previous to
transfer into McPharlin Collection in Detroit. See
Annals of the Poets; Ch Sci M Mag, Mr 30, 1946, p 12.
Pupp 15:3, 1944 and Pupp 12:3, 1941
Pupp J, 6(1):4-5, 1954, The McPharlin Collection, by
I. L. Zupnick.

Jack and Jill: U. S. A. (The Curtis Publ. Co.)
Very simple children's publication with much puppetry
material included.

Junior League Mag: U. S. A. (See Players and Puppets)
Periodical of the "Junior Leagues of America- Children's Theatre Division." Was published out of NYC
office of the Org. and often had much puppet material,
still carries some, but not as much as from 1933-
1950's.

Had a puppet page by puppet director of organization, Jean Starr Wiksell. Her work terminated, with
the position, about 1967 but the main office carries a
very long and complete line of original puppet plays
and helps or "packets" on puppetry. See also their
Catalogue on Marionettes and Puppet Plays, 1963-1968.

Junior Puppet News, The British: England
"British and Model Theatre Build-Junior Groups" peri-
odical and this is also the name of a page in the
"British Educational Puppetry Association's" Puppet
Post. This may cause some confusion in looking ma-
terial up. Try both places if it is not of an education-

al nature, although both are concerned with schools
of England rather than professional public work.

Der Komet: Germany
Periodical for puppet group, several issues are in the
McPharlin Collection.

Kuklapolitan Courier Yearbook: U. S. A.
From the television program, by Burr Tillstrom, in
Chicago, about his characters "Kukla, Fran and Ollie."
The first issue was edited by B. Tillstrom in 1951
and was an annual yearbook rather than monthly publication from indications of the Library of Congress records. I have not run across it.

Laienspieler, Der: Germany
Began as early as the 1950's.

Los Angeles Guild of Puppeteers News Bulletin: U. S. A.
(See Puppet Life, Los Angeles County Guild of Puppeteers
News Bulletin)
The first title was used by the "Los Angeles County
Guild of Puppetry," group No 4, of "Puppeteers of
America" as its very earliest publication, but very
shortly included the word "county."
Seemed to have been published monthly, 4-8 pages
starting around 1957 or earlier. It continues to date
under title Puppet Life, but now, although still mimeo.,
has become quite professional in approach, using snap-
shot illustrations, cartoons, free-hand drawings and
construction plans. It covers local news but includes
good general articles.
The editor for several years, especially during its
enlargement has been Bob Bromley, author of many
articles in the periodical. The word "county" was
dropped, officially, from the name of the group sponsoring it, in 1968. In 1969 it included the statement
"Printer, Dick Scott." In LA Pub Lib, and NY Pub Lib.
Pupp J, 11(5):29-30, 1960; 11(6):29, 1960

Loutkár: Czechoslovakia (See Cesky-Loutkár) Ceskowslö-
vensky Loutkár
Originally for an early Czech puppet group, and published by Dr. Jindrich Vesely at Chocen, correct full
name of the periodical was Ceskyloutkár but often written Cesky-Loutkár, or just Loutkár..
Summarizing many sources it appears that Loutkár
(The Puppeteer), usually edited by Dr. J. Vesely, be-

347

Loutkár: Czech. (cont.)
gan in 1900 and with slight title variations and several
different series numbers, continued until 1939. See
Loutkova, Scena, publ. now, Prage: Orbis.
In 1918 the "UNIMA International" group of Czech.
in Prague, seems to have begun using Loutkář as its
main periodical with Dr. Cesal doing some editing with
the title slightly altered to read Ceskowslovenský Loutkář, and the address written: Praha 12, Stalinova 3,
ČSSR. It is usually still referred to as Loutkář, by
the public and many sources.
The title changes again slightly, still under "UNIMA"
in 1939. See Loutkova, Scena (The Puppet Stage) but
still referred to generally as Loutkář by many.
See Zpravy-Loutkarskeho Soustredeni which was more
of a news sheet which went along with Loutkar, and
between it and Loutkova, Scena, and with Ceskowslovenský Loutkář.

Loutky, Nase: (our puppets) Czechoslovakia (See Nase
Loutky)

Loutkova, Scena: (The Puppet Stage) Czechoslovakia (See
Loutkář)
The continuation of Ceskowslovenský Loutkář and the
original periodical Cesky-Loutkář or Ceskyloutkar as
a monthly, about June 1939, came under full sponsor-
ship of "UNIMA International," in Prague, with Dr.
Jan Malik as editor. This is a highly professional
printed, illustrated magazine. It was interrupted in
1941 by the war, with only 6 issues to that date.
It began again in 1945-1947.
Some of these issues, by this name are in the Mc
Pharlin Collection.
Around 1945, Dr. Malik began a news letter called
Zpravy-Loutkarskeho Soustredeni. Then suddenly we
see no more Loutkova, Scena and c 1945, when the
State Government took charge of all puppetry, the
periodical is called Czechowslovensky Loutkar Magazine. According to a writer in Pupp, 17:54, 1946
and also in Pupp J, 7(5):5, 1956, this periodical has
had '40 years continued publication background.' This
indicates that all four periodicals given under this particular title are considered one and the same, historically speaking, despite the reference to the first given
name in Pupp Master, 2(6):173, 1949.
Pupp J, 1(3):12, 1949 (by M. B. McPharlin); Pupp J,
2(1):20-21, 1950; 7(5):5, 1956.

See also   A. R. Philpott's, Dictionary of Puppetry.
London, Macdonald, 1969

Lutkovni Oder: Yugoslavia
    The national periodical paper for Yugoslavian puppe-
    teers, the translation being "The Puppet Stage," was
    published from 1950-1952.   It had about six editions
    and was published from Slovenia.   The war was very
    disturbing to puppet work and periodicals because they
    were considered as a political tool to get messages to
    the people; sometimes used by the underground.   Edi-
    tors were imprisoned, periodicals stopped, perform-
    ances were supervised or halted.
       Perhaps this periodical appeared many years previ-
    ous to the war with a slightly different title, and the
    group has a periodical with a similar title from 1955
    to date.
    See   Obzornik: Yugoslavia.

Marionette Magazine, The: Italy   (See   Marionettes, Tonight at 8:30)
Marionette   and   The Marionettes

Marionettes, Tonight at 8:30:   Italy
    Gordon Craig's famous art puppet publication for all
    international puppeteers speaking the English language,
    much as Loutkář was for European's.   It began about
    April 1918, but was erratically numbered at first and
    unfortunately lasted only one year because of the war
    situation in Italy.   It was published in Florence, and
    grew out of the art periodical, The Mask which car-
    ried much puppet material.   It is confusingly referred
    to in different sources as Marionettes, Tonight at
    12:30, The Marionette Magazine, The Marionette and
    just plain Marionette.
       To simplify matters in this bibliography it is called
    by the last shortened name, Marionette, published but
    erratically numbered monthly, 12 issues.   N Y Publ
    Lib. has had to put it on microfilm since moving to the
    new Lincoln Center location.   It was in the original
    state in Cleveland, O. , Publ. Library, and in the Mc
    Pharlin Collection.
    See also   Mask, and A. R. Philpott's, Dictionary of
    Puppetry.   London, Macdonald, 1969, p 149-50, ex-
    cellent summary of its history is given.

Marionette Theatre: Belgium (See Het Poppenspiel)

Marionetten Theater: Germany (See Der Puppentheater)
This is also the name of a particular theatre, first in
Baden-Baden, under Ivo Puhonny, then in Munich (a-
bout 1918) with Paul Bronn directing. This periodical
could have been published by these theatres as a news
letter instead of being a different name for Der Puppentheater.

Marmouset-Mensuel Nomore: (Special) France
A special number of an account of puppet shows given
at the Exposition Internationale in Paris, 1937. Published as the Jan 1938 issue. In McPharlin Collection.
Other issues carried puppet items.

Mask, The: Italy
See Marionette Magazine, No 3, May, 1918, p 95-96,
which lists all puppet articles given in this more theatrical magazine published by Gordon Craig for 23 years,
1908-1929, 15 vols.
See also "The Voice Behind the Mask," by Paul Mc
Pharlin in Playgoer, Mr 16, 1930
See also Theatre Arts, D 1917, p 62 and Theatre
Arts, Summer, 1918, p 163
Special note: In the McPharlin Collection there is
one very small bound volume, much different in size
than the large Marionette Magazine volumes which were
found elsewhere, with title Marionettes Tonight at 8:30,
perhaps this was a special issue of Mask and not the
same as Marionette Magazine; done in one of these
seemingly 'lost' years of The Mask.

Meister Des Puppenspiels: Bochum, Germany (Theater Der
Welt)
This seems to be individual, erratically published, issues about Master Puppeteers published with text in
Dutch, English, German, by Fritz Wortelmann, starting
c 1959 out of Bergstr, Germany, sponsored and published by Deutsches Institut fur Puppenspiels. It was
supposed to have had 16 issues. The N Y Publ Library
file is incomplete and the McPharlin Collection has one
issue only.

Messenger, The: Belgium
The magazine of the "National Federation of Belgian
Puppeteers" started in Antwerp in 1947 and had nine

350

extremely interesting issues, when the organization disbanded.

Mitteilungen: Germany
 Started in Kiel, Germany about 1934. McPharlin Collection has one issue.

Model Stage, The: England
 One of the early titles for the publication of "English Model Theatre" Groups. The early publisher was Messrs. John Readington and Benjamin Pollock, Ltd. (Pollock Toy Theatre Shop). There was a new quarterly in 1950's which was replaced completely by the publications of the two British Puppet Organizations.
 Brit Pupp Thea, 1(5):7, 1951
 Pupp Master, 3:99-100, 1950

Le Montreur Des Marionettes: France
 A mimeo. magazine of the "Union Cooperative et National des Montreurs de Marionette" group. Started c 1948 and continued into the 1950's, perhaps longer. Printed in Paris, there arc a vew copies in McPharlin Collection.
 Pupp, 17:56, 1946
 See Theatre of Marionettes des Champ Elysee (issues mention this) Revue L'Historie Du Theatre (issues mention this)

Nase Loutky (Our Puppets): Czechoslovakia (See Loutkár)
 This puppet publication was published monthly, had 12 volumes by 1936. It seems to have ended in 1938. The sponsoring group is not known.
 Pupp, 5:32, 1934.

Natya: India
 A puppet periodical. A few issues are in N Y Pub Library.

National Capitol Puppetry Guild Newsletter: U.S.A. (See Puppetimes and Newsletter of National Capitol Puppetry Guild)
 This name was adopted when it was edited by June Sylvester. It was then shortened to Puppetimes, which seems to have been used as early as 1965. No articles, two pages, mimeo.

News Bulletin of Los Angeles Guild of Puppeteers: U.S.A. (See Puppet Life) and Los Angeles County Guild of Puppeteers News Bulletin.

News and Notes: England   See   Notes and News as the
title used most often.

Newsletter of the Detroit Puppeteers Guild: U. S. A.
      Periodical used by the group mentioned in title
      Pupp J, 4:26, 1953

Newsletter of Greater New York Guild of Puppeteers, Inc. :
U. S. A.
      Sometimes "Newsletter" comes at the end of the title
      in more recent issues.   This periodical runs about 4
      to 5 pages, some illustrations and very few articles,
      but of great value in following New York and eastern
      puppet life and showings.   Started about 1964 by Rod
      Young it has become more sophisticated in form from
      simple mimeo. to form of off-set and is published a-
      bout 6 times a year.

Newsletter of Chicagoland Puppeteers Guild: U. S. A.
(See   Puppet Patter)
      Has become quite a professional periodical starting
      c 1960 with Jay Marshall as editor, now quarterly,
      formerly was more of simple mimeo news letter to
      members.
      Pupp J, 15(4):20, 1965; 15(6):29, 1964

New York Staatz-Zeitung: U. S. A.
      An early American newspaper listing much German-
      American puppet material in the early 1950's.   A few
      copies of it are in McPharlin Collection.

Ningyo-Shibai: Japan
      Japanese magazine of the Marionette Theatre.   Started
      c 1930 and edited by Jiro Nan (Kyoto-fu).   Published in
      Osaka, Japan.   Vol 1(1), 1931, is in the McPharlin
      Collection.   He also had a few additional issues, but
      they do not name the sponsoring group.
      Pupp, 5:36, 1934

Nos Marionettes (The Puppeteers): France   (See Artistique
Revue)
      This is also the title of a book which may have started
      from this periodical.   The book is by Marcel Temporal.
      The periodical was published first in Paris with Gaston
      Cony as editor, c 1918 and seems to have continued at
      least till 1924.
      Pupp 9:39, 1938

Notes and News: England (See Puppet Master)
This was probably the first periodical of the British
Puppet and Model Theatre Guild in London. It started
about a year after the founding of the organization,
1926. A. R. Philpott's Dictionary of Puppetry, London,
Macdonald, 1969, talks of it under the organization
heading. He says the Press Secretary was G. Morice
but H. W. Whanslaw says the paper was edited by Seymour Marks in his, A Bench Book of Puppetry, p 194.
It continued from O 1926 till June 1927 and then O
1936-Aug 1939.

The War Time Bulletin became the title of the mimeo
Notes and News from No. 1-6, 1940-1941 during World
War II and those issues are in the McPharlin Collec-
tion. No. 12-17, 1942-1945, were edited by G. C. T.
Morice and were in the New York Publ. Lib. H. W.
Whanslaw remarks that "the War-Time Bulletin was
sometimes called Puppet Post around 1945; " which would
of course have been confusing since the British Educa-
tional Puppet Association's periodical was called Puppet
Post.

British Puppet Theatre was the title used for a short
time, until it became confused with another group's
periodical.

British Puppet and Marionette Guild Theater Magazine
was another title used in one of the change-over periods. For a short time, Monthly News was used as
newsletter.

Junior Puppet News, a branch publication, published erratically and now seems to be included in Puppet
Master, as a section.

British Puppetry Yearbook. The first publication was issued by Eric Brammall, according to the title page of
that issue. It resembled the McPharlin, American
Yearbook and was expensive so was soon discontinued.
New York Publ Lib. has a few issues.

Puppet Master and British Puppet and Model Theatre
Guild Newsletter are the last of the titles used. These
titles are explained under their own headings in this
section.

Notes and Queries: England
Originally known as For Literary Men, Artists, etc.
London, Bell, 1850. Vol. 14 D 1967, is No. 12 (No
212 of continuous series).   Many unusual puppet items
by well known puppeteers of the world.   Early materi-
al on "Punch" and early puppet forms.   Address:
Oxford, J. C. Maxwell, English Faculty Library, Man-
or Road, Oxford, England.
See also A. R. Philpott's, Dictionary of Puppetry.
London, Macdonald, 1969, p 171.
In British Museum.

Obzernik: Yugoslavia
The Yugoslavian Cultural Magazine under the Soviet
regime.   From Ljubljani, Miklosiceva, Yugoslavia, at
least 1949-1950's.   Puppetry is discussed in every issue in a column called "Lutkiovani Odri."   Lists good
puppet films, book reviews, etc., has good illustrations.

Od Szopki Do Teatry Lajek: Poland
Published in Warsaw, c 1951 to date.   Well illustrated,
monthly, with some English summary articles at the
end of each issue.   The current puppet productions
discussed; much Czech. material is included.

Opal, The: Canada
The Ontario Puppetry Association Newsletter, began
c 1962 and is published six times a year.   Mr. and
Mrs. Joseph Clark as editors; processed at 417 E.
42nd St., Hamilton, Ontario.

Oracle, The: U. S. A.
The publication of the "International Brotherhood of
Ventriloquists" published from 33 W. Maple Ave.,
Ft. Thomas, Kentucky.   W. S. Berger was editor at
one time and had a large collection and library of ma-
terial on ventriloquism.

Orange County Guild Newsletter: U. S. A.
Periodical of Puppeteers of America Guild No. 10,
from 1961 to date.   Printed in Laguna Beach, Calif.,
but rather erratic and appears to be inactive after
1968.
P. C. A. Newsletter: U. S. A.
Sponsored by Puppeteers Club Association of Cromwell,
Conn., John S. Miner, Jr., editor.   Issued every two

354

months, 4 pages of short articles. Began in Jan. 1969.
In N Y Publ. Lib.

Pelpup News: England
Periodical of the Pelham Puppet Club which was started
1949 in Marlborough, Wiltshire, England with Robert
Pelham as editor. About 50 copies published monthly,
then twice a year (1966). Worldwide circulation, large,
much variety in articles and material.

Perlicko-Perlacko: Germany
Edited by Dr. Hans Purschke in Frankfurt. Published
for more or less private circulation, 1950 into 1960's.
Back issues available from editor, M21, Hadrianstrasse,
3, Frankfurt. Some copies in N Y Publ. Lib.

Players and Puppets: U. S. A.
Periodical was published by the American Bureau of
Jr. Leagues, with Jean Star Wiksell and Helenka Adam-
owska as early editors. Published irregularly from
NYC office of the organization and starting c 1930, un-
der Children's Theatre Division, discontinued in 1940's.
Some copies in McPharlin Collection.

Players Magazine, The: U. S. A.
American theatre magazine with much college material
and which has a regular puppet page for many years by
different puppet masters. See Jero Magon's work in
this periodical, given in "Lighting" Section; (about Nov
1936). Jean Star Wiksell writing in 1938.
    Players, Jan 1942, has a bibliography by P. Mc
Pharlin on puppets and N-D, 1941 has another bibliography.
    Players, 21: , 1945 has an article "Special Empha-
sis on Puppetry Articles."
    Romain Procter wrote page from 1941-1947; Jero
Magon from 1952-1957. Rod Young in late 1950's.
See also Pupp Bulletin 1938, p 72; Pupp J, 1(1):7,
1949

Het Poppenspiel: Belgium
Periodical first published in Bochelen, by L. Contryn
as a mimeo. publication for Belgian puppeteers, c 1947.
After the war it was a printed periodical, published in
Antwerp, in 1960's, and is still active.
    Sometimes it is referred to as The Marionette Theo-
ater, because there is an English summary translation

appearing at end of each issue. In this bibliography
it will always appear as Het Poppenspiel with a note
if the article is in translated section. Because of this
translated title, do not confuse with Marionetten Theatre of Germany, or Gordon Craig's, Marionettes
published only in 1918-1919.
It is well illustrated and now contains serious medical and educational, as well as entertainment, material. Many copies are in N Y Publ. Lib.

Punch and Judy's Children's Annual: England
No information except that copies are in British Museum, London.

Punch and Judy: England
Published by Ernest Nister in London around 1869-
1870, some copies in British Museum.

Punchinello: England
Punch
Several copies in British Museum but this is not about
puppets, it is a satiric comment on life of the times.
They very seldom if ever have true puppet material.

"Punch and Puppetry" page in Weekly Fair: England
Very important regular puppet weekly column by Gerald Morice, the English puppet historian. Listing of
puppet activities, articles, discussions and reviews of
puppet books. Started before 1940, continuing into
1970's.

Punch Line: U. S. A.
Periodical of the Phoenix Puppet Guild of Phoenix,
Ariz. Began c to 1960's.

Puppenspiel und Puppenspieler: Switzerland
Copies are in the N Y Publ. Lib. It is well illustrated.

Die Puppenbuhne: Germany
A short lived periodical which ran for 7 issues and
seems to have been absorbed by Das Puppenspieler,
which seems to have also absorbed Der Puppentheater
and Die Puppenspieler, which is connected to this particular periodical in some way as indicated by its publishers.
This periodical tried to absorb Das Puppenspieler

for a very short time but being unsuccessful was dissolved. It was for a general "Marionetten Fellowship"
like Org. and was published from Sept 1933-Mar 1934.
These issues are in the McPharlin Collection.

Die Puppenspieler: Germany (See Der Puppenspieler and
Der Puppentheater)
A monthly periodical 1930-1931, of a group called
"Die Puppenspielers" it became bi-monthly, Jl 1931-
Je 1932 and then quarterly in 1933, stopped issues in
Jl 1933. It was published by the "Deutscher Bund für
Puppenspiele" under F. Wortelmann. For a short
while it absorbed Das Puppentheater, from N 1931.
See Die Puppenbuhne. A few copies in NY Publ Lib
and a few more in Harvard Univ. Lib.

Der Puppenspieler: Germany. Der Puppenspieler Und
Monats Hefts (this was full title)
A German art magazine with much puppetry included
and sponsored by the group, "Deutscher Bund für Pup-
penspiele" with Fritz Wortelmann as editor when it was
absorbed into Das Puppentheater in N and D, 1931.
It was suspended in Jl 1933 to blend into still another
puppet magazine.
This periodical started again in 1949 at Braunschweig
Germany. Pupp J, 1(1):13, 1949
Originally it was monthly, then bi-monthly in 1931
and then quarterly in 1935. In British Museum.
See Meister Des Puppenspiels, Der Puppentheater,
Die Puppenbuhne and Deutsche Buhne

Das Puppentheater: Germany (See Der Puppentheater)
Its history is confusing but it was published in Leipzig. According to Paul McPharlin it started in 1926
but I found an issue in NY Publ Lib as early as 1923
and as late as 1931, under slightly different title. The
original, Das Puppentheater seems to have stopped
in July of 1933. Indications are that it was for a
group called "The Puppentheater Forderung Der
Deutschen Theater Kulture" and that early editors were
Dr. Alfred Lehmann and Dr. Schuppel.
Copies may be found in British Museum and N Y
Publ Lib with the German wording "Verband zur Förd-
erung der Deutschen Theaterkultur-Abteilung Puppentheater."
See Die Puppenspieler, Das Deutsche Puppenspiel,
Die Puppenbuhne.

357

Der Puppentheater: Germany (See Das Puppentheater and Die Puppenbuhne)

According to H. W. Whanslaw's, Bench Book of Puppetry, No. 1. London, Wells, 1957, p 197, the periodical began Vol 1, no 1, 1930, but other sources give other dates and history; one saying it began as early as 1918 and another saying it started in 1923. It seems to have combined with another periodical in 1931-32, with a slight change from Das Puppentheater, to Der Puppentheater and then it may have changed again into Die Puppenspieler in Nov or Dec 1931 for only 3 volumes, and then ceased for the war years. Dr. Alfred Lehmann and Dr. Schuppel were early editors, for "The Puppentheater Forderung der deutschen theater Kulture." Pupp 2, 1931, p 124 and Pupp 3, 1932, p 14
Pupp Th Am, by Paul McPharlin p 391

An additional note indicates the periodical was for a group called "Deutscher Bund fur Puppenspiel" originally started 1930-1933 and began again 1948-1950 with Fritz Wortelmann as editor in 1951 and published in Bochum Germany: Puppenspieler Verlag. Volumes 1-3 of this issue are in McPharlin Collection but here it is called Die Puppenbuhne and under that title had only 7 issues in all.

A few sources seem to call it Marionetten Theatre, which is not indicated as a correct title by any of the regular historians.

It is still in publication during the 1970's and copies at the N Y Publ Lib have small sections in English and other languages at the end of each issue. It resembles the American Pupp J in material and illustrations.

The periodical publishers had some special issues. See Meister Des Puppenspielers, which has texts in various languages.

Puppet, The: U. S. A.

Published monthly by the Carnegie Institute of Technology, Dec 1921-23 in Pittsburgh. There are a few copies in N Y Publ Lib.

Puppet Club News: U. S. A.

Bulletin published by the Scattergood Y. M. C. A. Puppetry Club in Pasadena. Editor was John Sweers, when it started in the early 1950's.
Pupp J, 5(6):30, 1954

Puppet Master, The: (England and Hungary seem to have
used same name for a periodical)
   English: See Notes and News, British Puppet Theatre
   Limited and British Puppet Theatre; British Puppet and
   Model Theatre Newsletter
      Changes in size and printed form quite often in its
   history. Published as the Journal of "British Puppet
   and Model Theatre Guild" quite irregularly but supposed to come out quarterly. It became the official
   name for the publication of the "British Puppet and
   Model Theatre Guild" in the early 1940's. Stopped and
   started and finally became quarterly about 1948.
      Starting in Vol 1-new series in 1953, rather large
   size. In 1967 it became much smaller in size and irregular again. In N Y Publ Lib.
   See also Dictionary of Puppetry, by A. R. Philpott,
   p 210.

Puppet Master (or Puppet News): Hungary
      Having the same name as the English periodical of
   British Puppet and Model Theatre Guild, but published
   in Hungarian and sponsored originally by the Hungarian
   State Puppet Theater.
   Pupp J, 2(1):20-21, 1950.

Puppet Patter: U. S. A.
      Periodical of the "Chicagoland Puppet Guild." It was
   called a Newsletter at one time.
   Pupp J, 16(5):32, 1965

Puppet Post, The: England. See British Puppet Theatre
      Limited which may have been an offshoot.
   Official periodical of the Educational Puppetry Association of England.   A. R. Philpott publisher-editor from
   about 1950's.   It began about 1944 with Ellen Marks as
   editor, quarterly by 1946 with B. Tublin as editor and
   continued quite regularly.   It became biannual, September and March, from about 1952.   Rich material on
   educational puppetry and therapy work around the world.
      It was called The Puppet Post Journal around 1962
   but usually has the shortened name.   Partial set in NY
   Publ Lib.
   Pupp, 15:36-37, 1944; 17:54, 1946
   Pupp Master, 7(2):28-30, 1962

Puppet Show, The: England
      It is more like the periodical Punch, with satiric arti-
   cles but is of value to puppet student in that the illus-

Puppet Show, The: (cont.)
    trations are of puppet work of that time.   It is written
    from a puppeteer's angle more than the Punch materi-
    al was.   It began in 1848 as a London weekly paper,
    continued at least 3 years.   Vol 1, No. 3 was Mar 18,
    1848.   Volume for Dec 16, 1848 is called Puppet
    Show Almanac and is very interesting to a puppet his-
    torian.   In British Museum, Harvard Univ. Lib. and
    N Y Publ Lib.

Puppet Show, The: U. S. A.
    This was an occasional bulletin of the Yale Puppeteers
    theatre in California.   The theatre was called "The
    Turnabout Theatre".
    See also "Theatre" Section
    Pupp, 2:122, 1931

Puppet Tales: U. S. A.
    Mimeo. bulletin of the "Seattle, Washington, Puppet
    Club."   It started c 1954.
    Pupp J, 5(5):27, 1954

Puppet Teaching News Bulletin: U. S. A.
    Weekly mimeo. news bulletin of the Works Project
    Administration Theatre, Puppet Group, Division of
    Education and Recreation in NYC. Project no. 7501.
    It began about 1937 and continued to 1939 and was pub-
    lished from the Puppet Center, 78 Fifth Ave. , NYC.
        Very difficult to locate copies.   Some issues in
    NY Publ. Lib. and McPharlin Collection.

Puppet Theatre: England
    Seems to have been a very short lived publication in
    England in 1950.   No copies located.

Puppet Times (or Puppetimes): U. S. A.   (See National Capitol Puppetry Guild Newsletter)
    New title for the periodical of the Washington, D. C.
    Puppet Guild, beginning close to 1965 under this title.
    Mimeo. newsletter.

Puppet Tree, The: U. S. A.
    A junior puppeteer group publication of the Puppeteers
    of America which stops and starts; changes names
    slightly, and editors, but is not a recognized journal
    of the national group.   First began c 1938 in Ottawa,
    Ill.   N Y Publ Lib has a few issues of it.
    Pupp J, 5(2):3, 1953

Puppeteer, The: U. S. A.

Periodical of the Burroughs Marionette Theatre Guild, in Detroit. Began around Oct 1930-Jan 1931. Same title seems to be later taken over by Lewis Parson as editor for an American Sub-teenage puppeteers group started at Shelby, Michigan, c 1950's.

Puppeteers Newsletter (of St. Louis Guild): U. S. A.
(See Grapevine and Puppetry and St. Louis Guild Newsletter)
St. Louis, Mo. Puppet Guild Newsletter started c 1965, succeeding St. Louis Guild Newsletter. It is about six pages of mimeo. material. Once had name of Grapevine.

Puppeteers of America Membership Directory: U. S. A.
Yearly publication for members only, but found in many libraries along with the Puppetry Journal, August issues. Began close to the Fall of 1952.
In NY Publ Lib.

Puppetry Bulletin: U. S. A. (This is a part of the Puppetry International Yearbook)
The bulletin is sometimes referred to in sources as if it were a separate publication of the early group of Puppeteers of America. It is really the advertisement or commercial part of Puppetry yearbook. It may occasionally have been found separately but not after 1941 in the McPharlin Collection. It was published by Mr. McPharlin. In Harvard Univ. Lib. , N Y Publ Lib. , and the McPharlin Collection.

Puppetry Handbooks: U. S. A. (or Puppetry Imprints)
Published by Paul McPharlin, as editor, some at the Detroit Inland Press c 1931 and continued irregularly for 12 copies. Each dealt with a different aspect of puppet art. This grew out of reprinting articles, in pamphlet or short book form, which he had used in his Yearbook or written for publication elsewhere rather than a planned regular publication. They are difficult to locate now. Most are still in his collection.

Puppetry Journal: U. S. A.
This is the present official periodical of the Puppeteers of America group since July and Aug. 1949. It is the outgrowth of Grapevine, Grapevine Telegraph, Puppetry, and the Puppetry Yearbooks. Standard printing work is done.

Puppetry Journal: (cont.)
Beginning in 1949 with George Latshaw as editor
for one year, it was taken over by Vivian Michael and
Peg Blickle. Mrs. Michael has remained as its editor for 17 years without interruption, until 1967-18.
Then Herman London became editor for one year, publishing from Peekskill, N. Y. In 1969 the Journal returned to Ashville, Ohio under Mrs. Michael.
It is issued six times a year, carries fine articles
and has good illustrations as well as national news
notes on the membership. Puppet booklets are also
published by the Journal, often in mimeo form. The
Journal office store in Ashville, can usually locate any
standard puppet book.
Pupp J, 6(5):3, 1955 - a partial history of periodical
Pupp J, 19(1):43, 1967 - concerns Mrs Michael's work
Pupp J, 11, 3-4, Jl 1959

Puppetry Journal Photo Issue: U. S. A.
Pupp J, 22(3): N, & D, 1970 entire issue.

Puppetry Magazine, or Puppetry: U. S. A.   (See International Yearbook of Puppetry
At first issued by the American puppet group, "Marionette Fellowship of America" in Detroit.   The group
gradually developed into Puppeteers of America (See
"Organization" Section.)   This paper was first issued
Oct 15, 1930 by Paul McPharlin and announced the
"Fellowship" group, the mimeo. paper had an irregular career as a newsletter at first, but became the
name of the Yearbook for the group in 1936.   The
newsletter became Grapevine Telegraph, or Grapevine.
See St. Louis Guild Newsletter.

Important Notes
(a)   Because of the confusion, I have chosen (with Mr.
McPharlin) to call all material given from the early
Puppetry Magazine publication and the Yearbook publication under the one title of Puppetry (Pupp) starting
with Vol 1: in 1930 and continuing right up to Vol 18:
1947.
The Houghton Building of the Harvard Univ. Lib.
has almost all of these issues. N Y Publ Lib. has several; also McPharlin Collection.
(b)   Puppetry, an International Yearbook of Puppetry: USA
The new title combination given the yearbook in 1936.
Some sources will call it Vol 1.   I do not.

(c) Title often shortened to **Puppetry Yearbook: U. S. A.**
or **Puppetry.** It continued as a yearbook but was in
conjunction with **Grapevine** and **Grapevine Telegraph** as
a newsletter.

(d) **Puppetry, a Yearbook of Puppets and Marionettes:** USA
(1930-34). Same periodical but this title was sometimes cited. All are the same and were published by
Paul McPharlin, Birmingham, Michigan, from 1930 to
1942, then from Columbus, Ohio for a year.

(e) **Puppetry,** 1933 to 1941 (In the McPharlin Collection at
least) were printed with 26 "extra illustrated" copies,
not for sale, but as special gifts. They were lettered
A to Z and also numbered 1 to 26. Copies of these
special gift copies in the McPharlin Collection originally.

(f) **Puppetry,** 1946-47 - is sometimes entitled **The Annals
of the Poets: U. S. A.** on the cover page, Hastings
House, New York City, Paul McPharlin, editor." This
copy was in his private collection and may not be the
one distributed. **Puppetry,** 18: 1947, usually called
Annals of the Poets.
Pupp J, 6(6):3, 1955 - has partial history of this peri-
odical.
Thea Arts, 14:1070, D 1930; 17:162, Feb 1933; 18:1,
Feb 1934; 19:315, Feb 1935

Puppetalk: U. S. A.
Newsletter of "San Diego County Guild of Puppetry."
Edited in 1960's by Patricia Platt and others.
Pupp J, 15:30, 1964

Puppet Yearbook, or Puppetry Yearbook of England, The:
England (See Puppet Master)
Early publication of the British Puppet Model Theatre
Guild, previous to its change of name. See "Organization" Section. Do not confuse with U. S. A. **Puppetry;**
An International Yearbook which is indicated as **Pupp**
in this bibliography. Material in this bibliography, if
known to come from this particular yearbook are always given as from **Puppetry Yearbook.**

Puppets: U. S. A.
Periodical published by the "Hamburgh Guild, N. Y."
Seems to have started from 1935 with Ken Worthy as
editor.

Puppets and Poets: England
This seems to have been a monthly miscellany, published in London in 1800's and then again in early
1900's and Edward Gordon Craig seems to have de-
voted the entire issue of No 20 of The Chapbook,
Feb, 1921, to this title. The special issue was published by Poetry Bookshop, London. The McPharlin
Collection has one or two issues, but they have no
dates.

Puppetimes: U. S. A. (See Puppet Times p 360)

Puppet Life: U. S. A. (See Los Angeles Guild of Puppetry
News Bulletin or News Bulletin of Los Angeles Guild of
Puppeteers)
Started c 1956 with about 9 pages of mimeo material
and has become regular periodical under leadership
of Bob Bromley. It is the later name for the Los
Angeles County Guild of Puppeteers, which has now
dropped the word "County." Well illustrated. Has
some regular puppet articles. Wide circulation over
U. S. A. See Vol. 12, no 4, 1968.
Pupp J, 11(5):29-30, 1960; 11(6):29-30, 1960; 20(1):27,
1968

Quaker Village Puppeteers' Report: U. S. A. (See Report,
Puppeteers' Report, Report or Q. V. R.
The periodical has been called by all three names and
is still referred to under any one of them. It is the
periodical of the No 1 Guild of the Puppeteers of
America group. It started c 1940, or earlier as a
newsletter and continues to date. Emma Warfield was
editor. It is usually a single page of local puppet news
and announcements of the "New England Guild of Puppetry."

Report, The: U. S. A. See (Quaker Village Puppeteer's
Report)

La Revue Des Comediens De Bois: France
Published in Paris, Jan 1925, the first copy indicates
A. Crinon, A. Hardy, P. Jeanne and G. Moyses were
the editors. The copy in McPharlin Collection does
not give which particular org. used it as a periodical,
if there was one.

Revue Regionaliste De La Flandre Franciase: Belgium
  Published in Brussels, one of its issues was found in
  the McPharlin Collection, (N-D, 1932, No. 24). Indications were that the organization backing the publication
  of the periodical was "Le Lion De Flandre. This issue was completely on puppetry.

Ri-Wi-Puppen Post: Germany
  The magazine published by Richard Winzer for German
  puppeteers previous to 1940's and during the 40's.
  Some issues are in the McPharlin Collection. It is a
  periodical report of German puppetry. Auebeck-Schlutup,
  Schleswig-Holstein.

Rundbriefs: Germany
  Magazine for German Puppeteers, editor was Walter
  Kipsch, and it started c 1936. Some issues in Mc
  Pharlin Collection.

St. Louis Guild Newsletter: U.S.A. (See Puppeteers News-
letter) and Puppetry and Grapevine)
  The periodical was named for the Puppet Guild of St.
  Louis, No 17.

San Francisco Bay Area Puppeteers Guild Newsletter: U.S.A.
Known as SFBAPG Newsletter
  Periodical of from one to two mimeo pages with Lewis
  Mahlmann as editor. Personal data and announcement
  of play dates. Started c 1960 to date.
  N Y Publ Lib. has several copies.

Der Schattenbrief: Germany
  A newsletter about the German Shadow Theatres, edited
  by Margaret Cordes c the 1930's to the 1950's.
  Pupp J, 2(5):24, 1951

Scena, Loutkova: Czechoslovakia. (See Loutkova, Scena)

School Arts Magazine, The: U.S.A.
  Primarily for art departments it has always contained
  material about all forms of puppetry. It is published
  by the American Crayon Company of Sandusky, Ohio
  and runs c 1922, to date. The earlier issues handled
  more puppet material than those of 1950's and 1960's.

Showmen's Year Book: England
  London, World's Fair Press, 1951-to date, yr. ed. by

Showmen's Year Book (cont.)
      T. Murphy.   Much puppet information as it is official
      publication of the "Showmen's Guild of Great Britain."

Spotlight, The: England (See   E. P. A. Spotlight)
      Newsletter of British Educational Puppet Association.
      H. W. Whanslaw's, First Bench Book.   London, Wells-
      Gardner, 1957, p 195.

Staatl. Puppentheatersammlung Dresden: Germany
      Staatliches Museum für Volkskunst.   Dresden, Abteilung
      Puppentheatersammlung, Radebeul 4, Barkengrasse 6
      Deutsche-Ost.   Active in 1960's.   Copies in N Y Publ
      Lib of very recent issues.

Strings: U. S. A.
      Periodical of the Mid-Western Puppeteers which became
      "S. P. A. C." organization.   (See "Organization" Section)
      It began about 1939 when the group organized with Ro-
      main Proctor sponsoring the editing.   It continued pub-
      lication 1948, with many interruptions.   It was pub-
      lished in Chicago.

Sunset: U. S. A.
      A west coast of America periodical which carries a
      great deal of theatre and puppet information, play dates
      and reviews of puppet books and productions from time
      to time.   It has had much puppet information since
      1960.

Suffloren: Denmark
      The Denmark Puppet periodical which was in issue be-
      fore 1949.   It is sponsored by the Danish Model The-
      atre Association with headquarters in Copenhagen, at
      least in its early history.

Tanglestringed Talk: U. S. A.
      Very hard to find as it was a publication of the Feder-
      al Theatre of Oklahoma puppet division.   This was a
      rather vagabond puppeteer group which traveled about
      under "W. P. A." projects and was not closely organ-
      ized.   It was published around 1938 with Alma Shaw
      as one of the editors.   State records should help with
      finding it.   Stopped with end of W. P. A. Federal Pup-
      pet Theatre Work.

T. C. P. Notebook: U. S. A.   See Twin City Puppeteers Notebook.

Teatry Lalek: Poland (See Od Szopki)

Theatre Arts, The: U. S. A.
American theatre periodical carrying many very fine
articles about puppetry since 1915, by many American
puppet masters. The entire number of Thea Arts, July
1928, was given over to puppetry.

Theatre and School: U. S. A.
American periodical with much puppetry material as
early as 1930's. The Thea and Sch, 11: Ap 1933,
was all puppetry.

Theatre De Guignol: Belgium
Periodical for the "Society Des Amis De Guignol" in
Lyons. Started c to 1929 and by that time there were
at least 20 issues.
Harvard Univ. Lib. and Univ. of Calif. Lib.

Theater Der Welt: Germany (See Meister Des Puppenspiels)

Theatre Japonais De Poupee: Japan
Periodical of the central groups of puppetry in Japan
since the early 1930's, at least. Obtainable through
the Embassy of Japan.
Pupp, 2: 1931

Theatre De Marionettes des Champs Elysee: France
(See Magazine le Montreur De Marionettes)
A paper for French, (Paris) puppet organization called
"Union Corporative et National Des Montreurs De
Marionettes." The director and editor in 1950 was
Hubert Gignoux. In McPharlin Collection.

Titirimundo Imprints: (World of Puppet Imprints) Argentina
This is a periodical which has special issues of "Imprints." It is published three times each year in
Buenos Aires, with Javier Villafano as editor. It has
reprints of new or old works about puppetry.

"Les Trois Petite Tours:" France
Organ. 1960's, in Paris as a very expressionistic, and
active young group in the Vincennes suburb, at a
Youth Center.
Director not known.
Periodical not known.

"Les Trois Petite Tours:" (cont.)
   Unima France Marionnettes, No 28:18-19, O-D, 1968
      (article by R. Cheiney)
   Pupp Mast, 9(3):26, 1965

Twin City Puppeteers Notebook: U. S. A.   (See TCP Notebook)
   Periodical of the Twin City Puppeteers, a guild of the
   "Puppeteers of America." This publication started
   much earlier under different titles.
   Pupp J, 15(1):32, 1963

UNIMA-France Marionnettes: France
   This periodical appears four times a year and was
   started in 1966. It is well illustrated and is con-
   cerned with the work of French members of the inter-
   national group. It is published, 21 Blvd. De Port
   Royal, Paris 13.
   Pupp J, 19(1):41, 1967
   G N Y Pupp G Newsl, 5(3):5, 1968

UNIMA Loutkar: Czechoslovaki
   A puppetry journal of the 1930's which was probably
   another name for Loutkar. Although it may have been
   just for the "UNIMA" work rather than the national
   puppet work of the one country.

Union Internationale De La Marionnette: Czechoslovakia
   This is the full name for the international group of
   UNIMA, but it seems an entirely different publication
   of the UNIMA group for the entire world and all the
   many smaller groups of UNIMA. Published in Prague
   from central office of the club.
      Many pamphlets, books and lists are sponsored and
   published by this group, as are international festival
   programs which are put out yearly.

UNIMA, U. S. A. :   U. S. A.
   The periodical newsletter of the U. S. A. group, is
   edited by Mollie Falkenstein, the Sec. Gen. for the
   group in this country. It comes out irregularly since
   1960, usually about twice a year and contains listings
   of international meetings, important announcements and
   publications. Now and then repeats parts of important
   speeches and a review of the International Meeting in
   Europe and at the Puppeteers of America Convention.
      The group also published a pictorial and commentary
   Puppetry Calender, Aug. 1968, under the editorship of
   Mrs. Falkenstein but it did not appear in 1969.

Union for Promoting German Theatre Culture Journal:
Germany
Started in 1923 and had a special "Puppet" Section. It
was published by Lehmann and Schuppel in Leipzig.

Verband Deutscher Puppenspieler: Germany
Official publication of the "Union of German Puppet
Players" which was published monthly.

War-Time Bulletin: England (See Notes and News)
This was the Newsletter which took the place of other
publications for the "British Puppet and Model Theatre
Guild" during the second World War.

West Coast Conference News: U. S. A.
San Francisco Bay Area Puppeteers and the Los Ange-
les County Guild of Puppetry had this mimeo. paper
for a short time; rather irregular in publication. John
Seers was an early editor. This was before 1961.
Pupp J, 13(6):21, 1962

Wij Poppenspeler: Netherlands
Official publication of the "Netherlands Organization for
the Puppeteers." It is bi-monthly and started c 1960
with several issues. In N Y Publ Lib., 1965-66. Vol.
12 was in 1967.

World's Fair, The: England
"Punch and Puppetry Pars" was the name of a column
in this Showman's publication, which was written for
many years by Gerald Morice. It started in 1937 and
has continued almost continually at least till 1965. It
is published at Oldham, England and has both English
and International puppet items. See G. Speacht's,
History of English Puppet Theatre. London, Harrap, 1955, p. 308, but he recommends the material highly.

Pupp, 11:34, 1940
World's Fair special puppetry material: S 17, 1938,
p 4; S 24, 1938, p 45; O 1, 1938, p 12; O 8, 1938, p
16; O 15, 1938, p 4.

World Theatre: U. S. A.
A UNESCO organization periodical, two special puppet
numbers and many puppet articles. Purchase from
British Educ. Assn.

369

Young Puppeteer: England
    During World War II years this periodical was edited
    by Gerald Morice in the 1940's.

Zpravy Loutkarskeho Soustredeni: Czechoslovakia
    (News of the Puppeteer's Center) is the translation of
    this periodical, which indicates it is a Newsletter from
    Prague, edited by Dr. Jan Malik.   No. 1 to No. 9
    (1939) and one issue in 1947 are in the McPharlin Col-
    lection.
    Pupp 10:35, 1939

II-C.   Festivals, Exhibits and Conventions

Note: This division is a sample of the type of articles
that are to be found on these subjects and of the general locations of such material.

The Section is arranged alphabetically. First, in a
General Division if the group was not indicated in any
way and the author or country was not significant, then
under the country and organization, when the group was
indicated or known; again alphabetically; then by year.

General.   Festivals, Exhibits and Conventions

Albu, Erna.   "That Magic World of Puppets," Pupp J,   16(5):
9-10, 1965
"Asilomar Convention." "Puppeteers of America" -1961, p. 381.

"Antique Puppet Exhibit," Lib J, 55:830, O 15, 1930

"Art of Puppetry, Jr. Museum Exhibition," Balt Mus N,
10:3, Jan 1947
"Articles on Puppet Shows, Groups, Exhibits," N Y Times,
My 21, 1950, 5:11
Batchelder, Marjorie. "Festivals of the Future," Pupp J,
20(3):3-6, 1968
"Bochumer, Germany, Figurentheaterwoche-1952," Pupp J,
18(5):31-33, 1967.   These exhibits are still given annually.
Brown, Betsy. "Children's Theatre Conference, Puppet
Workshop," San Fernando Valley State College, North-
ridge, Calif. Pupp Life, Jl 1968, p 11.
"Chicago Fair-1931-'32," Pupp, 2:13, 32, 1931; 3:10, 1932;
4:5, 1933
Chicoineau, Jacques C. trans. , "Pierre Pedroff and his
Puppet Collection," Pupp J, 20(1):9-11, 1968. Held in
Geneva, Switzerland.
"Children's Theatre Conference Puppet Exhibit," Pupp J,
10(2):31, 1958.   By McPharlin and Latshaw Co.   This is
probably Marjore Batchelder McPharlin and George Lat-
shaw's work rather than Paul McPharlin.

Clipping File. "Exhibitions, Festivals, Museums, Conventions, Organizations," in the N Y Publ Lib.

This is a very large collection from all over the world but sometimes a bit vague on source of the clipping.

Colwyn Bay - See British

Crouse, E. "Dedication at Stoney Creek, Conn. of Grace Weil's International Puppet Museum for Sicilian Puppets," Pupp J, 15(2):3-5, 1953

See also "International" Section, Sicily, the Manteo family, moved the exhibit after Mrs. Weils' death in 1954 or 1956.

"Cultural International Society of United Nations Secretarit Puppet Festival-New York City," G N Y Pupp G Newsl, 5(1):1, 3, 1967

Daniels, George. Eighteenth Century Shows. Boston, Harvard Univ. Library Collection of exhibits, playbills, etc. "Puppet Material"

"Exhibit of Puppets at Cooper Union Museum," Interiors, 109:12, Jan 1950

Falkenstein, Mollie. "World Festivals for 1969-1972," UNIMA-Newsl, U. S. A. S 1969

"Impressions of Czechoslovakian UNIMA Festival-1969," UNIMA Newsl, U. S. A. , S 1969, and also Pupp Life, Aug 1969.

"Festivals, Exhibits and Fairs," Pupp, 7:14, 33, 37, 1936; 11:3-4, 5-7, 1940.

Most other issues of Pupp will give worldwide material from 1930-1949. Very brief items as a general thing.

Gamble, Jim. "Reflections on Prague Intern. Festival 1969," Pupp Life, S 1969, p 7-8

"Giant Puppets Exhibited at New York World's Fair of 1939," Life, 6:6-8, My 1, 1949

--- N Y Times, Ap 28, 1939, illus.

Grafett, Guy. "Master Peter's Puppet Show Exhibit," Music and Musicians, 5:19, Jl 1947.

This would concern the opera about "Don Quixote." Master Peter gives a puppet show within this opera.

"Independent Early Puppet Shows and Exhibits Discussed," New York Journal, Mr 26, 1767; Ap 2, 1767; My 1767.

This is rare and sig. m. for the historian and would probably be located either in Yale Univ. Lib. or downtown N Y Publ Lib.

"International Puppet Festival of New York City," G N Y Pupp G Newsl, 5(1):1, 3, 1967, by A. Brewer.

This is not connected with UNIMA but was under UNESCO org. of NYC.

--- "New York Guild of Puppetry sponsors International Puppet Festival as UN Benefit - Sept. 1967," G N Y Pupp G Newsl, 4(6): 1967
See also N Y C newspapers of this time
"Laguna Beach Art Festival and Rene's 'Fiesta in Miniature'," Pupp Life, Jl 1968, p 4, illus.
See also "Theatre" Section
"Laguna Beach Conference," Pupp J, 12:26-27, 1961 (probably No 5) as the date for the meeting was Feb. 11, 1961. This may be a Regional meeting of "P. of A." group. See that organization, this section.
"Largest Historical Exhibit of Puppets in America," Pupp J, 11(5):29, 1960
--- Ch Sci M, Jan 1960
--- Catalogue of Los Angeles County Museum. Sponsored by Los Angeles County Guild of Puppeteers in O 1960. See also their periodical for that year.
Llords, Daniel. "International Notebook" - Festival dates, 1969-1970, Pupp J, 21(2):29, 1969
Long, Charles J. "Puppets and the HemisFair (World Fair, Texas)," Pupp J, 20(1):5-6, 1968
Mahlmann, Lewis. "Macy's Grand Tour Puppet Exhibit," Pupp J, 18(3):36, 1966
    This was at San Francisco Municpal Museum in the Fall of 1966.
McPharlin, Marjorie Batchelder. See M. Batchelder

McPharlin, Paul. "Exhibition of Puppets at Marshall Field Co., Chicago, 1933," and "Exhibitions"(elsewhere) Pupp Th Am. 1949, p 364-86
--- McPharlin Collection - See I. L. Zupnick
--- "Puppets of the Arthur Maury Collection," Pupp, 10: 55-56, 1939
Malik, Dr. Jan. "Festivals, Pro and Con," Pupp J, 17(4): 3-6, 1966
"Museum Collections of Marionettes in U.S.A.," Pupp, 1: 23-28, 1930. This is very sig. m.
"Museums With Puppets," Pupp 20:52-53, 1949

"Nassau County, East Meadow, L.I., N.Y. -2nd Annual Puppet Festival," 1968. This was, and still is, sponsored by the Public Parks Dept. of the city, about June 1 of each year.
"National Puppet Fair and World's Fair of Puppets, at Chicago," June 25-27, 1948. This was sponsored by "S. P. A. C. Puppet Club" of Chicago. Local newspapers will carry material.

373

"New York Exhibits of Puppets," See Puppet Exhibits,
New York City
"New York World's Fair of 1964 and 1965, Exhibits, Shows,"
Pupp J, 15(5&6): 1964, scattered throughout issues.
Note: All World Fairs will have Puppet Exhibits and will
be much advertised and discussed in periodicals of
those years which carry puppet material and in local
newspapers. Large, usually illustrated, articles are
common since they serve to arouse interest in the
Fairs. This applies to the very earliest European
country fairs, that can be located through historical or
theatrical bibliographies, as well as to modern fairs.
"Northwest Drama Conference-Puppets Included." - Univ.
of Washington, Seattle. Pupp J, 18(5):45-47, 1967
O'Donnol, Shirley. "Brander Matthew's Collection," Columbia Univ., Pupp J, 12(5):12-13, 1961
"Pandora's Box Festival," See Los Angeles County Guild

"Paris Fair Puppets of 1937-1938," Pupp 8:6, 1937

"Paris Festival of Puppet Shows-1959," see local news-
papers and French Puppet periodicals of that year.
"Paris Theatre Exhibits of 1908, April to October," Pupp,
12:51-52, 1941
--- Catalogue of Exhibits, Paris, 1908. Section 6, no date.
In McPharlin Collection
Paul, Bernard. "First Exhibits of Puppets in America,"
Pupp, 10:7-8, 1930
Performing Arts Collections. Paris, Editions du Centre
National de la Recherche Scientifique, 1960.
Philpott, A. R. Dictionary of Puppetry. London, Macdon-
ald, 1969. "Performing Arts Collection," p 185 and
passim.
"Puppet Exhibit," Printers Ink, 169:40, D 13, 1934
"Puppet Exhibits in New York City," (these are usually
listed under a title very similar, if not the same. Usu-
ally in the Sunday or Saturday night theatre sections.
N Y Times, Jan 7, 1934, Sect 11, pt 1, p 10; Feb. 5,
1935, p 21; Mr 31, 1935, Sect. 2, p 2; Ap 30, 1935 p 12;
N Y Times, Ap 2, 1940, 29:3; S 28, 1941, 50:6; D 5, 1941,
30:2; D 30, 1942, 20:17
Quijada, Louis. "Long Beach Hobby Show--Worldwide Pup-
pet Hobby," Pupp Life, Jl 1968, p 2-3
"Santa Barbara Museum, Calif. Has Exhibit," San F. B. A. P.
G. Newsl, S 1969 p 1.
Sayre, J. W. "Complete Bookings and Exhibits, and Shows
of Puppets Given at Seattle Playhouse," unpublished list-

ing in mimeo. Seattle, Wash. , Seattle Publ. Lib. , Puppet File.
"Show on Strings, The Greatest International Exhibit of Puppeteers," Pupp J, 17(3):34, 1965
--- Pupp J, 16(5):9-10, 1965 - by E. Albo. This was at Palo Alto, Calif. , Jl 1-S 30, 1965, and was by Alan Cook, Betsy Brown and Roberto Lago.
Speaight, George. History of the English Puppet Theatre. London, Harrap, 1955. See also "History Section
Stevens, Martin. "Puppets and Marionette Performances and Exhibits," Cincinnati, O. , Art Museum Bulletin, 6:112-114, O 1935
"Shadow Puppet Exhibits at the Following Museums," in Olive Blackman's book, Shadow Puppets. New York, London, Rockliff, 1960, p 25
Whanslaw, H. W. A Bench Book of Puppetry. London, Wells, 1957, p 201-204
--- A Second Bench Book of Puppetry. London, Wells, 1958.
Willicate, V. "Puppets on Exhibit," Sch Arts, 40:314-15, My 1941
Zupnick, Irving L. "Report on the McPharlin Collection," Pupp J, 6(1):4-5, 1954

Exhibits, Festivals and Conventions by Country
and then by organization (given alphabetically, then by yr.

British Isles: England, Scotland, Ireland, Wales, etc.
"Birmingham Juvenile Dramatic Festival," Brit Pupp Thea, 1(4):15, 1950.
There are a great many small educational groups and they are very active. Usually the group belongs to "British Educational Puppet Assn." and material will be located in Pupp Post. However, Pupp Master is also used for educational notices.
--- "Birmingham," Pupp Master, 3(7):241-242, 1955
--- "A World of Their Own, Exhibit," Pupp Master, 8(2): 21, 1964
"British Educational Puppet Association. "
"Punch and Puppetry Pars, 1964 City of London Festival," by Gerald Morice, in his puppet column, World's Fair, June 11, 1964, p 50
"Whitechapel Art Gallery Giant Puppet Exhibition," by Elizabeth Blandine, Pupp Master, 8(2):20-21, 1965
"At Whitechapel Art Gallery," Pupp Master, 8(3):20-21, 1965

"British Puppet and Model Theatre Guild. "
(Much of this was a co-operative effort of both large puppet groups.)
"Festival of Britain," Pupp Master, 3(3):84-86, 1950
"Festival of Britain," Brit Pupp Thea, 2(1):2, 1951
"Puppet Convention," Illus Lon N, 225:799, N 6, 1954
"29th Annual Convention," Pupp Master, 4(2):240-41, 1955; 4(7):207, 1956
"British Puppet and Model Theatre Festival," Pupp Master, 7(2):24, 1968
"British Guild Weekend School Meetings and Exhibits," See all S. and O. issues of British Puppet and Model Theatre Guild Newsletters, by all their various war and peace names.
"British International Festival at Colwyn Bay, Wales," May 20-25, 1968 - See "Czechoslovakia," "Unima," as well as this heading.
"British Festival, May 20-25 at Colwyn Bay" by Mollie Falkenstein, Pupp J, 19(3):6-8, 1967
British Puppet Centre, Colwyn Bay, North Wales. Museum, Literary, Theatre, Shop sponsored by Borough Council opened 1967. Eric Bramall, Director has teaching course and films, as well as exhibits to loan.
"England's Colwyn Bay Festival Program" Brit Pupp and M Thea G Newsl, No 145, 1968, p 8. Held at first permanent puppet theatre in Wales.
"Punch Tercentenary Celebrations and Exhibits," by Jane Phillips. Pupp Master, 8(1):22-25, 1962. The entire issue is about the celebration in London.
"Punchiana Exhibits," Pupp Master, 7(1):26, 1962
Speaight, George. History of English Puppetry. London, Harrap, 1955
"Welsh International Puppet Festival," Pupp Master, 8 (2):22, 1965. See also "Harlequin Theatre" in "Theatre" Section, under England.
"Whitechapel Art Gallery Exhibit," See "British Educ.."

Canada
"Canadian Expo '67 Festival International de la Marionettes," Jl 9-16, 1967, by Lewis Mahlmann. Pupp J, 19(1): 35-36, 1967. Held in Montreal.
"Canadian First Puppet Conference-May 1939, Hamilton, Ontario. Paul McPharlin's book, Pupp Th Am, 1949, p 349
"Exhibit at Waterloo, Univ. Puppet Festival," by E. McKay,

<u>Pupp J</u>, 19(1):37-39, 1967
See also "Puppeteers of America" under United States
of America, as this was a National Convention held by
that group at invitation of Canadian puppeteers.
"Toronto Festival," <u>Pupp J</u>, 9(1):30, 1957

Czechoslovakia
"UNIMA International-regarding Festivals and like material,"
by Max Jacob, in the book, <u>Puppet Theatre of the</u>
<u>Modern World</u>. Boston, Plays, 1967, sponsored and
collected by a committee of this organization under M.
Niculesco, p 49-51.
The First Festival, in Paris-Nov, 1929 after the organiza-
tion meeting in Prague in May, 1929.
The Second Festival in Liege in 1930 and the 3rd Congress.
See also "International" Belgium and Czech.
The Third Festival was in Ljubljana, Yugoslavia in 1933
with Joseph Skupa as Pres. See also that country,
"International" Section
<u>Pupp Master</u>, 9(4):17, 1967
The Fifth Congress and Festival was in Prague in 1957.
Resumed after the war.
"Report on Bucharest, 6th Congress and International Festi-
val of Puppet Theatres," by R. Proctor, <u>Pupp J, 10</u>
(2):3-5, 1958
"International News," by M. B. McPharlin, <u>Pupp J</u>, 9(6):
10, 1958
"International Festival," by M. Batchelder McPharlin,
<u>Pupp J</u>, 10(1):8-12, 1958
"International Puppet Festival," <u>Thea Nbk</u>, 13(1):5-6,
Fall 1958
"International News," <u>Pupp J</u>, 9(1):6, 1957
"International Puppet Festival," by R. Proctor, <u>Players</u>,
35(2), N 1958, and <u>Players</u>, 35(3):57-58, D 1958
"La Festival De Bucharest," Spectacle, D 1958, p 64
"Bucharest Festival," <u>Players, 35(4):77</u>, 92, Jan 1959
<u>Pupp J</u>, 11(5):10-11, 12-13, Mr 1959
"Report on 1959 UNIMA Convention in Paris, preparations
for 1960 Congress," by R. Proctor, <u>Pupp J, 11</u>(2):5-
10; 12(1):10-11, 21-22, 1960
It was to be two days at Bochum, Germany for a Festi-
val and then two days at Braygsweig, Germany at another puppet Festival.
"Festival, International," <u>Thea Nbk,</u> 14(3):77, Spring 1960

"Planning the 8th UNIMA Festival in Rome for 1961 UNIMA
Puppet Congress," <u>Pupp J</u>, 13(2):33, 1961

Czechoslovakia (cont.)
"International News," Pupp J, 14(2):8-9, 1962

"UNIMA Congress-Warsaw-1962," by G. Morice, Pupp
Master, 7(2):14-15, D 1962
"Impressions of Warsaw, UNIMA '62," by C. M. McDonald,
Pupp Master, 7(2):16-17, 30, D 1962
"International News," by M. B. McPharlin, Pupp J, 14(2):
8-9, 1962
"International News," and Report on Convention," by Mollie
Falkenstein, Pupp J, 18(1):22-25, 1966
"International News," Pupp J, 18(5):29, 1967

"UNIMA Presidium and Festival of Puppet Theatres to Be In
Dresden, E. Germany on Nov. 8 and Nov 21-25, 1968,"
by M. Falkenstein, Pupp J, 19(3):7, 1967
"UNIMA News of European Festivals," by Mollie Falken-
stein, Pupp J, 19(3):6-8, N 1967. About Colwyn Bay,
Wales.
"UNIMA News of European Festivals," by Mollie Falkenstein,
Pupp J, 19(5):26-28, 1968
"International Festival at Colwyn Bay," UNIMA U. S. A.
Newsl, Je 1968. In NN, probably in Puppet File.
"Permanent Exhibit of International Puppets Committee,"
Pupp J, 20(4):5, 1969
"Prague Host to UNIMA 1969," Pupp J, 20(5):27, 1969

UNIMA Praha '69, An event of Puppeteers of the World,
June 23-July 7, 1969. A mimeo announcement and ex-
planation edited Prague, UNIMA Headquarters, 1969.
A copy in NY Publ Lib, Puppet Clipping file, probably
under "UNIMA. "
This was for the International Festival and Puppet
Congress and the Festival was sponsored by the follow-
ing groups:
Czech Group of UNIMA
Czech Theater ITI
Czech Center ITI (Intl. Theatre Institute)
District & local Nat. Committee in Chrudium
Czech Regional Natl. Committee in Hradec Králevé
Adult Ed. Institute in Bratislava
Union of Czech. Theatre Artists
Central House of Folklore in Prague - This group is
included to show what types of groups are often in-
volved in large international conventions and who
might furnish bulletins and information on such con-
ventions of puppeteers in Europe.

Festival Tour, UNIMA International, June 17-July 1, 1969.
Gilpin Travel Service Booklet, 1969
"Czech. Amateur Marionettists and Puppet Theatre XVIII
Puppet Festival," Brit Pupp and M Th G Newsl, 145:
6, 1968
"The 1969 Festival at Chrudium, Czech," trans. by M.
Falkenstein, UNIMA U. S. A. Newsl, S 1969
"Czech. Amateur Puppet Festival-Sept. 4-11, 1960,"
See Loutkár puppet periodicals near these dates.

France
"International De Marionettes-11th Festival" (at Le Creusot,
France on June 23-July 7, 1968) Brit Pupp and M Th
Newsl. 145:6, 1968

Germany
"Verband Deutscher Puppenspieler Festival in Russian Zone,"
Pupp J, 2(6):28-29, 1951
"National Museum-Munich Puppet Collection, G N Y Pupp
G Newsl, 6(6):1, 1969

Hungary
Hungarian Amateur Puppet Theatre III Festival - June 19-23,
1968," Brit Pupp and M Th G Newsl, 145:7, 1968

Poland
"Poland at Lodz, Festival of State Theatre," Pupp J, 19(3):
7, 1968. Held in My 1960

Portugal
"Portuguese Festival of Puppets, May 27-28, 1969, Pupp J,
20(5):8, 1969

Switzerland
"Switzerland, International Festival, Zuricher Woche 1968,"
at Zurich Brit Pupp and M Th G Newsl, 145:7, 1968

United States of America
"The Puppeteers of America," organization, its regional and
National Conventions collected by the year, rather than
location of item title.
"Puppet Exhibits and Performances," by Martin Stevens,
Cincinnati, O. , Art Museum Bulletin, 6:112-14, O
1935. This is where first real convention was held.
"Text of Speeches at First American Puppetry Confer-
ence in Detroit and Organization," Pupp, 7: 1936
"First Puppetry Convention," Thea Arts, 20:562, Jl 1936

U. S. A. (cont.)
"First National Puppet Exposition," N Y Times, Jan 15,
   1937, p 4; and N Y Times, Jan 23, 1937, p 4
"Reports of 2nd Puppetry Conference," Pupp, 8: 1937
"Festival Report," Players, 15:19, S 1938; 16:21-22, O
   1939
"Fifth Annual Puppet Festival," Players, 17:23, O 1940,
   by Jean Starr Wiksell.
"Sixth Annual Festival of Puppets," by R. Proctor,
   Players, 18:17, O 1941
"Seventh Annual Festival of Puppets," by R. Proctor,
   Players, 19:21, O 1942
"Twelfth Annual Puppet Festival," by R. Proctor,
   Players, 24:38, N 1947
"Thirteenth Annual Festival of Puppeteers of America,"
   by E. Hogan and C. Cruce, Players, 25:12, O 1948
"Festival News," Grapev, S 1948, p 3
"Fourteenth Festival," Grapev, Feb 1949, p 2; Ap 1949,
   p 2; Pupp J, 1(1):2, 24, 18, 1949
___"Puppetry Festival," by Margo Rose, Pupp J, 2(1):
   3-4, 1950
"Fifteenth Convention and Puppetry Institute, Two Weeks
   Study Course," Pupp J, 2(1):4-5, 1950
---"Impressions of Puppet Institute," Pupp J, 2(1): 1950
---"First Puppet Institute at Western College, Oxford,
   Ohio," N Y Times, Jl 2, 1950, 27:5
"National Festival Again at Oxford, Ohio, Mrs. Wiksell,
   President," N Y Times, Jl 30, 1951, 9:2
--- "Puppets Bob to Festival Time in U. S. A." by R.
   Johnson, Ch Sci M, 43(197): Cent. Ed. 2nd Sect, Jl
   18, 1951. This was at Oxford second time.
--- "Report on 16th Convention," Pupp J, 2(6):22, 24, 27-
   8; 3(1):10-11, 1951
"History of Festivals and Organizations," by Peg Blickle,
   Pupp J, 5:3-6, 1953
"Festival in Hiawatha Land, Minnesota," Pupp J, 4(4):
   22, 1953
"Report on McPharlin Collection, Detroit," by I. Zupnick,
   Pupp J, 6(1):4-5, 1954
"The Puppeteers of America Festival of 1956," by Rod
   Young, Players, 33(6): M 1957
"Festival in Calif. , Creative Puppetry," by M. H. Hei-
   stein, Pupp J, 8(4):21, 1957
"Festival-1957 in Univ. of Calif. , Los Angeles; Showman-
   ship is the Theme," Pupp J, 8(6):11, 1957. These may
   be more National but the titles do not suggest it, so
   will be cross-indexed. See also Regional and local
   area.

"Puppet Festival," by Rod Young, Players, 34(1):8-9,
   O 1957; 34(2):25, N 1957
"Festival Report in No. Carolina," by R. Young, Players,
   35(2):40-41, N 1958
---"Puppeteers of America Festival at Chapel Hill, No.
   Carolina," by B. G. Merten, Pupp J, 9(6):28-9, 1958
---"Exhibit at Chapel Hill, No. Carolina," Pupp J, 10
   (6):28-9, 1958
"Festival Issue-1959," Pupp J, 11(2): 1959
"Puppet Festival," by R. Young, Players, 36(1):10-11,
   1959
"The 1960 Festival Preview at Detroit," by Dorothy Oden,
   Pupp J, 11(5):26-27, 28-29, 1960
---"Festival at Detroit," Pupp J, 11(6):12-13, 1960
"Pacific Coast Regional Conference," Pupp J, 11(6):27-
   29, 1960
--- "Puppeteers Festival Report," by R. Young, Players,
   37(1):9, O 1960
---"Puppet Cavalcade, '65 Convention, Detroit," Pupp J,
   17(1):14, 1966
"Puppeteers of America 1960 Festival Program," Pupp J,
   11(6):23-25, 1960. There is to be a Festival Store un-
   der Vivian Michael. Festival Programs and Workshop
   Notes can be purchased from about this year to date
   from Pupp J Office, Ashville, O. Some years a regu-
   lar workshop was not given.
"Festival Plans and Program for Pacific Grove, Calif. ,"
   Asilemar, Pupp J, 12(5):29-30, 1961; 12(6): 1961.
"St. Louis Regional Festival-1961-July and Aug, 1961,"
   Pupp J, 14(2):25, 1962
"New England Guild of Puppetry Festival at Sturbridge,
   Mass. ," Pupp J, 14(3):11, 1962
"Convention at Asilemar." "National Convention at Asile-
   mar," Pupp J, 12(5):29, 1961
"The 29th Florida P. of A. Festival-Miami," Pupp J, 15
   (5):9-13, 1964, by J. Magnon
---Pupp J, 15(6):3-12, 1964
--- "Festival in Paradise," Pupp J, 16(1): 1964
--- The 29th Annual Puppetry Festival Program, Miami,
   Fla. , 1964. Held June 29th, July 5, 1964. Chairman
   was Jero Magnon. Program in NN, puppet file.
--- "Puppeteers of America Festival," Miami News,
   (The Land of Pretend), Jl 2, 1964
--- "If I Sneeze, You Better Too," by M. Lane, Miami
   News, Je 28, 1964, p 6
--- "Summit Meeting Here on Puppetry's Kings," by T.
   Crail, Miami Beach Daily Sun, Je 26, 1964, p 7, 11,
   in the "On the Go" section.

U. S. A. (cont.)
--- "Puppeteers of America Festival," Miami Herald,
    Jl 2, 1964
        "They Found Secrets of Puppetry," Miami
    Beach Daily Sun, Ap 24, 1966. Concerns Miami Guild's
    Third Festival.
"St. Louis holds 27th Puppet Carnival - May 9, 1966,"
    Pupp J, 17(6):10, 1966
"Festival (No. 31) 1966 in San Diego, Calif." Pupp J,
    17(4):12, 13, 25, 1966
"Memory of a First Festival," by Al Wallace, Pupp J,
    17(6):3-4, 1966
--- "Personal Impressions of My First Festival," by G.
    W. Ludwig, Pupp J, 18(1):5-7, 1966

"The Puppeteers of America" Organization. (Regional or
    local Areas)
"Los Angeles Guild's Annual Puppet Pageant - "Wonderful
    World of Puppets," Mar 12, 1966," Pupp J, 17(6):10,
    1966
"Plans for Canada Festival to be July 1-8, 1967," Pupp J,
    17(5):29-31, 1966
"Exhibit at Waterloo, Canada Festival," by E. McKay,
    Pupp J, 19(1):37-39, 1967
"First Festival of 'P. of A.' in Canada," by Mollie Falk-
    enstein, Pupp J, 19(1):13-21, 1967. Other authors as-
    sisted in play reviews. Held at Waterloo Univ. , Water-
    loo, Ontario. See local newspapers as many foreign
    puppeteers visited and TV and papers gave good cover-
    age.
"New York Guild sponsors Intl. Festival for UN Benefit,"
    N Y Pupp G Newsl, 4(6): 1967
"Northwest Drama Conf. , Puppet Festival," Pupp J,
    12(5):45-47, 1967.
"Convention at Asilemar, Calif." (Regional) Pupp J, 19
    (5):29, 1968
"Los Angeles Districts Regional Convention," and the

"San Fran. Bay Region," SFBA P G Newsl, Jan 1968,
p 12
"Meet Me in St. Louis - 'P. of A.' Festival 1968," by
Don Avery, Pupp J, 19(5):13-14; 19(4):4, 1968; 19(6):
14-17, 1968; 20(2):5-15, 1968
"National Festival at St. Louis," by Don Avery, Pupp J,
20(2):5, 1968
"Minifest," by Joe Ayers, Pupp J, 20(3):15, 1968
Regional for New York Area;
"Impressions - St. Louis Festival" UNIMA-France No 28,
D 1968, p 27
"San Francisco Regional Convention, Asilemar, Calif.,"
in Jan 1968. Pupp Life, 19(6):2-3, 1968
Note: Puppet Life and the earlier Bulletin of the Los
Angeles group will have much material on early region-
al conventions and much on their yearly festival, es-
pecially since 1966. I do not list it all.
"Regional Conference sponsored by Los Angeles Guild in
Ojai Valley, 1969 - Olga Stevens, supervisor," Pupp
Life, Jan 1969 issue.
---"Ojai Festival," Pupp Life, Mr 1969, p 2-4
"Northeastern Regional Minifest, Binghamton, N. Y. ," by
Rod Young. (New directions is program.) Pupp J, 21
(1):33-35, 1969
"Minifest," G N Y Pupp G Newsl, 6(5):1, 1969, held
May 2-4, 1969
--- New Directions Program, Binghamton, N. Y. 1969
Copy in NN, Puppet Clipping file.
"Festival Program for 1969 National Convention at Univ.
of Utah, Salt Lake City," Pupp J, 20(6):31-35, 1969
--- "Detail Day by Day of 1969 Program Plans," Pupp J,
21(1):28-32, 1969
--- "Tid Bits From 1969 Festival," by Leona Madsen,
N Y Pupp G Newsl, 8(1):1, O 1969
--- "Festival Review - Day by Day," Pupp J, 21(2):6-12,
1969, articles by J. Gamble, M. Samanisky, N. Lav-
erick, B. Bromley, K. McKay and V. Stanford.
Almost entire issue concerns Utah Festival.

Yugoslavia
"Yugoslavia 8th Festival Djeteta," (Children's Puppet Festi-
val) Brit Pupp and M Th G Newsl, No 145:6, 1968
Held at Sibeniki, June 25-July 5, 1968, for profes-
sionals.
"Yugoslavia International Puppet Theatre Festival at Bled,"
Brit Pupp and M Th G Newsl, No 145, 1968, p 7
Held for an invited group only, by puppet players in

Yugoslavia (cont.)
>Esperanto Oct 3-10, 1969.   Contact Esperanto League,
NYC.
>Sponsored by Institute Par Oficialige De Esperanto,
Sagreb, Yugoslavia; Director, Mr. Tisljar Zlakto,
Kultura Fake par Jugoslavia, Amrueseva 5/1, Pf 213
zagreb, Yugoslavia

Author Index

The few known presidents of some puppet organizations and a few editors are also listed here because they usually were the authors of their group's periodicals. They do not usually sign their names to each item.

Every effort has been made to eliminate the misspelling of names; corrections will be welcomed because many sources differ on this particular point. Sometimes we will list last names with initials which indicate that the same person may have written both items listed, yet when we were the least in doubt as to whether it was the same person writing, we gave both authors.

Each volume of The Puppeteer's Guide will carry page numbers from the previous volumes where an author's work may be found, in addition to those of that particular volume.

Publishers' and Booksellers' Address Key

Note: An attempt has been made to compile this list as completely as possible, but constant changes make inaccuracies and omissions impossible to avoid. The addresses and full names of publishers are given as found in the listed sources and are the most complete that the compiler could locate with the available facilities. For small and/or obscure companies, especially foreign, and those out-of-business, extreme difficulty is encountered in hunting addresses.

Universities, institutions of learning, museums, departments of governments which have printing presses, and other very well known or easy to locate places in large cities do not always have street addresses identified.

Many early French publishers are now merely "librairies" and are so listed in the publisher directories. Many of the compilers' sources evidently had incorrect spellings for these publishers; with care, these sources may be located in the present, or other, address lists. Corrections, additions, and suggested better addresses will be welcomed for supplementary printings.

The author takes full responsibility for errors or omissions, unavoidable as many have been, and only gives this Key as an assistance to our readers and not as any authentic advertisement.

Sources for Addresses

Sources used, in addition to all those already given in the regular Source Key, and which are directly concerned with the publishers only, are as follows:

American Book Trade Directory. 18th ed., New York: Bowker, 1969-70. Helpful for "Dealers in Foreign Books," p. 15-22, and "Former Publishing Companies merged or out of Business," p. 122-137. Indicates foreign libraries and headquarters in New York City where assistance might be given to locate material. Ed. for 1968-69 also consulted.

American Book Publishing Record. New York: Bowker, annual.

Authors' and Printers' Directory. ed. by F. H. Collins, New York: Oxford Univ. Press, 1956.

Deutsches Bucherverzeichnis. Leipzig: Borsenvereins, 1968 and earlier editions.

Dictionary of Booksellers & Printers of England, Scotland and Ireland (1688-1780) by H. R. Plomer, Oxford Univ. Press, 1922.

Editor & Publishers' International Yearbook. New York: annual.

English Catalogue of Books. London: Sampson-Low-Marston, annual and supplementary sets to 1970.

Five-Year Cumulative Book List. (British), London: Whitaker, annual.

French, and other Foreign Book Sellers' Modern Catalogues.

Kayser's Bücher-Lexikon. Leipzig: Herm Tauchnitz.

Publishers' International Directory. Comp by K. G. Saur, Munich: Verlag Dokumentation, 1967.

Publishers' International Yearbook. London: Wales, annual.

United States Booksellers Catalogues.

The actual books themselves gave many addresses and the bibliographies of modern puppet books supplied much of the material.

Publishers' and Booksellers' Addresses

Abbot (C. S.) -- New York, N. Y.

Abenland (Hans P.) Verlag -- 9 Genügsamkeitstr. , Wupper-
tal-Elberfeld, West Germany.

Abingdon-Cokesbury -- 201 Eighth Ave. S. , Nashville, Tenn. ;
and, 150 Fifth Ave. , NYC 10022.

Abrams (Harry N.), Inc. -- 6 W. 57th St. , NYC 10019.

Adamson (James), Co. -- Dates from 1686, at the Angel &
Crown, St. Paul's Churchyard, London, as late as 1800.

Adonis & Terre -- Usually given as Terre & Adonis, (Terre
Retrouvée, Soc. de les Editions; 12 Rue de la Victoire,
Paris 9e.

Affiliated Publishers -- 630 Fifth Ave. , NYC 10020.

Aico (or Alco) -- NYC.

A. L. A. -- See: American Library Association.

Alberts Drukkeryen -- 16-22 Putsroat, Postbus 4, Sittard,
The Netherlands.

Aldine Publ. Co. -- 320 W. Adams St. , Chicago, Ill. ,
60606; or, 22 S. Audley, London, W. 1. See: J. M.
Dent & Sons, London.

"Aldredor del Mundo" (Imp. de) -- Madrid.

Alicke (P.) -- Dresden, East Germany.

Allard-Chantelard et Cie. -- 111 Rue du Mont-Cenis, Paris
18^e.

Allardin -- Paris; See: Allard-Chantelard.

Allgemeiner Verein für Deutsche Literatur -- Berlin.

Allen & Unwin, Ltd. -- Ruskin House, 40 Museum St.,
    London, W. C. 1.

Allhems (N.) Forlag -- Malmö, Sweden.

Allman & Sons Publ., Ltd. -- 50 Grafton Way, Fitzroy Sq.,
    London, W. 1.

Allyn & Bacon, Inc. -- 11 E. 36th St., NYC; and, 470 At-
    lantic Ave., Boston 02210.

Amalthea Verlag -- 2 Akazien-Strasse, 8008 Zürich.

Amandus Verlag -- 10 Weihburggasse, Vienna 1; or,
    Kierling bei wieu, Büro, 65 Franz-Joseff-Kaiserstr.
    1010 Vienna.

American Antiquarian Society -- 185 Salisbury St., Wor-
    cester, Mass.

American Book Company -- 55 Fifth Ave., NYC 10003.

American Library Association -- 50 E. Huron St., Chicago,
    60611.

American-Russian Institute for Cultural Relations, Inc. --
    58 Park Ave., NYC 10016.

Las Americas Publishing Co. -- See under: Las.

"Ancora" (Editrice) -- See: Librara "Ancora"

Andrews (Max) Co. -- London.

Appleton-Century-Crofts, Inc., -- 440 Park Ave. S., NYC,
    10016.

L'Arche -- 8 Rue Bonaparte, 75 Paris 6^e.

Arco Publ. & Staples Press, Ltd. -- 1-3 Upper James St.,
    London, W. 1.

Ardant (Les Editions) -- 17 Rue Mirabeau Limoges, Haute-
    Vienne, France.

Argos (Libreria Editorial), S. A. -- 30 Paseio De Gracia, Apdo. No. 52-57, Barcelona 7, Spain.

Argus Books, Inc. -- 434 S. Wabash Ave., Chicago; See: Mitchell Kennerly Co. ; and, Argus Press, Ltd.

Argus Press, Ltd. -- Temple Ave. & Tudor St., London, E. C. 4.

Arnold (E. J.) & Son, Ltd. -- Butterley St., Leeds 10, England.

Arras Academie Des Science -- Lyons, France.

L'Arte Soc. Ed. -- 2 Piazza Stuparich, Milan, Italy.

Artia [foreign language publ.] -- 65 Bultofta-Vägen, Prague, Czechoslovakia; or, Nové Město Ve Směchách 30, Prague.

Arts Inc., Publ. -- 667 Madison Ave., NYC 10021. (for Golden Griffin Bks.).

L'Auteur (Editions de) -- 9 Rue Fessart, Boulognes sur Seine, France; also, Auteurs réunis (Editions d') -- 11 Rue de Sevres, Paris 6e.

Avio (Armando A.) -- 60 Via Della Gensola, Rome.

Bacon & Vincent -- Buffalo, N. Y.

Bailey Bros. & Swinfen, Ltd. -- Warner House, 48 Upper Thames St., London, E. C. 4. ; or, 46 Saint Giles High St., London, W. C. 2.

Baker Book House -- 1019 Wealthy St. S. E. , Grand Rapids, Mich.

Baker (J. John), Ltd. -- 5 Royal Opera Arcade, Pall Mall, London, S. W. 1.

Baker Street Irregulars, Inc. -- "Sycamores," Spring Valley Rd. , Morristown, N. J. , 07960.

Baker (Voorhis) -- 30 Smith Ave. , Mt. Kisco, N. Y.

Baker (Walter A.) -- 100 Summer St. , Boston, 02110.

Bakker (B.) -- Uitgoverijen, (Drukkerij n. v. S. J. B. , Bad-
hoeredorp), 144 Jan Van Gentstraat, The Hague, The
Netherlands.

Balai Pustaka -- Dinas Penerbitan Balai Pustaka. Djl. , Dr.
Wahidin II, no 2, Djakarta v /5 (Batavia), Indonesia.

Banter (George) Publ. Co. -- Menasha, Wisc.

Bärenreiter (Karl Votterle) Verlag -- 29-37 Heinrich-
Schutz-Alee, 3500, Kassel-Wilhelmshöne, West Germany.

Barnemann -- Paris.

Barnes (A. S.), Inc. -- now; Sportsman Press, Box 421,
Cranbury, N. J. 08512; and, The Yoseloff Ltd. , in Eng. ;
and Smithers Ltd. , in Canada.

Barnes & Noble Inc. -- 105 Fifth Ave. , NYC 10003.

Barre Publishers -- South St. , Barre, Mass. 01005.

Barrie & Rockliff -- 2 Clement's Inn, London, W. C. 2.

Basler Marionetten Theater Verlag -- Basel, Switzerland.

Batsford (B. T.), Ltd. -- 4 Fitzharding St. , Portman Sq. ,
London, W. 1.

Bauche, M. (Imp.) -- 39 Rue Chartraine, Evreux, France.

Bauer (M.) -- now: Bauer (Heinrich) Verlag, 11 Buchard-
strasse, 2000 Hamburg, West Germany.

Baurer -- 55 Rue St. , Lazare, Paris, ; but this may be
Baurer Editions (Alfred) -- 75 Rue Charles-Renouvier,
Paris 20^e.

Beaumont (Cyril W.), Ltd. -- 75 Charing Cross Rd. , London, W. C. 2.

Beckley-Cardy (Benefic Press) -- 1900 N. Narraganset,
Chicago, 60639.

Beginner Books -- See: Random House.

Bell (G.) & Sons, Ltd. -- York House, 6 Portland St. ,
    London, W. C. 2.

Bell-Daldy Co. -- See: Bell (G.).

Bemporad (R.) & Figlio Co. -- now: Bemporad-Marzocco
    Co. , 33a-35-37 Via Scipione Ammiraato, Florence, Italy.

Benn (Ernest), Ltd. -- Bouverie House, 154 Fleet St. ,
    London, E. C. 4.

Bennett-Sylvan Press, Publishers -- See: Sylvan Press.

Bentley's Codes, Ltd. -- 11 Bury St. , London, E. C. 3.
    (Formerly Richard Bentley Co.)

Berger-LeVrault -- 5 Rue Auguste-Comte, Paris 6e.

Berneuxet (Cumin) -- Lyons, France.

Best-in-Children's Books -- Garden City, N. Y. 11531.

Beysen -- See: Boysen & Maasch.

Bharatiya Natya Sangh Org. -- New Delhi, India.

Bible House -- See: Holt, Rinehart & Winston.

Les Bibliophiles de France -- See under: Les.

Bideri (Ferdinando) Tipografia Editrice -- Vettica Maggiore,
    Prajano, Salerno, Italy.

Binfords & Mort -- 2505 S. E. Eleventh Ave. , Portland,
    Oregon 97202.

Binny & Smith Press -- 380 Madison Ave. , NYC 10017.

Black (Adam & Charles), Ltd. -- 4/6 Soho Sq. , London,
    W. 1. [Formerly S. W. Partridge Co.]

Black (Parbury & Allen), Ltd. -- now: A. & C. Black, Ltd. ,
    -- 4, 5, 6, Soho Sq. , London, W. 1.

Blackie & Sons, Ltd. -- Kirkintilloch Round, Bishopbriggs,
    Glasgow, Scotland.

Blackwell (Basil) & Mott, Ltd. -- 48-51 Broad St., Oxford, England. See also: Davis Publications Inc.

Blackwell (Basil) (H.) -- W 44th St., NYC, See: Blackwell-Mott Ltd.

Bles (Geoffrey), Ltd. -- 52 Doughty St., London, W.C. 1.

Blom (Benjamin), Inc. -- 2521 Broadway, NYC 10025.

Bloud & Gay (Librairie) -- 3 Rue Garanciere, Paris, 6^e.

Blue Book Company -- 47 Biddulph Rd., S. Croydon, England. See also: Studio Vista, Ltd.

Blue Ox Press -- 575 Madison Ave., NYC 10022.

Blue Ribbon Books -- See: Random House.

Boardman (T.V.) & Co., Ltd. -- 3rd Floor, Gulf House, 2 Portman St., London, W. 1.

Bobbs-Merrill Co., Inc. -- 4300 W. 62nd St., Indianapolis, Indiana 46206.

Bochum -- Erfurt, East Germany.

Bodley Head (The), Ltd. -- 10 Earlham St., London, W.C. 2.

Boekhuis, Uitghet -- See: Vitghet Boekhuis.

Boekull en Karveel Uitgaven -- See: Uitghet Boekhuis.

Böhm (Anton) & Son -- 26 Lange Gasse, Augsburg 2, West Germany.

Boni & Liveright -- now: Liveright -- 386 Park Ave. S., NYC 10016.

Book Center (British), Ltd. -- 242 Marylebone Rd., London, N.W. 1; or, N. Circular Rd., Neasden, P.O. Box 30, London, N.W. 10. See also: British Book Centre.

Books for Libraries, Inc. -- 50 Liberty Ave., Freeport, N.Y. 11520.

Bordas (Editions) -- 37 Rue Boulard, 75 Paris 14e.

Borfenvereins -- Leipzig, East Germany.

Borna -- Leipzig, East Germany.

Bornemann (S.) -- 15 Rue de Tournon, Paris 6e.

Boston Book Co. -- now: Boston Book & Art Shop, Inc. --
657 Boylston St., Boston 02130.

Bouchery (Albert) -- 11 Square Marre-José, Ostende,
Belgium.

Bouverie House -- 154 Fleet St., London, E. C. 4.

Bowker (R. R.) Co. -- 1180 Ave. of the Americas, NYC
10036.

Boyer Co. -- Munich, West Germany.

Boysen & Maasch -- 25 Gerhofstrasse, 2000 Hamburg 36,
West Germany; or, 61 Ferdinandstr, Hamburg 1.

Brackman -- London.

Bradbury & Evans, Ltd. -- now: Evans Bros., Ltd.,
Montague House, Russell Sq., London, W. C. 1.

Branden Press, Inc. -- 221 Columbus Ave., Boston 02116.
[Has Silver Series Plays.]

Branford (Charles T.) Co. -- 28 Union St., Newton Center,
Mass. 02159.

Breslau -- Berlin.

Briasson -- Paris.

Brigg (Die) Verlag -- 43 Hermannstrasse Postfach 205,
8900 Augsburg, West Germany.

Brill (E. J.) -- now: E. J. Brill Verlag, 6-12 Antwerpener
St., Cologne, West Germany.

Brill (E. J.) De N. V. en Drukkerij. v. h. Boekhandel --

Brill et Gautier Imprints -- 38 Blvd. du Collège, Narbonne,
France.

23 Minderbroederstraat, Leuven, Belgium; and,
33a-39 Oude Rijn, Leiden, The Netherlands.

Bristol-Thirars -- Paris.

British Book Centre, Inc. -- 996 Lexington Ave. , NYC
10021. [This is a very practical way to send for any
British book; they charge no more, money exchange is
made easier, and air mail shortens the delivery time
by 5 weeks.]

British Educational Pupp. Inst. Press -- See: British
Puppet & Model Theatre Guild.

British National Bibliography, Ltd. -- 7-9 Rathbone St. ,
London, W. 1.

British National Museum Press -- Great Russell St. ,
London, W. C. 1.

British Puppet & Model Theatre Guild Org. -- 23a Southampton Pl. , London, W. C. 1.

Brockhampton Press, Ltd. -- Corridor Chambers, Market
Pl. , Leicester, England.

Brown Book Co. -- 239 Fourth Ave. , NYC 10003.

Bruckmann (B. F.) KG -- Abholfach, Nymphenburgerstr. ,
Munich 20, West Germany.

Brython Press -- Montague House, Russell Sq. , London,
W. C. 1.

Buchdr. Zollikofer & Co. , Verlag -- 122 Furstenlandstr. ,
St. Gallen, Switzerland.

Buchhandlung Lehmkuhl, Konzertvorverkauf und Schallplatten
-- Leopoldstrasse 45, 8 Munich 23, West Germany.
[This is a very good source for foreign puppet books.]

Bugbee (Willis N.) Co. -- 428 S. Warren St. , Syracuse,
N. Y.

Bühnervolfsbundes -- Frankfurt am Main, West Germany.

Bureau of American Ethnology -- Washington, D. C.

Burns & Oates, Ltd. -- [For Washbourne & Thomas Co.]
     8-10 Paternoster Row, London, E. C. 4. ; and,
     28 Orchard St. , London, W. 1.

Cabinet Press -- 12 Granite St. , Milford, N. H. 03055.

Callwey (G. D. W.) Verlag -- 35 Streitfeldstr. , Munich,
     West Germany.

Calmann-Lèvy -- [Most recent name for various Lèvy pub-
     lishers] 3 Rue Auber, Paris 9e.

Cambridge Book Co. -- 45 Kroft Ave. , Bronxville, N. Y.
     10708.

Cambridge Univ. Press -- Bentley House, 200 Euston Rd. ,
     London, N. W. 1. ; and, 32 E. 57th St. , NYC 10022.

Campitelli (F.) -- Rome.

Canadian Library Association -- Room 606, 63 Sparks St. ,
     Ottawa 4, Can.

Cape (Jonathan) [& Harrison Smith] -- 30 Bedford Sq. ,
     London, W. C. 1; or [NYC] contact Harcourt & Brace
     Co.

Capelia Corp, Polish Arts & Crafts -- Polish Institute of
     Arts and Sciences in America, 39 E. 35th St. , NYC
     10016.

Capitol Publishers Inc. -- Box 6235, Washington, D. C.
     20015; or, 5306 Belt Rd. , N. W. , Washington, D. C.
     20015.

Carlton Press Inc. -- 84 Fifth Ave. , NYC 10011.

Carmanne (Vaillant) Imp. -- 4 Place St. Michel, Liège,
     Belgium.

Carnier -- Paris.

Carwall Ltd. -- Grosvenor House, Manor Rd. , Wallington,
     (Surrey) England.

Casa Editrice Italia -- See: Signorelli.

Casey, Lea & Blanchard Co. -- See: Lea Bros. and Co.

Casilla-Correocentral -- Buenos Aires, Argentina.

Casini (G.) -- See: Casini S. R. L. (Edizione).

Casini S. R. L. (Edizione) -- 46 Viale Mazzini, Florence,
   Italy.

Caspar (C. N.) Co. -- 437 E. Water St., Milwaukee, Wisc.,
   [For the G. Soule Art Co., of Boston.]

Cassell & Co., Ltd. -- 35 Red Lion Sq., London, W. C. 1.

Cassirer (B.) Co., Ltd. -- now: Bruno Cassirer Co., Ltd.,
   31 Portland Rd., Oxford, England [U. S. distributors
   are Faber & Faber Co.].

Castle Book Co., Ltd. -- 27 Castle Arcade, Cardiff, Wales.
   See also: Castle Press.

Castle Press -- 50 Old Brompton Rd., London, S. W. 7.

Centrale Lausanne (Imp.) -- 7 Poute de Genève, Lausanne,
   Switzerland.

Century Crofts, Inc. -- See: Appleton-Century-Crofts.

Century House Inc. -- Ivy Museum, Watkins Glenn, N. Y.
   14891.

Century Publishing Co. -- Salt Lake City, Utah.

Cercle de la Librairie -- 117 Blvd. St. Germain, Paris 6e.

Cercle (Le) du Livre de France, Ltée -- 3300 Blvd., Rose-
   mont, Montreal 36, P. Q.

Champion (Ancienne Librairie Honoré) -- 5 et 7 Quai Mala-
   quais, 75 Paris 6e.

Champs Elysées (Librairie Des) -- 2 Rue de Barigan, 75
   Paris 8e.

Chaney (A.) -- Paris.

Chapman & Hall, Ltd. -- 11 New Fetter La., London,
   E. C. 4.

Charpentier (G.) -- now: Librairie Charpentier, 30 Rue de L'Université, 75 Paris 7e.

Charpentier (R.) -- 6 Rue Jean, Montdidier, France.

Chatto Educ. Ltd. -- 40-42 William IV. St. , London, W. C. 2. [Formerly Chatto & Windus, Ltd.]

Chester House Publications -- 2 Chester House, Pages La. , London, N. 10.

Chilton Book Co. (The) -- 401 Walnut St. , Philadelphia, Pa. 19106.

Ciordia (Editorial) S. R. L. -- 2271 Ave. Belgrano, Buenos Aires, Argentina.

Ciudad Trujillo (Editora Libreria) -- Dominican Republic.

Clark (H. G.) & Co. -- See: T. & T. Clark; Irwin Clark.

Clark (Irwin) & Co. -- 791 St. Clair Ave. W. , Toronto.

Clark (T. & T.) Ltd. -- 38 George St. , Edinburgh 2, Scotland.

Clarke (James) & Co. , Ltd. -- 31 Queen Anne's Gate, London, S. W. 1.

Classen (Werner) Verlag -- 21 Genferstr, Zürich, Switzerland.

Clowes (W.) & Son, Ltd. -- 14-16 Lower Regent St. , London, S. W. 1.

Coach House Press, Inc. -- 53 W. Jackson Blvd. , Chicago, 60604.

Colin (Librairie Arman) -- 103 Blvd. St. Michel, Paris 5e.

Collect Holdings Ltd. -- See following entry.

Collects' Russian Bookshop Press Ltd. -- 40 Great Russell St. , London, W. C. 1.

College & University Press -- 263 Chapel St. , New Haven, Conn. 06513.

College of the City of New York, Div. of Teacher Educ.,
Publication -- 535 E. 80th St., NYC 10021.

Collier (P. F.) -- 866 Third Ave., NYC 10019. [Subs. of
Crowell, Collier & Macmillan, Inc. q.v.]

Collins (William) Sons & Co. -- 215 Park Ave. S., NYC
10003; also: 14 St. James Pl., London, S.W. 1; and
also: 144 Cathedral St., Glasgow, Scotland.

Colombo, Dept. of Cultural Affairs Press -- Colombo, Ceylon.

Colombo (Francisco A.) Press -- 1889 Piso, 5, Sarmiento,
Buenos Aires.

Columbia University Press -- 440 W. 110th St., NYC
10025.

Comet Press -- See: Carlton Press and Random House.

Commissie Voor De Folkslectuur -- Weltevreden, The
Netherlands.

Commission du Folklore de la Saison Liegeoise -- Liège,
Belgium.

La Concarde (Imprimerie) -- 4 Rue Jumelles, Lausanne,
Switzerland.

Concordia Publishing House, Ltd. -- 42 Museum St.,
London, W.C. 1.; also, 3558 S. Jefferson Ave., St.
Louis, Mo. 63118.

Constable & Co., Ltd. -- 10-12 Orange St., Leicester Sq.,
London, W.C. 2.

Consulate General of the Federal Republic of Germany --
460 Park Ave., NYC 10022.

Continental Publishing & Distributors, Ltd. -- See: Hachette.

Cooper (C. L.) -- Tulsa, Okla.

Cooper Square Publishers, Inc. -- 59 Fourth Ave.,

NYC 10003.

Coptic House Press, Ltd. -- 7 Coptic St., London, W. C. 1.

Cornell University Press -- 124 Roberts Pl., Ithaca, N. Y. 14850.

Cornely -- Paris, France.

(Council of) British National Bibliography, Ltd. -- 7-9 Rathbone St., London, W. 1.

Courteline -- Voy, France.

Coutan-Lambert -- now: Lambert Co., 23 Rue Léningrad, Paris 8e.

Coward-McCann, Inc. -- 200 Madison Ave., NYC 10016.

Cowell (W. S.), Ltd. -- 28 Percy St., London, W. 1.

Cowes (William) & Sons -- Stamford St. & Charing Cross, London.

Cranbrook Institute of Science -- 380 Pine Rd., Bloomfield Hills, Mich. 48013.

Creative Educational Society, Inc. -- 515 N. Front St., Mankato, Minn. 56001.

Crothers (J. Francis) -- 81 Flagg Rd., W. Hartford, Conn. 06117.

Crowell Collier & Macmillan Inc. -- (Formerly, T. Y. Crowell),   -- 866 Third Ave., NYC 10022.

Crown Publishers, Inc. -- 419 Park Ave. S., NYC 10016. [For Allen; Towne & Heath; Lothrop & Covici; Bell; Arcadia; and many other discontinued houses in U. S. A.]

Cultural Information Publications -- Moscow.

Cumin et Masson (P.) -- See: Massonet Cie.

Daimond (A. Titanti) Press -- Castle Hedingham, Essex, England.

Daldy-Bell -- <u>See</u>: Virtue and Co.

Daragon (H.) -- 10 Rue Fromentin, Paris 9e.

Darton & Hodge, Ltd. -- <u>See</u>: next entry.

Darton, Longmann and Todd, Inc. -- 64 Chiswic High Rd.,
    London, W. 4.

Davin De Champelos -- Voy, France.

Davis Publications, Inc. -- 50 Portland St., Worcester,
    Mass. 01608.

Day (John) Co., Inc. -- In text Educational Publishers, 280
    Park Ave., NYC 10017.

Dealey & Lowe Co. -- Dallas, Texas.   Contact: Regional
    Publishing Co., c/o Genealogical Pub. Co. Inc., 521-
    523 St. Paul Place, Baltimore 21202.

Dean & Son, Ltd. -- 41-43 Ludgate Hill, London, E. C. 4.

Deane (H. F. W.) & Sons, Ltd. -- 31 Museum St., London,
    W. C. 1.

De Graff (John) Inc. -- 34 Oak Ave., Tuckahoe, N. Y. 10707.

De Jong (D.) -- The Hague, The Netherlands.

Delagrave, (Librairie) -- Sometimes written De LaGrave --
    15 Rue Soufflot, 75 Paris 5e.

Delahaye (A.) Librairie Classique -- 22 Chaussée Thièrs,
    Le Havre, France.

Dell Publishing Co. Inc. -- 750 Third Ave., NYC 10017.

De Magneet -- Antwerp, Belgium.

Demailly (Y.) -- Lille, France.

Dendolat -- Budapest, Hungary.

Denison (T. S.) & Co., Inc. -- 5100 W. 82nd St., Minneapol-
    is, Minn. 55431.

Denöel (Robert) Editions -- 12 Rue Amélie, Paris 7e.

Dent (J. M.) & Sons Publishing Co. , Ltd. -- Aldine House, 10-13 Bedford St. , Strand, London, W. C. 2.

Dentu -- Paris, France.

Den Verfasser -- Frankfurt am Main, West Germany.

De Pojl (S. V.) -- Leuven, Belgium.

"Deposito Edizioni" -- Florence, Italy.

Design Publishing Co. , Inc. -- 32 Warren St. , Columbus, Ohio.

Desvernay -- Lyons, France.

Detroit Institute of Art Press -- 5200 Woodward Ave. , Detroit, Mich. 48202.

Deutsch (André) Ltd. -- 105 Great Russell St. , London, W. C. 1.

Deutscher Kunstverlag, G. M. B. H. -- 1 Vohburger Str. , 800 Munich, 42, West Germany.

Deutscher Lainespielverlag -- 18/22 Kongsberger Str. , Weinheim, West Germany.

Devereaux Foundation -- Devore, Pa. 19333.

Devlet Matbaasi & Druckerei Universum -- Istanbul, Turkey.

Didier (Librairie Marce) -- 4 Rue de la Sorbonne, Paris 5e.

Didier Publishing Co. -- 660 Madison Ave., NYC 10021.

Didot-Bottin Editions -- 56 Rue Jacob, Paris 6e; and, 1 Rue Sebastian-Bottin, 75 Paris 7e.

Diederichs (Eugene) Verlag -- 1 Brehmstr. , Düsseldorf 1, West Germany.

Dielmas -- Bordeaux, France.

Dissigig Co. -- Freiburg, West Germany.

Disszain [Diszain, or Diszin] -- Paris.

Le Divan Cie. -- 37 Rue Bonaparte, Paris 6^e.

Djambatan, Penerbit (N. V.), Djambatan, Djl, Jrh. -- 9
    Djilosari, Djakarta, Indonesia.

Dobson (Dennis), Ltd. [Dobson Books, Ltd.] -- 80 Kensing-
    ton Church St. , London, W. 8.

Documentation Verlag -- Munich, West Germany.

Dodd, Mead & Co. , Inc. -- 79 Madison Ave. , NYC 10016.

Doran (George H.), Inc. -- See: Doubleday Co.

Dorrance & Co. , Inc. -- 1809 Callowhill St. , Philadelphia
    19130.

Doubleday & Co. , Inc. -- 277 Park Ave. , NYC 10017;
    orders to: 501 Franklin Ave. , Garden City, N. Y. 11530.

Dougherty (G. W.) -- NYC.

Dragon (A.) -- 3 Place des Précheurs, Aix-en-Provence,
    France.

Dreyers Forlag -- 7 Arbiensqt. , Oslo, Norway.

Dryad Press, Ltd. -- 22 Bloomsbury St. , London, W. C. 1;
    or, Northgates Leicester, England.

Dryden Press -- now see: Holt, Rinehart & Winston Inc.

Dubisson (Imp.) -- 15 Rue de Fesche, Liège, Belgium.

Duckworth (Gerald) & Co. , Ltd. -- 3 Henrietta St. , London,
    W. C. 2.

Duell, Sloan & Pearce Inc. -- orders to: Meredith Press,
    1716 Locust St. , Des Moines, Iowa 50303.

Dulau Co. , Ltd. -- 29 Dover St. , London, W. 1.

Dun & Bradstreet Corp. -- 99 Church St. , NYC 10008.

Dunetz & Lovett Co. -- NYC.

Dupret -- Paris.

Dutton (E. P.) & Co. , Inc. -- 201 Park Ave. S. , NYC
10003.

Eclaireurs Unionistes De France (Editions des) -- 94 Rue
St. Lazare, Paris 9ᵉ.

Ediciones Culturales Argentinas -- address "Cultura," 502
Medrano, Buenos Aires; or, "Cultural Argentina," 430
Lavalle 1, Buenos Aires.

Ediciones T. L. A. T. -- Buenos Aires.

Edirions (Editions) du Cercle d'Art -- 188 Blvd. de Smet
de Naeyer, Brussels 9, Belgium.

Editor & Publisher Co. , Inc. -- 850 Third Ave. , NYC
10022.

Editorial Ciordia, S. R. L. -- 2271 Belgrano, Buenos Aires.

Editorial Futuro, S. R. L. -- 2390 Sarmiento, Buenos Aires.

Editrice Del Fieramasca -- Florence, Italy.

Edizioni Radio Italiana -- See: E. R. I.

Education Press Inc. -- 1201 S. E. Second St. , Fort Lauder-
dale, Fla. 33301. Also, contact, Multimedia Biograf.
Co. , Shelton Towers, Room 436, 527 Lexington Ave. ,
NYC 10017.

Ehrenwirth (Franz) Verlag -- 8 Vilshofenerstr. , Munich 27,
West Germany.

Eichler (A.) -- now: Eichler & Roth (Imp.), 33 Speicherg,
Bern, Switzerland.

Elam (Charles H.) & Publ. -- Detroit Museum of Art Press,
Detroit.

Elton & Perkins Co. -- now: W. B. Perkins & Co. , 13
Astor Pl. , NYC.

Ely House -- 37 Dover St. , London, E. C. 4.

Engeroff (J.) -- Sweden.

English Book Centre, Ltd. -- See: British Book Centre,
    Inc.

English Chapbooks -- 60 St. Martin's La., Charing Cross,
    London; See also: Johnson Publications, Ltd.

English Universities Press, Ltd. -- 102 Newgate St.,
    London, E. C. 1.

E. P. A. -- Educational Puppet Association Press (British) --
    23a Southampton Pl., London, W. C. 1. Also, address
    Educational Supplies Assn. Press, 17 Little Russell St.,
    London, W. C. 1.

Epworth Press & Methodist Publ. House -- 25-35 City Rd.,
    London, E. C. 1.

E. R. I. -- Edizioni Della Radio-televisione Italiana, 21 Via
    Arsenale, Turin, Italy.

Erlenbach -- Zürich, Switzerland.

L'Ermite [Editions] -- Paris.

L'État Moderne (Editions de); 35 Rue Bonaparte, Paris 6e.

Ethnographical Museum of Sweden (Publications) -- Stock-
    holm. [Bokforlags Aktiebolaget Thule Press.]

Etrangères (Editions en Langues) -- Moscow.

Etzold & Co. -- Munich, West Germany.

European Publishers Representatives, Inc. -- 36 W. 61st
    St., NYC 10023

Evans Brothers, Ltd. -- Montague House, Russell Sq.,
    London W. C. 2. [For Hugh Evans & Son, See: Brython
    Press.]

Exposition Press Inc. -- 50 Jericho Turnpike, Jericho,
    N. Y. 11753.

Faber & Faber, Ltd. -- 3 Queens St., London. [Distributors for many publishers that have discontinued; helpful.]

Fahrmann-Verlag (Verlag des Kathol) -- Jugendwerkes, 13 Mahlerstrasse, 1015 Vienna.

Falkenstein (Mollie) -- 132 Chiquita St., Laguna Beach, Calif. 92651. (For UNIMA, (q.v.)

Fantemania -- Paris; See: Fatima Editions.

Farrar, Straus & Givoux, Inc. -- 19 Union Sq. W., NYC 10003; [for Pellegrini & Cudahy books].

Fatima Editions -- 3 Rue Gabriel-Peri, 31 Toulouse, France.

Faust (G.) -- Liège, Belgium.

Faxon (F.W.), Inc. -- 515-25 Hyde Park Ave., Boston, 02131; or, 15 Southwest Park, Westwood, Mass. 02090.

Federal Theater Projects Publishing Division -- U.S. Gov. Printing Office, Washington, D.C. [not currently active]; or, contact Bureau of Nat. Affairs, 1231 25th St. N.W., Washington, D.C. 20037.

Ferdinando (Editrice) -- Bideri, Naples, Italy.

Fiefield (A.C.) -- See: Jonathan Cape, Ltd.

Field Museum of Natural History Press -- Roosevelt Rd. & Lake Shore Dr., Chicago 60605.

Fieramosca (Editrice del) -- now: Fiere, (E.) Mostre-Casa Editrice, 14 Via G. B. Bazzoni, Milan, Italy.

Filser (B.) -- F. F. Filser-Verlag, 36 Pippingerstrasse, Munich, West Germany.

Firmin-Didot et Cie -- See: Didot-Bottin Cie.

Fischbacher -- 33 Rue de Seine, Paris 6^e.

Fischer (H.W.) & Bros., Inc. -- 214 S. 15th St., Philadelphia.

Fischer (S.) Verlag -- 10/12 Mainzer Landstr. , Frankfurt
am Main 1, West Germany.

Fischgrund Publishing Co. -- Mexico City, Mexico.

Fisher (T. S.) Co. -- See: Unwin (T. Fisher).

Fisher-Unwin (T. S.) -- See: Unwin (T. Fisher); and, Benn
(Ernest), Ltd.

Flaccorie -- See: Flaccovio.

Flaccovio (S. F.) -- 37 Via Ruggero Settimo, Palermo,
Italy.

Flamma (Editions) -- 16 A, Odos Amerikis, Athens.

La Flamma -- 5 Via Tranquillo Cremona, Milan 20145,
Italy.

Flammarion et Cie. -- 26 Rue Racine, 75 Paris 6e.

Fletcher (C. and I. K.), Ltd. -- 22 Buckingham Gate, London, S. W. 1. [Not a publ. but very helpful for rare
o. p. puppet books.]

Fleurus (Editions) -- 31 Rue de Fleurus, 75 Paris 6e.

Flore (Editions de) -- 22 Bis, Passage Dauphine, Paris 6e.

Focal Press -- See: Pitman Press.

Folk-Lore Academy Press -- Folklore Soc. , c/o University
College, Glower St. , London, W. C. 1; see also: Folklore Association, Inc.

Folklore Association -- Div. of Gale Research Co. , Book
Towers, Detroit, 48226.

Folklore Commission -- Liège, Belgium.

Folklore Library Publishers, Inc. -- 116 E. 27th St. , NYC
10016.

Folklore Publishing Co. -- 1010 W. Washington Blvd. ,
Chicago 60607.

Follett Publishing Co. -- 201 N. Wells St., Chicago 60606.

Fontemoina -- Paris

Foreign & International Book Co., Inc. -- 100 E. 42nd St.,
    NYC 10017.

Foreign Policy Association Publishing Co. -- 345 E. 46th
    St., NYC 10017.

Fortress Press -- 2900 Queen La., Philadelphia 19129.

Four Continents Book Shop -- See: Humphries Publishing
    Co.

Four Seas Co. -- See: Humphries Publishing Co.

Four Seasons Co. -- See: Humphries Publishing Co.

Four Winds Press -- 50 W. 44th St., NYC 10036.

Foyer (Editions du) -- 4 Rue Madam, Paris 6^e.

Foyle (W. & G.), Ltd. -- 119 Charing Cross Rd., London,
    W. C. 2.

Frageralle -- Paris.

Framont (E.) -- Rue D'Anjou, Paris.

Franklin Watts -- See under: Watts.

French & European Publications, Inc. -- Rockefeller Center,
    610 Fifth Ave., NYC 10020.

French (Samuel), Inc. -- 25 W. 45th St., NYC 10036.

Frensdorf (Ernest) -- Berlin.

Fromontier (M.) Editions -- Rue Féron, 75 Paris, 6e.

Funk & Wagnalls Co., Inc. -- 380 Madison Ave., NYC
    10017.

Furman (A. L.) -- See: Lantern Press.

Furrow Press (The) -- 1273 E. Tenth St., Brooklyn,

N. Y. 11215.

Gaebler (E.) -- Berlin.

Galler (O.) -- Munich, West Germany.

Gallimard (L.) -- 5 Rue Sebastien-Bottin, Paris 7e.

Gandoein -- Paris.

Garden City Publ. -- See: Doubleday.

Gardner Publishing Co. -- 723 Selby Ave. , St. Paul, Minn.
    55104.

Gardner-Wells Co. See: Wells, Gardner, Darton Co.

Gardnier (Arnould) Frères, Editions -- 19 Rue des Plantes,
    Paris 14e.

Gashet (W. M.) & Co. -- Langen (near Frankfurt am Main),
    West Germany.

Gehly (P.) -- Cologne, West Germany.

Geisler (F. A.) -- Leipzig, East Germany.

Geneva Book Co. -- contact: Westminster Press, Wither-
    spoon Bldg. , Juniper & Walnut Sts. , Philadelphia 19107.

Georg & Cie -- 5(10) Rue Corraterie, Geneva, Switzerland;
    see also: Georg (Paul).

Georg (Paul) -- Instituteur aux Charbonniers, St. Maurice-
    sur-Moselle, France.

Gérente -- Aix-les Baines, France.

Gessler (E. ?) Co. -- [Formerly Paris] now: Geneva,
    Switzerland.

Giant Education Co. , Ltd. -- 12 Corsitor St. , London,
    E. C. 4; or, 91-93 Union St. , Glasgow, Scotland.

"G. L. M. " Editions -- 6 Rue Huygens, Paris 14e.

Gold Label -- 257 Park Ave. S., NYC 10010.

Golden Press, Inc. -- 850 Third Ave., NYC 10022; but:
    orders to 1220 Mound Ave., Racine, Wisc. 53404.

Goldmann (Wilhelm) Verlag -- 22 Neumarkterstr., 8000
    Munich 8, West Germany.

Gorham (Edwins), Inc. -- See: Morehouse-Gorham-Barlow
    Co., Inc.

Gouncuilhou (G.) -- Bordeaux, France.

Government Theatre Bureau Press -- Moscow.

Gowans & Gray Co., Ltd. -- 5 Robert St., Adelphia,
    W. C. 2; and, 58 Caogan St., Glasgow, C. 2. Scotland.

Grafton (Frank H.) & Co. -- Coptic House, 105-51 Great
    Russell St., London, W. C. 1.

Graficznc (Wydawnictwo Artystyczno-) RSW "Prasa" --
    Krakow, Poland.

Grasset (Bernard) Editions, S. A. -- 61 Rue des St. Pères,
    Paris 6e.

Gravesend Press -- Lexington, Ky.

Greenburg -- NYC; contact: The Chilton Book Co., 401
    Walnut St., Philadelphia 19106.

Greystone Corp. -- 225 Park Ave. S., NYC 10013.

Greystone Press -- See: Hawthorn Books, Inc.

Grosset & Dunlap, Inc. -- 51 Madison Ave., NYC 10010.

Grove Press, Inc. -- 214 Mercer St., NYC 10012.

Grunow (F. W.) -- Leipzig, East Germany.

Guillot (Editions Georges) S. A. R. L. -- 39 Rue du Paradis,
    Paris 10e.

Guptil -- See: Watson-Guptil Publications, Inc.

Guptill-Watson -- See: Watson-Guptil Publications, Inc.

Guyot (E.) Imprimerie -- 25 Rue Ransfort, Brussels, Belgium.

Guyot (H. D.) -- 7 Rue de L'Éperon, Paris 6ᵉ.

Gryphon Books, Ltd. -- 50 Albemarle St., London W. 1.

Gryphon Press -- 220 Montgomery St., Highland Pk., N. J. 08904.

Haase -- Prague, Czechoslovakia.

Habbel (Josef) -- 17 Gutenburgstr., Regensburg, West Germany.

Hachette (Librairie) -- 79 Blvd. St. Germain, Paris 6ᵉ. [U. S.: Hachette, Inc., 301 Madison Ave., NYC 10017.]

Hadden Best & Co., Ltd. -- Westminster, London, S. W. 1.

Haddon Craftsman -- Scranton, Pa.

Hafner (Adolf) Verlag -- 2/4 Kapuziner-Strasse, 8000 Munich 15, West Germany.

Hafner Publishing Co., Inc. -- 260 Heights Rd., Darien, Conn. 06820.

Hall (G. K.) & Co. -- 70 Lincoln St., Boston 02111.

Haller Verlag -- 70 Münsingerstri, Starnberg, West Germany.

Hamilton & Co. (Stafford), Ltd. -- 108 Brompton Rd., London, S. W. 3.

Hamilton (Hamish), Ltd. -- 90 Great Russell St., London, W. C. 1.

Hamlyn (Paul), Ltd. -- Drury House, Russell St., London, W. C. 2.

Hammar (T.) -- Paris.

Hammond-Harwood House Association, Inc. -- 19 Maryland Ave., Annapolis, Md. 21401.

Happy Hours Co. -- absorbed by A. Point & A. Maussott Co. and moved from U. S. A.

Happy Publications -- 5451 Laurel Canyon Blvd., N. Hollywood, Calif. 91607.

Harcourt Brace Jovanovich, Inc. -- 757 Third Ave., NYC 10017.

Harmsworth Press, Ltd. -- 8 Stratton St., London, W. 1.

Harper & Row, Publishers -- 49 E. 33rd St., NYC 10016, but send orders to Scranton, Pa. 18512.

Harrap (George G.) Ltd. -- 182 High Holborn St., London, W. C. 1.

Hartman Handpress -- [formerly Mill Valley, Calif.] -- 4390 Mission St., San Francisco 94107.

Harvard Univ. Press -- 79 Garden St., Cambridge, Mass., 02138.

Harwaey (A.) -- 37 N. Rd., Bedfont, Middlesex, Eng.

Haskell House Publ. Ltd. -- 280 Lafayette St., NYC 10012.

Hasse (Otto) Hass, (Otto) Heinz, W. -- [formerly Prague] seems two names are used: O. Hasse, 6 Blankenseerstr., 2400 Lübeck, West Germany; and, Otto Hass (W. Heinz), 18 Arnold-Heise Str., Hamburg 20, West Germany.

Hastings House Publishers, Inc. -- 10 E. 40th St., NYC 10016.

H. A. U. M. Monarch House -- 58 Long St., Kaapstad (Capetown), S. Afr.

Haupt (Paul) -- 1/14 Falkenplatz, Bern, Switzerland.

Hawthorn Books, Inc. -- 70 Fifth Ave., NYC 10011; and, Andrew Hall, 30 Fleet St., London, E. C. 4.

Haye, La -- Paris, France.

Heffer (W.) & Sons, Ltd. -- 3-4 Petty Cury, Cambridge,
    England.

Heijnis, Tsxl, Jl, Zaandijk Lagedijk -- Amsterdam, The
    Netherlands.

Heimeran (Ernst) Verlag -- 14 Dietlindenstr. , Munich,
    West Germany.

Heineman (James H.), Inc. -- 19 Union Square West, NYC
    10003.

Heinman (William S.) -- 200 W. 72nd St. , NYC 10003 [Im-
    ported books.]

Heinemann (William), Ltd. -- 15-16 Queen St. , London,
    W. 1.

Heinemann (William) Medical Books, Ltd. -- 23 Bedford
    Sq. , London, W. C. 1.

Heinemann & Zsolnay, Ltd. -- 15-16 Queen St. , London,
    W. 1.

Hellinikes (Technes) -- Athens.

Helmshaus -- Zürich, Switzerland.

Hendel (O.) -- Halle (an der Saaiel), East Germany.

Hennseelverlag (K. H.) -- 29b Am Kleinen, Wahnsee, Berlin,
    39.

Hennsel (Karl Heinz) -- See: Hennseelverlag (K. H.)

Henschel Verlag-Kunst und Gesellschaft -- 67/68 Oranien-
    burger Strasse, 104 Berlin.

Herbig (F. A.) Verlag -- West Berlin

Het Institute -- Amsterdam, The Netherlands.

Hetzel (J.) & Co. -- 18 Rue Jacop, Paris.

Heye Foundation Press -- Museum of the American Indian,

NYC.

Hilaire -- Paris.

Hinkel & Gackeleia -- Oldenburg, West Germany.

Hinrichs (J. C.) Verlag -- 2 Scherlstr., Leipzig, C. 1.,
    East Germany.

Hispanic Society of America -- 613 W. 155th St., NYC
    10032; sometimes given as "at Broadway, between 155th
    and 156th St.," NYC 10032, U. S. A.

Hlavata (A.) -- Prague, Czechoslovakia.

Hobbies Publ. -- Lightner Publishing Corp., 10061 S.
    Michigan Ave., Chicago 60605.

Hobby House Press -- 461 Ben Franklin Station, Washington,
    D. C. 20044.

Hodge (William) & Co., Ltd. -- 12 Bank St., Edinburgh 1,
    Scotland.

Hoffman (Raymond A.) -- 509 S. Wabash Ave., Chicago

Höfling (Val) Verlag -- 11 Thierschstr., Munich 22, West
    Germany.

Holiday House Inc. -- 18 E. 56th St., NYC 10022.

Holt (Henry) & Co. -- See: Holt, Rinehart & Winston, Inc.

Holt, Rinehart & Winston, Inc. -- 383 Madison Ave., NYC
    10017. Send orders for educational books to 400 N.
    Michigan Ave., Chicago.

Hone (W.) -- London.

Hopkins Syndicate, Inc. -- Hopkins Bldg., Mellott, Ind.
    47958.

Houghton Mifflin Co. -- 2 Park St., Boston 02107; orders
    to: 53 W. 43rd St., NYC 10036.

Hubbard Press -- 2855 Sherimer Rd., Northbrook, Ill.
    60062.

Hubert (M.) Press -- 29 Rue Vandermaelen, Brussels, Belgium.

Huebsch (B.W.) -- 625 Madison Ave., NYC 10022.

Humphries (Bruce) Publishers -- 68 Beacon St., Somerville, Mass. 02143.

Huré -- Paris.

Hutchinson & Co., Publishers, Ltd. -- Hutchinson House, 178-202 Great Portland St., London, W. 1.

Hyperion-Verlag (Hermann Luft) -- 6 Lagenhardstr., Freiburg im Breisgrau 7800, West Germany.

Illman & Son -- Philadelphia.

Imprimerie National -- 27 Rue de la Convention, Paris 15e.

Imprimeries (Librairies) Réunies -- 23 Ave. de la Gare, Lausanne, Switzerland; or, 7 Rue St. Benoit, 75 Paris 6e.

Imprimerio Pan Americana -- Montevideo, Uruguay.

Indiana Univ. Press -- 10th & Morton Sts., Bloomington 47401; the Indiana Univ. School of Education Press Bulletin is at Ballantine Hall, No. 915, Bloomington 47401.

Ingram (H.) & Co. -- absorbed by Oxford University Press.

Insel-Bücherei -- Leipzig, East Germany.

Insel-Verlag -- 38 Feldbergstrasse, Postfach 3001, 6000 Frankfurt am Main, West Germany.

Insel-Verlag (Anton Kippenberg) -- 8 Mottelerstr., Leipzig, N22 East Germany; and, 38 Karlstr., Wiesbaden, West Germany.

Institute Belgique d'Information et de Documentation -- 3 Rue Montoyer, Brussels, Belgium.

Instituto De Estudios Madrilenos -- Duque de Medenaceli, Madrid 4, Spain.

Instituto de los Españoles en los Estados Unidos -- NYC.

Institute Masaryk -- c/o"UNIMA Organization Headquarters
for Czechoslovakia," Prague.

Invert -- Amiens, France.

Italian Information Center -- 686 Park Ave., NYC 10021.

Iversen (C. G.) -- Copenhagen.

Jager (C. V.) -- 1-3 St. Jansstraat, The Hague, The Netherlands.

Jaker Co. -- Surakata, Indonesia.

Janssen (G.) -- 9 Kerkstraat, Antwerp, Belgium.

Janssen Verlag -- 34 Elfstri, Werner, Bad Godesberg,
West Germany.

Japan Publications Trading Co. -- 1255 Howard St., San
Francisco, 94103.

Java Institute Press -- Weltevreden, The Netherlands.

Jay, Le -- Paris.

Jay Marshall Bookseller (Punch & Judy Bookshop) -- 5082
North Lincoln Ave., Chicago 60625. [By appointment
only; rare and out-of-print material.]

Jehebers (J. H.) S. A. -- 6 Rue du Vieux Collège, Geneva,
Switzerland.

Jena Publishing Co. (Max Kebler) -- Dusseldorf, West Germany; see also: Lichfenstein; and, Wartburg Verlag.

Jenkins (Herbert) Ltd. -- 3 Duke of York St., London,
S. W. 1.

Jeune, Europe (La) -- 51 Rue Vavin,, Paris 6e.

Jeunet -- Amiens, France. [See: Jeune?]

Joel' -- Paris.

Johns Hopkins Press -- Baltimore. 21218.

Johnson Publications, Ltd. -- 60 St. Martins La., Charing
    Cross, London; or, 11 Stanhope Mews West, London,
    S.W. 7.

Joly (André) Publications -- 164 Rue du Faubourg-St.
    Honoré, 75 Paris 8e; or, 215 Blvd. St. Germain Paris
    7e.

Jonathon Cape -- see under: Cape.

Jorel -- Paris.

Joseph (Michael), Ltd. -- 26 Bloomsbury St., London,
    W.C. 1.

Jugend und Volk (Verlag für) -- 7-9 Tiefer Graben, 1014
    Vienna.

Junge & Sohn -- 8/10 Brucker Strasse, 8520 Erlangen,
    West Germany.

Junior Leagues of America (Assn. of) -- 301 Waldorf Astoria,
    Park Ave., NYC 10022.

Junker und Dunnhaupt -- now: Axel Junker Verlag, 2
    Eisensch Str., Berlin, W. 30, Germany.

Juven (Félix) -- Rue Reaumour, Paris. [Believe discon-
    tinued; obtain books at "Madam Z" in Paris; see:
    "Madam S. Zlatin."]

Juventa-Verlag -- Nordl Auführtsallee, Munich 19, West
    Germany.

Kahn (Robert-Paul) Imp. -- 14 Rue de la Faiencerie, Epinal,
    France.

Kapelusz, S. A. -- 372 Moreno, Buenos Aires.

Karveel (Bookuilen) -- Antwerp, Belgium.

Kegan, Paul, Trench, Trubner & Co., Inc. (booksellers) --

43 Great Russell St. , London, W. C. 1.

Kelly & Walsh, Ltd. -- Box 76, Hong Kong; or, Box 1109,
    Singapore 1.

Kemper Verlag -- 16 Mühlensleig, Heidelberg, West Ger-
    many.

Keniks (Editions de) S. P. R. L. -- 87 Ave. du Roi, Brussels,
    Belgium.

Kennikat Press, Inc. -- PO Box 270, Port Washington,
    N. Y. 11050.

Kent State Univ. Press -- Kent, Ohio 44240.

Kepzomüveszeti Alap Kladóvallatta -- 15 Rakocziut, Buda-
    pest, Hungary.

Kidd (Steward) -- now: John G. Kidd & Son, 626 Vine St. ,
    Cincinnati, Ohio 45202.

Kimber (William) & Co. , Ltd. -- 46 Wilton Pl. , London,
    S. W. 1.

King's Crown Press -- [Division of Columbia Univ Press,
    g. v.]

Kinkel & Gackeleia -- Oldenburg, West Germany.

Klasse -- Munich, West Germany.

Kleinmann -- Paris.

Klett (Ernst) -- Rotebühlstr. , Stuttgart, West Germany.

Klopp (Fritz) Verlag, G. M. B. H. -- [E. Klopp Verlag]
    26 Wittelsbacherstri, Berlin-Wilmersdorf, Germany.

Knauss (O. P.) -- Macungie, Pa.

Knopf (Alfred A.) Inc. -- 201 E. 50th St. , NYC 10022;
    orders to Random House (same address).

Kodansha International Press -- 19 Otowacho, 3 Chome
    Bunkyoku, Japan.

Kolff (G.) & Co. -- 74 (Weltevreden) Weteringschans, Amsterdam, The Netherlands.

Kohlhammer (W.) Verlag -- 12 Urbanhstr., Stuttgart, West Germany.

Der Konegen -- Vienna.

Der Koniglich Academy der Wissenschaften -- Munich, West Germany.

Körner (W.) -- Stuttgart, West Germany.

Lacy (Bailes T.) -- 89 Strand St., London.

Lafaire (Heinz) Orient Buchhandlung -- Hanover, West Germany.

Lafolye Frères -- 1 Place des Lices, Vannes, France.

Lafolye (Joly Tournaire) -- see above.

Laiblin -- Ensslin, Reutlingen, West Germany.

Lambert Co. -- 23 Rue Léningrad, Paris 8e.

Lanchester (Waldo & Murel) -- Author-Publisher, The Puppet Centre, 39 Henley St., Stratford-on-Avon, England.

Lane (Allen) -- See: Penguin Books.

Langdon (John), Ltd. -- 1 Norfolk Pl., London.

Lankamp & Brinkman -- 19 Spiegelgracht, Amsterdam, The Netherlands.

Lantern Press, Inc., Publishers -- 257 Park Ave. S., NYC 10010.

LaPlace et Sanchez -- See: Sanchez.

Lardanchet (A.) (Librarie) -- 10 Rue du Président-Carnot, Lyon, France.

Las Américas Publishing Co. -- 152 E. 23rd St., NYC 10010.

Laterza Giuseppe & Figli -- 51 Via Dante Alighieri, Bari,
   Italy.

Laurence (G.) Enterprises -- NYC.

Laurens (Henri) -- 6 Rue de Tournan, Paris 6e.

Lawrence Publishing Co. -- 8615 Fifth Ave., N. Bergen,
   N. J. 07047.

Lawrence Publishing Co. -- 617 S. Olive St., Los Angeles,
   Calif. 90014.

Lawrence (Seymour) Inc. -- 90 Beacon St., Boston 02108.

Lea Bros. & Co. -- 706-708 Sansom St., Philadelphia.
   [Formerly Henry C. Lea's Son & Co.] See: Casey,
   Lea, & Blanchard.

Lea & Febiger -- Washington Sq., Philadelphia 19106.

League of Workers Theater Press -- NYC.

Lécene et Oudin -- Paris.

Lechte (Heinrich) & J. Co. -- 16 Schulstr., Emsdetten 4407,
   West Germany.

Lehigh University Reading & Study Clinic, School of Education -- 230 Racher Ave., Bethlehem, Pa. 18015.

Lehmann Books -- 1559 48th St., Brooklyn, NY 11219.

Lehmanns (J. F.) Verlag -- [formerly Lehmann & Schuppel]
   8 Agnes-Bernaver-Platz, 8000 Munich, West Germany.

Lehmkuhl (Buchhandlung) -- See under Buchhandlung Lehmkuhl . . .

Leiter-Nypels, N. V. Drukkerij En Uitgeverij -- 12 Wolf-
   straat, Maastricht, The Netherlands.

Le Jay -- Paris.

Lemerre (Alphonse) -- 23 Passage Choiseul, Paris 2e.

Leningrad State Press -- (U. S. S. R.). [Puppet books available.]

Le Rouge et le Noir -- 186 Blvd de la République à la Mad-
eleine-les Lille (Nord); and, 6 Rue de Clichy, Paris 9e.

Le Roux-at-the-Sorbonne -- Francis Roux-Devillas, 12 Rue
Bonaparte, Paris 6e.

Les Bibliophiles de France -- 85 Ave. Henri-Martin, 75
Paris 16e.

Lesort (André) Editions -- 10 Rue de L'Eperon, Paris 6e.

LeTort (Lambert) -- London.

Levrault -- [Paris]; See: Berger-Levrault

Lèvy frères -- See: Calmann-Lèvy.

Leyede -- Paris.

Librairie Ancienne Honoré Champion -- See: Champion.

Librairie de France -- 79 Blvd. St. Germain, Paris 6e.

Librairie Des Bibliophiles -- See: Les Bibliophiles de
France.

Librairie Française -- 27 Rue de L'Abbé Grégoire, 75
Paris 6e.

Librairie Hachette -- (See under: Hachette).

Librairie National d'Art et d'Histoire (G. Van Oest & Co.) --
Brussels, Belgium.

Librara "Ancora" -- 8 Via G. B. Niccolini, Milan, Italy.

Librara de Milan -- See: Majocchi.

Librario Editorial, Argos -- See: Argos.

Library Association [Britain] -- 7 Ridgemont St. & Store
Sts. , London, W. C. 1.

Lichfenstein (Eric) -- Jena, East Germany; see: Wartburg
Verlag.

Liègeoise (Commission de Folklore de la Saison, Musée de la Vie Wallon) -- 136 Rue fer Orisree, Liège, Belgium.

Lieutier (O.) -- Paris.

Lightner Publ. Corp. -- 1006 S. Michigan Ave. , Chicago 60605.

Limited Editions Club -- 207 W. 25th St. , NYC.

Lippincott (J. B.) Co. -- E. Washington Sq. , Philadelphia 19105; and, 521 Fifth Ave. , NYC 10017.

Little, Brown & Co. , Inc. -- 34 Beacon St. , Boston 02106.

Little (J. J.) & Ives Co. , Inc. -- 745 Fifth Ave. , NYC 10022.

Little Paul's House -- Warwick Sq. , London, E. C. 4. [For Univ. of London Press.]

Liveright Publishing Corp. -- [Formerly Boni & Liveright Co.] 386 Park Ave. S. , NYC 10016.

Lodzkie Wydawnictwo -- Poland; See: Ludowa Spoldzielnia.

London Library Association -- See: Library Association [Britain].

Longmans, Green & Co. , Ltd. -- 74 Grosvenor St. , London, W. 1.

Looker (John) Ltd. -- 82 High St. , Poole, Dorset, England.

Lordanchet -- Lyon, France.

Low (Sampson), Marston & Co. , Ltd. -- Gulf House, 2 Portman St. , London, W. 1.

Ludgate Circus House -- See: Chester House Publications, Ltd.

Ludowa Spoldzielnia Wydawnicza -- 4/8 Ulica Grzybowska, Warsaw, Poland.

Lust (B.) -- 124 E. 41st St. , NYC. [See next entry.]

Lust (Benedict) Publications -- 1390 E. Sixth St. , Beaumont,
    Calif. 92223.

Lust und Leid -- NYC [See previous entry.]

Lutheran Church in America, Publ. Dept. Press -- 231
    Madison Ave. , NYC 10002; 2900 Queen La. , Philadelphia.

Lutheran Publishers Group -- See: Concordia Publishing
    Co. , Inc.

Lux (Sebastian) -- 8110 Murnau/Obb Seidlpark 1, Munich,
    West Germany.

Luzac & Co. , Ltd. -- 46 Great Russell St. , P. O. Box 157,
    London, W. C. 1.

McClelland & Stewart, Ltd. -- 25 Hollinger Rd. , Toronto
    16, Canada.

MacDonald & Co. , Publishers, Ltd. -- 49-50 Poland St. ,
    London, W. 1.

McDowell -- [NYC] See: I. Obolensky.

McGraw-Hill Book Co. , Inc. -- 330 W. 42nd St. , NYC
    10036.

McKay (David) Co. , Inc. -- 750 Third Ave. , NYC 10017.

McKay Publishing Co. -- P. O. Box 66, Lyndon, Ky. 40222.

MacKay Publishing Co. , Inc. -- Box 1167, Cape Coral,
    Fla. , 33904.

McLead Co. -- 73 Bathurst St. , Toronto, 2B, Canada [for
    Lantern Press].

McPharlin (Paul) -- (Puppetry Imprints) discontinued; many
    of his books obtainable through Puppetry Journal Publi-
    cations, Ashville, Ohio.

McPharlin (Paul) Lib. Coll. -- Detroit Museum of Art Li-
    brary, 5200 Woodward Ave. , Detroit 48202.

MacUngie Press -- [Unable to locate; suggest contact:

Germantown Academy Store, Mr. Frank Cornell, Morris Rd. , Fort Washington, Pa.

"Madame S. Zlatin" -- 46 Rue Madame, Paris 6^e. [Very fine selection of out-of-print puppet material.]

"Magic" (Editions et Jouets) -- now: Editions et Jouets, 68 Ave. des Gobelins, Paris 13^e.

Magic House -- 120 W. 42nd St. , NYC 10036.

Majocchi (Serafine) Ditta -- 7 Via Meravigli, Milan, Italy.

Malvern College Press -- Malvern, Worcester, England.

Marboro Books, Inc. -- 56 W. Eighth St. , NYC.

March Bros. Publishing Co. -- [Lebanon, Ohio] now: Paine Publ. Co. , 40-44 E. First St. , Dayton, Ohio.

Marks (O. L.) Co. -- Longlane, Smithfield, London.

Marston-Searle-Rivington's Press Inc. , Ltd. -- now: Rivingtons Publishers, Ltd. , Montague House, Russell Sq. , London, W. C. 1.

Marten (D.) -- Fountain Court, Strand, London.

Maryknoll Publications -- Maryknoll, N. Y. 10545.

Masaryk Institute -- Prague, Czechoslovakia.

Masson (Pierre) -- 81 Rue de L'Hotel-de-Ville, Lyon, France. [See next entry.]

Masson et Cie. -- 120 Blvd. St. Germain, 75 Paris 6^e.

Maxwell (I. R.) & Co. , Ltd. -- 4-5 Fitzroy Sq. , London, W. 1.

Mayer & Hagen Grafische Wekstatt -- 36 Markusstrasse, Verlagsdruckerel, Trier, West Germany.

Mayer & Müller -- [Berlin. Changed to just Müller, not located.]

Mayer: sche (I. A.) Buchhandlung -- 5 Buchkremerstrasse,

Postfach 467, 5100 Aachen, West Germany.

Mazo (A. C.) et Cie. -- 15 Rue Guenegaud, 75 Paris 6^e.

M. B. K. -Verlag für Missions und Bibelkunde, G. m. b. H. --
14 Hermann-Lons-Strasse, Postfach 508, 4902 Munich,
West Germany.

M. B. K. Verlag, G. m. b. H. -- 2 Herforstr., Bad Salzuflen,
West Germany.

Melrose (Andrew), Ltd. -- 178-202 Great Portland St.,
London, W. 1.   See: Hutchinson & Co.

Menaglia (G.) -- Rome.

Mendel (Charles) Co. -- Paris.

Mera -- Lyon, France.

Mering -- London.

Merritt College Press -- Oakland, Calif.

Methuen & Co., Ltd. -- 11 New Fetter La., London, E. C.
4.

Mexican Dept. of Fine Arts, Ediciones Encuadernables de
el Nationale -- Mexico City, Mexico.

Michel (Albin) Editions -- 22 Rue Huyghens, Paris 14^e.

Michigan State University Press -- Box 550 E. Lansing,
Mich. 49923.

Midwinter (Daniel) Publ. -- [1757, no longer in existence;
old records have it listed as located at St. Paul's
Churchyard, London.]

Milford House -- absorbed by Oxford University Press (q. v.)

Miller (J. Garnet), Ltd. -- 1-5 Portpool La., London,
E. C. 1.

Mills & Boon, Ltd. -- 50 Grafton Way, P. O. Box 1, Fitzroy Sq., London, W. 1.

Mir Izdatelstvo -- 2 Rizskij Perculok, Moscow 1-278,
U. S. S. R.

Mitchell-Kennerly -- 333 S. Dearborn St., Chicago; also,
c/o Edward P. Gray Co., 8 Kensington Park Rd.,
London. [For Argus Books, Inc.]

Model Theatre Society [British] -- See: British Puppet &
Model Theatre Guild.

Molière Editions -- changed to 43 Ave. Maréchal-Foch,
06 Nice, France.

Morehouse-Gorham-Barlow Co., Inc. -- 14 E. 41st St.,
NYC 10017.

Morgan -- [Philadelphia] See: Morgan & Morgan, Inc.

Morgan und Abenland -- [Hannover] See: Hans P. Abenland Verlag.

Morgan & Morgan, Inc., Publishers -- 400 Warburton Ave.,
Hastings-on-Hudson, N. Y. 10706.

Morgan Bros., Publishers -- 28 Essex St., London, W. C.
2.

Morgan Buchverlag -- 48 Taubenstr., Berlin W. 8, East
Germany.

Morgan Cie -- 4 Rue Cassette, Paris 6e.

Morgan Rusand -- [Not identified.] Lyon, France.

Morgin-Russand -- See: Morgan Rusand.

Moring (Alexander) Co., Ltd. -- now: either Richards
Press, or The De La More Press, 8 Charles II St.,
London, S. W. 1.

Morrow (William) & Co., Inc. -- 105 Madison Ave., NYC
10016.

Moses -- [Boston; no longer active.]

Muhlenberg Press -- [formerly of Philadelphia] Rock Island,
Ill., 61201. See also: Lutheran Church Press, and,

The Fortress Press.

Mülhausen -- Mulhouse, France.

Müller (Albert) Verlag, KG. -- 69 Bahnhofstr., Rüschlikon.,
    Zürich.

Muller (Frederick), Ltd. -- Ludgate House, 110 Fleet St.,
    London, E. C. 4. [Contact for inactive Mayer &
    Müller firm books].

Müller (Harms G.) -- 45 Morgarstenstr., Krailling Post
    Planegg, Munich, West Germany.

Multimedia/Biograf. -- 174 Fifth Ave., NYC 10010; but,
    orders to 151 North Moison Rd., Blauvelt, N. Y. 10913.

Mulvelt Nep -- Budapest, Hungary.

Murray (John), Publishers, Ltd. -- 50 Albemarle St.,
    London, W. 1 [Includes Elder Smith Pub. Co.]

La Musée du Livre -- 9 Rue Ravenstein, Brussels, Bel-
    gium.

Musée National, (City of Paris) Press -- Palais du Louvre,
    Paris 1e.

Museum Press -- Milwaukee Public Museum Press, Mil-
    waukee, Wisc.

Museum Press, Ltd. -- 38-9 Parker St., London, W. C. 2.

Myers (A. N.) & Co. -- 4957 High Holborn, London.

Nasza (Naszej) Ksiegarnia Publishing Co. -- Inst. Wydaw-
    niczy; Ulica Spasowskiego, Warsaw, Poland.

Nathan (Fernand) et Cie. -- 18 Rue Monsieur le Prince,
    Paris 6e.

National Cultural Institute -- Ediciones Culturales Argen-
    tinas, Ministry of Education and Justice, Buenos Aires.

National Imprimerie -- 27 Rue de la Convention, Paris 15e.

Neale & MacKenzie Co. -- [formerly NYC; no longer in existence].

De Nederlandische Boekandel, N. V. -- 7 St. Jacobsmarkt, Antwerp, Belgium.

Nelson (C. C.) Publishing Co. -- Box 229 Appleton, Wisc. 54911.

Nelson (Thomas) Inc. -- Copewood & Davis Sts., Camden, N. J. 08103.

Neue Darmstadter Verlagsonstalt -- 117 Heinrichstr., Darmstadt 2, West Germany.

Neues Verlagshaus für Volksliterature -- 30 Markgrafenstrasse, 108 Berlin, East Germany.

Neues Verlagshaus für Volksliterature -- 2 Humboldtstrasse, Bad-Pyrmont, West Germany.

Newnes (George), Ltd. -- Tower House, Southampton St., London, W. C. 2.

Niemeijer (Halle) A. S. M. -- [now: J. Niemeijer Co., 4 Rodeweeshulsstraat, Groningen, The Netherlands.]

Nijhoff's Uitgevers-Mus., N. V. Mart. -- 9-11 Lange Voorhout, The Hague, The Netherlands.

Nimmo (John C.) -- [London; inactive since 1903] See: Routledge & Kegan Paul, Ltd.

Nisbet (James) & Co., Ltd. -- 22 Berners St., London, W. 1. and, Digswell Pl., Welwyn Hertfordshire, England.

Noble & Noble, Publishers, Inc. -- 750 Third Ave., NYC 10017.

Nonesuch Lib. Ltd. -- 10 Earlham St., Cambridge Circus, London, W. C. 2. [See: Penguin Press for U. S.]

Northwestern Press [For Northwestern College] -- c/o T. S. Denison & Co., Inc., 5100 W. 82d St., Minneapolis, Minn. 55415.

Northwestern Publishing House -- 3616/32 W. North Ave.,
   Milwaukee, Wisc. 53208.

Northwestern University Press -- 1735 Benson Ave., Evanston, Ill. 60201.

Nourrity, Plon & Nourrity Cie. -- Paris. See: Plon
   (Librairie).

Novello & Co., Ltd. -- 27-28 Soho Sq., London, W. 1.

Nutt (David), Ltd. -- 212 Shaftesbury Ave., London, W. C.
   2. [Uses The Acorn Works, Stanningly, Leeds (Yorkshire), England, for handling of many books.]

Oak Publications -- 33 W. 60th St., NYC 10023.

Oak Tree Press, Inc. -- 71 Park Ave., NYC 10016.

Oakwood Press -- Bucklands, Tandridge La., Lingfield,
   (Surrey) England.

Obolensky (Ivan), Inc. -- 341 E. 62nd St., NYC 10021.
   [Absorbed McDowell Co. books.]

Oest (G. Van) -- Brussels; See: Librairie National d'Art.

O'Galler -- Munich, West Germany.

Ohio State University Press -- Hitchcock Hall, Room 316,
   2070 Neil Ave., Columbus, Ohio 43210.

Ohio University Press -- Administrative Annex, Athens,
   Ohio 45701.

Old West Publishing Co. -- 1228 E. Colfax Ave., Denver,
   Colo. 80218.

O'Maier -- Ravensburg, West Germany.

"Ombres Haase" -- Prague Czechoslovakia.

Orbis Publishing Co. -- 66 Kenway Rd., London, S.W. 5;
   also, 46 Vinohradská tr, Prague II, Czechoslovakia.

Orellana (I. T.) Co. -- Mexico City, Mexico.

Orient Buchhandlung Heinz Lafaire -- Hannover, West Germany.

Osterrichischer Bundesverlag -- [Vienna]; see: Verlag des Osterrichischer.

Osvĕta -- 29 Ulica Cs. Armady, Bratislava, Czechoslovakia.

Oxberry (William) Press -- London.

Oxford Book Co., Inc. -- 387 Park Ave. S., NYC 10016.

Oxford University Press -- Ely House, 37 Dover St., London, W. 1.

Oxford University Press, Inc. [U. S.] -- 200 Madison Ave., NYC 10016; but, order from: 1600 Politt Dr., Fairlawn, N. J. 07410.

Pädagogischer Verlag Schwann -- 80186 Charlottenstrasse, 4000 Düsseldorf, West Germany.

Pageant Books, Inc. -- 128 Oliver St., Paterson, N. J. 07501.

Pageant Press International, Inc. -- 101 Fifth Ave., NYC 10003.

Palm & Enke Verlagsbuchhandlung -- 16 Universitätsstrasse, Postfach 41, 8520 Erlangen, West Germany.

Pantheon Books, Inc. -- 201 E. 50th St., NYC 10022; but, order from Random House, Inc., Westminster, Md. 21157.

Paravia (G. B.) & C., S. P. A. -- 16 Corso Racconigi, Turin, Italy.

Park (A.) -- Finsbury, England.

Partridge (S. W.) -- [London] See: A. & C. Black, Ltd.

Paul (H.) Press Ltd. -- Spitalfield, England. [No longer active.]

Paul (Stanley) & Co., Ltd. -- 178-202 Great Portland St., London, W. 1.

456 Publishers Index

Paul Trench, Trubner & Co. , Ltd. (booksellers) -- See under: Kegan, Paul, et al. See also: Routledge & Kegan Paul, Ltd. (publishers).

Paulus (Karl G.) Verlag -- 14 Paulustr. 7000 Stuttgart, West Germany.

Paxton (W.) & Co. , Ltd. -- 36-38 Dean St. , London W. 1. [For T. A. Pantomusik.]

Payatard Cie. -- Lausanne, Switzerland; perhaps see next entry.

Payot Cie. -- 5 Rue de Bourg, Lausanne, Switzerland; also, Payot-Paris Editions, 106 Blvd. St. Germain, 75 Paris 6e.

Payot (Librairie) S. A. -- 1 Rue de Bourg, Lausanne, Switzerland.

Pelham Books, Ltd. -- 26 Bloomsbury St. , London, W. C. 1.

Pellegrini & Cudahy -- See: Farrar, Straus, & Giroux, Inc.

Penguin Books Ltd. -- 7110 Ambassador Rd. , Baltimore, Md. 21207; and, 3984 W. 55th St. NYC 10019.

Penhoet (Oliver) & de Tannequy, Paris.

Pennsylvania Historical Association -- Pennsylvania State Univ. , University Park, Pa. 16802.

La Pensée Française -- 35 Rue Gayet, St. Etienne France.

People's Art Publishing Co. -- Peking, China.

Pepler & Sewell -- St. Dominic's Press, Ditchling, Hassocks (Sussex), England.

Pequot Press -- 10 West Ave. , Essex, Conn. 06426.

Perrin (Librairie Académique) -- 35 Quai des Grands-Augustins, Paris 6e.

Philip & Tracey, Ltd. -- 69-79 Fulham High St. , London,

S. W. 6.

Phoenix House, Ltd. -- 10-13 Bedford St., London, W.C. 2.

Phoenix Publications -- 25 Marktgasse, Bern, Switzerland.

Piglannier (Editions du) -- St. Felicien (Ardèche), France.

Pilgrim Press -- 1505 Race St., Philadelphia 19102.

Pilgrim Press of the Congregational Publications Society --
    14 Beacon St., Boston 02108; and, 19 La Salle St.,
    Chicago.

Pincebourse -- Paris [inactive].

Pioneer Press -- 114 E. Second St., Little Rock, Ark.
    72201.

Pioneer Press -- 301 N. Parton St., Santa Ana, Calif.
    92701.

Pioneer Press -- Harriman, Tenn. 37748.

Pitman Medical Publishing Co. Ltd. -- 46 Charlotte St.,
    London, W.C. 1.

Pitman Publishing Corp. -- 6 E. 43rd St., NYC 10017;
    and, 31 Fitzroy Sq., London, W. 1.

Pitman (Sir Isaac) & Sons, Ltd. -- 39 Parker St., Kingsway,
    London, W.C. 2.

Pixie Co., Publishers -- Ripon, Wisc. [Status uncertain,
    contact: Ripon College Book Store, Ripon, Wisc. 54971.]

Plays, Inc., Publishers -- 8 Arlington St., Boston 02116.

Ploma. -- Palermo, Italy.

Plon (E.) & Nourrit (or Nourrity) -- [Paris] See: Plon
    (Librairie).

Plon (Henri) -- (Rue Garancière, Paris 8e)
    now see: Plon (Librairie).

Plon (Librairie) -- 8 Rue St. Placide, Paris 6e.

Poeschel (C. E.) & Trepte -- [Leipzig] N̲o̲w̲:   Kererstr. ,
Stuttgart, West Germany.

Point (A.) & A. Mousott, Cie. -- Paris.

Polst (A.) -- Saltzburg, West Germany.

Polygraphic Co. of America -- 304 E. 45th St. , NYC.

Popular Mechanics Press -- 224 W. 57th St. , NYC 10019;
but, order from: Hawthorn Books, Inc. , 70 Fifth Ave. ,
N̅Y̅C 10011.

Popular Science [publications] -- 355 Lexington Ave. , NYC
10017.

Poulet-Melassis Cie. -- Paris.

Powell & White Co. -- 909 Edwards Bldg. , Cincinnati, Ohio.

Premier (E. I.) Press, Ltd. -- 30 Osborne St. , London, E. 1.

"Prasa" (Wydawnictwo Artystyczno-Graficzne RSW) --
Cracow, Poland.

Presses Editions Modernes (Les) (Pouzet et Cie.) -- 10 Rue
St. Roch, Paris 1er; o̲r̲, 22 Passage des Petites-Ecuries,
Paris 10^e.

Presses Universitaires de France (Les) -- Universitaires de
France, 90 Blvd. St. Germain, Paris 5^e.

Prior (V.) -- Copenhagen.

Pro Juventute Verlag -- Zürich, Switzerland.

Prowett (S.) Co. -- Church St. , London.

Publishers International Year Book -- 18 Charing Cross Rd. ,
London, W. C. 2.

Publishers' Weekly -- R. R. Bowker Co. , 1180 Ave. of the
Americas, NYC 10036.

Puhl (C. J.) -- Opole [Oppein], Lubelskie, Poland.

Puppet Theatre Press -- 26 Albert Rd. , Manchester, England.

Puppetry Centre -- 39 Henley St., Stratford-on-Avon, (Warwickshire), England.

Puppetry Journal Publications and Book Store -- 5013 W. Union St., Ashville, Ohio 43013.

Puppetry Journal (publication of periodical and special material) -- c/o Don Avery, Editor, 2015 Novem Dr., Fenton, Mo. 63026.

Putnam's (G. P.) Sons, Inc. -- 200 Madison Ave., NYC 10016.

Quarre -- Lille, France.

Quickborn-Verlag, G.m.b.H. -- 14 Dommtorstr., Hamburg 36, West Germany.

"R. A." Publ. Co. -- [London; no record, may be "R. B. A." (Royal British Art Club Press).]

Raftanis -- Athens, Greece.

Random House, Inc. -- 201 E. 50th St., NYC 10022; but, order from: Westminster, Md. 21157.

Random House, Ltd. -- 3 Golden Sq., London, W. 1. (For Knopf, Pantheon, Vintage, Blue Ribbon, and Beginner Books.)

Ravengate Press, Inc. -- Box 103, Cambridge, Mass. 02138.

Reeves (William): Booksellers, Ltd. -- 1A Norbury Crescent, London, S.W. 16. [May handle many discontinued puppet books.]

Regional Press Inc. -- Order from: Genealogical Publishing Co., Inc. 521-23 St. Paul Pl., Baltimore, Md. 21202.

Reimer (Dietrich, Andrews & Steiner) Buchhandlung -- 40 Drakestr., Berlin 45, West Germany.

Reimer (G.) -- [Munich]; see: other Reimer entry.

Reinhold Publishing Corp. -- See: Van Nostrand-Reinhold Books.

Reise-und Verkehrsverlag -- 21 Gutenberstrasse, Postfach 730, 7000 Stuttgart, West Germany.

Reiss (E.) -- Berlin.

Religious Education Press, Ltd. -- 85 Manor Rd. , Wallington (Surrey), England.

Religious Tract Society -- [London] See: Religious Education Press.

Rembrandt-Verlag, G. m. b. H. -- 1 Tauentzienstr. , Berlin 30, West Germany.

Remington-Putnam's Sons -- See Putnam's (G. P.) Sons, Inc.

Rencontre (Editions) S. A. -- 29 Chemin D'Entre-Bois, 1018 Lausanne, Switzerland.

Rentsch (Eugen)Verlag, A. G.-- 48 Wiesenstrasse, Erlenbach-Zürich; and, 20 Räpplenstrasse, 7000 Stuttgart, West Germany.

Revell (Fleming H.) Co. -- Old Tappan, N. J. 07675.

Revista de Occidente, S. A. -- 12 Bárbara de Broganza, Madrid, Spain.

Rey (A.) (Imp.) -- 4 Rue Gentil, Lyon, France.

Rhode Co. -- Rhodes-Livingston Institute, Box 900 Lusaka, Zambia.

Rhosne -- Lyon, France.

Ribadeneyra (Imp.) -- Madrid.

Richard (A.) -- 38 Rue de Laparde, Paris 8^e.

Richards Press -- 8 Charles II St. , London, W. W. 1.
   [For A. Moring Co. , Ltd. , and De La More Press.]

Ridge Press, Inc. -- 17 E. 45th St., NYC 10017. [Affiliated with Rutledge Books, Inc.]

Rimington & Hooper -- absorbed by Doubleday & Co., Inc., g. v.

Rinn (Hermann) G. m. b. H. -- 39 Shellinstr., Munich 13, West Germany.

Ritter (Elfenbein) -- now: Paul Ritter Buchdruckerei und Verlag -- 29 Zietenstr., Berlin-Lankwitz, Germany.

Rivers (Alston) Ltd. -- Walter House, 52 Bedford St., London, W. C. 2.

Rivingtons Ltd. -- Montague House, Russell Sq., London, W. C. 1.

Roberts Press -- 241 N. W. 196th St., Miami, Fla. 33169.

Roberts Print Co. -- Frankfort, Ky. 40601.

Roberts Publishing Corp. -- 136 William St., NYC 10038.

Rockliff Publishing Corp. -- See: Barrie & Rockliff.

Rockwell -- London.

Roger (Pierre) -- 140 Blvd. St. Germain, Paris 6^e.

Röhrscheid (Ludwig) -- 28 Am Hof, Bonn, West Germany.

Rohsne -- Lyon, France.

Romig (Walter), Publisher -- 979 Lake Pointe Rd., Grosse Pointe, Mich. 48230.

Ross (Alan), Ltd. -- 30 Thurice Pl., London, S. W. 7.

Rouge (F.) & Cie. -- 6 Rue Haldimond, Lausanne, Switzerland.

Le Rouge et Le Noir -- 186 Blvd. de la République (à la Madeleine les-Lille) Paris; and, 6 Rue de Clichy, Paris 9e.

Routledge & Kegan Paul, Ltd. -- 68-74 Carter La., London,

E. C. 4.

Rouveyre (Edouard) -- Paris.

Row & Peterson Co. -- merged with Harper & Row, Publishers (q. v.)

Rowe (H. M.) Co. -- 624 N. Gilmore St. , Baltimore, Md. 21217.

Roy Publications -- 29 Quai St. Michel, Paris 5e; and, 10 Rue Casimir-Delavigne, Paris 6e.

Roy Publishers, Inc. -- 30 E. 74th St. , NYC 10021.

Royal Asiatic Society of Great Britain & Ireland -- 56 Queen Ann St. , London, W. 1.

Royaux D'Art et Historie Musées -- Brussels, Belgium.

Ryerson Press -- 299 Queen St. W. , Toronto 2B, Ontario.

Sadler-Rowe -- [NYC] See: H. M. Rowe Co.

Sadlier (William H.), Inc. -- 9-11 Park Pl. , NYC 10007.

"Sagitta" -- Brussels, Belgium.

Sagittaire, (Editions du) -- 56 Rue Rodier, Paris 9e.

St. Dominic's Press -- Ditchling Common, Hassocks (Sussex), England.

St. Joseph College, Dept. of Publications -- Asylum Ave. , West Hartford, Conn. 06107.

St. Paul Public, (Soc. of) -- 2187 Victory Blvd. , Staten Island, N. Y. 10314.

St. Paul's House -- Middle Green Langley, Buckinghamshire, England.

St. Victor, (Editions de) -- Alsemberg, Belgium.

Samson Low-Marston & Co. -- See: Low (Sampson), Marston & Co. , Ltd.

Sanchez (Leon) -- 10 Rue Gay-Lussac, Paris 5e.

Sansoni (G.) C. S. P. A. -- 46 Viale Mazzini, Florence, Italy.

Sansot -- Champs Elysées, Paris.

Santa Fe Folklore Museum Bulletin Press -- Santa Fe, New
Mex. 87501.

Sapiens (Librairie) -- 4 Impasse Sainte-Léonie, Paris 14e.

Sapin -- [Paris] See: Sapiens.

Sarrazin -- Paris.

Saunders (W. B.) Co. -- West Washington Sq., Philadelphia
19105; and, 12 Dyott St., London, W. C. 1.

Scarabée (Editions du) -- 3 Rue de la Montagne-Sainte-
Geneviève, Paris 5e.

Scarecrow Press, Inc. -- 52 Liberty St., P. O. Box 656,
Metuchen, N. J. 08840.

Schauberg (M.) Verlag (Du Mont) -- [Cologne] See: M.
Schauenberg Verlag.

Schauenberg (Moritz) Verlag, KG. -- 13 Schillerstr., 7630
Lahr, West Germany.

Scherpe Verlag, G. m. b. H. -- 140 Glockenspitz, Krefeld,
West Germany.

Scheuring (N.) -- Lyon, France.

Schirmer (E. C.) Music Company -- 600 Washington St.,
Boston 02111.

Schmidt (E.) -- 32-34 Rue des Oranges, Amiens, France.

Schmidt (J.) -- 45 Rue Laffitte, Paris 9^e.

Schmit (Gaston) -- 45 Vannes-sur-Cosson, France.

Die Schönen Bucher Verlag KG. -- 11 Friedhofstrasse,
Postfach 1124, 7000, Stuttgart, West Germany.

Schöningh (Ferdinand) Verlag KG. -- Postfach 1020, Pader-
born, West Germany.

Sch. Arts Press -- 50 Portland St., Worcester, Mass.
01608.

Schreiber (J. F.) Verlag -- 40/48 Schelztorstr., Esslingen
am Neckar, West Germany.

Schulzesche hef-Buchundlang -- Leipzig, East Germany.

Schwartz (Richard) KG. -- 36 Eckenheimer Landstr.,
Frankfurt am Main, West Germany.

Scott (Thomas) -- Norwick Court, Holburn, Covent Gardens,
London.

Scott (William R.), Inc. -- See: Young Scott Books.

Scotti (G.) -- Rome.

"S. C. R." -- 14 Kensington Sq., London, W. 8.

Scribner's (Charles) Sons -- 597 Fifth Ave., NYC 10017;
and, 23 Bedford Sq., London, W. C. 1.   Orders from:
Vreeland Ave., Totowa, N. J. 07512.

Secker (Martin) & Warburg, Ltd. -- 14 Carlisle St., London, W. 1.

Seven Seas Publ. -- 13 Glinkastr., Berlin, W. 8, Germany.

Sheed & Ward, Ltd. -- 33 Maiden La., London, W. C. 2.

Siam Comm. Press -- National Culture Institute, Thailand
Culture Series, Bangkok, Thailand.

Sidgwick & Jackson, Ltd. -- 1 Tavistock Chambers, Bloomsbury Way, London, W. C. 1.

Signals Press -- 39 Wigmore St., London, W. 1.

Signorelli (Casa Editrice) -- 16 Via Botta, Milan, Italy.

Sikkel (Editions de) -- 116 Lamorinierestraat, Antwerp,
Belgium.

Simon & Schuster, Inc. -- 630 Fifth Ave., NYC 10020;
[For Golden Books; Trident Press; and, Pocket Books.]

"Sint Joris" Katholieke Jeugdbeweging -- 113 Jan Van Nas-
saustraat, The Hague, The Netherlands.

Small, Maynard, & Co. -- [No longer in existence; for
play collections, see: Dodd, Mead & Co.]

Smith (Elder) Publ. Co. -- See: John Murray Co.

Smith (Richard R.) & Ray Long Co. -- [formerly 12 E. 41st
St., NYC] now: Peterborough, N.H. 03458.

Smithers & Bonellie, Ltd. -- 266 King St. W., Toronto 2B,
Ontario.

S.N.T.L. -- (Státní Nakladatelstvi Technícké Literatury) --
51 Spalena, Prague, Czechoslovakia.

Soccer Association Press -- P.O. Box 634, New Rochelle,
N.Y. 10802.

Sociedad Folklorica de Mexico -- Mexico City.

Societé d'Editions Littéraires et Artistiques -- See: next
entry.

Societé d'Editions Scientifiques, Techniques et Artistiques --
19 Rue la Fayette, Paris 9e.

Societé de St. Victor -- Plancy, France; see: St. Victor
(Editions).

Soule (G.) Art Co. -- [Boston] absorbed by C.N. Caspar
Co., 437 E. Water St., Milwaukee, Wisc.

Southwest Book Service -- Francisco Plaza, 321 W. San
Francisco, Santa Fe, New Mex. 87501.

Southwest Press -- 2007 Brian St., Dallas, Tex. [For
Turner & Fisher books.]

Southworth (F.W.) Press -- Portland, Maine.

Spearight -- London.

"S. P. E. D." Editions -- ["S. P. E. G." Editions] 28 Rue du Four, Paris 6e.

S. P. E. L. D. (Societé Pour d'Exportation Des Livres De Droit) -- 29 Rue Rousselet, Paris 7e.

Spemann (W.) Verlag -- 5/7 Pfizerstr., Berlin, West Germany.

Springer-Verlag, KG. -- 3 Heidelberger Platz, Berlin 33, West Germany.

Stagecoach Press -- Box 4422, Albuquerque, N. Mex. 87106.

Stanford University Press -- Stanford, Calif. 94305.

Starr Bull. Press -- Honolulu; [may be the Starr Press of Okla., q.v.]

Starr Press -- Chickasha, Okla.

Státní nakladatelství krasne literatury a umeni Lido -- (State Publishing House of Literature and Art) -- Smíchov, Staropramenná, ul 12, Prague, Czechoslovakia.

Státní Pedagogícké Nakladatelstvi -- 30 Ostrovní, Prague 1, Czechoslovakia.

Stechert-Hafner, Inc. -- See: Hafner Publishing Co., [U. S.]

Stechert-Hafner, Inc. -- 16 Rue de Condé, Paris 7e.

Sterling Publishing Co. -- 419 Park Ave. S., NYC 10016.

Stern (J. W.) Co. -- [NYC; no longer in existence.]

Stock (D. ?) -- 6 Rue Casimir-Elavigne, Paris 6e. See also (perhaps): next entry.

Stock (Editions) -- 4 Rue des Six Aunes, Brussels, Belgium.

Stock (Elliot) Co. -- 7 Paternoster Row, London, E. C. 4.

Stockdale (J. J.) -- London.

Stockwell (Arthur H.), Ltd. -- Elms Court, Torris Park,

Ilfracombe (Devonshire), England.

Stokes (E. A.) Ltd. -- Aldine House, 10-13 Bedford St.,
London, W. C. 2. [For orders see: J. P. Lippincott
Co.]

Storck (A.) -- Lyon, France; perhaps see: D. Stock.

Strauch (Von Arwed) Verlag -- Leipzig, East Germany.

Stravech (A.) Co. -- Leipzig, East Germany.

Studio Books -- imprint of The Viking Press, Inc. (q. v.)

Studio Editorial Moderno -- Catania, Italy.

Studio, Ltd. -- See: Studio Vista, Ltd.

Studio Publications Co. (Viking Distributors) -- 625 Madison Ave., NYC 10022.

Studio Vista, Ltd. -- Blue Star House, Highgate Hill, London, N. 19.

Suebarno (Keluraga) -- Sala, Sweden.

Sylvan Press -- 5 Museum House, 24-25 Museum St., London, W. C. 1.

"Sztuka" -- Warsaw, Poland.

Tallandier (Jules) (Librairie) -- [Lille] now: Societé
d'Editions et de Publications; at, 17 Rue Remy-Dumoncel,
Paris 14e.

Tannen (Louis) -- 120 W. 42nd St., NYC 10036. ["Magic
House."]

Taplinger Publ. Co. Inc. -- 29 E. 10th St., NYC 10003.

Tauchnitz (Bernard) Verlag, G. m. b. H. -- 94 Leibnizstr.,
Stuttgart, West Germany.

Tawney (M. M.) Co. -- London.

Taylors' (Foreign) Press -- 37 Furnival St., London, E. C. 4.

Teachers' College Press of Columbia University -- 525 W.
120th St., NYC 10027.

Technes (Hellinikes) -- Athens, Greece.

Technischer Verlag -- 50 Linzergasse, Salzburg, Austria.

Tegg (W.) & Co. -- [London] See: A. N. Myers Co.

Temple University, Publications Division -- Broad & Montgomery Ave., Philadelphia. 19122.

Terrie & Adonis -- Paris.

Terre Retrouvée Societé (Les Editions) -- 12 Rue de la
Victoire, Paris 9e.

Théâtrale (Librairie) -- Rue de L'Echiquier, Paris 10e.

Theatre Arts Press, Inc. -- now: Theatre Arts Books,
333 Ave. of the Americas, NYC 10014.

Theatre Institute -- Valdstejnské /Nám 3, Prague 1, Czechoslovakia. [A very valuable source for out-of-print or
other puppet books.]

Thieme (W. J.) & Cie. -- 15 Greenmarkt, Zutphen, The
Netherlands.

Thule Press -- (Bokforlags Aktiebolaget Thule) Stockholm,
Sweden.

Tijdschrift Van Het-Java Inst. -- Jogjakarta, Indonesia.

Tokyo News Service, Ltd.   -- Kosoku Doro Bldg., Ginza
Nishi, 8 Chome Chu-Ku, Tokyo, Japan.

Tonson (Jacop & Richard), Ltd. -- Shakespeare's Head,
opposite Catherine St., London.

Toth (J. P.) Co. -- Hamburg, West Germany.

Tourelle (Editions de la) -- 24 Rue de la République, 94 St.
Mandé (Seine), France.

Tracey & Philips -- [London] See: Philip & Tracey, Ltd.

Trench, Trubner & Co., Ltd. -- See: Kegan, Paul, Trench, Trubner & Co., Ltd. (booksellers).

Tresse & Stock -- now: Editions Stock (q.v.)

Tri-Jas Co. -- Surakarta, Indonesia.

Truchet, -- -- 73 Rue Paul Frédéric, Belgium.

Truchy -- [Paris].

Tudor Press Ltd. -- 75 Carter La., London, E. C. 4.

Turkische Bibliothek -- Berlin.

Turner Company -- 4640 Harry Hines Blvd., Box 870, Dallas, Texas 75221.

Turner & Fisher -- [Philadelphia, and NYC] absorbed by Southwest Press, located at 2007 Brian St., Dallas, Texas.

Tuttle (Charles E.) Co. -- 28 S. Main St., Rutland, Vt. 05701.

Twinkle Books, Inc. -- Box 13426, Atlanta, Ga. 30324.

Twinkle Press -- Box 6, Roanoke, Va. 24001.

Twinkle Records -- 356 W. 40th St., NYC.

Uitgevers, Nederlandsche Vereniging Voor het Poppenspel -- Amsterdam, The Netherlands.

Uitghet Boe Khuis -- 113 Haringodestroot, Antwerp, Belgium.

Ullestein Taschenbücher Verlag -- 50 Kochstrasse, Berlin 61, Germany.

Umění Lído -- see: Státní Nakladatelství Krasne Literatury à Umění Lído -- 36 Narodní, Prague 1, Czechoslovakia.

"UNIMA" [France] Press -- 228 Blvd. Raspail, Paris 14e.

"UNIMA" Press (Union Internationale des Marionnettes) --
c/o Dr. Jan Malik, Sect. Générale; 28 Namestî M.
Gorkeho, Nove Mesto, Prague 1, Czechoslovakia.

"UNIMA [U.S.A.]" Press -- c/o Miss Mollie Falkenstein,
132 Chiquita St., Laguna Beach, Calif. 92651.

United Lutheran Publications -- See: Fortress Press or
Muhlenberg Press, or Lutheran Church Press.

Universal Book & Bible House -- 34 Beech St., London,
E. C. 1.

Universal Publishing & Distributing Corp. -- 235 E. 45th
St., NYC 10017.

Universitaires de France (Les Presses) -- See: Presses,
Universitaires de France.

Universidad de Mexico (Director of Graduate Publications) --
Mexico City.

Universidad de Oriente (Dept. de Publicaciones) -- Santiago
de Cuba.

Universidad National del Litoral -- Santa Fe, N. Mex.

University of London Press, Ltd. -- Little Paul's House,
Warwick Sq., London, E. C. 4.

University of Michigan Press -- 615 East University St.,
Ann Arbor, 48106.

University of Nebraska Press -- 901 N. 17th St., Lincoln,
68508.

University of Oklahoma Press -- 1005 Asp Avenue, Norman
73069.

University of Southern California Press -- University Park,
Los Angeles 90007.

University of Washington Press -- Seattle   98105.

University Press of Washington, D. C. -- 927 15th St. N. W.,
Washington, D. C. 20005

Unwin (Arthur) Co. -- 53 Glenmore Rd., London, N. W. 3.

Unwin, Ltd. -- See: Allen & Unwin, Ltd.

Unwin (T. Fisher) -- See: Allen & Unwin, Ltd.

Vaillant-Carmanne (Imprimerie) -- 4 Place St. Michel, Liège, Belgium.

Van In (J.) Inc. -- Lier, Belgium.

Van Nostrand-Reinhold Books -- 450 W. 33rd St., NYC 10001.

Van Oest (G.) (Editions) -- [formerly of Brussels] 3-5 Rue Du Petit-Point, Paris 5e.

Vawser & Niles, Ltd. -- 356/8 Kilburn High Rd., London, N.W. 6.

Veeder & Leonard -- Janesville, Wisc. 53545.

Verlag Des Oesterrichischer Gewerkschaftsbundes G.m.b.H. -- 1 Rennwag, Vienna.

Verlag für Buch und Bibliotheksweson, VEB. -- 26 Gerichtsweg, 701 Leipzig, East Germany.

Verlag für Der Verfasser -- Frankfurt am Main, West Germany.

Verlag für Jugend und Volk G.m.b.H. -- 7-9 Tiefer Graven, 1010 Vienna.

Verry (Lawrence), Inc. -- 16 Holmes St., Mystic, Conn. 06355.

Verschoyle Co. -- See: Deutsch (André).

Viking Press, Inc. -- 625 Madison Ave., NYC 10022.

Vilimek (Jos. R.) -- Prague, Czechoslovakia.

Vintage Books, Inc. -- See: Random House.

Virtue & Co. -- 19-21 Thavies Inn, Holburn Circus, London, E.C. 1.

Vitzetelly Bros. & Co. -- London.

Volksverlag Weimar -- 1 Puschkinstr., Weimar, East Germany.

Von Paulnoff Verlag -- See under: Paulus (Karl G.) Verlag.

Von Shröder (Marion) Verlag, G. m. b. H. -- 22 An Der Alster, 2000 Hamburg, West Germany.

Vowinckel (Kurt) Verlag -- 5 Jul-Menger-Str., Neckarsulm, West Germany.

Wahlström & A. B. Widstrand -- 83 Regeringsgatan, Stockholm, Sweden.

Wales (Alexander P.) -- 18 Charing Cross Rd., London, W. C. 2.

Walker (H.) -- See: H. E. Walter Co.

Wallis (E.) -- London.

Waltener (A.) -- Lyon, France.

Walter (H. E.) Co. -- 26 Grafton Rd. Worthing (Sussex), England.

Wancura (Edward) Verlag, G. m. b. H. -- 32 Beatrixgasse, Vienna III.

Ward, Lock & Co., Ltd. -- Warwick House, 116 Baker St., London, W. 1.

Ward (Marcus) -- absorbed by Ward, Lock & Co.

Wartburg Verlag -- 11 Inselplatz, 69 Jena, East Germany.

Washbourne & Thomas Co. -- See: Burns & Oates, Ltd.

Washington Univ. -- No longer called Wash. Col., St. Louis, Mo., U. S. A. (Do not confuse with Univ. of Washington in Seattle, Wash., U. S. A.)

Watson-Guptill Publications Inc. -- 165 W. 46th St., NYC 10036.

Watts (C. A.) & Co. , Ltd. -- 39 Parker St. , London, W. C.
2; but, order from Book Centre Ltd. , or, 5-6 Johnson
Court, London, E. C. 4.

Watts (Franklin) Inc. -- 845 Third Ave. , NYC 10022.

Webster Division (of McGraw-Hill Book Co.) -- Manchester
Rd. , Manchester, Mo. 63011.

Webster Publishing Co. -- 1154 Reco Ave. , St. Louis, Mo. ,
63126.

Weidmann's Buchhandlung -- 11 Georgstr. , Hannover 1,
West Germany.

Wells Gardner, Darton & Co. -- 49 Brighton Rd. , Redhill
(Surrey), England. [See also: Gardner Publishing Co. ;
sometimes not clear at source which company desired.]

Werl (A.) -- Leipzig, East Germany.

Westermann (B.), Inc. -- 18-20 W. 48th St. , NYC [possibly
connected with following entry].

Westermann (George) Verlag -- No. 66 George Westermann
Allee, 20b Braunschweig, West Germany.

Wheaton (A.) & Co. -- 143 Fore St. , Exeter, England.

Whitaker (J.) & Sons, Ltd. -- 13 Bedford Sq. , London,
W. C. 1.

Willems (J.) -- [formerly of Verviers, Belgium] now: 9
Ave. Galilée, Brussels.

Wilson (H. W.) Co. , Inc. -- 950 University Ave. , Bronx,
N. Y. 10452.

Windsor (A. G.) -- 801 Randolph St. , San Francisco 94132.
[For Popular Mechanics trade books.]

Windsor Books -- Box 280, Bright Waters, N. Y. 11718.

Windsor & Newton, Ltd. -- Wealdstone, Harrow (Middlesex),
England.

Wissen, Volk und -- VEB; 54a Lindenstrasse, 108 Berlin.

Wissenschaften und Werbung -- 8a Schobergstrasse, 7800
    Freiburg 50, Berlin.

Wolff (K.) -- See perhaps: next entry.

Wolff (Oswald), Ltd. -- 12 Fitzroy St. , London, W. 1.

Woman's Day Magazine -- NYC.

Woman's Home Companion Press -- 250 Park Ave. , NYC.

World's Fair Press -- London.

Wortelmann (Fritz) -- 115 Bergstrasse, 463 Bochum, West
    Germany.

Wydawnictwo Artystyczno-Graficzne RSW "Prasa" -- Cracow,
    Poland.

Yale University Press -- 149 York St. , New Haven, Conn.
    06511; but, order from: 92A Yale Station, Conn. 06520.

Yoseloff (Thomas), Ltd. -- 18 Charing Cross Rd. , London,
    W. C. 2; and, 352 Fourth Ave. , NYC 10010. [Selling
    very old English puppet books.]

Young Scott Books -- (imprint of) Addison-Wesley Publish-
    ing Co. , Reading, Mass. 01867.

Zanichelli (Nicola) -- 34 Via Irnerio, Bologna, Italy.

Zeff (M.) -- Buenos Aires.

Zlatin, Madam -- 46 Rue Madam, Paris 6^e.